Q: How do I force a formula's cell references to stay th

A: The key is to use dollar signs, which denote absolute references. Type a dollar sign in front of each row number or column letter that should stay fixed (for example, $A$1:$C$3). *See Chapter 9.*

Q: I entered a date, but it shows up as a number. How do I fix it?

A: You need to apply a Date number format to the cell. Select the cell, then choose Format, Cells. Click the Number tab, and select Date from the Category list; then click OK. *See Chapter 10.*

Q: How do I prevent the gridlines from printing?

A: Choose File, Page Setup. Click the Sheet tab, and then deselect the Gridlines check box. *See Chapter 13.*

Q: My printouts always say Sheet 1 at the bottom. How can I change or remove that text?

A: Excel is placing the sheet name in the footer. You can change the sheet name by double-clicking on the worksheet tab and typing a new name. Or you can modify the footer so that nothing at all appears there by choosing File, Page Setup, clicking the Header/Footer tab, and choosing None from the Footer drop-down list. *See Chapter 13.*

Q: I try to drag a chart object to move it, but the chart graphic image moves around inside the chart box rather than the whole box moving.

A: You have accidentally selected the chart graphic rather than the whole chart box. You must click the outside edge of the chart box first to select it, before you drag the object. *See Chapter 15.*

Q: I need more clip art! Isn't there any more than what shows up in the Clip Gallery?

A: There is a lot more clip art available from the Microsoft Web site. Click the Web button in the Chart Gallery to jump to the Web page from which you can select it. *See Chapter 16.*

Q: I sorted a list of names and addresses on a sheet, and now my column headings have disappeared.

A: You probably accidentally included the column headings in the sort. Choose Edit, Undo to reverse the sort. Then select the sort area again, this time without the heading row, and try again.

Q: Why can't I rotate the text in an AutoShape?

A: Excel's AutoShape feature has limited text rotation capabilities, but you can work around it like this. Select the AutoShape containing the text, and then choose Format, AutoShape. In the dialog box that appears, click the Alignment tab. Set the orientation for the text in the Orientation box, then click OK.

Q: Are there any functions in Excel 97 that work like Lotus 1-2-3 functions?

A: Excel 97 includes a new set of functions that are designed to be 100% compatible with a similar set of functions in Lotus 1-2-3. They are called the "A" functions because their names all end with A: AVERAGEA, MINA, MAXA, STDEVA, STDEVPA, VARA, and VARPA. *See Appendix C for the arguments for these functions.*

Q: What versions of Quattro Pro files can I open in Excel?

A: This can be confusing because the online help information on the subject is incorrect. Excel 97 can open Quattro Pro for MS-DOS files (*.WQ1) and Quattro Pro for Windows versions 5.0 and earlier (*.WB1) files. However, Excel cannot open Quattro Pro DOS, version 6.0, files (*.WQ2) or Quattro Pro for Windows, version 6.0, files (*.WB2).

How to Order:

For information on quantity discounts contact the publisher: Prima Publishing, P.O. Box 1260BK, Rocklin, CA 95677-1260; (916) 632-4400. On your letterhead include information concerning the intended use of the books and the number of books you wish to purchase. For individual orders, turn to the back of this book for more information.

The Essential Excel 97 Book

The Get-It-Done Tutorial

Faithe Wempen

with Donna Payne

PRIMA PUBLISHING

Acquisitions Manager: Alan L. Harris
Managing Editor: Tad Ringo
Product Marketing Specialist: Julie Barton
Acquisitions Editor: Deborah F. Abshier
Assistant Acquisitions Editor: Jill Byus
Development Editor: Joyce Nielsen
Project Editor: Geneil Breeze
Editorial Coordinator: Stacie Drudge
Technical Reviewers: Dave Maguiness, Robert Affleck, Brent Parrish
Interior Design and Layout: Claude Bell, Chad Dressler, Steve Esarey,
Karen Fields, Dennis Clay Hager, Tina Trettin
Cover Design: Vanessa Perez
Cover Illustration: Mike Tanamachi
Indexer: Sharon Hilgenberg

IMPORTANT: If you have problems installing or running Microsoft Excel 97, notify Microsoft Corporation at (206) 635-7056. Prima Publishing cannot provide software support.

ISBN: 0-7615-0428-1
Library of Congress Catalog Card Number: 97-65764
Printed in the United States of America
97 98 99 DD 10 9 8 7 6 5 4 3 2 1

To Margaret

Contents at a Glance

Contents

Hands-On Topics

Acknowledgments

I was really blessed in writing this book with a first-rate editorial team. First and foremost, I would like to thank Debbie Abshier at Prima Publishing for hiring me to write this book. She's not only one of the greatest acquisitions editors in the business, but a real friend to her authors. Thanks also to Donna Payne, who possesses an amazing knowledge of Excel, for stepping in and writing some of the more advanced chapters. Good job, Donna! And thanks to Joyce Nielsen, a great development editor, for a strong content editing pass. You didn't miss a thing, girl! And finally, thanks to Geneil Breeze, who edited out my inconsistencies and spelling mistakes and coordinated the project successfully through various crises and impossible deadlines. Great work, everybody.

About the Authors

Faithe Wempen (M.A. English) is the owner of Wempen Editorial Services, an Indianapolis-based company that provides writing and editing support to computer book publishers and OEM software developers. Faithe also teaches hardware and software classes, provides one-on-one computer tutoring, and troubleshoots and repairs computers. She has written more than a dozen computer books and edited over 250 more.

Donna Payne is President of Payne Consulting Group (PCG), a computer consulting firm in Seattle, Washington. She is a Microsoft Certified Trainer for Excel and Visual Basic for Applications and a three-time recipient of the Microsoft Most Valuable Professional award. She has developed applications and provided training for Microsoft, Northern Telecom, the U.S. Postal Service, Davis Wright Tremaine and Perkins Coie. Donna is a contributing author to many titles for several publishers. She is a featured columnist for *Microsoft Office Advisor* magazine and the originator of a networking group for women programmers.

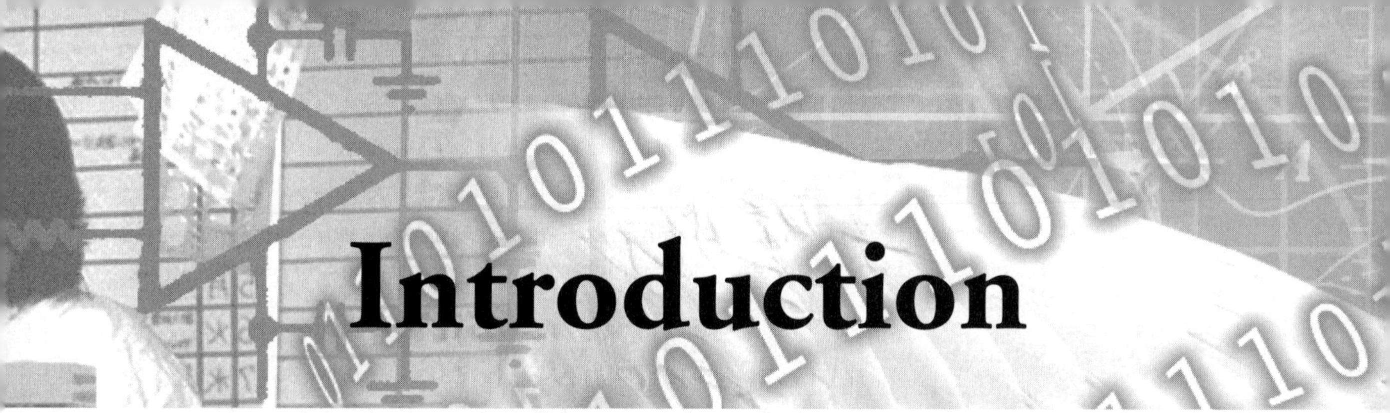

Introduction

Besides being an author, I'm also a software instructor, and I talk to businesspeople every week who are struggling with Excel. Their complaints are nearly always the same: "I want to know more about the program, but I don't have any time to spend figuring it out!"

It's ironic. The software developers, in the race to make their product the easiest to use, add more and more time-saving features to their products with every release. But the average user doesn't have the time to spend learning the new versions and understanding the new commands, so some of the best time-saving features seldom get used. This is especially true with Excel users because they tend to be business professionals interested in number-crunching and bottom-line results—and people like that seldom have much spare time at the office.

Excel is a tool—like a hammer or a briefcase. It doesn't have any value except in how it can help you manage your data. You don't need to know every little detail about Excel to use it effectively, just as you don't have to know what kind of thread holds your briefcase together, or what its maximum capacity is, to carry your papers around in it. That's why in this book, I won't bog you down with useless trivia. In *The Essential Excel 97 Book*, I'll focus only on the most important, useful features of the program and will show you the easiest method of getting things done, not every single method Excel includes.

Is This Book for You?

This book is designed for business professionals, not computer scientists. I won't try to make you into a computer guru, because I know you have other goals to reach. Instead, I'll guide you through the features of Excel that you will most likely need to use it effectively as a tool toward your *real* goals: like figuring out that bottom-line cost estimate or making an attractive chart that shows your division's profitability.

That doesn't mean that you won't come away with a thorough understanding of Excel when you're finished with the book. If you learn everything in this book, you will have knowledge equivalent to almost an entire week of intensive Excel in-lab training. You won't have to humble yourself and seek out your company's Excel expert nearly as often, and people in your office may actually start coming to *you* for help with Excel!

Whether you are a first-time Excel user or an experienced user of a previous version, this book is for you:

- *New users* should check out the first few chapters, to get grounded in some basic skills like using the Excel interface, working with files, and understanding worksheet organization.
- *More experienced users* will appreciate the intermediate-level discussions toward the middle and end of the book on topics such as database management, the Internet, and file sharing.
- *All levels of users* will appreciate the "real-world" focus of each chapter, including not only how to use each feature but why and under what circumstances.

Conventions Used in This Book

The conventions used in this book should help you learn Excel quickly and easily. Most Excel commands can be selected with either a mouse or the keyboard. The instructions in this book are written in a way that enables you to choose the method you prefer. For example, if the instruction reads "Choose File, Open," you should point the mouse to the word File on the menu bar and click the left mouse button, and then click on the word Open in the drop-down menu.

Notice that in each menu command, there is an underlined letter, both on the screen and in the book. That's the *selection letter*. If you prefer to use the keyboard instead of the mouse, you can hold down the Alt key and press the underlined letter in the menu name to open it. For example, to open the File menu, press Alt+F. After a menu is open, press the underlined letter in the command name to select a command. For example, once the File menu is open, press O to select the Open command.

Two keys to be pressed in sequence are separated with a comma. For instance, the End key is often pressed before pressing another key. "Press End, Home" means to press and then release the End key, and then press and release the Home key.

When two keys are to be pressed together (that is, you hold down the first key while you press the second key), a plus sign (+) is used to show the combination: Alt+F or Ctrl+Z.

Often the quickest way to access a feature is by clicking a button on the toolbar. (You'll learn all about the toolbar in Chapter 1.) In the text, I'll refer to the button using the same name that appears on-screen when you point to a toolbar button.

Bold text is used to indicate text that you should type in. On-screen messages appear in `monospace text`.

Throughout the book I'll assume that you're familiar with certain common mouse actions:

- **Point.** To move the mouse so that the tip of the pointer on-screen touches the object.
- **Click.** To press and release the left mouse button once.
- **Double-click.** To press and release the left mouse button twice quickly in succession.
- **Right-click.** To press and release the right mouse button once.
- **Drag.** To press and hold down the left mouse button while pointing at an object and then move the mouse until the object moves to a new location.
- **Right-drag.** Same as drag but with the right mouse button.

Special Elements

Along the way, you will find several special elements that will make using this book easier:

Hands On: Accomplishing a Specific Task

Occasionally you'll find that it's easier to begin learning a feature by following a specific example rather than learning a general procedure. For example, in Chapter 2 you'll learn about custom views by creating one that you can use right there in the worksheet you're creating.

Tips are short hints that provide shortcuts or recommendations on the best way to use a feature.

***Notes* provide further information — often of a more technical nature — on how a feature works or its uses or limitations.**

As you might expect, *cautions* tell you what to watch out for when using a feature.

If there's information or goodies to be found on the Internet that relate to a certain topic, I'll call your attention to it with a Find It Online icon.

A GRAY BOX IN THE MARGIN INDICATES WHERE ADDITIONAL INFORMATION CAN BE FOUND.

Sidebars for That Extra Touch

You'll see sidebars through the text that provide discussions about how you can best use a particular feature. For example, in Chapter 2 you'll find a sidebar that explains exactly what happens "behind the scenes" when you use the Zoom feature to view your worksheet at a different magnification.

PART I
Finding Your Way Around Excel

1

Introducing Excel

In This Chapter

- Starting Excel
- The Parts of the Excel Interface
- Using Dialog Boxes
- Getting Information from the Built-In Help System
- Exiting Excel

Excel is the best-selling spreadsheet program in the world – and with good reason. It's the perfect combination of power and ease-of-use. If you've never used Excel before or are unfamiliar with how Windows programs work, this chapter is the place to start.

Starting Excel

Before you can use Excel, you must start the program. (Of course, the program must already be installed on your computer or on a network that your computer is connected to; if you need help installing, see Appendix A.)

There are many ways to start Excel, but here is the easiest method:

1. Click the Start button.
2. Slide the mouse pointer up to Programs. A submenu appears.
3. Slide the mouse onto the submenu and then up or down to Microsoft Excel (see Figure 1.1).
4. Click on Microsoft Excel. Excel starts.

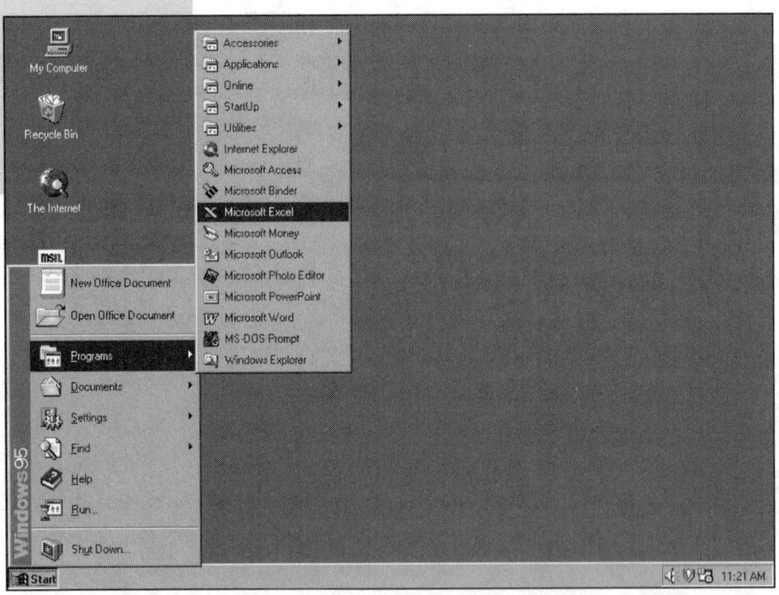

Figure 1.1 Choose Excel from the Start button's menu system to start the program.

Here are some other ways to start Excel from Windows 95:

- Double-click the Excel program file (Excel.exe) in the My Computer or Windows Explorer window. (It's in the Program Files folder, in a folder called Microsoft Office or Microsoft Excel, depending on your installation.)

- To open an existing Excel workbook and start Excel at the same time, double-click on the workbook's name in the My Computer or Windows Explorer window.
- Create a shortcut for Excel on your desktop and then double-click on that shortcut to start the program. To create a shortcut for Excel, find the program file (Excel.exe) in Windows Explorer or My Computer and right-drag it to the desktop. Choose Create Shortcut(s) Here from the shortcut menu that appears.
- If there is a particular workbook that you open frequently, create a shortcut for that workbook file on your desktop, as described previously, and then double-click on that shortcut to start Excel and open that workbook at the same time.

FOR MORE INFORMATION ABOUT STARTING A NEW DOCUMENT OR OPENING AN EXISTING DOCUMENT WITH THE SHORTCUT BAR, SEE CHAPTER 3.

If you use Microsoft Office 97, you have access to the Shortcut Bar if you installed it. Here are some ways to start Excel using the Shortcut Bar:

- Click the New Office Document button. Select Blank Workbook from the New Office Document dialog box that appears, and click OK.
- To start Excel and open an existing document at the same time, click the Open Office Document button. In the Open Office Document dialog box that appears, select the workbook to open and click OK.
- Add a button to the Microsoft Office Shortcut Bar for the Excel program and then click on that button to start the program. An easy way to do this is to drag an icon from the desktop to the Shortcut Bar.

Note

If the Shortcut Bar feature is not installed, rerun the Microsoft Office 97 Setup program, choose the Custom installation, and make sure that you place a check mark beside Microsoft Office Shortcut Bar. For more information about the installation program, see Appendix A.

Finding Your Way Around the Screen

In many ways, Excel is much like any other Windows program; it contains the standard elements that users expect to see, such as a title bar, toolbars, a menu bar, and window control buttons (Minimize, Maximize, and Restore). If you are already familiar with these controls, feel free to skip this section. Figure 1.2 shows the initial Excel screen and points out some of its parts; these parts are explained further in the following sections.

Figure 1.2 This is the default Excel screen, the one you see when you start the program.

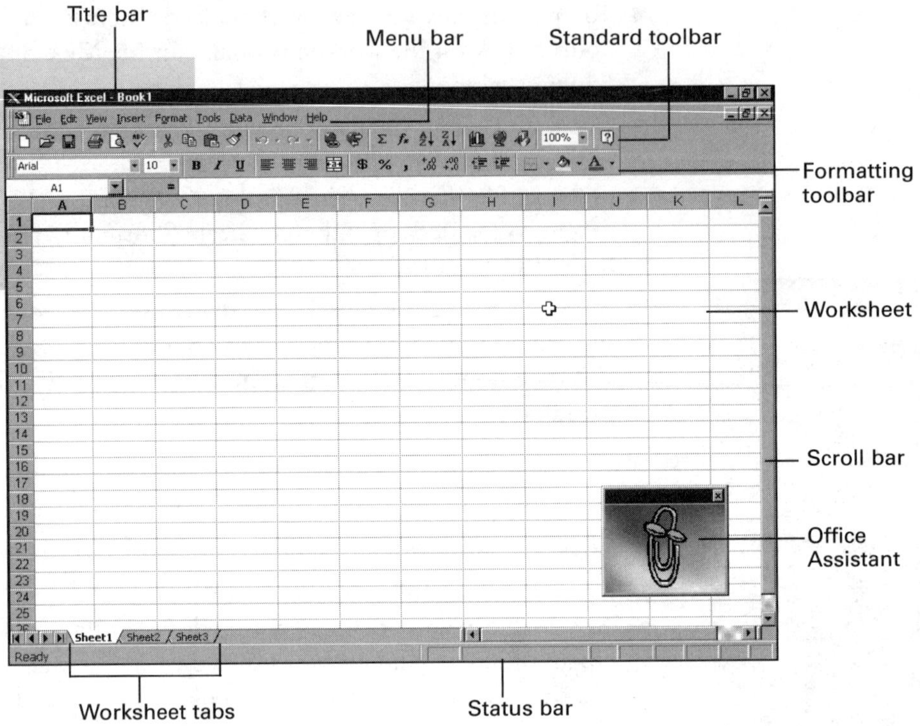

Note

The first time you start Excel, the Office Assistant may ask you if you need help. Just click Start Using Excel Now; the Office Assistant is discussed in detail later in this chapter.

Worksheets

YOU LEARN MORE ABOUT WORKSHEETS IN CHAPTER 5.

The *worksheet* is the heart of the Excel screen. Worksheets are like pages in a book (or *workbook*, as the case may be in Excel). Each workbook contains three worksheets by default, and you can add more later as needed, as you learn in Chapter 5. Figure 1.2 points out the worksheet tabs across the bottom of the workbook window; to see a worksheet, click on its tab.

Each worksheet consists of a grid of rows and columns. At the intersection of each row and column is a *cell*. A cell's name is derived from its position in the grid: for instance, the cell at the intersection of Row 2 and Column B is cell B2. In Chapters 7 and 8, you learn how to enter text, numbers, and formulas into the cells of a worksheet.

Title Bar

YOU LEARN HOW TO MAXIMIZE WINDOWS IN CHAPTER 2.

Every Windows program has a *title bar,* the colored bar across the top of the application window. It's called the title bar because, obviously, it contains the title of the program (Microsoft Excel). When a workbook is maximized, as it is in Figure 1.2, the workbook's name also appears in the title bar.

Where did that Book1 window come from? When you start Excel, a new workbook opens automatically, and its default name is Book1. You can change the name when you save the workbook, as you learn to do in Chapter 3.

Menu Bar

Immediately below the title bar is the *menu bar.* All Windows programs use drop-down menus to help you issue commands to the program. The menu bar contains the names of the menus you can open. To open a menu, simply click on its name. Figure 1.3 shows an open menu. When a menu is open, click on a command to choose it (this also closes the menu). If you open a menu and then decide not to choose a command from it, press the Esc key or click anywhere outside the menu.

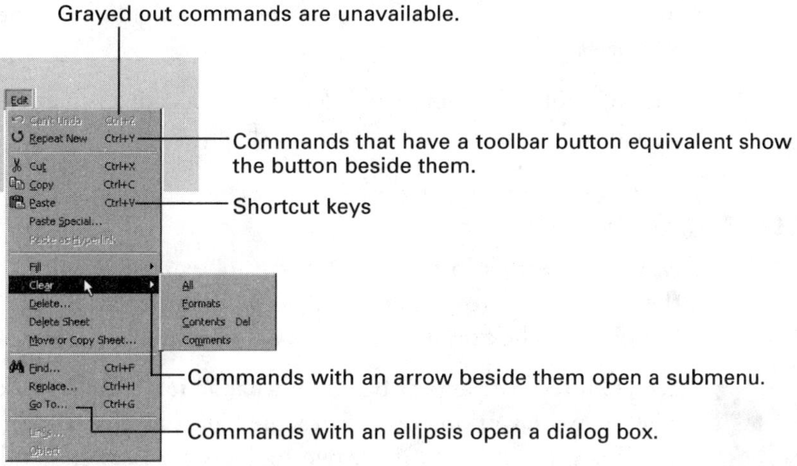

Figure 1.3 A typical menu in Excel.

Here's a quick look at the features you may find on a menu:

- Some commands have shortcut keys listed beside them. For example, in Figure 1.3, the Paste command has Ctrl + V next to it. That means that instead of opening the Edit menu and choosing Paste, you can simply hold down the Ctrl key on the keyboard and press the V key (without opening the menu).

- Some commands may not be available at the moment. Unavailable commands are grayed out—that is, they appear in gray letters rather than black. For example, in Figure 1.3, the Paste as Hyperlink command is unavailable.
- As you learn in the following section, many commands have toolbar button equivalents. If a command corresponds to a toolbar button, a picture of the button appears to its left. For instance, in Figure 1.3, the Cut, Copy, and Paste commands all have toolbar button equivalents.
- Commands that have right-pointing arrows next to them open submenus with more commands. For instance, in Figure 1.3, the Fill and Clear commands both open submenus. The Clear command's submenu is open because the mouse is pointing at it.
- Commands that have ellipses following them (…) open *dialog boxes,* which are special windows requesting more information about the action you want to take. You learn about dialog boxes later in the chapter.

Opening menus with the mouse is the easiest way, but there is also an alternative way. Hold down the Alt key and press the underlined letter (the *selection letter*) in the menu's name. For instance, to open the File menu, hold down Alt and press F. Then to choose a command, press the underlined letter in the command's name, or use the ↓ key to move the highlight to the command you want and press Enter.

Throughout this book, the selection letters for each menu and command are underlined, in case you want to use them.

Toolbars

As you saw earlier in Figure 1.2, there are two rows of little pictures (icons) across the top of the screen. Those are *toolbars,* and each picture is a button. To use a button, just click on it.

CHARTING IS COVERED IN CHAPTERS 14 AND 15.

Different toolbars appear based on what action you are performing. For example, when you are working on a chart, the Chart toolbar appears. But when you first start Excel (as in Figure 1.3), two toolbars are visible: Standard and Formatting.

Not all toolbar controls are buttons; some are drop-down lists—text with a down-pointing arrow to the right. To open a drop-down list, click the down-pointing arrow. A list of choices appears; just click on your selection.

Some controls are a combination of a button and a drop-down list—buttons with down-pointing arrows next to them. If you click on the button portion, the current setting is executed. For instance, if you click on the Font Color button (the rightmost button on the Formatting toolbar), the current font color is applied. To change the current setting (for instance, the current font color), click the down-pointing arrow to open a drop-down list of available settings.

Tables 1.1 and 1.2 show the buttons on the Standard and Formatting toolbars and explain what each one does. Don't worry if you don't understand the explanations fully now; all these buttons will be covered later in the book.

Tip

You may want to mark this page with a sticky note for easy reference later to Tables 1.1 and 1.2.

Table 1.1 Controls on the Standard Toolbar

Button	Name	Purpose
	New	Starts a new workbook.
	Open	Opens an existing workbook.
	Save	Saves the active workbook to disk.
	Print	Prints the currently displayed page of the active workbook.
	Print Preview	Enters Print Preview mode to preview a print job on-screen.
	Spelling	Runs a spelling check.
	Cut	Moves the selected data to the Clipboard.
	Copy	Copies the selected data to the Clipboard.
	Paste	Pastes the Clipboard contents into the worksheet.

continues

Table 1.1—continued

Button	Name	Purpose
	Format Painter	Copies the formatting of the selected text and applies it to the text you select next.
	Undo	Reverses the last action. Open its drop-down list to choose multiple previous actions to undo.
	Redo	Redoes the last reversed action. Open its drop-down list to choose multiple "undos" to redo.
	Insert Hyperlink	Opens the Insert Hyperlink dialog box.
	Web Toolbar	Displays or hides the Web toolbar.
	AutoSum	Quickly sums a column or row of numbers.
	Paste Function	Opens a dialog box that helps you build a function.
	Sort Ascending	Sorts a list of items from A to Z.
	Sort Descending	Sorts a list of items from Z to A.
	Chart Wizard	Opens a dialog box that helps you create a chart.
	Map	Opens the Microsoft Map program, enabling you to create a map that helps graphically display your data.
	Drawing	Displays or hides the Drawing toolbar.
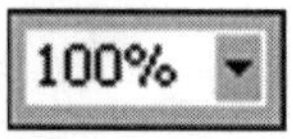	Zoom	Open this drop-down list to choose a magnification at which to view your worksheet.
	Office Assistant	Opens the Office Assistant, which provides program help information.

Table 1.2 Controls on the Formatting Toolbar

Button	Name	Purpose
	Font	Open this drop-down list to choose a font.
	Font Size	Open this drop-down list to choose a font size.
	Bold	Toggles the Bold attribute on/off.
	Italic	Toggles the Italic attribute on/off.
	Underline	Toggles the Underline attribute on/off.
	Align Left	Aligns text to the left side of the cell.
	Center	Centers text in the cell.
	Align Right	Aligns text to the right side of the cell.
	Merge and Center	Combines two or more adjacent cells and centers text in the combined cell.
	Currency Style	Applies currency formatting to the selected number.
	Percent Style	Applies percent formatting to the selected number.
	Comma Style	Applies comma formatting to the selected number.
	Increase Decimal	Moves the decimal place to the left in the selected number.
	Decrease Decimal	Moves the decimal place to the right in the selected number.

continues

Table 1.2—continued

Button	Name	Purpose
	Decrease Indent	If text is indented, moves it toward the left.
	Increase Indent	Indents text (moves it toward the right).
	Borders	Click to apply the selected border, or open the drop-down list to select a different border.
	Fill Color	Click to apply the selected background color, or open the drop-down list to select a different color.
	Font Color	Click to apply the selected font color, or open the drop-down list to select a different color.

Tip

If at any time you need a quick reminder of a button's name, just point the mouse pointer at it, and a ScreenTip box pops up to tell you, as shown in Figure 1.4. You can also get information about a tool with the What's This? feature described later in this chapter.

Figure 1.4 ScreenTips remind you what a button's name is, so you don't have to refer back to Tables 1.1 and 1.2 if you forget a button's purpose.

In Chapter 2, you learn how to display or hide various screen elements, including toolbars. In Chapter 6, you learn to customize the toolbars with different buttons and even create your own toolbars.

Formula Bar

SEE CHAPTER 8 TO LEARN HOW TO ENTER FORMULAS.

The *formula bar* is the bar immediately beneath the toolbars. You may not completely understand it now, but when you get to Chapters 8 and 9 its usefulness will become more apparent.

When you enter text or numbers into a cell, the exact characters you enter are displayed in the cell. However, when you enter a formula into a cell, the result is displayed in the cell. The formula bar is the place where you can see the formula behind the displayed answer. For instance, if I entered **=1+2** into a cell, the cell itself would display the answer, `3`, but the formula bar would display `=1+2`.

Status Bar

The *status bar* is the thin gray bar across the bottom of the Excel window. When Excel is ready to accept new data, it displays `Ready` on the left end, as shown in Figure 1.5. The status bar also displays special messages that help you figure out what's going on. For instance, if you have a circular reference in a cell (an improper reference, such as having `=E6+1` in cell E6), the status bar will report `Circular: E6` (as shown in Figure 1.5). The status bar also tells you the status of certain keys such as Caps Lock (CAPS) and Num Lock (NUM).

Figure 1.5 The status bar provides gentle reminders and information about the status of your workbook.

During certain operations, the status bar displays directions that guide you in using the feature. For instance, when you are using the Format Painter tool, the status bar displays `Use the mouse to apply the copied format to another object`. When you finish the operation, the status bar goes back to displaying `Ready`.

Scroll Bars

Each worksheet consists of up to 256 columns and thousands of rows. Obviously you can't see all the cells on the screen at once! You only see a tiny portion of the available cells at any given time, as shown in Figure 1.6.

Figure 1.6
You can see only a small percentage of the total available cells on a worksheet at once.

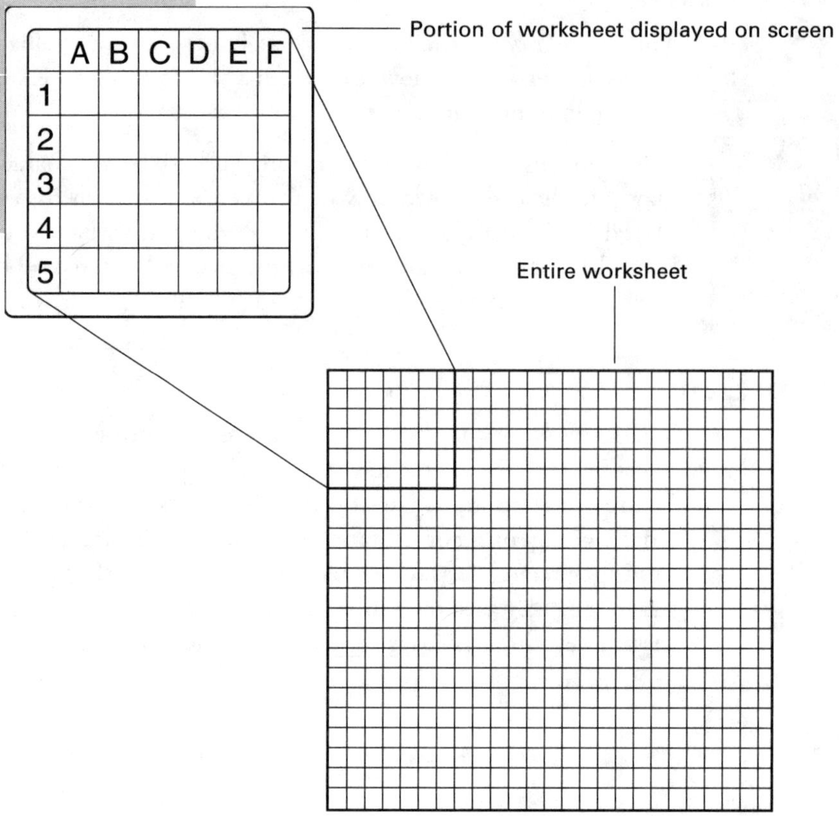

Scroll bars help you move different cells into view. You can think of your computer monitor as a viewport that slides over the top of the big worksheet, showing somewhere between 200 and 800 cells at once (depending on the screen resolution you're using). The scroll bars move the viewport.

CHAPTER 5 DISCUSSES MOVING AROUND WITHIN A WORKSHEET.

There are several ways to use scroll bars, as shown in Figure 1.7. The simplest is to click the arrow buttons at the ends to scroll the display up, down, to the left, or to the right one cell at a time. If you hold down the mouse button while pointing at one of the arrow buttons, the display scrolls quickly.

Another way to use a scroll bar is to drag the gray box (the *scroll box*) with your mouse. This moves through the worksheet more quickly. For instance, to scroll quickly to the top of the worksheet, drag the scroll box on the vertical scroll bar to the top of the scroll bar.

Figure 1.7 Use scroll bars to change which cells are displayed.

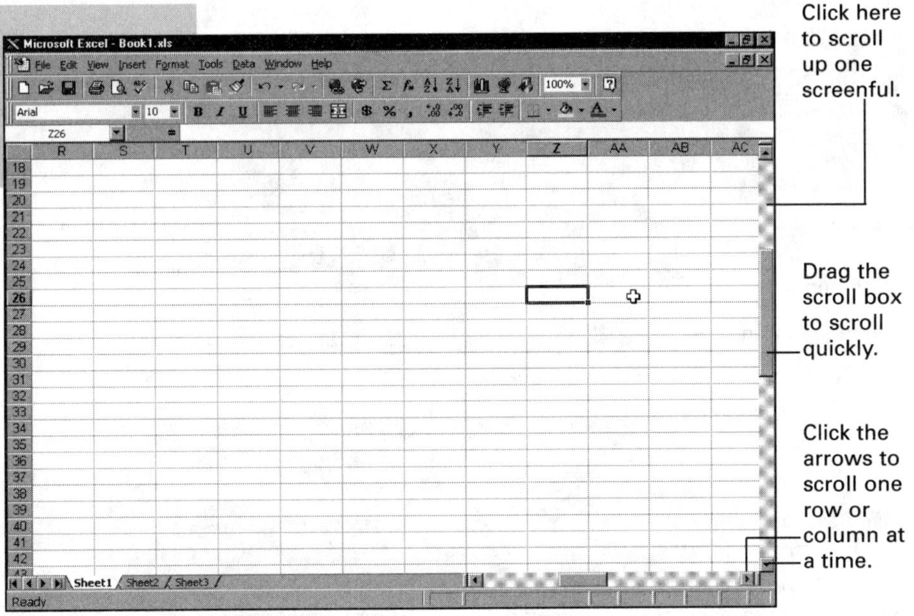

You can also scroll one screenful at a time by clicking on the scroll bar above or below (or to the right or left of) the scroll box. For instance, to move one screenful down, click in the space below the scroll box on the vertical scroll bar.

Using Dialog Boxes

As you learned earlier in this chapter, some menu commands and toolbar buttons open *dialog boxes*. Dialog boxes are simply requests for more information or opportunities for you to change default settings before a command is executed.

Figure 1.8 shows some common dialog box controls you may encounter. They are summarized in the following list:

- **Option buttons.** When you must choose one out of a group of options, these round option buttons appear. Like buttons on a car radio, only one can be selected at a time. When you click on one, the prior selection becomes deselected.
- **Text box.** Just type text into a text box.
- **Collapse Dialog button.** Text boxes in which you're supposed to type cell addresses contain a Collapse Dialog button. Click this button to temporarily minimize the dialog box so that you can select (with the mouse) the cells you want to reference.

Figure 1.8
Here are some of the most common dialog box controls you will need in Excel.

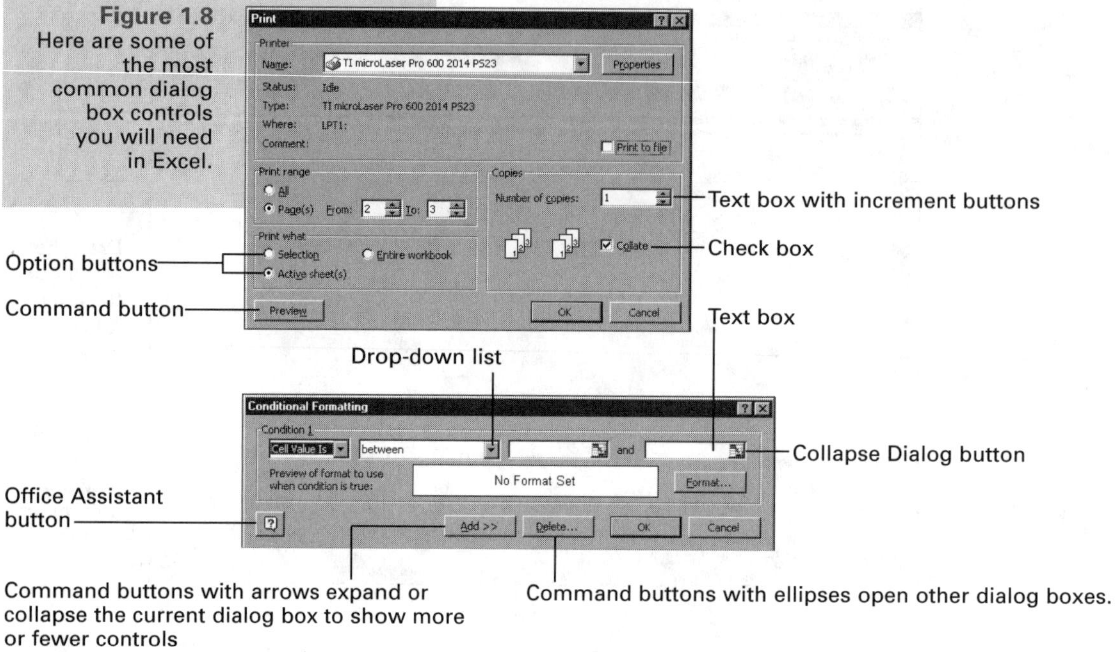

- **Increment buttons.** Text boxes in which you're supposed to enter a number often have increment buttons. Click the up arrow to increase the number by one (from 1 to 2, for instance); click the down arrow button to decrease the number by one.
- **Check box.** Check boxes are on/off switches for certain features. Click the box to place or remove the check mark.
- **Command buttons.** Command buttons take you somewhere else. Some buttons, such as the Preview button, take you to an entirely different screen and close the dialog box. Command buttons with ellipses (…) open other dialog boxes. Command buttons with >>> on them open additional sections of the same dialog box.
- **OK and Cancel.** Almost all dialog boxes have these two buttons. OK accepts your changes and closes the dialog box; Cancel rejects your changes and closes the dialog box.
- **Office Assistant button.** For certain tricky procedures, this button is available. Click on it to make the Office Assistant appear, described in the following section.

Using the Help System

Because every person is different, Excel offers many ways to get help with the program. Some of these Help methods will be familiar to experienced Windows users; others are brand-new for the Office 97 products. You can do the following:

- Ask the Office Assistant for help.
- Choose what you're interested in learning about from a series of Help Topics.
- Get help on a particular element you see on-screen with the What's This? tool.
- If you are connected to the Internet, access the Microsoft On the Web feature to view Web pages containing Help information.

The Office Assistant

The Office Assistant is that little paper clip character that popped up the first time you started Excel. It may look silly, but behind it is a powerful Help system.

Note

The Office Assistant has replaced the Answer Wizard feature from Excel for Windows 95.

By default, the Office Assistant starts whenever you start Excel and sits in a little box on top of whatever you're working on, as shown in Figure 1.9. You can turn it off by clicking the Close (X) button in its top right corner.

To turn the Office Assistant on again, click the Office Assistant button in the Standard toolbar or choose Help, Microsoft Excel Help.

If you don't like the paper clip, choose one of the other Office Assistants. Right-click on the Office Assistant and choose Choose Assistant from the shortcut menu. Then click the Back and Next buttons to find an assistant that you prefer; click OK to change the character. If you get a message telling you that the file cannot be located, put your installation CD in your drive and try again.

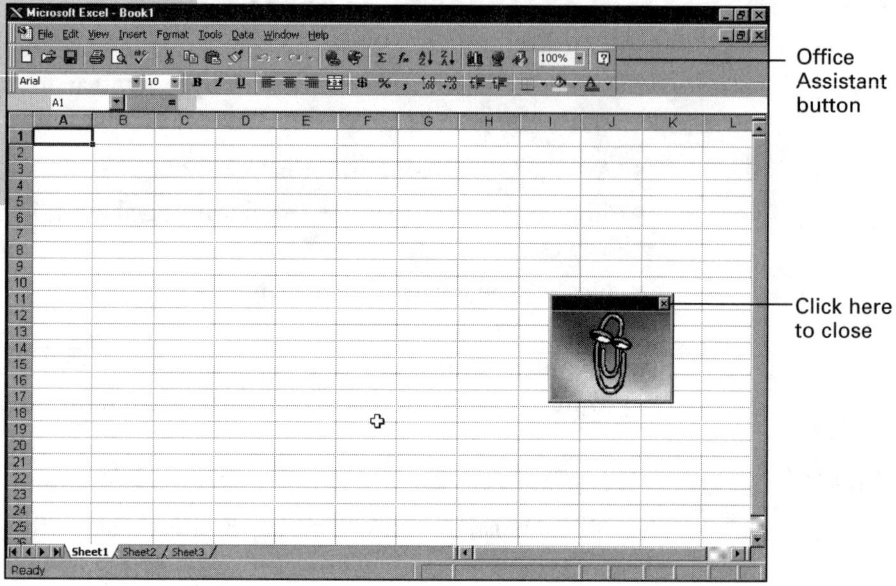

Figure 1.9 The Office Assistant appears in its own window on top of the Excel window.

When you turn on the Office Assistant, or when you click on it if it's already open, a bubble appears next to (or above) its box asking you what kind of help you want (see Figure 1.10). You can do any of the following:

- Type a question in the text box to tell the Office Assistant what kind of help you need.
- Select one of the Office Assistant's "guesses" about what you need help with, if any appear.
- Type what you want help on and click the Search button.
- Click the Tips button to get any tips that the Office Assistant can provide for the task you're performing.
- Click the Options button to customize the way the Office Assistant works.
- Right-click in the Office Assistant window to select options from a shortcut menu.
- Click Close (the word "Close," not the X button) to close the bubble (but leave the Office Assistant on-screen).

If you close the help bubble, you can reopen it at any time by clicking the Office Assistant button on the Standard toolbar; pressing F1; choosing Help, Microsoft Excel Help; or clicking on the Office Assistant window.

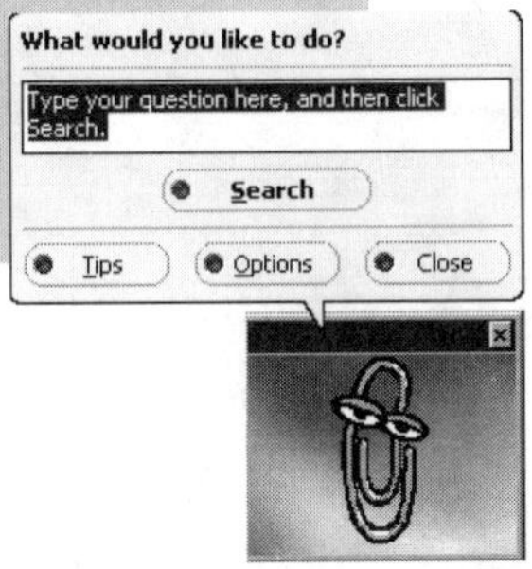

Figure 1.10
Office Assistant asks what you need help with.

Tip

If a light bulb appears next to the Office Assistant, it means that the Office Assistant has a suggestion for you. To get the suggestion, click the light bulb. Click the Close button when you're finished reading the suggestion.

Hands On: Asking the Office Assistant a Question

If you need help on a particular topic, simply type a question into the text box shown in Figure 1.10. Follow these steps:

1. If the Office Assistant's help bubble isn't on-screen, click the Office Assistant button on the Standard toolbar or click the Office Assistant window.
2. Type a question into the text box. For instance, you might type **How do I save?** to get help saving your work.
3. Click the Search button or press the Enter key. The Office Assistant provides some topics that might match what you're looking for. For instance, Figure 1.11 shows the Office Assistant's responses to the question "How do I save?"
4. Click the option that best describes what you're trying to do. For instance, I'm going to choose Save a Workbook from Figure 1.11. A Help window appears with instructions for the specified task. If none of the options describe what you want, click the See More arrow to view more options, or type in a different question in the text box.

The Help window that appears containing the task instructions is part of the same Help system that you can access with the Help, Contents and Index command. See "Working with Help Information" later in this chapter for information about navigating this window.

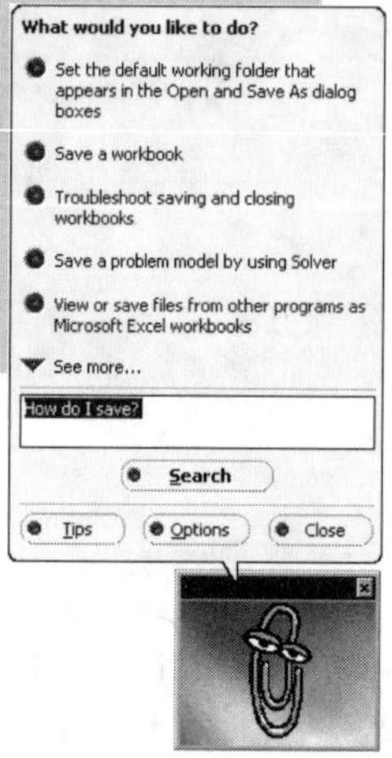

Figure 1.11 The Office Assistant attempts to narrow down exactly what you are trying to accomplish.

Help Topics

If you want a more conventional way to get help, try choosing the Contents and Index command on the Help menu. When you open the Excel Help system in this way, you move through the topics listed to find the topic you're interested in.

Several tabs are in the Help system, so you can use Help the way you want it. Click on a tab to display its options.

- **Contents.** This tab lets you browse the Help system as you would a reference book.
- **Index.** Use this tab to look up Help topics alphabetically.
- **Find.** Search for a certain word among all the topics in the system.

Complete the steps in the following sections to use the Contents, Index, or Find methods of getting help.

Contents

The Contents tab of the Help system is a series of "books" you can open. Each book has one or more Help topics in it. Some books contain other subbooks! It's like pulling a real book off the shelf and browsing through it for the topic you're interested in. Figure 1.12 shows a Contents screen.

Figure 1.12 The Help Contents screen presents books containing help topics and/or other books.

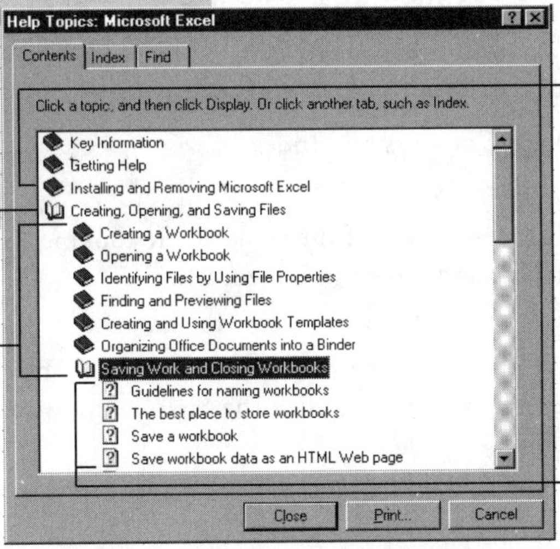

Hands On: Browsing the Help Contents

To select a help topic from the Contents screen, follow these steps:

1. Choose Help, Contents and Index.
2. Click the Contents tab.
3. Find the book that describes, in broad terms, what you want help with and double-click on it. A list of help topics appears below the book, as shown in Figure 1.12.
4. Double-click a help topic to display it.
5. When you finish reading a topic, click the Help Topics button to go back to the main Help screen; or click the Help window's Close button (X) to exit from Help.

Index

The Index is an alphabetical listing of all the Help topics available. It works well if you know the exact term you want to look up, like Saving or Printing, for instance. Use it as you would use the index in a real book (like this one!).

Hands On: Looking Up a Topic in the Help Index

To use the index, perform the following steps:

1. Choose Help, Contents and Index.
2. Click the Index tab.
3. Type the first few letters of the topic you're looking for. The index list jumps quickly to that spot (see Figure 1.13).
4. Double-click on the topic you want to see.
5. When you finish reading a topic, click the Help Topics button to go back to the main Help screen; or click the Help window's Close button (X) to exit from Help.

Figure 1.13 The Index tab enables you to browse alphabetically instead of by category.

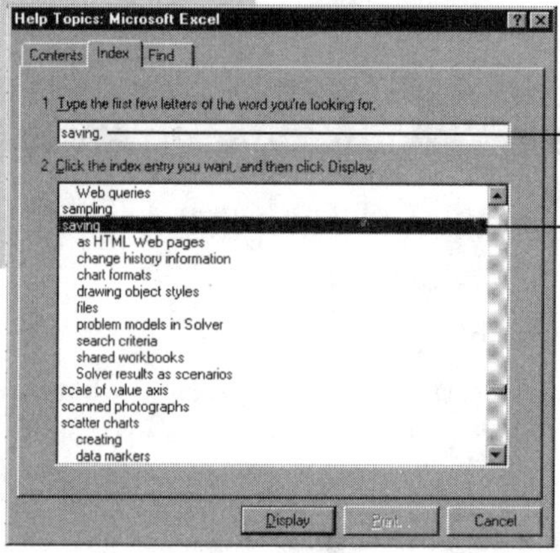

Find

What if you're not sure of the name of the feature you're looking for? Find works best in situations like that. Find searches not only the titles of Help topics, but also their contents, and retrieves all the topics in which the word(s) you typed appears.

Hands On: Finding a Help Topic in the Help System

To use Find, follow these steps:

1. Choose Help, Contents and Index.

2. Click the Find tab. The first time you use Find, it asks you to build the Find index. Click Next and then click Finish to create the list.
3. Type the topic you're looking for in the top box (1).
4. If more than one line appears in the middle box (2), click on the one that most closely matches your interest. Find considers uppercase and lowercase versions of a word to be different, so, for instance, in Figure 1.14 there are separate entries for "Save" and "save," as well as for other forms of the word ("saves" and "saved").
5. Browse the topics that appear at the bottom (3), and click on the one that matches the help you need (see Figure 1.14).
6. Click the Display button or press Enter to display the Help information.
7. When you finish reading a topic, click the Help Topics button to go back to the main Help screen; or click the Help window's Close button (X) to exit from Help.

Figure 1.14 Use Find to locate all the help topics that deal with a certain subject.

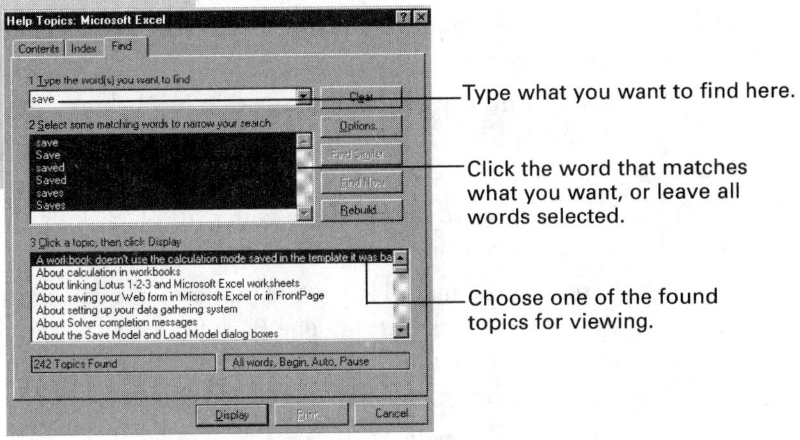

Working with Help Information

After you've located the Help topic you need—then what? Read it, of course. All the methods of getting Help described so far end up at the same place—only the journey is different. For instance, you could locate the "Save a workbook" information by any of the four methods I've told you about so far and get the same exact information, shown in Figure 1.15.

Figure 1.15 After you arrive at the information you need, you can read it on-screen, print it, or move to another Help topic.

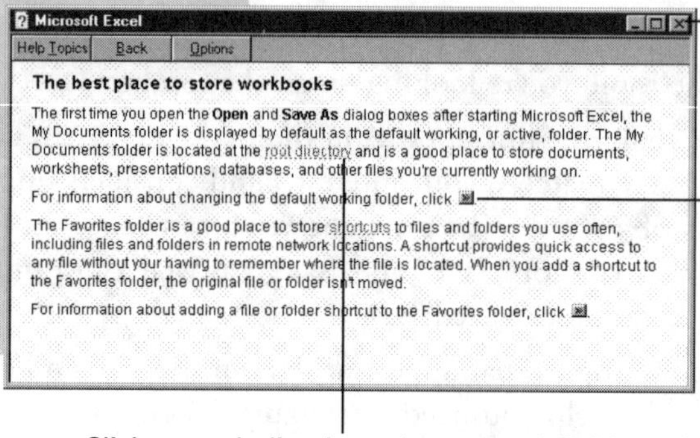

After you have a Help topic on-screen, here's what you can do with it:

- Click an underlined word to see a definition of it (for instance "root directory" in Figure 1.15).
- Click a button to jump to another Help screen. For instance, in Figure 1.15, two >> buttons are available to take you to screens of related information.
- Print a hard copy of the information by clicking the Options button and then choosing Print Topic.
- Copy the text to the Clipboard (for pasting into a program such as Microsoft Word or Windows Notepad) by clicking the Options button and then choosing Copy.
- Return to the main Help topic that brought you to this subtopic by clicking the Back button. The Back button is not available if you are viewing a topic that you arrived at directly from the Office Assistant, Contents, Index, or Find.
- Return to the main Help Topics screen by clicking the Help Topics button.
- Close the Help window by clicking the Close (X) button.

What's This? Help

Sometimes all the words and topics in the world can't help you—for instance, if you see something on the screen but you have no idea what it is. How do you look up a toolbar button when all you know is that it looks like a bunch of squiggly lines with a pencil? Or a globe with a piece of chain on it?

Hands On: Finding Out What an On-screen Element Does

The answer is the What's This? feature. You can point to an object on the screen and Excel will tell you what that object's purpose is. Here's how it works:

1. Press Shift+F1 or choose Help, What's This? Your mouse pointer turns into a big arrow with a question mark next to it.
2. Click on the object you want to know about. A box of information pops up telling you about it. For instance, Figure 1.16 shows the information I got when I clicked on a column heading.

Figure 1.16 What's This? Help spares you the trouble of figuring out the name of an on-screen element. Just press Shift+F1 and then click on the object.

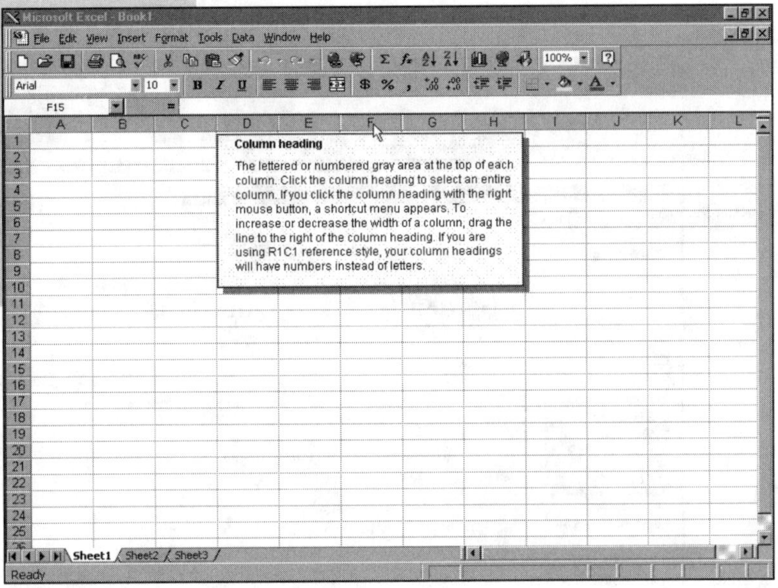

Tip

What's This? works well for screen elements in Excel, but it also works for individual rows, columns, and cells, as well as controls in dialog boxes. Try it any time and see what information you get!

Microsoft On the Web Help

All Microsoft Office 97 applications, including Excel, are tightly connected to the Internet. You get a closer look at the Internet features that Excel provides in Chapter 21, but here's an Internet feature you can take advantage of right away: Microsoft On the Web Help.

Simply put, Microsoft has made additional Help resources for Excel available at its Web site on the Internet. To access it, just choose Help, Microsoft on the Web, and the document you want to see. (You may have to dial up your Internet provider's computer first, unless you are already connected or you access the Internet through a LAN.) Your Web browser opens, and the document appears. Figure 1.17 shows the result of selecting the Frequently Asked Questions document.

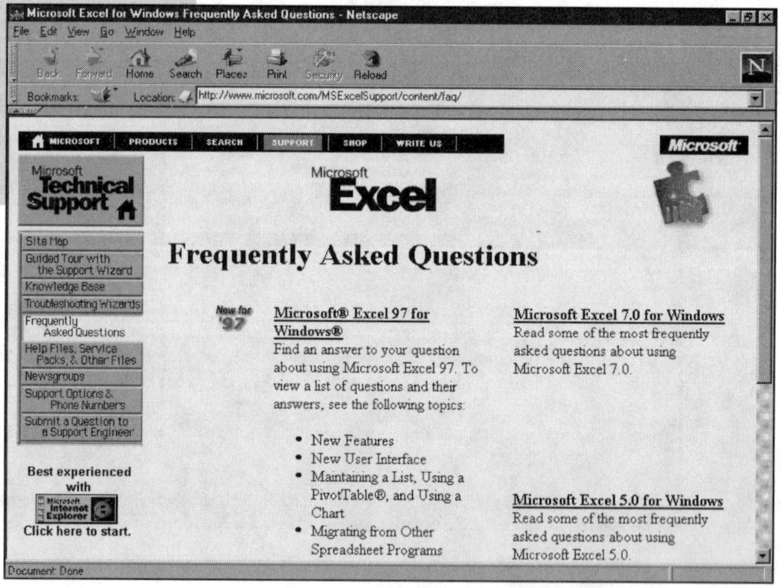

Figure 1.17 One of the many Help documents for Excel available at the Microsoft Web site.

Note

When you access the Web page, it may look different from what you see in Figure 1.17. That's because these pages are updated periodically with new information. That's the beauty of Internet-provided help—it is never out-of-date.

Exiting Excel

When you are finished working in Excel, you should close the program to free up system resources for other programs. You can exit Excel in any of these ways:

- Click the program's Close (X) button (in the title bar).
- Choose File, Exit from the menu bar.
- Press Alt+F4.
- Double-click the program's control icon (the icon at the left end of the title bar).

All these methods work equally well. If you have made any changes to a workbook, you'll be asked whether you want to save your changes. Click No. (Of course, if you really have made changes you want to save, click Yes and refer to Chapter 3 for more information about saving.)

2

Setting Up Excel to Work Best for You

In This Chapter

- Zooming In for a Different View
- Different Ways to View Your Workbook
- Working with Multiple Workbook Windows
- Splitting the Display into Two or More Panes
- Displaying or Hiding Screen Elements

This chapter is all about changing the way the Excel window looks on-screen. Most books about Excel save these topics for last or hide them away in the back of a chapter because they don't directly involve entering data. But in my opinion, that's a mistake. Why should someone learn the hard way of working first, before being let in on the secret easy way? There's no reason not to take control of Excel's interface right from the start.

Changing the View

Excel's default view works great for most people in most situations, but there may be times when it just won't do. In the following sections, you learn a bit about each of your viewing options and make some decisions about how you want those options to be set.

Zooming the View In and Out

Having trouble reading the fine print in your worksheet cells? Or wanting to see more rows and columns on the screen at once? In either case, you'll want to change the *zoom*. You can view the worksheet window at various magnifications on-screen, without changing the size of the surrounding tools or the size of the print on the printout.

If you haven't entered anything into a cell yet, you may not be able to gauge the appropriate zoom level for best viewing. To help with this, go ahead and enter some text now—just type a few letters and press Enter. The typed letters appear in the active cell on-screen. Data entry is discussed in more detail in Chapter 7.

Zoom is measured in percentages, from 10% to 400%. 100% is considered "normal" zoom, and adjustments you make are above or below that. For instance, zooming out to 50% makes the workbook cells one-half normal size, so you can see twice as many rows and columns on-screen at once. Zooming in to 200% makes the workbook cells twice normal size—you can see only half as many rows and columns, but they appear twice as large.

What Does Zoom Do?

In the Excel classes I teach, a common misconception that beginners have is that adjusting the zoom changes the size of the type on their printout. It doesn't. Zooming affects only the on-screen display and only the worksheet window. It's like holding a magnifying glass up to your monitor.

If you want to make the type larger or smaller on the printout, you must change the font size, a skill that is covered in Chapter 11.

If you have less-than-perfect eyesight, you may find yourself squinting to read the text and numbers in each cell. Zooming "in," which means increasing the zoom, will make each cell larger so that you can get a better look at it. Figure 2.1 shows a 200% zoom.

Figure 2.1
Zooming in makes for a close-up view.

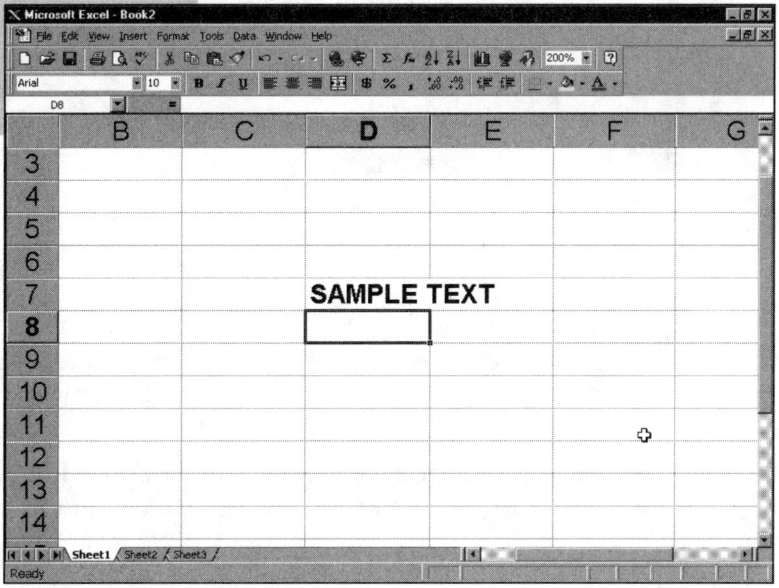

Zooming "out" goes the other way—it decreases the zoom, making everything on the screen smaller. The main advantage of zooming out is to fit more rows and columns on the screen at once. For instance, if I'm working with a long list of names, and I normally can see 25 rows on the screen at once, zooming out might let me see 35 or more rows at once. Figure 2.2 shows a 75% zoom.

Here's a simple way to remember which is "out" and which is "in"—think of how the view changes when you step toward or away from the monitor. When you step "out" (away), everything looks smaller; when you step "in" (toward the monitor), everything looks larger.

Figure 2.2 Zooming out gives you a birds-eye view in which you can see more of the worksheet.

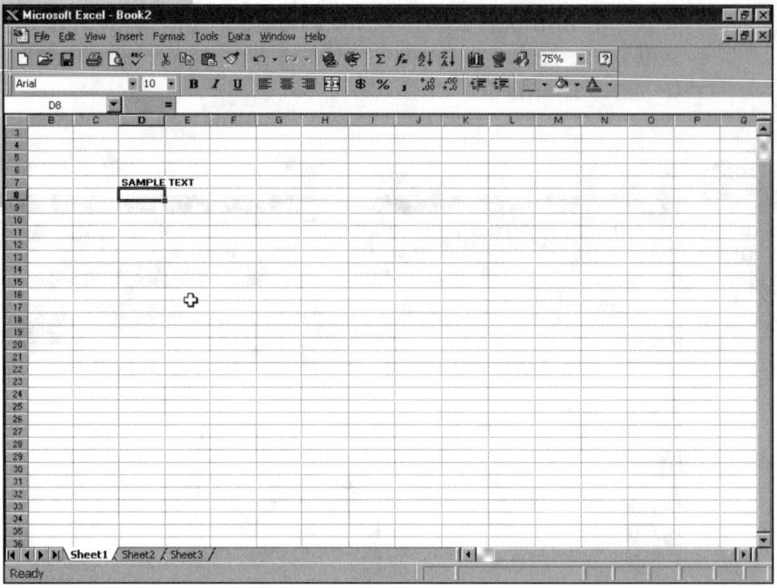

The easiest way to change the zoom is with the Zoom drop-down list on the Standard toolbar (see Figure 2.3). To change the zoom, just do this:

1. Click on the drop-down arrow next to the Zoom text box.
2. Select a different zoom level from the list.

You can also type a precise zoom number in the Zoom text box; for instance, I like to use 85% zoom, but 85% is not on the list, so I do the following:

1. Click on the current number in the Zoom text box. It becomes highlighted.
2. Type a new number.
3. Press Enter.

Figure 2.3 Use the Zoom drop-down list to change the zoom.

Besides the percentages on the Zoom drop-down list, you'll also find an option called Selection. This is a handy method of zooming in to show only the cells you're interested in, in as large a size as possible. The best way to understand Selection is to try it out. The following Hands On practice session involves selecting some cells, which you won't "officially" learn to do until Chapter 5, but if you follow the directions carefully, you should have no problem.

Hands On: Zooming to a Selection

To change the zoom to see only a particular range of cells, follow these steps:

1. Click on the top-left cell in the worksheet (the cell at the intersection of column A and row 1).
2. Hold down the Shift key.
3. Click on the cell at the intersection of column E and row 11. The block of cells between those two becomes highlighted (black).
4. Open the Zoom drop-down list on the Standard toolbar and choose Selection. The Zoom changes so that the selected cells are as large as they can possibly be while still fitting on the screen, as shown in Figure 2.4.
5. To return to 100% zoom, open the Zoom drop-down list again and choose 100%.

Figure 2.4 Zooming to a selection centers the selection and zooms it to fill the workbook window.

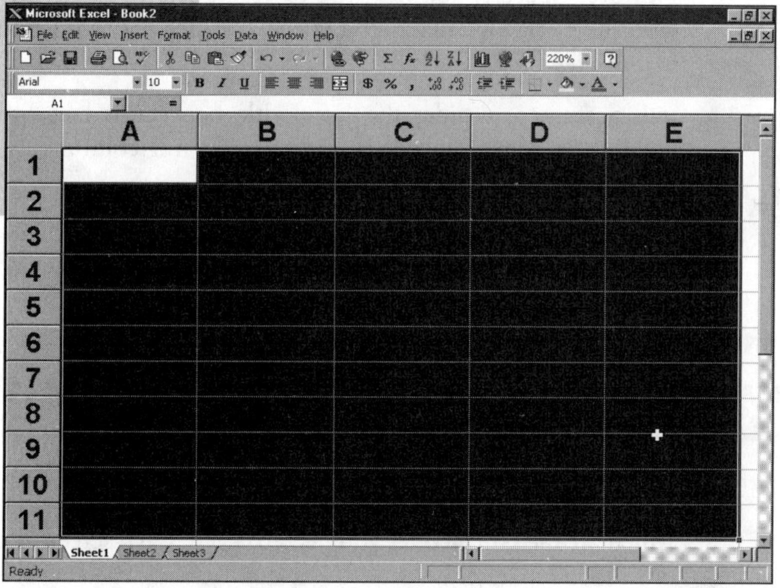

You can also change the zoom with a menu command: View, Zoom. When you choose this command, the Zoom dialog box shown in Figure 2.5 appears. Just make your selection by clicking on the appropriate button and then click OK.

The Zoom dialog box has a couple of things to notice:

- The Fit Selection option is the same as the Selection option on the Standard toolbar's drop-down list.
- There is a Custom setting, in which you can type a precise zoom percentage. This is the same as typing a percentage directly into the Zoom text box on the Standard toolbar.

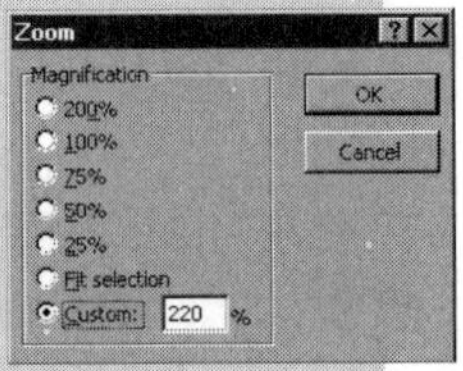

Figure 2.5 You can zoom with the Zoom dialog box rather than the Zoom drop-down list on the toolbar if you prefer.

Full Screen View

If you are trying to see as much of your worksheet on the screen at once, you are probably fairly satisfied after reading about zooming in the preceding section. However, there is another way to create more "real estate" on-screen for your worksheet without making anything smaller and harder to read. It's called Full Screen view.

Full Screen view hides the Excel title bar, status bar, and toolbars, making it possible to squeeze a couple more rows and columns on-screen, as shown in Figure 2.6.

To enter Full Screen view, choose View, Full Screen. To get back to normal viewing, click the Close Full Screen button that floats on top of the worksheet, or reopen the View menu and choose Full Screen again.

Displaying and Hiding Screen Elements

In the preceding section, you saw how you could temporarily hide some of the "nonessential" screen elements to make more room for your worksheet on-screen. But you're not limited to Excel's idea of which are the "essential" elements and which are the crucial ones you need to keep. Each screen element can be displayed or hidden separately.

Figure 2.6 In Full Screen view, certain screen elements are hidden to make more space for the worksheet.

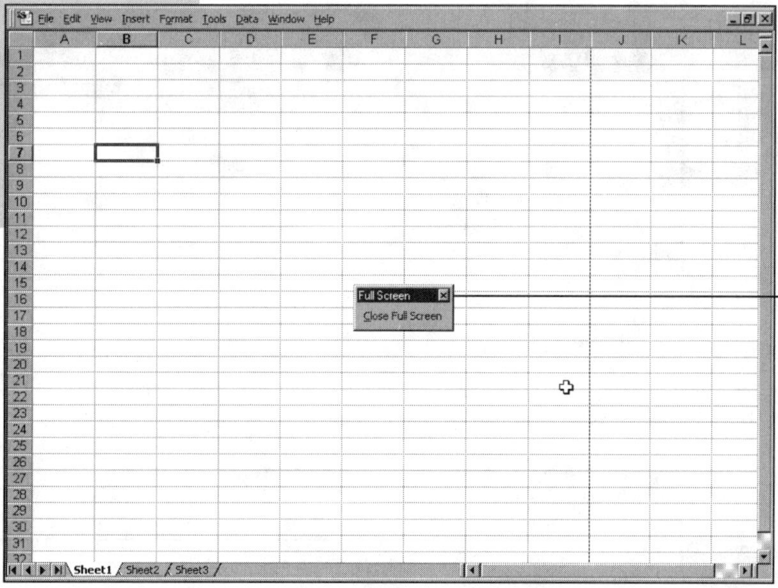

Formula Bar and Status Bar

The *formula bar* and *status bar* are considered by many to be nonessential screen elements. As you learned in Chapter 1, the formula bar tells you what formula is entered into the selected cell. If there's no formula (but merely some text or numbers), the formula bar simply repeats what's already displayed in the cell; so in the case of most cells, the formula bar doesn't offer any useful information.

The status bar similarly has limited usefulness. It tells you whether you have formula errors, but unless you are currently entering formulas, you already know that. It also tells you whether the Caps Lock and Num Lock keys are on, but that is not essential information.

To turn off one of these elements, open the View menu and choose either Formula Bar or Status Bar to remove the check mark next to one of them. Figure 2.7 shows how the screen looks without these elements displayed; on my monitor, I gained an extra two rows by turning them off.

DRAWING IS COVERED IN CHAPTER 16.

Toolbars

Excel comes with many toolbars, and you can create your own toolbars, too, as you learn in Chapter 6. By default, as you learned in Chapter 1, the Standard and Formatting toolbars appear on-screen. These can be turned on and off easily, and you can turn on/off some of the other toolbars too. For instance, if you frequently draw on your worksheets, you may want to have the Drawing toolbar turned on.

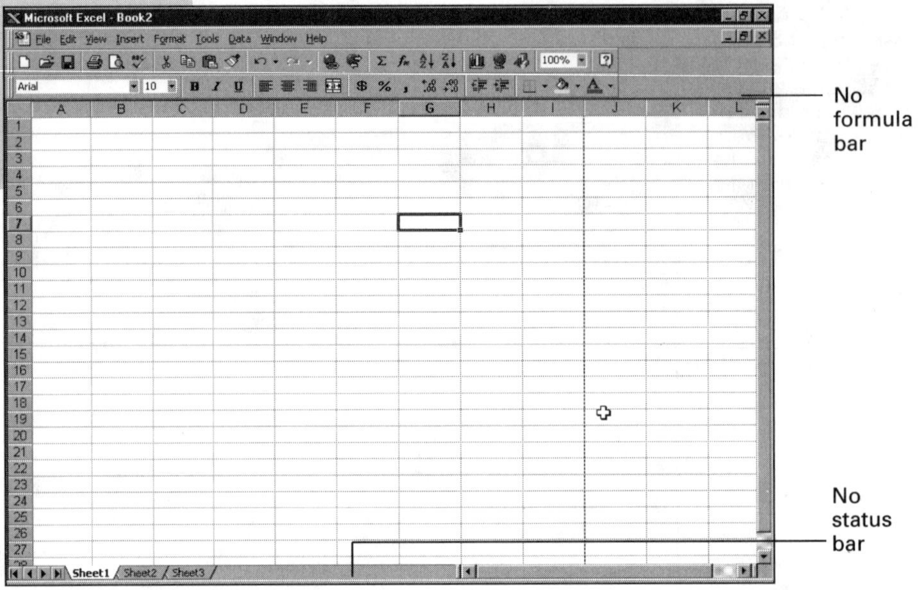

Figure 2.7 Many users will never miss the formula bar and status bar on their display.

> IN CHAPTER 6, YOU LEARN HOW TO CUSTOMIZE THE TOOLS ON EACH TOOLBAR.

To turn a toolbar off or on, choose View, Toolbars. A submenu appears, listing each of the available toolbars, as shown in Figure 2.8. Just click on the one you want to select or deselect it. You can also get this same list of toolbars by right-clicking on any toolbar; this is nice because it eliminates the step of opening the View menu.

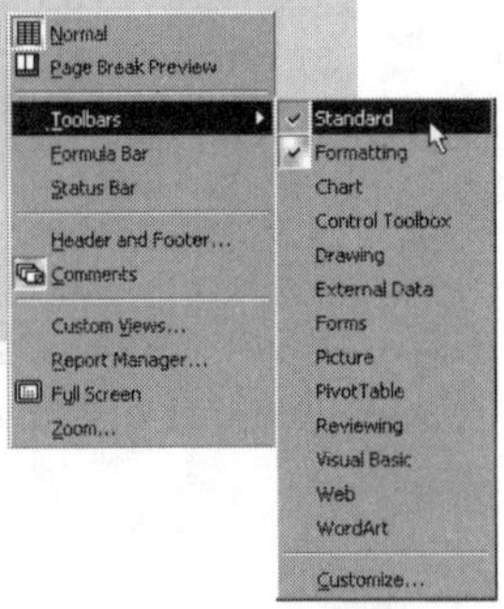

Figure 2.8 Turn any of Excel's toolbars on or off by selecting it from the list.

Other Screen Elements

Besides the formula bar, toolbars, and status bar, you can control many other on-screen elements. You select them from the Options dialog box shown in Figure 2.9; to open it, choose Tools, Options and click the View tab.

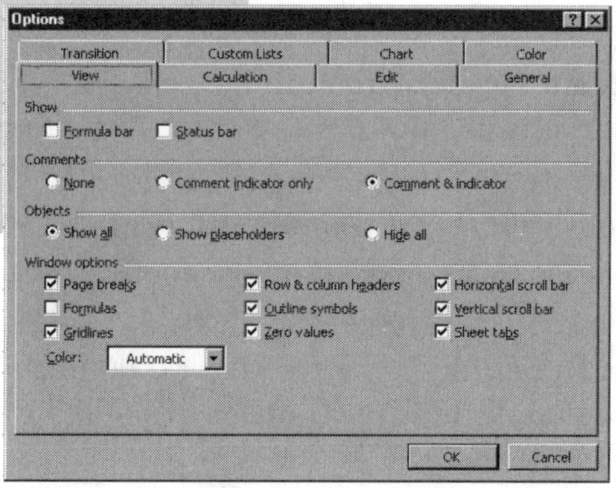

Figure 2.9 Set more display options from the View tab of the Options dialog box.

Here's a quick look at some of the options at your disposal on the View tab of the Options dialog box:

- **Formula Bar and Status Bar.** These check boxes are the same as the commands on the View menu that you learned about earlier in this chapter.
- **Comments.** In Chapter 7, you learn how to attach comments to cells. Here, you can choose to show or hide comments and/or their indicator.
- **Objects.** Here, "objects" refers to things that don't fit neatly into a single cell, like a drawing or a chart. You can choose to hide these or to show placeholders for them.
- **Page Breaks.** In Chapter 13, you learn how to insert page breaks. (These take effect only when you print.) You can choose whether to show the breaks on-screen here.
- **Formulas.** As I told you in Chapter 1 in the "Formula Bar" discussion, by default Excel shows the result of a formula in the cell, not the formula itself. Mark this check box to show the actual formula in the cell. This is good for troubleshooting.
- **Gridlines.** Gridlines are the thin gray lines that separate each row and column. You can hide these on-screen by deselecting this check box.

Note

When you print, gridlines show, even if you have their display turned off on-screen. If you don't want to show gridlines when you print, choose File, Page Setup, click the Sheet tab, deselect the Gridlines check box, and click OK.

- **Color.** This drop-down list controls the gridline color. You can open the list and select any color you want for them.
- **Row & Column Headers.** You can turn off the A, B, C across the columns and the 1, 2, 3 down the rows by deselecting this check box.
- **Outline Symbols.** This one is kind of obscure. You can't create the same sort of outline in Excel that you can in a word processor, but if you import an outline that you've created in another program (like Word), the outline symbols will show if this check box is marked.
- **Zero Values.** By default, if you type **0** (or **0.00** or any variation of that) in a cell, it shows up. To hide the contents of any cell whose value is 0, deselect this check box.
- **Horizontal Scroll Bar and Vertical Scroll Bar.** You can hide the scroll bars by turning off their respective check boxes.
- **Sheet Tabs.** This check box turns on/off the worksheet tabs at the bottom of the workbook that enable you to move quickly from worksheet to worksheet.

As with most other screen elements, turning off things like the sheet tabs and the scroll bars may buy you an extra line or two of worksheet cells on the screen. However, you should weigh carefully the cost of not having those features available for your use against that extra worksheet space.

Custom Views

After you get the view exactly the way that you want it, Excel lets you save your settings as a *custom view.* This is a great time-saver! For example, suppose that you have two people sharing the same computer. Each person has his own idea of what the ideal Excel display settings should be. So each person creates his own custom view and applies it whenever he sits down to work at the computer. When the next person comes along, he applies his settings and presto, Excel is set up exactly the way he wants it.

Even a single person can benefit from a custom view. Suppose that you have different display settings you like to use for certain workbooks; a custom view can preserve those special settings and apply them in one step.

Hands On: Creating a Custom View

To set up a custom view, follow these steps:

1. Set all your display settings exactly the way you want them, as you've learned to do so far in this chapter.
2. Choose View, Custom Views. The Custom Views dialog box opens (see Figure 2.10).

Figure 2.10 Set up and apply custom views from the Custom Views dialog box.

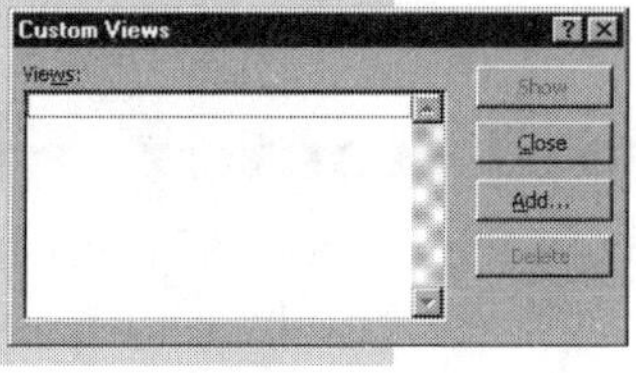

3. Click the Add button. The Add View dialog box opens.
4. Type a name for the view. If you're creating the view to distinguish your settings from someone else's, use your name; otherwise, use a descriptive name for the purpose of the view (such as "For Large Worksheets" or "Everything Hidden").
5. Leave the two check boxes marked unless you know that you don't want their information included in the view settings:
   - **Print Settings.** Includes any print options you've set, such as the default printer, in your custom view.
   - **Hidden Rows, Columns, and Filter Settings.** Includes those elements in the custom view.
6. Click OK to return to the Custom Views dialog box.
7. Click OK to save your settings.

Because all the settings for the custom view were already in effect when you created it, there is nothing more that you need to do now; your view is already in effect. However, if you later change any of the view settings, you can return to your custom view's settings by applying the custom view.

Follow these steps to apply a custom view:

1. Choose View, Custom Views to open the Custom Views dialog box.
2. Click the view you want to apply.
3. Click the Show button.

All the settings from that custom view are immediately put into effect.

Controlling Windows

If you are a long-time Windows user, you can safely skip this section; it's all about controlling the windows of Windows 95. I've included it here because without a basic knowledge of how to control a window, your Excel productivity can be severely hampered, especially when you begin working with more than one workbook at a time.

Minimizing, Maximizing, and Restoring

Before we can talk about how Excel uses windows, you must understand a few basic terms: *minimize*, *maximize*, and *restore*. These are standard Windows operations, but if you aren't sure what they mean, refresh your memory here:

A *minimized* window is reduced to an icon or a small rectangle. You minimize a window by clicking its Minimize button.

A *maximized* window fills the entire screen (or the entire space of the window in which it resides, if it's a window-in-a-window). You maximize a window by clicking its Maximize button.

If a window is already maximized, you *restore* it to the size and shape that it was before being maximized by clicking the Restore button.

Understanding Excel's Window Structure

Excel, like most Windows applications, uses windows-within-windows. The outer window is Excel itself. The inner windows are any workbooks you have open. For example, in Figure 2.11, the Excel application window is maximized; it fills my entire computer monitor. Within it, I have two workbook windows open: Book3 and excelbk.xls. The excelbk.xls window is minimized, and the Book3 window is restored (that is, not maximized). Contrast this to the maximized workbook window in Figure 2.12. Notice that when a workbook window is maximized, it shares a title bar with the Excel application window; when it's restored, it has its own title bar. Notice also in Figure 2.12 that when a workbook window is maximized within the Excel window, its window control buttons (Minimize, Restore, and Close) appear directly below those for the Excel window itself rather than in the title bar.

When a workbook window is minimized, it sits as a rectangular icon on the Excel window's *desktop*—the gray area behind the workbooks. To reopen a minimized workbook, you just double-click on it. If another window is obscuring it, press Ctrl+Tab to cycle through until it appears.

Figure 2.11 This Excel window has two open workbooks: one minimized and one restored.

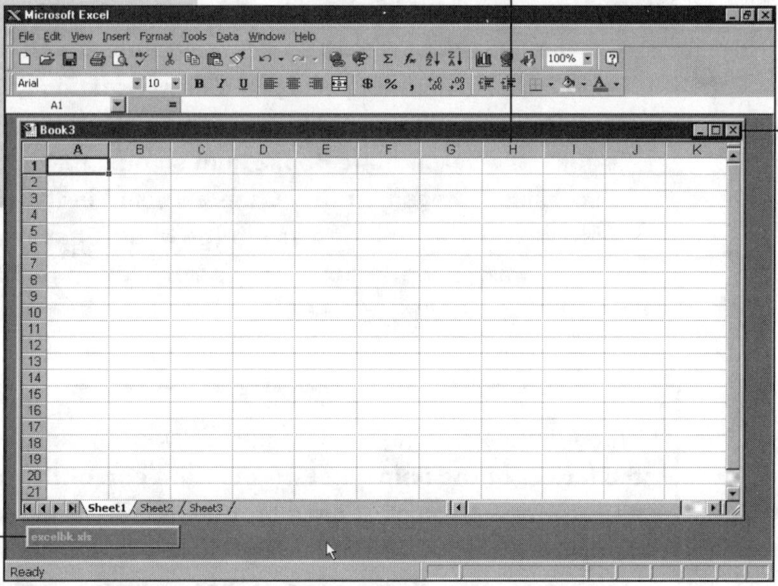

Figure 2.12 This Excel window has a maximized workbook.

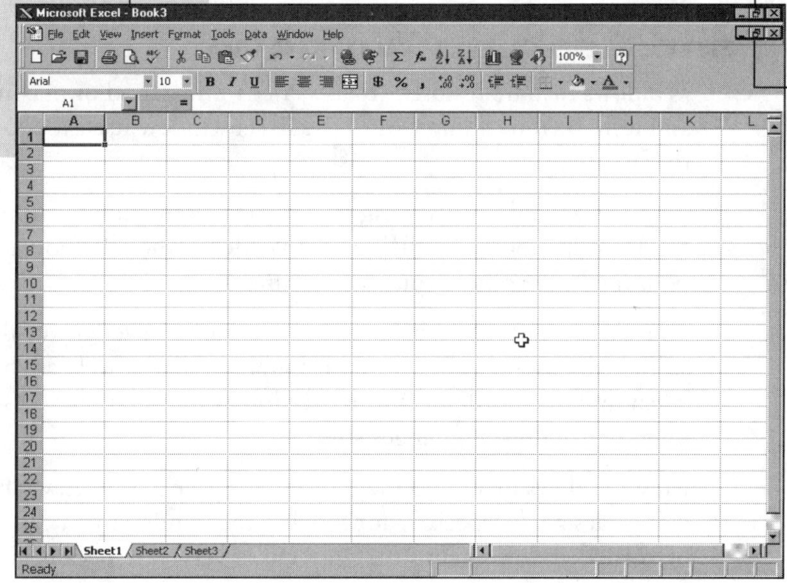

Note

If you've been following along carefully since Chapter 1, you may have noticed that the numbers in the workbook names have been creeping up. First it was Book1, then Book2, and now Book3. That's because when you open a new workbook, Excel assigns it a default name. The first one you open after you start the program is Book1, the second one Book2, and so on. I haven't exited from Excel since I began writing Chapter 1, and in the course of planning what I was going to say in the book, I have opened and closed several workbooks. That's why I'm up to Book3 now!

Caution

When double-clicking on a minimized workbook to open it, click on the letters of the name, not on the right end of the rectangle. That's because when you click once on the minimized workbook, window control buttons appear at the right end of the rectangle, and you may accidentally click on one of those controls that you don't want (like the Close button) if you click on the right end.

Moving and Resizing Windows

Windows that are restored (that is, aren't minimized or maximized) can be moved and resized. You can do this to the Excel window itself too, or to any window, for that matter.

To move a window, just drag its title bar. (Remember, I told you how to drag in the Introduction? Just click and hold down the left mouse button while you're pointing at the object you want to drag.)

To resize a window, position the mouse pointer over any of the window's borders, so that the pointer changes to a double-headed arrow, as shown in Figure 2.13. Then drag the border until the window is the size that you want it to be. As you drag the window, it changes size.

Most windows in Windows 95 programs have a little gray tab in the bottom right corner designed especially for resizing the window; you can drag any of the sides or corners, but dragging the gray tab is very easy because it is large and easy to position the mouse pointer over, and because it resizes both sides at once.

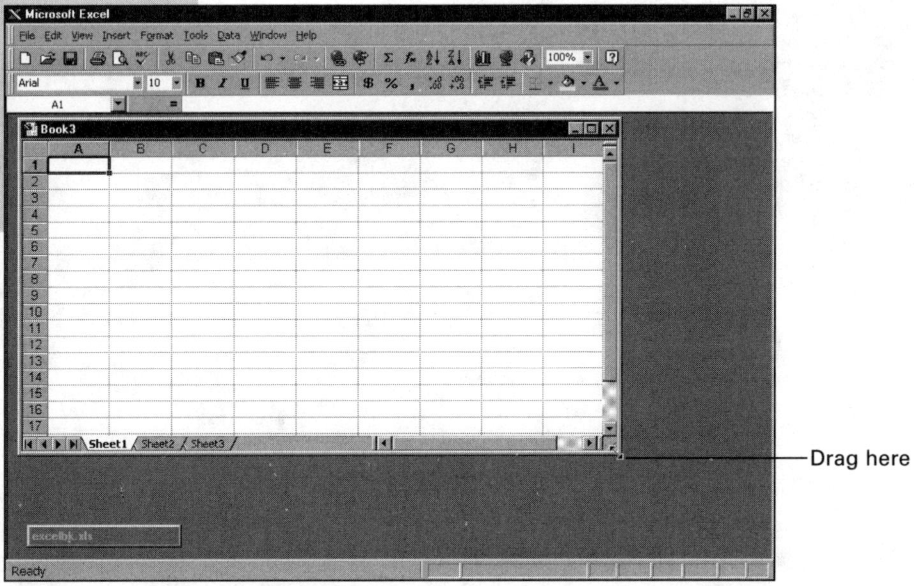

Figure 2.13 To resize a window, drag the gray tab in the bottom right corner, or any side or corner of the window.

Splitting the Display Window

Have you ever wished that you could be in two places at once? Well, in Excel, you actually can. Excel provides a way to view two different spots in a worksheet at the same time by splitting the worksheet window into two panes. Each pane has its own scroll bars so that you can move around in it independently. For example, in Figure 2.14, notice that the top pane shows rows 1 through 11, and the bottom pane shows rows 41 through 54. This is useful if you need to refer to one part of a worksheet while entering or checking data in another part. For instance, perhaps you need to copy ZIP codes from entries at the top of the worksheet to entries at the bottom; with both the "from" and "to" cells visible at once, the transfer is easy.

There are two split bar controls: one horizontal and one vertical. That means you can split your display into a total of four panes. The easiest way to split your view is to drag a split bar into the worksheet. When a split bar is not in use, it resides on the scroll bar. The horizontal split bar resides at the top of the worksheet window, right underneath the up-pointing arrow of the vertical scroll bar, as pointed out in Figure 2.15. The vertical one is right next to the right-pointing arrow button on the horizontal scroll bar. They aren't obtrusive; they're just little black lines. Drag one toward the middle of the worksheet to create an active split bar like the one shown in Figure 2.14.

Figure 2.14
This view has been split into two panes so that you can see two separate parts of the worksheet at once on-screen.

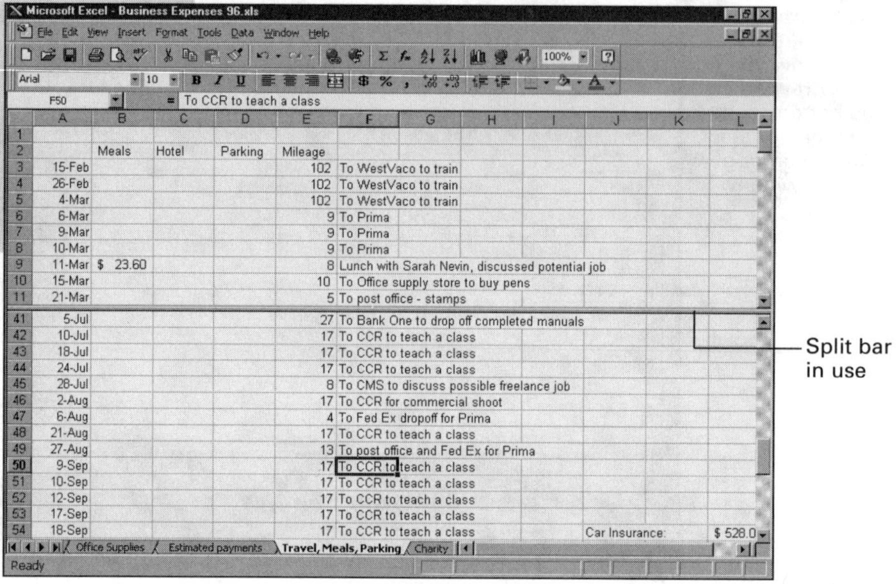

Figure 2.15
To activate a split bar, drag one or both of these controls into the worksheet area.

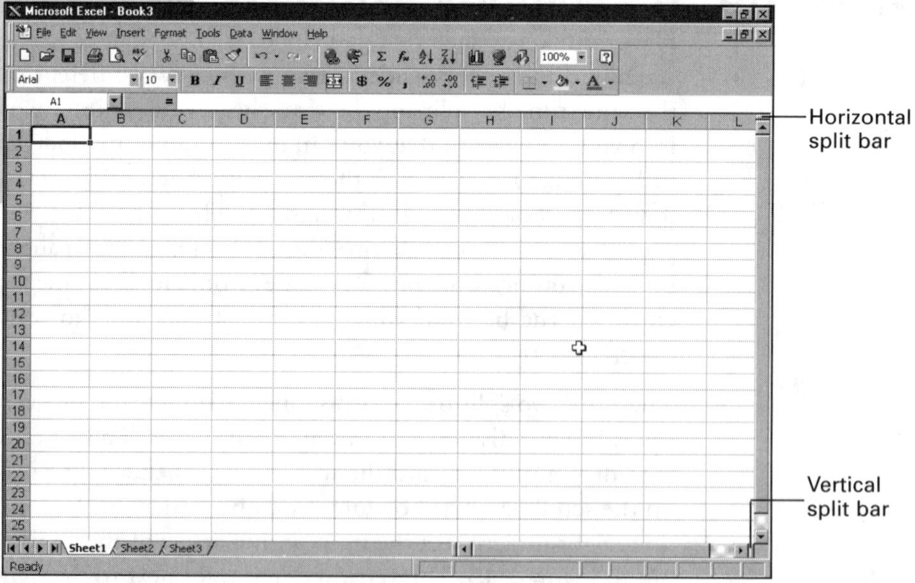

After a split bar is active, you can drag it wherever you want it. To get rid of it, drag it totally to one side or the other of the worksheet, or open the Window menu and choose Remove Split.

Note

You can also activate the split bar by choosing Window, Split. This activates both split bars and places them in the middle of the screen.

Tip

If you need to view two different worksheets from the same workbook at once, choose Window, New Window. You then have two windows containing the same workbook, each with its own worksheet tabs. Then see the "Arranging Windows" section that follows to arrange them so that both are visible.

Arranging Windows

Splitting windows is great for two views of the same workbook, but if you want to see two or more different workbooks on-screen at the same time, you need a different method.

Almost all Windows-based programs (at least the ones that allow you to have more than one data window open at once within them) have a Window menu with Cascade and Tile commands. In Excel, those commands are located behind another command: Arrange. When you want to arrange the open windows, do the following:

1. Choose Window, Arrange. The Arrange Windows dialog box opens (see Figure 2.16).

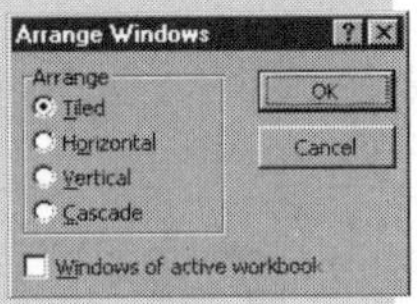

Figure 2.16 Use the Arrange Windows dialog box to choose the window arrangement you want.

2. Select the arrangement you want:
   - Tiled arranges the open, non-minimized windows into blocks so that each window has approximately an equal amount of space on-screen and no windows overlap, as shown in Figure 2.17.
   - Cascade arranges the windows with their title bars neatly cascading down the screen, as shown in Figure 2.18.

Figure 2.17
These workbook windows are tiled.

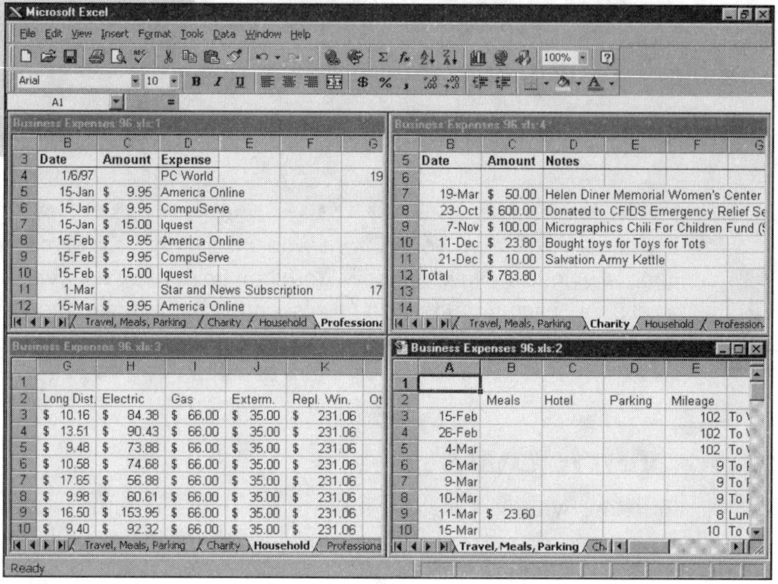

Figure 2.18
These workbook windows are cascaded.

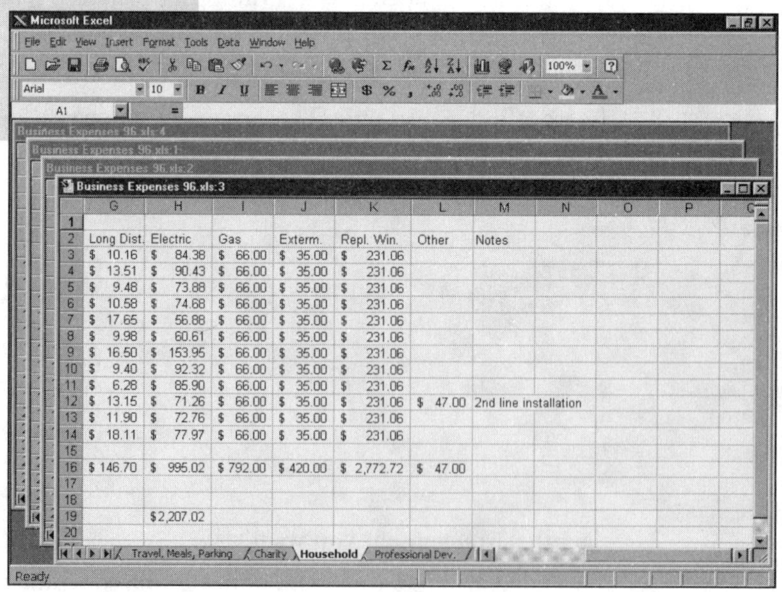

Note

Don't worry if you don't know how to open multiple windows yet; you learn all about it in Chapter 3. If you want some workbook windows to practice on now, click the New button on the Standard toolbar a few times to open some blank workbooks.

- H<u>o</u>rizontal is like <u>T</u>iled except that each window is in a strip the full width of the Excel window, as shown in Figure 2.19.
- <u>V</u>ertical is like H<u>o</u>rizontal, but each window is in a vertical strip the full height of the Excel window.

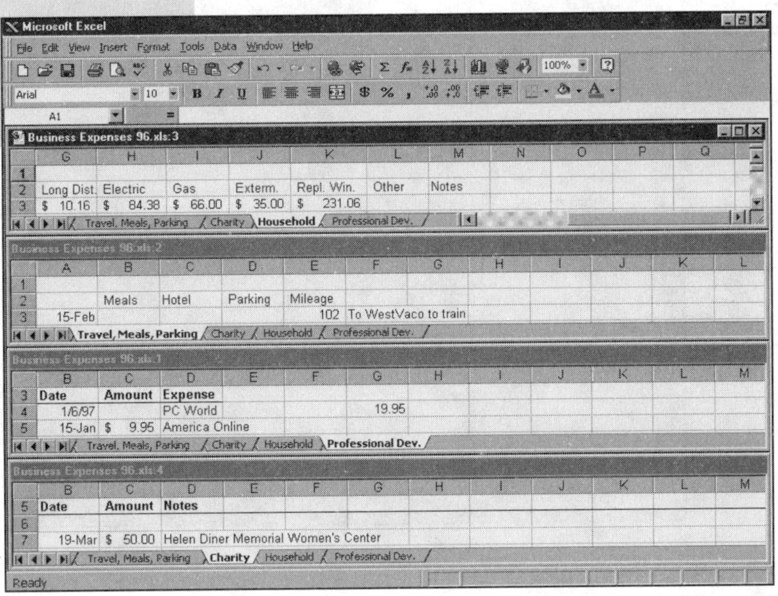

Figure 2.19
These workbook windows are horizontally tiled.

Caution

As you may have noticed from Figures 2.17 through 2.19, the Arrange Window commands do not apply to minimized windows. If you want to include an open workbook in the arrangement, make sure that you restore it from its minimized state first, if needed.

Switching Among Open Windows

If you have more than one workbook open and all the workbooks are at least partly visible on-screen, you can switch among them by clicking on any visible portion of the one you want to see. It moves to the top of the pile.

If you have one of the workbook windows maximized, however, or if another workbook is completely obscuring the one you want, you will have to resort to another method: the Window menu. Open the Window menu, and notice that at the bottom of it, all the open workbooks are listed (see Figure 2.20). Just choose the one you want to switch to from that list.

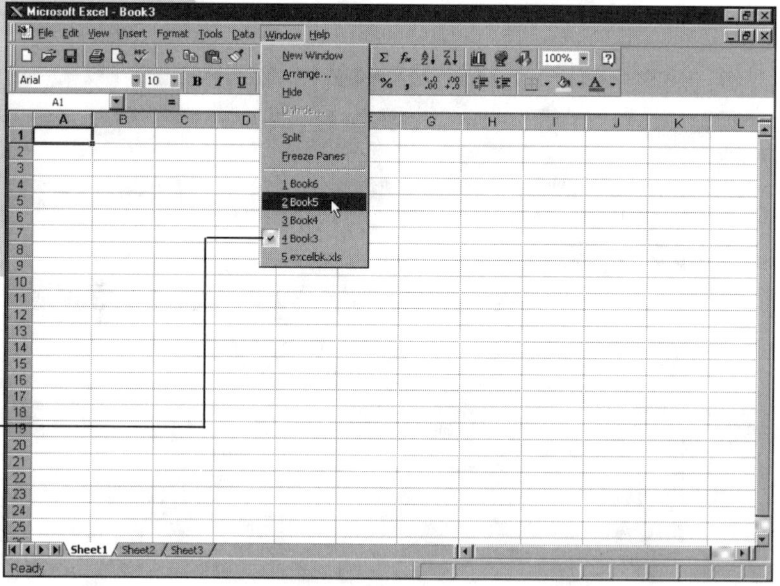

Figure 2.20 One of the best ways to switch among open workbook windows is to choose the one you want from the Window menu.

The currently active window has a check mark next to it.

3

Starting a New Workbook

In This Chapter

- Creating New Workbooks
- Saving and Opening Workbooks
- Opening a File from Another Program
- Duplicating a Workbook
- Deleting a Workbook

Workbooks are the heart of Excel; they're the files into which the program saves your data. Just as you must understand suitcases before you can pack your bags for an exciting trip, you must understand workbooks before you can begin your journey with Excel.

What Is a Workbook?

A *workbook* is a collection of worksheets saved under a common file name in Excel. As you saw in previous chapters, when a workbook is open on-screen, there are several worksheet tabs at the bottom; each represents a sheet in the workbook. All sheets are saved when the workbook is saved. You can think of the workbook as a ring-bound binder into which you insert and remove "pages" (worksheets).

You can have more than one workbook open at once, as briefly discussed at the end of the last chapter, and switch freely among the open workbooks. In the sections that follow, you'll learn all about the creation, care, and management of Excel workbooks.

Creating a New Workbook

Each time you start Excel, a blank workbook opens (called Book1, as you can see in the title bar). That's because Excel assumes that you want to create a new workbook. If that is indeed what you want to do, just start using Book1! You can save it under a more descriptive name later, as you'll learn later in this chapter.

If you wanted to create another new workbook, you could exit Excel and then reopen it, and another new workbook would appear. However, there is a much easier way to create a new workbook without exiting the program. (In fact, there are several ways.) Create a new workbook in any of these ways:

- Click the New button on the Standard toolbar.
- Press Ctrl+N.
- Choose File, New.

YOU LEARN MORE ABOUT TEMPLATES IN CHAPTER 4.

With the first two options, the new workbook simply appears on-screen. That's because the New button and Ctrl+N both create a new workbook based on the Normal template. As you'll learn in Chapter 4, a *template* is a set of specifications, such as the margins, column widths, number of worksheets, and other options, on which a new workbook can be based. New workbooks based on the Normal template are just that: fairly ordinary and normal, with average settings appropriate for a wide range of purposes.

The third method, choosing File, New, opens the New dialog box shown in Figure 3.1. As you can see, this dialog box has two tabs: General and Spreadsheet Solutions. These tabs contain the available templates.

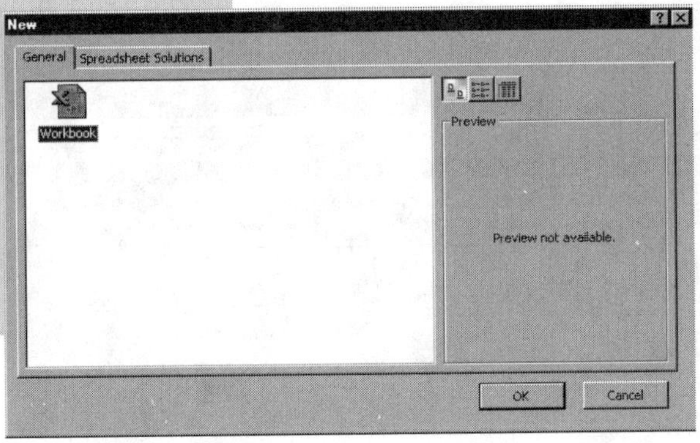

Figure 3.1 The File, New command opens the New dialog box, in which you can choose a template on which to base your new workbook.

The General tab contains only one template: the Normal one. It's labeled Workbook (a generic name). If you click on the Spreadsheet Solutions tab, you see several other templates, which you'll learn to use in Chapter 4.

For now, you just want a normal workbook, so click on the General tab to return to it and then click on the Workbook icon. Then click OK. A new workbook opens (Book2), the same as if you had clicked the New icon on the toolbar or pressed Ctrl+N.

As you might have guessed, the File, New method is not the best one to use if you are just creating a normal workbook because it takes so many more steps. Use the File, New command only if you are going to create a new workbook based on a different template than Book.

There is a fourth method for creating a new workbook if you have the Microsoft Office package's Shortcut Bar installed. Click the New button on the Shortcut Bar to open the New Office Document dialog box (see Figure 3.2).

From the New Office Document dialog box, click the Blank Workbook icon and then click OK. This starts Excel if it is not already started and also starts a new workbook.

Saving a Workbook

Let's skip ahead a moment and pretend that you have created something in your workbook worthy of saving. (That's what all the chapters from Chapter 6 to the end will help you do.) After you've entered something you want to preserve, you need to save it to disk.

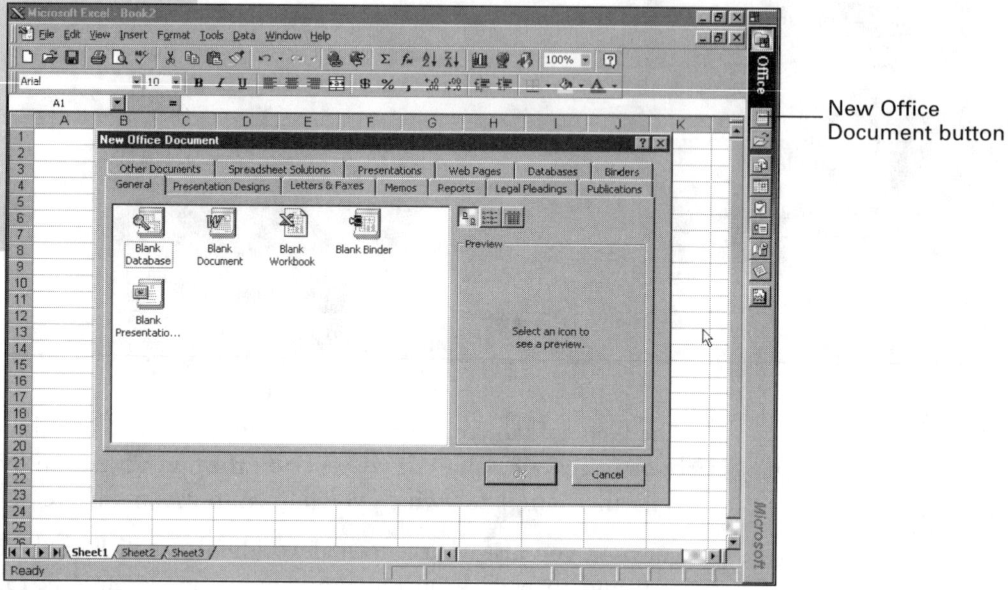

Figure 3.2 You can create any kind of Office document, including an Excel workbook, from the New Office Document dialog box.

What Happens When You Save?

You can think of your computer's memory as the top of your desk and your hard disk as a drawer in the desk. When you work in Excel, you're working on the top of the desk, just as you would when you wrote a letter or added numbers by hand. When you exit Excel or turn off your computer, it's like a janitor coming in and scooping everything from your desk surface into the garbage. Everything in memory is wiped out. If you want to preserve something you've been working on, you have to copy it to the hard disk, so that it's safely stashed away in a "drawer" where the "janitor" can't get it. Copying it to the hard disk is called *saving*.

As you're working with a new workbook, it has a generic name like Book1, Book2, and so on. Excel assigns these names to prevent you from getting confused when you have more than one unsaved workbook open at once. When you save a workbook, you give it a "real" name, something more descriptive that will help you remember its purpose.

Names can be up to 255 characters and can include spaces. For practical purposes, however, you should keep the names reasonably short, such as Invoice 4A or Henson Report. You can include spaces in your file names and most symbols (although not < > ? or *). You don't have to type .XLS on the end of the name, because Excel adds that automatically.

After a workbook has been saved, a copy exists on your hard disk that you can "open," which you'll learn to do later in the chapter. The copy stays on your hard disk until you delete it (also covered later in the chapter). Each time you make changes to a workbook, you must save it again for the changes to be reflected in the copy stored on your hard disk.

Save Versus Save As

There are two procedures for saving: Save and Save As. If you have never saved the workbook before, they are identical: they both ask for a name and location for the file. After you have saved the workbook, Save resaves the workbook with the same name and location that you initially entered, whereas Save As gives you the opportunity to save the workbook with a different name and/or location.

Hands On: Saving a Workbook for the First Time

The first time you save a workbook, you assign it a name and a location, so that you can retrieve it later. Follow these steps to save a workbook for the first time:

1. Do any of the following to open the Save As dialog box:
   - Click the Save button on the Standard toolbar.
   - Press Ctrl+S.
   - Choose File, Save or File, Save As. (They work the same if you have never saved this workbook before.)
2. In the Save As dialog box (see Figure 3.3), enter a name for the workbook in the File Name text box. (Type over the generic name that's there.)
3. (Optional) To save the workbook in a different folder, use the navigation buttons in the dialog box to change the folder and/or drive. (See the following section for help with this.) The default is the My Documents folder on the same drive on which Windows 95 is installed.
4. Click the Save button in the dialog box. The workbook is saved to disk, and the new name of it appears in the title bar.

Figure 3.3
Use the Save As dialog box to specify a file name and location.

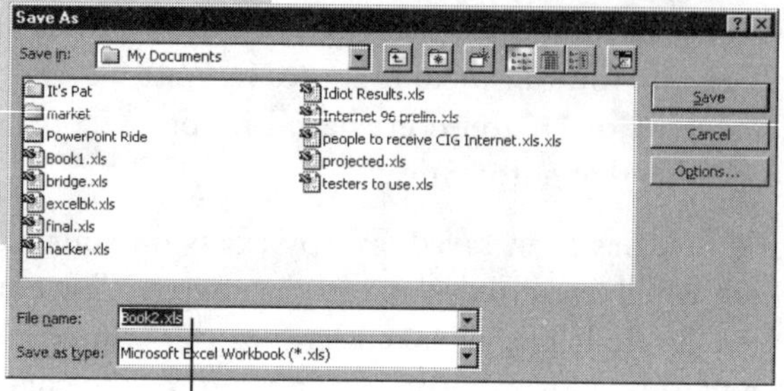

Type a name here, replacing the generic name.

Changing the Folder or Drive

If you have not used many Windows 95 programs, the file navigation system may seem foreign at first. You must use it whenever you need to change the drive and/or folder in a dialog box that saves or opens files. You'll encounter it in the Save As dialog box (see Figure 3.3) and also in the Open dialog box covered later in the chapter.

To change to a different drive, you must open the Save In or Look In drop-down list. (The name changes depending on whether you're saving or opening a file.) Figure 3.4 shows this drop-down list in the Save As dialog box. From it, choose the drive on which you want to save the file.

Next, you must select the folder where you want to save the file (or open it from). When you select the drive, a list of the folders on that drive appears. Double-click on the folder you want to select it.

Figure 3.4
Use this drop-down list to choose a different drive.

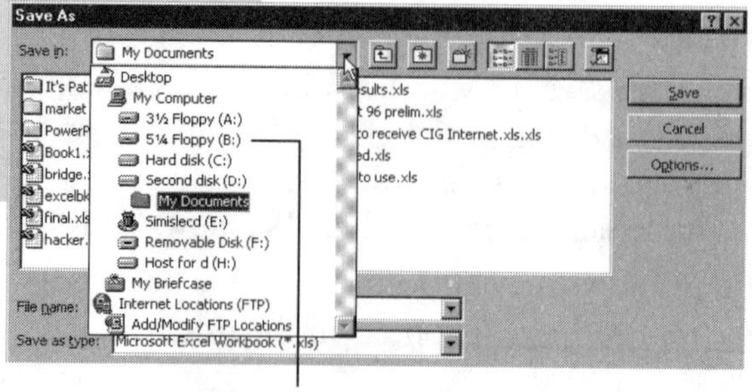

Select the drive from this list.

Table 3.1 explains the buttons and other controls you see in the Save As and Open dialog boxes, as well as in other Windows 95 dialog boxes you may encounter.

Table 3.1 Buttons for Changing Drives and Folders in Windows 95 Dialog Boxes

Button	Name	Purpose
	Up One Level	Moves to the folder "above" the one shown in the Save In box (that is, the folder in which the current one resides).
	Look in Favorites	Shows the C:\WINDOWS\FAVORITES folder, no matter which folder was displayed before.
	Create New Folder	Creates a new folder (Save As dialog box only).
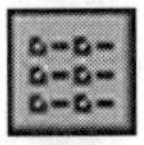	List	Shows the folders and files in the currently displayed folder in a list.
	Details	Shows details about each file and folder.
	Properties	Shows the properties of each file and folder.
	Preview	Shows a preview of the current file (Open dialog box only).
	Commands and Settings	Opens a dialog box of settings you can change that affect the dialog box.
	Add to Favorites	Adds a shortcut to the currently displayed folder to the Favorites list (Open dialog box only).
	Search the Web	Enables you to search the Internet for documents to open (Open dialog box only).

Tip

Notice in Figure 3.4 that you can select Internet Locations to save a file to from the Save In drop-down list. If you are connected to an Internet FTP site, you can save the file directly to that server's disk drive rather than your own hard drive. You learn more about this in Chapter 21.

Saving a Workbook Subsequent Times

After a workbook has been saved, you can resave it using the same file name and location by doing any of the following:

- Click the Save button on the Standard toolbar.
- Press Ctrl+S.
- Choose File, Save.

If you need to reopen the Save As dialog box, to specify a different name or location, for instance, choose File, Save As and then save the file as you did the first time.

Saving in Other Formats

You may have noticed in the Save As dialog box the Save as Type drop-down list. It enables you to save your Excel workbook in a variety of foreign formats, for use with other programs. For example, suppose that you have a coworker who uses only Lotus 1-2-3. You could export your workbook in 1-2-3 format so that your coworker could use it. You can export to more than a dozen formats, including 1-2-3, Text, Access, old versions of Excel, and dBASE IV.

To save in another format, save the file normally using the Save As dialog box, but before you click Save, open the Save as Type drop-down list and select a different type, as shown in Figure 3.5. Then click Save.

Tip

Some formats, on the surface, seem less helpful than others. For instance, what about Text (Tab Delimited)? Who would want a file like that? Well, Text formats are seldom anyone's first choice, but they can be useful if you need to open your work in a program that Excel does not directly export to—for instance, an old spreadsheet program like MultiMate. The Text format provides a link between the two because Excel can export it and MultiMate can import it. You can also use Text format to import into multifunction programs' spreadsheet components like LotusWorks and Microsoft Works.

Other Saving Options

You may have noticed the Options button in the Save As dialog box shown in Figure 3.5 and wondered about it. Let's check it out now. Click it, and the Save Options dialog box appears, shown in Figure 3.6.

Figure 3.5 You can save your work in other formats for compatibility with other programs.

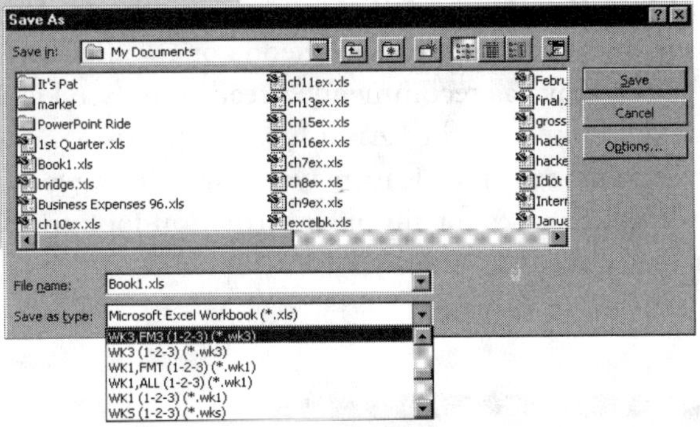

Figure 3.6 You can specify a few special save settings in the Save Options dialog box.

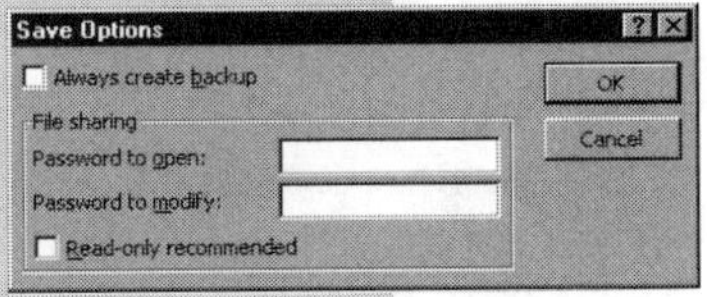

These options have one thing in common: protection. They offer various ways for you to protect your work from damage or snooping:

- **Always Create Backup.** If you mark this check box, every time you save this file subsequent times, the next-to-most-recent version will be saved in a file with the same name and an .XLK extension. For instance, if I saved the current file under the name MYFILE.XLS and then clicked the Save button to save it again, the original MYFILE.XLS would be renamed MYFILE.XLK, and the new version would be saved as MYFILE.XLS. This is handy if you are worried about making a change incorrectly and ruining your existing work. If you need to reopen the .BAK copy, refer to the section "Opening Files from Other Programs" later in this chapter.
- **File Sharing.** If you want, you can specify two passwords for this file. The first one, Password to Open, will be required to open the file. The second one, Password to Modify, will be required to save changes made to the

YOU LEARN MORE ABOUT PASSWORDS IN CHAPTER 22.

file. You can then tell the assigned password(s) only to the people who you want to have that access. For example, suppose that you have a group of computer experts who need access to your Invoices workbook; you could give them the Password to Modify. You could then give your salespeople the Password to Open, so that they can use the invoice form but not make changes to it that might confuse others.

- **Read-Only Recommended.** Marking this check box places a warning message on-screen each time someone opens the file, informing him that the file's creator has recommended read-only (see Figure 3.7). The user can then choose Yes (for Read-Only) or No (to ignore the recommendation). This feature works well for a workbook that the same user sometimes uses for simple information lookup (Read-Only) and other times needs to modify.

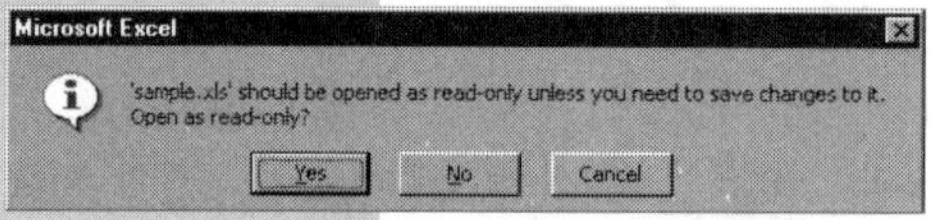

Figure 3.7 You can recommend Read-Only mode each time the workbook is opened.

Changing the Default Save Location

If you find yourself changing the location where you are saving your files each time, perhaps you should set a different folder to be the default folder where Excel saves. Normally it's My Documents, but you can change it to any folder. For example, I have mine set to a folder I've created called Books because the Excel files I work with are used in the books that I write.

To change the default file location, choose Tools, Options, and click the General tab. Then in the Default File Location text box, type the path to the folder you want to use and click OK.

Closing a Workbook

When you save a workbook, it remains on-screen so that you can continue to work on it. When you're finished working with the workbook for now, you can close it in either of two ways:

- You can exit Excel. The workbook closes when Excel closes.
- You can close the workbook and keep working in other Excel workbooks.

You already learned how to quit Excel in Chapter 1: choose File, Exit or click the Excel window's Close (X) button. To close a workbook and leave Excel open, do any of the following:

- Click the workbook window's Close (X) button. If the workbook window is maximized, the Close button is the lower of the two X's in the top-right corner. If the workbook window is not maximized, the X is at the right end of the workbook window's title bar.
- Choose File, Close.
- Press Ctrl+W.

When you close the workbook, if you have made any changes to it since you last saved it, you'll be asked if you want to save your work (see Figure 3.8). Click Yes or No, depending on what you want. If you click Yes and the workbook has not yet been saved, the Save As dialog box opens, which you learned about earlier in this chapter.

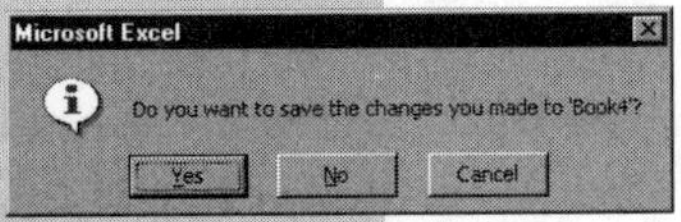

Figure 3.8 If you try to close a workbook without saving your changes, you'll get this warning.

Opening a Workbook

There's no point in saving your workbooks to your hard disk unless you are, at some point, going to open them again. When you open a file, you redisplay it on-screen, where you can modify it further if you want.

To open a saved Excel file, follow these steps:

1. Do one of the following to open the Open dialog box shown in Figure 3.9:
   - Click the Open button on the Standard toolbar.
   - Choose File, Open.
   - Press Ctrl+O.

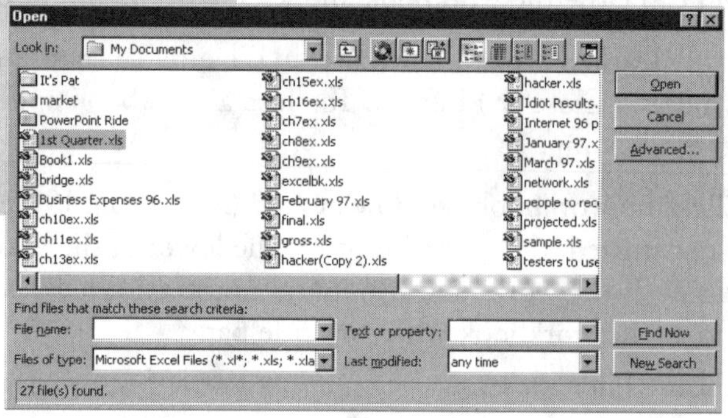

Figure 3.9 Choose the saved file you want to open and then click the Open button.

2. If the file you want to open appears, click on it. Otherwise, change the drive and folder displayed as needed to find it. (Refer to "Changing the Folder or Drive" earlier in this chapter for help.)
3. Click the Open button, or double-click the workbook file. The workbook opens on-screen.

Note

If you use the Microsoft Office Shortcut Bar, you can open a workbook from it. Click the Open Office Document button on the Shortcut Bar and then navigate through the drives and folders to find the file you want. When you've found and selected it, click Open.

Finding a Workbook to Open

If you're having trouble locating your workbook, Excel can help you look. Perhaps you forgot which folder you saved it in, or you have moved it in Windows 95 since you saved it. No matter what the reason, Excel's Find feature can rescue you.

Follow these steps to find a file:

1. Open the Open dialog box if is not already open.

2. In the File Name box at the bottom of the dialog box, type the name of the file you're looking for (see Figure 3.10).

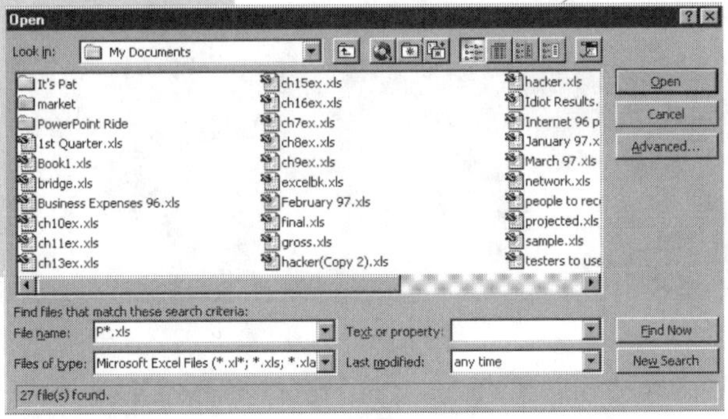

Figure 3.10
If you aren't sure where a file resides, search for it by entering the portion of the name that you know.

You can use wild cards if you don't know the entire name of a file. The asterisk (*) wild-card character stands in for any character or set of characters, and the question mark (?) wild-card character stands in for any single character. For instance, if you know the file begins with *P*, you could type **P*.xls**, as shown in Figure 3.10, to find all Excel files that begin with *P*.

3. (Optional) Enter other search criteria:
   - If you're looking for a different file type, choose it from the Files of Type drop-down list.
   - If you're looking for a file containing certain text, type that text in the Text or Property box.
   - If you know when you last modified the file, choose the time interval from the Last Modified drop-down list.
4. Click the Advanced button. The Advanced Find dialog box appears (see Figure 3.11).
5. In the Look In section at the bottom of the Advanced Find dialog box, narrow the search area as much as possible using these techniques:
   - If you are sure that the file is in a certain folder, type that folder's path (such as C:\WINDOWS) in the Look In box.
   - If you are sure that the file is on a certain drive, select that drive from the Look In drop-down list.
   - If you don't know which drive contains the file, select My Computer from the Look In drop-down list.

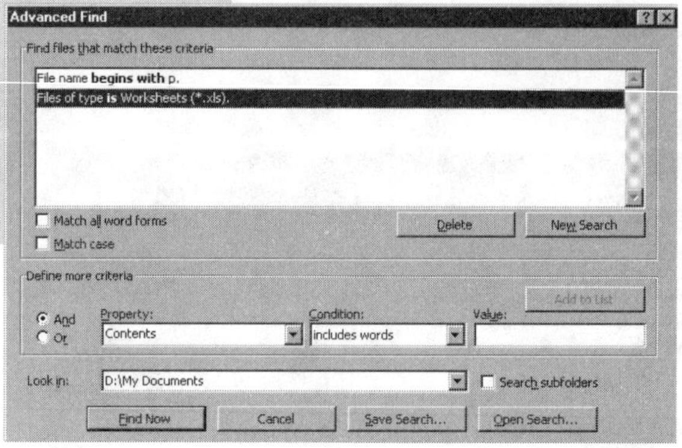

Figure 3.11 Use the Advanced Find dialog box to select the folders and drives you want to search.

6. Make sure that the Search Subfolders check box is marked. If it isn't, click on it.
7. Click the Find Now button. The Open dialog box reappears and displays the files that match your search criteria.
8. Double-click on the desired file to open it.

Note

As you may have noticed in Figure 3.11, many more complex search options are available—too many to cover here. See the Excel online help for more details. (You learned how to use the Help system in Chapter 1.)

Opening Files from Other Programs

Most of the time, you'll create a brand-new workbook and then enter new data into it. But occasionally you may need to import data from another source. That source could be a Lotus 1-2-3 worksheet, a Word document, a text file, an Access database, or some other file format.

Opening Spreadsheet Files from Other Programs

Opening files in other formats can be easy if the format is similar to Excel's. For instance, opening a file from another spreadsheet program, such as Lotus 1-2-3, is nearly automatic. Follow these steps:

1. If it is not open already, open the Open dialog box (choose File, Open).

2. Open the Files of Type drop-down list and choose the type of file you want to open.
3. If needed, change the drive and/or folder to the one where the file to be opened resides.
4. Double-click the file to open, or click it once and then click Open.

Caution

The files listed when you choose a particular file type from the Files of Type list are based wholly on their extensions. For instance, when you choose dBase Files (*.DBF), Excel does not check each file to see whether it actually is a dBASE file; it merely lists all the files with .DBF extensions. If a file is misnamed with the wrong extension, it won't appear on the list when you want it to. To rename a file, find it in the Windows Explorer, click on it, press F2, and type a new name.

Opening Text Files in Excel

Opening a text file in Excel is nobody's first choice. It involves a lot of work to whip a text file into spreadsheet shape. However, sometimes you don't have a choice. Perhaps you need to import data from a program that does not have any other common import/export paths with Excel, or perhaps you were given a disk with text data on it from an unknown source.

Note

By "import/export paths," I mean some common format between the export capabilities of the original program and the import capabilities of Excel. For example, the original program might not export to Excel format, but it might export to Lotus 1-2-3 format, which Excel can import.

Data in text files comes in two different versions: *space-delimited* and *tab-delimited.* Here's the difference:

- In a space-delimited file, data is separated by spaces. For example, in each row, column 1 might begin at character 1, column 2 at character 10, column 3 at character 20, and so on. Figure 3.12 shows some space-delimited text.

- In a tab-delimited file, columns are separated by tabs. For example, in each row, the text before the first Tab stop is column 1, before the second Tab stop is column 2, and so on. Figure 3.12 shows some tab-delimited text.

Tip

If you have a choice when you're creating the text file (that is, exporting it from the original program), choose tab-delimited rather than space-delimited. It makes for more accurate conversions in most cases.

Figure 3.12 Tab-delimited and space-delimited versions of the same file.

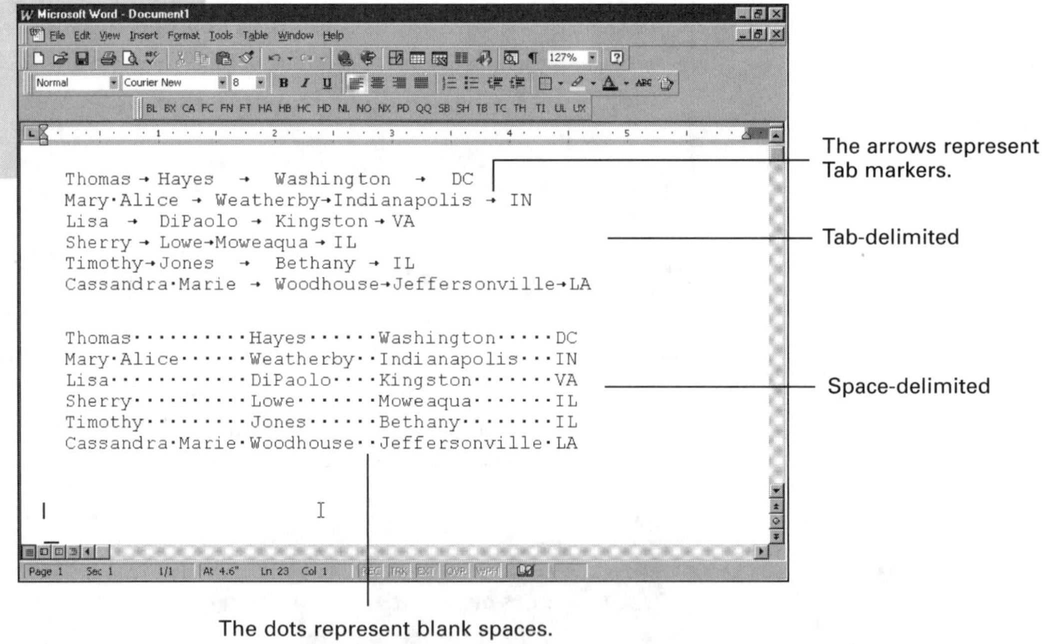

When you open a text file (either tab-delimited or space-delimited), the Text Import Wizard opens automatically in Excel, as shown in Figure 3.13.

To use the Text Import Wizard, follow these steps:

1. At the first Text Import Wizard screen (Step 1 of 3), check what format the wizard has determined your data to be: Delimited (tabbed) or Fixed Width (spaced). If the wizard has chosen incorrectly, click the correct option button.

Figure 3.13 The Text Import Wizard helps you figure out where the column dividers should be in your imported data.

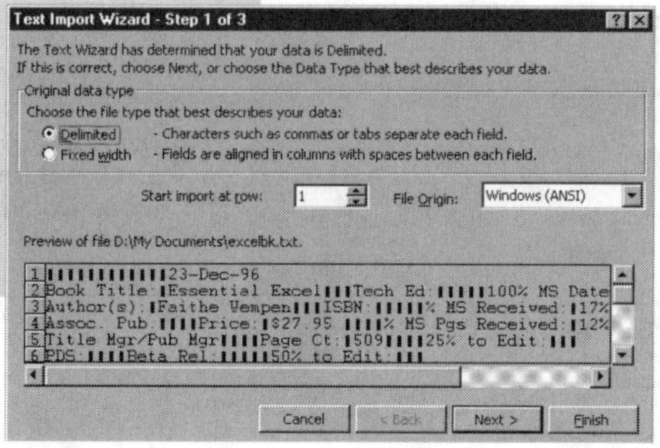

2. If you do not want the import to start with the first line of the text file, change the number in the Start Import at Row box to a number high enough to exclude the lines you want to exclude at the top.
3. Check the entry in the File Origin drop-down list. If it is not correct, change it. (Your choices are Windows, Macintosh, or OS/2. It should be clear which is right based on the computer from which the data came.)
4. Click the Next button to view the Step 2 of 3 dialog box.
5. In the Delimiters section, choose which type of delimiter was used in the file. The default is Tabs, but Excel can also accept files that use semicolons, commas, or even spaces as delimiters.

If you choose Space as the delimiter in step 5, this is not the same as in a fixed-width (space-delimited) file. If you choose Space as the delimiter character here, every time there is a space, Excel will start a new column. If you don't want this, click the Back button and make sure that Fixed Width is marked on the Step 1 of 3 screen.

6. If you might have several delimiting characters in a row in your data, and each one indicates the start of a new column, leave the Treat Consecutive Delimiters As One check box unmarked. However, if two or more delimiters in a row should result in only one new column, mark this check box.
7. Click Next to move on to Step 3 of 3.
8. Set the data format for each column, as shown in Figure 3.14, as follows:
   a. Click on the column for which you want to set the data format.

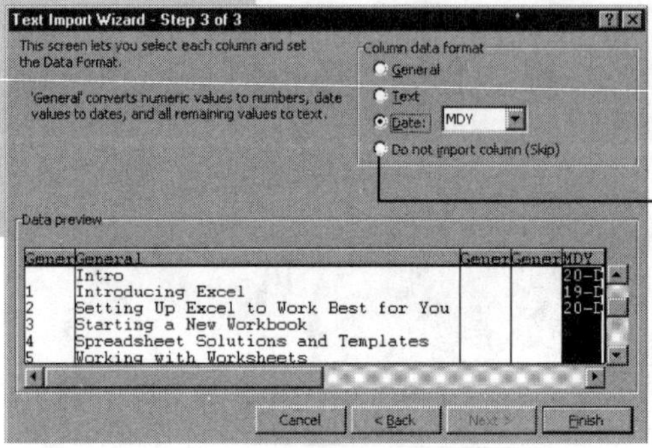

Figure 3.14 Choose a format for each column, or leave them set to General if you prefer.

To exclude a column from Excel import, choose Do Not Import Column.

b. Click on the button in the Column Data Format section at the top of the dialog box (General, Text, Date, or Do Not Import Column).

9. Click the Finish button to import your data into Excel.

Using the File Conversion Wizard

If you have several files that you need to import into Excel and they're all in the same format (for instance, Lotus 1-2-3 format), you can process them all in one batch. The following things must be true for this procedure to work:

- All the files must be in the same format with the same extension, and it must be a format other than Text.
- They must all be in the same folder. (Move them to the same folder, if needed, using Windows Explorer.)

If the above two conditions are true, follow these steps:

1. Choose Tools, Wizard, File Conversion. The File Conversion Wizard Step 1 of 3 dialog box appears.

Note

If you don't have a File Conversion option on the menu, rerun the Setup program and choose a Custom installation. Then choose the File Conversion component to install.

2. Enter the location of the files in the Drive and Folder text box. (Use the Browse button to locate it if needed.)
3. Open the File Format drop-down list and select the format that the files are currently in.

4. Click the Next button to move to Step 2 of 3 (see Figure 3.15).
5. In the Which Files Do You Want to Convert? box, click to place a check in the check box beside each file that you want to convert. You can select them all quickly by clicking the Select All button.
6. Click the Next button to move to Step 3 of 3.
7. In the Type or Select a Folder text box, enter the location for the converted files. The default is the same as the original file location, but you can change it if you want.
8. Click Finish. Excel opens a Conversion Wizard Report in a workbook window, detailing the results.
9. Read the conversion report and then close the window (saving it if desired, or discarding the changes.)

Figure 3.15
Click to place a check next to the files you want to convert.

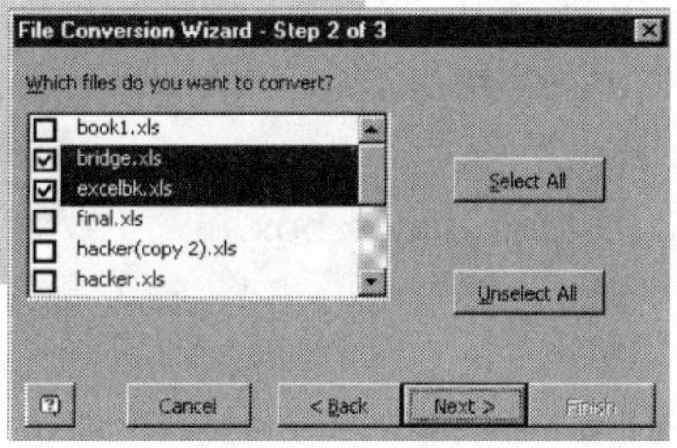

Switching Among Open Workbooks

In Chapter 2, I talked a little about workbooks and windows. When you have more than one workbook open at once, each has its own window. When a workbook is at the top of the stack, it becomes the *active* workbook. Any commands you issue or changes you make apply to the active workbook.

You can switch to a specific open window by following this procedure:

1. Open the Window menu.
2. Click on the name of the workbook whose window you want to see.

Another way to switch among the open workbooks is to press Ctrl+Tab. Each time you press Ctrl+Tab, the display toggles to the next workbook in the list of open ones. Keep pressing Ctrl+Tab until the one you want comes into view.

If the workbook windows are not maximized and you can see any part of a workbook "behind" another one, click on the part you can see to bring that workbook to the top of the stack.

Duplicating a Workbook

Suppose that you have a great workbook that you want to make a copy of. You could make a copy in Windows Explorer, but it might be easier to do the copying right here in Excel. Here's how to do it:

1. Choose File, Open to open the Open dialog box.
2. Change the drive and/or folder if needed to bring the file's name into view.
3. Right-click on the file you want to copy and choose the Copy command from the shortcut menu that appears.
4. Change the drive and/or folder if needed to display the folder into which you want to place the copy.
5. Right-click on any empty area of the folder window and choose the Paste command from the shortcut menu that appears. The copy is pasted into that folder.
6. (Optional) If you want to change the name of the copy, click on it once and then press F2 and type a new name for it. Press Enter when you're finished typing.
7. Click Cancel to close the Open dialog box.

Deleting a Workbook

Just as you can copy files from the Open dialog box, you can also delete them from there. This makes it very convenient to clean up unwanted files without leaving Excel.

To delete a file from within Excel, follow these steps:

1. Choose File, Open to open the Open dialog box.
2. Change the drive and/or folder if needed to bring the file's name into view.
3. Click on the file you want to delete and then press the Del key.
4. A warning appears asking whether you are sure that you want to delete the file. Click Yes. The file is gone.
5. Click Cancel to close the Open dialog box.

You can delete multiple files at once from the Open dialog box; click on the first one and then hold down the Ctrl key while you click on others. When they are all selected, press the Del key to delete them as a group.

If you accidentally delete something you shouldn't have, you can get it back in Windows 95. Double-click the Recycle Bin icon on the desktop and then click the file you want to retrieve. Then open the Recycle Bin's File menu and choose Restore.

4

Spreadsheet Solutions and Templates

IN THIS CHAPTER

- Understanding Templates
- Creating Your Own Templates
- Using the Spreadsheet Solutions

Although Excel can be fun to use, nobody uses it for the sheer joy of using a spreadsheet program. Everyone is in a hurry; everyone needs to get things done quicker and better than the competition. One of the greatest features Excel offers is the capability of creating *templates* that preserve the boilerplate settings that you use over and over. That way, you spend less time setting up margins and more time getting value out of your worksheet. Excel even comes with some premade templates, called *Spreadsheet Solutions,* that help automate some common but difficult jobs.

Templates

Have you ever seen a professional sign painter at work? When one of his signs must include some standard lettering, he doesn't attempt to paint it freehand, measuring out each letter separately. Instead, he uses a stencil for each letter, a pattern with the exact height and width of the letter predetermined. This saves the professional sign painter a tremendous amount of time by making the ordinary and boring part of the job go faster. That way, he can focus his attention on the special or tricky parts of the particular job.

That's exactly what a template does for an Excel user. A template helps you zoom quickly through the mundane parts of worksheet creation, so that you have more time to focus on the special parts. For example, suppose that every week you create a worksheet for your supervisor that contains the sales figures. You could create a template that contains the parts of the report that stay the same from week to week, and then each week you could base the new report on that template. Figure 4.1 shows such a template blank, and Figure 4.2 shows it filled in with the sales figures. Notice that to get to the finished product in Figure 4.2, I only had to enter the date and the numbers themselves—the headings and formatting were already in place.

Figure 4.1 This template is ready to accept this week's sales figures.

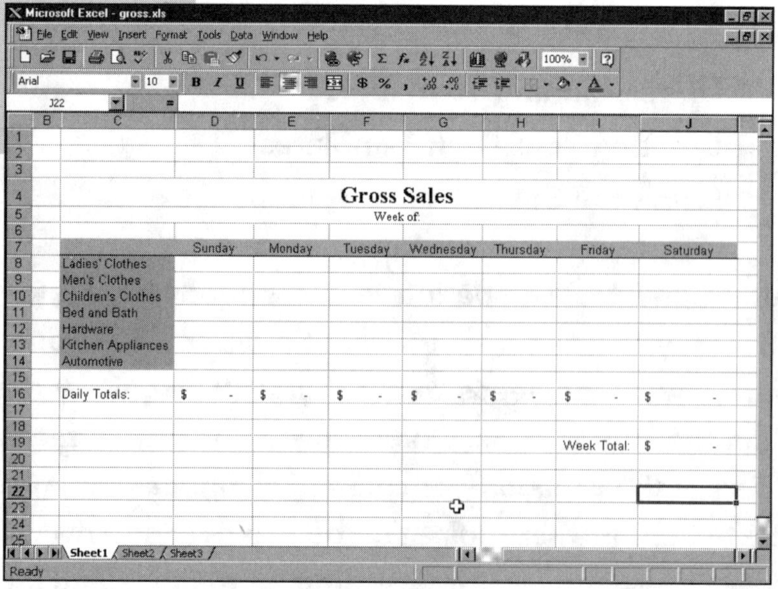

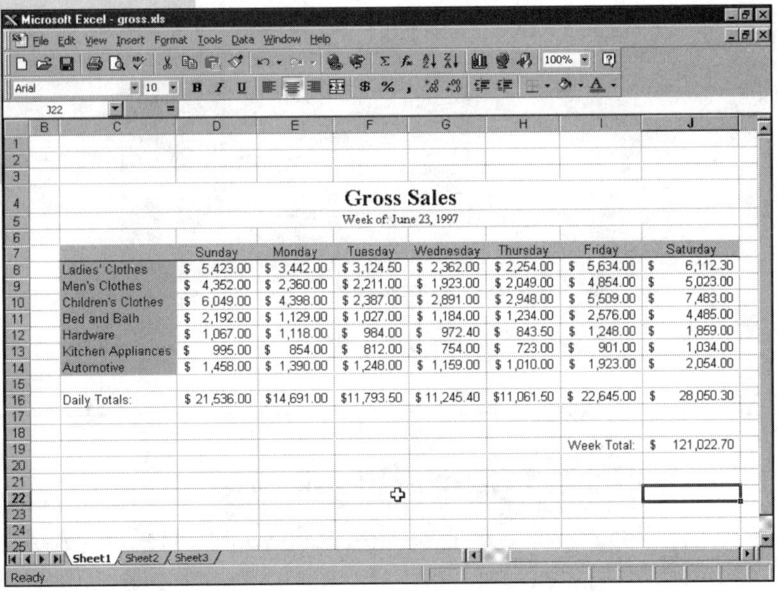

Figure 4.2 To complete the report, I simply filled in the date and sales figures for the week.

Making Your Own Templates

A template is nothing more than a workbook that has been saved in template format. You can save any workbook in template format, no matter how much or how little it contains. After you have created a template, you use the template by starting a new document based on that template. (You learned to do this in Chapter 3, and I'll go over it again later in this chapter.)

You can easily create your own templates that contain the "setup" for any job that you do frequently in Excel. It could be a report like the one shown in Figures 4.1 and 4.2, a chart, a list of names, or anything else that you might do in Excel.

The basic procedure for creating a template is this:

1. Set up the workbook the way you want it to be in the template.
2. Choose File, Save As. The Save As dialog box appears.
3. Open the Save as Type drop-down list and select Template (*.xlt), as shown in Figure 4.3.
4. Type a name for the template in the File Name text box. You do not need to add an extension—Excel adds .xlt to the end automatically.
5. Click Save. The workbook is saved as a template.

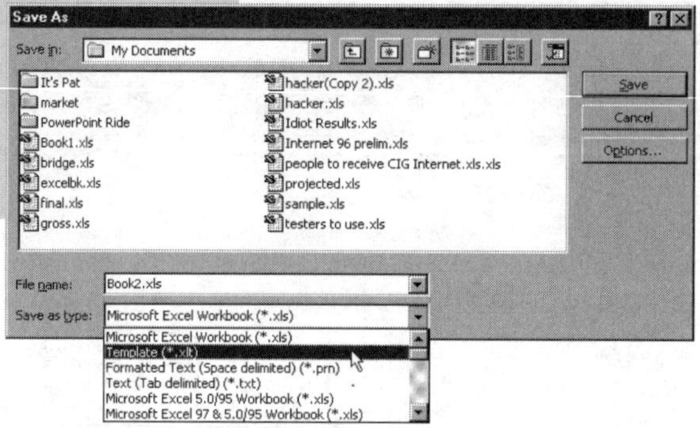

Figure 4.3 Change the file type to Template to save a workbook as a template.

First Things First ...

To create your own templates, you need to have an understanding of everything you want to put into the template. That means you may need to read ahead in the book and learn some more Excel skills before you can create the templates you need. The following list can help you find the information you want:

- To learn how to enter text and numbers in cells, see Chapter 7.
- To learn how to enter formulas and functions in cells (to do calculations), see Chapter 8.
- To learn how to format the text in cells, see Chapters 10 and 11.
- To learn how to set the margins for a worksheet, see Chapter 13.
- If you want to include a chart in your template, see Chapter 14.
- If you want a drawing or other graphics in your template, see Chapter 16.

Hands On: Creating a Template

The following example doesn't require you to know very much about entering worksheet data (which you'll learn in upcoming chapters) but still illustrates the template concept. You will use this template later in the chapter, so make sure that you follow along here if you want to work through later tutorials.

Suppose that you want to put your name at the top of the first worksheet in every workbook you create. You could create a template with your name already entered and then base each of your new workbooks upon it. Follow these steps to create a template containing your name:

1. Click the New button on the Standard toolbar to start a new workbook.
2. Type the following in cell A1, replacing my name with yours: **Created by Faithe Wempen**.
3. Press Enter. The text you entered appears in cell A1 (overflowing into one or more cells to the right).
4. Choose File, Save As. The Save As dialog box appears (refer to Figure 4.3).
5. Open the Save As Type drop-down list and select Template (*.xlt).
6. In the File Name text box, type **Name**.
7. Click Save. Notice that the name in the title bar now reads `Name.xlt`.
8. Choose File, Close to close the template.

Using a Template

As I explained earlier, the whole purpose of creating a template is to be able to base new workbooks upon it. So let's take a look at how to do that.

Be judicious with template use; a template is not always appropriate. For some regularly updated workbooks, you might want to simply update the original workbook each time. For example, suppose that you keep a list of personnel in Excel. (You'll learn more about keeping such lists in Chapter 17.) Each week you delete the names of employees who have quit and add the names of new employees. If you created a template based on the current list and then created a new workbook each week based on it, you would not retain the changes you made in previous weeks. It would be better to just open the same workbook file week after week and make changes to it.

In Chapter 3 you learned how to create a new workbook based on the Book.xlt template; the procedure for using a different template is not much different:

1. Choose File, New. The New dialog box opens, and you see the names of the templates you've saved on the General tab, as shown in Figure 4.4.

2. Select the name of the template you want to use.
3. Click OK.

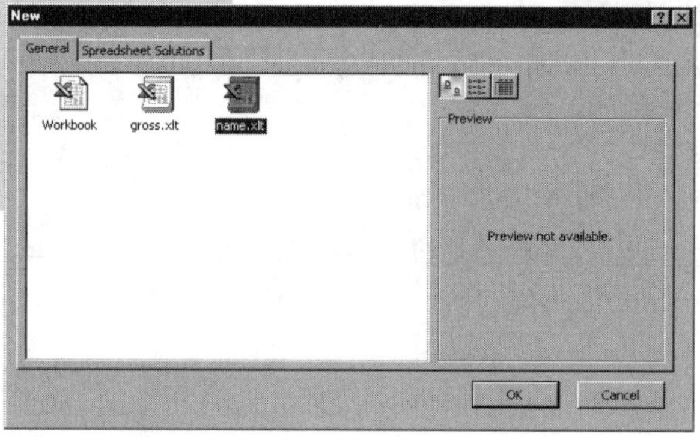

Figure 4.4
You can create a new workbook based on any of the templates you've created.

If you want to practice this, complete the Hands On tutorial that follows.

Hands On: Starting a New Workbook Based on the Name Template

If you created a template called Name in the tutorial earlier in this chapter, you can now use it to start a new workbook. Follow these steps:

1. Choose File, New. The New dialog box appears (see Figure 4.4).
2. Click on the Name icon and then click OK (or just double-click on the Name icon).

A new workbook opens, called Name1. (It's called that rather than Book1 because it is based on the Name template.) As you can see in Figure 4.5, the contents of the Name template—the `Created by` message—appear in cell A1.

Tip

Another useful template you can create for yourself is one with more worksheets than the normal three that each workbook starts out with. Open a new workbook and then add more worksheets to it (see Chapter 5). Then save it as a template, and use that template whenever you need to start a workbook with that number of worksheets.

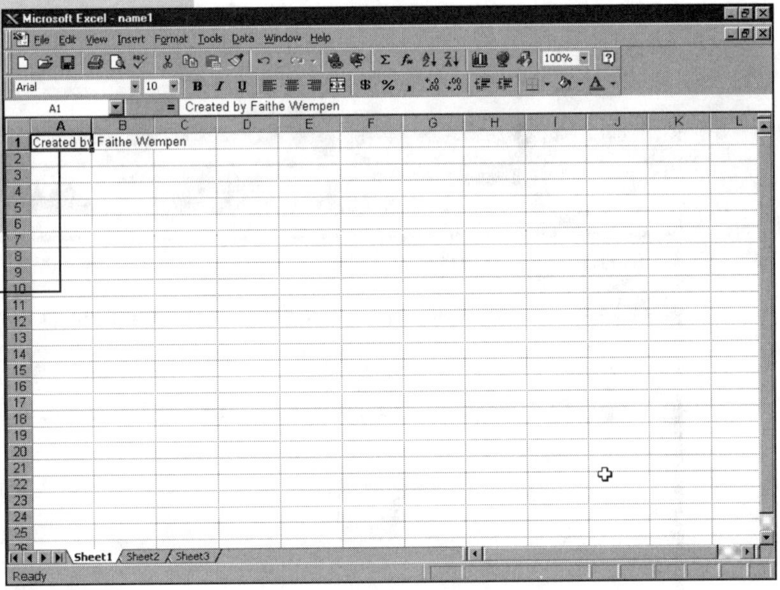

Figure 4.5 When you base a new workbook on a template, the new workbook takes on all the properties of the template.

This text came from the template.

Spreadsheet Solutions

Back in Chapter 3, when you learned about creating new workbooks, I pointed out the Spreadsheet Solutions tab in the New dialog box and promised to discuss it later. Well, I always keep my promises.

Spreadsheet Solutions are fancy templates. They provide the text, formatting, and formulas that you need to create good-looking expense statements, invoices, and purchase orders without a lot of fuss or complicated setup.

A Look at the Spreadsheet Solutions

Excel comes with three Spreadsheet Solutions templates, and you can download many more from the Microsoft Web site (as I'll explain later in this chapter). These are commonly used business forms that involve calculations (Excel's forte) that business people often use again and again. For example, the average businessperson doesn't generate one invoice—she generates ten, or twenty, or hundreds. That fact makes the Invoice a prime candidate for a template because a template's purpose is to help automate repetitive creation.

The three Spreadsheet Solutions that come with Excel are:

- **Expense Statement.** This template helps you create a professional-looking record of expenses incurred by you or other employees. It's shown in Figure 4.6.

- **Invoice.** This template helps you create invoices with which to bill your customers for goods or services delivered (see Figure 4.7).

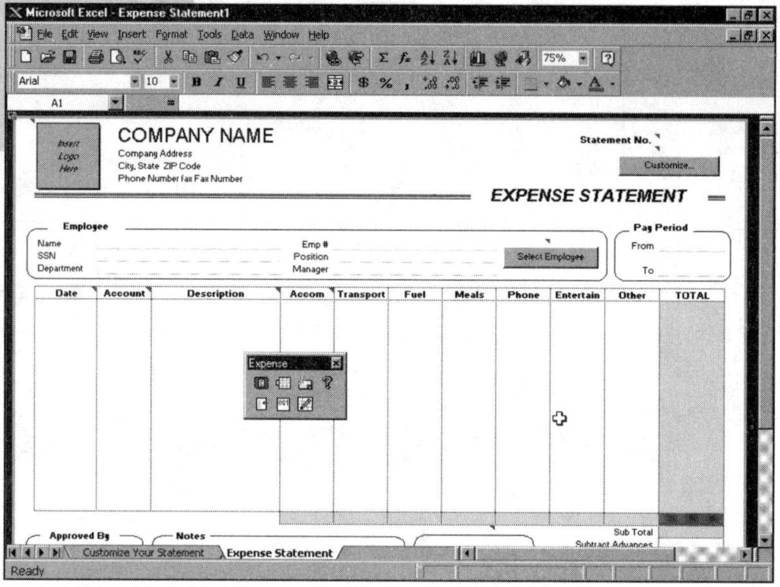

Figure 4.6 This workbook is based on the Expense Statement template.

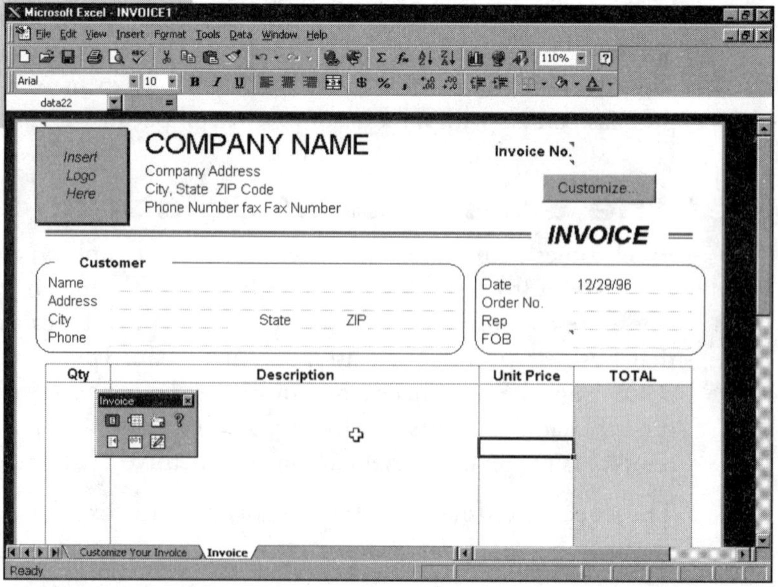

Figure 4.7 This workbook is based on the Invoice template.

- **Purchase Order.** This template helps you generate a purchase order to use internally in your company to tell your accounting or buying department what you want to buy and how much it costs (see Figure 4.8).

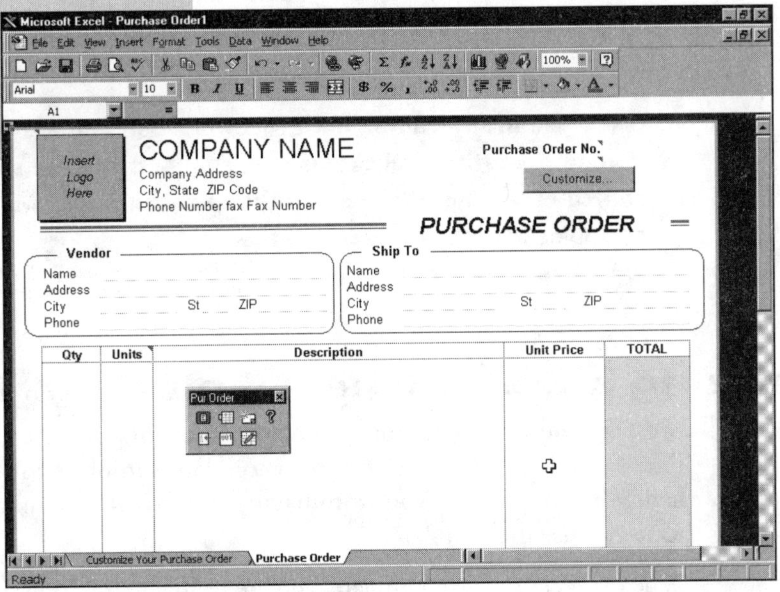

Figure 4.8 This workbook is based on the Purchase Order template.

Note

If you do not see all three of these on the Spreadsheet Solutions tab of the New dialog box, perhaps they are not installed. Rerun the Excel installation program, as described in Appendix A, and make sure that you select all the templates to be installed.

Find it Online

Many more templates are available on Microsoft's Web site in the Free Stuff section. Choose Help, Microsoft on the Web, Free Stuff to jump directly to the Web page that lists what's available for download, as explained later in this chapter.

Hands On: Creating a New Workbook with a Spreadsheet Solutions Template

To use any of the Spreadsheet Solutions, create a new workbook based on it, as described in the following steps:

1. Choose File, New. The New dialog box opens.
2. Click the Spreadsheet Solutions tab.
3. Double-click on the template you want to use.
4. If you see a warning message about macros containing viruses, click Enable Macros. (It's okay because you are confident of the source of this template: Microsoft itself.) A new workbook based on the template appears.

Caution

If you see the warning about macros when you are opening a file, don't automatically click Yes every time. If you are unsure of the source of the file, click No, and then select Tools, Macro, Macros to see a list of the macros in the file.

Customizing a Spreadsheet Solutions Template

Most Spreadsheet Solutions templates (including all the ones that come with Excel) enable you to enter your own company's information and graphics. This is handy because it saves you from having to retype this standard information each time you use the template.

When you customize a template, you are really just entering information on a separate sheet of the workbook. Various fields on the main (first) sheet of the workbook are linked to that sheet, so entering your company's name on the customization sheet makes the name appear on the main sheet. For example, information you enter on the Customize Your Expense Statement sheet appears on the Expense Statement sheet in a workbook created with the Expense Statement template.

To display the customization sheet in a Spreadsheet Solutions template, click the Customize button at the top of the worksheet. The customization sheet appears. (The one for the Expense Statement is shown in Figure 4.9.)

On the customization sheet, the row and column lines and headings are hidden, but it's really just a worksheet. To change information in a cell, just click on the cell and type the new information.

Here are some tips for working with the customization sheet:

- For information about the customization you can do, point at one of the little red triangles on the customization sheet. A comment box appears with some help.
- To change a graphic, click on the appropriate button. For example, to change the logo, click on the Select Logo button at the bottom of the

CHANGING FONTS IS COVERED IN CHAPTER 11.

customization screen (scroll down if you need to) and then choose a different logo from the graphic files on your hard disk.

- To change a font, click the Change Plate Font button at the bottom of the customization screen. This opens the Format Cells dialog box, from which you can select a different font.

Figure 4.9 Customize the template by filling in your own information.

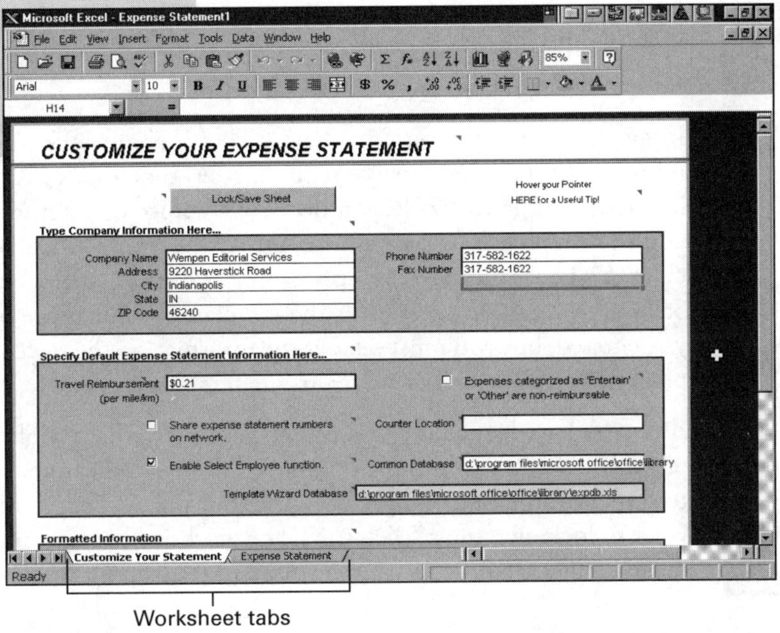

When you are finished entering your customization, you can return to the main worksheet by clicking its tab at the bottom of the Excel window. However, you will probably want to lock and/or save your changes before you do so. To lock and/or save your changes, click the Lock/Save Sheet button on the customization sheet. The Lock/Save Sheet dialog box appears (see Figure 4.10). This is a special feature found only in templates supplied by Microsoft (or in templates that somebody builds based on them). It enables you to prevent accidental changes to important information.

Figure 4.10 You can lock out changes and save your customization to the template itself from here.

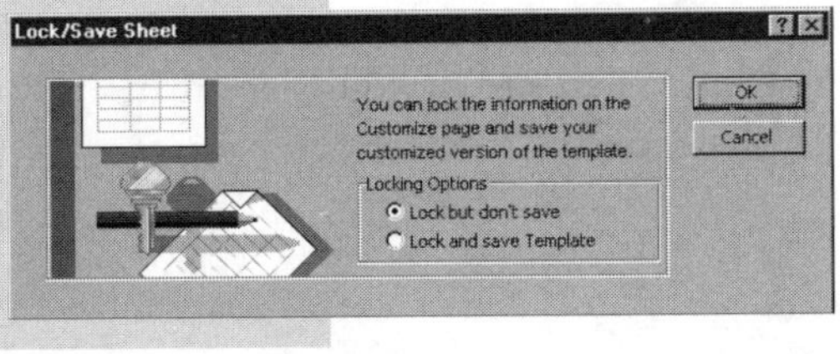

YOU LEARNED HOW TO USE TOOLBARS IN CHAPTER 1, AND YOU'LL LEARN HOW TO CREATE YOUR OWN CUSTOM TOOLBARS IN CHAPTER 6.

Locking and saving are two different things and are not necessarily related:

- *Locking* prevents changes from being made to the customized information. This ensures that you do not accidentally change your company name, address, and so on. Locking does not affect the cells on the worksheet that are designed to be changed frequently, such as the amount on a purchase order; it affects only the customized information you entered.
- *Saving* transfers the customized information you entered from this workbook (which is based on the template) to the template itself so that when you use the template in the future, your information (company name, address, and so on) is already filled in.

If you want to save, you don't have a choice about locking—you must lock the information. (You can easily unlock it later, though, as I'll show you momentarily.) However, if you lock, you do have a choice of whether you want to save. If you want to use the same information in the future when you use this template, click the Lock and Save Template option button. If not, click Lock But Don't Save. (Selecting the latter locks the template for this usage only with the settings you entered, but you must reenter the information the next time you use the template.) Then click OK to return to the template.

YOU LEARNED ABOUT ZOOMING IN CHAPTER 2. COMMENTS ARE COVERED MORE FULLY IN CHAPTER 7.

After you have locked the customizations, the Lock/Save Sheet button changes to read Unlock Sheet. To unlock the sheet, so that you can make changes to the customized information, simply click that button. At the warning box that explains what unlocking entails, click OK. The worksheet is now unlocked, and you can make further changes to your customized information.

Using the Spreadsheet Solutions Toolbar

Each of the three Spreadsheet Solutions templates that Excel provides comes with a custom toolbar that floats in its own little box on-screen. You may have noticed it in some of the earlier figures. The buttons on this toolbar correspond to built-in macros in the templates that you can use to further improve your efficiency with the template. Click on these buttons to use them, just like the buttons on any other toolbar. They are shown in the table on page 83.

Getting More Templates on the Internet

Besides the Spreadsheet Solutions templates that come with Excel, many more are available from Microsoft's Web site. If you have an Internet connection, you can access them right from Excel. Follow these steps:

Button	Description
	Toggles the zoom between full-screen view (entire page fits on-screen) and normal view (whatever zoom percentage was in use before jumping to full-screen view).
	Toggles between displaying and hiding comments (the red triangles that indicate a comment is available). These comment triangles do not print, regardless of their displayed/hidden status.
	Adds a new comment and attaches it to the cell that was selected when you clicked the button. Comments are helpful when you want to annotate a worksheet without interfering with its readability.
	Opens a Help window that further explains this template.
	Toggles between displaying and hiding an example of how to fill out the form in this template. This can be helpful if you do not understand what kind of information should go in a particular field.
	Assigns a number to the worksheet. For example, if you are working with the Invoice template and you click this button, after a dialog box warning, a number is placed next to the words Invoice Number at the top of the worksheet, starting with 1 for the first one and incrementing up each time you use the template.
	Captures the data from the form in a database. You might do this, for instance, to save the contact information for everyone you sent an invoice to into an Access database that recorded customers. After clicking this button, you have the choice of creating a new database or using an existing one. Just follow the prompts.

Hands On: Downloading Additional Templates

1. If you have a dial-up Internet connection, establish the connection. (If you have a LAN-based connection, you're already connected.)
2. In Excel, choose Help, Microsoft on the Web, Free Stuff. Your Web browser opens and displays the appropriate page at the Microsoft Web site (see Figure 4.11).

Find it Online

You can go to this Web site anytime, even if you are not in Excel. It's at http://www.microsoft.com/OfficeFreeStuff/Excel/.

3. Click on the hyperlink for the template you want to download; for example, Business Planner.

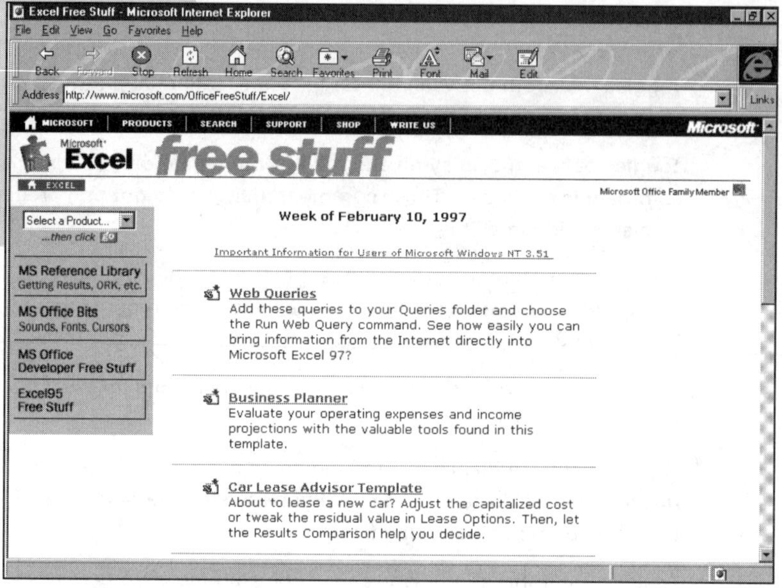

Figure 4.11 Microsoft's template offerings may change a bit over time, but you will always find a good selection here.

4. If you use Internet Explorer as your Web browser, the dialog box shown in Figure 4.12 appears. (A similar one appears in other browsers, such as Netscape.) Click Save It To Disk and then click OK.
5. Internet Explorer's Save As dialog box appears, shown in Figure 4.13. Open the Save In drop-down list and select the drive containing the folder that you typically use to temporarily hold downloaded files, such as C:\DOWNLOAD or C:\WINDOWS\DOWNLOAD.

Tip

If you do not have a folder where you can store temporary files, choose the drive on which Excel is installed and then click the New Folder button in the Save As dialog box (refer to Figure 4.13). Type **DOWNLOAD** for the name and click OK. Then choose that folder for the destination.

6. Click Save. The download begins. It may take several minutes, depending on the template you chose and your modem speed.
7. Wait for the download to complete.
8. Repeat steps 3 through 7 for each template you want to download.
9. When you are finished downloading templates, close Internet Explorer and terminate your Internet connection (if it's a dial-up connection).

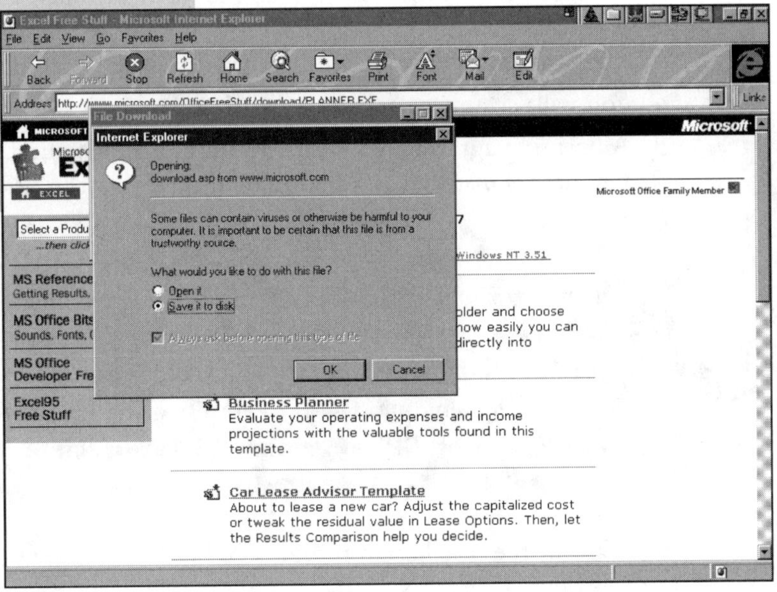

Figure 4.12 Internet Explorer asks what you want to do with the template. In this case you want to save it.

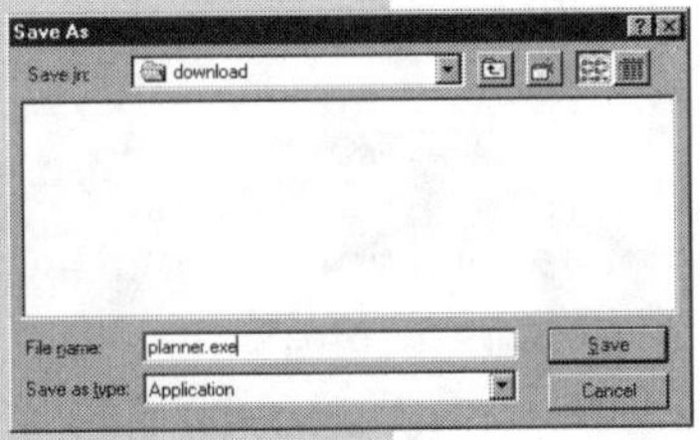

Figure 4.13 Select a folder where you normally store temporary files. If you don't have one, create one by clicking the New Folder button.

Next, you must install each template that you downloaded. Each file you downloaded is an executable file (ending in .EXE) that contains both the template you want and an installation program. To install the template, you run the installation program, as follows:

Hands On: Installing a Downloaded Template

1. Click the Start button and point to Programs. Then click Windows Explorer on the submenu. Windows Explorer opens.
2. Navigate to the folder where you put the downloaded file(s) (for instance, C:\DOWNLOAD).

3. Double-click on the downloaded file (for example, Planner.exe) to start the template installation program. You can identify the downloaded file by its icon—it looks like an open box with a window behind it.
4. You will see a message asking whether you want to continue. Click Yes.
5. A licensing agreement appears. Read it and then click Yes. The new template is installed automatically in the correct location.

Note

The exact location depends on how you installed Excel and whether you have the Office version or the stand-alone. It will probably be in the Program Files folder on the drive where Windows is installed—for example, mine is C:\Program Files\Microsoft Office\Templates\Spreadsheet Solutions.

6. Wait for the installation to finish. When it is finished, you see a notice that it is done. Click OK.

That's it! The new template is fully installed. You can use it just as you use any of the other Spreadsheet Solutions templates.

Note

If you do not see the template on your Spreadsheet Solutions tab, you may have installed it in the wrong folder. The installation program is good, but it's not infallible. Find it by clicking the Start button, pointing to Find, and then clicking on Files or Folders. Type `*.xlt` **in the Named box and then click the Find Now button. A list of all the Excel templates on your hard drive appears.**

Make a note of the location of the missing template and then use Windows Explorer to move it to the Spreadsheet Solutions folder. (If you have Windows Explorer open at the same time as the Find window, you can drag the file from the Find window's results pane directly into the appropriate folder in Windows Explorer.)

5 Working with Worksheets

In This Chapter

- Choosing Which Worksheet to Work On
- Assigning Meaningful Names to Worksheets
- Selecting Multiple Cells and Worksheets
- Adding and Removing Rows, Columns, and Cells
- Moving and Copying Worksheets

The spreadsheet landscape has changed a lot over the past decade. In early versions of Excel, a spreadsheet file (a work-book) consisted of a single worksheet, with only two dimensions (rows and columns). Nowadays, as you've seen in earlier chapters, a workbook contains a stack of work-sheets and is three-dimensional. Managing this stack of worksheets in your workbook is the subject of this chapter.

The Workbook Metaphor

Microsoft picked an excellent metaphor for describing the three-dimensional aspect of Excel's files: the workbook. Surely everyone is familiar with a three-ring binder containing a stack of reports. Each report is on a separate two-dimensional sheet containing rows and columns, and the reports are neatly stacked in a single binder. This is exactly how an Excel workbook file operates. You have a stack of worksheets neatly arranged in your workbook.

When you start a new workbook in Excel based on the default template, the workbook contains three worksheets, as shown in Figure 5.1. Each worksheet has its own tab, like tabs in a three-ring binder that mark off the sections. The only difference is that in an Excel workbook, every single page (worksheet) is tabbed, not just each section of pages.

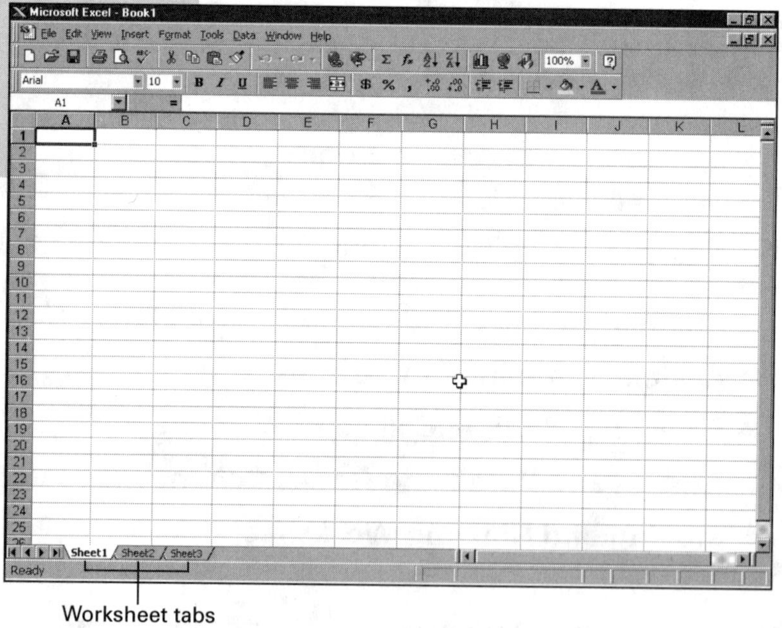

Figure 5.1 This workbook, based on the default template, has three worksheets.

Note

A workbook created with a different template than the default Workbook template might have a different number of worksheets in it. In Chapter 4, for example, I suggested that you might want to create a template containing more than three worksheets if you find yourself continually needing more than three in every workbook.

TEMPLATES ARE COVERED IN CHAPTER 4.

They may look unobtrusive, but these little tabs hide some very powerful features, as you'll see in some of the following sections. You can use them to move a worksheet to the top of the pile (a.k.a. switch to it), rename a worksheet, rearrange worksheets, and more.

Switching Between Worksheets

When you are working with a three-ring binder, you open the binder to a particular section by grabbing its tab and flipping the pages to that section. In Excel, it's even easier than that to flip to a particular page. Just click on the desired tab. That worksheet moves to the top of the pile. Figure 5.2 shows what happens when you click on the Sheet2 tab. The rows and columns for Sheet1 are hidden, and the ones for Sheet2 are displayed, or *active.*

Figure 5.2
Sheet2 is now on top (active). The rows and columns displayed are Sheet2's.

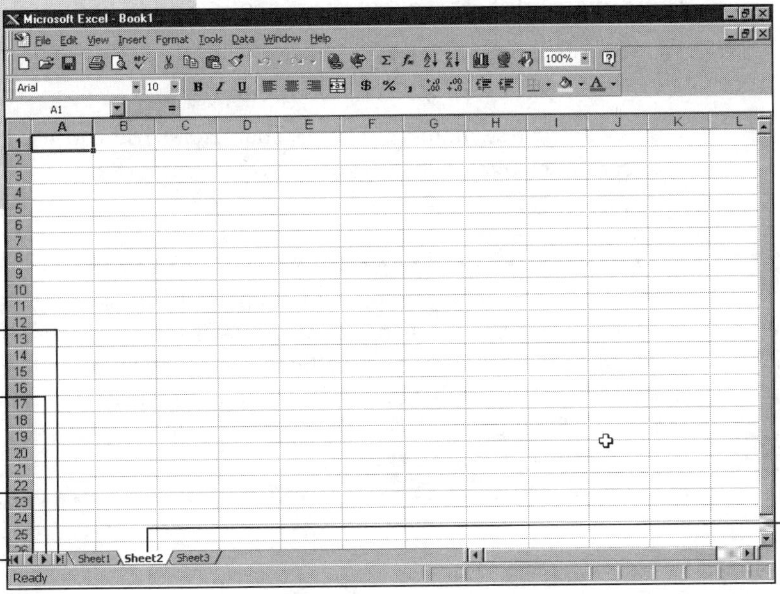

With only three worksheets using the default names, you can easily see all the tabs on-screen at once. But if you add more worksheets or change their names to longer names, the area allotted for tabs may become full. In that case, you can scroll left and right to see other tabs by clicking the Tab Scrolling buttons, pointed out in Figure 5.2. Use the Previous Sheet and Next Sheet buttons to scroll the tabs by one worksheet, or the First Sheet or Last Sheet button to scroll all the way in one direction or the other.

One of the most common mistakes beginners make is to think that they've lost all their data when they accidentally click on a worksheet tab. If you have entered all your data on Sheet1, for example, and then you click on the Sheet2 tab, you won't see your data on-screen. That's because it's on Sheet1, and Sheet1 is not currently displayed. To get back to it, just click the Sheet1 tab. If your data ever unexpectedly disappears, check the worksheet tabs to make sure that you are still on the correct sheet.

Naming a Worksheet

The default names of the worksheets (Sheet1, Sheet2, and so on) don't tell you anything about the sheets except their original positions in the workbook. For most situations, you will want more descriptive tab names, such as 1997 Budget, 1998 Estimates, Revenue Chart, and so on. Fortunately, it's easy to change the name of a worksheet. Follow these steps:

1. Double-click on a tab you want to rename. The name becomes highlighted (white letters on a black background).
2. Type the new name, up to 31 characters. You can use spaces and any special characters you want.
3. Press Enter.

There is a 31-character limit on the length of the name you give to a tab, but try to keep the names shorter than that. Why? Take a look at Figure 5.3. The first two worksheets in the workbook have been assigned names so long that you can't see the third tab at all without scrolling with the Tab Scrolling buttons. If you don't want to spend a lot of time scrolling the tabs, make the names short enough so that all the tabs can be displayed at once.

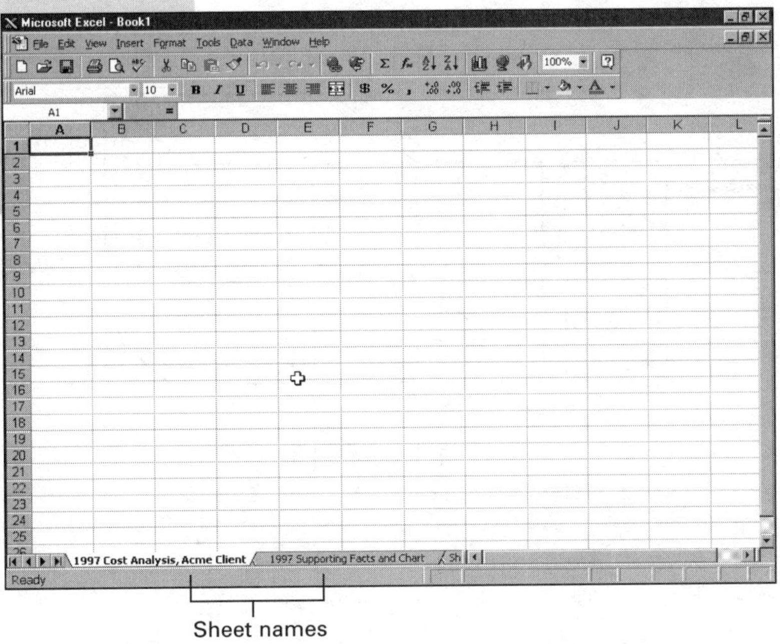

Figure 5.3
The sheets have been assigned such long names that not all the tabs are visible without scrolling.

Understanding Cells

Cells are the individual boxes on a worksheet into which you enter your text and data. A good way to envision cells is as a stack of cardboard boxes, with their openings all facing out toward you, as shown in Figure 5.4. Each cell is a separate entity by itself, with its own sides, name, and format settings. This cardboard-box metaphor will become useful later, when you start doing things to cells (like moving them and formatting their contents), so file it in the back of your mind for now.

Cells take their names from the row number and column letter in which they reside. This name is called a *cell address*. For example, in Figure 5.4, the top row contains cells A1, B1, C1, and D1, from left to right. The second row contains cells A2, B2, C2, and D2.

Row and column letter and number designations are strictly determined by their position. For example, if you moved Column A to the right of Column D, it would no longer be Column A; it would be Column D, and all the columns to the left of it would shift up one letter (B would become A; C would become B; D would become C). The row numbering and column lettering, therefore, serves no purpose except to help you identify where you are on a worksheet at any given time.

Figure 5.4
A useful metaphor for thinking about cells in a worksheet is a stack of cardboard boxes.

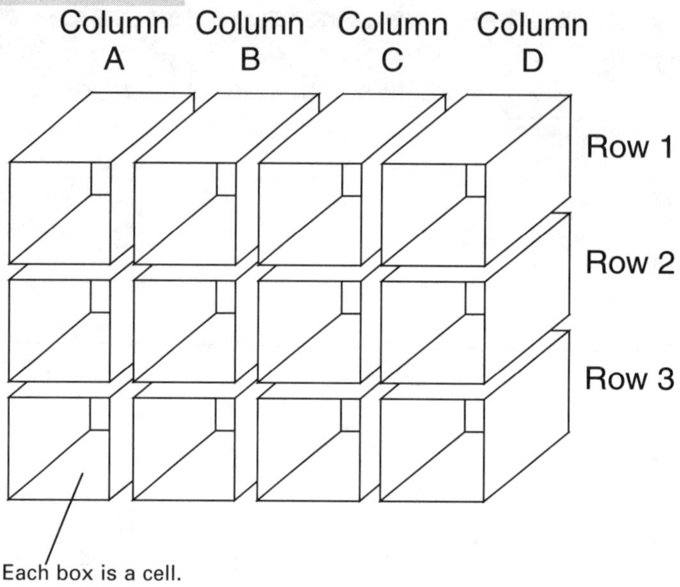

Moving Around on a Worksheet

By "moving around" on a worksheet, what I really mean is moving the *cell cursor*. The cell cursor is the dark outline that rests on the *active* cell (see Figure 5.5). For example, when you first open a new workbook, the top-left cell is active (cell A1). It's important to know which is the active cell because the characters you type go into whatever cell is active.

The simplest way to select a cell (making it the active one) is to click on it with the mouse. You can also move the cell cursor to a cell by pressing one of the keyboard arrow keys. This moves the cell cursor one cell in the direction of the arrow you pressed.

Table 5.1 shows some of the many ways to move the cell cursor around on the worksheet.

Note

In some of the examples in Table 5.1, you may see columns identified by multiple letters, such as IV. When Excel runs out of single letters (there are only 26, and there are hundreds of columns on a worksheet), it starts with AA, then AB, and so on, until it gets to AZ. Then it starts with BA, BB, and so on. The last column in an Excel worksheet is IV.

Figure 5.5 The active cell is the one with the cell cursor's black border around it at the moment.

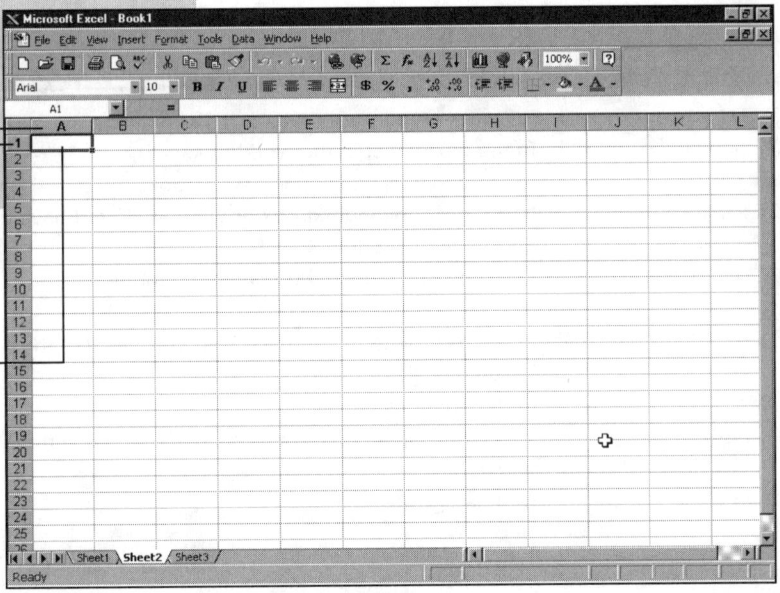

The row number and column letter of the active cell appear bold.

Cell cursor

Table 5.1 Cell Cursor Movement

Key	Moves ...
←	Left one cell.
→	Right one cell.
↑	Up one cell.
↓	Down one cell.
Ctrl+→	To the last column of the active cell's row. For example, if the active cell is A1, Ctrl+→ makes the active cell IV1.
Ctrl+←	To the first column of the active cell's row (column A).
Ctrl+↓	To the last row of the active cell's column. For example, if the active cell is B3, Ctrl+↓ makes the active cell B65536.
Home	Same as Ctrl+←.
Ctrl+Home	To cell A1.
Ctrl+End	To the bottom right corner of your data area. For example, if you have data in cells A2, B4, F8, and D16, pressing Ctrl+End makes cell F16 active (because the last column used is F, and the last row used is 16).
Pg Dn	Down one screen.
Pg Up	Up one screen.
Alt+Pg Dn	Right one screen.

Table 5.1 Continued

Alt+Pg Up	Left one screen.
Ctrl+Pg Dn	To the next sheet in the workbook.
Ctrl+Pg Up	To the previous sheet in the workbook.
Ctrl+F6 or Ctrl+Tab	To the next open workbook or window (if you have more than one workbook opened).
Ctrl+Shift+F6 or Ctrl+Shift+Tab	To the previous open workbook or window.
F6	To the next pane, if you have split your view of the workbook (see Chapter 2).
Shift+F6	To the previous pane.
Ctrl+←Backspace	Scroll the display to show the active cell, if it is not already displayed on-screen.
End, then Home	Same as Ctrl+End.

What if you can't see the cell on-screen that you want to make active? You can use some of the methods in Table 5.1 to move quickly to different parts of the worksheet, and then click on the exact cell you want. Alternatively, you can use the scroll bars to bring that cell into view, and then click on it to make it active.

If you're using the scroll bars to locate a cell, don't forget to click on a cell after you've found it to make it active. Simply bringing a cell into view with the scroll bars does not make it active. Many people have made the mistake of scrolling to a particular cell and then immediately typing, thinking that they were typing into the visible cell. Actually, they were typing into the previously selected active cell.

CHAPTER 3 COVERS OPENING MULTIPLE WORKBOOKS AT ONCE.

The following list describes how to scroll the display up or down, but it works the same way when using the horizontal scroll bar to scroll to one side or the other.

- Click the arrows at the top or bottom of the vertical scroll bar to move the display up or down one cell.
- Click above or below the scroll box on the vertical scroll bar to move the display up or down one screen.

- Drag the scroll box. A pop-up box appears next to it telling you which row will be at the top of the display if you release the mouse button at that point. For example, in Figure 5.6, if I were to release the mouse button, the top row would be 14.

Note

Dragging the scroll box will take you quickly to the last or first row or column in which there is something entered, but won't take you all the way to the last row or column on the worksheet. You must use one of the other methods for that.

Figure 5.6 You can scroll the display by dragging the scroll box.

YOU LEARNED ABOUT SCROLL BARS IN CHAPTER 1.

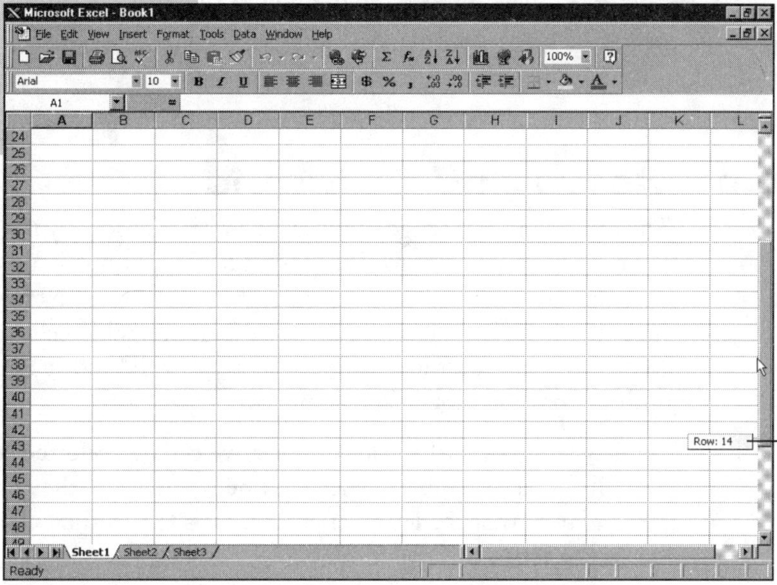

This tells what cell will be at the top if I release the mouse button now.

Selecting Ranges

When you move the cell cursor around, as you learned to do in the preceding section, you are selecting which cell will be active. Anything that you do—any command you enter or button you click—affects the active cell. For example, when you type text, it always goes into the active cell.

Sometimes, however, you might like to affect more than one cell at a time. For example, perhaps you want to format an entire row to show dollar signs next to the numbers it contains. In cases like this, you select a *range* of cells. A single cell is still active, but other cells are included in a grouping with it too, so that commands you issue to affect the active cell also affect the other selected cells too.

When referring to a range, it is customary to refer to it in this way: the top-left cell address, followed by a colon, and then the bottom-right cell address. For example, the range of B2, B3, C2, and C3 would be B2:C3.

Remember that selecting is always a prelude to some other action, such as formatting, moving, or copying. When you select a range of cells, you're saying to Excel: "Please apply the command I'm about to issue to this group of cells." Later in this chapter, you'll learn how to take that second step: issuing a command that affects the selected range.

Note

You can work with a range when issuing almost any command, but you cannot enter text into more than one cell at a time. When you type text, it always goes in the active cell, regardless of how many other cells are selected.

Selecting Rows and Columns

The most common range that most people occasionally need to select is an entire row or column. To do so, just click on the column letter or row number. The entire column or row becomes highlighted (black, with any contents that may be there in white letters) except for the leftmost visible cell in it. The first cell in a selected row or column becomes the active cell, and it remains white to distinguish it from the others (see Figure 5.7).

Here's where it gets a bit tricky: the active cell in a selected row is the leftmost visible cell—that is, visible on-screen when you select the row. If you had scrolled the display so that the leftmost column was C and then clicked on the 5 to select row 5, the active cell would be C5.

If you were to type some characters while a row was selected, as in Figure 5.7, the text would be placed into the active cell, and the rest of the selected cells would be ignored. If you were to issue any command, however, such as a formatting directive, it would affect all the cells in the entire row or column.

Figure 5.7
Click on the row number to select the entire row.

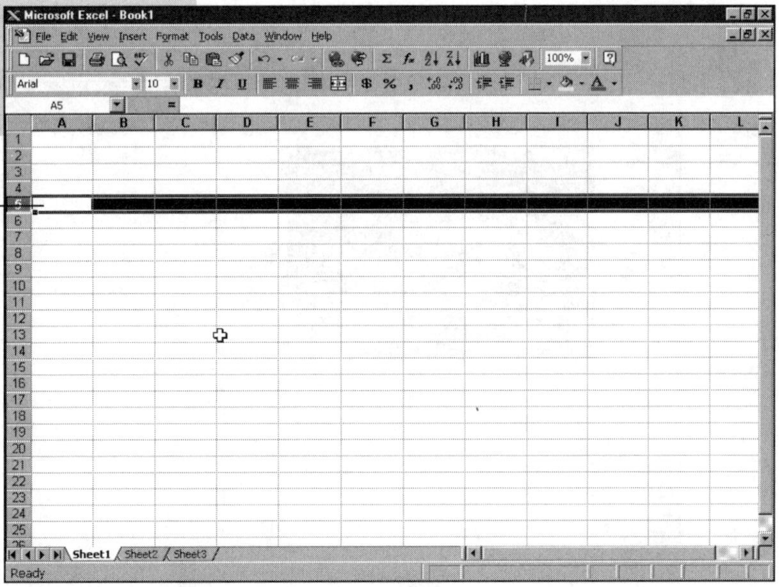

The active cell is A5, the leftmost visible cell in the row.

Selecting Ranges of Cells

Selecting a range of cells is a bit more involved than simply clicking on a row or column indicator. You must drag your mouse across the cells you want to select. For example, to select the range of cells B2:F14 (that is, the cells in a block with B2 in the upper left corner and F14 in the lower right), follow these steps:

1. Position your mouse pointer over B2.
2. Hold down the left mouse button.
3. Drag the pointer to cell F14.
4. Release the mouse button. That range of cells is selected (highlighted), as shown in Figure 5.8.

Notice that the cell you started with, B2, is the active cell. You could have started with F14 and dragged to B2 if you had wanted F14 to be the active cell instead.

Tip

To select a large range, where some of the cells are not in view, click on the first cell of the range. Then scroll to the last one (opposite corner) and hold down the Shift key while you click on it.

Figure 5.8 The range B2:F14 is selected here.

The active cell is a different color than the rest, but it is still part of the range.

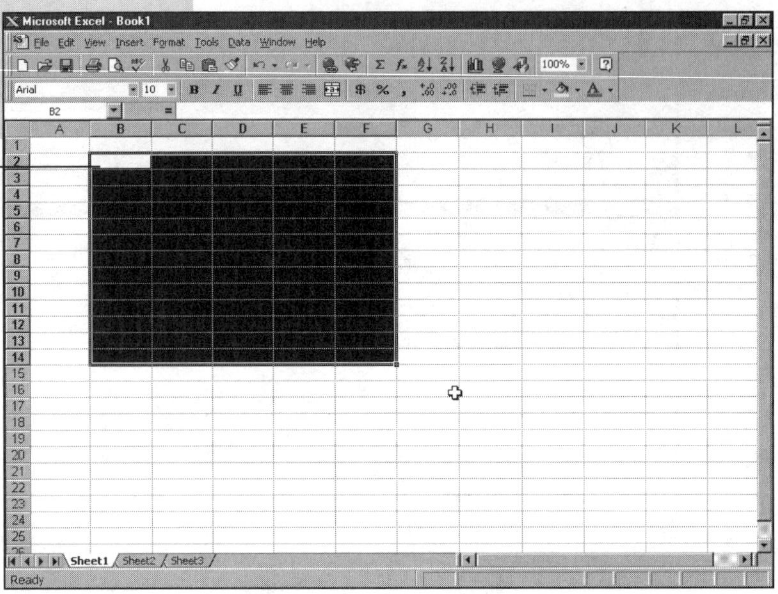

Note

Most of the time when you select a range, you are selecting it to issue a command that affects the entire range. Therefore, most of the time it does not matter which is the active cell of the range.

You can also select blocks of cells with the keyboard if you prefer. Follow these steps:

1. Move the cell cursor to a cell that should be in one corner of the range.
2. Hold down the Shift key.
3. Press the arrow keys to extend the highlight from the active cell to other cells.
4. Release the Shift key when the desired range is selected.

Tip

You can combine the movement keys from Table 5.1 with the preceding procedure. For example, to quickly jump the selection to the last column of the worksheet, hold down the Shift key and then press Ctrl+→.

Selecting Noncontiguous Ranges

Usually you will want to select a contiguous range of cells—that is, a rectangular block where all the cells lie together in one spot. But occasionally you may need to select cells or blocks of cells in several spots on a worksheet. (For example, perhaps you want to set up special formatting for some headings, and they are scattered all over the worksheet.) To select noncontiguous cells, do the following:

1. Select the first cell or range of cells, using any of the methods you learned in the preceding section.
2. Hold down the Ctrl key.
3. Select additional cells or ranges with the mouse.
4. Release the Ctrl key.

Figure 5.9 shows several noncontiguous blocks selected. (The group of blocks forms a single range.) If you want to practice selecting, see whether you can duplicate the look of Figure 5.9.

Figure 5.9 Try to duplicate the selections shown here.

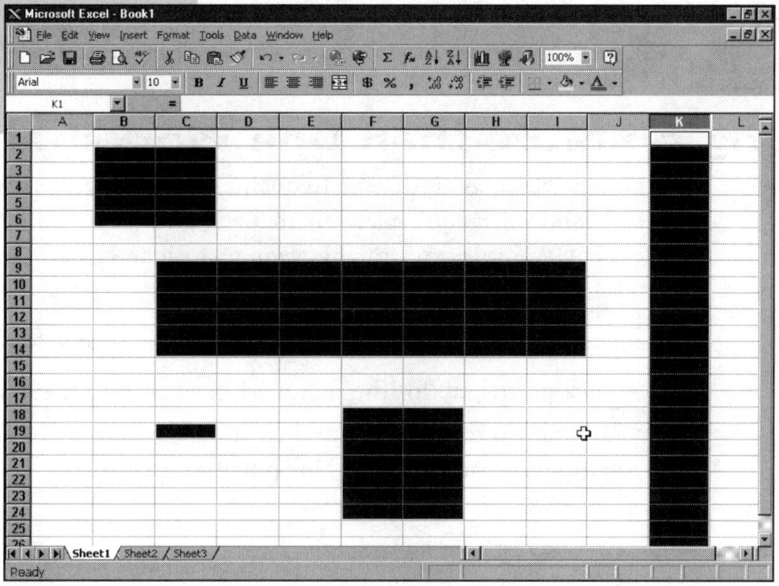

Hands On: Selection Practice

You can try selecting multiple ranges on your own, or follow these steps:

1. Select the range B2 through C6.
2. Hold down the Ctrl key.
3. Drag the mouse across the range C9 to I14.
4. Click on cell C19. (A range can be a single cell.)
5. Drag across F18 through G24.
6. Click on the heading for column K. (A range can also be a column or a row.)
7. Release the Ctrl key.

When you're finished practicing, click on any cell to undo the range selection. To undo a range selection, all you have to do is click away from it.

Tip

If you release the Ctrl key and then decide you want to select more ranges, just press it again and continue selecting.

Selecting on More than One Worksheet

Although they may not occur frequently, there may be times when you want to make a noncontiguous selection that includes cells from more than one worksheet. For example, you might want to format cell A1 on every sheet in your workbook in a certain way.

To make the same cells highlighted on multiple sheets, follow these steps:

1. Click on the tab for the first worksheet you want to include.
2. Hold down the Ctrl key and click on the tabs of the additional worksheets, one-by-one. This puts the selected worksheets in Group mode; you see `Group` in the title bar.
3. Release the Ctrl key.
4. Select the range with the mouse on the currently visible worksheet. The range is highlighted on every worksheet that you included.
5. When you are finished working with the range, click on any tab that's not part of the worksheet group to turn off Group mode, or Shift-click the active worksheet's tab.

You can test the preceding steps by clicking on the tab for each selected worksheet. Notice that no matter which tab you click on to display, the same range is selected.

You can also include multiple worksheets in irregular, noncontiguous ranges. For example, perhaps you want to select A1:C3 on Sheet1 and D5:F14 on Sheet2. Follow the steps in the preceding section for selecting noncontiguous blocks as a range, and release the Ctrl key and click on Sheet2's tab to jump to it. Then hold down the Ctrl key again and select its range(s).

Selecting an Entire Worksheet

Now that you've run the gauntlet of range selections, selecting an entire worksheet should be a piece of cake. See that blank gray box where the row numbers and column letters intersect? It's called the Select All button. Just click on it. The entire worksheet becomes selected (see Figure 5.10). To remove the selection, click any cell in the worksheet.

Note

Be careful when you have the entire worksheet selected. An accidental press of the Del key can wipe out your entire worksheet's contents. (Of course, you can still choose Edit, Undo to reverse a mistake.)

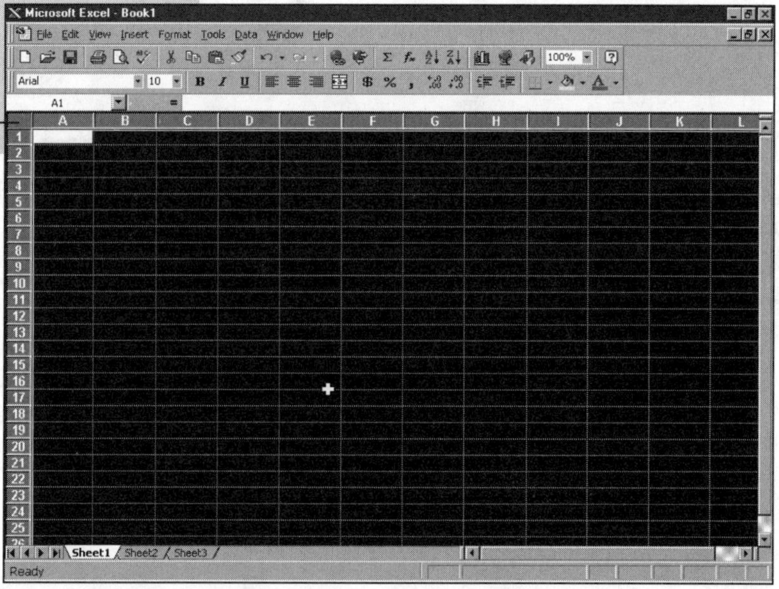

Select All button

Figure 5.10 To select the entire worksheet, click on the Select All button.

Inserting and Deleting Cells

Remember earlier, in Figure 5.4, when I said you should think of the grid of cells as boxes? Well, now is an excellent time to bring out this metaphor again.

When you insert or delete a cell, it's like pulling its entire box out of the stack, except that the stack has sort of a "reverse gravity"—When you pull a box out of the stack, the remaining boxes fall either up or to the left to close up the space. So, for example, If I delete cell C2, Excel asks me whether I want to close up the space by shifting the cells up or by shifting cells to the left, as shown in Figure 5.11.

Figure 5.11 When you remove a cell, Excel needs to know which way the remaining cells should shift to close up the space.

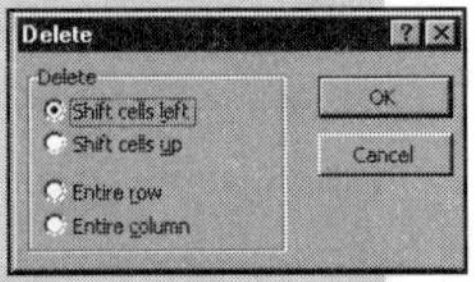

If I choose Shift Cells Up, all the remaining cells in column C move up: C3 becomes C2, C4 becomes C3, and so on. If I choose Shift Cells Left, all the remaining cells in row 2 move to the left: D2 becomes C2, E2 becomes D2, and so on.

It's the same thing when you insert a cell. Excel needs to know which cells should move over to make room for the new box in the stack. For example, if I insert a new cell at position C2, the existing C2 must either move down to C3 or across to D2.

Caution

Inserting and deleting individual cells can throw off the alignment for the rest of the worksheet. Cells that used to be in the same row with each other may not be together anymore after you insert or delete a cell from one of their columns. For this reason, you will usually want to insert and delete entire rows and columns instead of individual cells, or remove the contents of a cell rather than the cell itself.

Inserting a Cell

To insert a cell, follow these steps:

1. Select the cell that is currently in the position where you want the new cell to go. (The existing cells will move to make room.)
2. Choose Insert, Cells. The Insert dialog box appears (see Figure 5.12).
3. Choose Shift Cells Right or Shift Cells Down to indicate what should happen to the existing cells.
4. Click OK. The new cell is inserted.

Figure 5.12 Use the Insert dialog box to specify where the existing cells should shift.

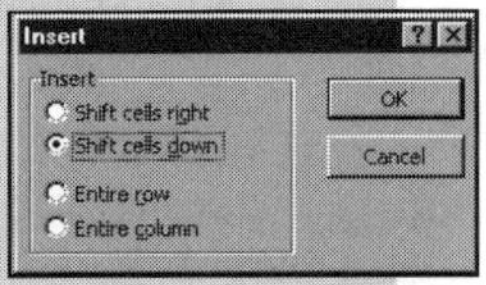

You can insert more than one cell at once by selecting more than one cell before you begin. For example, to insert four cells in column C, starting right below C1, select C2 through C5 in step 1 and then choose Down in step 3.

Deleting a Cell

To delete a cell (or more than one cell), follow these steps:

1. Select the cell(s) you want to delete.
2. Choose Edit, Delete. The Delete dialog box appears (refer to Figure 5.11).
3. Choose Shift Cells Left or Shift Cells Up to indicate what should happen to the existing cells.
4. Click OK. The cells are removed.

Note

There is a big difference between clearing a cell and deleting it. Clearing a cell removes its content; it's like taking everything out of the box. (Select the cell and press the Del key to clear it.) Deleting a cell is like taking the entire box out of the stack.

Inserting and Deleting Rows and Columns

Compared to deleting and inserting cells, deleting and inserting rows and columns are a snap. Just follow these steps to insert a row or column:

1. Select the row or column before which you want the new one inserted. If you want to insert multiple rows or columns at once, select an equivalent number to begin with; for example, to insert three columns to the left of the current column B, select columns B, C, and D.
2. Open the Insert menu and choose either Columns or Rows, depending on which you want. The new rows or columns appear, and the existing ones move to the right or down to make room.

You can perform step 2 without step 1 if you are inserting just a single row or column. For example, if you want to insert a new row before row 6, make sure that the active cell is in row 6 and then choose Insert, Rows. The row or column is inserted relative to the active cell, so make sure that an appropriate cell is active before you choose the command.

Deleting a row or column works just like deleting individual cells. Select what you want to delete (a single row or column or multiple ones) and then choose Edit, Delete.

Note

In some programs, notably word processing ones, pressing the Del key on the keyboard is a shortcut for the Delete command. Not so in Excel. In Excel, the Del key is a shortcut for the Edit, Clear, Contents command, which clears the contents of a cell without removing it from the worksheet. You must use the Edit, Delete menu command to completely remove the cells, rows, or columns from the worksheet.

Inserting and Deleting Worksheets

Excel's workbooks are flexible; you can have as many or as few worksheets in a workbook as you want, from 1 to 255.

Having no more worksheets than are required makes the saved file smaller and quicker to open and close. Therefore, if you know you will not use more than one sheet in the workbook, you could delete the other two default ones to trim your workbook. Conversely, if you run out of worksheets in a workbook, you can add more.

Inserting Worksheets

As you learned in Chapter 3, each workbook starts with three tabbed worksheets. You can easily add hundreds more to meet the needs of any size project, if you have enough memory in your computer. (In reality, a computer with an average amount of memory gets bogged down when more than a few dozen worksheets are used.)

To insert a single worksheet, follow these steps:

1. Click the tab for the worksheet before which you want the new one inserted. For example, to insert a worksheet before Sheet1, click the Sheet1 tab.
2. Choose Insert, Worksheet. A tab for the new sheet appears.

When you insert a new sheet, it takes on the name "Sheet" followed by the next available number in your workbook. For example, if you already have Sheet1, Sheet2, and Sheet3, the new sheet is Sheet4. Notice in Figure 5.13 that the existing sheet names have not changed—the new sheet has the name "Sheet4" even though it is now the first worksheet in the workbook. (You can rename any sheet at any time, as you learned earlier in this chapter.)

Figure 5.13 The new sheet's name does not reflect its position in the workbook.

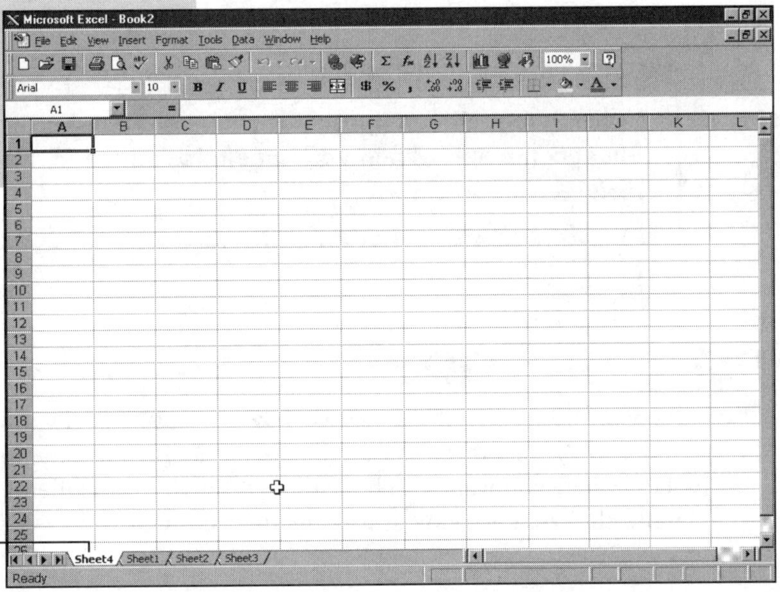

New sheet

You can add more than one worksheet at a time. Select the number of worksheet tabs that represents the number of sheets to add. For example, to add two worksheets before Sheet2, click on the Sheet2 tab and then hold down the Ctrl key while you click on the Sheet3 tab. Then choose the Insert, Worksheet command.

Tip

Need to add many sheets to the workbook? Select all the existing sheets before you insert, to insert the maximum number possible. Then choose Insert, Worksheet; reselect all sheets; and keep inserting until you have the number you need. To select all sheets at once in a workbook, right-click any worksheet tab and choose Select All Sheets from the shortcut menu that appears.

You can't insert a new worksheet in "last place" in a workbook because the new sheet is always placed before the selected sheet. However, you can insert a new sheet and then move it to the position you want, as described later in this chapter in "Moving and Copying Worksheets."

Deleting Worksheets

There is a special command for deleting a worksheet: Edit, Delete Sheet. Choose that command, and you'll see a warning box reminding you that you are permanently deleting that sheet. Click OK to continue and remove the sheet.

As with inserting, you can delete more than one sheet at a time. Click on the tab of the first sheet you want to delete; then hold down the Ctrl key and click on the tabs for each of the other sheets you want to delete. When you've selected all the sheets, choose Edit, Delete Sheet to wipe them all out at once.

Caution

Unlike many other commands, you cannot undo the Edit, Delete Sheet command. When you issue this command, make sure that it's really what you want.

Moving and Copying Worksheets

As with most tasks, there are two ways to move or copy a worksheet: 1) the easy way and 2) the powerful way. The easy way is to use the mouse to just drag the sheet where you want it. The harder way involves the menu system and gives you more choices. Let's look at each method individually.

Moving or Copying with the Mouse

Moving a sheet is easy—just drag its tab. The mouse pointer looks like a sheet of paper as you drag. You will also see a little black triangle showing where the sheet will be positioned if you released the mouse button at that moment (see Figure 5.14). When you are satisfied with the position, release the mouse button to drop the sheet into its new location.

Figure 5.14
To move a sheet, drag the sheet tab and drop it in the new position.

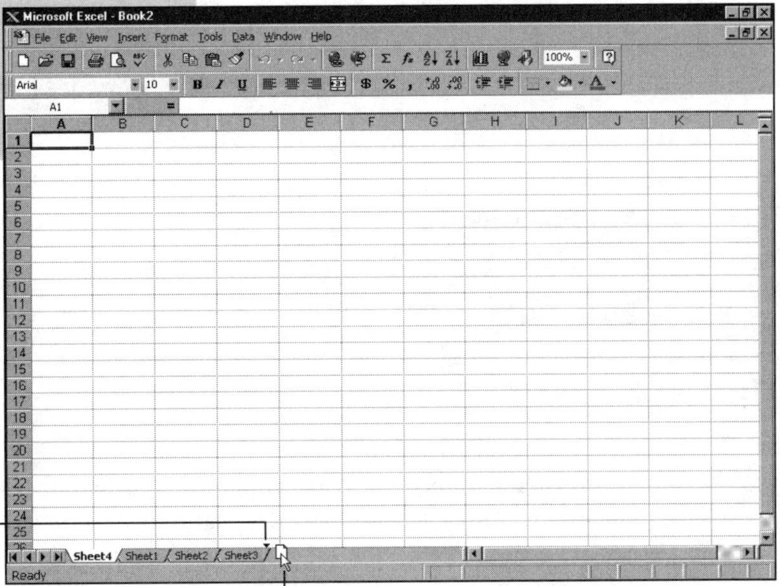

This marker shows where the sheet will be positioned.

Mouse pointer

You can move sheets from one workbook to another in this same way. Open both workbooks and arrange the windows so that they are both visible (choose Window, Arrange, Horizontal—see Chapter 2). Then drag the worksheet tab from one workbook's window to the other.

To copy a sheet by dragging it, hold down the Ctrl key as you drag the sheet tab. If you're dragging the sheet tab within the same workbook, the new tab will have a (2) in the name (or some other number, if you've made more than one copy). For example, if you copy Sheet1, the copy will be named Sheet1 (2). You can rename the new sheet as you like.

Moving and Copying from the Menu

Excel offers an alternative to dragging the mouse—the Edit, Move or Copy Sheet command. When you use this command to move or copy a worksheet, you get a dialog box of choices, a few of which are unavailable or unwieldy in the dragging method. Follow these steps:

1. If you want to move or copy into a different workbook, make sure that both the source and destination workbooks are open.
2. Click the tab of the sheet you want to move or copy to ensure that it's the active sheet.
3. Choose Edit, Move or Copy Sheet. The Move or Copy Sheet dialog box appears (see Figure 5.15).

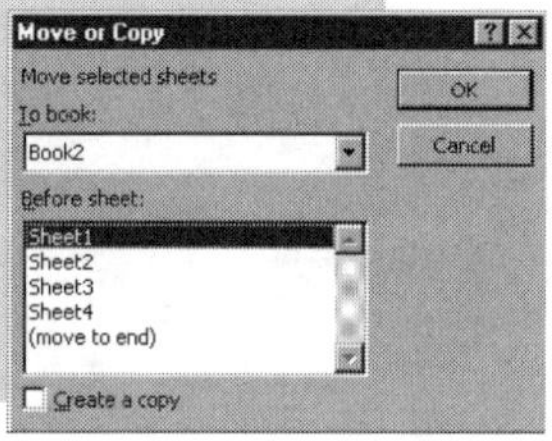

Figure 5.15 This dialog box contains all the controls you need to move or copy a worksheet.

4. If you want to move or copy into a different workbook, open the To Book drop-down list and select the destination workbook.
5. On the Before Sheet list, click the worksheet before which the new one should be placed. Or, to place it at the end of the workbook, select Move to End.
6. If you want to copy rather than move, select the Create a Copy check box.
7. Click OK. The move or copy is executed.

6

Customizing Excel Settings

In This Chapter

- Changing the Toolbar Buttons
- Creating Your Own Toolbars
- Changing How Excel Operates
- Specifying File Locations

This chapter is for the dial-turners, the button-tweakers, the folks (like me) who aren't content until every little control is set to their exact specifications. In this chapter, you'll look at the contol panel behind Excel's interface and learn how to change the system settings for your own preferences.

Toolbars

The toolbars you see at the top of the screen change in Excel depending on what you're doing. Most of the time, the Standard and Formatting toolbars appear; when you do special things like edit charts (see Chapter 14), other toolbars appear instead containing tools appropriate to the task at hand. In Chapter 2, you learned to display and hide toolbars. (Remember: right-click on any visible toolbar and then select the toolbar you want to display or hide from the menu that appears.)

Changing What Buttons Appear on a Toolbar

SEE CHAPTER 1 TO LEARN HOW TO USE TOOLBAR BUTTONS FOR COMMON TASKS LIKE PRINTING, SAVING, AND SO ON.

Not all Excel users use the program in the same way, and you may find that you frequently use a few commands for which there are no buttons on the Standard or Formatting toolbars. In cases like that, you may want to add a button to one of the default toolbars that will perform the action you need.

To add a new toolbar button, the general procedure is this:

1. Right-click any toolbar and choose Customize from the shortcut menu that appears. The Customize dialog box opens.
2. Click the Commands tab.
3. Select a menu or toolbar from the Categories list. All the buttons, commands, and options available from that menu or toolbar appear on the Commands list to the right (see Figure 6.1). For example, many commands on the Format menu open dialog boxes full of options. When you select Format in the Categories list, a complete list of all the options from all those dialog boxes appears on the Commands list.
4. Scroll through the Commands list and select the command you want. Some of the commands have ellipses (…) after their names. If you choose one of these, the button you add to the toolbar will open a dialog box.

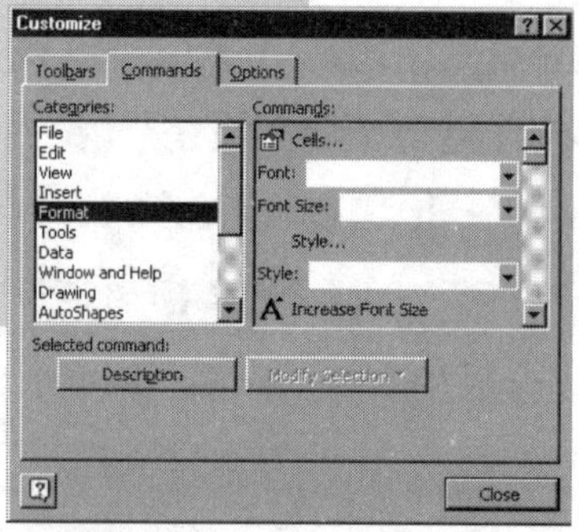

Figure 6.1 From the Commands tab, you choose what command you want to make into a button.

Others (for example, Font in Figure 6.1) have a drop-down list after their names. Choosing one of these will place the drop-down list on the toolbar.

5. Drag the command you want from the Commands list to a toolbar. As you drag onto a toolbar, your pointer becomes a bold vertical line that indicates where the new button will go. When you release the mouse button, the command becomes a button on that toolbar.
6. Repeat steps 3 through 5 to add more buttons if you want. Click Close when you're finished.

When the Customize dialog box is open (refer to Figure 6.1), you can not only add buttons to toolbars but also remove them simply by dragging them off the toolbar. You can also rearrange buttons by dragging them from one toolbar to another or from one spot to another on the same toolbar.

When the Customize dialog box is open, none of the menu commands and toolbars work normally—instead they respond to your dragging them around. So don't try to use any of the menus when the Customize dialog box is open (for instance, don't try Edit, Undo to reverse a button-dragging action you just performed), or you might accidentally make a change to the menu itself.

The easiest way to learn how to add and remove buttons to a toolbar is to "just do it," so perform the steps in the following "Hands On" section to try one out.

Hands On: A Double Underline Button

Let's say that your boss wants you to double underline certain cells on your worksheet so that they will be more easily noticed. There is no double underline button on either of the default toolbars, so each time you want double underline, you have to go through the arduous process of opening the Format menu, choosing Cells, clicking the Font tab, opening the Underline drop-down list, selecting Double, and clicking OK. Whew!

A much easier way to go is to add a Double Underline button to the Formatting toolbar, right next to the regular Underline button. Follow these steps to do it:

1. Right-click on any toolbar and choose Customize.
2. Select the Commands tab.

3. Scroll down the Categories list and select Format.
4. On the Commands list, scroll down and select Double Underline.
5. Drag the words "Double Underline" up to the Formatting toolbar and drop them immediately to the right of the Underline (U) button.
6. Click Close. Your new button appears on the toolbar, as shown in Figure 6.2.

Figure 6.2 The Double Underline button has been added to the Formatting toolbar.

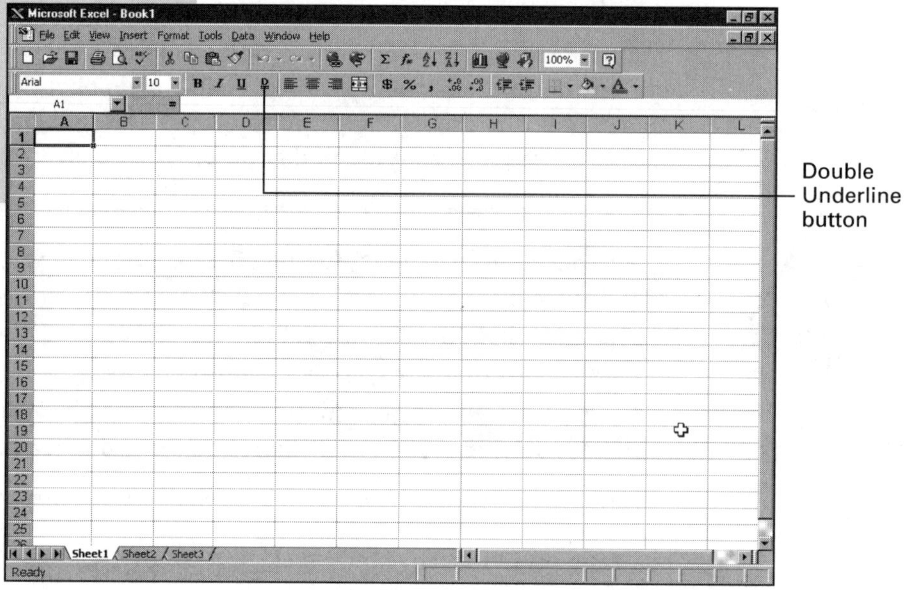

To try out your button, type some text in a cell, and then click the new Double Underline button. It toggles the double underline attribute on or off each time you click on it.

Suppose that you want to place that Double Underline button elsewhere—perhaps at the far left of the Bold button. Follow these steps to do so:

1. Right-click on any toolbar and choose Customize.
2. Drag the Double Underline button from its current location to the right of the Bold button (see Figure 6.3).
3. Release the mouse button. The button moves to its new location.
4. Click Close.

Now let's say that you change your mind and you don't want that Double Underline button anymore. (Perhaps you get a new boss who doesn't care about double underlining!) Follow these steps to get rid of the button:

1. Right-click on any toolbar and choose Customize.
2. Drag the Double Underline button down and away from the toolbar. Your mouse pointer turns into a gray box with an X (see Figure 6.4) when the button is far enough away from the toolbar to be removed.
3. Release the mouse button. The button disappears.
4. Click Close.

Tip

If you make mistakes in customizing one of Excel's toolbars, you can undo your changes by selecting the toolbar from the Toolbars tab of the Customize dialog box and then clicking the Reset button. This works only with the toolbars that come with Excel, not with toolbars you have created yourself (which you'll learn to do in the following section).

Creating New Toolbars

SEE CHAPTER 2 TO LEARN HOW TO WORK WITH MULTIPLE WINDOWS.

Sometimes a nip and tuck at an existing toolbar just isn't enough. Perhaps you need to add ten buttons to a toolbar, for instance—there won't be enough room for all the buttons on one line! In cases like that, it's best to create a brand-new toolbar. For example, if you do a lot with multiple windows, frequently splitting and arranging the panes for various purposes, you might want to create a window-controlling toolbar.

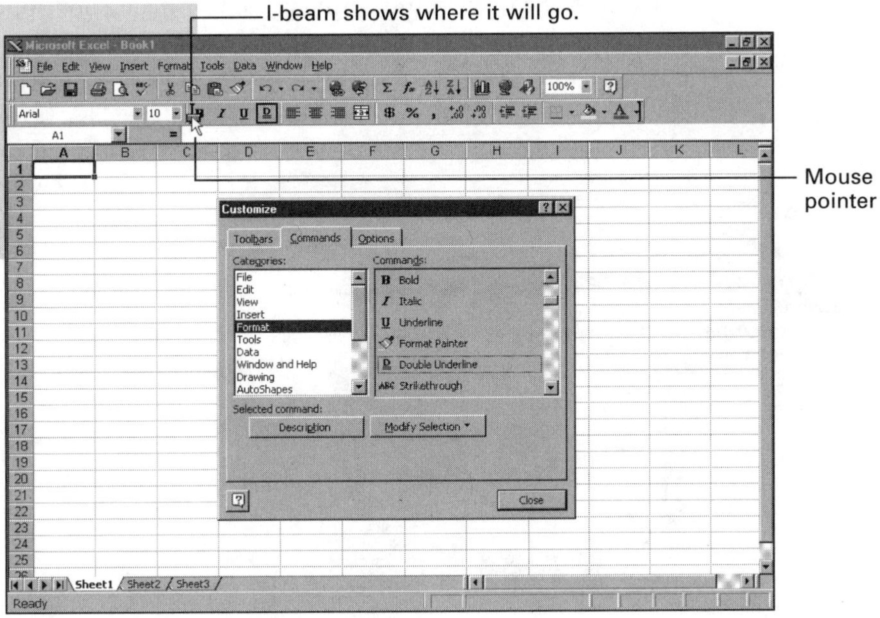

Figure 6.3 You can move a button by dragging it to a different spot while the Customize dialog box is open.

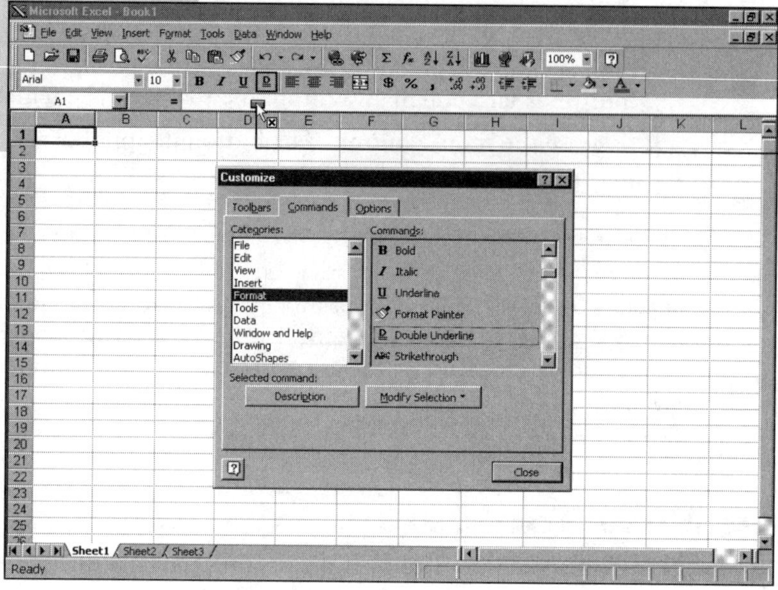

Figure 6.4 Drag a button away from the toolbars to remove it.

Mouse pointer shows an X under it.

To create a toolbar, follow these steps:

1. Right-click any toolbar and choose Customize.
2. Select the Toolbars tab (see Figure 6.5).
3. Click the New button. A New Toolbar dialog box appears.
4. Type the name for the new toolbar in the Toolbar Name text box (for example, **Window Controls**) and click OK. A little floating window appears alongside the Customize dialog box. This is your new toolbar (see Figure 6.6).

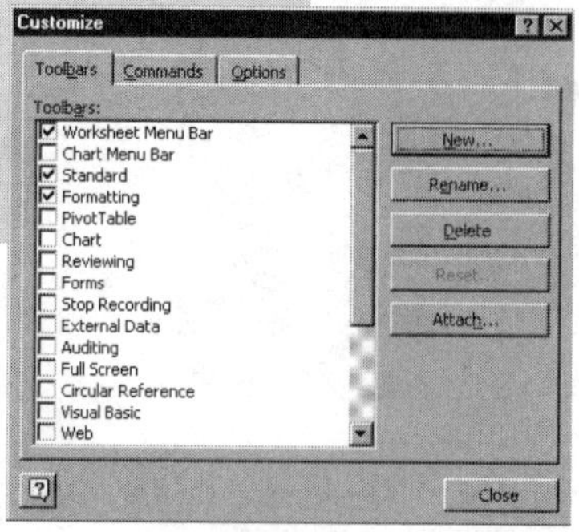

Figure 6.5 You can create your own toolbars from here.

Figure 6.6 Your new toolbar is empty, so it is very small. It will get bigger as you add buttons to it.

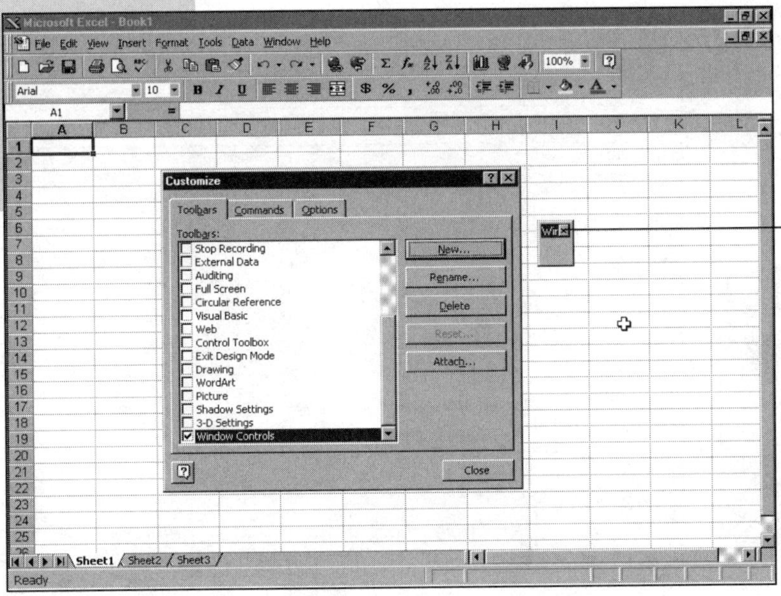

Note

If you don't see the new toolbar floating alongside the dialog box, drag the title bar on the dialog box to move it slightly to the left. The floating toolbar may be behind it.

5. (Optional) If you want the toolbar to be anchored at the top of the screen, like the other toolbars, drag its title bar up to the position where you want it (see Figure 6.7).

If you plan on using the toolbar in its docked position at the top or bottom of the screen, drag it into place (step 5) first, before you add buttons to it (step 6). That way you can gauge how many buttons will fit on the toolbar without running off the screen.

6. Add buttons to the new toolbar, as you learned earlier in this chapter.
7. When you are finished, click Close.

Figure 6.7 When the toolbar is anchored at the top, it no longer has a title bar.

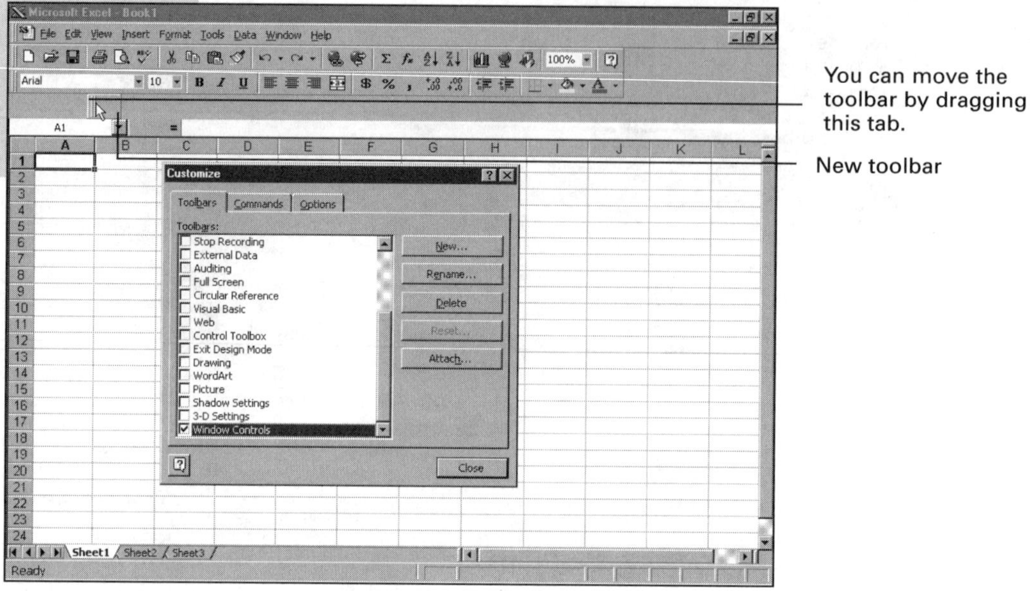

SEE CHAPTER 2 TO LEARN ABOUT DISPLAYING AND HIDING TOOLBARS.

Choosing Which Toolbars to Display

You have already learned how to display and hide toolbars—just right-click any toolbar and select the one you want to display or hide. A check mark means the toolbar is displayed.

In Figure 6.5, you saw another way to choose which toolbars to display or hide. Each toolbar listed on the Toolbars tab of the Customize dialog box has a check box beside it. Click to place or remove check marks to display or hide each toolbar.

Deleting a Toolbar

You cannot delete the toolbars that come with Excel, but you can delete the custom toolbars you have created yourself. To do so, click the check box next to the toolbar's name on the Toolbars tab of the Customize dialog box and then click the Delete button.

Renaming a Toolbar

Like deleting, renaming works only with toolbars you've created yourself. To rename a toolbar, select it from the Toolbars tab of the Customize dialog box and then click the Rename button. The Rename Toolbar dialog box appears. Type a new name in the Toolbar Name text box and click OK.

Attaching a Toolbar to a Workbook

The custom toolbars that you create are available only in your copy of Excel on your computer. If you give your workbook to a friend or colleague on a different computer, he or she will not have access to your toolbar.

To solve this problem, you can attach the toolbar to the workbook. That way, when you send the workbook to someone else, you send the toolbar too.

To attach a toolbar to a workbook, follow these steps:

1. Open the workbook to which you want to attach the toolbar.
2. Right-click any toolbar and choose Customize.
3. Click the Toolbars tab.
4. Click the Attach button. The Attach Toolbars dialog box appears (see Figure 6.8).
5. In the Custom Toolbars list, select the custom toolbar you want to attach.
6. Click the Copy button to attach that toolbar to the active workbook.
7. Click OK.

Figure 6.8 Use this dialog box to attach the toolbar to a workbook.

Customizing Menus

Customizing menus is a lot like customizing toolbars, but for some reason many people are more afraid of doing it. It's not complicated, really. When the Customize dialog box is open, the menus become customizable, just like the toolbars. With the Customize dialog box open, you can:

- Drag a menu from one spot to another to rearrange the order in which menus appear.
- Drag a menu away from the menu bar to remove it (not recommended because you won't have access to its commands anymore if you do that).

- Click on a menu to open it, and then drag a command to a different spot on the menu (or off the menu completely to remove it).
- Rename a menu by right-clicking it and typing a new name in the Name text box on the shortcut menu.

You can also create your own menus and add commands to them. To create a new menu, follow these steps:

1. If the Customize dialog box is not open, right-click any menu and choose Customize to open it.
2. Click the Commands tab.
3. Select New Menu at the bottom of the Categories list.
4. Drag the words "New Menu" from the Commands list to the spot on the menu bar where you want the new menu. The new menu appears with the name New Menu.
5. To change the menu name, right-click on it and type a new name in the Name text box, pressing Enter when finished.
6. To add commands to the menu, locate the command you want to add on the Commands list (after choosing a different category) and drag it up to the new menu. When the mouse pointer touches the new menu, the menu opens so that you can drag the command onto it. Release the mouse button.
7. Repeat step 6, filling your new menu with the commands you want.
8. Click Close when finished.

If you right-click on one of Excel's default menu's names, you can see that the name of a menu has an ampersand (&) in it. The ampersand precedes the letter that should appear underlined. (Remember, the underlined letter can be pressed along with Alt to open the menu.) For example, *F&ormat* means that the *o* will appear underlined. When you are naming menus that you create yourself, don't forget to add an ampersand in the name to indicate which letter should be underlined. Make sure that you choose a letter that none of the other menu names are currently using as their underlined letter.

Let's take a quick look at the Options tab of the Customize dialog box (see Figure 6.9) before moving on. There are a few options here you might find useful.

- Select the Large Icons check box to make the buttons on the toolbars larger. This is helpful if you have poor eyesight, but it makes fewer icons fit on the screen at once.

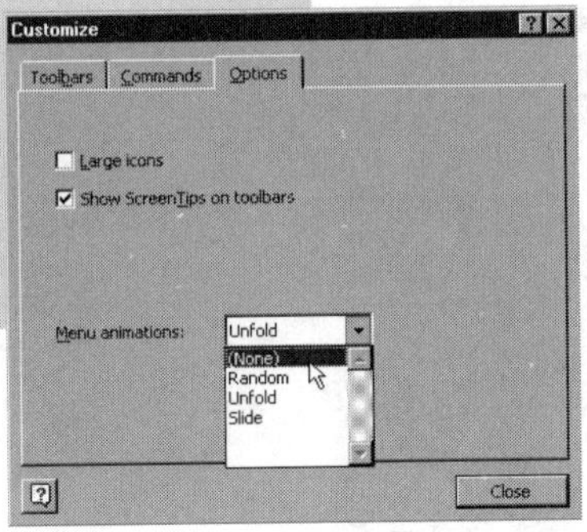

Figure 6.9 The Options tab contains a few miscellaneous settings for menus and toolbars.

- Deselect the Show ScreenTips on Toolbars check box if you don't want the ScreenTips popping up whenever you position your mouse pointer over a toolbar button.
- Open the Menu Animations drop-down list and choose an animation type if you like. (The default is None.) This makes the menus open with more of a flourish, but it may make slower computers run even more slowly.

Setting Excel Options

Besides the settings for menus and toolbars that you've seen so far in this chapter, there are many, many other settings you can choose. Some of them are purely cosmetic, whereas others enable timesaving or safety features. Think of this dialog box as Excel's "control panel," where you can adjust the default settings to your own preferences.

To access the options, you must open the Options dialog box by choosing Tools, Options. The Options dialog box has eight tabs, each with a different category of settings on it; let's look at each tab individually.

View Options

The View tab (see Figure 6.10) contains options that affect how Excel appears onscreen. Here's what each one does:

- **Show.** This section contains check boxes that let you turn on/off the Formula Bar and Status Bar. These are the same as the Formula Bar and Status Bar commands on the View menu, so you will seldom use them from here.

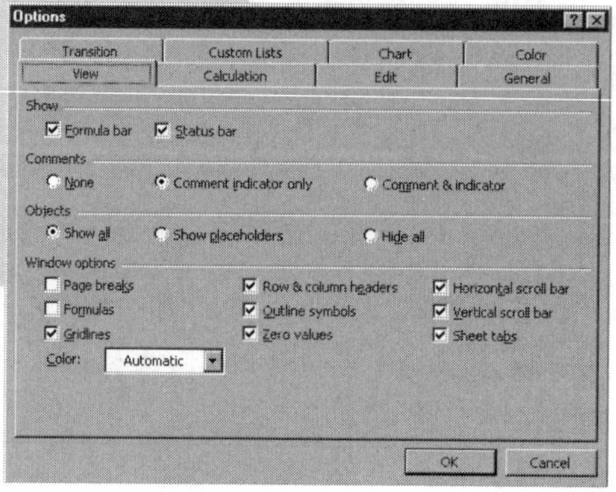

Figure 6.10 The View tab of the Options dialog box controls which elements are visible on-screen.

COMMENTS ARE COVERED IN CHAPTER 7.

- **Comments.** In this section, you choose whether (and how) you want any comments attached to cells to appear.
- **Objects.** Here you choose whether (and how) you want any objects in the worksheet to appear. Objects are items like imported graphics and drawings that do not neatly fit into a single cell.
- **Window Options.** The check boxes here each refer to a screen element that you can turn on/off. In most cases, you will want to leave all of them on except the first two, but feel free to turn any element off that you never use. The Color drop-down list refers to gridline color—use it to set the color for the gridlines if the Gridlines check box is marked.

Transition Options

The Transition tab (see Figure 6.11) contains settings that help users of other spreadsheet programs (notably Lotus 1-2-3) make the transition to using Excel for their spreadsheet needs.

YOU LEARN HOW TO IMPORT GRAPHICS AND DRAW OBJECTS IN CHAPTER 16.

- **Save Excel Files As.** Open this drop-down list and select a different format if you want Excel to save its files in a different format by default. For example, if you share files with 1-2-3 users, you may want to save all files in 1-2-3 format for their convenience.
- **Settings.** A variety of options that work together to help 1-2-3 users become accustomed to Excel's commands. Here's how they work: first you enter a character in the Microsoft Excel Menu or Help Key box. (The default is /, which opens the menu system in Lotus 1-2-3.) Then you choose one of the following:

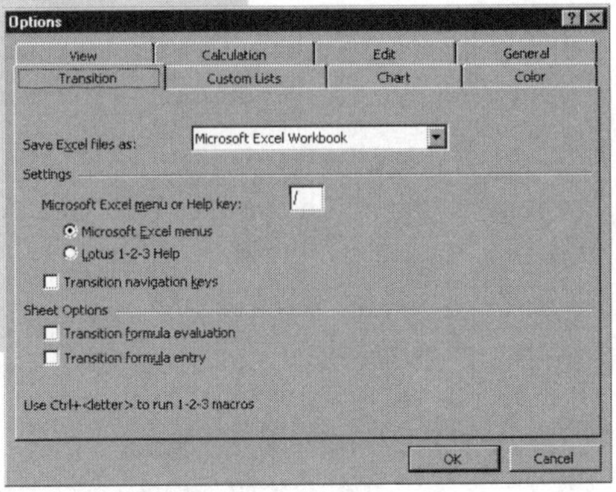

Figure 6.11 The Transition tab of the Options dialog box offers features to help 1-2-3 users become accustomed to Excel.

> TO SAVE A FILE IN ANOTHER FORMAT AS A ONE-TIME THING, INSTEAD OF MAKING THAT FORMAT THE DEFAULT, SEE CHAPTER 3.

Microsoft Excel Menus. When you press the key you specified, the menu system becomes activated (just like in 1-2-3).

Lotus 1-2-3 Help. When you press the key you specified, the Excel Help system opens with information about how Lotus 1-2-3 commands translate to Excel commands.

- **Sheet Options.** Two more check boxes that also help 1-2-3 users:

Transition Formula Evaluation. When this is checked, Excel opens 1-2-3 worksheets with the formulas intact and functional. (1-2-3 uses a different method of writing formulas than Excel does, and with this check box unmarked, Excel does not recognize them.)

Transition Formula Entry. When this is checked, you can enter formulas using Lotus 1-2-3 syntax, and Excel will convert them to Excel syntax.

Custom Lists

Lists are a great timesaving feature. As you'll see in Chapter 7 when you begin entering text in your worksheet, when you start a list that Excel recognizes, like the days of the week or months, Excel's AutoFill feature can fill in the rest of the list for you.

> AUTOFILL IS COVERED IN CHAPTER 7.

By default, Excel can recognize number series and also days of the week and months of the year. You can create your own lists on the Custom Lists tab, such as the names of departments or employees, and then later use AutoFill to fill in the list.

To create a custom list, follow these steps:

1. If the Options dialog box is not open, choose Tools, Options.
2. Select the Custom Lists tab.
3. Select NEW LIST on the Custom Lists list.
4. Type the list you want to create in the List Entries column (see Figure 6.12), with the entries separated by pressing Enter.
5. Click the Add button to create your custom list.
6. When you are finished, click OK.

Note

If the entries you want to make into a custom list already appear in a row or column on the worksheet, enter the range in the Import List from Cells text box, or click the Collapse Dialog button to temporarily move the dialog box out of the way so that you can select the cells you want with the mouse. When you press Enter after selecting cells, the dialog box reappears with the range you selected entered in the text box. When the range you want appears in the text box, click the Import button.

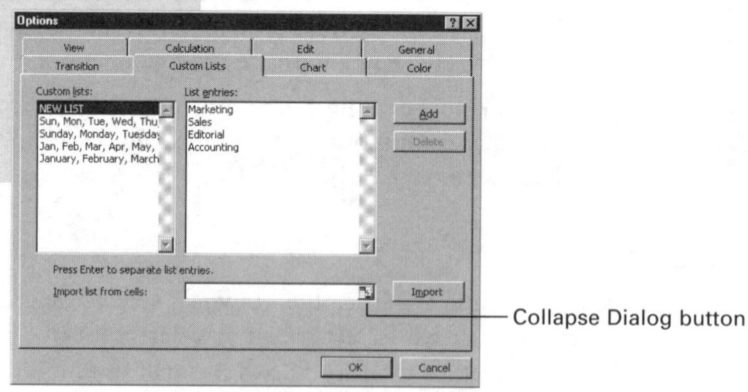

Figure 6.12 Type in your own custom lists for later use with the AutoFill feature.

Calculation Options

As you might imagine, the Calculation options have to do with how formulas are calculated in your worksheet.

The most important calculation option for most people is Recalculation. Normally, each formula is recalculated automatically whenever you change a number

YOU LEARN HOW TO CREATE FORMULAS IN CHAPTER 8.

in a cell to which the formula refers. For example, suppose that I have a formula in cell C3 that reads =C1+C2. C1 contains a 5, and C2 contains a 10, so C3's result is 15 (5 plus 10). If I changed the contents of C1 to 6, the value in C3 would automatically change to 16 (6 plus 10). That's because recalculation is set to Automatic by default.

However, sometimes you may not want your formulas to recalculate automatically. This is primarily a speed issue—the slower your computer, the longer it takes for your formulas to recalculate. It's not so bad when you have a simple, single formula, but suppose that you have 20 formulas that refer to one another's results. When the result of the first formula changes, it causes the result of the second formula to change, which in turn causes the third formula to change, and so on. This recalculation can take several seconds on some slower computers, so people in that situation may choose Manual recalculation instead. When you choose Manual recalculation, calculation takes place only when one of the following happens:

- You press F9 (the Calculate key).
- You click the Calc Now button on the Calculation tab of the Options dialog box.
- You save the workbook.

If you set recalculation to Manual, make sure that you recalculate before you print your work, or the printout may be inaccurate.

To set the recalculation, just click Manual or Automatic, whichever you prefer (see Figure 6.13). To calculate the entire workbook now, click the Calc Now (F9) button; to calculate the active worksheet only now, click the Calc Sheet button.

Several other calculation options are available on this tab, but they are primarily for advanced users. If you are interested in finding out exactly what each one does, click the What's This? (?) button in the top right corner of the dialog box, and then click on the option you are interested in. A Help window pops up explaining that option.

Editing Options

On the Edit tab (see Figure 6.14), you'll find a variety of options that affect the way Excel works as you enter and change data in cells. Setting these options the way you feel most comfortable with can be a big time-saver and frustration-eliminator. Some examples:

- **Edit Directly in Cell.** When this is on, you can click in a cell and type, and the text goes immediately into that cell. When this is off, the entry goes into the formula bar as you type and then is transferred into the cell when you press Enter. Most people prefer this to be on.
- **Allow Cell Drag and Drop.** Drag and drop is a great feature that enables you to move the contents of cells from place to place by dragging with the mouse. Most people leave this feature turned on; however, if you don't use the feature and find yourself accidentally moving things when you didn't mean to, turn off the feature. Unless you never make mistakes (and everyone does!), you should leave the Alert Before Overwriting Cells feature on; this prevents you from overwriting existing data with dragged-and-dropped data.

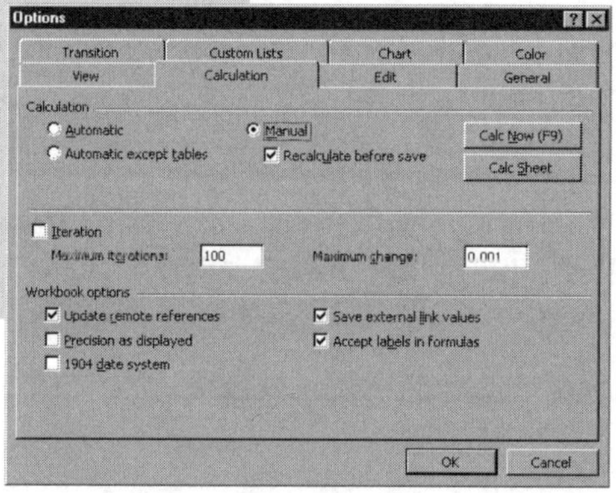

Figure 6.13 Choose between Automatic and Manual calculations here and set several other minor calculation options.

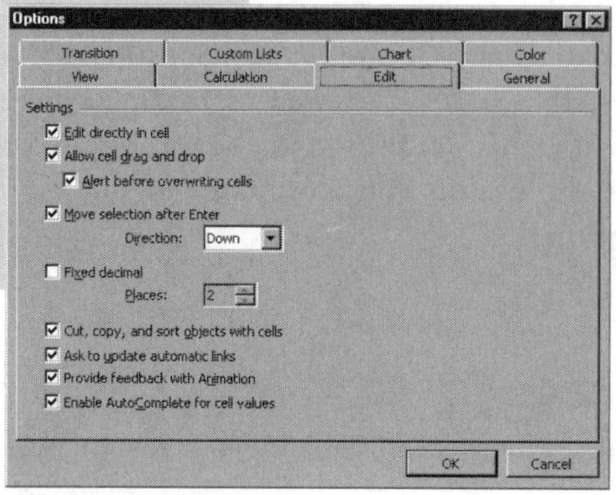

Figure 6.14 Use the Edit tab's options to set up how Excel will behave when you are entering and editing in cells.

- **Move Selection After Enter.** When you press Enter after typing in a cell, the cell cursor moves down to the next cell in that column by default. You can deselect the check box so that the cell cursor doesn't go anywhere, or change the direction that it moves by selecting a different direction from the Direction drop-down list.

  Several other, less-common options are on this tab too; check them out by clicking the What's This? (?) button and then clicking on the option you're interested in.

Charting Options

CHARTS ARE COVERED IN CHAPTERS 14 AND 15.

The options on the Chart tab (see Figure 6.15) have to do with the charts you create in Excel. (Unless you have a chart in the active workbook when you select this tab, most of the options will be grayed out, so yours may not look exactly like Figure 6.15.) These are less common options, and most people will never change them. However, just in case you need to, here's a brief explanation of each:

- **Plot Empty Cells As.** Lets you choose how you want Excel to handle any empty cells in a range that you're charting. You can choose not to plot them at all, to plot them as 0, or to have Excel interpolate them (take an average of the points before and after them and fill in a reasonable guess).
- **Plot Visible Cells Only.** Automatically changes a chart when some of the cells that it is based on become hidden. For example, if you have a chart based on three columns and you hide one of the columns, the chart will change to show only the two columns that are not hidden.
- **Chart Sizes with Window Frame.** Expands the chart to fill the available space in the window. (This is available only for chart sheets, not charts

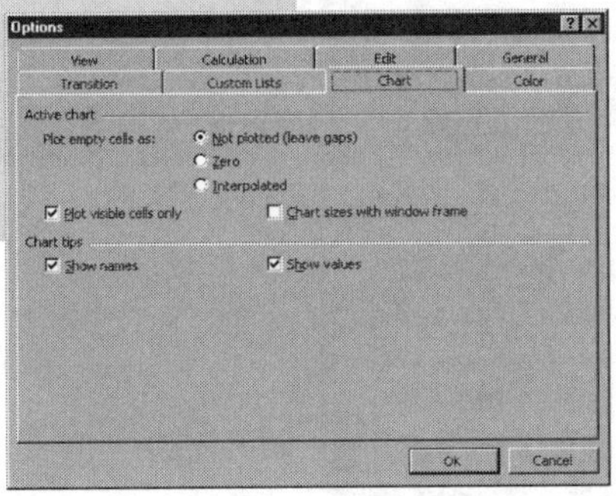

Figure 6.15
Use the chart tab to set up how your charts appear

that float on top of a sheet. This will make more sense after you've read about charts in Chapter 14.)

- **Show Names.** Displays the chart name when you rest your mouse pointer over it.
- **Show Values.** Displays the value of a bar or data point when you rest your mouse pointer on it.

General Options

Most of the customization I personally do to Excel is done on the General tab (see Figure 6.16). It contains the features that I most want to tinker with. This may be the case for you too! Let's take a look at what the General tab offers:

- The Settings area has a list of check boxes that turn on/off various features:

  R1C1 Reference Style. By default, Excel uses the A1 method of identifying cells—that is, column letter, and then row number. You can change to the R1C1 style, where cell A1 would appear like this: R1C1, for compatibility with very old versions of Excel that used this.

  Ignore Other Applications. Prevents exchanging data with other OLE-enabled programs. (Don't worry if you don't know what this means now; you learn about OLE in Chapter 20.)

  Macro Virus Protection. Some computer viruses embed themselves in Excel macros. If you open a workbook that contains macros, Excel will warn you of that fact if you leave this feature turned on.

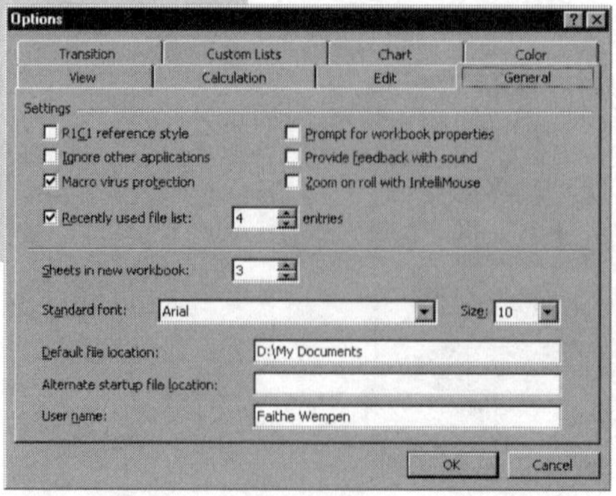

Figure 6.16 General options affect the way Excel operates in general, rather than in a specific area.

Prompt for Workbook Properties. The first time you save a file, you are asked for a name and location, as you learned in Chapter 3. If you also want to be prompted for additional information at that point, turn on this feature.

Note

> **To enter the workbook properties for a workbook at any time, choose File, Properties. The dialog box that appears is the same one that appears when you save a workbook for the first time when the Prompt for Workbook Properties feature is turned on.**

SEE APPENDIX B FOR MORE INFORMATION ABOUT THE INTELLI-MOUSE.

Provide Feedback with Sound. When this feature is on, Excel plays the sounds associated with various system events. (You set these up from the Windows 95 Control Panel's Sound feature.) Most people find these annoying after the first ten minutes and leave this feature turned off.

Zoom on Roll with IntelliMouse. The IntelliMouse is a new type of mouse that comes with some versions of Microsoft Office. To enable its capability to zoom and move around on-screen with its special control wheel, turn on this feature.

Recently Used File List. As you learned in Chapter 3, one way to open a file that you have recently used is to select it from the bottom of the File menu. The File menu, by default, lists the four most recently used files. To increase or decrease this number, change the number in this text box. Or turn off the feature completely by deselecting the check box.

- **Sheets in New Workbook.** As you learned in previous chapters, the default number of sheets in a workbook is three. You can change this by changing the number in this box.
- **Standard Font and Size.** Change the default font and font size with these drop-down lists.
- **Default File Location.** You can type a different drive and folder path here to change what folder Excel's Save As dialog box opens into.
- **Alternate Startup File Location.** If you have worksheets or templates that you want opened every time you start Excel, you should enter their location here.
- **User Name.** Fill in your name here if it doesn't already appear. Excel uses this information in several ways, including placing it on the Properties sheet (File, Properties) and filling it in on certain forms and templates.

The Default File Location setting, even though it's buried in a mass of other settings on this tab, is very important and useful. Changing it to the folder where you keep most of your files can save you many keystrokes and mouse clicks in the future. For example, I keep all the files for the books I write in C:\Books, and I have a folder within Books for each book. I set the Default File Location in Excel to C:\Books, and then all I have to do when using the Save As dialog box is double-click on the folder for the project I happen to be working on.

Colors

The final tab is Color. This tab won't necessarily increase your productivity or efficiency, but it might make your experience with Excel more pleasing to your eyes.

Excel starts you out with 56 colors. Most computer monitors these days, however, are capable of displaying at least 256 colors. That means you are missing out on 200 colors. The Color tab enables you to specify which colors are included in that palette of 56. To use it, follow these steps:

1. If the Options dialog box isn't open, choose Tools, Options.
2. Click the Color tab (see Figure 6.17).
3. Select on one of the colors that you don't particularly like.
4. Click the Modify button. The Colors dialog box appears (see Figure 6.18).

Figure 6.17 Use the Color tab to change the palette of 56 standard colors.

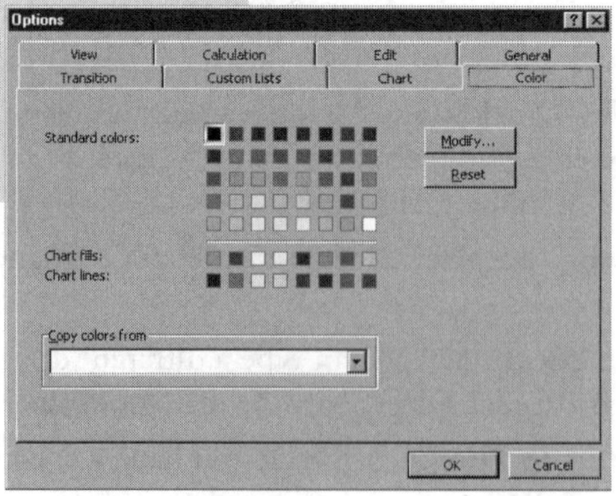

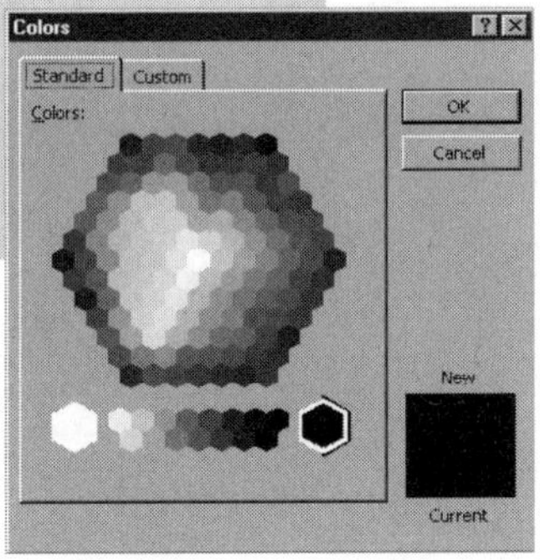

Figure 6.18 Choose a different color to replace one that you don't like.

5. Select a color that you would prefer using.
6. Click OK. That color replaces the one you selected in the palette.
7. Repeat steps 3 through 6 for any other colors you want to change.
8. Click OK to close the Options dialog box.

Notice in Figure 6.18 that the Colors dialog box has two tabs: Standard and Custom. On the Custom tab, you have a much broader range of color choices. If you don't find the color you want on the Standard tab, try Custom.

PART II

Putting Your Data into Excel

7

Entering Text and Numbers into Cells

In This Chapter

- Entering and Editing Data in Cells
- Data Entry Shortcuts
- Editing and Clearing a Cell
- Freezing Rows and Columns
- Moving and Copying Cell Contents
- Correcting Your Spelling
- Undoing Mistakes

If using Excel is like driving a car, then you can think of this book as your Driver's Education course. In this chapter, you'll get behind the wheel and take to the open road. You learn how to enter and edit data, correct your mistakes, and move data around.

Entering Text and Numbers

MOVING THE CELL CURSOR IS DISCUSSED IN CHAPTER 5.

Data entry on a worksheet is actually rather anticlimactic after all the buildup in the previous chapters. Move the cell cursor to the cell where you want to enter text and then type. Press Enter when you're finished.

As you type, the characters appear both in the cell and in the formula bar, as shown in Figure 7.1. In the formula bar, you'll see two buttons as you type: a check mark and an X.

- The check mark button works the same as the Enter key on your keyboard. Click it (or press Enter) when you are finished typing that cell's contents.
- The X button works the same as the Esc key on your keyboard. If you decide to abort the data entry in that cell, click it (or press Esc) to cancel.

Figure 7.1
To enter text or numbers in a cell, just type and press Enter.

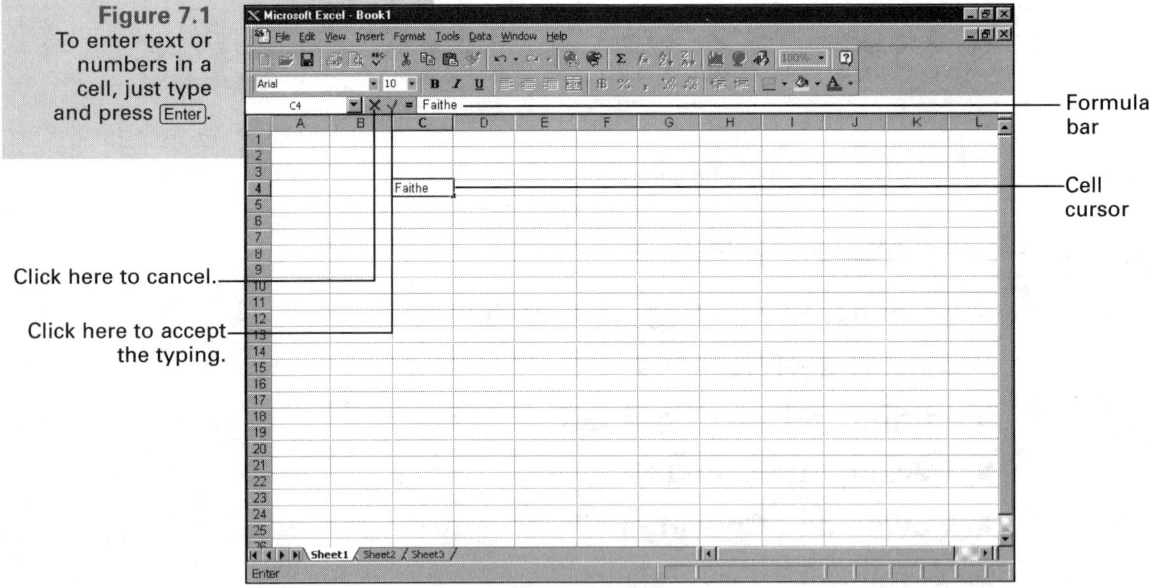

Some Useful Shortcut Keys

As you're entering text and numbers into the cells, you may find some of the following shortcuts helpful:

- You can start a new line in the same cell by pressing Alt+Enter.
- When you press Enter, you move to the next cell down. If you would prefer to move to the next cell up, or to the right or left, use the following instead of Enter: Shift+Enter for up, Tab for right, and Shift+Tab for left.

THERE IS MORE ON HYPERLINKS IN CHAPTER 21.

- You can insert the current date in a cell (based on your computer's clock) by pressing Ctrl+; (semicolon). Insert the time by pressing Ctrl+Shift+: (colon).
- You can insert a hyperlink in a cell by pressing Ctrl+K.
- You can copy the value from the cell above into the active cell by pressing Ctrl+Shift+ " (quotation mark).

How Text and Numbers Align in Cells

When you press Enter, the cell cursor moves down to the next cell in that column, and the data you entered aligns itself in the cell according to the following scheme:

- If Excel considers what you entered to be a number, it aligns it to the right edge of the cell. Numbers include digits, commas, decimal points, dollar signs, and percentage signs.
- If Excel considers what you entered to be text, it aligns it to the left edge of the cell. If a cell contains even one letter, or a non-math symbol (like a semicolon), the entire cell is considered text.

Figure 7.2 shows text and numbers aligned in their cells.

Figure 7.2 Data aligns in cells differently depending on whether Excel considers it text or numbers.

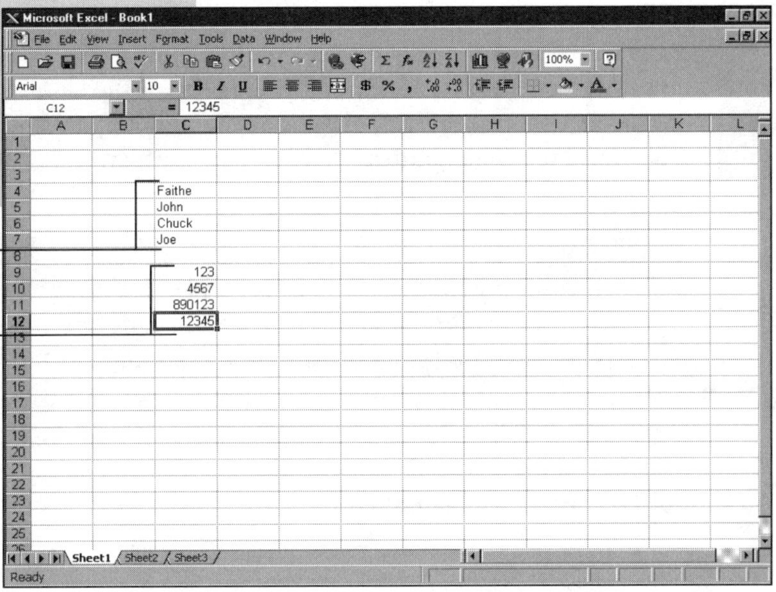

Text is aligned to the left.

Numbers are aligned to the right.

How Excel Distinguishes Between Text and Numbers

Excel, like most spreadsheet programs, makes a distinction between text and numbers. It's important that you understand this distinction before you get started.

The bottom line is simple: numbers can be calculated; text cannot. Excel can tell you what 34+59 is, but it can't tell you what Abner+Daryl is.

You're probably thinking "how dumb does she think I am? Of course I know the difference between letters and numbers!" Well, good for you, but it's not quite as simple as it sounds on the surface. For example, what about these?

1097 Walnut Street

720A

YOU CAN OVERRIDE A CELL'S "NATURAL" ALIGNMENT TO MAKE THE TEXT/NUMBERS ALIGN ANY WAY YOU WANT. SEE CHAPTER 11 FOR DETAILS.

These examples start out with a number, but some letters are mixed in. When Excel sees even one character that it can't identify as a number (or a number helper, like $), it automatically classifies that cell's content as "text." So the preceding two examples would both be text.

How about these?

46240-1097

317-555-1622

If you said "number" for these you probably were thinking of it as a mathematical formula (one number minus another). But in this case you are wrong: these are a ZIP code and a phone number. Because of the dash(es) in the middle, Excel considers them text. That's okay, though, because you would never perform calculations on phone numbers or ZIP codes anyway.

Note

If you really did want to enter a mathematical formula with a minus sign in it and have Excel calculate the result, you would start it out with an equals sign, like this: =46240-1097. You learn more about formulas in Chapter 8.

Okay, now for a final test:

46240

23409586723498

Excel considers these numbers, because there is no reason not to—they contain only numerals, and therefore don't have any "disqualifiers" (like text or symbols) that would force Excel to consider them text. However, in both cases, I want Excel to consider them text. The first one is a ZIP code; the second one is a credit card number. In cases like these, I would enter the numbers preceded by an apostrophe ('). This tells Excel that "the following string should be considered text, even if it contains only numerals."

When you enter an apostrophe before a number, the apostrophe does not show up in the cell—Excel is intelligent enough to know that it's merely an indicator and should be hidden. For example, in Figure 7.3, I have entered an apostrophe in front of the ZIP code 46240, to make it left-aligned like the other text in the column.

Figure 7.3
To force Excel to see a number as text, place an apostrophe in front of it.

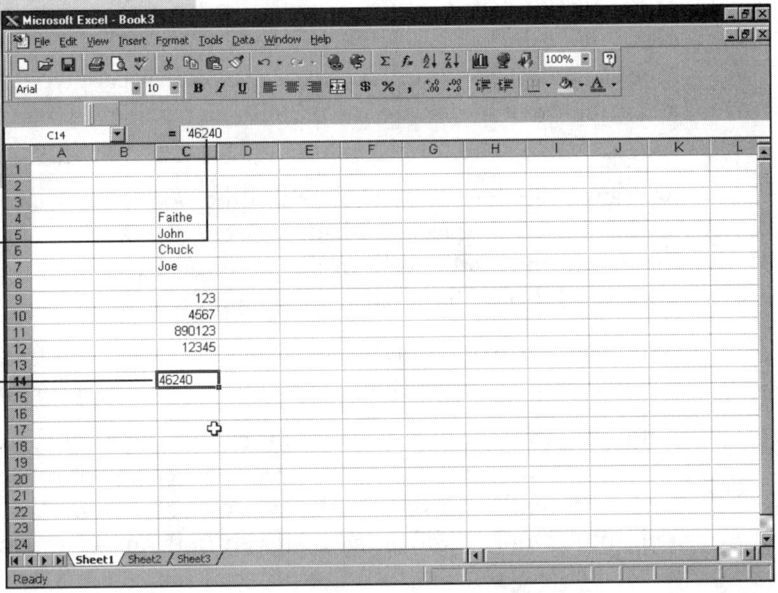

The apostrophe shows up in the formula bar...

...but not in the cell itself.

Filling Cells

One of the greatest shortcuts Excel provides is the capability to fill in cells for you. There are several ways to go about telling Excel to fill cells, depending on what you want.

- **AutoComplete.** Anticipates your typing if you have typed a similar bit of text in the same column before and completes the text for you.
- **Fill Command.** Fills in the same value in multiple cells or fills in a series of values, depending on what command you choose.

- **AutoFill.** Tries to guess what kind of Fill you want and provides it. AutoFill is quicker than the Fill command but is useful only if your wishes coincide with Excel's guess in that instance.

Even though AutoFill is the easiest, and is probably the method you will end up using most often, let's look at the other fill methods first. Understanding them will help you understand how AutoFill makes its guesses about what you want so that you can know more precisely when AutoFill is likely to give the results you are looking for.

Saving Time with AutoComplete

If you type the same text in more than one cell in a column, Excel can help you be more efficient. For example, suppose that I type **Wempen Editorial Services** (my company's name) in cell A1, and then I start typing the same thing in cell A2. As soon as I type the **W** in cell A2, Excel guesses that I am typing the same phrase again and completes it for me. Instead of finishing typing the phrase, I can just press Enter.

It took Excel only one letter (W) in cell A2 for it to make its guess, because I don't have any other cells in that column of the worksheet whose contents begins with W. It was an easy guess. If I had, for example, Widener, Welding, and Wempen Lumber in three other cells in that column, Excel would wait until I had typed **Wempen E** before it completed the typing for me.

AutoComplete works only within a column; if you have typed some phrase in, for example, cell A1, Excel won't try to AutoComplete it for you in cell D6.

AutoComplete isn't perfect, so it can't always know when you want to type something different. If AutoComplete kicks in when you don't want it, keep typing the new entry until it becomes different from the one in AutoComplete's memory, and AutoComplete will go away. If you find AutoComplete to be annoying, or just unhelpful, you can turn it off by choosing Tools, Options and clicking the Edit tab; then deselect the AutoComplete check box.

REFER TO CHAPTER 5 IF YOU NEED A REFRESHER ON SELECTING RANGES OF CELLS.

Hands On: Filling Several Cells with the Same Entry

If you know in advance that several contiguous cells are going to need the same entry, you can use the Fill feature to save time. Follow these steps to try it out:

1. Type the entry into the first cell where you want it. For example, type your name in cell B2.
2. Select that cell and the other cells where you want that entry to appear. For example, select B2:B8 (see Figure 7.4).

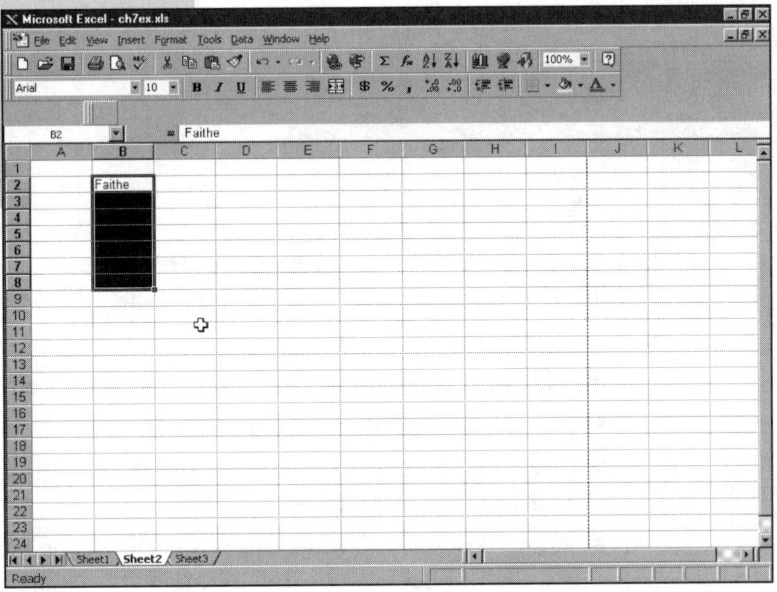

Figure 7.4 Select the range that includes both the original cell and the other cells to be filled.

3. Select Edit, Fill, and from the submenu that appears, select the direction in which the cells to be copied into are from the original. For example, if the original is in cell B2 and you want to fill cells B3:B8, select Down.

You can use the preceding method to copy Down, Up, Left, or Right. Down and Right also have shortcut keys that you can use instead of step 3: Ctrl+D and Ctrl+R, respectively.

Hands On: Filling Cells with a Series

Instead of filling a range of cells with the same value, you might want to increment the value. For example, you might want the days of the week listed, or numerals from 1 to 9, or the dates of all the Sundays from now till November.

Follow these steps to try out a filled series:

1. Enter the first entry in the first cell. For example, if you want to fill in a series of numbers starting with 100, type **100** in the first cell.
2. Select the cell you just typed in plus the other cells where you want to fill the series. For example, if you entered 100 in cell B2 and you want eight more cells filled in below it, select B2:B10.
3. Select Edit, Fill, Series. The Series dialog box appears (see Figure 7.5).

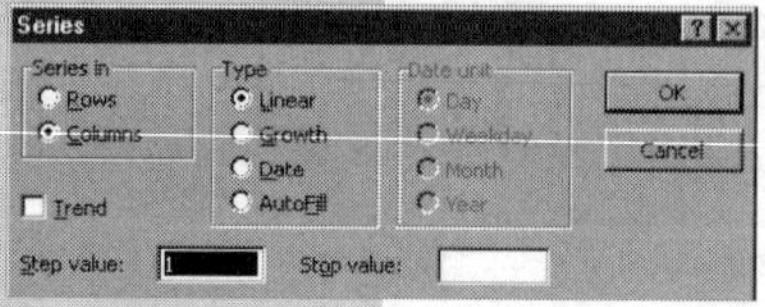

Figure 7.5 Use the Series dialog box to choose how you want the series filled.

4. Select Rows or Columns in the Series In area. This should already be selected correctly for you because you selected the cells beforehand.
5. Select an increment type:
   - The most common is Linear, which works for almost all numbers.
   - Growth is a geometric progression that most casual users will not use.
   - Selecting Date opens up the options in the right-hand column, which you'll see in the next step.
   - AutoFill ignores all other options in the dialog box and fills based on Excel's best guess of what you want. If you want to use AutoFill, this is a rather roundabout way to do it; it's much easier to follow the steps in the following section.
6. If you selected Date in step 5, choose what kind of increment you want from the Date Unit section.
7. Enter a Step Value to indicate how you want the series to progress. For example, if I want to start with 100 (see step 1) and fill by multiples of 200, I would enter **200** in the Step Value text box.
8. Click OK. Your series is filled in. Figure 7.6 shows the results I got using the examples listed in these steps.

Creating Series with AutoFill

Now that you know how to fill the "hard way," let me introduce you to the easy way: AutoFill. With AutoFill, you enter enough information to give Excel something to guess with and then drag with the mouse to do the filling.

AutoFill can fill the same text in all cells, or it can fill a series, depending on how you use it. (More on this shortly.)

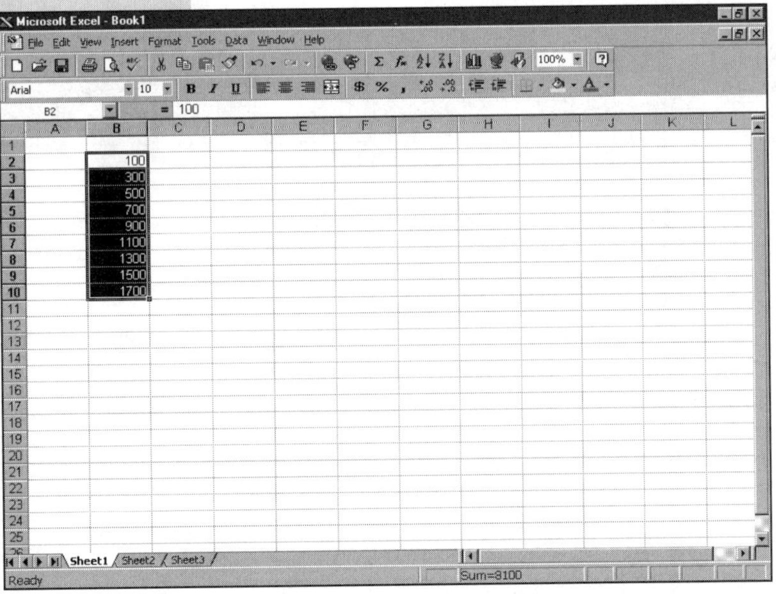

Figure 7.6 I used the Series dialog box to fill in a series beginning with 100 and incrementing by 200 with each entry.

Hands On: Filling a Series with AutoFill

The best way to become acquainted with the feature is to try it out. Follow these steps:

1. Enter the starting entry in a cell and press Enter. (For example, enter **January** in cell C5.) Then move the cell cursor back onto that cell.
2. Notice in the bottom right corner of the cell cursor, there is a little black box. Point your mouse at that black box until the mouse pointer becomes a crosshair.
3. Holding down the left mouse button, drag the mouse pointer to select all the cells you want to fill. For example, drag down to C16. A ScreenTip box tells you what the final cell in the range will contain, as shown in Figure 7.7. (More on this shortly.)
4. Release the mouse button. The cells are filled.

Experiment with AutoFill, and you'll notice that sometimes it fills the same value in all cells, and other times it increments. In the preceding steps, it incremented the month from January to December. How do you know what you're going to get, then?

Figure 7.7 Here, I am filling in the months of the year with AutoFill.

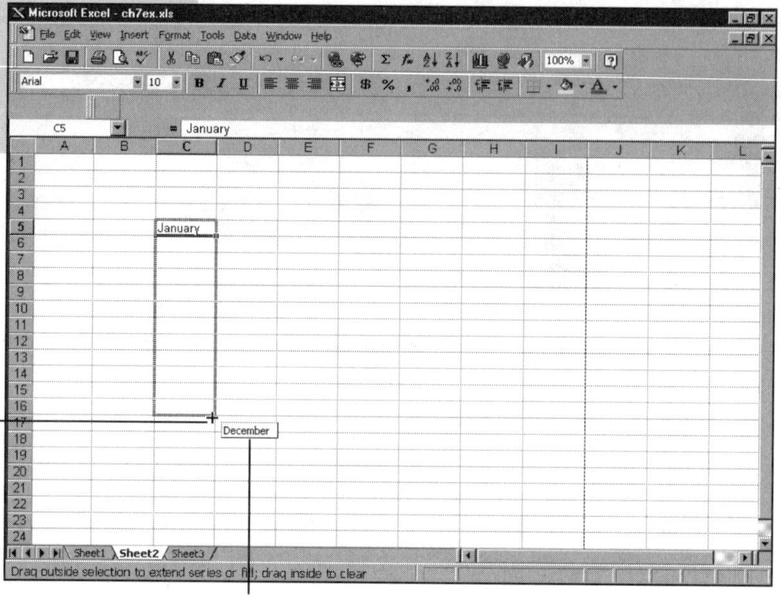

CHAPTER 6 COVERS SETTING UP YOUR OWN CUSTOM LISTS.

AutoFill has some rules it follows:

- If you place a single entry in a cell that happens to be the first item on one of Excel's Custom Lists, it fills in that list. That's what happened in the preceding steps—Excel maintains a list of months as one of its Custom Lists.
- If you place a single entry in a cell and it's *not* the first item on one of Excel's Custom Lists, it fills in that same entry in all the selected cells. It doesn't matter whether it's text or a number.
- If you place a single number in a cell and hold down the Ctrl key as you drag in step 3, Excel increments the number by 1 in each of the cells it fills. The Ctrl key has no effect if the content of the cell is text rather than a number.
- If you fill in a number in one cell and then another number in the next cell, and then you select them both instead of a single cell in step 1, Excel increments the fill according to the relationship between the two. For example, if the first number is 2 and the next one is 5, it increments each filled cell by 3.
- If you fill in some text in one cell and then different text in the next cell, and select both of those cells instead of step 1, Excel alternates the fill between those two text strings.

Editing Cell Contents

How you edit a cell's contents depends on what kind of editing you want to do. The simplest kind of editing is to just replace what's already there. To do this, do the following:

1. Move the cell cursor to the cell.
2. Type the new text. It replaces what's there.
3. Press Enter.

Hands On: Editing Existing Text in a Cell

If you want to change the existing text without typing over it, do the following instead:

1. Move the cell cursor to the cell. The cell's contents appears in the formula bar.
2. Press F2, double-click the cell, or click on the text in the formula bar. An insertion point (a vertical line) appears in the text (see Figure 7.8), showing where any new text you type will be placed. The insertion point appears in the formula bar if you clicked there and in the cell if you pressed F2.

Figure 7.8 Pressing F2 or clicking in the formula bar places an insertion point in the text.

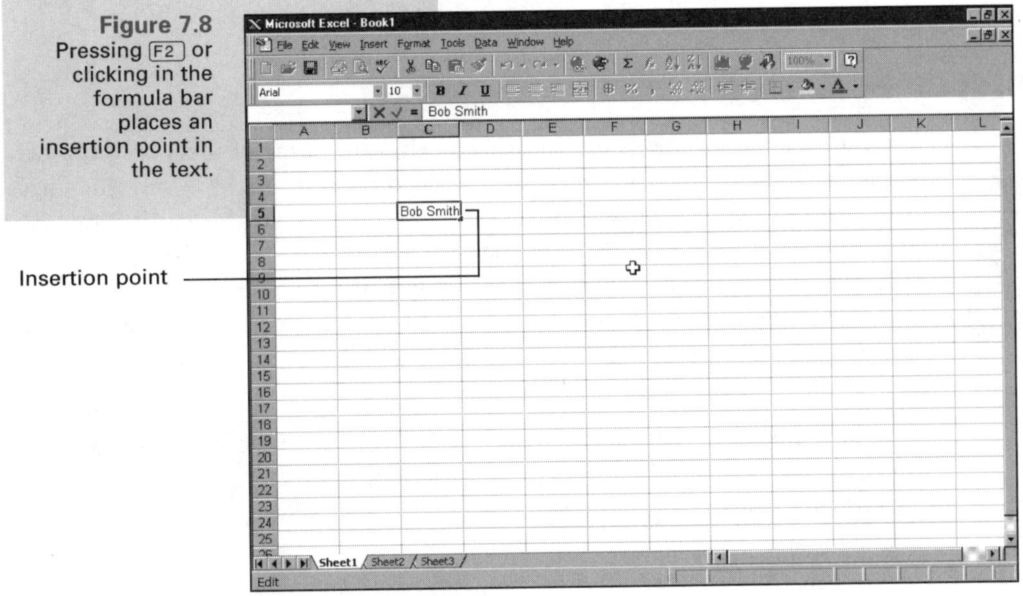

3. Move the insertion point with the keyboard's arrow keys (or by clicking with the mouse where you want it to go).

> **Tip**
>
> A quick way to move the insertion point to the beginning of the text is to press the [Home] key.

4. Remove any text you want to get rid of by pressing the [←Backspace] key (to remove to the left of the insertion point) or the [Del] key (to remove to the right).

> **Tip**
>
> Instead of steps 3 through 5, you can drag the mouse over the text you want to replace and then type the new text. The new text replaces whatever text was selected in that cell.

5. Type the new text you want to add.
6. Press [Enter] or click the check mark in the formula bar to accept your changes.

> **Tip**
>
> As you're editing, you can delete all the text from the insertion point to the end of the line by pressing [Ctrl]+[Del].

Clearing a Cell

BOLD, AS WELL AS OTHER TEXT FORMATTING, IS COVERED IN CHAPTER 11.

There are several meanings for "clearing a cell," and some of them are not obvious at first. The simplest meaning is to remove the text you have entered. That's called *clearing the contents.* When you clear the contents, any formatting you may have applied to the cell remains in that cell and attaches itself to whatever new contents you put into the cell later. For example, if the text in a cell was bold and you cleared the cell's contents, the bold attribute remains dormant in that cell, waiting for you to put some other text into the cell. When you do, the new text receives the bold attribute.

To clear the contents of a cell, move the cell cursor to the cell or select a range. (You can clear several cells at once if you select them as a range before you start.) Then do any one of the following:

- Press the [Del] key.
- Select Edit, Clear, Contents.

- Drag the little black box in the lower right corner of the cell cursor inward toward the center of the cell (or selection area). Release the mouse button when the mouse pointer is well inside the cell or the selected area.

Besides this kind of cell clearing, there are several other kinds you can do.

YOU LEARN HOW TO ADD COMMENTS TO A CELL LATER IN THIS CHAPTER.

- You can clear only the formatting from a cell, leaving the contents intact. To do this, select the cell(s) and then choose Edit, Clear, Formats.
- You can remove only the comments attached to a cell by selecting it and then choosing Edit, Clear, Comments.
- You can clear the formatting, the contents, and the comments, leaving it in its default, blank state. To do this, select the cells and then choose Edit, Clear, All.

Freezing Rows or Columns

As you create your worksheet masterpiece, you may have certain rows and columns that contain labels or headings. For example, in Figure 7.9, Row 1 and Column A contain labels that describe the rest of the data. When I scroll across or down to enter more data in rows and columns that are out of view, however, the labels scroll away too, leaving me trying to remember which column was for Bob's sales figures and which was for Ted's.

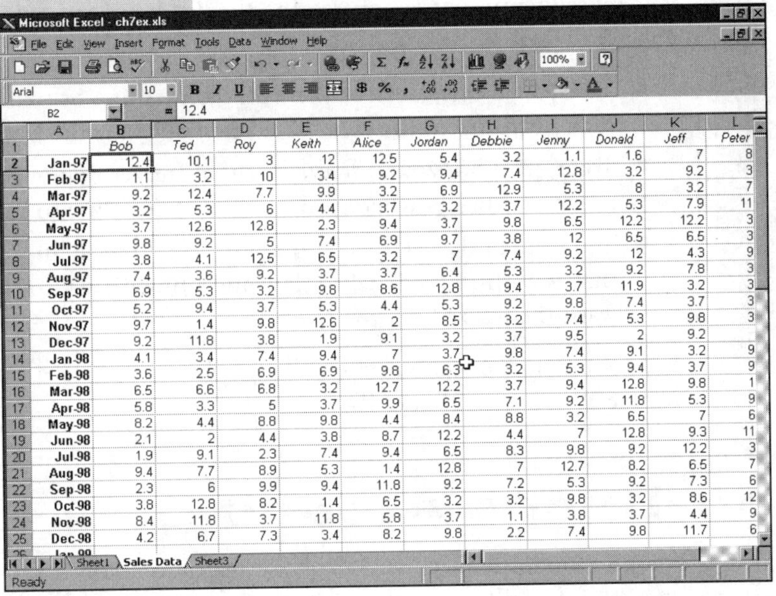

Figure 7.9 Row and column headings are great, but when you scroll some distant rows and columns into view, you won't be able to see the headings anymore.

Luckily, Excel provides a way of "freezing" certain rows and/or columns so that they stay on-screen even when the others scroll, as shown in Figure 7.10.

Figure 7.10 With a freeze line separating the row and column headings from the data, the headings will remain on-screen even when the rest of the worksheet scrolls.

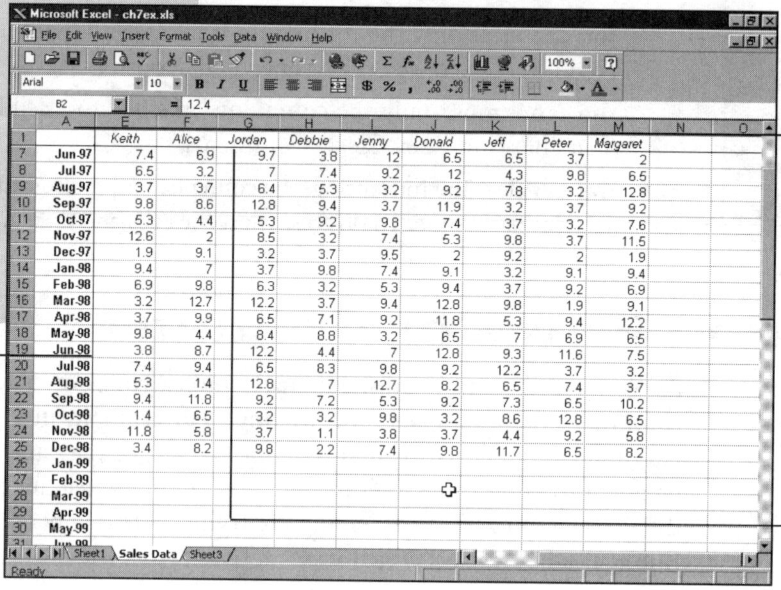

IN CHAPTER 2 YOU LEARNED ABOUT SPLITTING A WINDOW, WHICH IS AN ALTERNATIVE TO FREEZING PANES.

The most important part of freezing the display is to accurately select where you want the freeze line to be placed.

- To create a vertical freeze line that freezes one or more columns, select the entire column to the right of where you want the freeze line to appear.
- To create a horizontal freeze line that freezes one or more rows, select the entire row below where you want the freeze line to appear.
- To create both a vertical and a horizontal freeze line, select the single cell that is both immediately below and immediately to the right of where you want the freeze lines to appear.

After you've made your selection, choose Window, Freeze Panes. To undo a freeze, choose Window, Unfreeze Panes.

Moving Things Around

Another kind of editing you might want to do involves moving and copying the contents of a cell to another cell. Perhaps you have decided that your headings need to start in a different row or column, or that a number is out of place. No need to delete and retype; just move it.

There are two ways to move and copy cell contents on a worksheet. Drag-and-drop is the easiest way, and it involves using the mouse. Cut-and-paste is the more traditional way, and it involves the Windows Clipboard.

Note

As you move or copy, you are moving or copying both the contents of the cells and the formatting. This is an exception to the rule I told you about in Chapter 5, that formatting stays with the cell rather than with the contents.

Hands On: Using Drag-and-Drop

After you master drag-and-drop, you may never move and copy any other way. It's very convenient. Here's how it works:

1. Select the cell(s) you want to move or copy.
2. If you are copying, hold down the Ctrl key.
3. Position the mouse pointer at the edge of the selected range so that the mouse pointer turns into an arrow. If you are copying, a plus sign appears next to the pointer as you drag.
4. Drag the cell or range of cells to a new position in the worksheet. When you release the mouse button, you "drop" the contents into the new cells.

Cut, Copy, and Paste

The older, more traditional way to move and copy is with the Cut, Copy, and Paste commands. These use the Windows Clipboard.

When you move cell contents, you are really using a two-step operation: 1) Cut and 2) Paste. When you copy cell contents, you are using a different two-step operation: 1) Copy and 2) Paste. If you cut without pasting, it's the same as clearing the content and formatting from the cell with Edit, Clear, All. The data is on the Clipboard, but it must be pasted before you cut or copy something else, or it is lost.

What Is the Windows Clipboard?

The Windows Clipboard is a storage area in Windows 95 that all Windows programs share. When you use the Cut command in any Windows program to remove a bit of data from your work (text or graphics), it gets placed in the Clipboard. Then when you use the Paste command, the contents of the Clipboard is pasted into the active application. The Copy command copies the selected text or graphic to the Clipboard, leaving the original in place.

Some examples will make this clearer. Suppose that you wanted to move the contents of cells A1 through A6 elsewhere in your worksheet. You would select that range and then choose Edit, Cut. Cells A1:A6 are cleared (both content and formatting), and whatever was in them is now on the Clipboard. Then you select the new range where you want to paste—say, C2:C7—and choose Edit, Paste. The data from the Clipboard is pasted into the new location.

There are a few things you should know about the Clipboard. One is that when you Paste from it, the data remains on the Clipboard so that you can paste multiple times. For example, after I pasted into C2:C7, I could select D1:D6 and choose Edit, Paste again to paste that same material into yet another location. The only way to get rid of something on the Clipboard is to cut or copy something else to the Clipboard. When you cut or copy something else, it replaces the previous Clipboard contents.

Another important fact is that the Clipboard is not an Excel feature; it's a Windows feature that all Windows programs share. That is important because you can cut, copy, and paste among different applications. For example, you could cut some text from Microsoft Word and paste it into Excel. You can even cut, copy, and paste among programs that do not ordinarily accept one another's data.

Hands On: Cut and Paste

To cut or copy the contents of one or more cells to the Clipboard and then paste it elsewhere, follow these steps:

1. Select the cell(s) whose contents and formatting you want to cut or copy.
2. Do one of the following:

- To cut, click the Cut button on the toolbar, or press Ctrl+X, or choose Edit, Cut.
- To copy, click the Copy button on the toolbar, or press Ctrl+C, or choose Edit, Copy.

3. Select the cell(s) to receive what's on the Clipboard. If you selected multiple cells to cut or copy in step 1, you must either select the same range size and shape to paste into, or you must select a single cell (which will become the top left corner of the paste range).

To copy the contents of a single cell into many cells at once, select a single cell in step 1 and then select many cells in step 3.

4. Click the Paste button on the toolbar, or press Ctrl+V, or choose Edit, Paste.

Adding Comments to Cells

THE PASTE SPECIAL COMMAND ON THE EDIT MENU HELPS YOU LINK OBJECTS BETWEEN FILES. YOU LEARN ABOUT THAT IN CHAPTER 20.

If you've been reading all the chapters in order, you may recall the discussion of the Spreadsheet Solutions templates in Chapter 4. There were little red triangles on some of the cells, indicating comments. When you positioned your mouse pointer over these cells, comment boxes popped up providing you with information about the template.

You can create your own comments, just like the big guys. Comments are useful whenever you need to annotate a worksheet without making your comments a full-time part of the worksheet. For example, suppose that I need to make a comment about Bob's sales performance in February 1997, informing the reader that Bob's performance was so bad because he was sick most of that month. I could attach a comment to that effect to that cell, as shown in Figure 7.11. When the reader positioned his or her mouse pointer over that cell, the comment would appear.

Hands On: Attaching a Comment to a Cell

To create a comment, follow these steps:

1. Move the cell cursor to the cell for which you want to add a comment.
2. Right-click on the cell and choose Insert Comment from the shortcut menu that appears, or choose Insert, Comment from the regular menu system. A text box appears next to the cell, into which you can type.

Figure 7.11 Comments pop up when you position the mouse over them; otherwise, they're hidden.

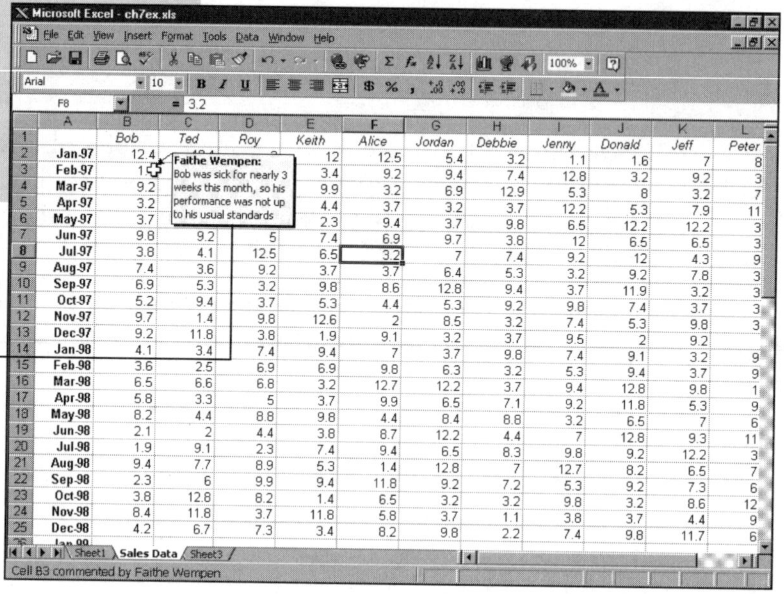

This comment pops up because my mouse pointer is over the cell.

3. Type your comment (see Figure 7.12). It can be as long or short as you like and can include paragraph breaks (by pressing Enter as you type).

Figure 7.12 Type your comment into the text box provided.

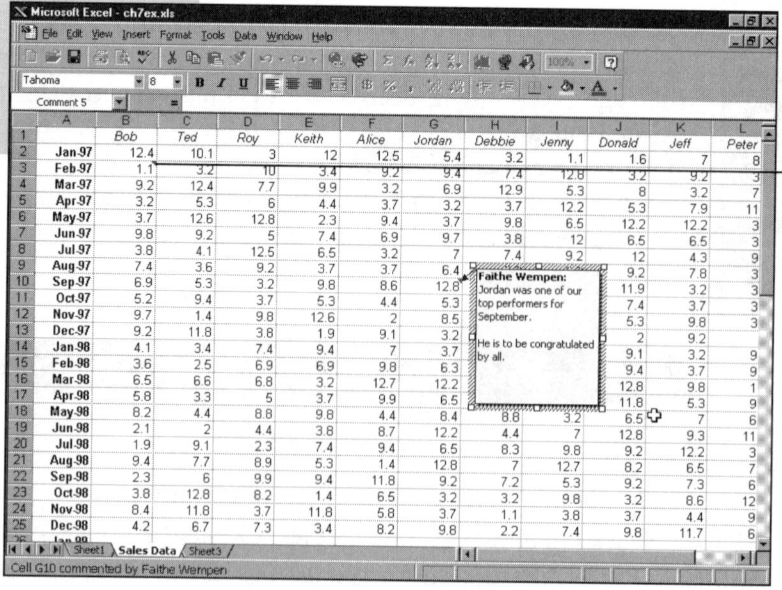

A red triangle indicates a comment is there.

Note

If you type a lengthy comment, it scrolls up, but you can manually resize the box by dragging its sizing handles so that you can see the entire note as you type if you prefer.

4. When you are finished typing your comment, click the mouse anywhere outside the comment box.
5. To view the comment, position your mouse pointer over the cell to which it is attached.

To edit a comment, select the cell and press Shift+F2, or right-click the cell that contains it and choose Edit Comment from the shortcut menu that appears. An insertion point will reappear in the comment box, and you can make your edits just as you did when you were typing it originally.

To remove a comment from a cell, right-click the cell and choose Delete Comment from the shortcut menu. Or, alternatively, you can select the cell and then choose Edit, Clear, Comments. You can remove the comments from multiple cells at once by selecting the entire range before you right-click.

Checking Your Spelling

Like other Microsoft Office programs, Excel comes with a powerful spelling program that can check your work for you at any time, minimizing the number of embarrassing spelling mistakes. (Of course, the spelling checker can't catch an inaccurate number, so the spelling checker isn't as useful in a number-intensive program like Excel as it is in a text-intensive program like Word.)

The Office programs use the same spelling checker, so if you are familiar with it in another Office program, you should be able to breeze through a spell check in Excel with no problem.

Note

When Excel marks a word as "misspelled," it really means that the word is not in its dictionary. Many words, especially proper names, are perfectly okay to use and yet not in Excel's dictionary, so don't believe Excel against your own good judgment.

To begin the spelling check of your worksheet, click the Spelling button on the Standard toolbar, or choose Tools, Spelling, or press F7. If you have no misspelled words, Excel presents a dialog box telling you that your spell check is complete. Click OK to close the dialog box.

If, on the other hand, Excel finds a misspelled word, as it did in Figure 7.13, you can choose from the following options:

- **Ignore.** Skips over this occurrence of the word.
- **Ignore All.** Skips over all occurrences of the word in this worksheet.
- **Suggestions.** Lists words that Excel thinks may be what you meant instead of the word you actually typed. Choose the correct one by clicking on it.
- **Change To.** Shows the word that you selected from the Suggestions list. If none of the words on the Suggestions list are right, you can type your own correction into this text box instead.
- **Change.** Changes the word in the cell to the word listed in the Change To text box. (Don't click this button until you've put the correct word in the Change To text box.)
- **Change All.** Changes all occurrences of the word in the entire worksheet to the word listed in the Change To text box.

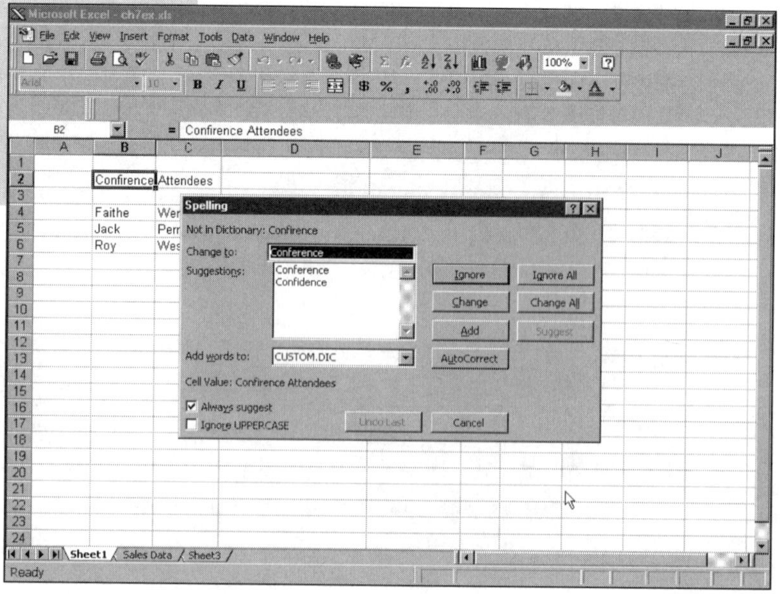

Figure 7.13 If Excel finds a word that is not in its dictionary, this dialog box asks you what to do about it.

- **Add.** Adds the word to Excel's dictionary so that it will recognize it in the future.
- **AutoCorrect.** Adds the word to the AutoCorrect list so that if you misspell it the same way in the future, Excel automatically corrects it as you type.

Don't click the AutoCorrect button for misspellings that you may sometimes want to change to some other word, or you may introduce embarrassing mistakes into your worksheet. For example, if you often type "pian" instead of "pain," but sometimes you accidentally type "pian" instead of "piano," don't tell Excel to always AutoCorrect to "pain," or you may find that Excel has corrected your attempt at typing piano and made it a pain!

When the spell check is over, Excel displays a dialog box to that effect; click OK.

Using AutoCorrect to Prevent Common Mistakes

With AutoCorrect, Excel can correct certain common misspellings automatically as you type. One way to put a word on this AutoCorrect list, as you saw, is to click the AutoCorrect button in the spelling checker. Another way is to directly access the AutoCorrect feature.

To access AutoCorrect, choose Tools, AutoCorrect. The AutoCorrect dialog box appears, as shown in Figure 7.14.

At the top of the dialog box is a series of check boxes that help you fine-tune some other corrections that AutoCorrect makes:

- **Correct TWo INitial Capitals.** If you accidentally hold down the Shift key too long and get two capital letters in a row, such as *MIcrosoft*, Excel corrects this if you leave this check box marked.
- **Capitalize First Letter of Sentence.** Leave this check box marked to have Excel capitalize the first word that comes after a sentence-ending punctuation mark, such as a period, or that occurs at the beginning of a paragraph.
- **Capitalize Names of Days.** Leave this check box marked to make sure the names of days, like Sunday, Monday, and so on, are capitalized.

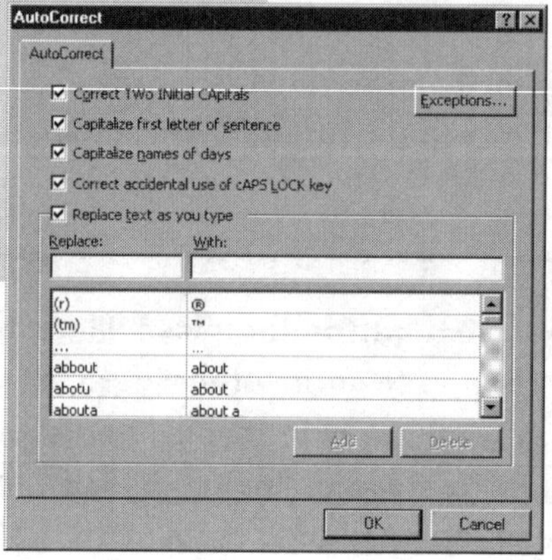

Figure 7.14 The AutoCorrect dialog box enables you to edit the list of AutoCorrections that Excel makes.

- **Correct Accidental Use of cAPS LOCK key.** If you leave the Caps Lock on, Excel can sometimes detect it and fix the problem. For example, if you had a sentence like "hE WAS GLAD TO SEE US," Excel could conclude that the Caps Lock was inappropriately on and would turn it off for you.
- **Replace Text as You Type.** This check box enables the main portion of AutoCorrect: the word list. You must leave this check box on if you want AutoCorrect to correct the words on the list.

On the list in this dialog box, you'll see a number of word pairs. To the left is the common misspelling, and to the right is the word that Excel substitutes in its place. Scroll through this list to get a feel for the corrections Excel makes.

If Excel insists on making a correction that you do not want, you can delete it from the list. Simply select it on the list and click the Delete button. For example, my editors like me to code certain headings with (c) in front of them, so the first thing I do in any Office program is remove the AutoCorrect entry that specifies that (c) must be converted to a copyright symbol (©).

To add your own entries to the list, type the misspelling in the Replace text box and the correction in the With text box, and then click the Add button.

When you are finished, click OK to close the AutoCorrect dialog box.

Using Undo and Redo

Everyone makes mistakes as they work. It's inevitable. In Excel, there's an easy way to reverse the last action you have taken, whether you have accidentally typed over important information in a cell or moved the wrong thing to the wrong place. It's called Undo.

Use Undo immediately after the mistake. Click the Undo button on the Standard toolbar, or choose Edit, Undo from the menu. (The exact wording of the Undo command varies depending on what the action was; it might be Undo Typing, Undo Bold, or something else.)

There are some actions that you cannot undo, such as saving and printing. Be careful when you perform these actions because there is no going back.

If the action that you want to undo occurred several actions ago, you can still undo it, but you must undo all the actions that you have done since then too. To do this, click the down arrow next to the Undo button on the Standard toolbar. This opens a drop-down list of the actions you've taken, from most recent at the top to earlier actions at the bottom. Move the mouse pointer down to the action you want to undo; all the actions above it become selected too, as shown in Figure 7.15. Then click, and Excel "undoes" all the actions back to that point.

Figure 7.15 Here, I've selected the last nine actions to undo.

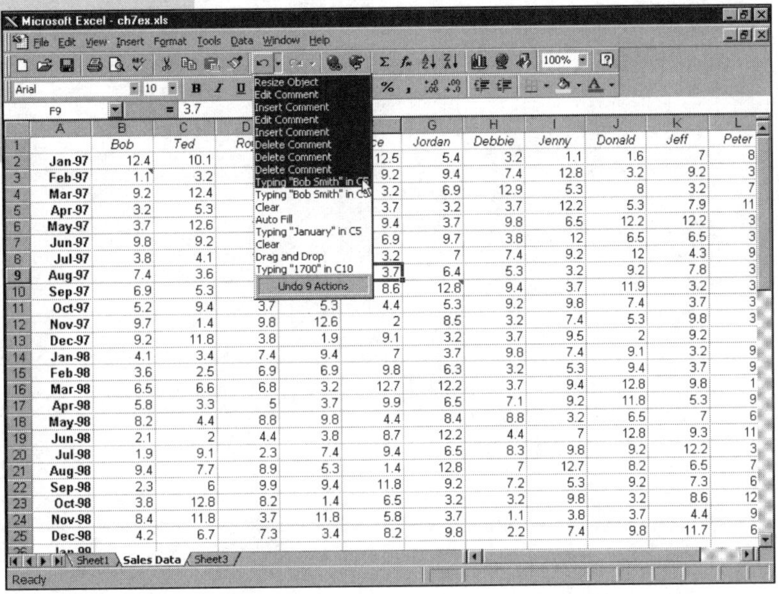

A related command, Redo, works the same way, except forward. If you have undone a series of actions and you now want to "undo the undoing," it's considered *redoing*. The Redo button, immediately to the right of the Undo button, enables you to do just that. Click on it to redo the most recent undone action, or select a number of undone actions to redo from its drop-down list.

8

Entering Formulas and Functions

In This Chapter

- What Formulas Can Do for You
- Quick Adding with AutoSum
- Naming Ranges
- Using Functions

In the preceding chapter you learned how to type text and numbers into cells. But if that were all Excel was good for, you could just as easily use a word processor! Excel's real power lies in its capability to perform calculations on numbers. These calculations come in two forms: *formulas,* which are simple mathematical phrases you create, and *functions,* which employ sophisticated built-in formulas.

What Is a Formula?

Simply speaking, a formula is an expression that calculates a value. The following are Excel formulas you might already be familiar with:

=2+2

=72/9

=6*7

=500-45

CREATING AN ELECTRONIC FILING SYSTEM IS DISCUSSED IN CHAPTER 22.

All these formulas are simple—they use basic math operators and regular, whole numbers. The equals sign at the beginning of each formula is an Excel requirement that tells Excel "the following is a formula." If you were to put one of them in a cell in Excel, the formula bar would show the formula you entered, and the cell itself would show the result. Figure 8.1 shows an Excel sheet with the preceding four formulas entered in cells C3 through C7.

Note

If you enter a formula into a cell but the cell shows the formula itself rather than the answer, make sure that you typed an equals sign at the beginning of the formula. If you are sure that you did, try pressing Ctrl+` (single left quotation mark, on the far left on most keyboards) to toggle the display between showing formulas and showing results.

Figure 8.1
When you enter a formula into a cell, the cell shows the answer.

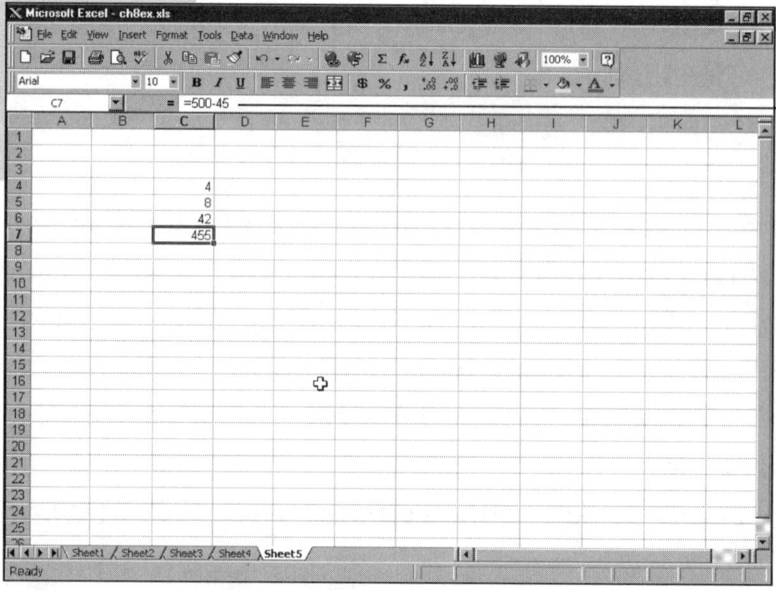

The formula bar shows the formula in the active cell.

Excel uses the basic math operators that most computer programs do:

Operator	Meaning
+	Addition
-	Subtraction
/	Division
*	Multiplication
^	Exponentiation

All the preceding should seem familiar, except perhaps exponentiation. That's when you raise the value to the *n*th power. For example, 2^3 is 2 to the 3rd power, or 2x2x2, or 8.

Besides doing basic math, you can also refer to the contents of other cells in a formula. For example, say that you have entered **15** in cell A1 and **20** in cell A2. Then in cell A3, you enter:

=A1+A2

Cell A3 would then display `35`, the answer to the formula. If you changed the number in A1 to **40**, cell A3 would change to display `60`.

Let's look at some more examples. Suppose that you entered the following values in the indicated cells in column B:

B1: **35**
B2: **20**
B3: **15**
B4: **12**

Table 8.1 shows some example formulas you could enter into any other cells and the results you would get.

Table 8.1 Formula Examples

Formula is ...	Which means ...	Result is ...
=B1+B2	35+20	55
=B2+B4	20+12	32
=B2/B4	20/12	1.666667
=B4*B1	12*35	420
=B3	15	15
=B1+B2+B3	35+20+15	70
=B2-5	20-5	15

Notice in Table 8.1 that a single cell reference can be a formula, as in =B3. When you enter a formula like that into a cell, it simply repeats the contents of the referenced cell. Notice also that you can mix in regular numbers with cell references, as in =B2-5.

Understanding Order of Precedence

If you use more than one math operator in a formula, Excel handles them in a particular order. The order is this:

- Exponentiation first
- Multiplication and division second
- Addition and subtraction third

These are the same rules that mathematicians follow, so if you have had any math classes lately you are probably already up on this. For example, let's say that you used the following formula:

=12+5*6-2^3

Here's how Excel would work that out:

1. Do the exponentiation first: 2^3 is 8. So now you have =12+5*6-8.
2. Do the multiplication: 5 times 6 is 30. So now you have =12+30-8.
3. Because all remaining operators are of the same precedence, you can do them in any order (left to right is fine). 12+30 is 42, minus 8 is 34.

If you want the order of precedence to occur differently than the default, use parentheses to show which math operations should be done first. For example, to do the addition first and then the multiplication in this formula:

=A1+6*C4

You would write it with parentheses around the addition formula like this:

=(A1+6)*C4

Entering a Formula into a Cell

You can type formulas into cells in the same way as you type regular text and numbers. Just remember one important thing: type an equals sign first. This signals to Excel that whatever you type after it should be considered a formula. Remember in Chapter 7 I told you that if your entry had even one letter in it, Excel would consider it text rather than a number and not calculate it? Cell references like A1 have letters in them. The equals sign before a formula containing a cell reference is necessary to tell Excel that it's not intended to be text, even though it has a letter in it.

Another way to enter a formula in a cell is with a mixture of typing and mouse clicking. For example, if you wanted to create a formula that referred to a certain cell, you could start out typing the equals sign and then click on that cell to place its address in the formula you're building. For example, suppose that you want to add the contents of cells C3 and C4 and put the result in C5. You would do the following:

1. Click in C5 and type an equals sign.
2. Click on C3.
3. Type a plus sign.
4. Click on C4.
5. Press Enter.

Note

If you begin entering a formula and then change your mind, you can press Esc to cancel the entry anytime before you press Enter.

Hands On: Entering Formulas

The following tutorial walks you through entering some formulas in cells. If you feel like you need some practice entering formulas, take the following steps, starting with a blank worksheet:

1. Enter the following values in the indicated cells. Do not skip the labels in column B! It is important to get into the habit of labeling each number you enter, so that you will not forget what it represents.

A1:	**15**
A2:	**7**
A3:	**8**
A4:	**6**
B1:	**Gross Sales**
B2:	**Other Income**
B3:	**Administrative Expense**
B4:	**Sales Expense**

2. In cell C7, enter **=A1+A2** and press Enter. C7 should display `22`. Enter **Total Revenue** in D7 as a label.

Note

If you enter the formula and the result doesn't appear (the formula appears instead), make sure that you typed the equals sign. If you did, select Tools, Options, click the View tab, and make sure that the Formulas check box is unmarked.

3. In cell C8, enter **=A3+A4** and press Enter. C8 should display `14`. Enter **Total Expenses** in D8 as a label.
4. In cell C9, enter **=C7-C8** and press Enter. C11 should display `8`. Enter **Profit** in cell D9 as a label. You now have a simple worksheet that calculates the profit you make by subtracting your expenses from your income (see Figure 8.2).
5. Now change the value in cell A2 to **2**. Notice that the Total Revenue (cell C7) changes to `17`. And because the Profit (cell C9) depends on the values in cells C7 and C8, its value changes to `3`.

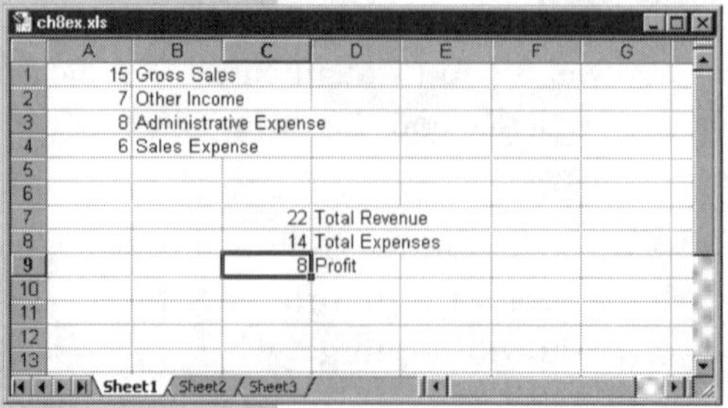

Figure 8.2 This worksheet adds the income categories together, adds the expense categories together, and then subtracts the expense total from the income total.

Tip

You can use a formula to combine the contents of two cells in a third cell. For example, suppose that cell A1 contains a first name and cell A2 contains a last name, and you want cell A3 to contain the first and last names together with a space in between. In A3 you would enter this formula: **=A2&" "&B2**. The *&* sign concatenates, or combines, the cells' contents. The " ", a space between two quotation marks, inserts a space between the two cells' contents.

Using AutoSum

One of the most common uses for a formula is to sum a row or column of numbers. For example, in Figure 8.3, I have the gross sales for each of my salespeople in December. I would like to total up the sales at the bottom of the list.

One way to total the numbers would be to enter the following formula in cell C10:

=C3+C4+C5+C6+C7+C8+C9

That works just fine, but it's rather tedious to type in. A better way is to use AutoSum. AutoSum uses the Sum function, one of Excel's built-in functions (which you'll learn about later in this chapter). Because the Sum function is the most commonly used one, Excel has given it its own button on the toolbar.

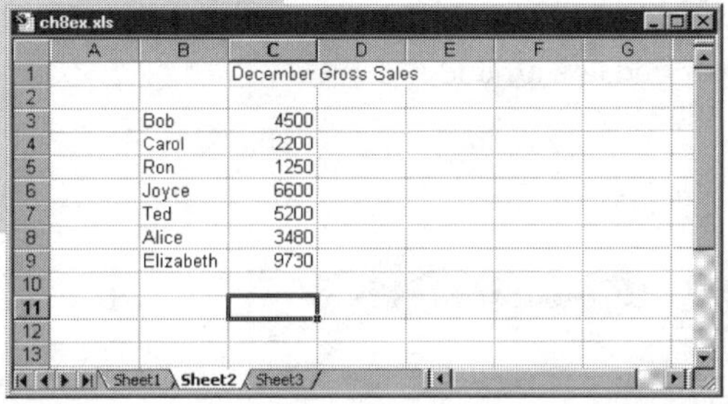

Figure 8.3 I would like to sum all the sales figures for a grand total.

Hands On: Adding with AutoSum

To use AutoSum, follow these steps:

1. Click in the cell into which you want the result to go. For example, in Figure 8.3, I would click in cell C10.

2. Click the AutoSum button on the toolbar or press Alt+= (equals sign). Excel enters =SUM in the cell, followed by its best guess of what range you want to add up in parentheses. For example, if summing the numbers in Figure 8.3, it would enter =SUM(C3:C9), as shown in Figure 8.4.
3. If the range Excel chose is correct, press Enter. You're finished! Otherwise, drag your mouse across the correct range. That range's address replaces Excel's guess. After you've indicated the correct range, press Enter.

You can also type the correct range in step 3, but most people find it easier to drag across it with the mouse. You can also type the =SUM function directly into a cell instead of using AutoSum, but if you do so, you must type the parentheses and the range yourself; Excel does not put them in automatically when you type the function manually.

You can sum more than one range with a single =SUM formula. Select the first range and then hold down the Ctrl key as you select other ranges. They'll be separated in the function with commas.

When you select a range, the sum of the cells in the range appears on the right side of the status bar.

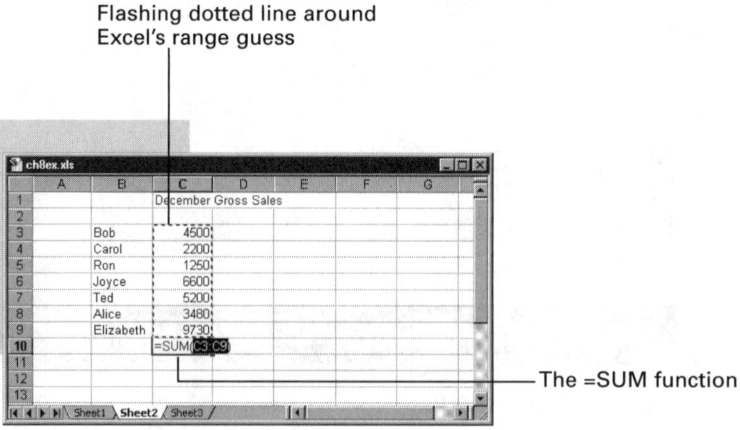

Figure 8.4 AutoSum enters the =SUM function and guesses at what you want summed.

Working with Ranges

Before you go much deeper into functions, you will need a firm understanding of ranges. That's because most functions do their work based on ranges of cells.

As you learned earlier in the book, a *range* is a group of cells, usually contiguous. A range can be as small as a single cell or as large as an entire workbook. Ranges are named according to their top left and bottom right cells, with a colon in-between, like this: A1:B6. When you are working with functions, you will almost always indicate what range you want the function to act upon.

When the worksheet name is part of the range, it appears at the beginning of the range name, separated from the rest by an exclamation point. For example, if you were referring to A1:B6 on Sheet1, the full name of the range would be Sheet1!A1:B6. However, unless you are working with more than one sheet in the workbook, you don't have to worry about the sheet name.

Naming a Range

Sometimes it is more convenient to refer to a range of cells by an alias rather than its cell addresses. For example, in Figure 8.4, the range C3:C9 might be easier to remember if it were called Individual_Totals. Assigning range names is optional, but in some cases it can make a worksheet easier to use. The name you assign is just an alias; you can continue to use the old name (the row and column address) whenever you prefer it.

Range names can be any length up to 255 characters, but they cannot contain spaces; that's why there is an underscore character (_) separating the words in my example, Individual_Totals. They also cannot contain any symbols except a period, dash, or underscore, and they must start with a letter or an underscore. The name must also not be the same as a cell reference (for example, you can't name cell A1 "A2.")

Hands On: Naming a Range

To assign a meaningful name to a range, follow these steps:

1. Select the range to which you want to assign a name.
2. Click in the Name box at the left end of the formula bar.
3. Type a name for the range.
4. Press Enter.

If you want to name a range that contains more than one sheet, you can't do it this easy way; you must use the Define Name dialog box. Use these steps instead:

1. Choose Insert, Name, Define. The Define Name dialog box appears, shown in Figure 8.5.
2. Type a name for the range in the Names in Workbook text box.
3. Click the Collapse Dialog button (at the right end of the Refers To box). The dialog box disappears except for a single bar that shows what you've selected (see Figure 8.6).

Figure 8.5
Enter a name for the range and specify what it refers to.

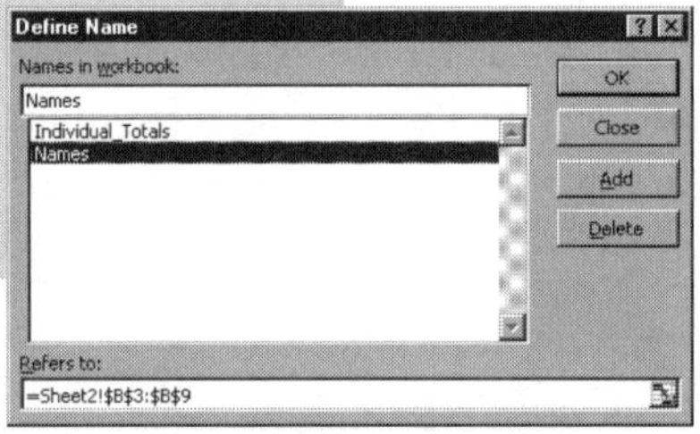

Figure 8.6
The range you select is also selected on all the other sheets you've chosen.

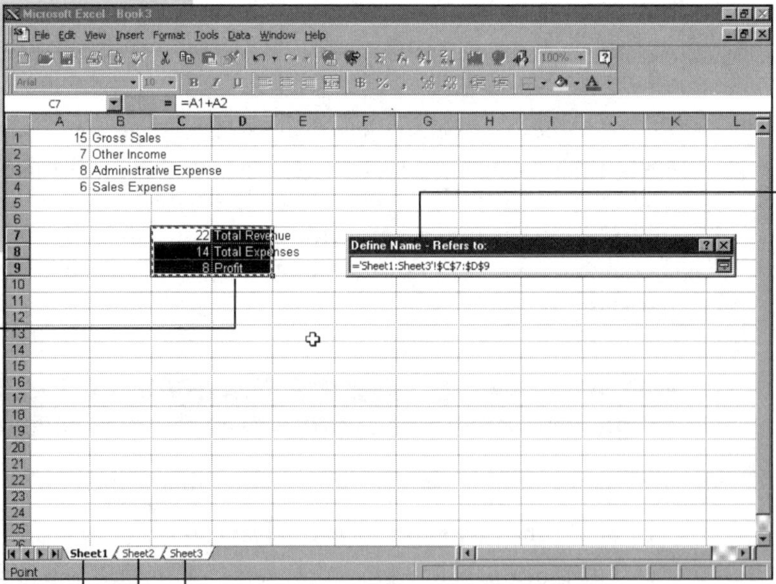

Select the range you want.

The dialog box is collapsed; press Enter to reopen it.

All the tabs are white, meaning they are all selected.

4. Hold down the Shift key and click on the tab for the last worksheet you want to include in the range. All the tabs for the worksheets in-between are selected too.
5. Still holding down the Shift key, select the cells you want to include in the range. The same range of cells will be selected on each sheet of the range.
6. Release the Shift key and press Enter to return to the dialog box. The range you chose appears in the Refers To text box.
7. Click OK. The dialog box closes. Your 3-D range is named.

Quickly Creating a Series of Named Ranges

Suppose that you have a list of names and corresponding numbers, as in Figure 8.4. It would be nice to assign the person's name to the figure next to it, so that you could more easily refer to the figure in formulas. For example, if you wondered what Bob's and Carol's sales totals added together equaled, you could look up the addresses of the cells containing their totals and enter:

=C3+C4

or you could spare yourself the trouble of looking up the references by entering:

=Bob+Carol

It would take longer than it's worth to individually name a single-cell range for each person, but you can do it quickly with the following procedure:

Hands On: Creating Automatic Range Names

1. Select the entire range for which you want to create names. Make sure that the text you want to use for the names is on one edge of the range (top, bottom, right, or left).
2. Choose Insert, Name, Create or press Ctrl+Shift+F3. The Create Names dialog box appears (see Figure 8.7).

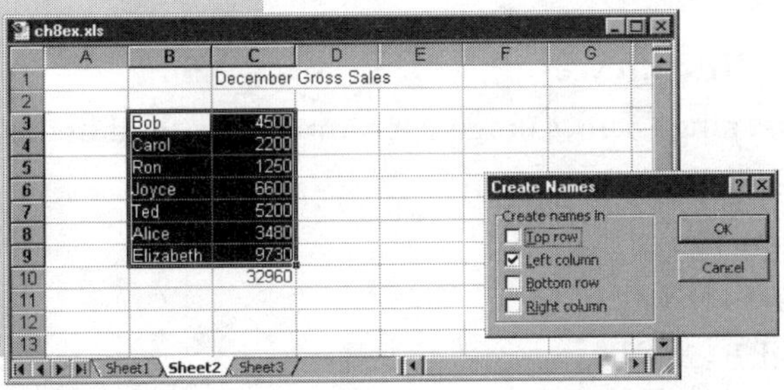

Figure 8.7 Choose a check box that represents where in the selected range the text lies that should be used for range names.

3. Click the appropriate check box for the side of the range containing the labels. Excel may have already tried to guess for you, in which case a check box may already be marked.
4. Click OK. Each range is named.

To test your work, click on one of the cells containing the data to which you assigned a name. Notice that in the Name box on the formula bar, the name now appears.

Changing What Cells a Name Refers To

If you later need to make a change to the range defined by a name, follow these steps:

1. Choose Insert, Name, Define. The Define Name dialog box opens (refer to Figure 8.5).
2. Click on the name you want to change.
3. Type a new range in the Refers To text box; or click the Collapse Dialog button, reselect a range, and press Enter.
4. Click Close.

Referring to a Named Range in a Formula or Function

The payoff for naming a range comes in using the name in a formula or function. Even though the name you chose may be longer than the original name (for example, *Carol* takes longer to type than *C4*), the new name is easier to remember, so you won't have to look it up every time you want to refer to it.

Use a named range just as you would a regular range. For example, if you wanted to sum the first four salespeople on your list (Bob, Carol, Ron, and Joyce), instead of entering:

=SUM(C3:C6)

you could enter:

=SUM(Bob:Joyce)

You can use range names in regular formulas too, and in the same formulas as regular cell references:

=Bob+100
=Div1+Div2
=Ted*E12

If you aren't sure what the exact name is of the range that you want, you can paste from a list by doing the following:

1. Start the formula by typing an equals sign, and type the formula up to the point where the name should be inserted.
2. Press F3. The Paste Names dialog box appears.
3. Choose the range name you want from the list.
4. Click OK.
5. Continue typing the formula and then press Enter.

Named ranges are certainly not a requirement, and many experienced Excel users don't use them at all. However, many people find them handy at least occasionally, as an easy way to remember an otherwise-cryptic cell reference that they use frequently.

What Is a Function?

SEE APPENDIX C FOR A COMPLETE LIST OF FUNCTIONS AND THEIR ARGUMENTS.

You have already had a good look at a function in this chapter: =SUM. It's simple, but it has all the basic components of a function that you should know about:

- It starts with an equals sign (as all functions and formulas do).
- It contains the function name in all caps.
- It is followed by parentheses containing *arguments*.

Arguments is a scary sounding word, especially for those of us who were never very good at algebra, but it's really quite simple. Remember in Chapter 1 I told you that dialog boxes are Excel's way of asking for additional information before it executes a command? An argument is the same thing. An argument is additional information that clarifies how you want the function to behave.

One of the most common arguments is to tell what range of cells you want the function to act upon. You saw this with the =SUM function earlier. In the function =SUM(A1:A6), the range of cells to be acted upon—A1 through A6—is the argument. Some functions use other arguments too, but we'll get to those later.

Here are some examples of handy functions Excel provides. You'll see more examples in Chapter 9 too.

```
=AVERAGE(number1,number2,...)
```

The =AVERAGE function averages a group of numbers. The arguments are the ranges of cells you want to average. For example, to average the numbers in cells B4:B12, you would type **=AVERAGE(B4:B12)**. (That's just one argument, even though there are nine cells referenced in the range.) You could average two or more ranges at once by typing something like **=AVERAGE(A1:A5,B2:B4)**.

Note

The words *number* and *value* in the argument placeholders are a bit confusing because each argument can actually be a range of numbers or values. For example, when you enter *=AVERAGE(A1:A5,B2:B4)* it's considered to have two arguments. The same thing could be written as *=AVERAGE(A1,A2,A3,A4,A5,B2,B3,B4)*, but it would be considered to have eight arguments in that case because you are listing eight separate ranges.

```
=COUNT(value1,value2,...)
```

The =COUNT function counts the number of cells in the specified range that contain *numbers*. For example, suppose that you have a worksheet in which cells containing data are interspersed with cells containing text, as in Figure 8.8. If you wanted to know how many cells actually contain data, you could use the =COUNT function. For example, in Figure 8.8, I would enter the following formula in cell G13 (or any other empty cell) to count the number of man-months (one man-month being one salesperson working for one month): **=COUNT(A4:G11)**. The result would be 17.

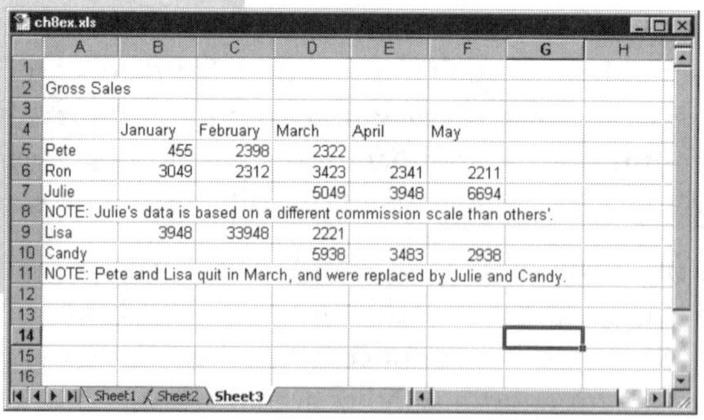

	A	B	C	D	E	F	G	H
1								
2	Gross Sales							
3								
4		January	February	March	April	May		
5	Pete	455	2398	2322				
6	Ron	3049	2312	3423	2341	2211		
7	Julie			5049	3948	6694		
8	NOTE: Julie's data is based on a different commission scale than others'.							
9	Lisa	3948	33948	2221				
10	Candy			5938	3483	2938		
11	NOTE: Pete and Lisa quit in March, and were replaced by Julie and Candy.							

Figure 8.8 You could use the =COUNT function to count the number of cells containing numbers in this worksheet.

```
=MAX(number1,number2)
```

The =MAX function finds the highest value from a list. For example, suppose that you wanted to know at a glance which salesperson had the highest sales. You could use the =MAX function to find out. Specify the entire range of data as the argument—for example, in Figure 8.8 it would be B5 through F10. Then enter the function in the cell where you want the value to appear: **=MAX(B5:F10)**. The result in this example would be `33948`, which appears in cell C9.

Using the Paste Function Button

Now that you've seen a few things that functions can do, you are probably eager to get started entering them.

In the old days of spreadsheets, functions were difficult to use because you had to remember what arguments each function needed. Spreadsheet programs often came with thick books of function reference information that nobody wanted to use. The result was that even though functions are one of the most powerful features of a spreadsheet, few people used them.

Fortunately, Excel 97 makes it easy to use functions. The built-in Paste Function feature walks you through each step and helps you provide the correct arguments in the right spots.

Hands On: Pasting a Function

Let's try pasting a function, starting with the =AVERAGE function that you learned about in the preceding section. Say that you wanted to average a column of numbers but you weren't sure how to use =AVERAGE. You would follow these steps:

1. (Optional) Type the label **Average** in a cell beside the one where you're planning to place the function. It is always a good idea to provide labels for each function and each number you enter.
2. Click in the cell where you want to place the =AVERAGE function.
3. Click the Paste Function button on the Standard toolbar. The Paste Function dialog box appears (see Figure 8.9).
4. The most recently used functions appear on the Function Name list. If you see AVERAGE on that list, click on it. If you don't see it, click Statistical in the Function Category list, and then click on AVERAGE in the Function Name list. When you've selected AVERAGE, click OK to proceed. The Paste Function dialog box disappears, and the Formula Palette opens at the top of the worksheet, as shown in Figure 8.10.

Tip

If you already know the name of the function you want to use, you can bypass the Paste Function dialog box. Type an equals sign and the function name in the cell, and then press Ctrl+A to jump to the Formula Palette. Or, if you are *really* experienced, you can bypass the Formula Palette too and work directly with the function's arguments by typing the formula name and then pressing Ctrl+Shift+A.

The equals sign appears in the cell when you open the Paste Function dialog box.

Figure 8.9 Choose which function you want to use from the Paste Function dialog box.

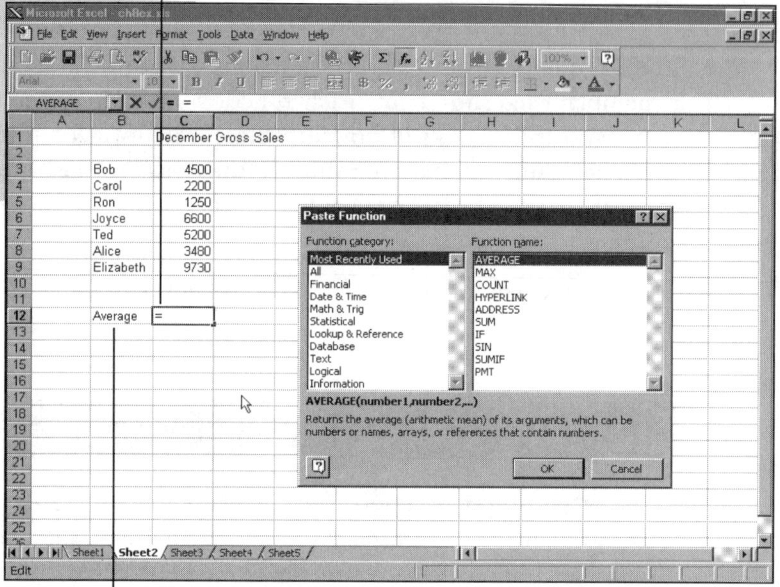

Enter a label in the cell next to the one where you're placing the function.

Figure 8.10 Excel's Formula Palette provides some help for entering the needed arguments of the function.

Function drop-down list

Office Assistant button

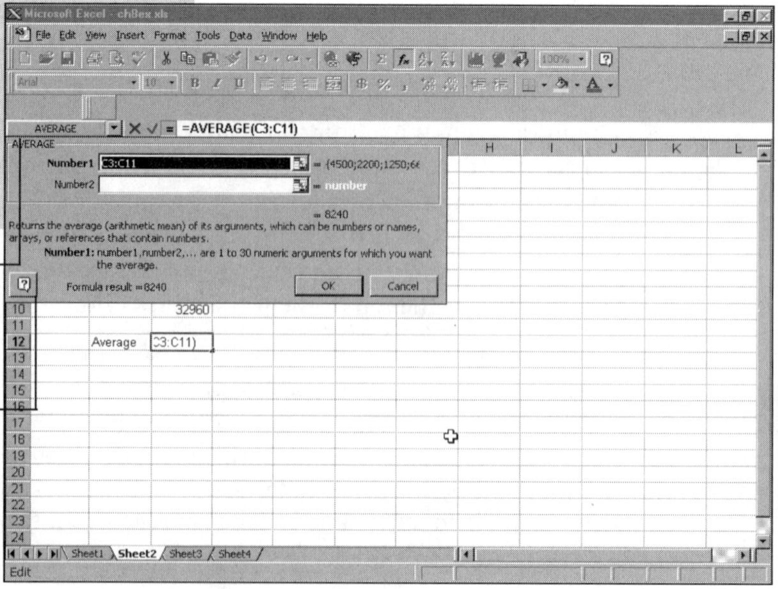

5. If you know the range you want to enter for the argument, type it in the Number1 text box. Excel may have already entered the correct range for you.
6. If you don't know the range without looking at the worksheet, click the Collapse Dialog button at the end of the Number1 text box to move the Formula Palette out of the way while you select the range. When you're finished selecting the range, press Enter to return to the Formula Palette.
7. Because we're only going to enter one range right now, click OK to finish up. The =AVERAGE function appears in the cell you specified. To take a look at it, click on that cell and then look in the formula bar.

Now that you've survived your first function, take another look at the procedure with an eye toward future exploration:

- Notice the Function drop-down list box in Figure 8.10. If you decide you've chosen the wrong function, you can select a different one from this list anytime before you click that final OK button on the Formula Palette.
- If you would like more information about the function you've chosen, click the Office Assistant button (also shown in Figure 8.10). When the Office Assistant appears, click Help With This Feature, and then click Help on a selected function. A screenful of information about that function appears, with examples included. Very handy! *All* spreadsheet programs should have this feature—but many don't.
- Notice in Figure 8.10 the line at the bottom of the Formula Palette that says Formula Result. This shows what the result will be if you click OK now with the current arguments entered. This can be helpful because if the result is nowhere near what you expected, perhaps you have incorrect arguments chosen or perhaps you are using the wrong function.
- Notice that each argument line has its own Collapse Dialog button. And, although you can't see it in Figure 8.10, if you were to click in the second argument line, a third line would appear. Click in the third line and a fourth one appears, and so on, up to 30 argument lines. This works with all functions that can have a variable number of arguments.
- When you enter a range as an argument, as in Figure 8.10, the individual numbers in that range appear to the right of the text box. Of course, in Figure 8.10 there are too many, and the display cuts off, but you can at least see the first few. This can be helpful if you're wondering whether you chose the right range.

There is much more to learn about formulas and functions, but hopefully this chapter has whetted your appetite for more. In the following chapter, you'll learn how to edit, move, and copy formulas and functions, as well as learn about the important concept of absolute versus relative cell references.

9

Moving and Changing Formulas

In This Chapter

- Editing a Formula
- Moving and Copying Formulas
- Relative and Absolute References
- Finding and Fixing Mistakes

Entering formulas is only half the battle. It's kind of like when you write a report in your word processor. The first time through, you just try to get your thoughts down on paper. Then you reread it and begin editing, rearranging, cutting, and so on to make it the best report it can be. That's exactly what you need to do with your Excel worksheets too. After you've entered all your numbers and formulas initially, take a cruise through and make sure that everything works.

Making Changes to a Formula

Changing a formula is much like changing any other text; you select the cell and then either click in the formula bar or press F2 to begin your editing. A formula is not something mystical and untouchable—it's just a string of text, symbols, and numbers that Excel happens to recognize as a signal that you want something calculated.

An additional risk is involved in editing formulas and functions, however, that you don't get with editing text. If you change some text and introduce a typo, it may cause some embarrassment, but the data presented will still be accurate. However, if you accidentally change a formula or function, it may give a result that you do not intend. When editing formulas and functions, be careful that you do not inadvertently remove a parenthesis or math symbol.

To change a formula, click in the cell and press F2, or select the cell and then click in the formula bar, or double-click the cell. Then type your changes, using the ←Backspace and Del keys as needed to delete existing text and the arrow keys to move the insertion point.

Hands On: Changing a Function

SEE CHAPTER 8 FOR A FULL EXPLANATION OF HOW TO USE THE FORMULA PALETTE.

If you want to change a function, you can type in your changes manually, as with a formula, or you can reopen the Formula Palette. To do so, follow these steps:

1. Click in the cell containing the function.
2. Click the Paste Function button on the Standard toolbar, or click the equals sign button on the formula bar. The Formula Palette reappears onscreen, as shown in Figure 9.1.
3. Make changes to your arguments as needed.
4. Click OK to close the Formula Palette.

When you click the equals sign button on the formula bar while a cell that does not contain a function is active, you get a special editing palette (see Figure 9.2) that looks sort of like an abbreviated version of the Formula Palette. It provides one main benefit—it lets you see the result of your formula while you are editing it. When you finish editing, you can click the OK button to finish up or the Cancel button to reject your changes.

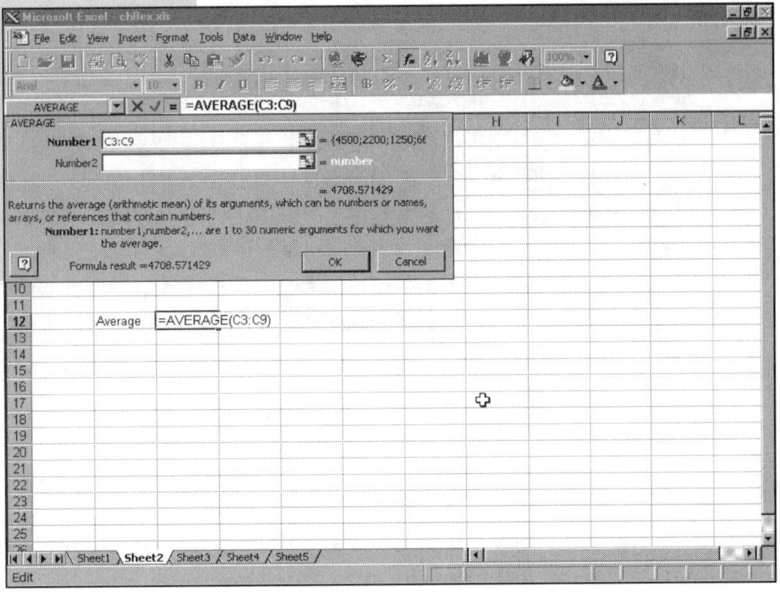

Figure 9.1 When you click the Paste Function button while a cell is active that already contains a function, the Formula Palette reappears.

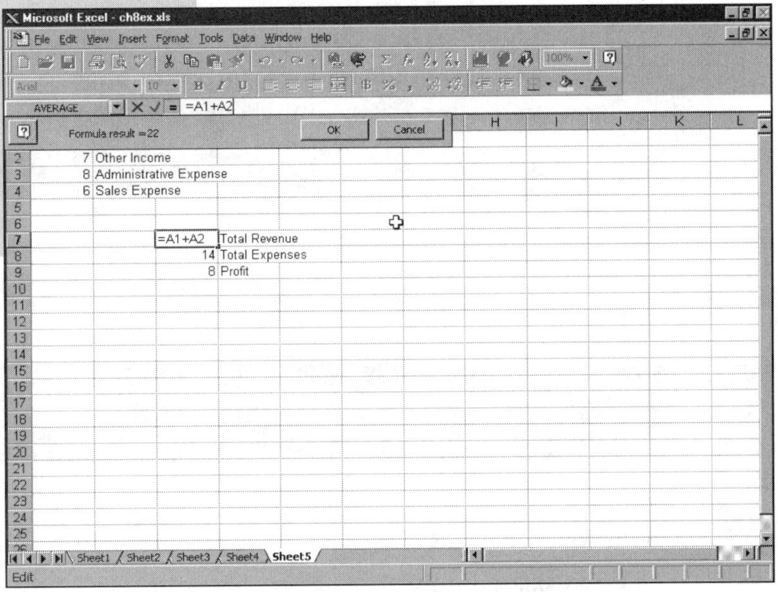

Figure 9.2 Clicking the equals sign on the formula bar opens these controls if the active cell does not contain a function.

Note

If you change a formula, or the contents of a cell referenced in the formula, but the result shown doesn't change, perhaps you have somehow inadvertently set recalculation to manual. With manual recalculation, results are updated only when you request it, not automatically. If you have recalculation set to manual, you can press F9 to recalculate all the sheets in all open workbooks, or Shift+F9 to recalculate only the active sheet. To turn automatic recalculation back on, choose Tools, Options, click the Calculation tab, and make sure that Automatic is selected.

Moving and Copying Formulas

To move or copy a formula, you use the same procedure as you do when moving and copying text. You can drag and drop or cut and paste—it's your choice. You can also use shortcut keys, which I'll explain as we go along.

Note

I'm going to explain the physical mechanics of moving and copying formulas and functions here, but to understand exactly what gets moved or copied, you will need to read the discussion of "Absolute and Relative References" later in this chapter.

Moving and Copying with Drag and Drop

SEE CHAPTER 7 FOR INFORMATION ABOUT MOVING AND COPYING TEXT.

Hands On: Moving or Copying a Formula or Function with Drag and Drop

To move or copy a single formula or function, the easiest way is to drag and drop. Do the following:

1. Select the cell containing the formula or function that you want to move or copy.
2. If you are copying, hold down the Ctrl key.

3. Position the mouse pointer at the edge of the selected cell, so that the mouse pointer turns into an arrow.
4. Drag the cell to a new position in the worksheet. An outline shows where it is going (see Figure 9.3). When you release the mouse button, you "drop" the contents into the new cell.

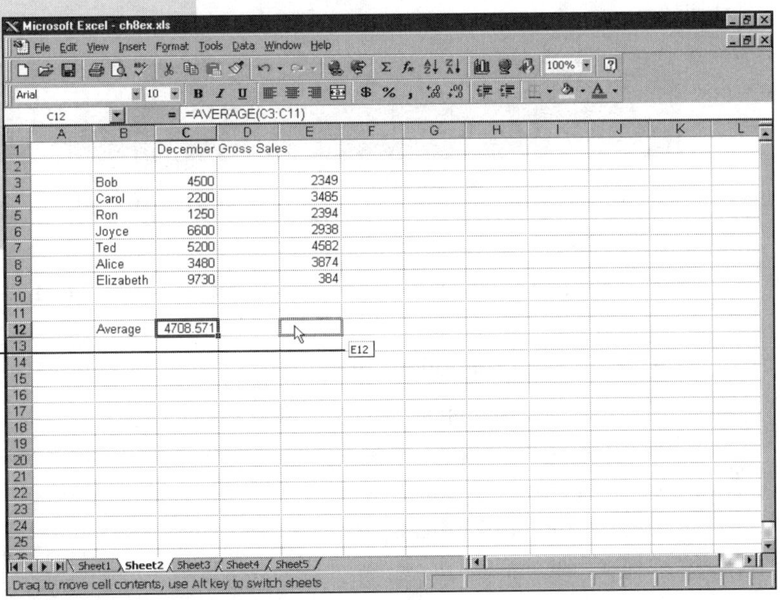

Figure 9.3
Drop the outline where you want the formula or function you are moving or copying to appear.

A ScreenTip shows the address where it will go.

When you copy a formula or function, the copy refers to different cells than the original. For example, if you have a formula in cell A3 that reads =A1+A2, when you copy that formula elsewhere, the formula changes to refer to whatever two cells are above its new position. This is because of relative references, and it's explained fully later in this chapter. In contrast, when you *move* a formula, it does *not* change the cells to which it refers.

Cut, Copy, and Paste

Another way to move and copy formulas is with the Cut, Copy, and Paste commands. These commands use the Windows Clipboard. Although it might seem

SEE CHAPTER 7 FOR MORE INFORMATION ABOUT THE CLIPBOARD.

that you would never bother with this method because drag and drop is so easy, don't discount it outright. I'm an experienced user, and I rarely use any method to move and copy other than the Cut (Ctrl+X), Copy (Ctrl+C), and Paste (Ctrl+V) shortcut keys. Nothing else is quite as quick.

As explained in Chapter 7, when you move cell contents, you are really using a two-step operation: 1) Cut and 2) Paste. When you copy cell contents, you are using a different two-step operation: 1) Copy and 2) Paste.

Hands On: Moving or Copying a Formula or Function with the Clipboard

To cut or copy a formula or function to the Clipboard and then paste it elsewhere, follow these steps:

1. Select the cell containing the formula or function that you want to cut or copy.
2. Do one of the following:
   - To cut, click the Cut button on the toolbar, or press Ctrl+X, or choose Edit, Cut.
   - To copy, click the Copy button on the toolbar, or press Ctrl+C, or choose Edit, Copy.
3. Select a cell to receive the formula or function. If you are copying, you can select multiple cells, and a copy will go into each one. If you are moving, you can select only a single cell because you selected only a single cell in step 1.
4. Click the Paste button on the toolbar, or press Ctrl+V, or choose Edit, Paste, or press Enter. The formula or function is copied or moved to the new location.

Here is one more keyboard shortcut: you can copy the formula from the cell above the active cell by pressing Ctrl+' (apostrophe).

Absolute and Relative References

Now you know the mechanics of moving and copying formulas, but do you understand what you're doing? Probably not. Excel's system of relative and absolute references can tie you in knots the first time you encounter it.

Here it is in a nutshell. When you copy a formula, say from A3 to B3, Excel is smart enough to know that you don't want an exact copy of it. If the formula in A3 was =A1+A2, chances are good that you don't want that same formula in B3. Instead, you probably want to add =B1+B2. That capability to change the formula to match the location where you copy it is called *relative referencing*. The references to cells in the formula are *relative* to the position of the formula itself in the worksheet.

On the other hand, when you move a formula, say that same one (=A1+A2), Excel guesses that you probably don't want to change the formula to match the new location. So it doesn't change the content of the formula as you move it. =A1+A2 is still the same =A1+A2, no matter where you move it. This is a type of *absolute referencing*, because the values (A1 and A2) remain constant even though the formula itself is changing position.

In that case, where you're moving the formula, Excel figures out that absolute referencing is needed and makes it happen. However, that formula is not permanently absolute. If you turned around and copied it somewhere, the copy would be relative, like any other copy.

You can force a formula's references to be permanently absolute by placing dollar signs in front of each letter and each number that you want to stay the same when copied. For example, suppose that you wanted the entire formula to be the same no matter where you copied it. You would insert dollar signs like this:

=$A$1+$A$2

If you wanted only the column letters to stay fixed, but not the row numbers, you would omit the dollar signs from in front of the row numbers, like this:

=$A1+$A2

If you wanted only one of the cell references to remain fixed, you would use dollar signs only for that cell reference:

=$A$1+A2

Hands On: Absolute Versus Relative References

This is an exercise in three parts. First, set up your worksheet by following these steps:

1. In cell A1, enter **5**.
2. In cell A2, enter **6**.
3. In cell B1, enter **100**.

4. In cell B2, enter **400**.
5. In cell B4, enter **12**.
6. In cell B5, enter **9**.

When you're finished, your worksheet should look like Figure 9.4.

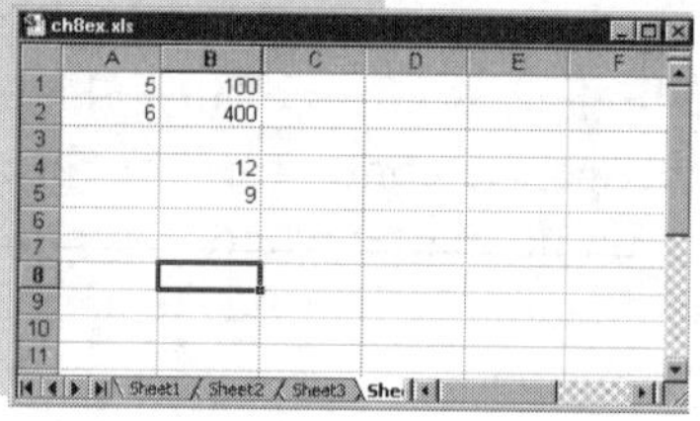

Figure 9.4 Enter these numbers as preparation for completing the following exercise.

Next, complete the following quiz. If each of the following formulas is typed into cell A3 and then copied to cell B6, predict how each formula will read when it's in cell B6 and what the result of that formula (displayed in B6) will be.

Formula in A3	Formula Copied to B6	Result Shown in B6
A. =$A$1+$A$2	____________	____________
B. =A1+A2	____________	____________
C. =$A$1+A2	____________	____________
D. =A$1+A$2	____________	____________
E. =$B4+B$5	____________	____________

Ready for the answers?

The first one (A) would be the same when copied to B6 as it was in A3. That's because every column letter and row number in the formula contains a dollar sign, so every one is absolute. The formula stays the same: =$A$1+$A$2. The result, both in A3 and B6, is 11.

In B, there are no dollar signs, hence no absolute references. Therefore, this formula is fully relative. Because in A3 it added the numbers in the two cells directly above (A1 and A2), when you copy it to B6 it will add the numbers in the cells directly above that location (B4 and B5). The formula would be =B4+B6, and the result would be 21.

In C, the first cell is fully absolute ($A$1), and the second is fully relative (A2). Therefore, when the formula is copied to B6, the first one will remain $A$1, but the second one will move to its counterpart in the new location, B5. The result of =$A$1+B5 would be 14.

In D, the row numbers are absolute, but the column letters are not. That means when the formula is copied to B6, it will take on the new column letter (B), but the row numbers will be fixed at 1 and 2, respectively. The formula would therefore be =B$1+B$2, and the result would be 500.

The last one, E, is tricky. B4 is one down and one to the right of the formula in A3. The letter stays frozen because of the dollar sign in front of the B, but the number changes. So with the formula copied to B6, the first reference becomes B7 (one row down from the formula). The second reference, B5, changes column but not row because of the dollar sign in front of the 5. It becomes C5. So the new formula is =$B7+C$5. Both of these cells are blank, so the result is 0.

To enter absolute references, type in the $ signs where appropriate in the formula. Don't forget that $ signs refer to whatever comes *after* them, so put the $ sign *before* the letter or number that you want to affect.

Tip

You can toggle between relative and absolute (and between various mixed references) by pressing the F4 key. Try it!

Auditing Worksheets

It's a rare individual (having a really good day) who gets all his formulas correct the first time. Most likely, you will end up with at least one problem in your worksheet, especially if you are putting together a complicated network of formulas that depend on one another. *Auditing* is the process of identifying errors in your formulas so that you can correct them.

For example, the worksheet in Figure 9.5 has a couple of errors: the formula in cell H15 has a circular reference, and Excel doesn't understand the formula in cell F18. Excel's Auditing features can help fix inadvertent errors like these. (You'll see how to fix both problems in the following sections.)

Note

Even if you make some mistakes, you won't always end up with any auditable errors in your worksheet. Why? Because of Excel's Formula AutoCorrect feature. This great little feature helps correct the most common data entry problems that beginners run into, such as leaving off the ending parenthesis in a function. Best of all, this feature is automatic—you don't have to do anything but sit back and enjoy it.

Figure 9.5 This worksheet shows two formula errors.

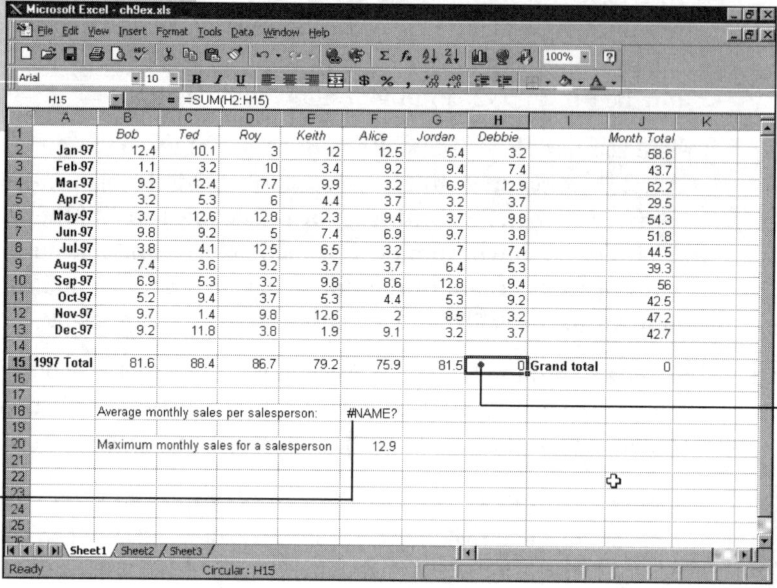

The blue dot next to the 0 means there is a circular reference.

Errors begin with #.

The Auditing Toolbar

Before you begin auditing for errors, it's best to turn on the Auditing toolbar. That way, you'll have all the auditing tools you need at your fingertips, and you won't have to fumble with the menu system.

To turn on the Auditing toolbar, choose Tools, Auditing, Show Auditing Toolbar. Don't worry if you don't understand all these tools immediately; you'll use them in the sections that follow, so by the time you complete this chapter, they will all make perfect sense.

Note

Unlike other toolbars, the Auditing toolbar cannot be accessed by right-clicking another toolbar and selecting it from the menu. You must access it from the menu system.

The buttons on the Auditing toolbar are listed and described in Table 9.1.

When you're finished using the Auditing toolbar, click the Close (X) button in its corner. If you've dragged it up to the top of the screen with the other toolbars, you'll need to drag it back to a floating toolbar before you can close it; unlike other toolbars, you can't right-click on it and select its name from the shortcut menu that appears to remove it from the screen.

Table 9.1 Buttons on the Auditing Toolbar

Button	Name	Description
	Trace Precedents	Draws lines showing where the faulty formula gets its data.
	Remove Precedent Arrows	Removes the lines drawn by the Trace Precedents button.
	Trace Dependents	Draws lines showing where the faulty formula's result is called for in other formulas.
	Remove Dependent Arrows	Removes the lines drawn by the Trace Dependents button.
	Remove All Arrows	Removes all lines drawn, including those drawn by the Trace Precedents, Trace Dependents, and Trace Error buttons.
	Trace Error	When a cell containing an error message is active, draws lines showing where that formula gets its data.
	New Comment	Just like the Insert, Comment command; attaches a comment to the cell.
	Circle Invalid Data	Shows cells that violate any data validation rules you have set up.
	Clear Validation Circles	Clears the marks made by the Circle Invalid Data button.

Tracing Formulas

When you have a faulty formula, it can affect many more formulas in the workbook that depend upon it. For example, suppose that (as in Figure 9.5) I have a formula in cell H15 that adds up the sales in 1997 for Debbie. Further suppose that I have another formula in cell J15 that adds up the totals in cells A15 through H15. If the formula in H15 is spitting out faulty results, the formula in J15 will have a faulty result too. That's what you see in Figure 9.5: both H15 and J15 read 0, which is obviously not the right answer.

What is wrong with cell H15? It has a *circular reference.* (I can tell that because Excel displays the message `Circular: H15` at the bottom of the screen (see Figure 9.5). A circular reference is a formula that refers to the cell that it's in. In this case, the formula in cell H15 is =SUM(H2:H15), which can't be calculated because it can't take into account its own value to calculate its resulting value.

Excel helps you prevent circular references. When you enter one, it not only gives you the `Circular` message in the status bar and the blue dot in the cell, but it also gives you a dialog box explaining what you've done. (I closed this dialog box before I shot Figure 9.5 so you could see the screen better.) The dialog box (see Figure 9.6) explains what you've done.

Figure 9.6 Excel warns you whenever you create a circular reference.

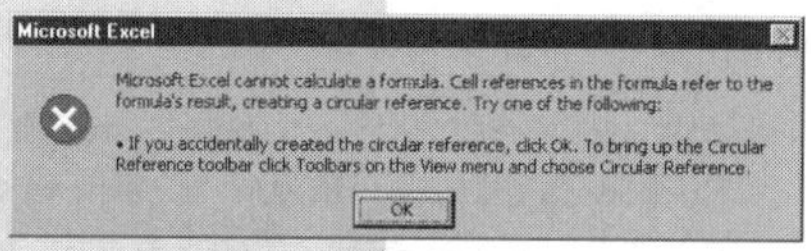

Note

Depending on the situation, you might see a slightly different dialog box than the one shown in Figure 9.6. It may have several buttons, including OK and Cancel. If so, clicking OK opens the Circular Reference toolbar automatically, and clicking Cancel closes the dialog box without opening the toolbar.

To track down your circular references, you may want to turn on the Circular Reference toolbar, as the dialog box in Figure 9.6 suggests. There are many ways to do so, but the easiest is to right-click on any toolbar and choose Circular Reference from the menu that appears. The Circular Reference toolbar contains buttons from the Auditing toolbar, so if you already have the Auditing toolbar turned on, you probably won't need the Circular Reference one.

Note

The one feature that the Circular Reference toolbar has that the Auditing toolbar lacks is a drop-down list of all the circular references in the workbook. You can move to the next circular reference quickly by opening the drop-down list and selecting it from the list.

Note

The Circular Reference toolbar is available only when you have one or more circular references in your workbook. That's why you never noticed it before on the shortcut menu—it was never there.

Most of the time, when you examine the formula in a cell that has a circular reference, the problem will be immediately apparent. For example, in Figure 9.5, obviously cell H15 contains a reference to H15. But just in case you want more information, you can use the following buttons from either the Auditing toolbar or the Circular Reference toolbar.

- Click the Trace Precedents button to draw a line showing the cells referenced in the formula.
- Click the Trace Dependents button to draw a line showing what other formulas use the result of this one.
- When you're finished looking at the lines, click the Erase All button to remove the lines.

Figure 9.7 shows the worksheet with both precedent and dependent lines. Excel can't correct the formula error for you, but it can make it extremely clear where the error lies so that you can correct it yourself.

Figure 9.7
Lines show the formula's precedents and dependents.

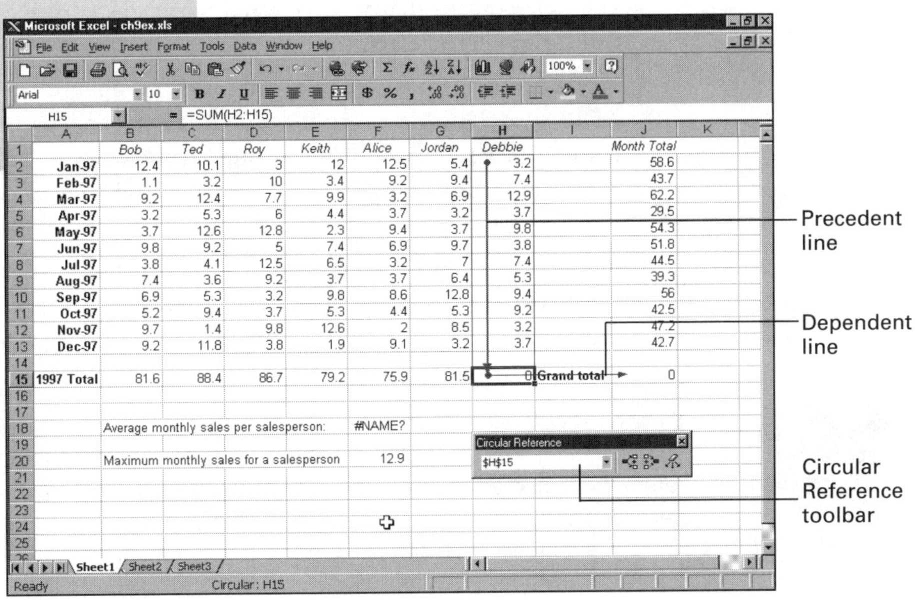

SEE CHAPTER 7 FOR MORE INFORMATION ABOUT COMMENTS.

In rare cases, you may want to leave an error in the worksheet. For example, if you can't figure out why an error is occurring, you might leave the error and make a copy of the worksheet file for a more experienced person to look at. In cases like that, you should insert a comment in the cell containing the error so that the person looking at it will know immediately where it is. The Auditing toolbar contains an Insert Comment button that works the same as the Insert, Comment command you learned about in Chapter 7. Click it to add a comment to the cell.

Correcting Worksheet Errors

Besides circular references, the most common type of audit item in a worksheet is an error message. You see these messages whenever Excel cannot understand what you want or whenever the result in a cell is invalid. For example:

- **#NAME?.** You have entered an invalid range name or function name, left out a quotation mark in a text string, or left out a colon in a range.
- **#DIV/0!.** Your formula divides something by 0. For example, if you have =C2/C3 in a cell, and the number in C3 is 0, you will get this error.
- **#NUM!.** Your formula uses an unacceptable number or numeric argument. For example, you may be referring to a number that is too large or too small for Excel to represent, such as -1*10^307 or 1*10^307.
- **#REF!.** You have a cell reference in your formula that is not valid. Perhaps you deleted cells that were referred to, or pasted some other cells over the cells originally referred to.
- **#NULL!.** You have used an incorrect range operator or cell reference. Make sure that if the formula contains two ranges, they are separated by a comma. If you leave out the comma, Excel tries to act on the cells common to both ranges, but if they have no cells in common, you get this error.
- **#N/A.** You get this one if a needed value is not available to a function or formula.

Some people use #N/A as a placeholder by entering it themselves. If certain cells on the worksheet will later contain data, but the data is not available at the moment, you can enter #N/A in those cells. That way, formulas that refer to those cells will return #N/A instead of attempting to calculate a value (and possibly giving inaccurate results). The #N/A will remind you that you need to make sure that the data gets entered eventually. You can place #N/A in a cell manually by entering the =NA function in it.

- **#VALUE!.** You have entered the wrong type of argument or math operator, or the Formula AutoCorrect feature cannot correct the formula. For example, you'll get this if you have a formula that sums the contents of two cells but one of the cells to be summed contains text rather than a number.

To get more information about a cell containing an error message, use the Trace Error button on the Auditing toolbar to add lines that show the cells where the formula is attempting to draw its data from (see Figure 9.8). You can clear the arrows when you're finished looking by clicking the Remove All Arrows button.

Figure 9.8
The Trace Error button draws a box around the range of cells referenced and a line from the top left cell in the range to the cell containing the formula.

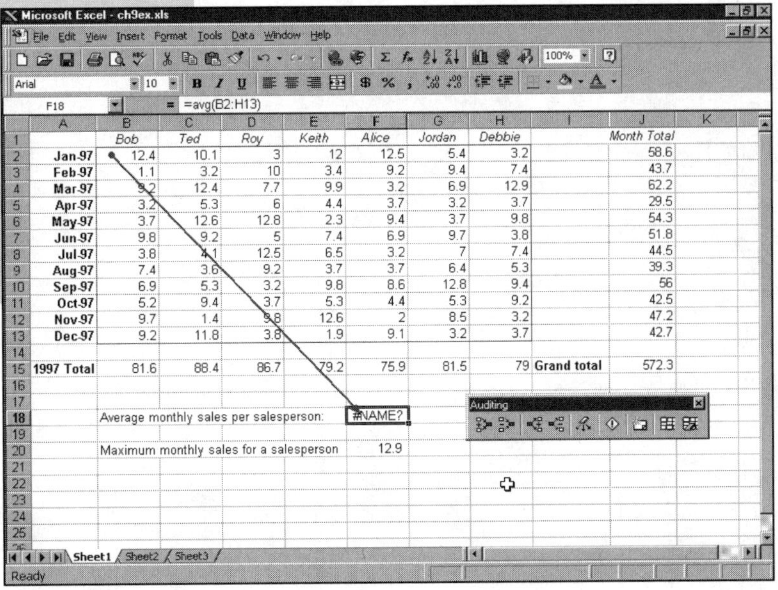

If you look closely at the formula in cell F18 (check out the formula bar in Figure 9.8), you'll see the problem immediately—I have tried to use a function called =AVG but there is no such function: its correct name is =AVERAGE. I'll simply edit the formula to use the correct name. If I hadn't known the correct name for the =AVERAGE formula, I could have looked it up by pressing F2 to edit the cell and then selecting the correct formula name from the Function drop-down list at the far left end of the formula bar.

PART III

Formatting and Printing Your Work

10

Formatting Numbers

In This Chapter

- Differences Between Text and Number Formatting
- Decimal Places
- Currency and Percentages
- Negative Numbers
- Dates and Times
- Fractions

In ancient theatre productions, you could tell the good guys from the bad guys by their traditional costumes. In Excel, number formatting gives you a way of assigning the appropriate costume to a number so that the reader can more easily understand your point. You can use Currency formatting, Percent formatting, Date/Time formatting, and much more, as you'll learn in this chapter.

Why Use Number Formatting?

A little formatting can make a big difference in your worksheet. For example, what do you see when you look at the following number?

12345.67

In its plain format, you'd be hard-pressed to tell what significance the number had. But if formatted in any of the following ways, its meaning becomes clear:

$12,345.67—the number is a dollar amount.

12345.67%—the number is a percentage.

1.23E+04—the number is in scientific notation.

000-01-2345—the number is a Social Security number.

10/18/1933 4:04 PM—the number is a date and time.

Some of these you would have never guessed from the original, eh? But that's the whole purpose of number formatting—to take a generic-looking number and fix it up so that the reader immediately can tell why it's there.

Note

Don't worry if you don't understand how some of these examples translate back to the original. The Date/Time example can be particularly puzzling to beginners. All will be revealed later in the chapter.

Figure 10.1 shows this number repeated many times in a worksheet, each instance formatted in a different way. You'll learn about these formats in the remainder of the chapter.

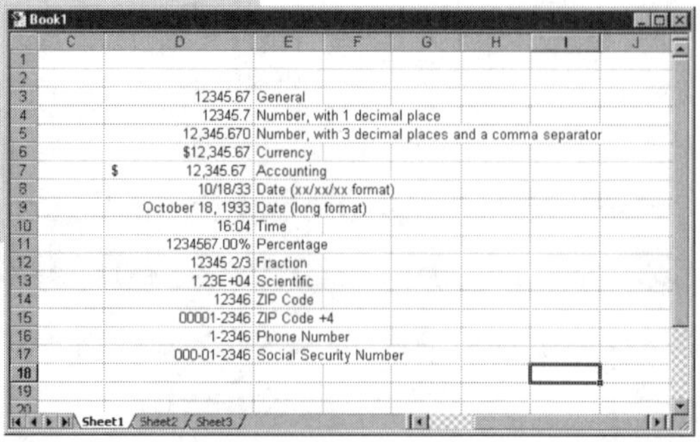

Figure 10.1 Excel offers a wide variety of number formats for every occasion.

Applying a Number Format

Before getting into a discussion of the various format types, you should know how to actually apply one. That way, if you see a number format that you want to use as I go through them, you can apply it right then, without wasting any time.

First, the quick way. If you want cells formatted as currency, a percentage, or with a comma, select the cell(s) you want and then click on the appropriate button on the Formatting toolbar.

Button	Name	Description
$	Currency Format	Applies the Accounting format with two decimal places
%	Percent Format	Applies the Percentage format with no decimal places
,	Comma Format	Applies the Number format with a Comma separator and two decimal places

Note

No, that's not a misprint—the Currency Format button applies the Accounting format, not the Currency format. The difference is the placement of the dollar sign. In Accounting format, the dollar sign is aligned at the left edge of the cell; in Currency format, the dollar sign is flush with the number.

Hands On: Choosing a Number Format

If you want any other number format or a different variation than you get with these buttons, follow these steps:

1. Select the cell(s) to which you want the format to apply.
2. Do any of the following to open the Format Cells dialog box:
   - Choose Format, Cells.
   - Right-click on the selection and choose Format Cells.
   - Press Ctrl+1.

3. If the Number tab is not active, click on it.
4. Click on the format category you want on the Category list. The controls in the dialog box change. For example, if you click on Accounting, you'll see the controls shown in Figure 10.2.
5. Use the controls to fine-tune the exact format you want. For example, in Figure 10.2 you would select the number of decimal places and the currency symbol.
6. Click OK to apply the format.

Figure 10.2 Use the Number tab of the Format Cells dialog box to apply a number format.

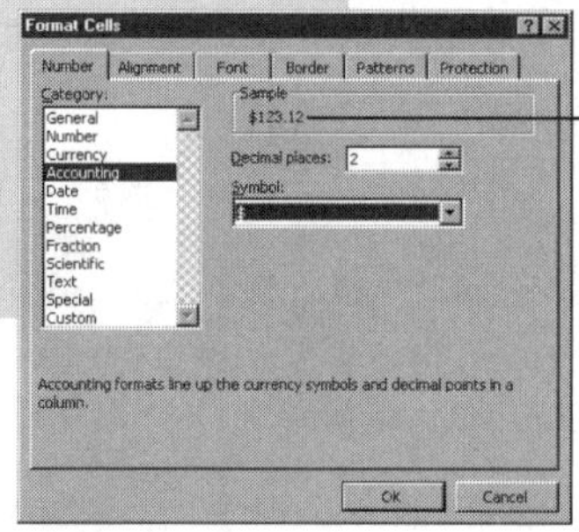

This same basic procedure works for almost all the number formats, with a few minor differences that I'll explain to you in the individual sections that follow.

Note

Some of the number formats let you specify a certain number of decimal places. If you want to change the number of decimal places without changing the number format itself that's in use, click the Increase Decimal or Decrease Decimal button on the Formatting toolbar.

General Format for Generic Entry

Sometimes the best format is no format. That's what the General format is—no format at all. In other words, whatever format you enter is the format used. If you enter a number with commas, decimal places, currency symbols, or whatever, the number uses them—otherwise, it doesn't.

General format is the default for each cell unless you change it. Unless you have a reason to want a particular number format applied to a cell (or group of cells), leaving it set to General is fine. You can also apply the General format to a cell to remove any existing number formatting in that cell.

Tip

To quickly apply the General format, select the cell(s) and press Ctrl+Shift+- (minus sign).

"Just a Number": The Number Format

The Number format is for those occasions when you need a "regular number"—that is, just digits and maybe some decimal places and commas. Its controls appear in Figure 10.3.

For number formatting, you have three choices to make:

- **Decimal Places.** Sets the number of decimal places your number will display. If your number is a whole number (that is, if it doesn't have a decimal point in it), or if your number does not have as many decimal places as specified, Excel will add zeroes on the end to make them up. For example, if your number is 123 and you set decimal places for 4, Excel displays **123.0000** in the cell.

Tip

Remember, you can change the number of decimals with the Increase Decimal or Decrease Decimal buttons on the Formatting toolbar, without even opening this dialog box.

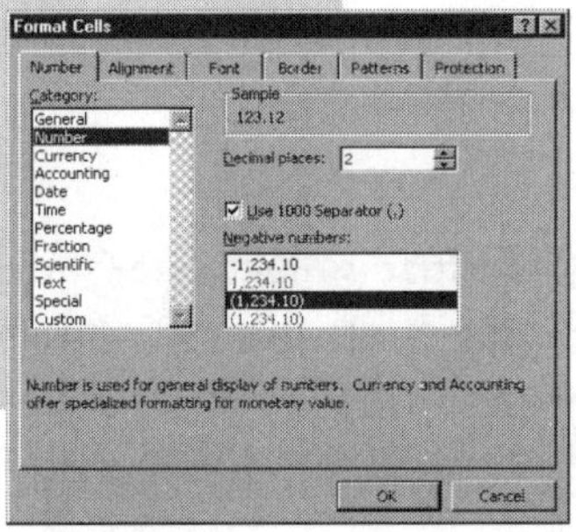

Figure 10.3 Use the Number format when you need a plain number, with or without commas and decimal places.

- **Use 1000 Separator (,).** Does just what the name implies: adds a comma between every three numerals to the left of the decimal place. For example, if your number is 12345.6789 Excel displays it as 12,345.6789.
- **Negative Numbers.** Provides a list of samples showing how negative numbers can be displayed. Choose any one you like. You can show them with a minus sign, in red, or in parentheses.

Money, Money, Money

The Currency Format options (see Figure 10.4) are similar to the Number Format options, with one exception. The Thousands separator is permanently "on," so you don't get to choose whether you want it. In its place in the dialog box is a drop-down list of currency symbols. (The default is $, for American dollars.) The list includes a mind-boggling number of countries and currencies!

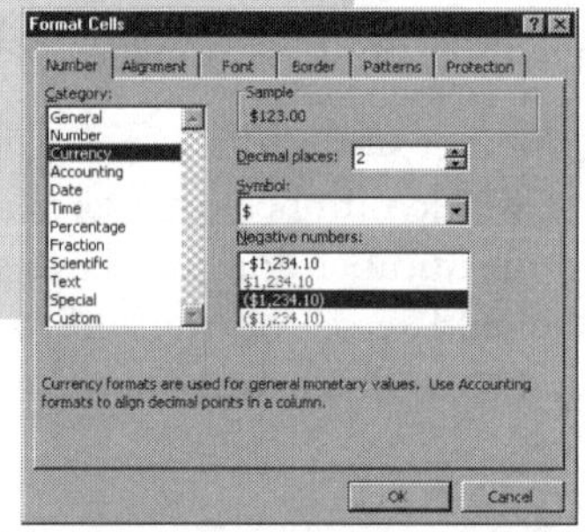

Figure 10.4 The Currency format enables you to choose a currency symbol, like $ or £.

To quickly apply the Currency format with two decimal places and negative numbers appearing in parentheses, press Ctrl+Shift+$ (dollar sign).

Adding It Up with the Accounting Format

As mentioned earlier, Accounting format is much like Currency format. The only difference is that Currency aligns the entire number and its symbol to the right, whereas Accounting aligns the currency symbol to the left, separate from the rest of the number. The Accounting format also aligns all decimal points together. Its controls are shown in Figure 10.5.

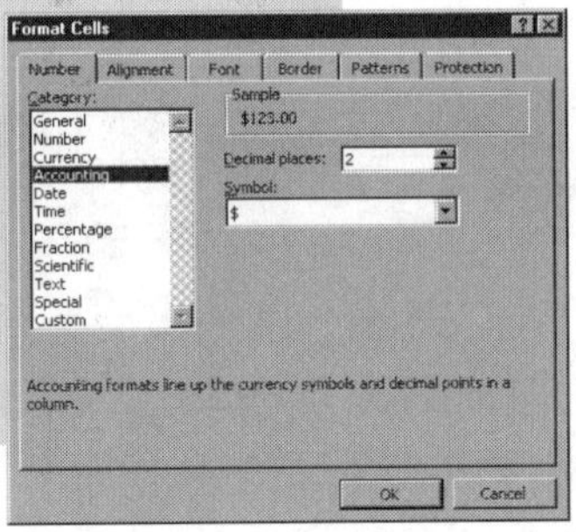

Figure 10.5 The Accounting controls are similar to the Currency ones, but with no selection area for negative numbers.

As you can see in Figure 10.5, you still have the Symbol drop-down list from which to choose your currency symbol, and you also still have the Decimal Places box. What's missing? The Negative Numbers list! That's because, apparently, accountants note negative numbers in only one way: with parentheses.

A Time Trip: Date and Time Formats

Dates and times are probably the hardest formats for beginners to understand. That's because most people don't realize that to Excel, a date is just another number. For example, the following date:

10/18/1933 4:04 PM

is really the number 12345.67 formatted as a date. How? It's the number of days that have passed since 12:00 AM on January 1, 1900. The numbers after the decimal place represent the time on that day—.67 means that 67% of the day has passed. Sixty-seven percent of the 24-hour period from 12:00 AM to 11:59 PM is 4:04 PM. Now you know.

Fortunately, you don't have to know the number that corresponds to the date you want. When you're entering a date into a cell, Excel recognizes it as a date and formats it as such. For example, you can enter 1/15/97 into a cell, and it will appear exactly that way, or in one of the other date variations available. Excel formats the cell as Date for you. It makes a "mental note" of the real number that the date represents, but it doesn't burden you with looking at it unless you reformat that cell to a number format other than Date.

On the Number tab of the Format Cells dialog box, when you choose Date from the list, you'll find a whole series of sample date and time formats. Choose the one you want (see Figure 10.6). Notice that not all of them contain all the information to be gleaned from the number. Some of them are just the day and month; others are just the month and year. Choose carefully.

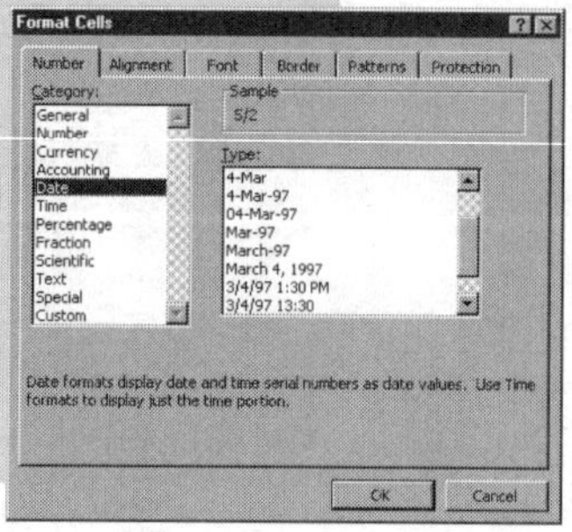

Figure 10.6 Choose the Date or Time format appropriate for the job at hand. Make sure that you get one that includes the information you need.

Note

If you enter a date as a date, such as 1/15/97, Excel stores it as a whole number. Why? Because remember that the numerals after the decimal place represent the time, and you have not entered a time. Therefore, there's nothing after the decimal place—Excel assumes 12:00 AM. If you choose a format that includes the time, make sure that you enter a time for it to display, or it will display 12:00 AM.

Tip

To apply the Date format quickly with the day, month, and year, press Ctrl+Shift+# (pound sign).

Although you can get a combination of date and time from some of the types on the Date format's list, to get the time alone you must choose the Time format. When you choose the Time format (see Figure 10.7), Excel considers only the numbers after the decimal point in the cell's content; any numbers before the decimal point are ignored.

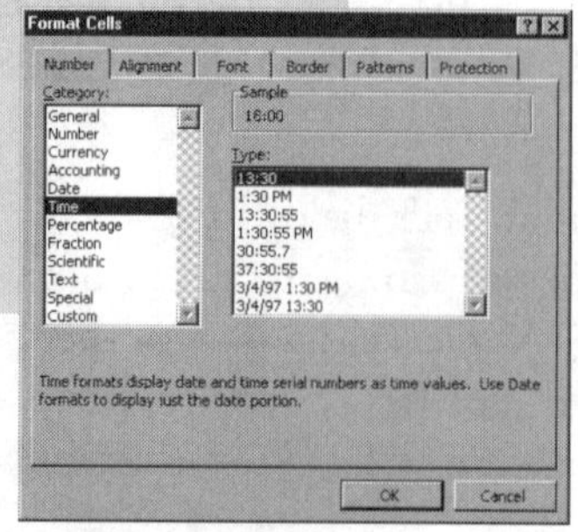

Figure 10.7 If you want the time by itself (without the date), choose the Time format.

The Time category's types include a couple that also include the date, just as the Date category's types have a few that include the time. Some time formats include the seconds as well as the hour and minutes.

Tip

To quickly apply the time format with a 12-hour clock (that is, the time with AM or PM), press Ctrl+Shift+@.

Hands On: Working with Dates and Times

If you're still not sure about how Excel formats dates and times, complete this exercise for a better understanding. Start with a new worksheet.

1. In cell C3, enter your birthdate in this format: *mm/dd/yy*. For example, 08/05/64. Note that it appears in the cell exactly as you entered it, except that Excel drops the leading 0 in the month if you have one (for example, it would drop the 0 in 08 for August).
2. Select C3 and then choose Format, Cells. The Format Cells dialog box opens. If the Number tab is not displayed, click on it. Notice that Excel has preset Date as the Category and chosen the appropriate date format in the Type column, to match what you entered.
3. Click on General and then click OK. Now that the Date format has been removed from the cell (by applying the General format), the number appears in its "true" form—a regular number. This number is the number of days between January 1, 1900 and the day you were born.
4. Click on cell C4 and enter the time that you were born in hours and minutes on a 24-hour clock (for example, 15:55) or in hours and minutes followed by AM or PM (for example, 3:55 PM).
5. Now format cell C4 in General format, to see what that time represents. Click on cell C4 again and choose Format, Cells to display the Format Cells dialog box.
6. Click General in the Category list. Notice the number in the Sample area —that's the number your birth time translates to.
7. Before leaving the dialog box, set C4 back to a time format. Click Time in the Category list and then choose one of the time formats in the Type column. Because you did not include a date (that is, nothing before the decimal point) in C4, don't pick one of the Time formats that includes the date—it will show up as January 1, 1900 if you do.

8. Click OK to close the dialog box.
9. Now practice on your own: enter the birthdates of your entire family in column C, and then display them in several different date/time formats.

What Percentage Is That?

As you saw at the beginning of this chapter, there's an easy way to apply the Percentage format—click the Percent Style button on the toolbar. It doesn't get much simpler than that.

To quickly apply the Percentage format with no decimal places, press Ctrl+Shift+%.

What happens when you click that button or press Ctrl+Shift+%? Well, when you apply the Percentage format to a cell that already has a number in it, Excel multiplies the number by 100 and then expresses it as a percentage. So:

562 becomes 56200%.

56.2 becomes 5620%.

56 becomes 5600%.

56 becomes 56%.

If you apply the Percentage format to an empty cell, the format lies in wait for the number you'll later enter into the cell. When you enter the number, the Percentage format attaches itself to that number for as long as the number is in the cell.

If you already have applied the Percentage format to a cell and then you enter a number (or change the number), things get a little tricky. That's because Excel tries to be intuitive and guess what you want.

If you enter a number into the cell that's 1.0 or more, Excel simply adds a percent sign on the end without multiplying it by 100. So:

562 becomes 562%.

56.2 becomes 56% (it rounds it off).

56 becomes 56%.

If, on the other hand, the number you enter is less than 1.0, Excel *does* multiply it by 100, because Excel figures that you meant for the number to be a percent of 1. So:

.56 becomes 56%.

Yes, that's right, you get the same result when you enter .56 as when you enter 56. Don't think about it too much—it will only make your head hurt.

The only control you have for the Percentage format is the number of decimal places. You can set it from the Number tab in the Format Cells dialog box, or you can use the Increase Decimal and Decrease Decimal buttons on the toolbar. It's your choice.

Fractionally Speaking

Most of the time, you'll express parts of a whole as fractions or percentages—that is, divided by 100. But occasionally you may need to use fractions in your Excel worksheets. Fortunately, Excel does a bang-up job at converting decimal numbers to fractions and vice-versa, just by changing the cell's formatting.

When you format as a fraction, you can force Excel to round up (or down) to the nearest increment that you choose. For example, as you can see in Figure 10.8, you can choose single- or double-digit fractions, or a particular fraction such as sixths or eighths.

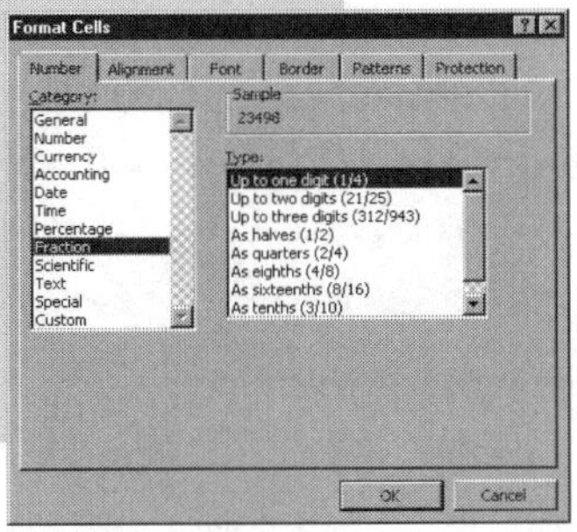

Figure 10.8 When you specify the Fraction format, you can tell Excel exactly what type of fraction you want.

Note

Back in Chapter 7, you learned that Excel uses the symbol / to mean "divided by." How does Excel know that you want a fraction rather than a formula here? Easy. Remember that all formulas begin with an equals sign. No equals sign—no formula.

The choices you have for fraction Type fall into two categories. The first type restricts the number of digits in the "bottom" of the fraction, to keep the fraction from getting too detailed for anyone to understand. For example:

- **Up to One Digit.** Such as 1/3, 1/5, and 1/9.
- **Up to Two Digits.** Such as 1/29, 1/67, and 1/91.
- **Up to Three Digits.** Such as 1/673, 1/382, and 1/997.

The second kind of format rounds the entered number up or down to fit a particular specification:

- **As Halves.** The bottom number must be 2, as in 1/2. That means the number in the cell will be either a whole number or a whole number followed by 1/2.
- **As Quarters.** The bottom number must be 4. The cell contents will be either a whole number or a whole number followed by 1/4, 2/4, or 3/4.
- **As Eighths.** The bottom number must be 8.
- **As Sixteenths.** The bottom number must be 16.
- **As Tenths.** The bottom number must be 10.
- **As Hundredths.** The bottom number must be 100.

> **If you use one of the formats like As Eighths or As Sixteenths, be aware that all your non-whole numbers will be in that format, not just the ones that need to be for precision. For example, you may end up with 8/16 or 2/8. That's okay, except that people aren't used to seeing those numbers expressed that way—they're used to them being simplified to 1/2 or 1/4. The casual reader may think you've made a mistake by not simplifying them.**

Eureka! Using Scientific Format

To be honest, I've never fully understood the value of the Scientific format. But then, I'm not a scientist. The purpose of the scientific format is to make numbers that are an obscenely large number of digits appear manageable in print. For example, suppose that you have this number:

56,000,000,000,000,000

In Scientific format with two decimal places, the number would look like this:

5.60E+16

Translated, that means "move the decimal place 16 places to the right, and you'll have the actual number." Here's another example:

465,555,555,555,555

In Scientific format, this time with four decimal places, the number would look like this:

4.656E+14

What happened to the other 5's? Excel rounded them up to make that last 6 right before the E. As you can see from this, the larger the number of decimal places, the more precise your number ends up. If someone were to expand the number from seeing the scientific notation of it, they would end up with:

465,600,000,000,000

YOU LEARN HOW TO WIDEN CELLS IN CHAPTER 11.

which isn't exactly right. But it's close. Scientific format is not very useful for the everyday user's view because of this imprecision. (The real number is stored in the cell and used for calculations.) But for someone who makes a career of working with huge numbers, it can be invaluable, saving him or her from having to widen all the columns to the point where the huge numbers display correctly.

When you apply Scientific format from the Format Cells dialog box, you have one choice: the number of decimal points.

Tip

To quickly apply the Scientific number format with two decimal places, press Ctrl+Shift+^. An easy way to remember this shortcut is to remember that the Scientific format is sometimes referred to as the Exponential format (even though it has nothing to do with exponents), and ^ is the mathematical operator in Excel for exponentiation.

When a Number Isn't a Number: The Text Format

Remember at the beginning of Chapter 7, when I explained the difference between text and numbers? Excel can usually figure out the difference based on the presence or absence of alphabet letters. If it doesn't have anything but numerals, Excel figures that it must be a number, and you must want to have it available for calculations.

But sometimes you might use numbers that you have no intention of calculating anything with—such as ZIP codes or phone numbers. Even though they look like numbers, you want Excel to realize that they should be treated like text. The Text format provides a way to do that.

Normally, numbers align to the right edge of the cell. (In Chapter 11 you'll learn to override that, though.) But when you format a number in Text format, Excel aligns it to the left, the same as other text. When you apply the Text format, Excel also strips off any remnants of previous number formatting you've applied, leaving the number in exactly the format that you entered it.

There aren't any format types for the Text format; select it from the Category list in the Format Cells dialog box.

Special-Use Formats

Excel's special-use formats are among the most helpful formats of all, because they help you with complicated formats that you probably use quite often. To use them, select Special from the Category list in the Format Cells dialog box (see Figure 10.9), and then select the Type that you need:

- **Zip Code.** Formats the number as one string, with no commas or decimal points. If the number is not at least five digits long, it adds zeros at the beginning to make it so.
- **Zip Code + 4.** If the number is not at least nine-digits long, it adds zeros at the beginning to make it so. Then it adds a hyphen separating the last four numbers from the others.
- **Phone Number.** If there are ten digits, it puts parentheses around the first three and a dash between the second three and the remainder. If there are less than ten digits, it plugs the numbers in from right to left.

A number that contains less than five digits formatted as a phone number looks just like a negative number with a minus sign. Make sure that you do not mislead your reader this way. Format numbers as phone numbers only if they have a correct number of digits to be recognizable as such.

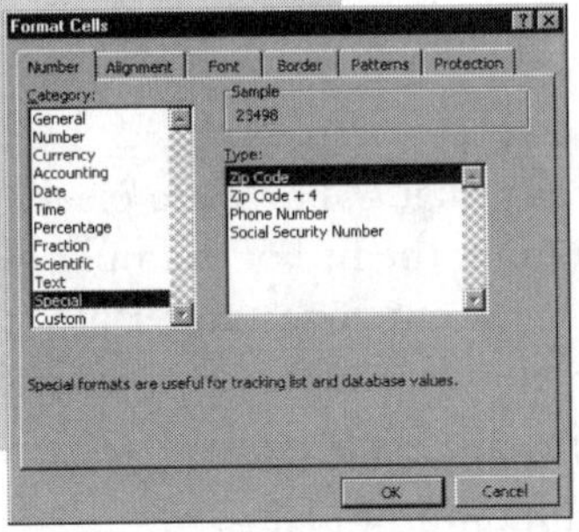

Figure 10.9 Excel's Special format types provide help for some common entry situations such as ZIP codes and phone numbers.

- **Social Security Number.** If the number is not at least nine digits, it adds zeros at the beginning to make it so. Then it adds a dash between the fourth and fifth numbers from the right, and another between the sixth and seventh from the right. (It always counts these from the right, never the left.) If there are excess digits, they appear at the beginning, like this: 345986-34-2384.

Designing Custom Number Formats

Perhaps your company uses part numbers or serial numbers with a special format, such as *xx-xxxxx*. Or perhaps you want to format telephone numbers in a different way than Excel uses. In cases like this, you can design your own number format.

When you select Custom in the Category list, the Type list shows every number format that you have used since you began using this copy of Excel (see Figure 10.10). The list may be very long. Why is that list there? It's there so that you can use one of the other formats as a jumping-off place for creating the new one.

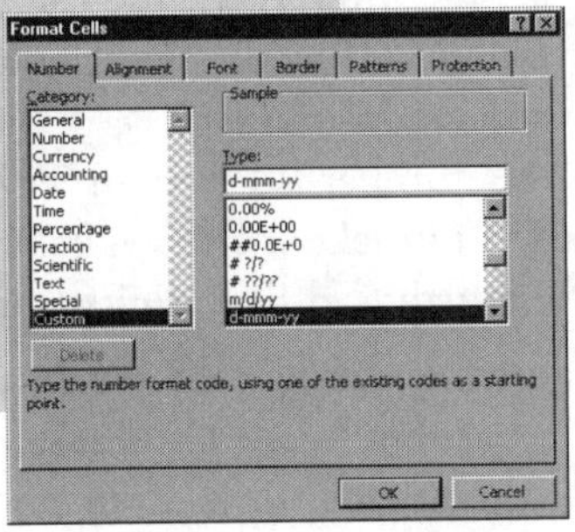

Figure 10.10 The Custom formats are the formats you have created yourself since you began using Excel.

Here's a quick decipher of the formats you may see on the list:

- When a format has a 0 or an # in it, it means any number, as in `#,##0.00`.
- The # stands for insignificant digits. These are places that can be left out if the number does not contain them. For example, `#.##` means to display up to two decimal places if the entered number uses them, but not to display those places if the number doesn't. For example:

  56, 56.0, and 56.00 would all display as `56..`

  56.1 and 56.10 would both display as `56.1`.

  56.11 and 56.112 would both display as `56.11`.
- The 0 stands for significant digits. These are places that must be filled, even if they are filled with 0. For example, `0.00` means to display the number with two decimal places always, even if the number does not contain them. For example:

  56, 56.0, and 56.00 would all display as `56.00`.

  56.1 and 56.10 would both display as `56.10`.

  56.11 and 56.112 would both display as `56.11`.
- Colors appear in square brackets, like this: `[Red]`.
- When there are two parts to the code separated by a semicolon, it means there are two different formats, one for positive numbers and the other for negative. For example, `$##,##0.00_);[Red]($##,##0.00)`. Some rare formats may have one or two additional parts separated by semicolons: formats for zeros and formats for text.
- A ? adds blank spaces for insignificant digits so that numbers align with others in the same column. For example, suppose that you had a column of numbers where the decimal places varied from 1 to 6 places. You could format the cells like this: `###.??????` so that all the decimal points aligned.
- To set number formats based on criteria, enclose the criteria in brackets. For example, to format five-digit ZIP codes without a hyphen and nine-digit ones with a hyphen, you could use this: `[<=99999]00000;00000-0000`. It says, in effect, "if the number is less than 99999, format it with leading zeros added as needed to make it five-digits. Otherwise, format it with a hyphen between the fourth and fifth digits from the right."
- To add a thousands separator (comma), add a comma to the format in the appropriate spot. To scale a number by 1000 (that is, to move the decimal point three places to the left), add a comma at the end of the format. For example, `##,###` adds a comma separator like this: `12,000`. But `#####` moves the decimal like this: `12`.

- Represent dates with m, d, and y:

  m is the one- or two-digit month number (as appropriate), such as 1 or 12.

  mm is the two-digit month number, such as 01 or 12.

  mmm is the three-letter month abbreviation, such as Jan.

  mmmm is the full name of the month, such as January.

  d is the one- or two-digit day number, such as 1 or 31.

  dd is the two-digit day number, such as 01 or 31.

  ddd is the three-letter day-of-the-week abbreviation, such as Mon or Sat.

  dddd is the full name of the day of the week, such as Monday or Saturday.

  yy is the last two digits of the year, such as 97 or 64.

  yyyy is the full year, such as 1997 or 1964.

- Represent times with h, m, and s:

  Use *h*, *m*, or *s* when you want the single- or double-digit number as appropriate, such as 1, 5, 12, or 59.

  Use *hh*, *mm*, or *ss* when you want a double-digit number, such as 01, 05, 12, or 59.

  Use AM/PM or am/pm when you want the a.m. or p.m. designation like this: 12:25 AM or 12:25 am.

  Use a/p when you want the a.m. or p.m. designation as a single letter, like this: 12:25 a.

  If a format contains an a.m. or p.m. code, the time is based on a 12-hour clock; otherwise, the time is based on a 24-hour clock.

Note

If you are a careful reader, you may have noticed that *m* is used to stand for two different things: minutes and months. How does Excel tell the difference? It's in the placement. If the *m* or *mm* code comes immediately after an *h* (hours) code or immediately before a *s* (seconds) code, Excel interprets it as minutes. Otherwise, Excel interprets it as a month.

To create a custom format, type the format string in the text box in the Type column. You can start with one of the existing formats by clicking on it first. After you type your format, press Enter to add it to the list of custom formats, and then select it from the list to apply it.

Hands On: Practicing Custom Formats

Now that you know the rules for creating custom number formats, try out these exercises. Then check out the answers that follow them to see how well you did!

For each of the following, figure out the Custom format code you would use to get the desired result:

1. Phone numbers that use a dash to separate the area code rather than parentheses, like this: 217-555-2222. Excel should *not* add zeroes if digits are missing.
2. A date format that includes the month, day, and year with the day of the week in parentheses afterward, like this: 8/5/97 (Monday).
3. A number format with no decimal places that contains commas and always displays at least ten digits, even if they are zeros, like this: 0,034,549,348 or 1,234,567,892.
4. A number format where the number must contain between three and seven digits, like this: 001 or 321 or 4321345.

Here are the answers to the preceding:

1. ###-###-####
2. mm/dd/yy (mmmm)
3. 0,000,000,000
4. ####000

11

Formatting Text and Cells

In This Chapter

- Adjusting Row Height and Column Width
- Aligning Text in a Cell
- Wrapping Text to Multiple Lines
- Merging Cells
- Changing the Font and Size of Text
- Borders and Shading

Which would you rather look at—a worksheet where everything is the same dull format, or one in which the headings and titles are bold and colorful, and the important information is shaded and boxed? The latter, of course, right? If you feel that way, then your potential readers probably do too. Attractive formatting helps to sell your reader on the idea that your worksheet is worth reading.

Why Bother with Formatting?

Some curmudgeons will tell you that you should never bother with formatting a worksheet. "Numbers are what's important," these people say, "The rest is just fluff." Granted, the formatting isn't as important as the accuracy or completeness of the information, but it does have definite value.

There are two sides to formatting: functionality and beauty. A worksheet's formatting can make it easier to read, and therefore more understandable and functional. It is certainly easier, for instance, to determine which rows are the headings when they are made bold and underlined.

The second part, beauty, is harder to pin down, but attractiveness can actually increase the success of your worksheet in your audience's eyes. Let's face it: people like to look at attractive things. If they didn't, we wouldn't have supermodel calendars. People spend more time looking at a worksheet that is visually pleasing than one that makes their eyes glaze over with boredom. By making your worksheet as attractive as possible, you increase the chances of your audience actually paying attention to what you're trying to present.

Changing Column Width

One of the biggest complaints that beginners have with Excel is that their text or numbers don't fit in the cell. As you've probably seen in your Excel work, one of these things happens when a cell is too narrow to display its contents:

- If you're entering text and the cell to the right is empty, the text spills into the next cell.
- If you're entering text and the cell to the right is not empty, the text is cut off on-screen.
- If you're entering numbers, the cell displays ###### rather than the number.

There are three possible solutions: you can decrease the font size, widen the cell, or make the cell taller (increase the row height) and set that cell so that the text wraps in it. By "wraps," I mean that when the text reaches the right edge of the cell, the text starts a new line in the same cell, and the row height increases to make room for it. Figure 11.1 shows the problems just described and the two possible solutions.

In the following sections, I'll explain various ways to make your cells wider. Then, later in this chapter in the section "Wrapping Text in Cells," you'll learn about wrapping text to multiple lines in a cell.

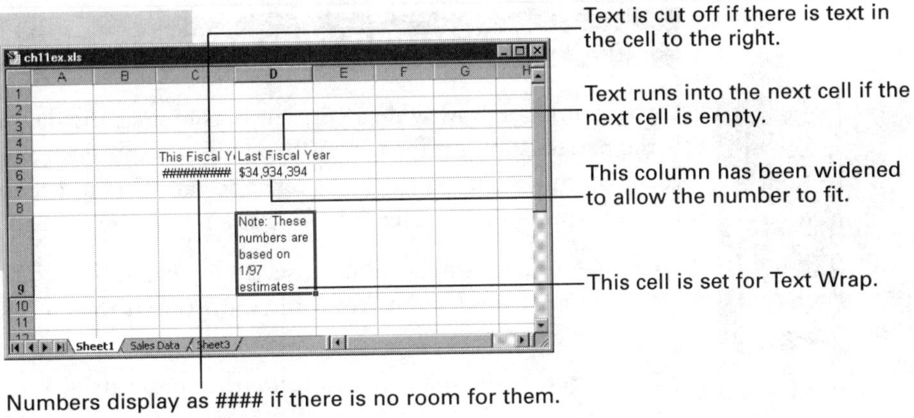

Figure 11.1 When text is too long for the cell, you can widen the cell or wrap the text onto multiple lines in the cell.

Hands On: Changing Column Width with the Mouse

The easiest way to make your text fit is to widen the column. There are many ways to do this, but the easiest way is to drag the column to make it wider. Follow these steps to do so:

1. Position your mouse pointer at the right edge of the column label for the column you want to widen. For example, in Figure 11.2, I'm getting ready to widen column E. The mouse pointer changes to a vertical line with left and right arrows coming out of it.
2. Hold down the left mouse button and drag the column's right edge to make it as wide as you want. Then release the mouse button.

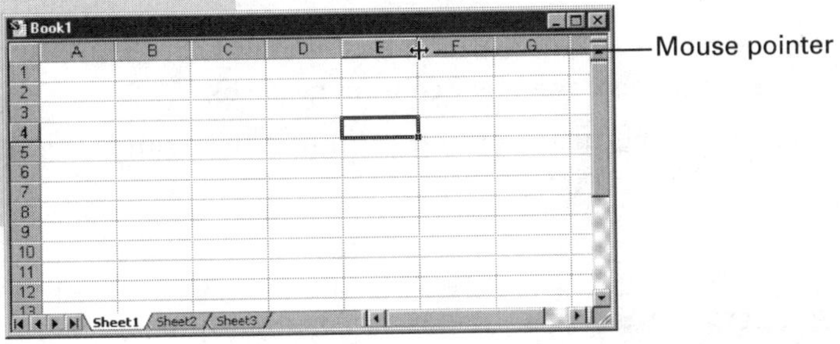

Figure 11.2 Position your mouse to the right of the column you want to widen.

Hands On: Resizing With AutoFit

SELECTING CELLS, COLUMNS, AND WORKSHEETS IS COVERED IN CHAPTER 5.

If you don't care how wide a column is as long as the data within it fits, AutoFit is the perfect solution for you. When you use AutoFit, Excel calculates how wide each column has to be for all its text and numbers to fit, and then it resizes each column appropriately. Here's how to use it:

1. To AutoFit a single column, select any cell in it. Or, to AutoFit multiple columns, select them. You can even AutoFit the entire worksheet at once by selecting it.
2. Do one of the following to resize the column(s):
   - Choose Format, Column, AutoFit Selection.
   - Position your mouse pointer at the right edge of the column label and double-click.

Tip

When you enter a number into a column and press Enter, Excel AutoFits the column automatically without your having to issue the command. This works only if you have not previously changed the width of that column yourself.

Hands On: Setting a Precise Column Width

The drag-and-drop method of widening (or narrowing) columns works great if you want to "eyeball it," but there may be times when you want the column to be a certain width. To be precise like that, you must use the following procedure:

1. Select the column(s) for which you want to change the width. You can change more than one column at once.
2. Choose Format, Column, Width. The Column Width dialog box appears (see Figure 11.3).

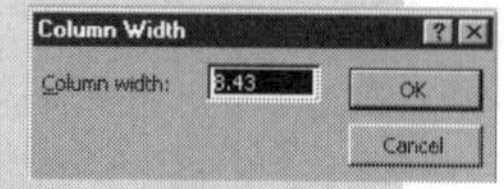

Figure 11.3 Use the Column Width dialog box to enter a precise column width, in characters.

3. Enter the exact width you want in the Column Width text box. The default is 8.43.
4. Click OK. The column width changes.

Note

Many people wonder what unit of measurement this column width is based on. No, it's not inches or centimeters! It's the average number of digits (0-9) of the standard font that can fit in that cell. The default is 10-point Arial type. If you change the standard font, the default column width will still be 8.43 but it will be wider or narrower in actual inches than the current default, depending on the new font and font size you chose. (You change the default font on the General tab of the Options dialog box, as you'll learn later in this chapter.)

Changing the Default Column Width

If you decide that the standard column width (8.43) is not right for your worksheet, you can change it. This procedure affects every column in the worksheet except ones for which you have already changed the width. After you change the width of a column, the default width no longer applies to it.

Do the following to change the standard width of columns:

1. Choose Format, Column, Standard Width. The Standard Width dialog box appears (see Figure 11.4).
2. The Standard Width text box shows the current default column width. Type a new width in the text box.
3. Click OK. All the columns that had not been resized before are resized to the width you specified.

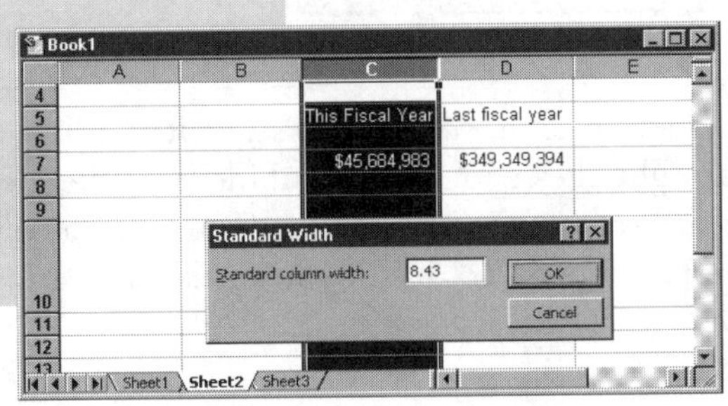

Figure 11.4 Use the Standard Width dialog box to change the default column width.

Hiding and Unhiding a Column

There are many reasons why you might want to hide a column. Perhaps you have a personnel worksheet that displays salaries, and you want to make a printout of the worksheet without that information. Or perhaps some columns refer to a survey that is already completed, and you don't need to see them anymore. Whatever the reason, Excel makes it easy to hide columns. Just set the column's width to zero. You can do this in any of several ways:

- Drag the right edge of the column to its left edge. This effectively "resizes" the column out of sight.
- Select the column(s) you want to hide and then choose Format, Column, Width and type **0** in the text box.
- Select the column(s) you want to hide, and then choose Format, Column, Hide.
- Right-click the column letter and choose Hide from the shortcut menu that appears.
- Press Ctrl+0 (zero).

When a column is hidden, Excel "skips over" its letter, as shown in Figure 11.5. This is different from deleting a column, as you learned to do in Chapter 5. When you delete a column, it's gone for good, and the column letters change so that there's no gap in the letter sequence. When you hide a column, it's still there—it's just not visible. Hiding a column is purely a formatting thing.

Figure 11.5 Column D is hidden.

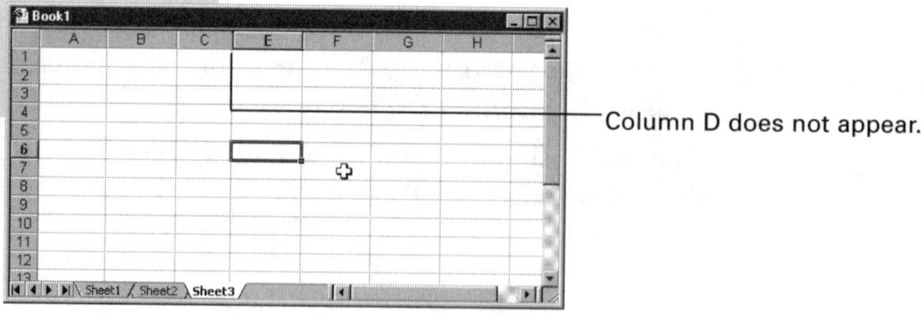

To display the hidden column, you have to select it and then choose Format, Column, Unhide, or right-click and choose Unhide from the shortcut menu, or press Ctrl+Shift+9. But wait a minute—how can you select a column when you can't see it? That's the tricky part. To do so, you must select a range of columns that includes the hidden one. For example, in Figure 11.5, to unhide column D, you would first select the range of columns C through E by clicking on column C's heading and dragging over to column E's heading. Now column D is selected too, even though you can't see it. Then choose Format, Column, Unhide, and Excel unhides all hidden columns in the selected range. Because C and E were not hidden, the command has no effect on them.

If you drag a column to hide it, you may not get it completely hidden, but only very narrow. If you look at the space where it should be and see a slightly thicker gridline there than usual, as in Figure 11.6, it means that the column is not hidden. When a column is hidden, the gridlines where it should be look completely normal. In such cases, the Unhide command won't work. To resize the column, you must select it and then drag it back open or resize it with the Format, Column, Width command. To select it, click on a cell in the column to the left of it, and then press the → on the keyboard. A cell in that column becomes active, and any commands you issue (such as Format, Column, Width) will apply to that column.

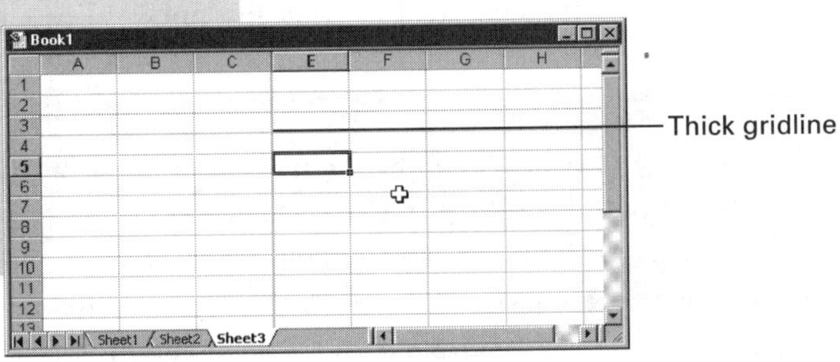

Figure 11.6
Column D is not really hidden—it's just very narrow. You can't use the Unhide command on it.

Wrapping Text in Cells

CHAPTERS 17 AND 18 COVER USING EXCEL AS A DATABASE.

When I first learned to wrap text in cells, it was a great breakthrough. No more obscenely wide cells in the interests of making a lengthy bit of text fit! Text wrapping is especially helpful when you are using Excel as a database to hold names and addresses, because street addresses can sometimes be very long.

Text wrapping is a cell property: by default this property is turned off for each cell. To turn it on for selected cells, follow these steps:

1. Select the cell(s) for which you want to turn on Text Wrap.
2. Choose F<u>o</u>rmat, C<u>e</u>lls. The Format Cells dialog box opens.
3. Click the Alignment tab (see Figure 11.7).

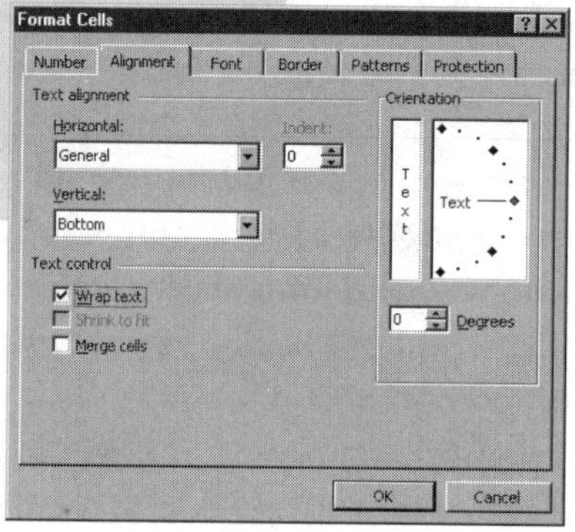

Figure 11.7 The <u>W</u>rap Text check box controls text wrapping.

4. Click the <u>W</u>rap Text check box to select this option.
5. Click OK.

Figure 11.8 shows the same text in two cells: one wrapped and one not wrapped.

If you wrap text in a cell and then change its column width, the wrapping won't look right. If you make the cell narrower, some text will be cut off; if you make the cell wider, the cell will be too tall. That's because when you wrap text, Excel calculates line breaks and row height based on the current width. When you change the width, Excel does not recalculate the wrap. And unfortunately, there is no way to force Excel to recalculate it, either. After you have made a height or width adjustment to a cell, Excel will no longer automatically adjust its height or width. You must adjust the column width and height manually for that cell (or use AutoFit) so that the wrapped text fits.

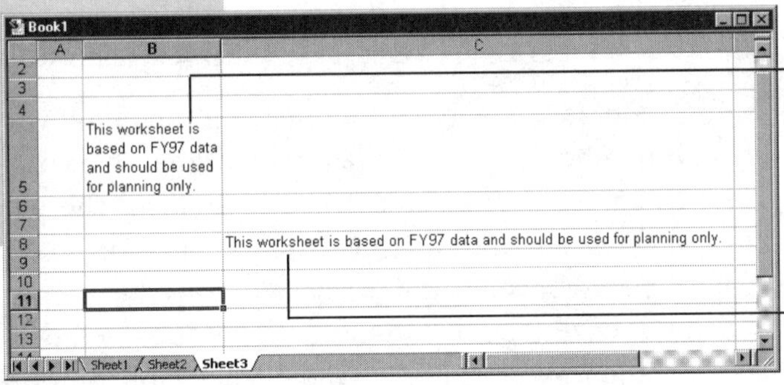

Figure 11.8 Text wrapping can make a dramatic difference in the readability of your worksheet.

Changing Row Height

After you've mastered column width, row height is a piece of cake. That's because in many cases, Excel adjusts the row height for you automatically. For example, when you reformat some text in a cell so that it appears in a larger font (covered later in this chapter), Excel makes the cell taller to accommodate the larger text. Similarly, when you set a cell to wrap text in it, Excel automatically makes the cell the height necessary to display all lines of the wrapped text. You will seldom want to manually change a row's height, because after you do, Excel will not automatically adjust that row's height for you anymore, and you miss out on that automation.

If you do need to change a row's height, however, there are several ways to do it. These are similar to the procedures for setting column width that you learned earlier in this chapter:

- Position the mouse pointer at the bottom edge of the row number and drag the row to the correct height.
- Position the mouse pointer at the bottom edge of the row number and double-click to AutoFit the row height.
- Choose Format, Row, AutoFit to AutoFit the row height.

If you are trying to AutoFit a multiline cell and it doesn't seem to be working, try changing that cell's vertical alignment to Top and then reapplying the AutoFit command. Vertical alignment is changed on the Alignment tab of the Format Cells dialog box, as you'll learn later in this chapter.

- Select the row and then choose Format, Row, Height, or right-click on a row number and choose Row Height from the shortcut menu. Type a row height in the Row Height dialog box and click OK.

How Is Row Height Calculated?

Row height is measured in points. Unlike column width, the row height number is a fixed measurement that does not depend on the font being used. One point is 1/72 of an inch. There is no fixed row height — each row's height is based on the fonts used in it. When you start a new worksheet, all the cells use 10-point type, so each row height is 12.75 (10 points plus 2.75 points for white space). When you change the font used in a row, the row height automatically changes to accommodate the largest font used in that row plus enough white space to make it readable. For example, if you change cell C3 to 48-point type, the row height for all of row 3 changes to 59.25 (48 points plus 11.25 points for white space). If you have multiple lines in that row (that is, if you have used Text Wrap on at least one cell in it), the row height will be based on multiple lines.

Hiding and Unhiding Rows

You might want to hide rows for the same reasons as hiding columns—to protect sensitive information or to eliminate extraneous data from the display. Hiding and unhiding rows works exactly the same as with columns, except you use a different command. Use Format, Row, Hide to hide a row and Format, Row, Unhide to unhide it.

A quick way to hide a row is to select it and press Ctrl+9. To unhide, press Ctrl+Shift+9.

Changing Vertical Alignment

By default, the text in each cell aligns at the bottom of the cell. This isn't usually an issue because each row is, by default, the exact height it needs to be to display its contents. Because there is no extra height in the row, it's a moot point where the extra height lies.

But as you begin to resize rows and change fonts, you may find that some cells have some white space at the top. If you would prefer the extra space at the bottom of the cell, or the text evenly floating in the center, you are free to change the vertical alignment. Figure 11.9 shows your choices for vertical alignment in a cell.

Figure 11.9 You can vertically align text in a cell to the top, middle, or bottom, or justify it.

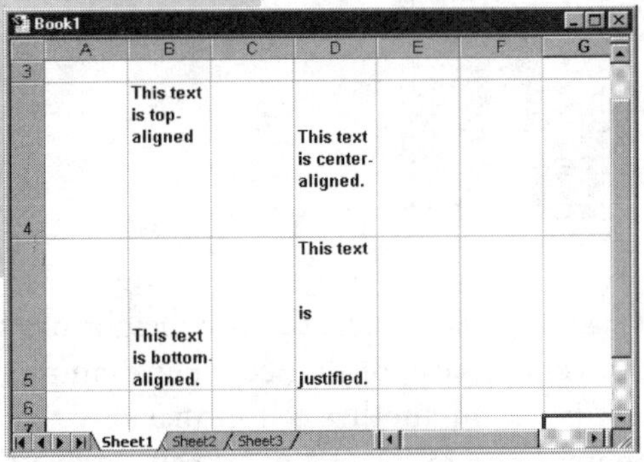

Note

Vertical and horizontal alignment are both set on a cell-by-cell basis. That means you can have a different alignment for cells that are in the same row or column with one another.

As you can see in Figure 11.9, you can justify text in a cell too. That means that the lines of text are evenly spread out across the entire height of the cell. Justify works only if you have multiple lines in the cell (with Text Wrap on). Otherwise, Justify is the same as Top.

To change the alignment of a cell, follow these steps:

1. Select the cell(s) you want to change the vertical alignment for.
2. Choose Format, Cells to open the Format Cells dialog box.
3. Click the Alignment tab.
4. Open the Vertical drop-down list (see Figure 11.10) and select the alignment you want.
5. Click OK. The text is aligned as you specified.

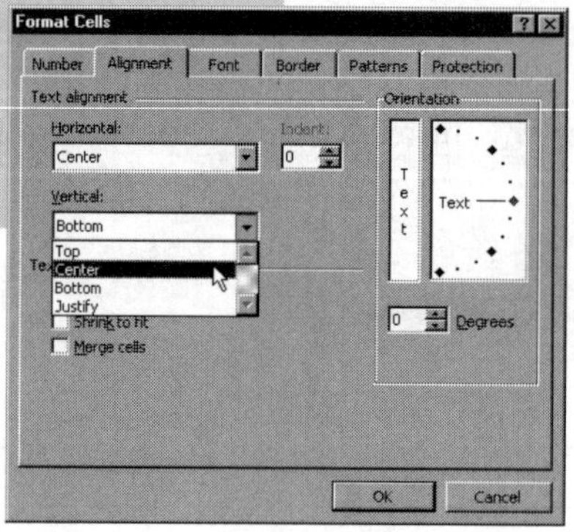

Figure 11.10 Choose a new alignment from the Vertical drop-down list.

Vertical alignment has no effect unless the row height has been changed so that the row is taller than is necessary for that cell. For example, if the text in the cell is 12-point but there is text in another cell in that row that is 48-point, the row height is larger than necessary for the 12-point cell, and vertical alignment will be noticeable for that cell. In contrast, it won't be noticeable for the cell containing the 48-point type, because Excel has sized that row to exactly fit the type in that cell because it's the largest type used in the row.

Changing Horizontal Alignment

Horizontal alignment is a much more common change than vertical for most users. That's because, whereas text in a row is commonly all the same height (the same font size), text in a column is seldom the same number of characters from cell to cell. Therefore, at least one cell in a column probably has some white space at the left or right of the text.

As you may recall from Chapter 7, by default text aligns to the left, and numbers align to the right. That's because Excel figures that you read text from left-to-right, but you will want your numbers aligned right so that you can easily add them up. (Remember math problems in school? You would always right-align the column of numbers to be added or multiplied.) These defaults can be changed as needed for each cell to make the worksheet nicer to look at.

For example, look at the worksheet in Figure 11.11. The default alignment makes the text look crowded and unattractive. Also, because the headings are text but the values in two of the columns are numbers (date and currency), the headings do not look aligned with the data they describe. But by applying different horizontal alignments, as shown in Figure 11.12, it looks much better.

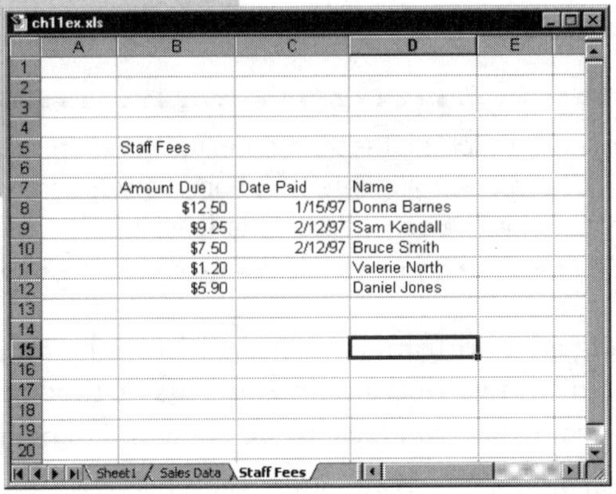

Figure 11.11 This worksheet suffers from unattractive alignment.

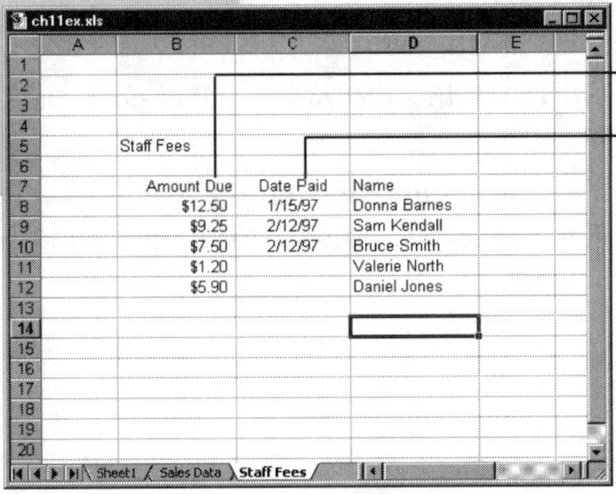

Figure 11.12 Some alignment changes make the worksheet easier to read.

The easiest way to change a cell's horizontal alignment is with the alignment buttons on the Standard toolbar. Just select the cell(s) and then click on the appropriate button:

Button	Name
	Align Left
	Center
	Align Right

There are several other alignments you can use, but to access them, you must use the Format Cells dialog box as described next.

Using toolbar buttons is much faster than opening the menu system. If you find yourself using one of the other alignment options very much, you might want to create a toolbar button for it. See Chapter 6 to learn how to create toolbar buttons.

You can also change the horizontal alignment from the Format Cells dialog box, the same as you did with vertical alignment. This method takes longer than using the alignment buttons, but you have more choices. Follow these steps:

1. Select the cells(s) you want to align.
2. Choose Format, Cells or right-click on the selection and choose Format Cells from the shortcut menu.
3. Click on the Alignment tab.
4. Open the Horizontal drop-down list and choose the alignment you want (see Figure 11.13).
5. (Optional) If you want any indentation at the left edge of the cell, enter how much in the Indent text box. This is applicable only if you have chosen Left alignment.
6. Click OK.

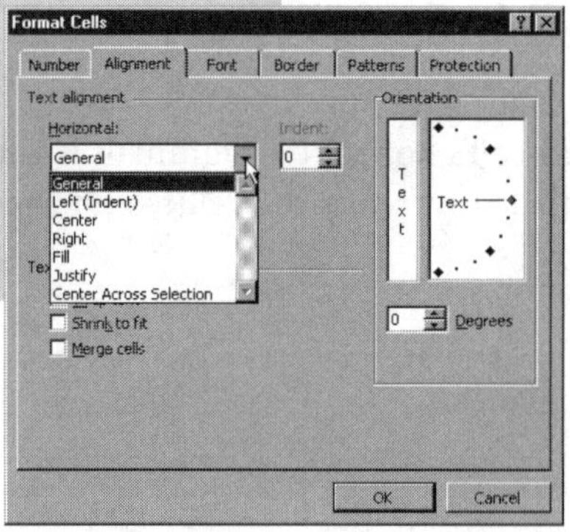

Figure 11.13 Use the Horizontal drop-down list to choose a horizontal alignment.

You are already familiar with Left, Center, and Right, but what about the other alignment options in the Format Cells dialog box (refer to Figure 11.13)?

- **General.** Removes all artificial alignment from the cell so that the contents align depending on its type (numbers to the right, text to the left).
- **Fill.** Repeats the contents of the cell so that the entire cell is filled with it. If you change the width of the column, the fill changes too. For example, you could enter **X** in the cell and set the alignment to Fill, and the cell would appear to have a whole row of Xs across its entire width (see Figure 11.14).

Figure 11.14 Use the Fill alignment to fill a cell's entire width with its contents.

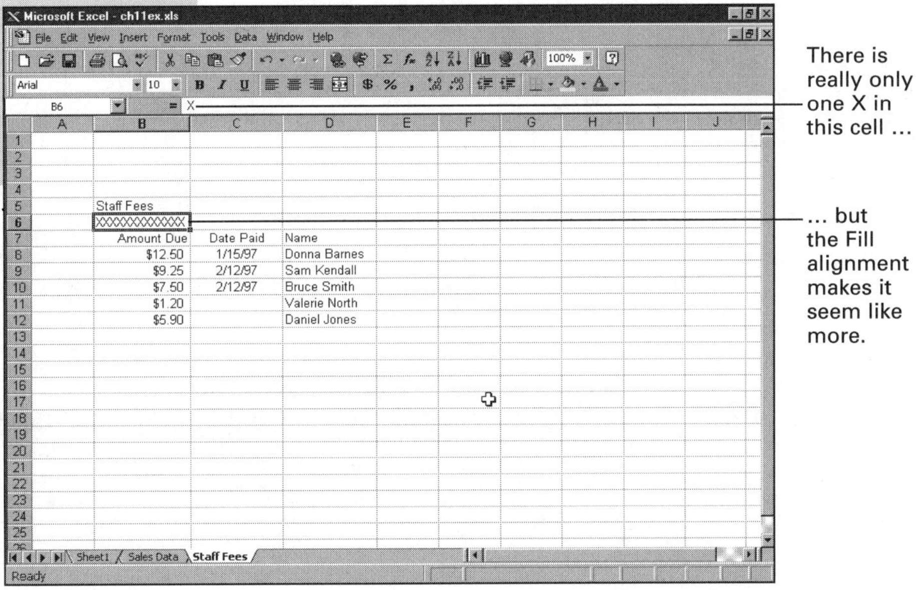

- **Justify.** Stretches out the cell contents, word-by-word, so that it fills the entire width of the cell. But there's a catch—it does not work on the last line in a cell. And unless you are using Text Wrap, you have only one line in the cell. If you do have more than one line in the cell (see Figure 11.15), however, all but the last line are justified.
- **Center Across Selection.** This is applicable only if you selected two or more contiguous cells in a row before you opened the dialog box. It takes the content of the leftmost cell and places it in the center of the selected range, as shown in Figure 11.16. Notice that cells B5:D5 are *not* merged into a single cell—they're each still individual cells. However, the content of B5 has been made to center across the range B5:D5, and that center point happens to be the middle of C5.

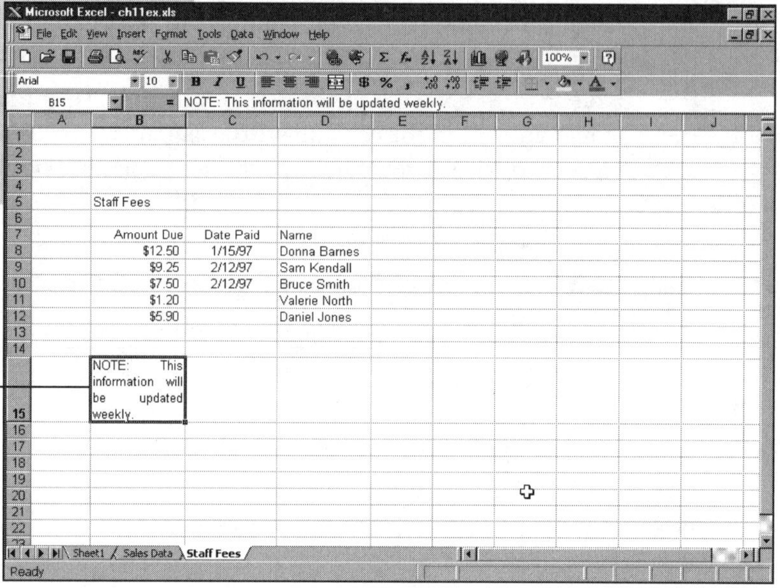

Figure 11.15 Use the Justify alignment to stretch out a multiline entry to fill the cell's width.

This is not particularly attractive in this case, but you get the idea.

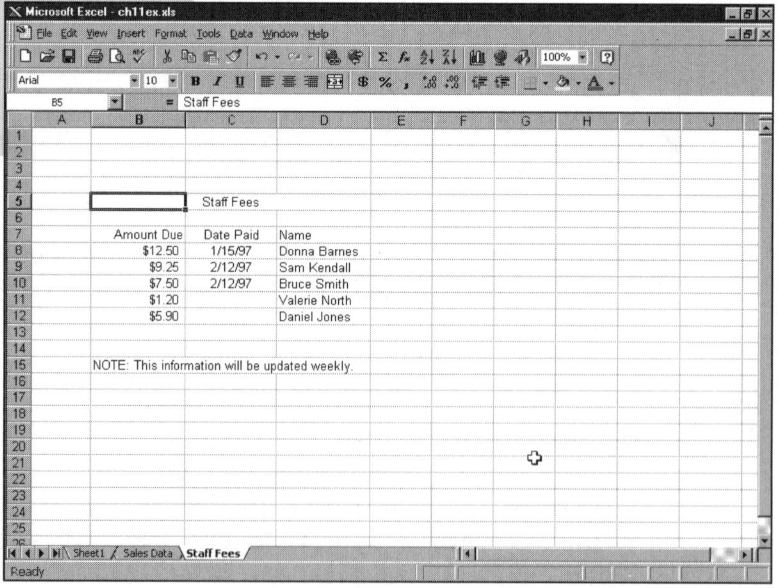

Figure 11.16 The content of cell B5 appears centered across the range B5:D5.

Rotating Text

You are not limited to horizontal text in a cell—you can have text at any angle. Normally, text runs straight across from left to right, but you can adjust the Degrees to make it run vertically or at an angle. Figure 11.17 shows some rotated text.

Figure 11.17 Rotated text is another way to dress up a dull worksheet.

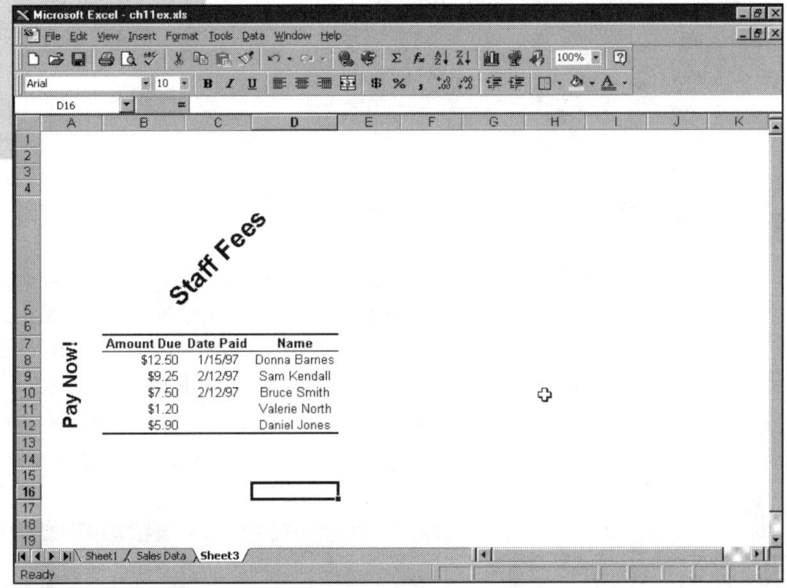

ANOTHER WAY TO MAKE TEXT AT AN ANGLE IS TO USE WORDART, WHICH IS COVERED IN CHAPTER 16.

Hands On: Rotating Text

Follow these steps to rotate some text:

1. Select the cell(s) containing the text to rotate.
2. Choose Format, Cells. The Format Cells dialog box appears.
3. Click the Alignment tab (see Figure 11.18).
4. In the Orientation area, drag the red diamond up or down along the curve to shift the text orientation.
5. Click OK.

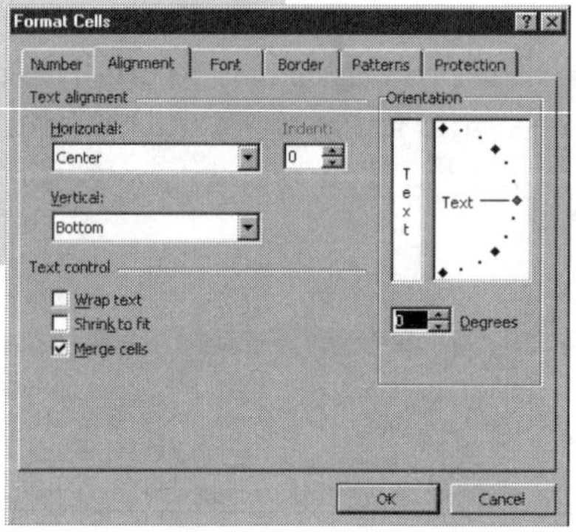

Figure 11.18 Drag the red diamond in the Orientation section of the dialog box.

Merging Cells

Sometimes Excel's rigid rectangular grid can get in the way of your creativity. For example, in Figure 11.19, I want to put the Name and Address into cells C4 and C5, respectively. But if I were to widen column C enough that the entries would fit, I would throw off column D. Besides, I don't need much room in C6 to enter the daytime phone number, so I don't want to widen column C.

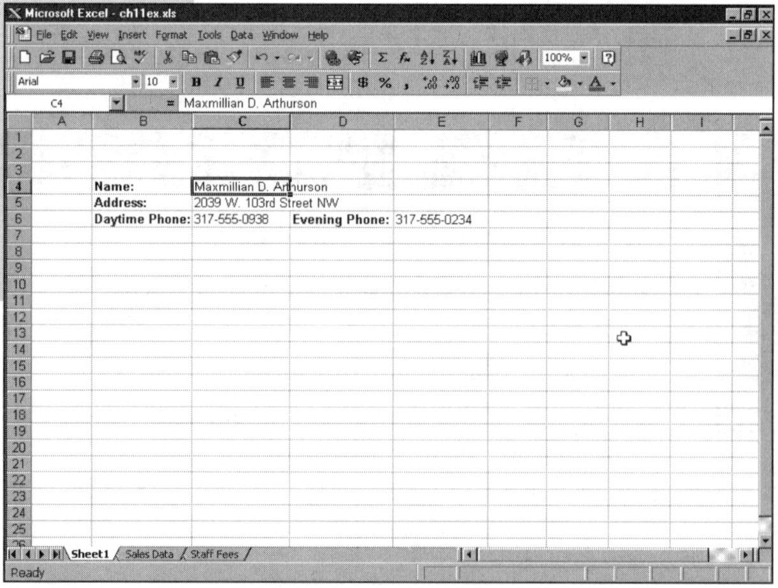

Figure 11.19 I'm trying to create a data entry form, but if I resize column C to hold enough data in C4 and C5, column D won't be in the right place for row 6.

What's the solution? Simple. Merge cells C4:E4 and C5:E5, as shown in Figure 11.20. This gives me plenty of room to enter long names and addresses without sacrificing the regular cell widths in row 6.

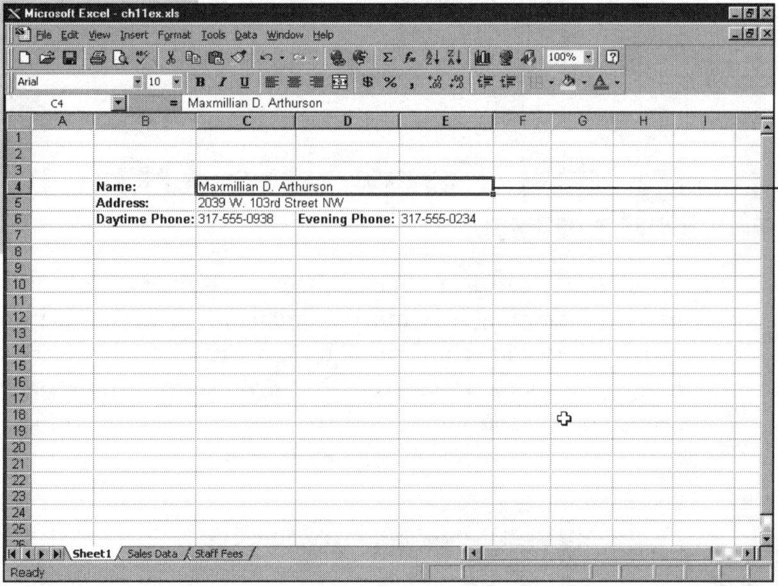

Figure 11.20 By merging cells C4:E4 into a single cell (named C4), I've created a large enough work area to enter the names.

Hands On: Merging Cells

To merge cells, do the following:

1. Select the cells you want to merge. They must be contiguous. You can merge from more than one row if you want.
2. Right-click on the selection and choose Format Cells. The Format Cells dialog box opens.
3. Click the Alignment tab.
4. Click the Merge Cells check box to select the option.
5. Click OK.

Excel offers a shortcut if you want to both merge cells and center across the selection at once: the Merge and Center button on the Formatting toolbar. Select the cells and then click that button to perform both actions: Center Across Selection and Merge Cells.

Note

Where did cells D4 and E4 go in Figure 11.20? They don't exist anymore, at least you can't access them anymore. If you want them to be accessible to you, you must turn off the Merge Cells formatting. Follow the preceding procedure and clear the Merge Cells check box in Step 4.

Changing the Font and Other Text Attributes

Of all the formatting you can do to a cell, changing the font is one of the most dramatic. It's amazing how much a different font makes text stand out. For example, turn back for a look at Figure 11.15, where everything is the same font. Pretty dull, isn't it? Now look at Figure 11.21, in which the same worksheet is enhanced with some different fonts and text attributes. It makes for a much nicer-to-read sheet.

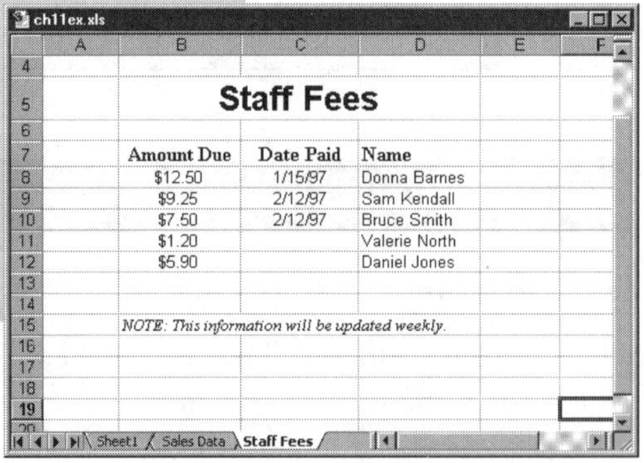

Figure 11.21 This formerly dull worksheet has been dressed up with some font changes and is much easier to read now!

Selecting a Different Font and Size

There are several ways to set a different font and/or font size for a cell. Among the easiest is to use the drop-down lists on the Formatting toolbar:

1. Select the cell(s) for which you want to change the font and/or font size.
2. If you want to change the font, open the Font drop-down list on the Formatting toolbar (see Figure 11.22) and make a new selection.
3. If you want a different font size, open the Font Size drop-down list and make a new selection.

Figure 11.22 Use the Font and Font Size drop-down lists right on the Formatting toolbar.

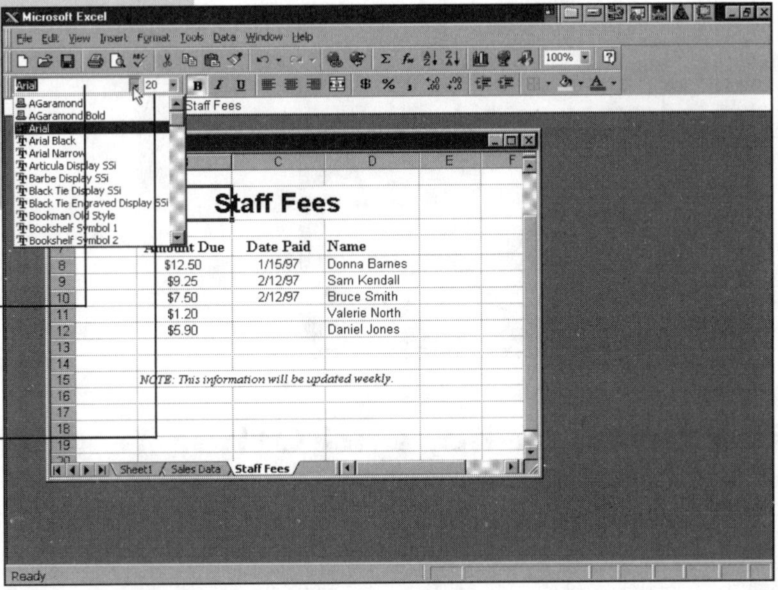

Font list; your fonts may vary.

Font Size list shows the available sizes for the selected font.

Note

You should always select the font first, and then the size. That's because not all fonts are available in all sizes, and the Font Size list shows the available sizes for the selected font.

Another way to change the font and font size is through the Format Cells dialog box. With this method, you can see a sample of a font before you apply it to your text, so this method is good if you aren't familiar with the fonts on your system. Follow these steps:

1. Select the cell(s) for which you want a different font or font size.
2. Choose Format, Cells, or right-click on the selection and choose Format Cells from the shortcut menu.
3. Click the Font tab (see Figure 11.23).
4. Select a font from the Font list. Check the Preview area for a sample of it.
5. Select a font size from the Size list.
6. While you're here, if you want to set any special text attributes, do so. (These are covered in detail in the following section.)
7. Click OK to close the dialog box.

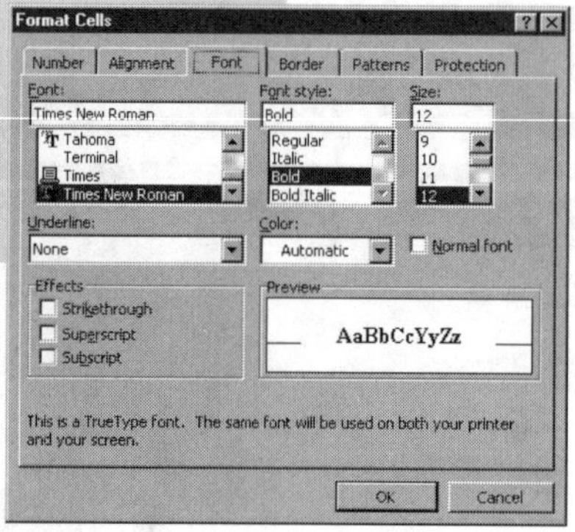

Figure 11.23 You can change the font and font size from here, and set text attributes too.

Applying Bold, Italic, and Other Text Attributes

Besides changing the font, you can also make more subtle changes that affect how the font appears, like making certain cells' contents bold, italic, or underlined. You can even make the text in a cell another color!

Note

In previous versions of Excel, you could only apply formatting to an entire cell, not to the text within it. That meant that you couldn't format one word in a cell differently from the rest in the cell. It was all or nothing. In Excel 97, you can format individual words or even individual letters by selecting them and then applying the format.

The most common formatting can be found on the Formatting toolbar. Select the cells to which you want to apply formatting, and then click one of the following buttons:

Button	Name
B	Makes the text in the cell bold
I	Italicizes the text
U	Underlines the text

These buttons are simple on/off toggle switches; when they're on, they look pushed in. They're not mutually exclusive; a cell can be formatted with all three (although it may not look very good that way). You can also activate these attributes with the following shortcut keys:

Ctrl+B for Bold

Ctrl+I for Italic

Ctrl+U for Underline

You can also change the text color from the Formatting toolbar, with the Text Color button. This button works in two ways. If you select the cells and then click on the button, it applies whatever color is currently showing. (The default is Red.) If you want to change the color displayed on the button, click the down arrow to the right of the button to open a list, as shown in Figure 11.24. Then click the color that you want.

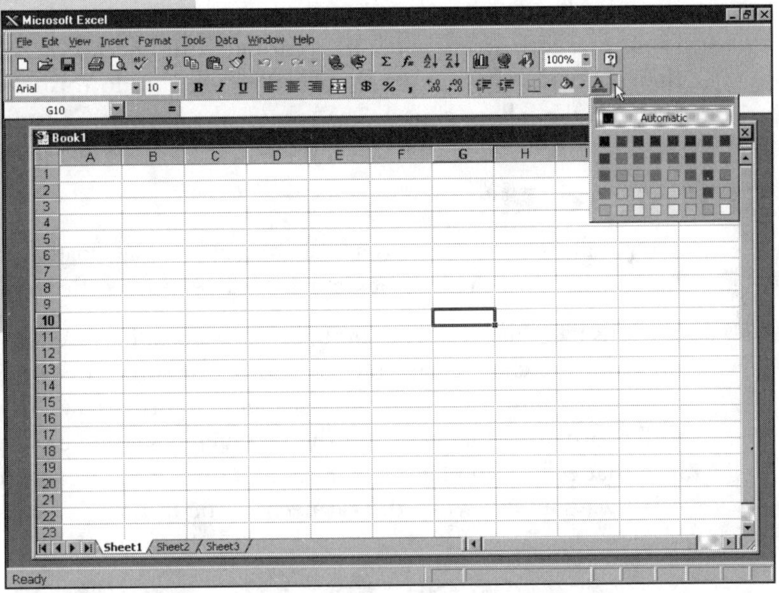

Figure 11.24 Choose the color that you want to use. That color then appears on the Text Color button, and you can apply the color to other selections by simply clicking the button.

For more choices than the toolbar provides, use the Format Cells dialog box:

1. Select the cell(s) you want to format.
2. Choose Format, Cells. The Format Cells dialog box opens.
3. Click the Font tab (see Figure 11.23).
4. From the Font Style list, select Regular, Bold, Italic, or Bold Italic. (Not all fonts have all these choices, but all have at least one style available.)
5. If you want underlining, select the underline type from the Underline drop-down list.

6. Open the Color drop-down list and select the text color you want. Or, if you want Excel to assign the color for you (usually Black), select Automatic.
7. If you want a special effect, like Strikethrough, Superscript, or Subscript, select the check box for one or more of those options.

Tip

Strikethrough can be set or removed without entering this dialog box; select the cell(s) and press Ctrl+5.

8. Check out the result in the Preview area. If you don't like what you see, make some more changes.
9. Click OK to accept your formatting.

If you make mistakes choosing your format options and want to return the cell(s) to normal formatting, click the Normal Font check box. If it is already selected, the text is already formatted normally. You can do this even if you have already clicked OK; follow steps 1-3 to reenter the Format Cells dialog box.

Using Shrink to Fit

Technically, Shrink to Fit is an "alignment" format, in that you set it up from the Alignment tab of the Format Cells dialog box. But its effect is to change the font size.

It works like this: you type some text into a cell, but the text is too long and won't fit. You can't change the column width (for some reason; perhaps you need the particular column width for something in another row), so you apply the Shrink to Fit format to that cell, and the text changes to be exactly small enough to fit into that cell. If you later widen that column, the text in the cell enlarges so that it is always exactly as small as it needs to be to fit.

Hands On: Shrinking a Worksheet to Fit a Certain Number of Pages

Now try shrinking a worksheet:

1. Select the cell(s) to which you want to apply the Shrink to Fit format.
2. Choose Format, Cells. The Format Cells dialog box opens.
3. Click the Alignment tab.
4. Select the Shrink to Fit check box.
5. Click OK. The text in that cell shrinks so that it fits.

Note

You can "shrink" an entire worksheet so that it fits on a specified number of pages. You learn to do this in Chapter 13, but here's a preview: choose File, Page Setup, and specify the number of pages in the Fit To text boxes.

Adding Borders Around Cells

Each cell has four sides: right, left, top, and bottom. And on-screen, each side of each cell is marked off by gray gridlines. But these gridlines are utilitarian in purpose—they show you where one cell ends and another begins, but they're not particularly attractive.

Borders, in contrast, are designed to improve the look and readability of your worksheet. You can assign a border to each side of each cell individually, for perfect control over their use. For example, look at Figure 11.25. Borders have been used to separate the headings from the text beneath them and to draw attention to a note. (I've turned off the on-screen display of gridlines so that you can see the borders better.)

Figure 11.25 Borders can improve the appearance and readability of your worksheet.

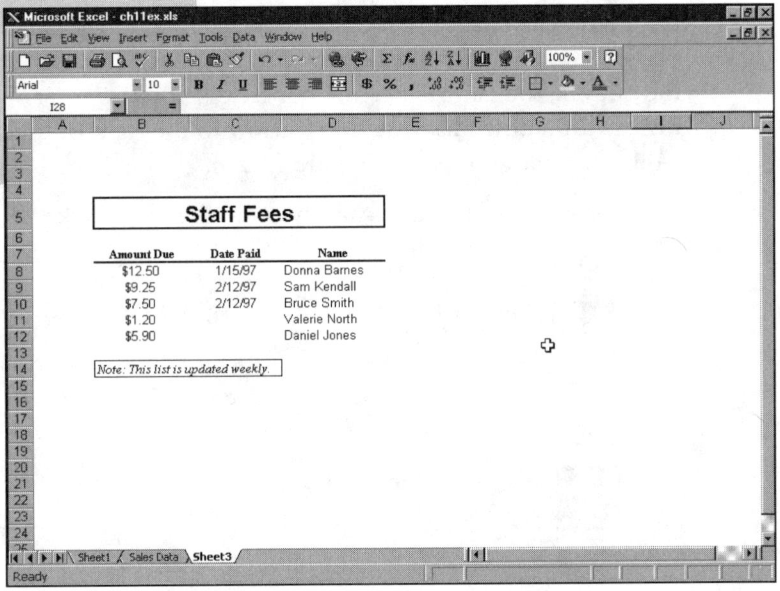

Take Control of Your Gridlines

By default, those gray gridlines on-screen on your workbook are turned off. When turned on they print as thin black lines on your printout. If you are using borders, however, you may want to turn off the gridlines, either on-screen, on the printout, or in both places. (However, if you can stand it, I recommend leaving gridlines turned on on-screen, because it's harder to tell where cells begin and end on-screen without them.)

To control the display of on-screen gridlines, choose Tools, Options. Click the View tab, and click in the Gridlines check box.

Gridlines do not print by default. You can have them print in that workbook by choosing File, Page Setup. Click the Sheet tab, and click in the Gridlines check box. (A check mark appears in the box.) If your worksheet uses many borders, it's a good idea to turn off gridline printing so that your printout doesn't look too line-bound.

The easiest way to set borders is with the Border button on the Formatting toolbar. Like some of the other buttons you've encountered, it works two ways. It displays a border type on the button; if you want that border, select the cell and click the button. You can change the border type that appears on the button by opening the drop-down list (the down arrow to the right of the button) and choosing a different border type (see Figure 11.26).

The Border button offers a variety of borders. Let's take a look at its offerings:

Button	Description
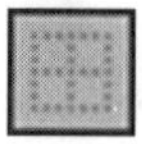	No border. Selecting this clears any borders that have been set for the selected cell(s).
	Thin bottom border.
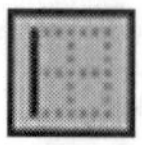	Thin left border.
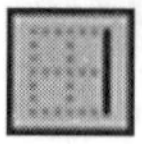	Thin right border.

Figure 11.26 Select a border from the Border button's drop-down list.

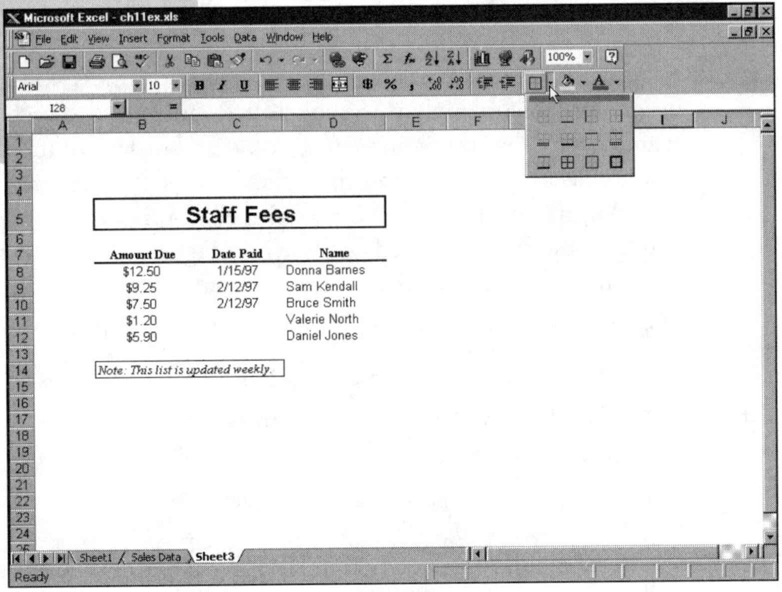

Button	Description
	Double bottom border.
	Thick bottom border.
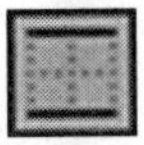	Thin borders at top and bottom.
	Thin border at the top and double border at the bottom.
	Thin border at the top and thick border at the bottom.
	Thin borders on all sides of all cells in the selected range.
	Thin border around only the outside of the selected range.
	Thick border around only the outside of the selected range.

You can also apply an outline border to the selected range by pressing Ctrl+Shift+7.

Keep in mind that when you apply a border, unless you specifically choose an inside border, you apply it to the selected range, not to each cell in the range. For example, suppose that you want to create a border around the range B2:E6. You would select that range, and then click one of the last two buttons shown in the preceding table, the *outside* buttons. Cell C4, because it is in the middle of the range, would be untouched, as shown in Figure 11.27. The simple act of creating the border around the selected range has actually done all the following:

- Placed a top and left border in cell B2.
- Placed a top border in cells C2 and D2.
- Placed a top and right border in cell E2.
- Placed a left border in cells B3:B5.
- Placed a right border in cells E3:E5.
- Placed a left and bottom border in cell B6.
- Placed a bottom border in cells C6 and D6.
- Placed a bottom and right border in cell E6.

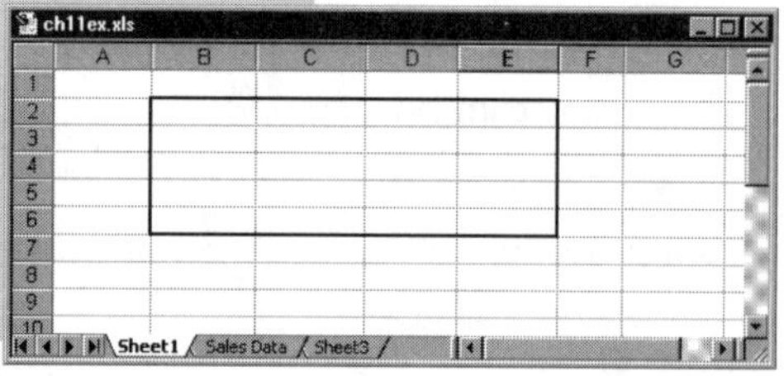

Figure 11.27 This border is the result of placing an outside border around the range B2:E6.

If you need more control over the borders than the Border button can provide, follow these steps to use the Border tab in the Format Cells dialog box:

1. Select the cell(s) you want to apply a border to.
2. Choose Format, Cells. The Format Cells dialog box appears.
3. Click the Border tab to display the Border controls (see Figure 11.28).
4. Select the line style you want to use from the Style list. You can use more than one line style in a worksheet, but you must apply each line style separately.
5. Select a color for the selected line style from the Color drop-down list.

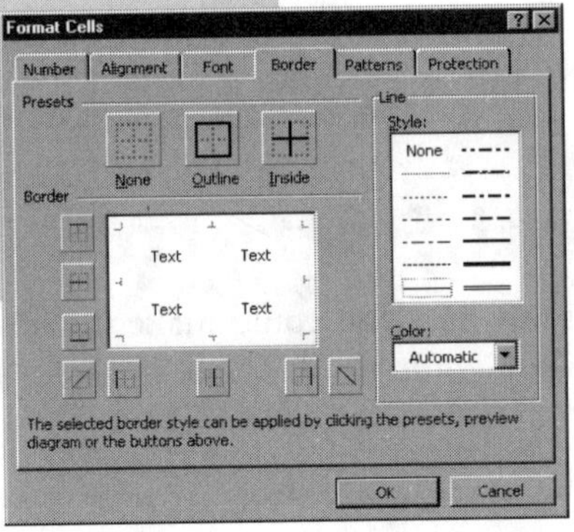

Figure 11.28 Use the controls on the Border tab to assign borders to individual sides of a cell.

6. Now you are ready to apply the line style. You can apply it in either of two ways:
   - Click one of the Presets buttons to apply the selected line to the Outside or Inside of the selected range. (Or, to apply it to both outside and inside, click one button, and then the other.)
   - Click on one of the buttons in the Border area. Some of these buttons are the same as the ones you saw on the Border button's drop-down list; here are the ones that are different:

If you make a mistake in setting borders, click the None button in the Presets area to clear all the borders in the dialog box and start over. You can remove all borders without opening the dialog box by selecting the cell(s) and pressing Ctrl+Shift+_ (underline).

Button	Description
	Adds an inside horizontal border in the range. For example, if there are two rows of cells in the range, it adds a horizontal line between them.
	Adds an inside vertical border in the range. For example, if there are two columns of cells in the range, it adds a horizontal line between them.
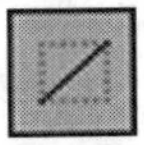	Adds a diagonal line through each cell in the range from the bottom left to the top right corners.
	Adds a diagonal line from the top left to the bottom right corners of each cell.

7. Check out the sample area to see how your borders will look. If you are satisfied, click OK. Otherwise, continue working with the borders. (You can click the None button to start over if needed.)

Color, Shading, and Patterns

IN CHAPTER 12 YOU'LL LEARN HOW TO PUT A BACKGROUND BEHIND AN ENTIRE WORKSHEET.

Earlier in the chapter you saw how you could make the text you type a different color. Did you know that you could do the same thing for the cell background?

Not only can you change the background color in a cell, but you can also apply some fancy special effects to it, such as creating a pattern with two colors or shading it.

The easy way to color a cell's background is with the Fill Color button on the Formatting toolbar. Like the Text Color button, you can use it in two different ways. You can apply the color shown on the button by selecting the cell(s) and clicking the button. Or, you can change the color shown by opening the drop-down list and selecting another color, as shown in Figure 11.29. To remove the color from a cell, select No Fill.

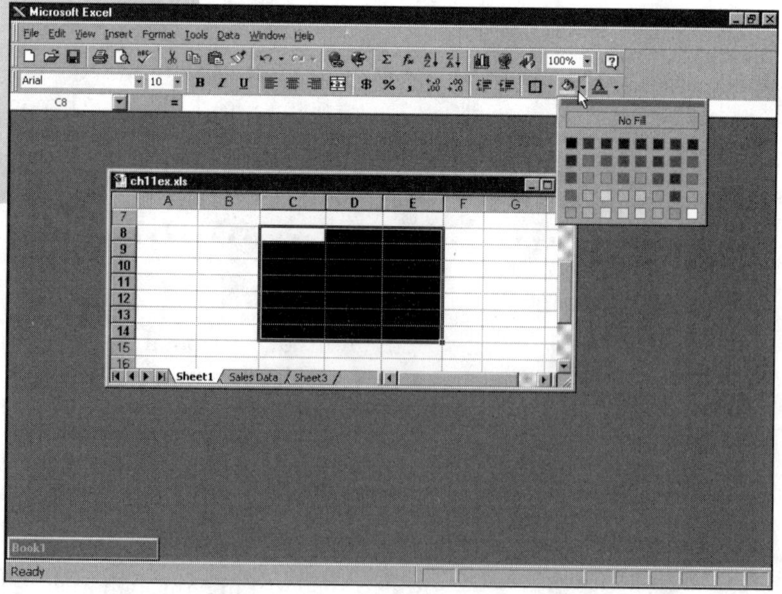

Figure 11.29 You can select a different background color to apply to cells from this list.

If you want special shading or other color options, you must use the Format Cells dialog box. Follow these steps:

1. Select the cell(s) you want to format.
2. Choose Format, Cells to open the Format Cells dialog box.
3. Click the Patterns tab to display the pattern controls (see Figure 11.30).

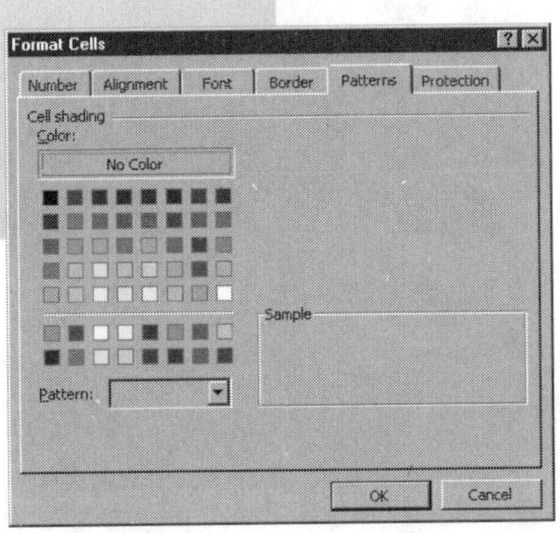

Figure 11.30 You can choose not only solid colors but also patterns here.

4. Select a color from the Color list. This will be the background color for the cell(s).
5. (Optional) If you want a pattern in the cell, open the Pattern drop-down list and select one from the top of the list (see Figure 11.30).
6. If you want the pattern to appear in a different color than black, open the Pattern drop-down list again, and this time select a color.
7. Check the Sample area. If you are not satisfied with the colors and pattern, repeat steps 4-6. When you are satisfied, click OK.

Do not use bright, high-contrast patterns for cells that will contain important text because it will be hard to read the text on such a background. Also, avoid using color backgrounds on worksheets that you plan to print and distribute unless you are using a color printer. Using gray backgrounds is better for printing on a black-and-white printer because what you see on the screen will more closely resemble what you'll see on the printout. If you do have a color printer and you want light text on a dark background, try bright yellow or light blue text on a dark blue background.

12

Worksheet Formatting

In This Chapter

- Hiding Worksheets
- Placing a Background Behind a Sheet
- AutoFormatting
- Conditional Formatting
- Styles

If you've read Chapter 11, you're up to speed on the basic formatting skills you need in Excel. Excel offers formatting options that some people consider "advanced," but I consider them big-time efficiency tools that are infinitely worth taking the time to learn about. With this chapter, and a little initiative to learn, you can discover these timesaving secrets for yourself.

Hiding and Unhiding Worksheets

IF YOU NEED TO HIDE A WORKSHEET AND ASSIGN A PASSWORD, SEE CHAPTER 22.

When you want to distribute a workbook to colleagues who have no interest in certain worksheets, you can hide those sheets. You sometimes can't just delete the unneeded sheets because calculations on other sheets may depend on them. So instead you hide the unneeded sheets, making the remaining sheets easier to find and work with.

Hands On: Hiding a Worksheet

To hide a worksheet, follow these steps:

1. Select the worksheet(s) you want to hide. To select a worksheet, click on its tab. To select more than one worksheet, hold down the Ctrl key while you click on multiple tabs.
2. Choose Format, Sheet, Hide. The selected worksheets are hidden.

Hands On: Redisplaying a Hidden Worksheet

When you want to see a hidden worksheet again, follow these steps:

1. Choose Format, Sheet, Unhide. The Unhide dialog box opens, listing all the hidden worksheets (see Figure 12.1).
2. Click on the worksheet you want to unhide.
3. Click OK. The sheet returns to view.

Note

You can unhide only one worksheet at once. If you want to unhide more than one, you must repeat the unhide procedure for each one.

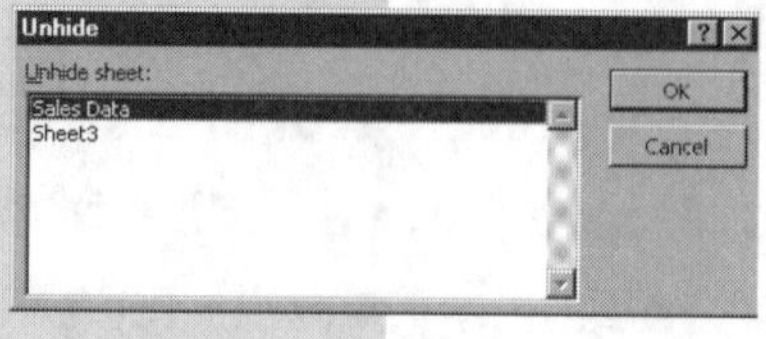

Figure 12.1 In the Unhide dialog box, choose which worksheet you want to unhide.

Placing a Background Behind a Worksheet

> **CHAPTER 11 COVERS DISPLAYING AND HIDING GRIDLINES.**

One way to dress up a worksheet is to hide the gridlines so that they don't display on-screen and/or don't print. Another way is to place a background on the worksheet. This background situates itself behind the cell contents and gridlines, as shown in Figure 12.2.

Hands On: Adding a Background to a Sheet

To place a background on a sheet, follow these steps:

1. Display the sheet that you want to add a background to.
2. Choose Format, Sheet, Background. The Sheet Background dialog box appears (see Figure 12.3).

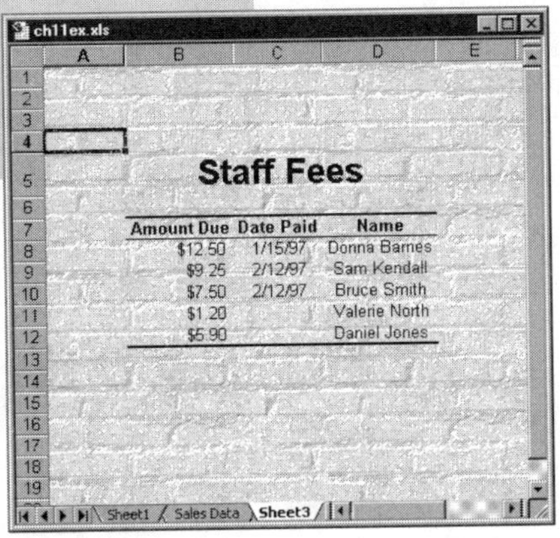

Figure 12.2 This background dresses up the worksheet a bit.

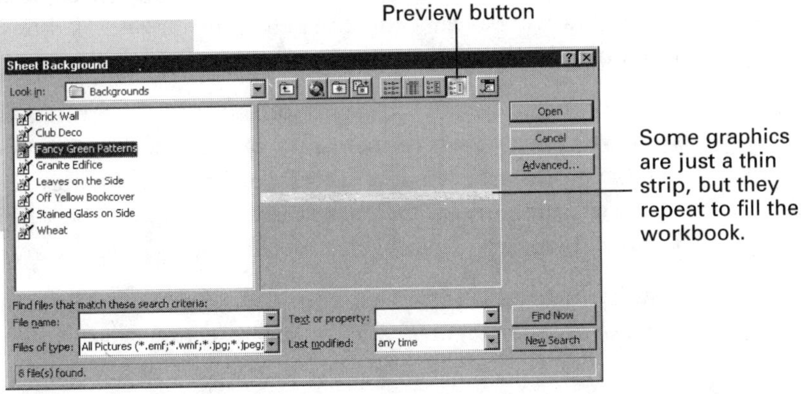

Figure 12.3 Choose a background from among all the graphics files on your computer.

3. Locate the file you want to use for a background. It can be any graphics file. If you have the Office 97 version of Excel installed, you can find some backgrounds in Program Files\Microsoft Office\Clipart\Backgrounds. (Those are the ones shown in Figure 12.3.)

Note

If you don't see a preview window like the one in Figure 12.3, click the Preview button in the dialog box to change the view to Preview. Some of the graphics in the Backgrounds folder look like narrow strips when previewed, but when you apply them to your worksheet, they tile themselves to cover the whole sheet.

4. Click Open to apply the background.

If you later decide to apply a different background, you must remove the existing background first. To remove a background, choose Format, Sheet, Delete Background.

Find it Online

Microsoft frequently posts free graphics files at its Internet site that you can download to use with Office programs like Excel. To check it out, start your Internet connection, and then choose Help, Microsoft On the Web, Free Stuff, or check out http://www.microsoft.com/OfficeFreeStuff/Excel to jump to the Web page where you can see what's available.

Applying Automatic Formatting with AutoFormat

Some people are born with an eye for style and decorating—some aren't. Similarly, some people seem to have this instinctive sense of what formatting will look good on a worksheet. Unfortunately, I'm not one of those people. That's why I often turn to Excel's AutoFormat feature to give me a hand.

AutoFormat consists of a variety of predesigned formats that you can apply to your worksheet. Each format takes care of the fonts, borders, and shading you need to produce an attractive sheet. For example, Figures 12.4 and 12.5 show two different AutoFormats applied to my example worksheet from Chapter 11. Much improved, don't you think?

AutoFormatting isn't perfect; you may need to tweak it some after it's finished. For example, in Figure 12.5 I chose to center-align some of the columns after

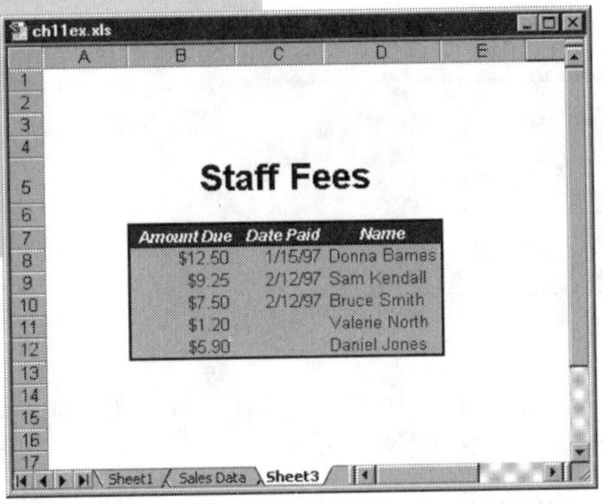

Figure 12.4 All the text under the title has been AutoFormatted with the Classic 3 format.

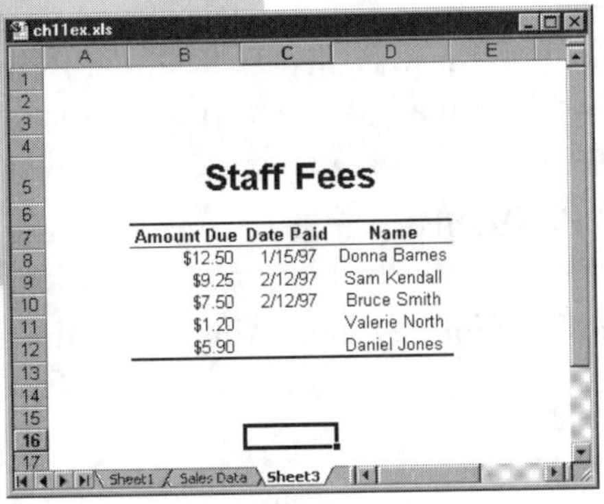

Figure 12.5 In this example, the text under the title has been AutoFormatted with the Simple format.

AutoFormat did its job. But AutoFormat gives you a head start, as well as some formatting ideas that might not have occurred to you.

Hands On: Formatting with AutoFormat

To use AutoFormatting, follow these steps:

1. Select the range that you want to AutoFormat. Include column and row labels but not the worksheet title (if it has one).
2. Choose Format, AutoFormat. The AutoFormat dialog box appears (see Figure 12.6).
3. Select one of the formats from the Table Format list. The sample in the dialog box changes to show what the formatting looks like.

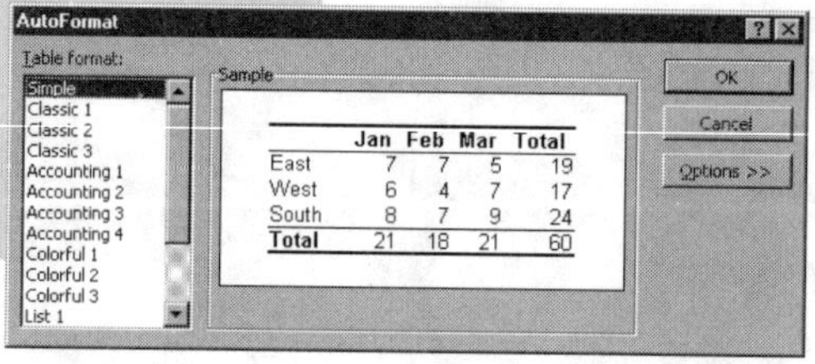

Figure 12.6 Select the format you want from the Table Format list.

4. When you have selected the format you want to use, click OK. Excel formats the range with that format.
5. Fine-tune the formatting using the tools you learned about in Chapter 11.

After you have become familiar with the various AutoFormat formats, you may decide that not all the attributes of a particular format are what you want. For example, you may not like the way that the Simple format aligns columns or changes the column width. If that's the case, you can turn off certain aspects of a format by following these steps:

1. While you are in the AutoFormat dialog box, click the Options button. Additional options appear at the bottom of the dialog box (see Figure 12.7).
2. Deselect the check box for any formatting aspect that you do not want to apply.

If you decide you don't like the AutoFormatting, click the Undo button on the toolbar or choose Edit, Undo immediately after you apply the format.

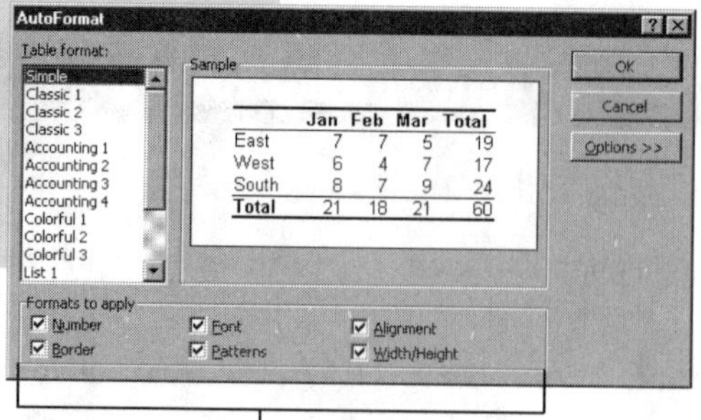

Figure 12.7 You can selectively apply each aspect of an AutoFormat format.

These extra controls appear when you click the Options button.

Conditional Formatting

Have you ever considered how Excel knows to format negative numbers in red when you set it up to do so? It's a type of *conditional* formatting. If the number is negative, Excel applies the format "red"—otherwise, it doesn't. It's as simple as that. With conditional formatting, if the content of a cell meets certain criteria, it is formatted a certain way; if it doesn't, the content is formatted differently.

There are many everyday business uses for conditional formatting. Suppose, for instance, that you create a daily list of delinquent accounts. If the account delinquency is greater than 30 days, you want to make that account stand out on the list, so that you can investigate the problem. You would apply conditional formatting to the cell that showed the date due. If the date due was more than 30 days from today, the cell contents would be made bold.

Another example: say that your organization has a list of bank accounts, and each bank has a certain minimum balance, below which the account is subject to service fees. You could set up a field for each organization listing that minimum, and then have a formula in another cell subtracting the current balance from that number. If the current balance is less than the minimum, you could make the balance formatted in bright green, or some other color that you will easily notice.

To set up a conditional format, first write out a sentence, at least in your mind if not on paper, that describes the condition and result. For example:

> If cell C3 is less than cell C4, format the cell in bold and italic, with a box drawn around it and a light blue background.

Hands On: Applying Conditional Formatting

Then follow these steps to fill your sentence information into the Conditional Formatting dialog box:

1. Select the cell(s) you want to format with this condition—for example, C3 from my example.
2. Choose Format, Conditional Formatting. The Conditional Formatting dialog box appears (see Figure 12.8).

Note

In step 2, if this is the first time you have used Conditional Formatting, the Office Assistant appears. Click Close to get rid of it.

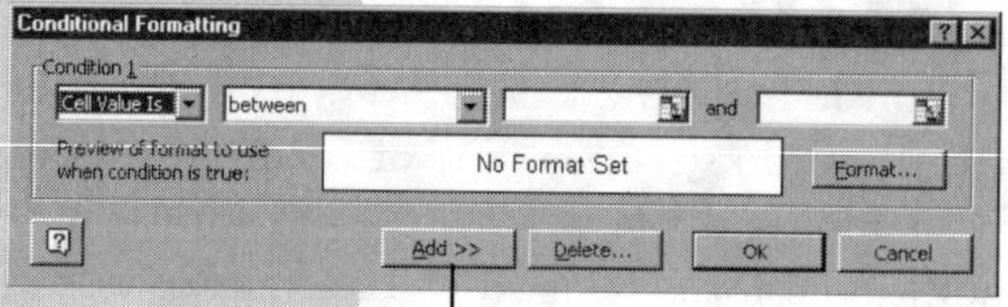

Figure 12.8 Use the Conditional Formatting dialog box to set up both the conditions and the formatting to be applied.

> **REFER BACK TO CHAPTER 11 FOR HELP WITH THE FONT, BORDER, AND PATTERN OPTIONS.**

3. In the Condition 1 drop-down list, select either Cell Value Is or Formula Is, depending on what you want to apply the condition to. (I'm choosing Cell Value Is.)
4. The next drop-down list to the right enables you to select the relationship. The default is Between, but you should change it to reflect your sentence (for example, Less Than in my selection).
5. Moving on to the right, there is a text box with a Collapse Dialog button. Either type the cell or value you want into that box, or click the Collapse Dialog button to select the cell from the worksheet. For my example, I'll type **C4**.
6. Now comes the part where you choose the formatting. Click the Format button to open the Format Cells dialog box (see Figure 12.9).

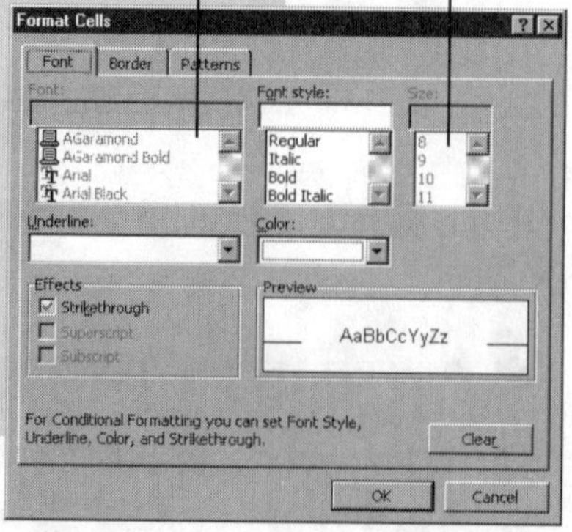

Figure 12.9 This Format Cells dialog box looks much like the regular one but has fewer tabs because it shows only the formatting that can be applied conditionally.

7. Use the options on the Font, Border, and/or Patterns tabs to set up the formatting you want. For example, for my sentence, I'll do the following:
   - On the Font tab, select Bold Italic on the Font Style list.
   - On the Border tab, click the Outline button.
   - On the Patterns tab, click a shade of light blue.
8. Click OK to close the Format Cells dialog box. A preview of the selected format now appears in the Conditional Formatting dialog box.
9. If you want to add a second set of criteria, click the Add button to open a second set of controls and repeat steps 3 through 8 for Condition 2. Keep clicking the Add button and filling in the controls until you have entered all the criteria you want.
10. Click OK to close the dialog box and apply the conditional formatting. If you do not see the formatting in the cell, type a value in the cell that meets the conditions you set up.

To remove all formatting from a cell quickly, including conditional formatting, choose Edit, Clear, Formats.

Working with Styles

If you are an experienced word processor user, you may already be familiar with the concept of styles. *Styles* are like AutoFormatting for individual cells. You set up in advance what formatting you want a style to contain, and then apply it to one or more cells to transfer that formatting automatically to the cell. For example, instead of going through all the steps to make several cells bold and italic with a blue background, I could create a style that contained that formatting and then apply that style to every cell that I wanted formatted that way.

Excel's styles are not as sophisticated as the ones found in Microsoft Word, but they work on the same principle. You have already used some of Excel's styles, in fact, if you have clicked on the Currency Style, Percent Style, or Comma Style buttons on the Formatting toolbar. These buttons are shortcuts for applying their respective styles.

Note

Remember in Chapter 10, when I told you that the Currency Style button actually applies the Accounting format? That's because the Currency Style button refers to a style that calls that format. The Currency Style and the Currency format have nothing in common except for their names. The Currency Style could just as easily have used a completely different format.

Understanding Excel's Styles

SEE CHAPTER 4 FOR MORE INFORMATION ABOUT TEMPLATES.

Styles are stored with templates, so the styles you have available for use depend on what template you used to create your workbook. With the Normal template, the Normal style has these properties:

- General number format
- General horizontal alignment
- Bottom vertical alignment
- Arial 10 font (or whatever you have the default font set to be)
- No borders
- No shading
- Locked protection status

SEE CHAPTER 22 TO LEARN MORE ABOUT A CELL'S PROTECTION STATUS.

The other styles included in the Normal template do not specify a font, alignment, or any of those other formatting options—they simply set a particular number format:

- The Comma style applies the Accounting number format with no currency symbol and two decimal places.
- The Comma (0) style applies the Accounting number format with no currency symbol and no decimal places.
- The Currency style applies the Accounting number format with a $ currency symbol.
- The Currency (0) style applies the Accounting number format with no decimal places.
- The Percent style applies the Percent format with no decimal places.

Applying a Style

As you learned in Chapter 10, you can apply certain styles by clicking a toolbar button:

Button	Description
	Applies Currency style
	Applies Percent style
	Applies Comma style

Hands On: Applying a Style

If you want any of the other styles, you must apply them by following these steps:

1. Select the cell(s) to which you want the style to apply.
2. Choose Format, Style. The Style dialog box appears (see Figure 12.10).
3. Open the Style Name drop-down list and choose the style you want to apply.
4. Click OK. The style is applied.

Did you notice the check boxes in Figure 12.10? Each style can apply any or all of six types of formatting. If a style applies a type of formatting, any formatting that the cell previously had of that type is gone. For example, if you apply the Normal style to a cell that uses 14-point Courier font, because the Normal style specifies its own font, the 14-point Courier is changed to the font and size specified in the style. However, if you apply a style that does not include a specific font, applying that style will not change the font used. (Normal style is the only preset style that changes all the types of formatting; the others just change the number format.)

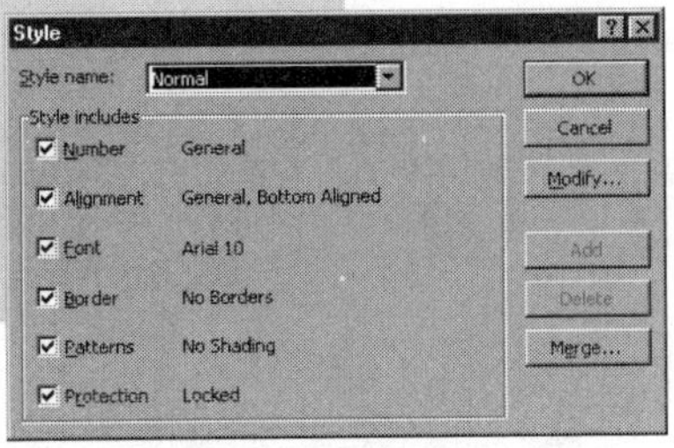

Figure 12.10 In the Style dialog box, you choose the style you want to apply.

Hands On: Adding a Style Control to the Toolbar

SEE CHAPTER 6 FOR FULL INFORMATION ABOUT CREATING TOOLBARS.

If you use styles frequently in your workbooks, you may want to add a Style control to one of the toolbars, or create a new toolbar containing style controls. This was covered in Chapter 6, but let's look at it again specifically with styles in mind:

1. Right-click on any toolbar and choose Customize from the shortcut menu. The Customize dialog box appears.
2. Click the Commands tab.
3. Click Format on the Categories list.
4. On the Commands list, you see the word `Style:` followed by a drop-down list box, as shown in Figure 12.11. Click on this and drag it to a toolbar. This creates a drop-down list on the toolbar from which you can select styles.
5. Click Close. The new drop-down list appears on the toolbar where you dropped it (see Figure 12.12).

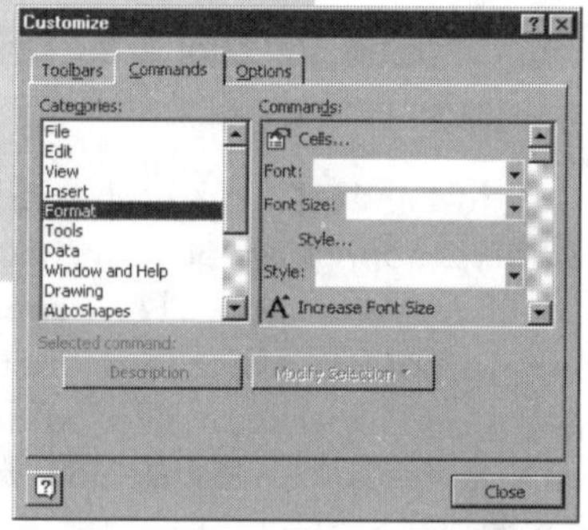

Figure 12.11 Drag the Style drop-down list control to a toolbar for easy access to styles.

If you later want to remove the toolbar control, reopen the dialog box (step 1) and drag the control off the toolbar. Then close the dialog box (step 5).

Modifying a Style

As you become more familiar with Excel's styles, you may find that one or more of the preset styles doesn't exactly meet your needs. Maybe you would prefer the Currency style to show no decimal places, for example, or maybe you want all percentages to appear in italics.

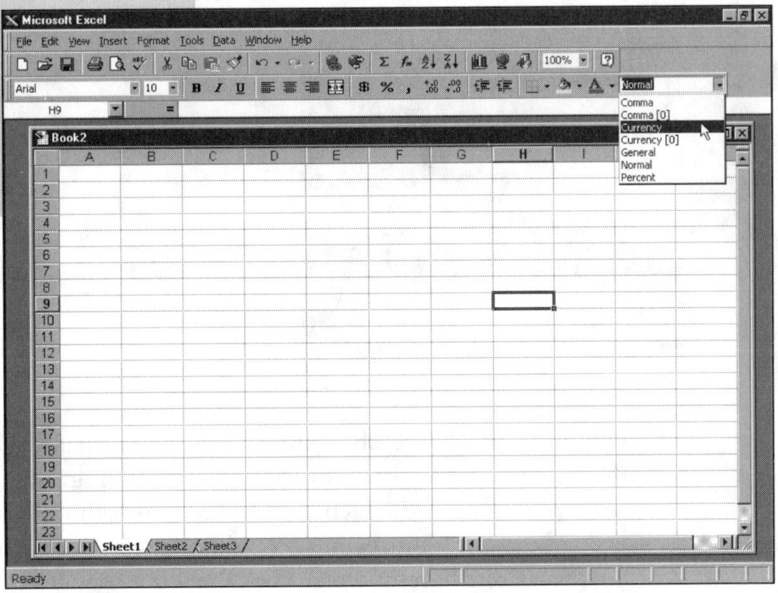

Figure 12.12 Now you can select the style directly from the toolbar, without the Style dialog box.

As you learned in the preceding section, each style can have up to six attributes. To activate an attribute for a style, select the appropriate check box in the Styles dialog box and then click the Modify button to choose the formatting you want.

Hands On: Making Changes to a Style

SEE CHAPTER 11 FOR MORE INFORMATION ABOUT THE FORMAT CELLS DIALOG BOX.

Follow these steps:

1. Choose Format, Style to open the Style dialog box.
2. Open the Style Name drop-down list and choose the style you want to modify.
3. In the Style Includes area, select or deselect check boxes as needed to specify what formatting options the style will control. When you select a check box, the default options for that item appear. For example, if you select Alignment, `General, Bottom Aligned` appears.
4. If the settings are not right next to any of the selected check boxes, click the Modify button. This opens the Format Cells dialog box (see Figure 12.13).

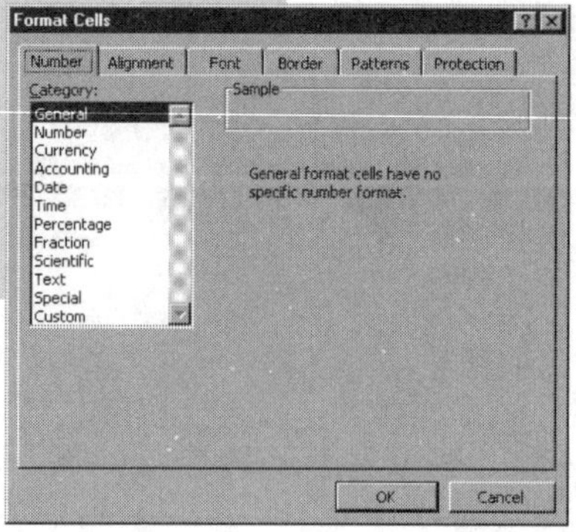

Figure 12.13 This version of the Format Cells dialog box applies only to the style you're modifying.

5. Use the options on each of the tabs in the Format Cells dialog box to select the formatting you want for the style. You can ignore the tabs for any of the format types for which you did not select the check box in the Style dialog box. For example, if you did not check Border in the Style dialog box, you don't have to worry about making changes to the Border tab of the Format Cells dialog box, because any changes you make there will not affect the style.
6. When you are finished modifying the style, click OK to return to the Style dialog box.
7. Click OK to close the Style dialog box, or click the Add button to modify the style without closing the dialog box (if you need to modify another style).

Creating New Styles

The styles that come with Excel are fine, except that they are fairly limited in scope. Most of them apply only a number format, for example. As you become more experienced, you might want to create your own styles that represent formatting you use frequently.

Hands On: Creating a Style

To create a style, follow these steps:

1. Choose Format, Style to open the Style dialog box.
2. Select the style that is most like the one you want to create. You'll base your new style on it.

3. Click in the Style Name text box and type a new name for the style. The words (By Example) appear after Style Includes, as shown in Figure 12.14.
4. Modify the style, as you learned in the preceding section.
5. When you are finished modifying, click the Add button to create the new style.
6. Repeat steps 2 to 5 to create another new style, or click OK if you are finished.

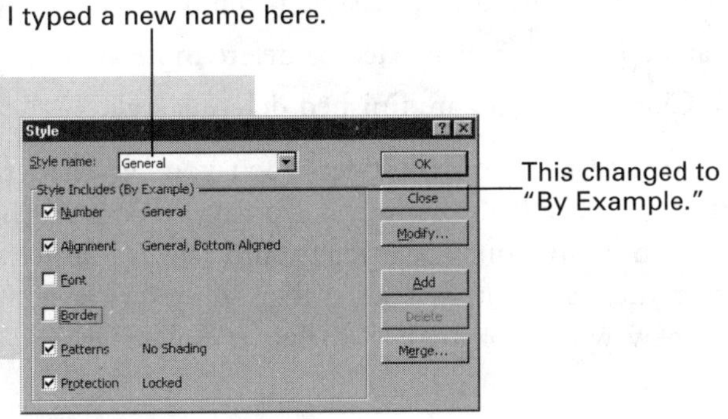

Figure 12.14 You can create a new style by starting with the example of an existing one and modifying it.

Here are some ideas for styles you can create:

- **Bottom Border.** You can apply this whenever you need to create an underline to separate column headings from their data. Base this on the Normal style, but remove all the checks from the check boxes except Border. Then click Modify and use the Border tab to set a thick bottom border.
- **Standout.** This formatting will really make a particular cell stand out from the rest. Base this on the Normal style and remove all the checks except for Patterns and Font. Click Modify and use the Patterns tab to set a shaded background for the cell. Then use the Font tab to set the font to 12-point and Bold.
- **Wrapped.** This style makes text wrap in a cell if it is too long to fit. (Of course you can set this up the normal way, as you learned in Chapter 11, but it's easier with a style, especially if you added the Style control to your toolbar as the procedure earlier in the chapter suggested.) Start with the Normal style and remove all the checks except Alignment. Then click the Modify button and the Alignment tab, and click to select the Wrap Text check box.

Deleting a Style

If you find that you have too many styles in your workbook, you may want to delete some of the ones that you never use. Keeping your style list lean and trim makes it easier for you to locate the style you want to use on the list.

To delete a style, follow these steps:

1. Choose Format, Style. The Style dialog box appears.
2. Select the style you want to delete from the Style Name drop-down list.
3. Click the Delete button. The style is removed.
4. Repeat steps 2 and 3 as needed to delete more styles.
5. Click Close when you are finished deleting styles.

You cannot delete the Normal style; when you select it, the Delete button is grayed out and unavailable. However, you can delete all the other preset styles from the workbook (Comma, Currency, and so on). Don't worry that you've lost them forever, though—you've deleted them only for the active workbook. When you start a new workbook based on that template, it will have all the original styles available.

If you want to change the styles that come with a particular template, open the template, as described in Chapter 4, and edit the styles from there. You can add or delete styles, or modify them—anything that you can do with a regular workbook. Then when you save your template, all future workbooks created with that template will contain the styles you specified.

13

Printing Your Work

In This Chapter

- Setting a Print Area
- Printing with Special Options
- Choosing Whether to Print Gridlines
- Creating Page Headers and Footers
- Repeating Headings on Each Page
- Adding Page Breaks

When you print a worksheet, it opens a whole new can of options. Where will the page breaks be? What information should be repeated on every page? Should the gridlines print? How many pages should it fit on? In this chapter, you'll learn to take your beautiful on-screen worksheet and turn it into a beautiful printout.

Setting the Print Area

Normally, when you print a worksheet, the entire worksheet prints, or a certain number of pages you specify (as you'll learn in "Printing with Options" later in this chapter). But if you prefer, you can set a *print area*, and only the cells in that range will be printed. This can be handy if you have several tables of information on a single sheet and you want to print only one of them.

Note

Print areas have been around for a long time. In fact, in older versions of Excel, you had to set a print area before you could print, even if your print area was the entire worksheet! This bedeviled many beginners, who couldn't understand why the Print command didn't work and who had no idea that they had to set a print range. Later versions of Excel fixed this by setting the default print range to the entire sheet.

Setting the print area is a matter of selecting the range and then issuing the command to make that range the print area. Follow these steps:

1. Select the range that you want to print.
2. Choose File, Print Area, Set Print Area.

Now when you print (see the following section), only the specified print area will print. You can test this by clicking the Print Preview button on the Standard toolbar. (There's more about the Print Preview screen at the end of this chapter.)

If you want to go back to using the entire worksheet as the print area, remove the print area setting by choosing File, Print Area, Clear Print Area. You don't have to select any particular range first; this command simply clears Excel's memory of any print area being set.

Simple Printing from the Toolbar

The easiest way to print is to click the Print button on the Standard toolbar. It doesn't get much simpler than that. When you click this button, the active worksheet prints on the default printer, one copy of the entire sheet.

Tip

How do you tell what the default printer is? Point the mouse at the Print button on the toolbar, and a ScreenTip pops up. It tells you that it's the Print button, and it also tells you what the default printer is. If you have more than one printer, you can change which printer is the default in the Print dialog box, which you'll learn about in the following section.

Printing with Options

The default print options work well if you want just the default settings, but many times you will want more than one copy, more than one sheet, or some other special settings when you print.

Hands On: Setting Print Options

To set your print options, use the Print dialog box:

1. Choose File, Print or press Ctrl+P. The Print dialog box appears (see Figure 13.1).
2. Set any options in the Print dialog box that you want. (These are covered in the following sections.)
3. Click OK to print.

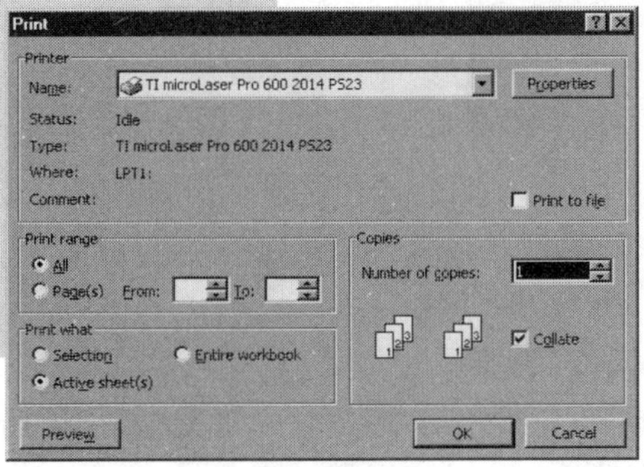

Figure 13.1 The Print dialog box enables you to choose nonstandard print settings like a different number of copies or pages.

Printer Properties

The first thing to do in the Print dialog box is check whether the printer that you want to use appears in the Name text box. If it doesn't, open the drop-down list and select it.

Note

If the printer you want to use doesn't appear on the drop-down list, it has not yet been set up in Windows 95, and you will need to set it up through the Control Panel before you can use it in any Windows program.

If the printer you want appears, the next thing to be concerned about is the printer settings. You don't have to check these every time you print, because once you set them the way you want them, they stay set. But the first time you use a particular printer, it is worth a look to make sure that everything is the way you like it. Click the Properties button next to the Name text box to display the printer's properties. Different printers show different tabs in the Properties dialog box; the ones for my printer (a PostScript laser model) appear in Figure 13.2.

Figure 13.2 Here are my printer's properties; yours may look somewhat different.

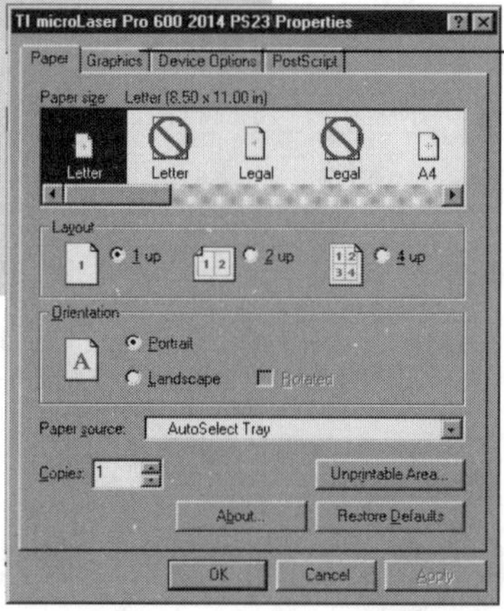

Following are some of the settings you may see on your printer's Properties dialog box and what to do with them:

- **Paper Size.** Choose what size of paper you are using in your printer. If your printer can't handle a certain size, it appears with a red circle and line (the international symbol for "anti"), as you can see in Figure 13.2.
- **Orientation.** You can choose between Portrait and Landscape. Beware, however, that if you set this to Landscape, you may get unintended Landscape printouts in other programs besides Excel; most people leave this set for Portrait and then set up Landscape for individual workbooks as needed within Excel. (You'll learn to do this later in the chapter.)

- **Copies.** As noted in the following sidebar, "Print or Properties: What's the Difference?," unless you always want more than one copy of every document you print in every program, leave this set to 1. You can always specify more than one copy of a particular printout in the Print dialog box.
- **Graphics Tab.** Almost all printers show a Graphics tab in their Properties dialog box, but the controls on it vary widely. Color printers have color controls; PostScript printers have Scaling. Most printers have something about halftoning too, which means how grayscale images are represented using black ink (with little screens of dots that represent shades of gray). You may also see settings for Resolution, Dithering, and Intensity. If you don't understand a setting, leave it as-is.
- **Device Options Tab.** Nearly all printers also have a Device Options tab, and again the options are different depending on the printer type. Again, if you don't understand a setting, it's best to leave it alone.

Some printers include a Print TrueType as Graphics check box or option button in their Properties. This has to do with the way that TrueType fonts are sent to the printer. If you are running into problems such as TrueType fonts not printing correctly or not thick or dark enough, or if you are getting `Out of Memory` error messages on your printer, try changing this setting to see whether it corrects the problem.

When you're finished with your printer's Properties dialog box, click OK to close it and return to the Print dialog box in Excel.

There is one last control in the Printer section of the Print dialog box: a little check box called Print To File. When you select this check box, instead of printing when you click OK, Excel opens a Print To File dialog box (see Figure 13.3) where you can specify a file name (with the extension .PRN) to print to. This is a handy feature if the printer that you want to print from is not attached to your computer or not available at the moment, but the computer to which the correct printer is attached does not have Excel. You print to a file, take the file on a floppy disk to a computer attached to that printer, and then copy the file to the printer.

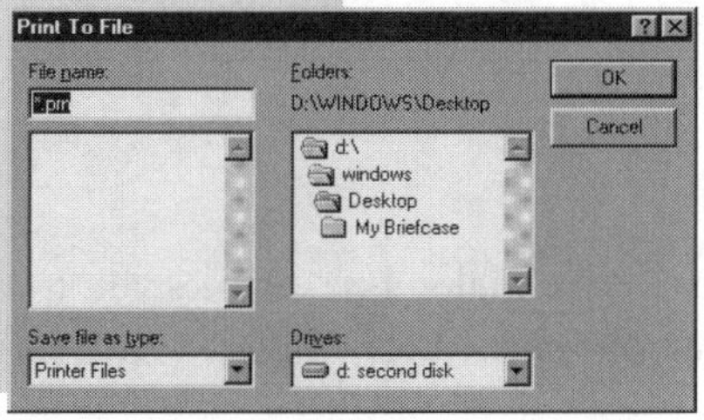

Figure 13.3 When you mark the Print To File check box, this dialog box appears when you click OK to print.

Print or Properties: What's the Difference?

Some options can be set in two places: in the Properties dialog box for your printer and in Excel's Print dialog box. Examples of this include page orientation and number of copies. It may seem like the same thing to set these in either spot, but it's not.

Keep this firmly in mind: when you make changes in the Properties dialog box for your printer, you are making base-level changes to the way that printer operates in Windows in general—and in all Windows-based programs. For example, if you set the number of copies to 2, your printer will print two copies of every single thing you print in every Windows program. If you set the orientation to Landscape, Landscape becomes the default orientation for every program that doesn't specify a particular orientation.

In contrast, when you set options in the Print or Page Setup dialog boxes in Excel, the settings are applicable only in Excel, and in some cases only in the active workbook.

Some settings build upon each other in ways you might not intend. For example, if you specify two copies in the Properties dialog box, and two copies in the Print dialog box, you will get a total of four copies. That's because Excel sends two copies of your work to the printer driver, and when they get there, the printer driver says "let's see, you want two copies of everything, so here's two copies of each of the two things you sent me."

Be mindful when making changes to the Properties dialog box for your printer! The settings are easy enough to change back if you decide you're unhappy with your settings (just click the Restore Defaults button), but if you forget you made those setting changes, you may find yourself with a problem that's hard to diagnose (like the extra copies issue just described or a printer that will print only in Landscape orientation).

Print Range

The Print Range area of the Print dialog box enables you to specify a certain number of pages to print from your worksheet, if the worksheet contains enough data

More About Printing to a File

Notice under the Name list in the Print dialog box, there are some settings you cannot change, like Status, Type, and Where. Where tells what port the printer is installed on, such as LPT1 or COM2. You can't change this from within Excel.

If it says FILE rather than a port, that means that someone has set up that printer to always print to a file. It's as if the Print To File check box in the Print dialog box were permanently marked (even though it may not appear to be marked at all when that printer is selected). If a particular printer is never directly available to your computer, for example, it would be appropriate for that printer to be set up this way.

If you need to change the port that a printer is on, you must change it from Windows 95. Choose Start, Settings, Printers to display a window with icons for each installed printer. Then right-click on the printer and choose Properties. You'll see the Properties dialog box again, but this time with more tabs to choose from. Click the Details tab, and then choose a different port from the Print to the Following Port dropdown list, as shown below.

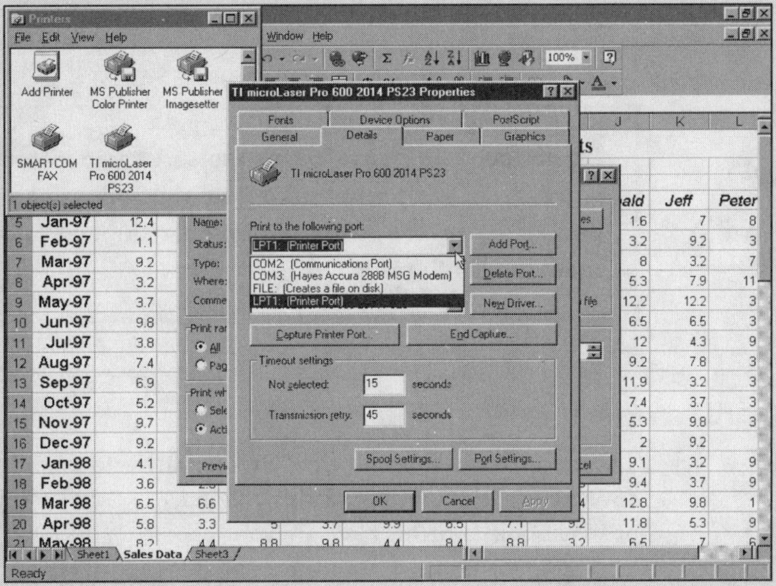

> After you have printed to a file, copy the file onto a diskette or other portable medium and take it to a computer that's attached to that printer. Then in Windows 95, open the Printers window (Start, Settings, Printers), open a window for the disk (My Computer/double-click on the drive), and then drag the file to the printer icon and drop it there. This adds the file to that printer's queue.

to fill more than one page. The default is All, which prints everything on the worksheet. You can enter a range of pages if you prefer in the From and To boxes.

This feature can be handy, but not unless you know where the page breaks are going to fall. Otherwise, you will have no idea what data will actually be on a given page. Therefore, you probably won't enter a range of pages to print unless you have done one of the following:

- Printed the worksheet before
- Viewed the worksheet in Print Preview (covered at the end of this chapter)
- Manually entered your own page breaks (also covered later in the chapter)

I use this feature most often after I have printed the entire worksheet once. Inevitably, I'll find a misspelling or error on one page and need to reprint that page after I've made the correction. Setting the Print Range to include only the page I've corrected saves me paper.

Caution

> **Do not confuse *pages* with *sheets*. A sheet is sort of like a page in a work-book, but for the purposes of printing, page refers to a printed piece of paper. The information on a single worksheet may require many pages to print.**

Print What

The Print What section offers an alternative to using the Print Area command covered at the beginning of this chapter to specify a certain part of a worksheet or workbook to print. Here are your choices:

- **Selection.** To use this, you must have selected a range of cells before you opened the Print dialog box. If you did and you choose Selection, only that range will print. This is kind of like using the Set Print Area command without the hassle of having to Clear Print Area afterwards.

- **Active Sheet(s).** To use this, you must either want to print only the active sheet (the one on top when you opened the Print dialog box), or you must have selected more than one sheet. (Remember, to select multiple sheets, hold down the Shift key while you click on their tabs.) This is the default.
- **Entire Workbook.** This prints every sheet in the workbook that has something on it. (It doesn't print totally blank sheets.)

Copies

The Copies options are pretty straightforward. How many copies do you want? One is the default. What's a little less straightforward is the Collate check box underneath. This feature is applicable only if both of the following are true:

- You are printing more than one copy.
- The selection you are printing has more than one page.

Collating means printing the copies so that they're ready to distribute, like this: Copy 1 page 1, Copy 1 page 2; Copy 2 page 1, Copy 2 page 2. If you deselect this check box, all the copies of each page will print in a row, like this: Copy 1 page 1, Copy 2 page 1; Copy 1 page 2, Copy 2 page 2.

Controlling Your Printout Appearance

Besides the print options you just learned about, there are several significant ways that you can enhance your printout's appearance. Strangely enough, these are not considered print options, even though they are applicable only when you print. Instead, they're called page setup options.

To access the page setup options, follow these steps:

1. Choose File, Page Setup. The Page Setup dialog box appears (see Figure 13.4).
2. Use the settings on each of the four tabs to set your page options. (See the sections that follow for details.)
3. Click OK to accept your settings.

You can jump quickly to one of three other screens with the command buttons available in the Page Setup dialog box:

- **Print.** Takes you to the Print dialog box (refer to Figure 13.1), useful if you're ready to print.

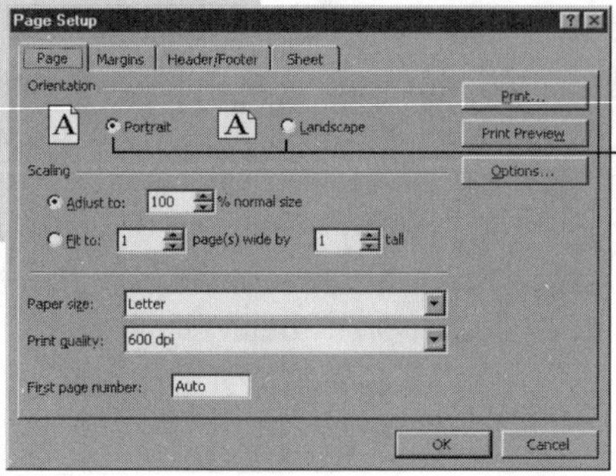

Figure 13.4 The Page Setup options enable you to enhance the look of the printed page.

- **Print Preview.** Takes you to Print Preview (covered at the end of this chapter), where you can check your work before printing.
- **Options**. Opens the Properties dialog box for the default printer (refer to Figure 13.2), so that you can change or confirm your printer's settings.

Setting Portrait or Landscape Orientation

The Page tab (see Figure 13.4) enables you to set options that affect how the information you print will appear on the printed page.

The most obvious of these is Orientation. Remember, you saw some orientation controls in the Properties dialog box for your printer, and I promised you would be able to set this in Excel instead? This is the place.

- **Portrait.** Taller than it is wide. This is the normal orientation for most business letters and textual reports. Use it if your worksheet has many more rows than columns.
- **Landscape.** Wider than it is tall. This is the normal orientation for slides, charts, and some reports. Use it if your worksheet has many more columns than rows.

Even if your rows outnumber your columns, you may still want to print in Landscape orientation. Why? Because columns are typically wider than rows are tall, so you can fit many more rows than columns on a page. For example, take a look at Figures 13.5 and 13.6. These show a worksheet printed in Portrait and Landscape orientations. Even though this worksheet had more rows than columns, it still looks better (and fits on fewer pages) in Landscape.

Figure 13.5 In Portrait orientation, this worksheet is split into two pages.

Acme Corporation Sales Results

	Bob	*Ted*	*Roy*	*Keith*	*Alice*	*Jordan*	*Debbie*	*Jenny*
Jan-97	12.4	10.1	3	12	12.5	5.4	3.2	1.1
Feb-97	1.1	3.2	10	3.4	9.2	9.4	7.4	12.8
Mar-97	9.2	12.4	7.7	9.9	3.2	6.9	12.9	5.3
Apr-97	3.2	5.3	6	4.4	3.7	3.2	3.7	12.2
May-97	3.7	12.6	12.8	2.3	9.4	3.7	9.8	6.5
Jun-97	9.8	9.2	5	7.4	6.9	9.7	3.8	12
Jul-97	3.8	4.1	12.5	6.5	3.2	7	7.4	9.2
Aug-97	7.4	3.6	9.2	3.7	3.7	6.4	5.3	3.2
Sep-97	6.9	5.3	3.2	9.8	8.6	12.8	9.4	3.7
Oct-97	5.2	9.4	3.7	5.3	4.4	5.3	9.2	9.8
Nov-97	9.7	1.4	9.8	12.6	2	8.5	3.2	7.4
Dec-97	9.2	11.8	3.8	1.9	9.1	3.2	3.7	9.5
Jan-98	4.1	3.4	7.4	9.4	7	3.7	9.8	7.4
Feb-98	3.6	2.5	6.9	6.9	9.8	6.3	3.2	5.3
Mar-98	6.5	6.6	6.8	3.2	12.7	12.2	3.7	9.4
Apr-98	5.8	3.3	5	3.7	9.9	6.5	7.1	9.2
May-98	8.2	4.4	8.8	9.8	4.4	8.4	8.8	3.2
Jun-98	2.1	2	4.4	3.8	8.7	12.2	4.4	7
Jul-98	1.9	9.1	2.3	7.4	9.4	6.5	8.3	9.8
Aug-98	9.4	7.7	8.9	5.3	1.4	12.8	7	12.7
Sep-98	2.3	6	9.9	9.4	11.8	9.2	7.2	5.3
Oct-98	3.8	12.8	8.2	1.4	6.5	3.2	3.2	9.8
Nov-98	8.4	11.8	3.7	11.8	5.8	3.7	1.1	3.8
Dec-98	4.2	6.7	7.3	3.4	8.2	9.8	2.2	7.4

Donald	*Jeff*	*Peter*	*Margaret*
1.6	7	8.5	9.4
3.2	9.2	3.7	12.4
8	3.2	7.1	11.9
5.3	7.9	11.7	7.4
12.2	12.2	3.2	5.3
6.5	6.5	3.7	2
12	4.3	9.8	6.5
9.2	7.8	3.2	12.8
11.9	3.2	3.7	9.2
7.4	3.7	3.2	7.6
5.3	9.8	3.7	11.5
2	9.2	2	1.9
9.1	3.2	9.1	9.4
9.4	3.7	9.2	6.9
12.8	9.8	1.9	9.1
11.8	5.3	9.4	12.2
6.5	7	6.9	6.5
12.8	9.3	11.6	7.5
9.2	12.2	3.7	3.2
8.2	6.5	7.4	3.7
9.2	7.3	6.5	10.2
3.2	8.6	12.8	6.5
3.7	4.4	9.2	5.8
9.8	11.7	6.5	8.2

Figure 13.6 In Landscape orientation, the same worksheet fits on a single page.

Acme Corporation Sales Results

	Bob	*Ted*	*Roy*	*Keith*	*Alice*	*Jordan*	*Debbie*	*Jenny*	*Donald*	*Jeff*	*Peter*	*Margaret*
Jan-97	12.4	10.1	3	12	12.5	5.4	3.2	1.1	1.6	7	8.5	9.4
Feb-97	1.1	3.2	10	3.4	9.2	9.4	7.4	12.8	3.2	9.2	3.7	12.4
Mar-97	9.2	12.4	7.7	9.9	3.2	6.9	12.9	5.3	8	3.2	7.1	11.9
Apr-97	3.2	5.3	6	4.4	3.7	3.2	3.7	12.2	5.3	7.9	11.7	7.4
May-97	3.7	12.6	12.8	2.3	9.4	3.7	9.8	6.5	12.2	12.2	3.2	5.3
Jun-97	9.8	9.2	5	7.4	6.9	9.7	3.8	12	6.5	6.5	3.7	2
Jul-97	3.8	4.1	12.5	6.5	3.2	7	7.4	9.2	12	4.3	9.8	6.5
Aug-97	7.4	3.6	9.2	3.7	3.7	6.4	5.3	3.2	9.2	7.8	3.2	12.8
Sep-97	6.9	5.3	3.2	9.8	8.6	12.8	9.4	3.7	11.9	3.2	3.7	9.2
Oct-97	5.2	9.4	3.7	5.3	4.4	5.3	9.2	9.8	7.4	3.7	3.2	7.6
Nov-97	9.7	1.4	9.8	12.6	2	8.5	3.2	7.4	5.3	9.8	3.7	11.5
Dec-97	9.2	11.8	3.8	1.9	9.1	3.2	3.7	9.5	2	9.2	2	1.9
Jan-98	4.1	3.4	7.4	9.4	7	3.7	9.8	7.4	9.1	3.2	9.1	9.4
Feb-98	3.6	2.5	6.9	6.9	9.8	6.3	3.2	5.3	9.4	3.7	9.2	6.9
Mar-98	6.5	6.6	6.8	3.2	12.7	12.2	3.7	9.4	12.8	9.8	1.9	9.1
Apr-98	5.8	3.3	5	3.7	9.9	6.5	7.1	9.2	11.8	5.3	9.4	12.2
May-98	8.2	4.4	8.8	9.8	4.4	8.4	8.8	3.2	6.5	7	6.9	6.5
Jun-98	2.1	2	4.4	3.8	8.7	12.2	4.4	7	12.8	9.3	11.6	7.5
Jul-98	1.9	9.1	2.3	7.4	9.4	6.5	8.3	9.8	9.2	12.2	3.7	3.2
Aug-98	9.4	7.7	8.9	5.3	1.4	12.8	7	12.7	8.2	6.5	7.4	3.7
Sep-98	2.3	6	9.9	9.4	11.8	9.2	7.2	5.3	9.2	7.3	6.5	10.2
Oct-98	3.8	12.8	8.2	1.4	6.5	3.2	3.2	9.8	3.2	8.6	12.8	6.5
Nov-98	8.4	11.8	3.7	11.8	5.8	3.7	1.1	3.8	3.7	4.4	9.2	5.8
Dec-98	4.2	6.7	7.3	3.4	8.2	9.8	2.2	7.4	9.8	11.7	6.5	8.2

Scaling: Making It All Fit

The next feature on the Page tab is Scaling. Scaling is such a great idea that it's a wonder someone didn't think of it back in the very first version of Excel. Instead of struggling with resizing columns and fonts to make your work fit on one page (or on a certain number of pages), you simply turn on scaling, and Excel resizes the print area as needed to fit the specified number of pages.

For example, say that the worksheet in Figure 13.6 had one more column added to it, but that that column printed on a subsequent page. You would click the Fit To option button (see Figure 13.7) and then type in **1** and **1** in the Wide and Tall text boxes.

The other way to use scaling is as a percentage of the actual size. The default is 100% of actual size, but you can type any percentage you want into the Adjust To text box. If you want to see the results of the setting before you print, use Print Preview (covered later in this chapter).

Figure 13.7 You can enter a percentage to scale to, or a number of pages.

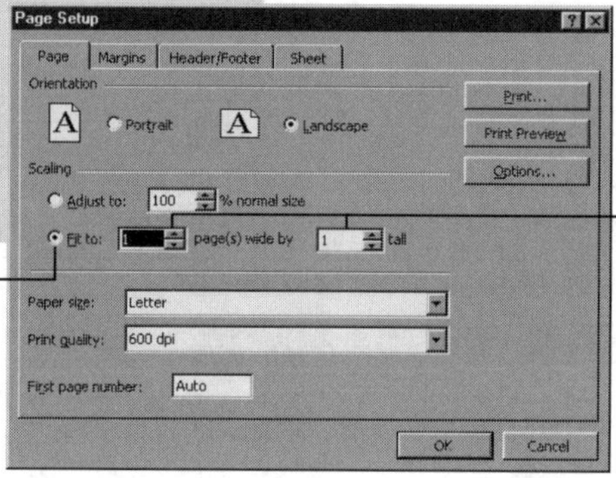

Setting the Paper Size and Print Quality

These two options you probably won't change very often. If you want to print a particular worksheet on a different size paper than usual, you select the different size from the Paper Size drop-down list. Keep in mind, however, that if your printer always uses a different size of paper, you should set it in the Properties dialog box for your printer (discussed earlier in the chapter) rather than here.

Some printers give you a choice of print qualities (such as 300 or 600 dots per inch, or dpi). If your printer does, you'll have a choice of resolutions in the Print Quality drop-down list. The general rule of thumb is to choose a lower number for faster printing and a higher number for better quality printing. However, with numbers above 300 dpi, the average person will not notice much difference in the printout quality. Graphic quality will be more noticeable than text. If your printer is fairly fast, set this to the highest number available; if you find yourself often waiting impatiently on your printer, set this to the lowest number available.

Setting Your Page Margins

On the Margins tab (see Figure 13.8), you can choose margins for your printouts. Margins refer to the amount of blank space at each edge of the printout—the distance from the edge of the page to the first bit of ink on each side.

Tip

If you print a worksheet that's smaller than will fit on the page, you may have additional white space at the right and bottom edges. This is normal. Also, if you use the Fit To feature described in the Scaling section earlier in the chapter, there may be additional white space on certain pages to conform to the number of pages you specified. You can't fix that problem by changing the margins here; you must adjust the number of pages you are trying to fit to.

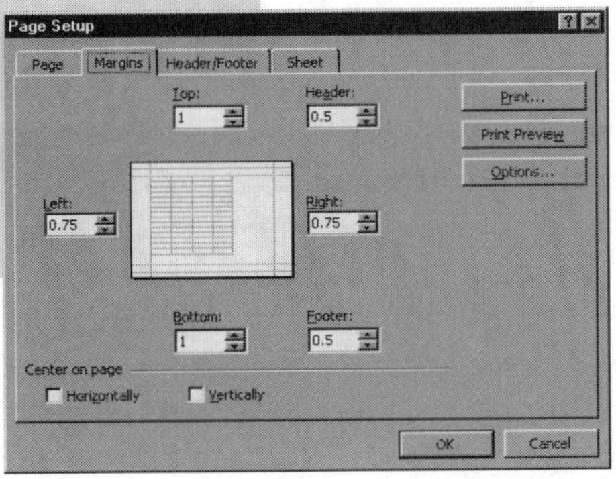

Figure 13.8 The Margins tab contains the margin settings for the workbook's printouts.

To set the margins, change the numbers in the Top, Bottom, Right, and Left text boxes.

Caution

Be aware that the sample shown in the middle of the dialog box (refer to Figure 13.8) does not change to reflect your new settings; you have to experiment with the settings and with Print Preview to get the look you're after.

A nice feature in Excel 97 is the capability to center the printout either vertically or horizontally (or both) on the page. Select the Vertically and/or Horizontally check box to make it so. This has no effect if the worksheet exactly fits on the page; it works only if there is extra white space either at the top or right edge.

If you use headers and/or footers on your printout (as you'll learn to do in the following section), you can specify their positions with the Header and Footer text boxes on this tab. Enter the amount of white space you want between the top or bottom edge of the page and the beginning of the header or footer.

Note

If your header or footer numbers are not sufficiently smaller than your top or bottom margin numbers, the areas will overlap, and your header or footer will print over the top of your data. A good rule of thumb is to make sure that your header and footer margins are at least 1/2-inch less than your top and bottom margins. If you use multiline headers or footers with large fonts in them, you may need to allow even more room.

Headers and Footers

You have no doubt seen headers and footers in use, everywhere from your daily newspaper to the novel that you're reading. They run across the top and bottom of each page, telling the name of the publication, the page number, and often extra information like the date of publication and the author's name. Including these on your Excel printouts adds a touch of class and also makes it much easier to reassemble a dropped stack of papers in the correct order (which you can't truly appreciate the value of until it's happened to you!). Figure 13.9 shows a page that uses a header and a footer.

In some spreadsheet programs (not naming any names, but if you've used others, you may know who they are), it is fairly difficult to set up headers and footers that contain variable information like the page number or the current date. You have to use many obscure codes like &p&d that you must look up in a thick reference manual. Not so with Excel—all that code business is built-in in plain English.

You set up headers and footers on the Header/Footer tab (surprise!) of the Page Setup dialog box, shown in Figure 13.10.

The easiest way to set up a header or footer is to choose one of the preset ones from the Header or Footer drop-down list. These presets contain the most common text and fields that the average person would want to use, including codes for the date, time, page number, document name, author name, company name, and so on.

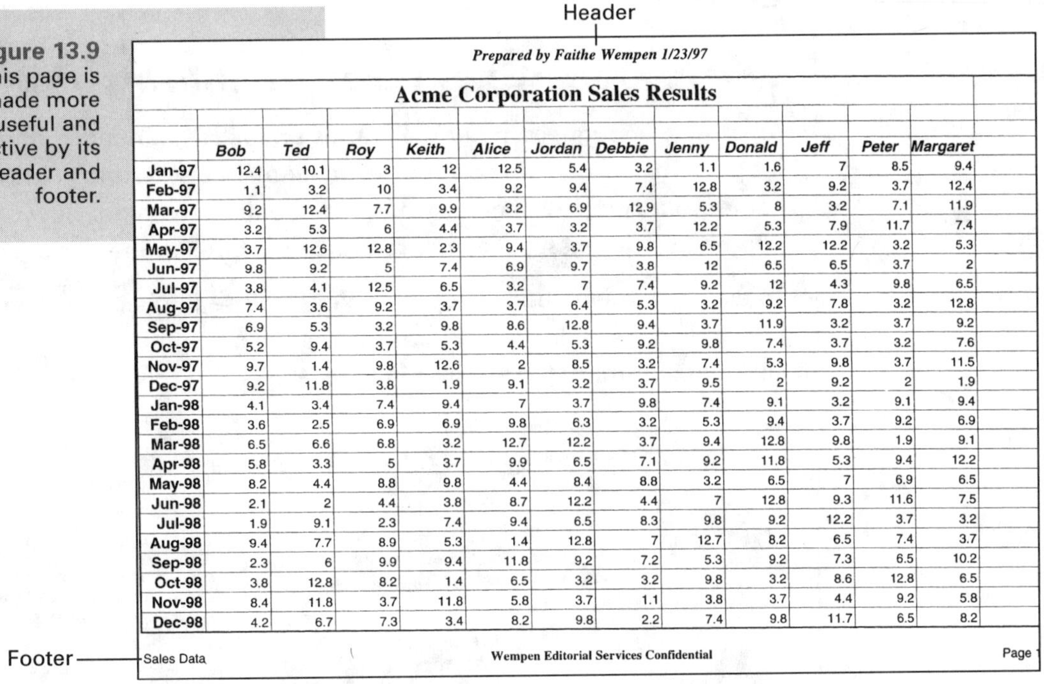

Acme Corporation Sales Results

	Bob	Ted	Roy	Keith	Alice	Jordan	Debbie	Jenny	Donald	Jeff	Peter	Margaret
Jan-97	12.4	10.1	3	12	12.5	5.4	3.2	1.1	1.6	7	8.5	9.4
Feb-97	1.1	3.2	10	3.4	9.2	9.4	7.4	12.8	3.2	9.2	3.7	12.4
Mar-97	9.2	12.4	7.7	9.9	3.2	6.9	12.9	5.3	8	3.2	7.1	11.9
Apr-97	3.2	5.3	6	4.4	3.7	3.2	3.7	12.2	5.3	7.9	11.7	7.4
May-97	3.7	12.6	12.8	2.3	9.4	3.7	9.8	6.5	12.2	12.2	3.2	5.3
Jun-97	9.8	9.2	5	7.4	6.9	9.7	3.8	12	6.5	6.5	3.7	2
Jul-97	3.8	4.1	12.5	6.5	3.2	7	7.4	9.2	12	4.3	9.8	6.5
Aug-97	7.4	3.6	9.2	3.7	3.7	6.4	5.3	3.2	9.2	7.8	3.2	12.8
Sep-97	6.9	5.3	3.2	9.8	8.6	12.8	9.4	3.7	11.9	3.2	3.7	9.2
Oct-97	5.2	9.4	3.7	5.3	4.4	5.3	9.2	9.8	7.4	3.7	3.2	7.6
Nov-97	9.7	1.4	9.8	12.6	2	8.5	3.2	7.4	5.3	9.8	3.7	11.5
Dec-97	9.2	11.8	3.8	1.9	9.1	3.2	3.7	9.5	2	9.2	2	1.9
Jan-98	4.1	3.4	7.4	9.4	7	3.7	9.8	7.4	9.1	3.2	9.1	9.4
Feb-98	3.6	2.5	6.9	6.9	9.8	6.3	3.2	5.3	9.4	3.7	9.2	6.9
Mar-98	6.5	6.6	6.8	3.2	12.7	12.2	3.7	9.4	12.8	9.8	1.9	9.1
Apr-98	5.8	3.3	5	3.7	9.9	6.5	7.1	9.2	11.8	5.3	9.4	12.2
May-98	8.2	4.4	8.8	9.8	4.4	8.4	8.8	3.2	6.5	7	6.9	6.5
Jun-98	2.1	2	4.4	3.8	8.7	12.2	4.4	7	12.8	9.3	11.6	7.5
Jul-98	1.9	9.1	2.3	7.4	9.4	6.5	8.3	9.8	9.2	12.2	3.7	3.2
Aug-98	9.4	7.7	8.9	5.3	1.4	12.8	7	12.7	8.2	6.5	7.4	3.7
Sep-98	2.3	6	9.9	9.4	11.8	9.2	7.2	5.3	9.2	7.3	6.5	10.2
Oct-98	3.8	12.8	8.2	1.4	6.5	3.2	3.2	9.8	3.2	8.6	12.8	6.5
Nov-98	8.4	11.8	3.7	11.8	5.8	3.7	1.1	3.8	3.7	4.4	9.2	5.8
Dec-98	4.2	6.7	7.3	3.4	8.2	9.8	2.2	7.4	9.8	11.7	6.5	8.2

Figure 13.9 This page is made more useful and attractive by its header and footer.

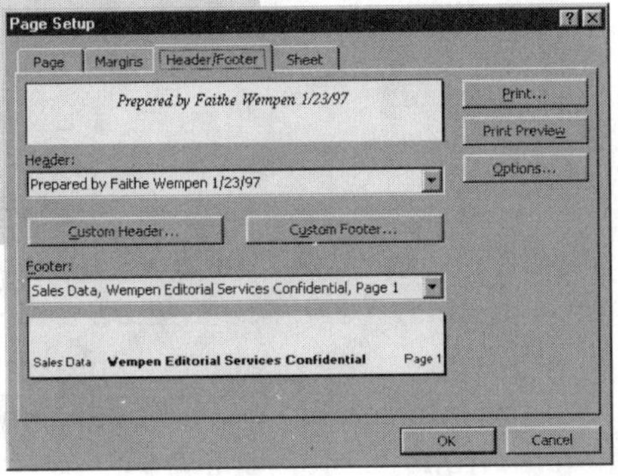

Figure 13.10 Create your headers and footers here, or use the preset ones.

If you don't like any of the preset headers or footers, or if you want to start with one of them and then make some modifications, select the one to start with and then click the Custom Header (or Custom Footer) button. The Header or Footer dialog box appears, as shown in Figure 13.11. (They both have the same controls.)

Where Does Excel Get Its Information?

Amazingly enough, many of the entries on the Header and Footer drop-down lists contain correct information about you, including your name, your company's name, the current date, and so on. How did that information get there? It came from the workbook properties sheet.

To display the workbook properties sheet, close the Page Setup dialog box and choose File, Properties. Then, if it isn't already displayed, click the Summary tab, as shown here:

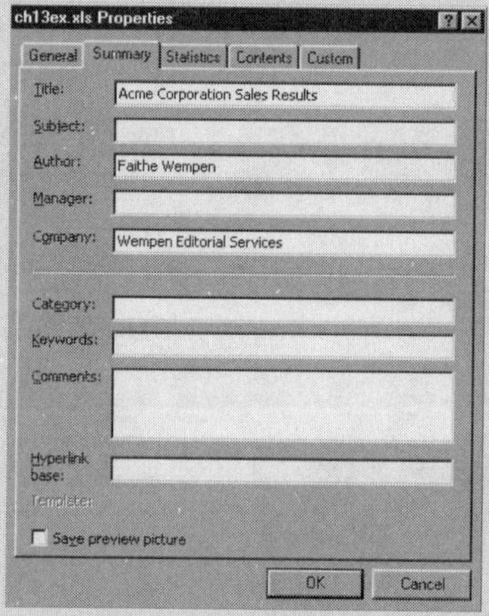

In particular, Excel pulls information from the Title, Author, and Company fields into the Header and Footer drop-down lists. The correct information may already be here about your name and company because you entered the information when you installed Excel. If not, or if the information is wrong, simply change it. You can enter other information here about the workbook too, but it won't transfer automatically to the Header and Footer drop-down lists.

As you can see in Figure 13.11, the header or footer is broken down into three sections: Left Section, Center Section, and Right Section. You can put information into any or all of them, or remove information if you don't want it there. For example, in Figure 13.11, I have removed the information from the Left and

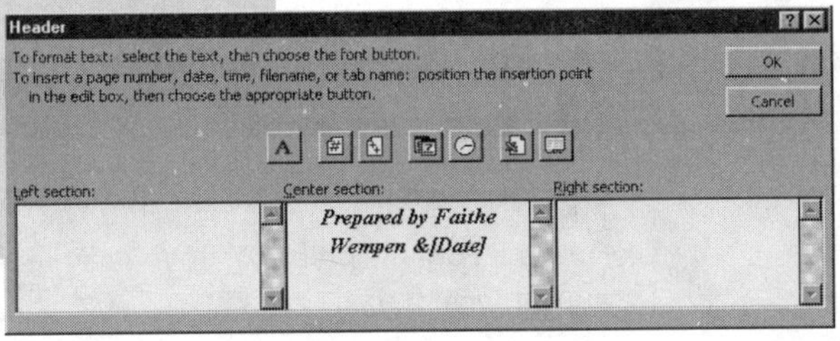

Figure 13.11 Set up a custom header or footer to say exactly what you want it to say.

Right sections, leaving information only in the Center. Look at the header in Figure 13.9 to see how this will look when printed. Each section will be aligned on the printout as its name implies (at the left or right margin or centered). Look at the footer in Figure 13.9 for examples of left and right section use.

There are two ways to put information in a section: type in regular text, or click buttons to insert codes. In Figure 13.11, you see both in use: the text **Prepared by Faithe Wempen** is regular typed text, and the code **&[Date]** has been inserted by clicking a button.

Typing text is straightforward: click in the desired text box and type. To insert a code at the insertion point, click one of the buttons shown in Table 13.1.

Hands On: Changing the Font for a Header or Footer

To change the font for part of a header or footer, follow these steps:

1. In the Header or Footer dialog box, select the text you want to format. This is important; merely having the insertion point in the correct text box is not enough to affect the already typed text. You must select it.
2. Click the Font button. The Font dialog box appears, as shown in Figure 13.12.
3. Select the Font, Font Style, Font Size, Underline, and other effects you want.
4. Click OK to return to the Header or Footer dialog box.
5. Repeat steps 1 through 4 to format different text until all the text is formatted the way you want it.
6. When you are finished setting up your custom header or footer, click OK to return to the Page Setup dialog box.

SEE CHAPTER 11 TO LEARN MORE ABOUT THE CONTROLS IN THE FONT DIALOG BOX.

Table 13.1 Header/Footer Icons

Icon	Name	Description
	Font	Opens a Font dialog box that you can use to change the appearance of the text.
	Page Number code	Prints the correct page number on each page.
	Total Pages code	Prints the total number of pages. This is useful in situations where you want something like "Page 1 of 12," "Page 2 of 12," and so on.
	Date code	Prints the date that the printout is being printed. It takes the date from your computer's internal clock.
	Time code	Prints the time that the printout is being printed.
	Workbook Name code	Prints the name of the workbook file.
	Worksheet Tab code	Prints the name of the worksheet tab. (Remember, you can change this by double-clicking on the tab and typing a new name.)

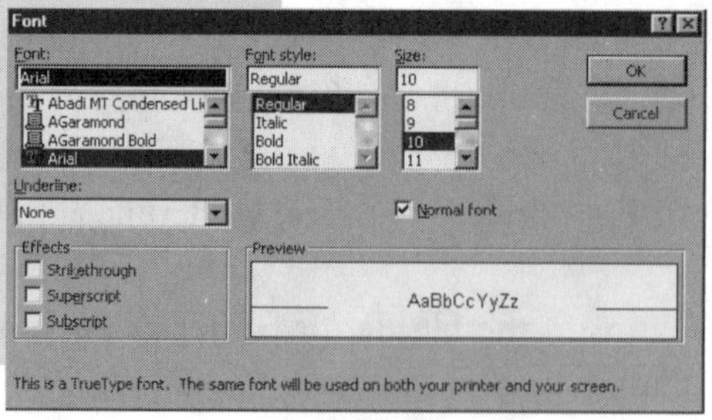

Figure 13.12 Use the Font dialog box to set the appearance of header or footer text just as you used it to format your cells.

Your header and/or footer is ready to go; you can check it out in Print Preview, discussed at the end of this chapter.

Print Area Revisited

When you look at the Sheet tab in the Page Setup dialog box, the first thing you see is the Print Area text box (see Figure 13.13). Now, where have you seen this before? That's right, at the beginning of this chapter, you learned that you could set the print area with the File, Print Area, Set Print Area command. If you do that, the range you choose appears in the Print Area text box on the Sheet tab. You can also enter the range directly into the Sheet tab, bypassing the File menu command.

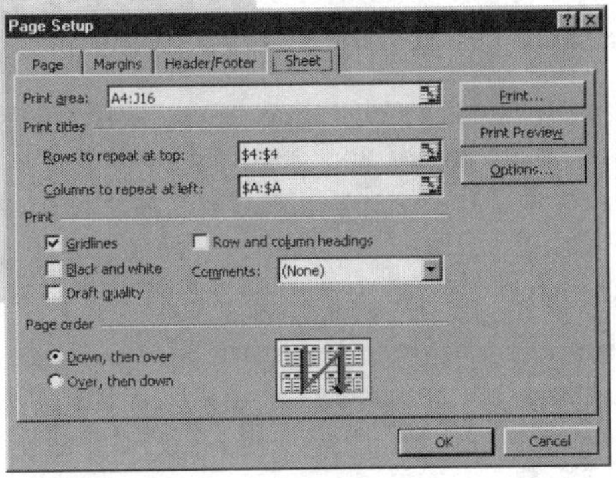

Figure 13.13 Use the Sheet tab to set print area, repeating rows and columns, gridlines, and more.

Printing Certain Rows or Columns on Every Page

SEE CHAPTER 7 IF YOU DON'T REMEMBER FREEZING ROWS AND COLUMNS.

Remember in Chapter 7, when you learned how to freeze the rows and columns that contained your titles so that you could always see them even when you scrolled far away from them? The same principle applies when printing. You can "freeze" the row and column titles so that they appear on every page of the printout. This is especially nice if you have many rows and columns on many pages because your reader doesn't have to turn back to the first page to see what each row and column represents.

To specify which rows and columns should be repeated on each page, enter them in the Rows To Repeat at Top and Columns To Repeat at Left text boxes, as shown in Figure 13.13. You must enter a range, even if it is only a single row or column. Excel also expects you to enter them in absolute reference format, and as you know from Chapter 9, that means dollar signs ($). So, as you can see in Figure 13.13, to repeat row 4 at the top of each page, you would enter **$4:$4**. To repeat column A at the left of each page, you would enter **$A:$A**.

Tip

Notice in Figure 13.13 that these first three text boxes have Collapse Dialog buttons. You've seen these before in Chapter 8: they shrink the dialog box out of the way so that you can select cells with the mouse instead of typing the range. Feel free to use these if you find them helpful.

Gridlines and More: What To Print?

In the Print section on the Sheet tab (refer to Figure 13.13), you'll find an assortment of controls that help you specify what you want included on your printout:

- **Gridlines.** I change this setting more frequently than any other in this dialog box. By default, gridlines are turned off, so that you don't see them on your printout. But many times you will want to turn them on so that you don't have to rely on the borders you've added to the worksheet to be your guiding lines.
- **Black and White.** If you don't want any shades of gray or any color on your printout, click this check box. This is useful if you are creating black-and-white transparencies. Shading will be represented by black-and-white patterns, rather than actual gray.
- **Draft Quality.** Turning on Draft Quality makes the printer use a draft font, which makes it print faster. You won't notice much difference with a laser or inkjet printer, but it makes printing much faster on some dot-matrix models.
- **Row and Column Headings.** These are different from the headings you type in yourself for each row and column; in this case, Excel is referring to the actual row numbers and column letters. Most people don't want these printed, but if you do, select this check box.

COMMENTS ARE COVERED IN CHAPTER 7.

- **Comments.** This drop-down list enables you to select whether you want any comments to print that you have attached to cells. You can choose None (the default), At End of Sheet, or As Displayed On Sheet.

In What Order Will Pages Print?

This another setting that is an issue only if you are printing a worksheet that is too big to fit on one page both vertically and horizontally. For example, it might be two pages' worth across and three pages' worth down. In a case like that, you can tell Excel in what order the pages should print. The default is Down, Then Over. (Refer to the diagram at the bottom of Figure 13.13.) You can change this to Over, Then Down if you prefer. It doesn't make much difference unless you need to collate them in a certain way; if that's the case, it can save you a tremendous amount of hand-collating work.

Inserting and Removing Page Breaks

While we're on the subject of multiple pages, let's talk about page breaks. As you have seen, when you have more information on your worksheet than will fit on one printed page, Excel automatically starts a new page for you. You can see these in Page Break Preview view.

To enter Page Break Preview view, choose View, Page Break Preview, and then click OK at the informational dialog box that appears. In it, as you can see in Figure 13.14, you can clearly identify where the pages will break.

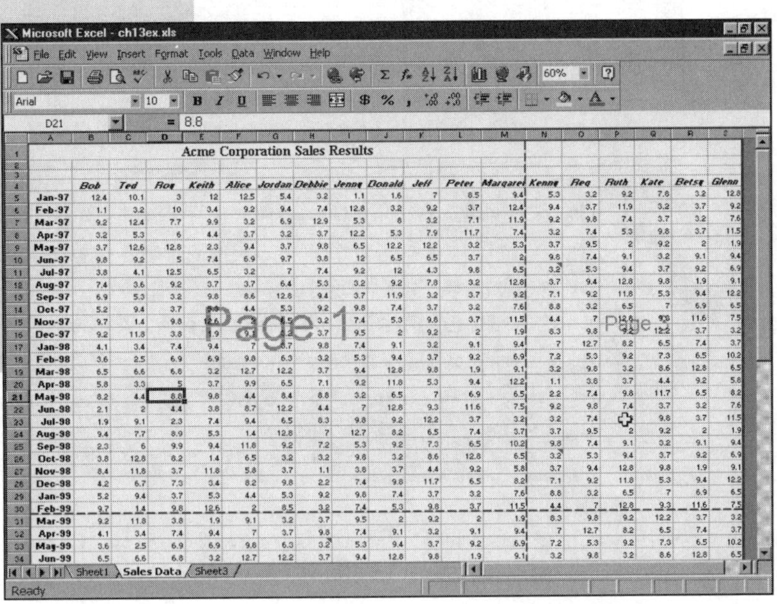

Figure 13.14 These dashed lines, which appear blue on-screen, show Excel's own page breaks. They are dynamic; they change when you change the margins or other page setup settings.

The dashed blue lines show where Excel's own page break decisions fall. You can adjust them by dragging these lines where you want the page breaks to be instead. To drag a line, follow these steps:

1. Position the mouse pointer over the page break line you want to move.
2. Drag the line to its new location.
3. Release the mouse button. The line becomes solid blue, indicating a user-specified page break (see Figure 13.15).

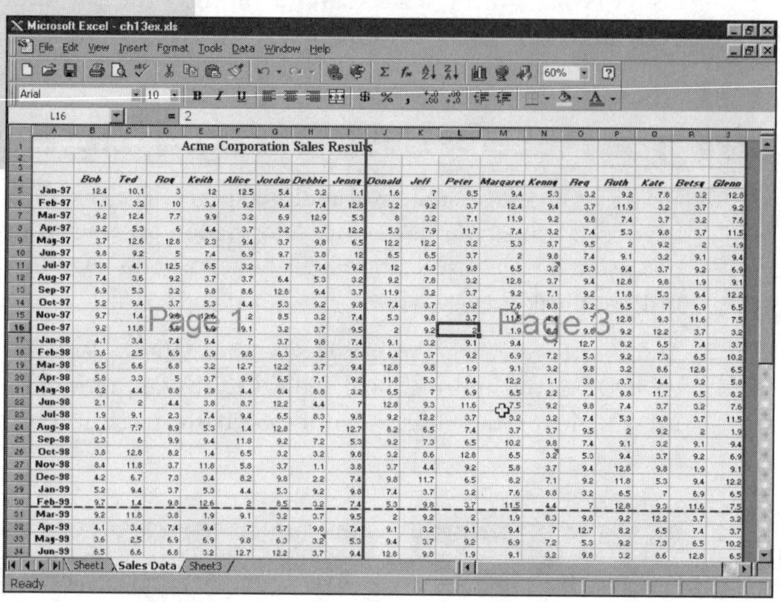

Figure 13.15 Solid blue lines indicate hard page breaks that I created myself.

Note

You can't drag these lines to put more on a page—only less. That's because Excel's own page breaks are based on the maximum that can fit on each page. If you drag a soft vertical page break to the right, Excel's page break will stay, and a new hard page break will be created in addition to it. If you want to fit more on a page, try some of the other techniques you have learned in this chapter, such as scaling.

When you move one of Excel's page break lines, you are in fact adding a "hard" page break of your own. Unlike Excel's "soft" page breaks, the hard page breaks you enter are fixed. If you change the margins or orientation, they won't budge. This means that you can potentially end up with a result you don't want, such as a few lonely rows or columns on a page all to themselves. Therefore it's important to check your work in Print Preview after you've set up page breaks. (I know, I keep promising coverage of that feature, and it's in the very next section.)

To remove a hard page break, right-click a cell below the horizontal page break or a cell to the right of the vertical page break, and then choose Insert, Remove Page Break. To remove all manual page breaks, right-click any cell on the worksheet, and then click Reset All Page Breaks on the shortcut menu.

You can also create and remove hard page breaks from Normal view. From Normal view, follow these steps to create page breaks:

1. Select where you want the page break to go:
   - To insert a vertical page break, select the column that you want to be the first one on the new page. The page break will appear to the left of the selected column.
   - To insert a horizontal page break, select the row that you want to be the first one on the new page. The page break will appear above the selected row.
   - To insert both a vertical and a horizontal page break, select a single cell. This cell will be the topmost, rightmost cell on the new page.
2. Choose Insert, Page Break. Excel adds your page break as a dashed line onscreen, as shown in Figure 13.16.

Note

If you don't see these lines on-screen where the page breaks should be, make sure that Excel is set up to show them. To check this, choose Tools, Options, and click the View tab. Make sure that the Page Breaks check box is marked. In Normal view, soft page breaks appear as dotted lines, and hard page breaks appear as dashed lines.

Figure 13.16
Page breaks appear as dotted or dashed lines in Normal view.

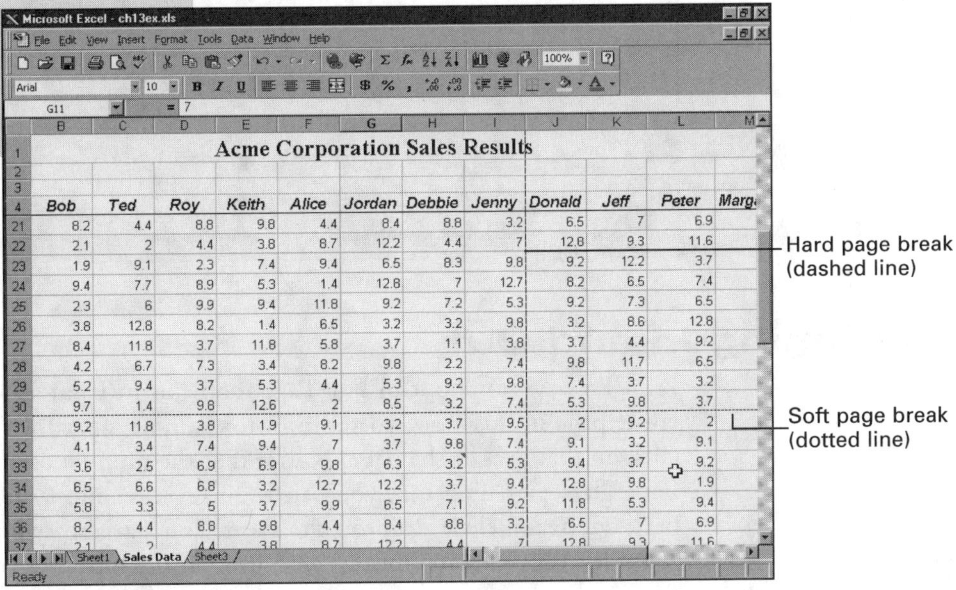

To remove a page break from Normal view, select the row, column, or cell that you selected when you created the page break, and then choose Insert, Remove Page Break.

Previewing Your Print Job

At last we come to this topic, after I've been promising it to you throughout the chapter! Print Preview is a great feature because it helps you save paper. You can try out your print and page setup settings on-screen, before you set your printer into action.

You can enter Print Preview (see Figure 13.17) in any of several ways: from the Print Preview buttons in the Page Setup or Print dialog boxes, by choosing File, Print Preview, or by clicking the Print Preview button on the toolbar.

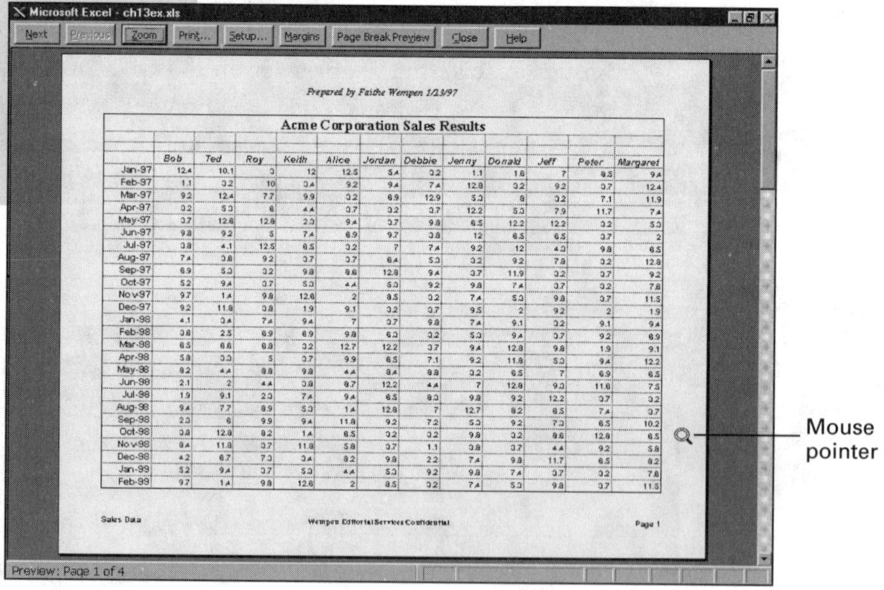

Figure 13.17 Print Preview lets you see exactly how the worksheet will look when printed.

Zooming In and Out

Print Preview starts out in Full Page mode, as in Figure 13.17. You can see one entire page in this view. To zoom in to examine a part of the page more closely, click on that part of the page. Notice that the mouse pointer looks like a magnifying glass, signaling that you can zoom by clicking. When you want to zoom back out again, click again on the sheet. You can also switch between these two zoom levels by clicking the Zoom button at the top of the screen.

Note

Unfortunately, unlike some other programs, such as Word, you cannot see more than one page at a time on-screen in Excel's Print Preview.

Modifying How the Printout Will Look

The bulk of the Print Preview controls have to do with modifying what you see on-screen. You can:

- Click the Setup button to open the Page Setup dialog box, covered earlier in the chapter.
- Click the Page Break Preview button to enter Page Break Preview view, which you learned about in the preceding section.
- Click the Margins button to show lines representing the margins on-screen, as shown in Figure 13.18. From here, you can position the mouse pointer over these lines and drag them to change the margins. (You can still change the margins in the Page Setup dialog box if you prefer that method.) Note that there are separate margin lines for the body of the printout and the header and footer.

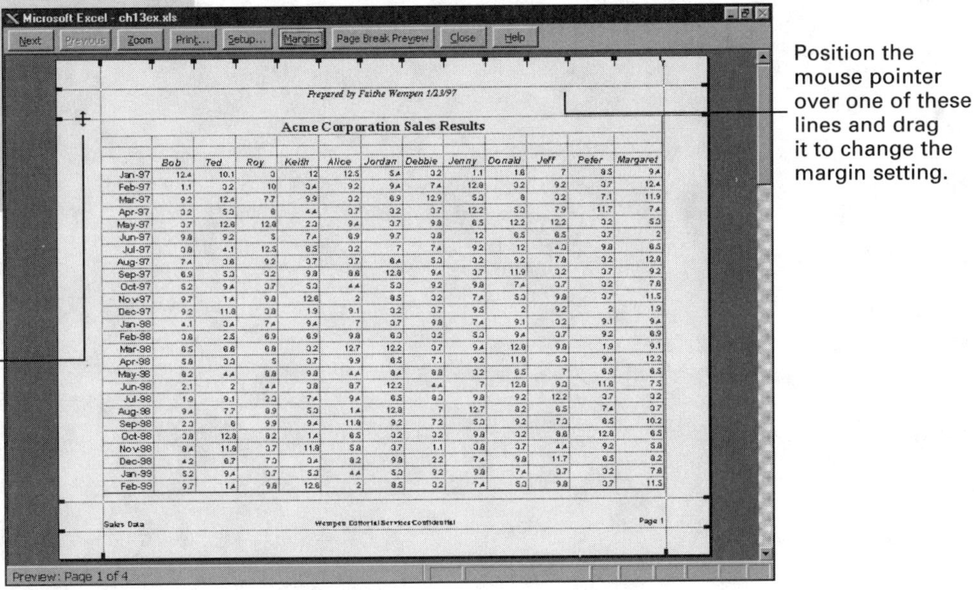

Figure 13.18 When you click the Margins button, lines appear showing the current margins.

Viewing Other Pages

If there is more than one page to print, the Next button is available at the top of the Print Preview screen. Click it to see the next page. If there are pages before the one you're currently viewing, the Previous button is also available. Click it to move to the previous page.

Closing Print Preview

There are two ways to close Print Preview:

- Click the Print button to enter the Print dialog box and then click OK to print.
- Click the Close button to leave Print Preview without printing (for example, if you realize that you need to do more editing before you print).

PART IV
Charts and Graphics

14

Creating Charts

In This Chapter

- Easy Charting with the ChartWizard
- What Types of Charts can Excel Create?
- Changing a Chart Type
- Choosing a Different Data Range
- Do You Want a Data Table with That?

Charting is a big subject in Excel, and its capabilities are powerful in this area. In this chapter, you'll ease into charting with Excel's ChartWizard and make some basic-level changes to a chart; then in the following chapter, you'll learn how to take control over the finer aspects of a chart.

Introducing ChartWizard

ChartWizard is another of Excel's "wish-come-true" features. Many users told Microsoft they wished they could just click a button and create a chart out of their data, and Microsoft listened—that's exactly what ChartWizard does.

The best way to see ChartWizard in action is to try it out, so you'll do that in the following Hands On sections. You'll create two different charts—a simple pie chart and a slightly more complicated bar chart.

Hands On: Creating a Pie Chart

Say that you need to make a simple pie chart showing the data in Figure 14.1. Enter the data in Figure 14.1 into a blank worksheet, and then perform the following steps to make the chart.

Figure 14.1 Enter this data in Excel for the example chart you're going to make.

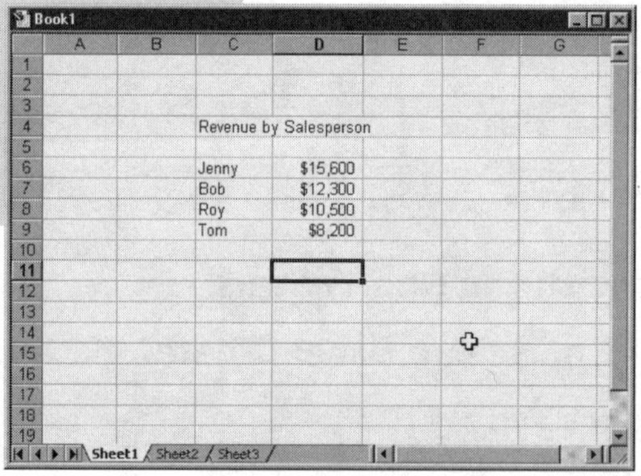

1. Select the range C6:D9.
2. Choose Insert, Chart or click the ChartWizard button on the toolbar. The ChartWizard - Step 1 of 4 dialog box appears.
3. Select Pie in the Chart Type list. The Chart Sub-Type list shows the various kinds of pie charts available (see Figure 14.2).
4. Click on the middle subtype in the top row (a 3-D pie). Then click Next to display the ChartWizard - Step 2 of 4 dialog box (see Figure 14.3).
5. Because you already selected the correct range (step 1), it appears in the Data Range text box, as shown in Figure 14.3. Click Next to display the ChartWizard - Step 3 of 4 dialog box (see Figure 14.4).

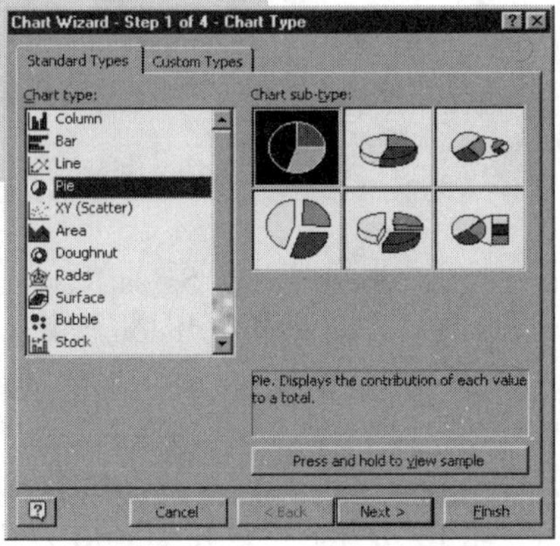

Figure 14.2
The first step is to choose a chart type.

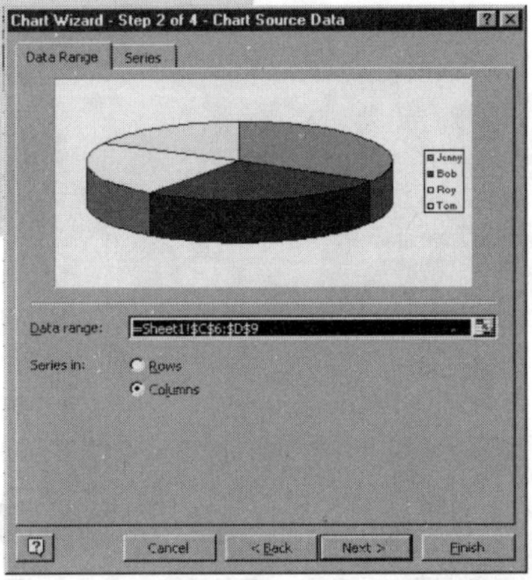

Figure 14.3
The second step is to make sure that the right data is selected to be charted.

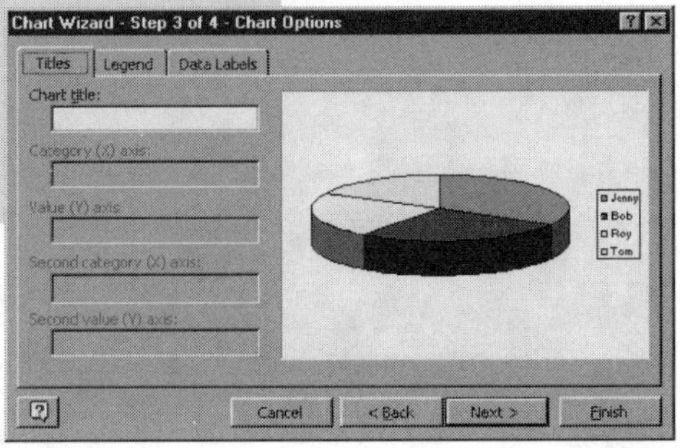

Figure 14.4
In this dialog box, you can enter a title for the chart.

Note

If the Data Range text box hadn't contained the correct range, you could have retyped it or clicked the Collapse Dialog button and selected the range from the worksheet.

6. In the Chart Title text box, type the title **Sales Revenue**. Then click Next to display the ChartWizard - Step 4 of 4 dialog box shown in Figure 14.5.
7. The last step is to choose the location for the chart. For this example, click As Object In.
8. Make sure that Sheet1 (or the sheet name where you originally typed the data you used) is selected from the drop-down list next to As Object In.
9. Click Finish. The chart appears floating on the worksheet, as shown in Figure 14.6. From here you can move it, modify it, and so on.

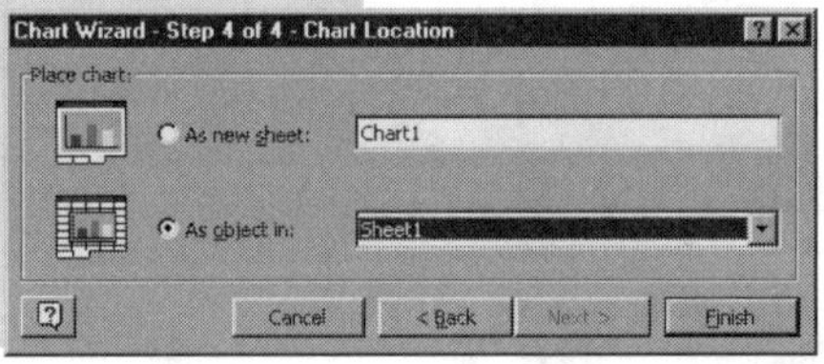

Figure 14.5 The last step is to decide whether the chart should be on its own sheet.

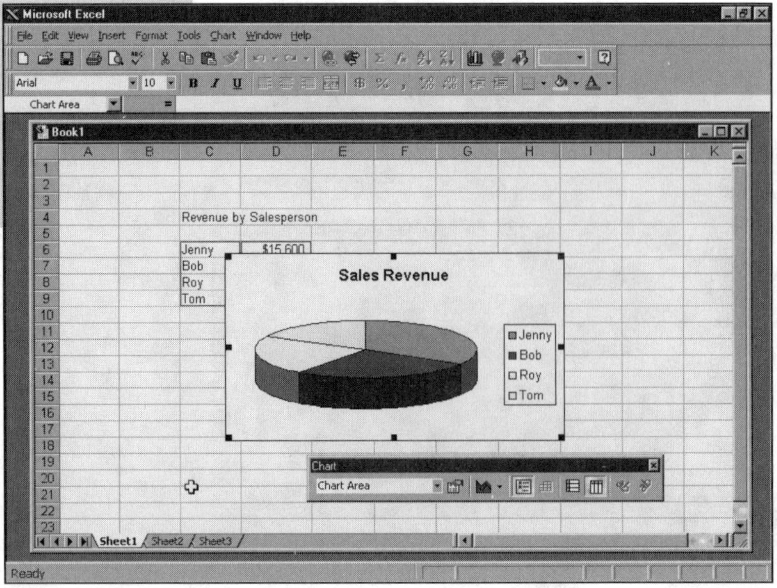

Figure 14.6 Because you chose As Object In in step 7, the chart appears as a floating object on the worksheet.

Note

Don't worry if the chart doesn't appear exactly where you want it on the sheet; later in this chapter you'll learn how to move and resize a chart on a sheet.

Hands On: Creating a Bar Chart

Now you'll tackle a slightly more complex chart—a bar chart showing multiple series. A *series* is the group of data points for one row or column. For example, in Figure 14.7, the information in each row—the data for each salesperson—could be considered series.

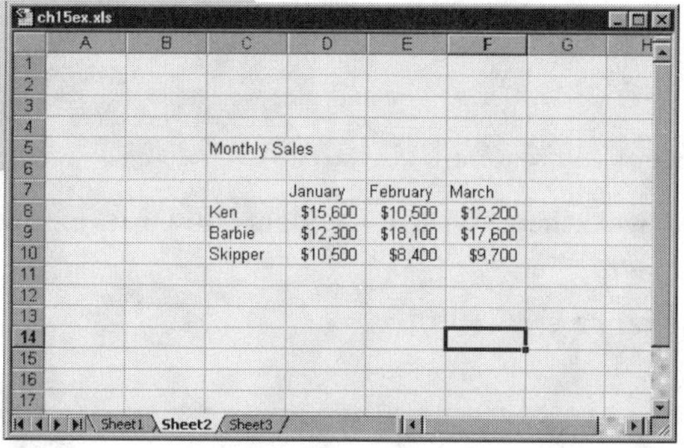

Figure 14.7 There are three series here, one for each person.

YOU'LL LEARN TO MANIPULATE AND MODIFY THE CHART IN THE REMAINDER OF THIS CHAPTER AND IN CHAPTER 15.

When you have a block of data that contains more than one row of data *and* more than one column of data, you have a choice to make. Do you want the series to be the rows or the columns? It makes a big difference in the message that your chart shows to your reader. For example, look at the two charts in Figure 14.8. The left one uses the data in Figure 14.7 to make a chart where the salespeople are the series, whereas the right one uses the same data to make a chart where the months are the series. In the left chart, the reader is invited to compare the performances of each salesperson against one another for each month. In the right one, the reader is invited to compare the performances of a particular salesperson against that salesperson's performance in other months. See the difference?

Figure 14.8 You can choose rows or columns as your data series, with very different results.

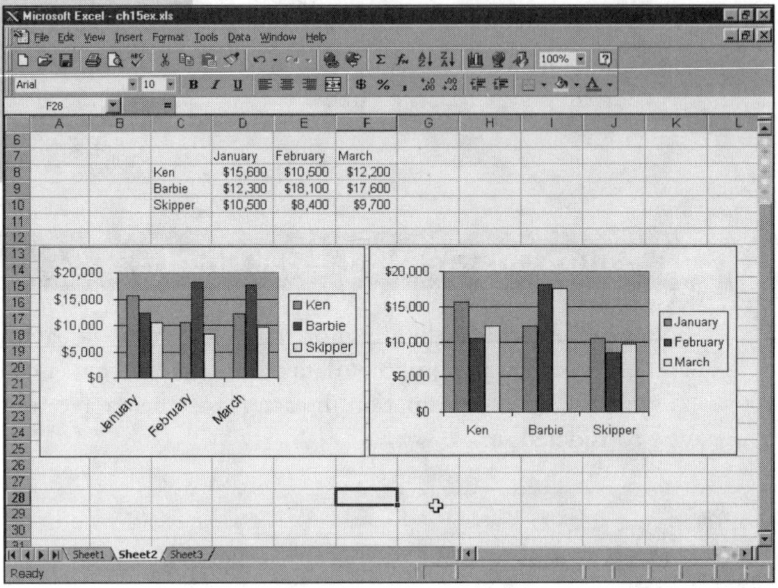

Follow these steps to create a bar chart now:

1. On a new worksheet, type in the data shown in Figure 14.7 in the same cells as shown.
2. Select the range C7:F10.

Note

Notice that you included the row and column labels in the range you selected in step 2. If you select them as part of the range, Excel can add them to the chart for you in the appropriate spots.

3. Choose Insert, Chart or click the ChartWizard button on the toolbar. The ChartWizard - Step 1 of 4 dialog box opens.
4. Select Column on the Chart Type list.
5. Click the first subtype in the second row of the Chart Sub-Type list (see Figure 14.9). Then click Next to continue. The Step 2 of 4 dialog box appears.

Figure 14.9 Choose the Column chart type and then choose the 3-D subtype.

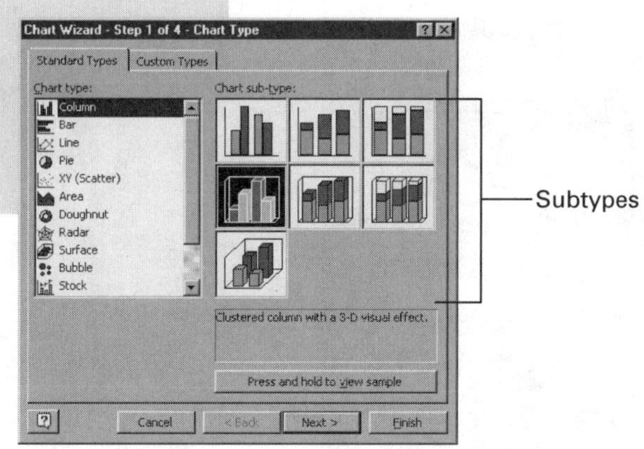

Note

Later, when you are working on your own charts, you may want to try out some of the other chart types. To see what a chart type looks like, select it and then click and hold down the mouse button on the Press and Hold To View Sample button.

6. Because you selected the data range beforehand, you don't need to change it, so leave the Data Range text box alone.
7. Click the Rows or Columns button, depending on which way you want the series to run (see Figure 14.10). For this example, choose Rows. The preview shows how the chart appears at this point.
8. Click Next to display the ChartWizard - Step 3 of 4 dialog box. More text boxes are available now than when you saw it earlier with the pie chart because this type of chart is more complex than a pie.
9. Type **Monthly Sales** in the Chart Title text box (see Figure 14.11).
10. The X axis is the horizontal one, which in this chart shows the months (because you chose Rows in step 7; if you had chosen Columns in step 7, the months would be on the vertical axis). Because months are self-explanatory, leave the Category (X) Axis text box blank.
11. The vertical axis in this chart shows the dollar amounts. To be clear on what that amount represents, enter **Gross Revenue** in the Value (Z) Axis text box, as shown in Figure 14.11.

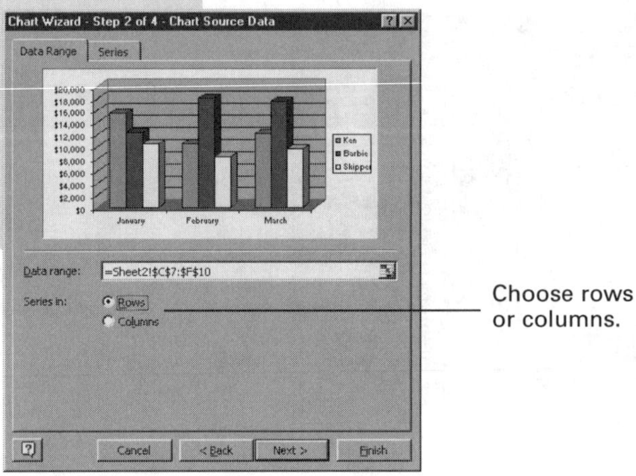

Figure 14.10 Make sure that the data range is correct and that the appropriate button (Rows or Columns) is selected.

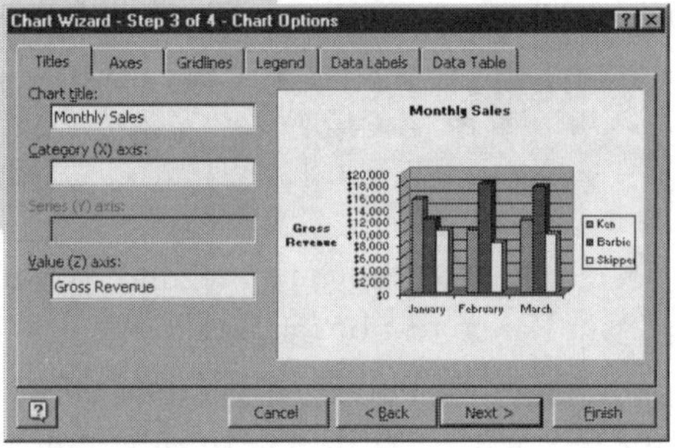

Figure 14.11 In this dialog box, you name the chart and the axes.

Note

X, Y, and Z? The horizontal axis is always X, but the vertical axis is sometimes Y and sometimes Z depending on what chart type you pick. On most charts (and probably in the Algebra class you took), the vertical axis is Y; but in Excel, Y represents the series, in this case the salespeople. That leaves Z for the vertical axis. Don't worry too much about the Y or Z name; it works the same no matter what it's called.

12. Click Next to move on to the ChartWizard - Step 4 of 4 dialog box.
13. Click the As New Sheet button. You're going to make this chart a sheet all by itself.
14. Type a name for the sheet's tab in the text box next to As New Sheet. Call it **Sales Chart**.
15. Click Finish. Excel creates your chart and places it on its own sheet, as shown in Figure 14.12.

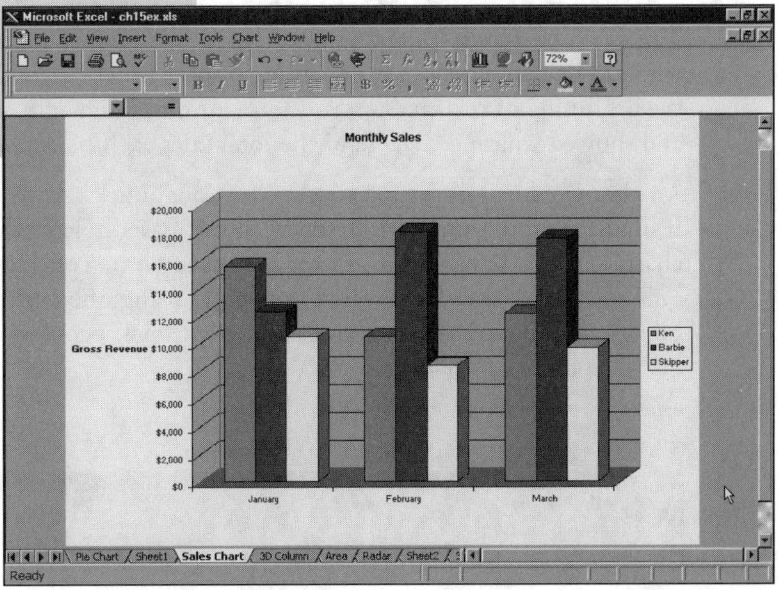

Figure 14.12 This finished bar chart appears on a sheet all by itself.

Hang onto this chart! Don't delete it right away. You can use it to follow along with the examples in Chapter 15, where you learn how to modify and format a chart.

Note

If you did want to delete a chart that's a sheet by itself, do you know how you would do it? I covered it earlier in the book—it's the same as deleting a regular worksheet. You display that sheet and then choose Edit, Delete Sheet. To delete a chart that's an object on a regular sheet, select the chart and press the Del key.

Exploring Chart Types

Now that you've created two sample charts, you may be wondering about the vast number of chart types and subtypes you saw in the ChartWizard dialog box. There's a chart type for every situation you can imagine, and several types for situations that the average person could *never* imagine! The following sections showcase the various chart types and offer some advice for when you might want to use them.

Charts That Show Percentages

The simplest type of chart is one that shows several pieces' relationships to a whole. The pie chart is a prime example of this; when you created a pie chart at the beginning of this chapter, you took information about four salespeople's sales and showed what percentage of the total sales each person's "slice" represented.

An alternate form of the pie chart is the doughnut chart, shown in Figure 14.13. It does the same thing as a pie chart, but it has a hole in the middle. Doughnut charts can also have multiple series, represented by concentric rings. If you have only one series, there's no real advantage to using one over the other, except that because a doughnut chart is not as conventional, people may be surprised by it and take more notice of it.

Figure 14.13 A doughnut chart is simply a variation of a pie chart.

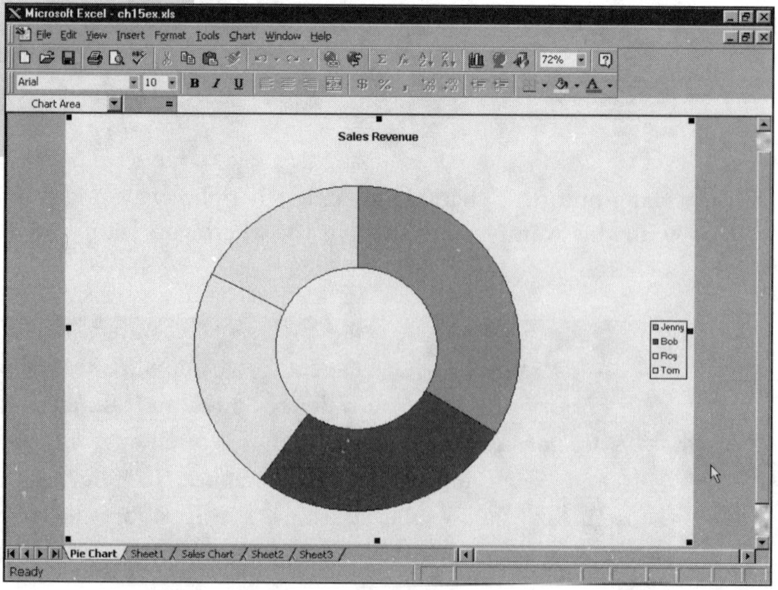

When you choose a pie or doughnut chart type (in step 1 of 4 of the ChartWizard), the subtypes offer two basic choices:

- **2D or 3D.** This is a purely cosmetic choice—it doesn't affect the data.
- **Exploded Slices or Not.** By exploding the slices, you can make the fact that each piece is separate a little clearer, but it becomes harder for the reader to evaluate the exact value of the slices in relation to the whole.

Figure 14.14 shows a 3-D exploded pie.

Figure 14.14 You can choose to have the slices exploded on a pie or doughnut chart.

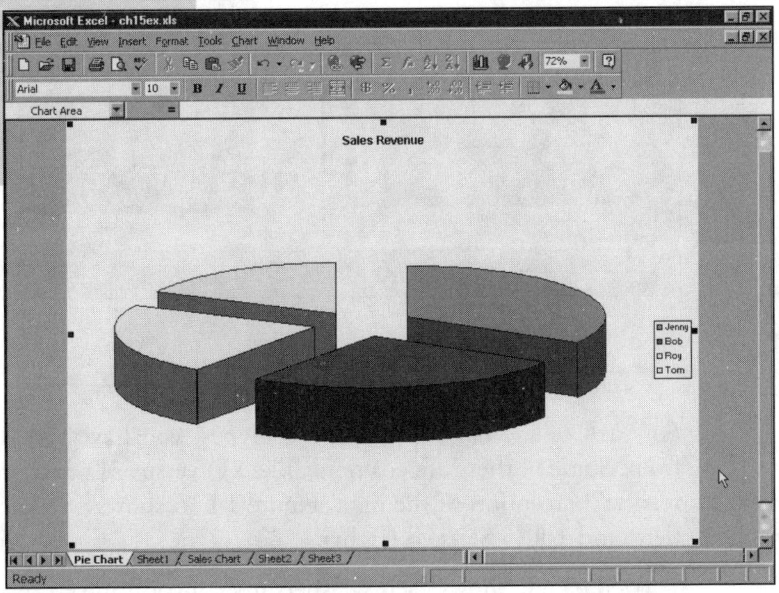

Column/Bar Charts and Their Relatives

You saw an ordinary column chart in the Hands On session earlier in the chapter, but there is a staggering array of variations on it that you can use. The simplest is the bar chart, which is simply a column chart on its side. In fact, "bar" is the more common name for charts of this genre, and you will likely hear charts like them called "bar charts" regardless of whether the bars run vertically or horizontally.

Several different chart types do the same job as a column chart but look a little different. Figure 14.15 shows the same data charted as (clockwise from upper left): bar, pyramid, cone, and cylinder. These variants can be used anytime for a fresh look without affecting the readers' understanding of the data.

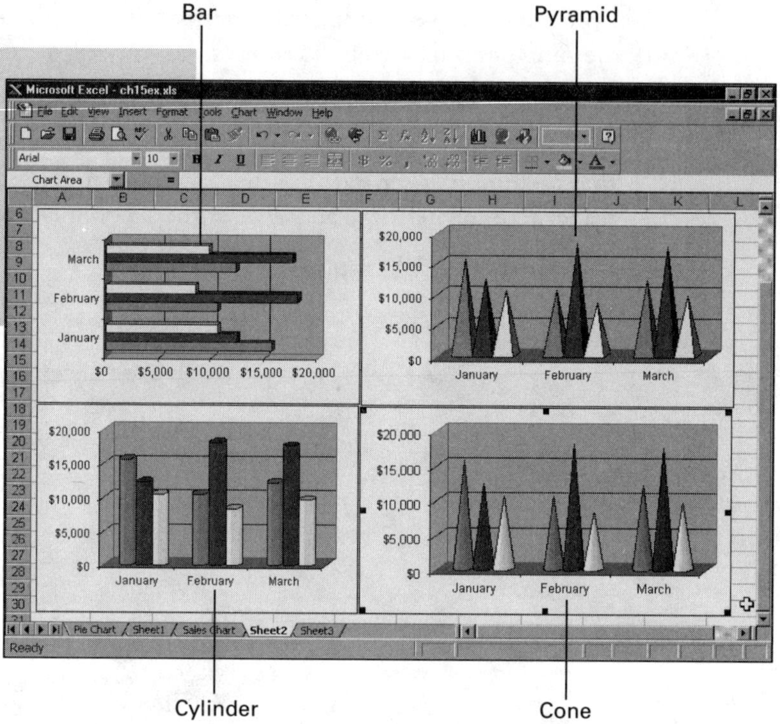

Figure 14.15 Here are some variations on the column chart. They're just cosmetic differences; the data is presented the same way.

For each of the bar/column related types, you have several subtypes to choose from. Some of these are cosmetic, like 2D versus 3D, but others can change your readers' perception of the data. Figure 14.16 shows two such variations: Stacked (left) and 100% Stacked (right).

- **Stacked.** Shows each salesperson's contribution to the entire sales amount for each month. The total height of the bar is determined by the combined total of all salespeople for the month, and each salesperson's contribution is represented by a different color.
- **100% Stacked.** Is like a series of pie charts molded into the shape of bars. Each bar is the same height, representing 100% (the whole pie). Each person's contribution to the whole percentage-wise is represented by a colored portion of the bar.

A third variation, 3D Column, is like a regular bar/column chart except that it shows each bar separately rather than in a cluster. It's shown in Figure 14.17.

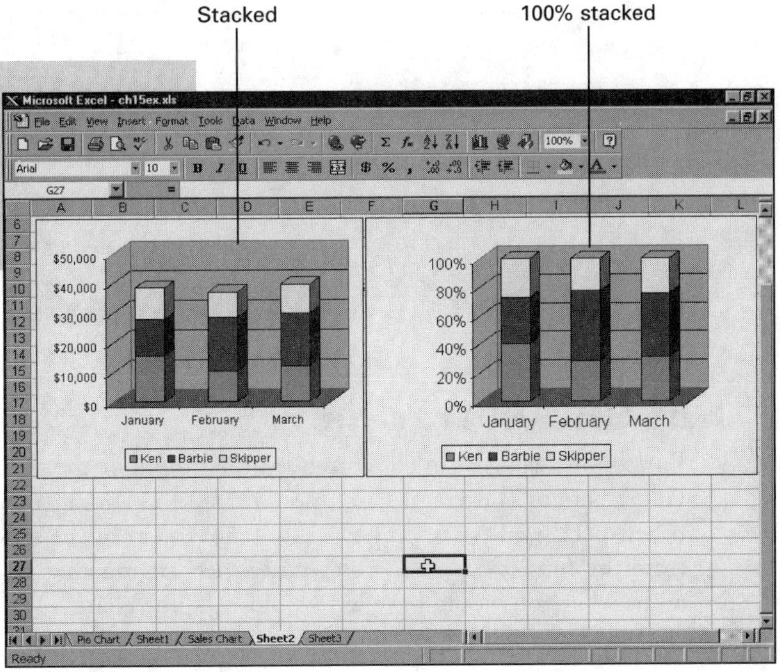

Figure 14.16 These subtypes can convey different messages with your data.

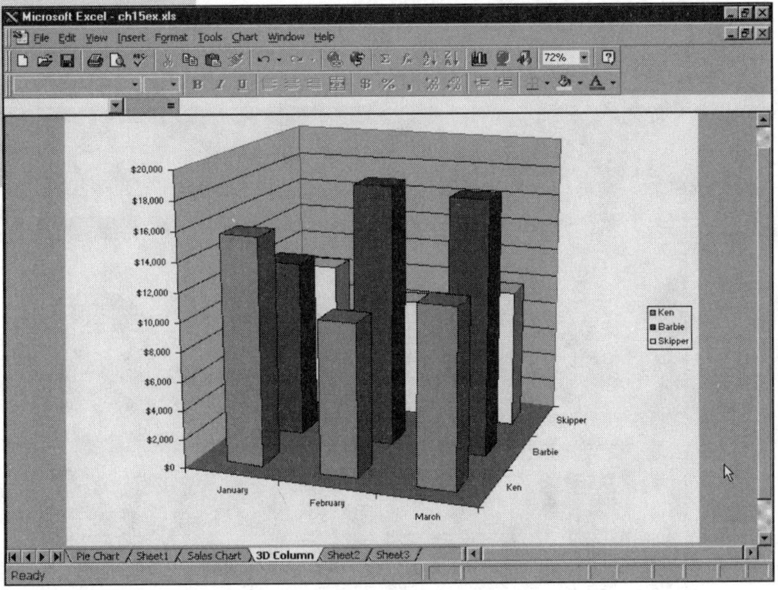

Figure 14.17 The 3D Column subtype shows each value as a separate bar on a 3-D grid.

Note

You don't want to use the 3D Column subtype if the later series have lesser values than the earlier ones, because the later series' bars get hidden behind the ones in front, as in Figure 14.17. Because Barbie's bars are so high, you can't see Skipper's bars well at all. Changing the order of the series, as covered in Chapter 15, might help somewhat, because then Barbie's bars would be behind Skipper's.

Charts That Show Trends

Bar/column charts can show trends over time, but the emphasis is on the individual bars or clusters of bars. In contrast, line and area charts, as well as some other specialized types, emphasize the movement of the series. If you drew a line from the tops of each bar, connecting the bars together, and then took the bars away, what you would have left would be a line chart.

For example, the chart on the top of Figure 14.18 shows a line chart that plots a single series over time. You aren't limited to one series, though; the chart on the bottom of Figure 14.18 shows a line chart tracking multiple series. Each series has its own different-colored line.

Figure 14.18 Line charts emphasize how the series changes over time (or over whatever is represented on the X axis).

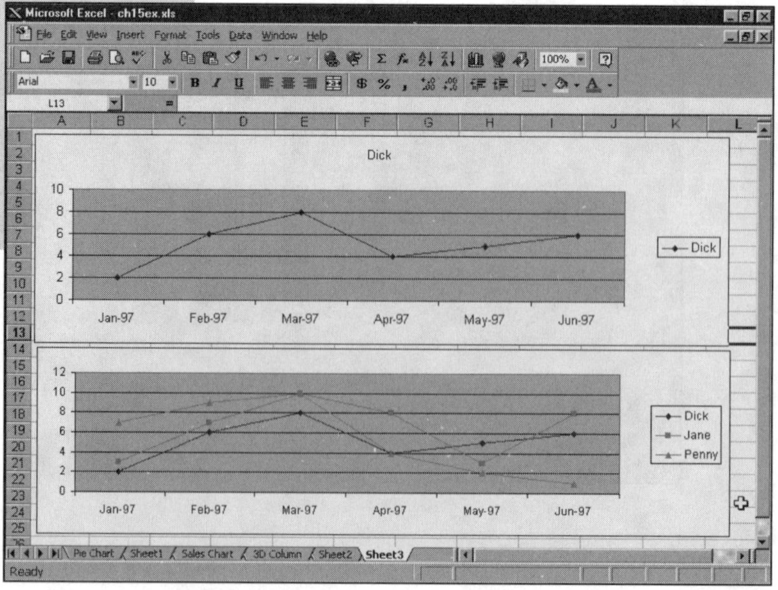

A 3-D line chart is called a *ribbon chart*, but many people find it hard to read. In general, when using line charts, stick to 2-D.

Less Common Chart Types

Excel comes with a variety of other chart types that the average user may not use as often as the ones I've told you about so far. Here's a look at a few of them:

- **XY (Scatter).** These charts show distribution trends by showing how data points (dots) fall on a two-axis grid. For example, suppose that you wanted to prove that the more expensive products in your line performed better and were therefore worth the extra cost. A scatter chart like the one in Figure 14.19 would show that, on the average, products with a higher cost had higher performance scores.

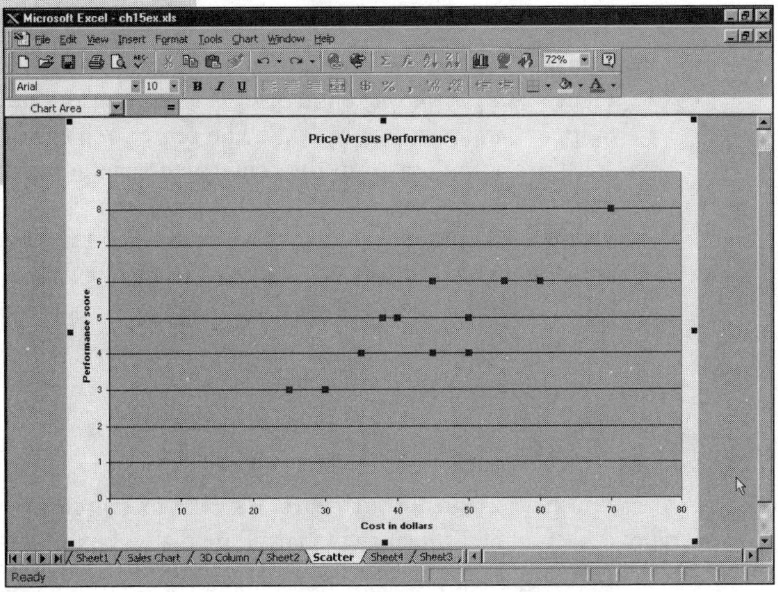

Figure 14.19 Scatter charts typically plot many data points to show an overall trend.

- **Area.** These charts, such as the one shown in Figure 14.20, are like line charts that have been filled in down to the bottom. They produce results that are a cross between the emphasis on values with a bar chart and the emphasis on movement with a line chart. You can have them where each series is its own bar, as in Figure 14.20, or where the series are stacked like a stacked bar chart.

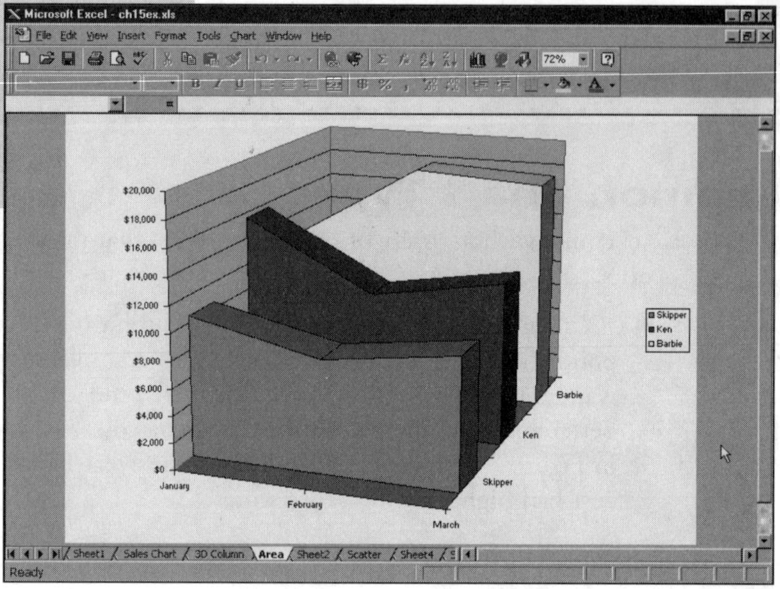

Figure 14.20 Area charts combine the benefits of line and bar charts into a single graphic.

- **Radar**. This kind of chart can be confusing to a beginner, but the one in Figure 14.21 is simple enough. It was made using the Barbie, Ken, and Skipper data from Figure 14.7. The center point is 0. There are three thin axis lines going out from the center: January (going toward the top), February (going out to the right), and March (going out to the left). Each data point is plotted on one of those axes, and the points for each person are connected (in this case to form a triangle because there are three axes, but it could be another shape like a square or pentagon if there are four or five axes).

Changing the Chart Type

After you have created your chart, it's easy to switch among the various chart types and subtypes. Open the Chart Type dialog box in any of these ways:

- Right-click on the chart (on a blank spot, not on a part of the chart) and choose Chart Type from the shortcut menu.
- If the chart is on its own sheet, display that sheet and then choose Chart, Chart Type.
- If the chart is an object on an existing sheet, click on the frame around the chart so that selection handles appear around it, and then choose Chart, Chart Type.

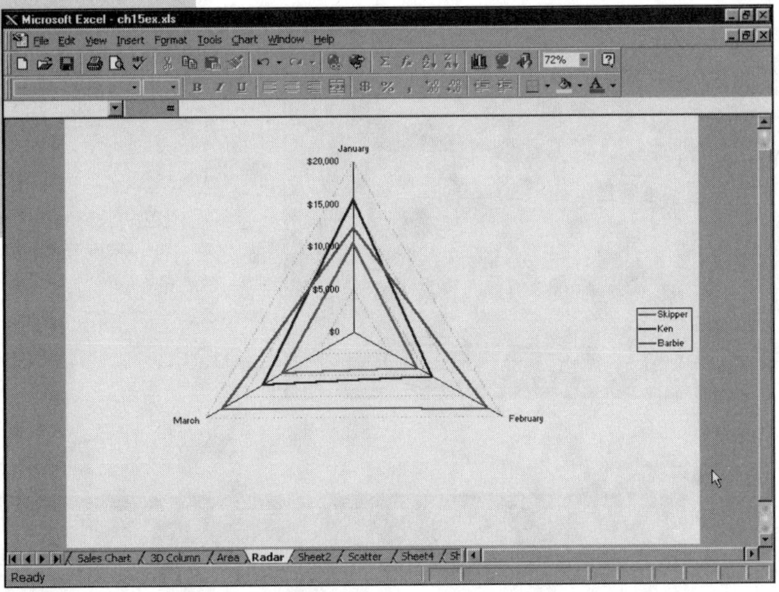

Figure 14.21 This simple radar chart shows how they work; the more data you have, the more complex it gets.

After the dialog box is open, simply select a different chart type and subtype. The dialog box contains exactly the same controls that you worked with when you used the ChartWizard to create the chart (refer to Figures 14.2 and 14.9).

While you are changing the chart type, you might want to check out the Custom Types tab in the Chart Type dialog box (see Figure 14.22). It contains some less-common chart variations that you can try out, such as black-and-white charts (great for printing using a black-and-white printer) and preformatted specialty charts with attractive backgrounds or special effects. Figure 14.23 shows a sampling of these interesting custom types.

Be aware of what message you are trying to present as you change the chart type. A different chart type or subtype can give the reader a very different message. For example, if you change your data from a bar chart to a pie chart, the emphasis shifts from the values to the percentage of the whole that each value represents. Watch that your intended meaning is enhanced, not lost!

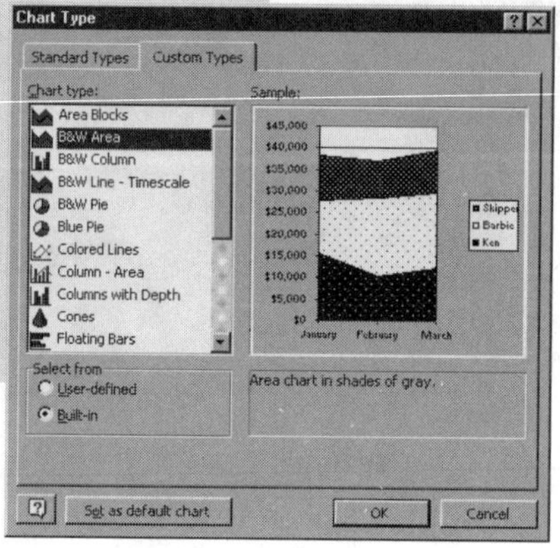

Figure 14.22 If you don't see the list of custom types on your screen, make sure that the Built-In option button is selected below the list.

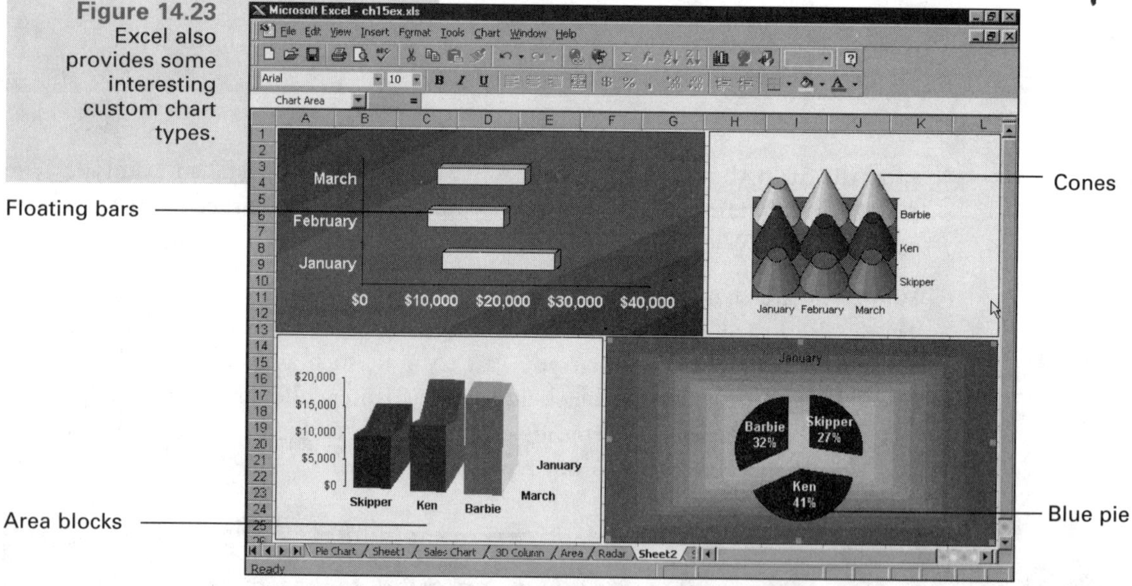

Figure 14.23 Excel also provides some interesting custom chart types.

Hands On: Creating Your Own Custom Types

In Chapter 15, you're going to learn how to format charts to look as good as (if not better than!) the custom charts shown in Figure 14.23. You can save any chart's formatting as a Custom Type, and apply that formatting as easily as you change the chart type. Here's how to do it:

1. Format the chart exactly the way you want it. You may need to read Chapter 15 first.
2. Right-click the chart and choose Chart Type from the shortcut menu.
3. Click the Custom Types tab.
4. Select the User-Defined button. An Add button appears.
5. Click the Add button. The Add Custom Chart Type dialog box appears.
6. Type a name and description for your custom type.
7. Click OK. Your new chart type appears on the Chart Type list.
8. Click OK again. Your new chart type is saved.

Then later, when you want to apply that custom type to another chart, do this:

1. Select the chart you want to format.
2. Right-click the chart and choose Chart Type from the shortcut menu.
3. Click the Custom Types tab.
4. Select the User-Defined button.
5. Select your chart type from the list.
6. Click OK to apply it.

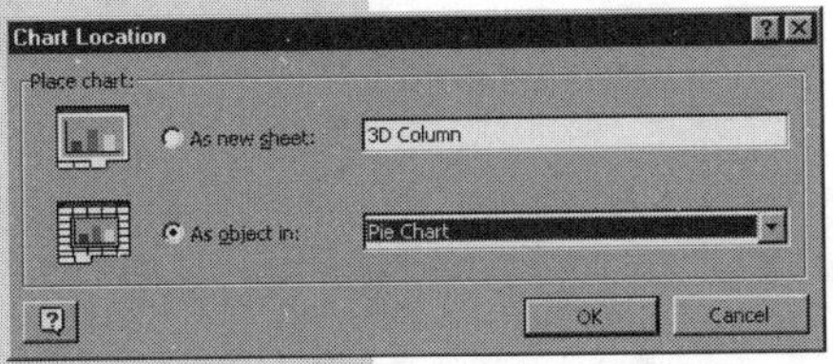

Figure 14.24 Right-click on a chart and choose Location to open this dialog box, where you can change where the chart resides.

Switching a Chart's Location

As you were creating the chart, you got to choose in the ChartWizard where you wanted the chart to appear. You could put it on its own sheet or have it float on top of an existing sheet. Remember that you made the pie chart float on the same sheet as the data, but you made the column chart a separate sheet. So if you followed along with the Hands On sessions earlier in the chapter, you now have one of each.

You can switch a chart back and forth between being on its own sheet and floating over a worksheet very easily. Right-click the chart (a white area, not a particular part of it) and choose Location from the shortcut menu. The Chart Location dialog box appears (refer to Figure 14.24). These are the same controls that you used on the ChartWizard - Step 4 of 4 screen, so they will likely seem familiar. To change where a chart is located, simply select the other option button (As New Sheet or As Object In) and then enter the appropriate location. Then click OK, and the chart moves where you specified.

Resizing a Chart

Each chart, no matter where it resides, has two windows. The outer one is the frame in which the chart appears. When a chart is on a sheet by itself, this frame is that entire sheet. When a chart is an object on a worksheet, that frame appears as the black box that surrounds the chart. But there is also an inner frame that you can't always see for each chart. That frame contains only the *plot area*—chart itself, and not special related elements like the title and legend. You select this plot area frame by clicking on a white area of the chart (see Figure 14.25).

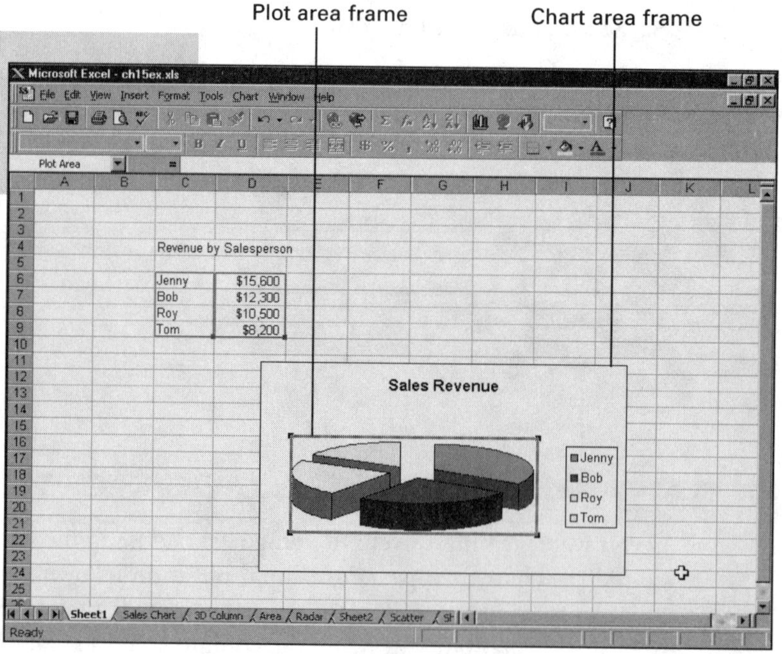

Figure 14.25 Each chart has an inner and outer frame.

I'm telling you this because you can change the size of either frame, but you'll get different results with each:

- If you resize a chart's outer frame on a worksheet, you resize the entire chart and all its elements such as the title, legend, and so on.
- If you resize the plot area on a chart, you resize only the plot area. Other related elements stay the same.
- The only way to resize a chart that's on its own sheet is to resize the plot area. You can also resize the related elements like the title and legend, but you must resize them independently.

Now, with that out of the way, try resizing.

You resize by dragging one of the *handles* (black squares in the corners) of the frame. When you position your mouse pointer over a selection handle, it turns into a double-arrow, as shown in Figure 14.26. From there, hold down the left mouse button and drag that edge of the frame where you want it. Hold down the Shift key while you drag to maintain the height-width ratio of the chart.

Figure 14.26
Drag a handle to resize the frame.

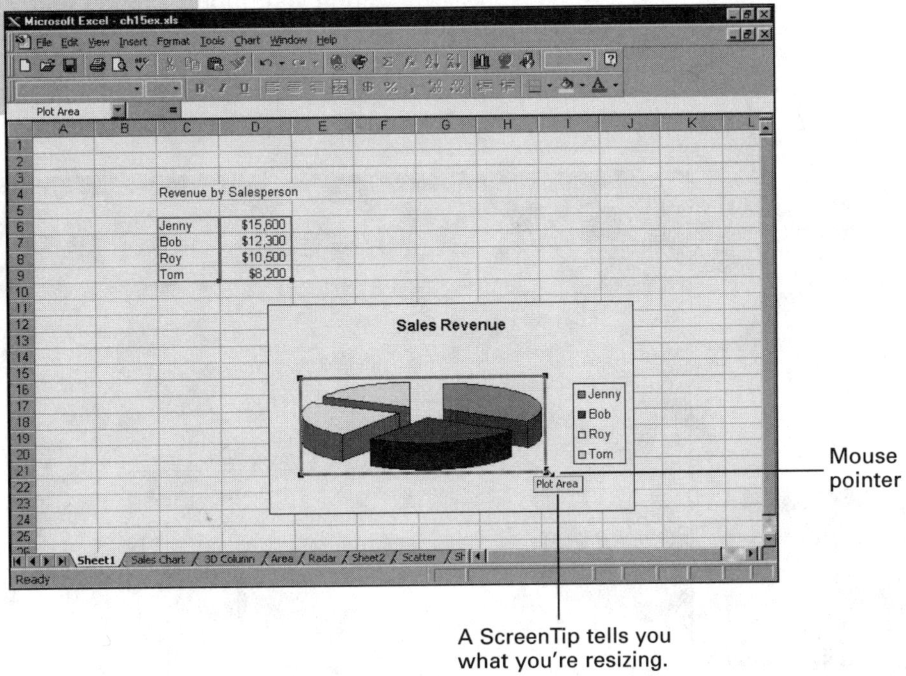

When you resize the frame, you can change its proportions—make it tall and thin or short and wide. This gives you a great deal of control over how the chart will look. However, make sure that you don't lose any axis labels by changing a dimension too much. For example, say that you have the names of your salespeople along the X (horizontal) axis. If you make the chart too thin, some of the names will disappear from the chart. They reappear again if you widen the chart enough so that they can be displayed. Your reader will not understand the chart if important labels are missing.

Moving a Chart

If your chart is floating on an existing worksheet, you can move it around on that sheet. (You can't move a chart that's on its own sheet except to move the entire sheet.) To move a chart, position your mouse pointer on the chart frame, but not on a selection handle. The mouse pointer turns into an arrow (rather than a thick plus sign), as shown in Figure 14.27. Then drag the chart where you want it.

Figure 14.27
To move a chart, drag the border while you are not pointing to a handle.

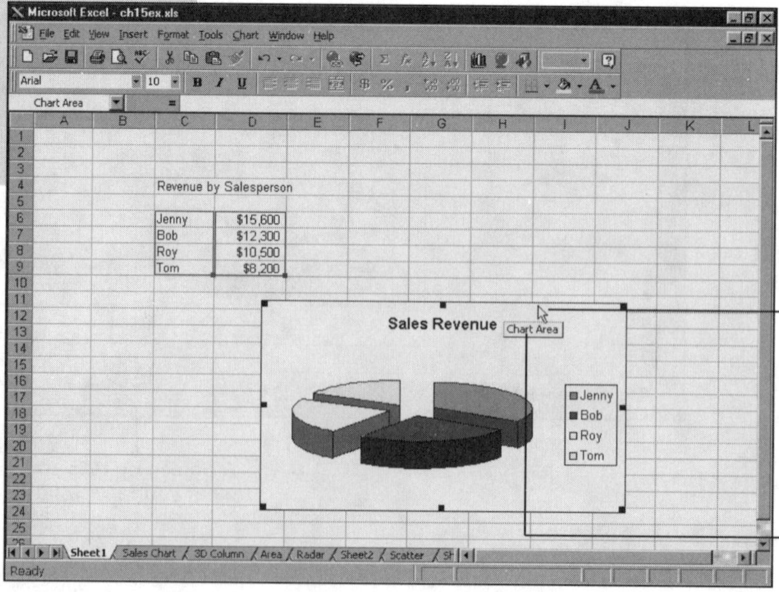

Mouse pointer becomes an arrow.

A ScreenTip tells you what you're pointing to.

CHAPTER 5 COVERS MOVING ENTIRE SHEETS IN A WORKBOOK.

You must position the mouse pointer over the chart frame border, not just anywhere within the chart window. That's because if you drag while the mouse pointer is pointing to the inside of the chart window, you will likely drag the plot area frame rather than the outer frame. This just moves the plot area around within the confines of the chart frame, and that's probably not what you want.

Changing What Data Appears in a Chart

Suppose that you make a beautiful chart and then decide that you want to include more data, or exclude some of the data you've chosen. Not a problem. Just change the data area. To do this, follow these steps:

Hands On: Changing the Chart Data

1. Right-click on the chart and choose Source Data from the shortcut menu. The Source Data dialog box appears (see Figure 14.28).

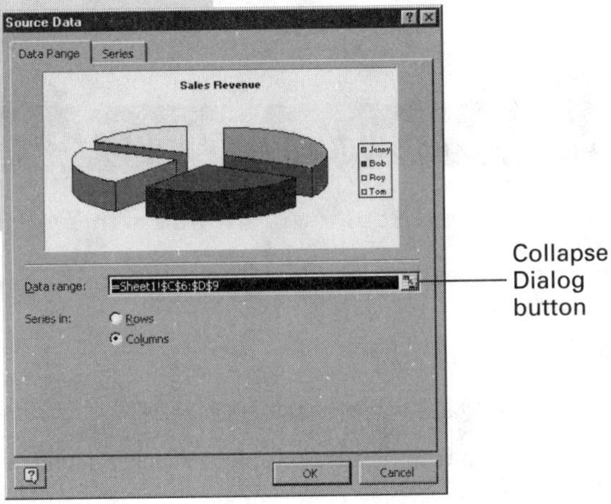

Figure 14.28 You can change what data appears in your chart from the Source Data dialog box.

2. Change the data range listed in the Data Range text box in one of these ways:
   - Click in the Data Range text box and type your corrections.
   - Click the Collapse Dialog button and reselect the data range; then press Enter to return to the dialog box.
3. (Optional) If you want to switch between Columns and Rows as the series, select the Columns or Rows button to make the change.
4. Click OK. Now the chart shows the new data range!

Tip

Advanced users may want to explore the Series tab in the Source Data dialog box. It gives you full control over what data series appear in the chart and in what order. However, most beginning and intermediate users will never need to make changes of that level of precise detail.

Including/Excluding the Data Table

When you place a chart on the same worksheet as its data, you have one advantage over placing it on its own sheet: you can put the chart right next to the data that it represents, so that the reader can see firsthand where the chart's data comes from. But thanks to the Data Table feature, you can include the data table from which the data came on a chart sheet too. Data Tables are not available for all charts (notably, they're missing for pie charts), but many chart types have them available.

Hands On: Displaying a Data Table

To display the data table next to the chart, follow these steps:

1. Right-click the chart and choose Chart Options from the shortcut menu. The Chart Options dialog box appears.
2. Click the Data Table tab.
3. Select the Show Data Table check box.
4. Click OK. Your data table now appears on the sheet with the chart, as shown in Figure 14.29.

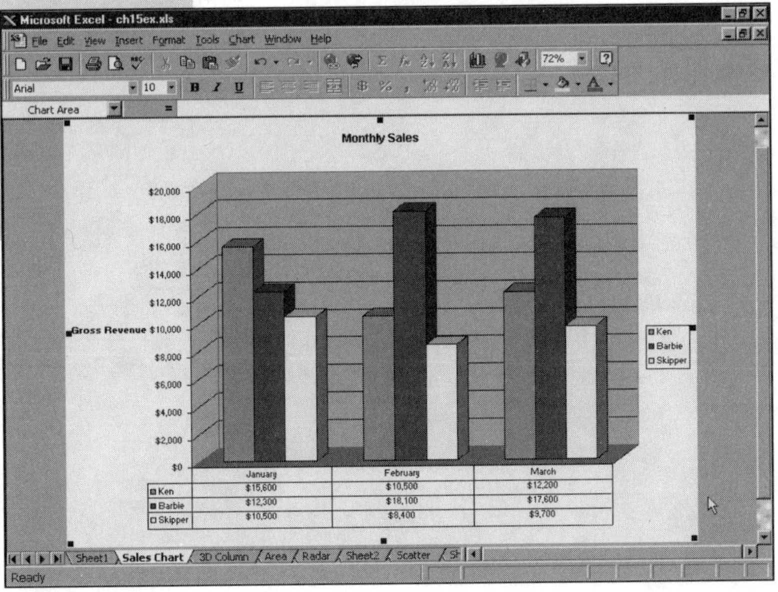

Figure 14.29 A data table on a full-sheet chart lets the reader see both data and chart without flipping sheets.

Is that all? Hardly. You can do much more with a chart to make it more attractive and clear, including changing the fonts, axes scales, background, and more. You'll take a look at those options in Chapter 15.

15

Improving the Look of Your Charts

In This Chapter

- Choosing Backgrounds
- Changing Axes
- Adding and Formatting Titles
- Working with Legends
- Controlling Data Labels

The whole point of a chart is to show information in an attractive format that invites the reader to pay attention. It stands to reason, then, that anything you can do to improve the appearance of your chart will help you achieve that same ultimate goal of helping your readers get your message. In the preceding chapter you learned how to create a chart, and in this chapter you'll learn to customize that chart to make it the best that it can be.

Understanding the Chart Elements

Before you can effectively edit a chart, you must understand the pieces that comprise one. That's because each piece has its own, separately set formatting. For example, if you want the background behind the chart to be set to blue, you must set it separately from the background behind the legend, because these are separate pieces.

Figure 15.1 shows the parts of a chart that are considered separate elements. You can move and resize these elements separately, as you learned to do in Chapter 14.

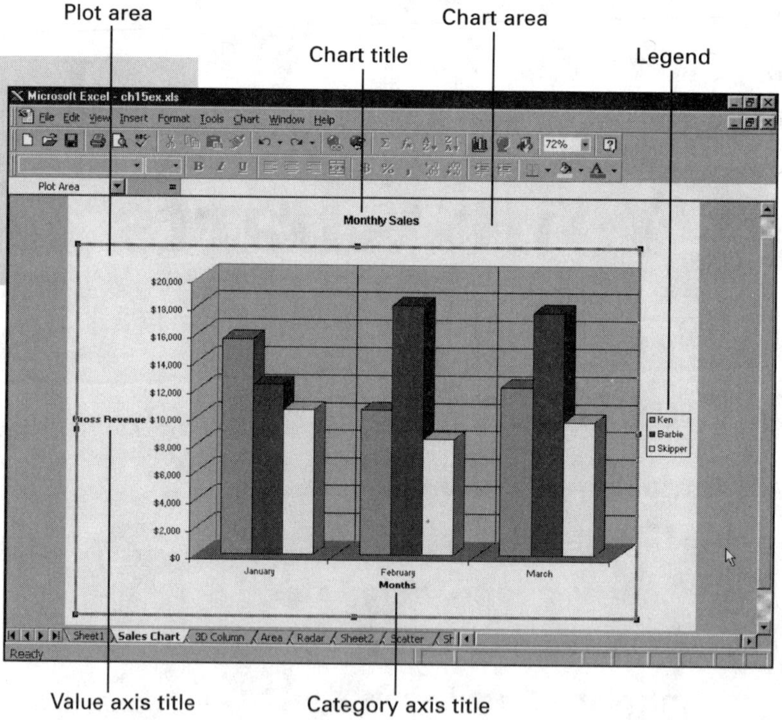

Figure 15.1 Certain chart elements are individual entities and have all their own formatting.

CHAPTER 14 INTRODUCED CHARTS.

- **Chart Title.** The text above the chart that tells what the chart as a whole represents.
- **Chart Area.** The area behind all the other elements. On a floating chart it's the framed area; on a full-sheet chart it's the sheet itself.
- **Plot Area.** The frame that contains the actual chart itself. The plot area is a "window-in-a-window" within the chart area.

- **Value Axis Title.** This optional title tells what the Y axis's units represent. It is separate from the plot area.
- **Category Axis Title.** This optional title tells what the X axis's categories represent. It too is separate from the plot area, although by default it sits on top of it.
- **Legend.** When you have multiple data series, as in Figure 15.1, the legend provides a color (or pattern) code telling which series is which.

In addition to the parts that are considered "separate," the plot area contains many individual elements that you can format too. You can't resize or move these elements separately, but you can apply certain formatting to them, such as background color. They're labeled in Figure 15.2.

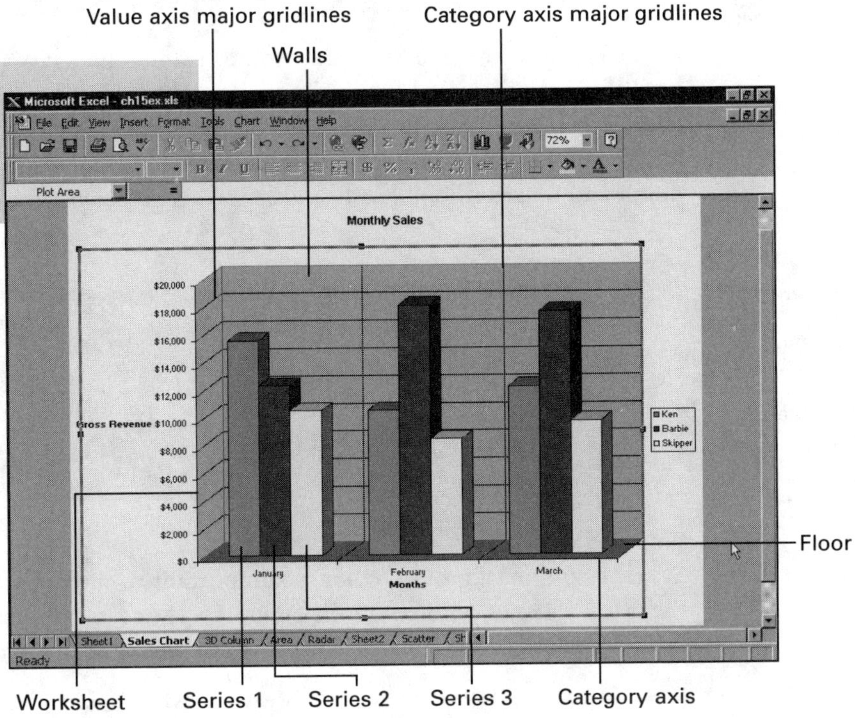

Figure 15.2 Formattable elements within the plot area.

- **Axes.** Each chart has at least one axis; all charts except pie and doughnut have last least two. You can format the scale of the axis (for example, start the numbering of the Value axis at $1000 rather than $0), change how the labels appear on it (for example, make the month names in Figure 15.2 appear bigger or bolder), and more, as you'll learn later in this chapter.

TURN TO CHAPTER 14 TO LEARN ABOUT CUSTOM CHART TYPES.

- **Gridlines.** Gridlines are the thin lines that run across the walls at even intervals. They are optional, but they do help the readers' eyes follow across the chart to determine what a bar represents.
- **Walls and Floor.** The plot area usually has shaded walls for most chart types. 3-D charts also have floors. You can change the color of these, or make them transparent so that the background set for the plot area shows through.
- **Series.** The series are the heart of the chart—they're the bars or slices or other elements that show the data values. You can format these to make them different colors or patterns.

Changing Chart Backgrounds

At the end of Chapter 14, you saw some custom chart types that contained backgrounds. A background can really make a chart look professional! For example, check out Figure 15.3. On the left, you see a plain chart; on the right is the same chart with a background applied. The textured background gives the chart more depth and makes it look less like a slapped-together-on-the-run affair.

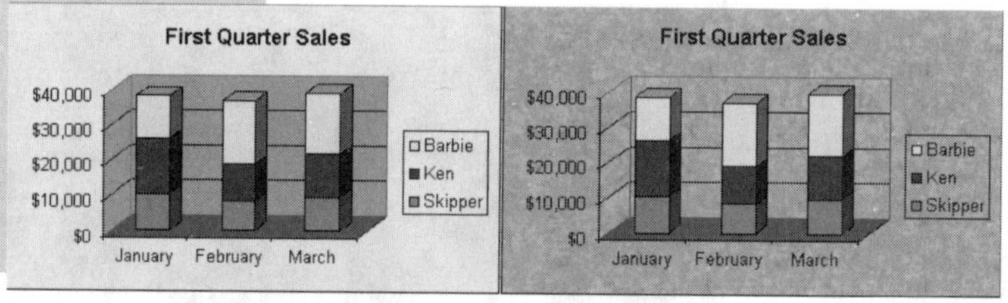

Figure 15.3 The chart on the right has a background applied; the one on the left is plain.

When setting background color, it's important to remember that each chart element (of the ones pointed out in Figure 15.1) has its own background color, also known as Area color. An element starts out with one of two defaults:

- **Auto.** Excel chooses its color (usually white). The chart area and legend start with this.
- **None.** The background is transparent, enabling the color of whatever is underneath it to show through. All the other chart elements (plot area, titles, and so on) start with this.

Note

What color is Auto, anyway? When you set the color of something to Auto, you are leaving it in Excel's hands to adjust. For example, say that your chart area is set to Auto, and you have a chart that has black lettering and lines. Excel will make the chart area white, so that the lettering shows up well. If you changed the lettering and lines to white, Excel would change the chart area to black so that you could see the white lines.

That means that you can have separate Area colors for all the elements shown in Figure 15.1 if you want. However, in reality, a chart with all those different backgrounds would not look very good. It's better to simply assign a background color to the chart area and legend and leave all the other elements (which are set by default for None, or transparent) to pick up that same background too.

Hands On: Changing the Background Color

In this exercise, start with any bar or column chart that you created in Chapter 14 (or any other chart), and follow these steps:

1. Right-click on the chart area (outside the plot area).

Tip

To make sure that you are pointing at the chart area, rest your mouse pointer a moment so that a ScreenTip pops up that says `Chart Area`. If the ScreenTip says anything else, you are not in the right spot.

2. Choose Format Chart Area from the shortcut menu. The Format Chart Area dialog box appears.
3. If needed, click the Patterns tab to bring it to the front (see Figure 15.4).
4. Click on a color in the Area portion of the dialog box. (Try a light blue; that usually looks nice.)
5. Click OK. The background is applied to all areas of the chart except the legend, which is still white.
6. Next format the legend with the same color. Right-click on the legend and choose Format Legend from the shortcut menu.
7. In the Format Legend dialog box, click on the same color that you chose previously.

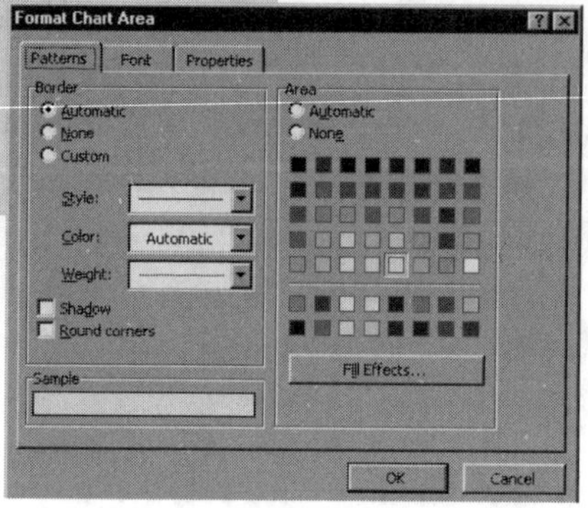

Figure 15.4
Use the Patterns tab to change the background color.

8. Click OK. The background of the legend now matches that of the rest of the chart area.
9. Now make the walls "disappear" by formatting them the same as the chart area. Right-click on the wall behind the bars and choose Format Walls from the shortcut menu.
10. In the Format Walls dialog box, click on the same color again.
11. Click OK.

That's all there is to it! Right-click on any chart element and then choose the Format command for it from the top of the shortcut menu that appears. Then on the Patterns tab, choose the color you want and click OK. This works with every element on the chart.

If you aren't sure what color you want to make your background and want to experiment, set the Legend and Walls' background colors to None. That makes them transparent, so that they pick up the chart area background color. Then you can change the chart area background repeatedly until you find exactly the right look without having to also change the Legend and Walls each time.

Using Special Fills and Patterns

Besides the normal colors that you saw in the Format Chart Area dialog box in the preceding Hands On section, you can also choose special patterns and blended colors for your backgrounds. These can give some professional-looking results, so don't discount them just because they involve an extra step or two. Try this out:

1. In the chart that you just set a background for, right-click again on the chart area and choose Format Chart Area from the shortcut menu.
2. On the Patterns tab, click the Fill Effects button. This opens the Fill Effects dialog box shown in Figure 15.5. There are four tabs here, each one for a different kind of background fill.

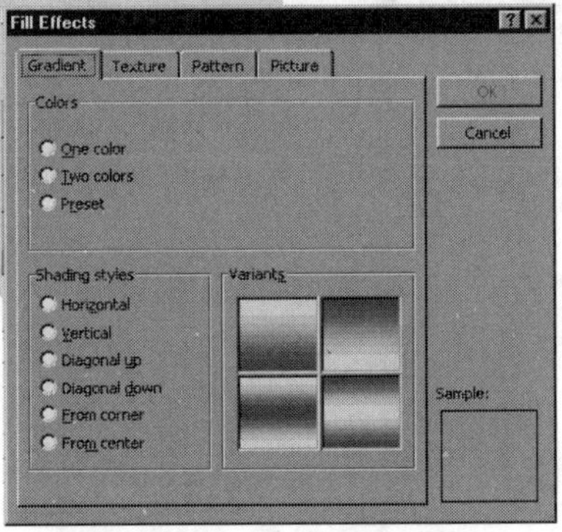

Figure 15.5 The Fill Effects dialog box provides access to built-in patterns and color blends.

3. Click the tab for the type of fill you want. I'll explain more about each of these shortly. Your choices are:
   - **Gradient.** These options blend two colors together to make a background that starts out one color and blends into another.
   - **Texture.** This tab offers a variety of premade textures that can make your background look like brick, marble, granite, or any of several other materials.
   - **Pattern.** Here you can pick a background pattern and then pick the two colors that will comprise it.
   - **Picture.** You can choose any graphic file on your system to be the background behind your chart. (Watch out, though—this can make the chart hard to read.)
4. Select the colors and options you want.
5. Click OK to apply the background.

The following sections explain each of the fill effects in more detail.

Using a Gradient Fill

The Gradient controls, shown in Figure 15.5, blend one color into another. This can really spice up a chart! For example, the chart shown in Figure 15.6 has a one-color gradient that fades blue into white. The lighter color toward the center of the chart emphasizes the bars and draws the readers' eyes toward them.

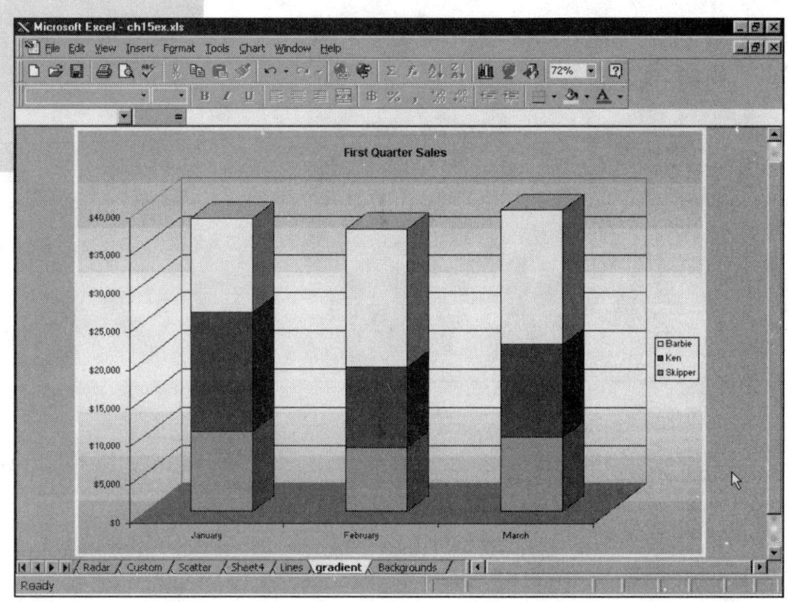

Figure 15.6 This gradient fill emphasizes the middle of the chart.

You have three choices for the type of fill to use:

- **One Color.** This blends a single color with either white or black. When you select the One Color button, a single drop-down list appears with a sliding bar under it. Choose the color from the drop-down list, and then move the sliding bar toward Light to blend with white or toward Dark to blend with black.
- **Two Colors.** This blends two colors that you choose. When you select the Two Colors button, two drop-down lists appear. Select the colors from these lists.
- **Preset.** When you select the Preset button, a drop-down list of preset color combinations appears. Choose any of these to use it.

After you choose the type of fill and the colors, move down to the bottom of the dialog box, where you see examples of various gradients. Some start with one color at the top (or bottom, or left, or whatever) and gradually shift the color toward the opposite side; others start with one color in the middle and move out from it with the other color. Choose the example that matches what you want.

Tip

A gradient fill draws the readers' eyes to the part of the background that's the lightest, so make sure that the fill pattern you choose puts the lighter color where the important information lies.

Using a Texture Fill

Click on the Texture tab in the Fill Effects dialog box (see Figure 15.7), and you'll see an array of texture samples. There are more than just the 12 that you see initially; use the scroll bar to the right of the first 12 to see the others. Each one has a picturesque name like "Pink Tissue Paper" or "Paper Bag."

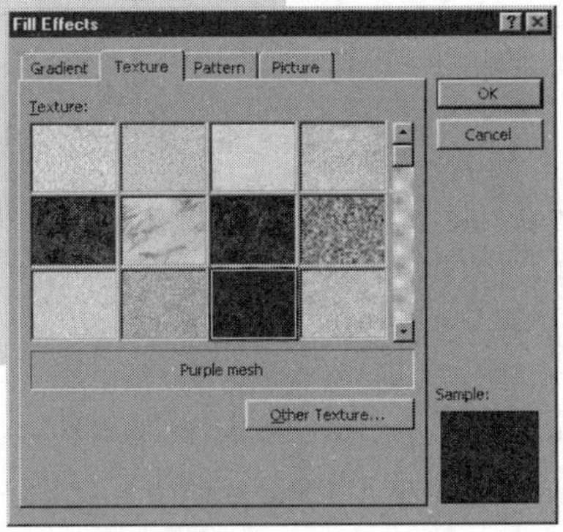

Figure 15.7 Choose a texture fill for an interesting background effect that looks like paper, wood, stone, or some other material.

Using a Pattern Fill

The Pattern tab has two features (see Figure 15.8). The first is the array of patterns at the top of the dialog box. Click on a pattern to choose it. The second is the drop-down lists of colors at the bottom. You can choose white for one of the backgrounds to have, essentially, a one-color pattern, or choose a second complimentary color for the pattern for something more colorful.

Caution

Be careful of loud or "busy" patterns. They can make parts of your chart more difficult to read, especially the small letters of the axis labels.

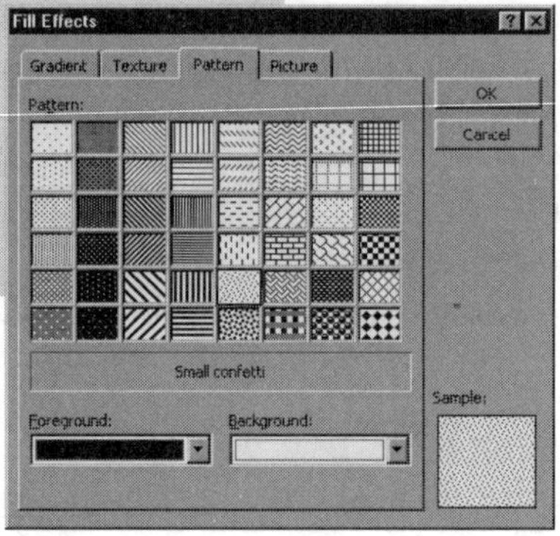

Figure 15.8 You can select from dozens of patterns and choose the colors that will form it.

Using a Picture Fill

> YOU CAN ALSO DOWNLOAD IMAGES FROM THE MICROSOFT WEB SITE, AS EXPLAINED IN CHAPTER 16.

Picture fills are my favorite. There's no limit to what you can do, with a little imagination and access to a color scanner. You could scan in a picture of your CEO, for example, and place it behind the chart that shows your record-breaking profits for the year!

Using a picture fill requires a few more steps than the other fills. Here's what to do:

1. If you are not already at the Fill Effects dialog box, right-click again on the chart area and choose Format Chart Area from the shortcut menu. Then on the Patterns tab, click the Fill Effects button.
2. From the Fill Effects dialog box, click the Picture tab. All the controls are grayed out because there's no picture selected yet.
3. Click the Select Picture button. The Select Picture dialog box appears. (It's just like any other dialog box that prompts you to select a file; you've seen these all over Excel in previous chapters.)
4. Navigate to the drive and folder containing the picture to use and double-click its name to select it.

If you don't have any pictures of your own to use, try using some of the MS Office 97 clip art. It's in the \Program Files\Microsoft Office\Clipart\Popular folder. More clip art also is on the Office 97 CD.

5. Back on the Picture tab, click OK to close the Fill Effects dialog box.
6. Click OK to close the Format dialog box and see your background picture in place.

Figure 15.9 shows a chart with a piece of MS Office clip art used as a background.

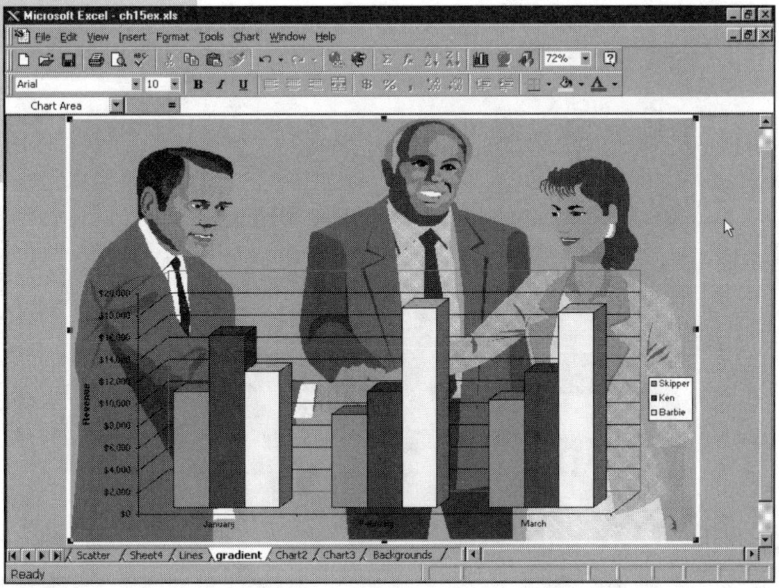

Figure 15.9
A picture like this one can imply "these sales were the result of teamwork."

Working with Titles

Let's look at titles next. When you created your chart, you had the opportunity to enter a chart title, but if you didn't do it, you can go back and add one later. You can also change an existing title by giving it a different font, making it larger or smaller, and more.

Besides the chart title, there are other titles you can work with on a chart. Each axis can have a title too (like `Months` and `Gross Revenue` in Figure 15.2.)

Adding a Title

If you need to add or modify a title (either an axis title or one for the entire chart), follow these steps:

1. Right-click on the chart area. (If you aren't sure where that is, point to the blank space just inside the chart frame. A ScreenTip should say `Chart Area`. If it doesn't, move the mouse to try a different spot.)
2. Choose Chart Options from the shortcut menu that appears. The Chart Options dialog box opens.
3. Click the Titles tab if it is not displayed already.

4. Enter the titles you want in the text boxes provided (see Figure 15.10), or edit the existing ones. For example, to enter a chart title, type one in the Chart Title text box.
5. Click OK.

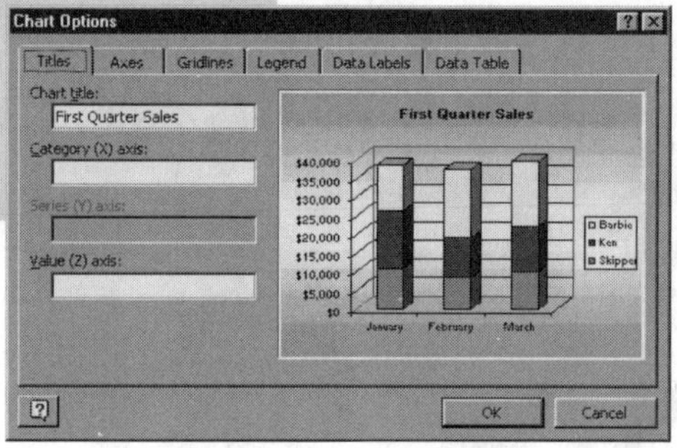

Figure 15.10 Create chart titles from the Chart Options dialog box.

When you add titles, you take away from the available space for the plot area in the chart frame. The chart in the plot area will appear smaller after you add titles, because Excel shrinks it so that it, along with the added titles, all fit in the chart frame.

Formatting a Title

After you have a title on your chart, the formatting fun begins. Right-click on the title you want to format and choose Format Chart Title (or whatever kind of title it is) from the shortcut menu. A Format dialog box opens with that title type's name (for example, the Format Chart Title dialog box, shown in Figure 15.11).

The first tab is Patterns (see Figure 15.11), which you saw in the "Changing Chart Backgrounds" section earlier in this chapter. You can set a background for a chart title the same as for any other element.

You can also set a border around the title. The default is None, which means the border frame blends in invisibly with the background on which it's placed. But if you prefer, you can place any color or thickness of border around it. Follow these steps:

1. From the Patterns tab of the Format Chart Title dialog box, select the Custom button in the Border area.

Figure 15.11 The Format Chart Title dialog box lists all the formatting you can do to a chart title.

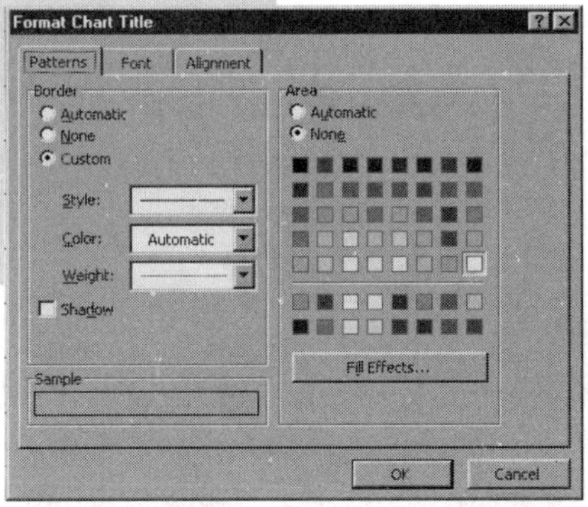

2. Open the Style drop-down list and choose a line style (solid or broken in any of a variety of ways).
3. Open the Color drop-down list and choose a line color.
4. Open the Weight drop-down list and choose a line weight (in other words, a thickness).

SEE CHAPTER 11 FOR HELP USING THE FONT CONTROLS.

Before you click OK to close the dialog box, look at the other two tabs to make sure that there aren't any more changes you want to make.

The next tab is Font (see Figure 15.12). It works exactly the same as the Font controls you have worked with in regular worksheet cells. Simply choose a font, font size, and any attributes. The only thing that's different is the Auto Scale check box at the bottom of the dialog box. Leave this marked; if you later resize the chart area, the font for the title will adjust itself in proportion as long as this stays marked.

Figure 15.12 These Font controls work the same as font controls you have used earlier, but they govern only the title you selected.

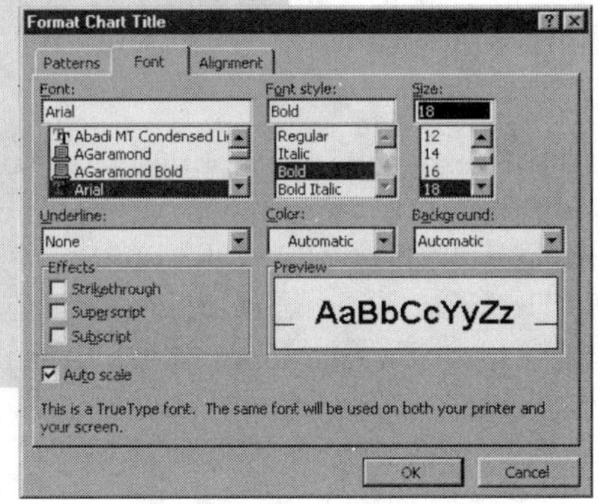

Tip

It's a good idea to make the chart title big—the biggest text on the chart. That way it gets noticed. Try 14 or 18 for the size and make it bold.

The final tab in the Format Chart Title dialog box is the Alignment tab (see Figure 15.13). In theory, these controls work the same as the Alignment tab for individual cells. You choose Left, Right, or Center for Horizontal alignment, and Top, Center, or Bottom for Vertical. However, alignment is a moot point with a title, because it is aligned only within its own frame, not within the whole chart area. And because its frame is exactly as big as it needs to be to hold the text, there is nowhere for the text to go in any direction. Therefore, no matter what alignment you choose, the text will look the same.

Figure 15.13 Set the alignment for the title within its frame.

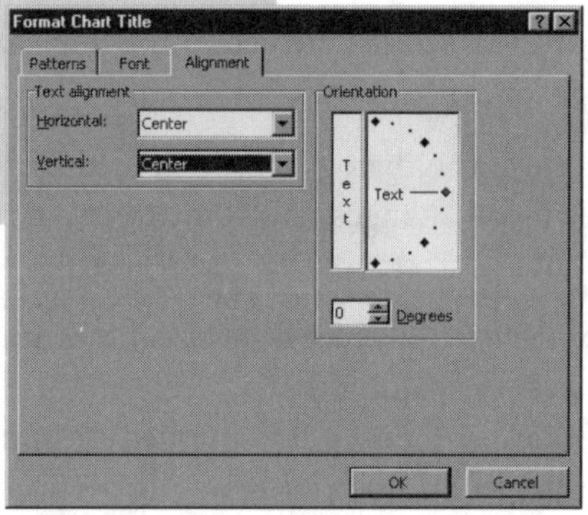

CELL ALIGNMENT WAS COVERED IN CHAPTER 11.

Now is a good time to check out the Orientation controls on the Alignment tab. These controls are available when you're formatting cells too, as you saw in Chapter 11. The feature is of limited usefulness in a cell, but on a chart, it can add real flair!

By default, all text starts out formatted horizontally, at 0 degrees of tilt. But it doesn't have to stay that way; you can rotate it to any number of degrees of tilt, from 1 to 359. (A full circle is 360, so 360 is the same as 0.) To do this, enter a number of degrees in the Degrees text box, or drag the red diamond in the Orientation panel to a different position (see Figure 15.13). Figure 15.14 shows the sample chart with some rotated text.

Figure 15.14 This chart's rotated title adds interest, whereas the rotated axis title makes the title take up less room, leaving more room for the plot area.

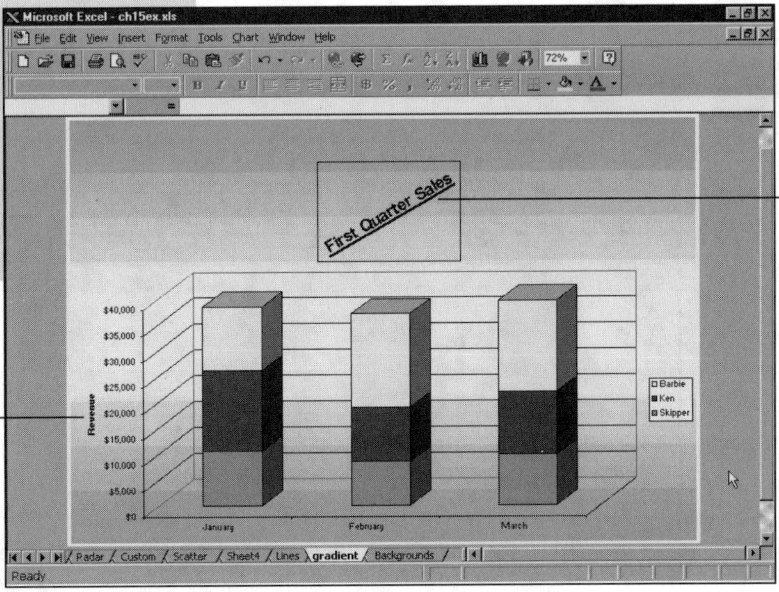

Tip

Remember, titles are separate elements from the plot area. That means you can drag their frames to reposition them anywhere within the chart area.

Changing How the Axes Appear

Every time I see the word "axes" I think of the axes that chop down trees, but in Excel, "axes" is the plural of axis, and an *axis* is a side of your chart containing the measurements that your data is plotted against. For example, in the chart you've been working with in this chapter, the Category (X) axis contains the months, and the Value (Y) axis contains dollar amounts.

You can do many things to an axis. The option with the biggest potential impact on the chart is changing the scale. For example, look at the chart in Figure 15.15. (It's the same chart that you've been working with throughout this chapter, but changed to a different subtype.) The bars are so close to each other in value that it is difficult to see the difference between them. Compare it to the same chart in Figure 15.16 with an adjusted scale. Because the scale is smaller, the differences are more dramatic.

Figure 15.15 This chart doesn't show the differences between values very well.

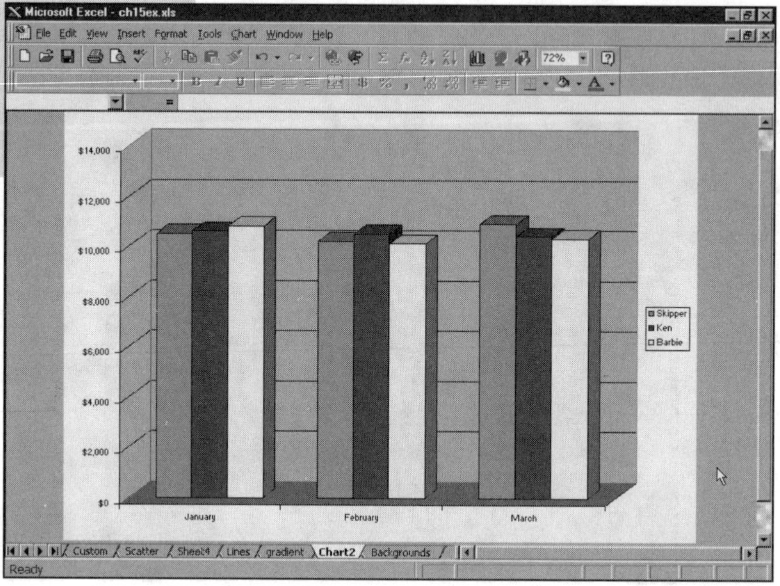

Figure 15.16 A change to the Value axis scale makes the differences easier to see.

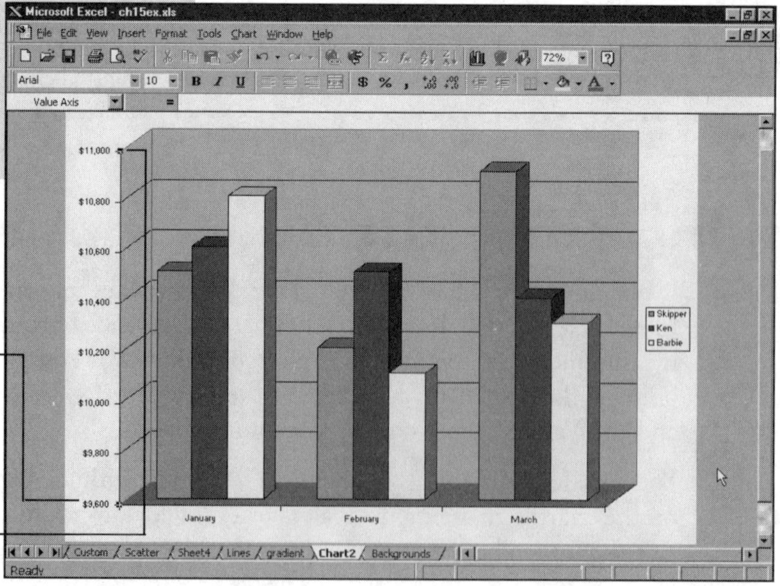

Scale now starts at $9,600 ...

... and ends at $11,000.

To set the scale for an axis, follow these steps:

1. Point your mouse at the axis to be scaled (probably the vertical axis) and wait for a ScreenTip to pop up telling you that you're pointing at the right spot.
2. Right-click, and choose Format Axis from the shortcut menu.

Tip

You can double-click on one of the axis labels (for example, any of the numbers along the Value axis in Figure 15.16) to open the Format Axis dialog box quickly.

3. In the Format Axis dialog box, click the Scale tab to display the scale settings (see Figure 15.17).

Figure 15.17 Set your scale numbers on the Scale tab.

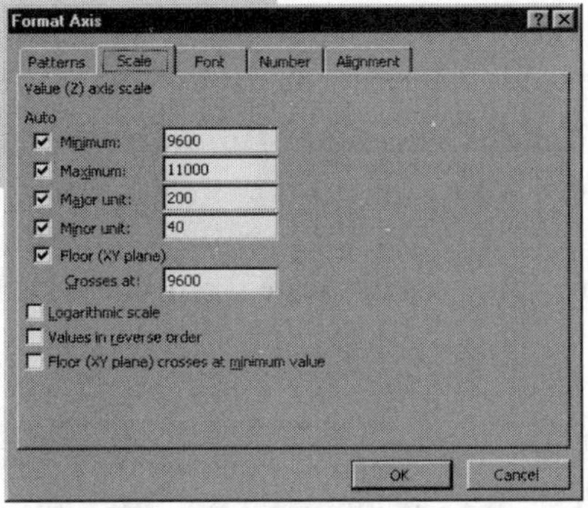

4. Enter the number you want at the bottom (or left) end of the axis in the Minimum text box, or leave its check box marked to have Excel calculate it automatically.
5. Enter the number you want at the top (or right) end of the axis in the Maximum text box, or leave its check box marked to have Excel calculate it automatically.
6. Enter the units you want counted off on the scale in the Major Unit text box, or leave its check box marked to have Excel calculate it automatically. (For example, in Figure 15.17 the major unit is 200.)
7. (Optional) If you want to show a minor unit between the major ones, enter it in the Minor Unit text box, or leave its check box marked to have Excel calculate it automatically.

Tip

Most charts look better without minor units shown. Minor units can make a chart look too cluttered. Excel can determine whether a minor unit would be useful and omit it when appropriate if you leave the Minor Unit check box marked.

8. If you want a specific number at the floor other than the number you entered under Minimum, enter it in the Crosses At text box. (This is rarely done; usually the floor shows the minimum value.)
9. If you want any of the following special features, select their check boxes:
   - **Logarithmic Scale.** Rarely used by ordinary folks, this check box recalculates the minimum, maximum, major units, and minor units according to a power of 10 for the value axis based on the range of data. (If that explanation doesn't make any sense to you, you're not the target audience for this feature.)
   - **Values In Reverse Order.** This check box turns the scale backwards so that the greater values are at the bottom or left.
   - **Floor (XY Plane) Crosses at Minimum Value.** This sets the Crosses At text box's value to the smallest value represented on the chart. For example, if the shortest bar on the chart were $10,100, the minimum value on the scale would be $10,100, and that bar would have no height.

Caution

Each of these check boxes recalculates the numbers in the Minimum, Maximum, Major Units, and Minor Units text boxes. Don't select them after you have entered specific values for any of these if you want to keep those entered values.

SEE CHAPTER 11 FOR INFORMATION ABOUT CHANGING THE FONT USING THE FONT DIALOG BOX.

10. Click OK when you're finished, and take a look at the results in your chart.

As you may have noticed in the Format Axis dialog box, several other tabs contain settings that you can change for your axis. These controls are all ones that you have seen earlier in the book, so you should be familiar with them:

- **Patterns.** You can set text and background colors and patterns the same as you can any other part of the chart. This is covered earlier in this chapter.
- **Font.** Changing the font used to display axis labels is the same as changing any other font.

- **Number.** You can change how the numbers on your Value axis appear using the same number formats that you used on cells in Chapter 10.
- **Alignment.** Just like the titles on the chart, the axis labels can be aligned. See Chapter 11 and the "Formatting a Title" section earlier in this chapter.

Legends

SEE CHAPTER 10 TO LEARN ABOUT THE AVAILABLE NUMBER FORMATS.

With a multiseries chart, the value of the legend is obvious—it tells you what colors represent which series. Without it, your reader wouldn't know what the various bars or lines meant.

You can do all the same formatting things to a legend that you can do to other chart elements you've seen so far. Right-click on the legend and choose Format Legend from the shortcut menu; then use the tabs in the Format Legend dialog box to do any of these things to it:

- Change the background. Use the Area controls on the Patterns tab.
- Change the border around the legend. Use the Border controls on the Patterns tab.
- Change the font, font size, and attributes. Use the controls on the Font tab.
- Change the placement of the legend in relation to the chart. These controls are on the Placement tab.

The only thing that's tricky here is that the alignment controls on the Placement tab do not mean the same thing for the legend as the Alignment tab does for other elements. For other elements, "alignment" refers to the text's alignment within its frame; but for the legend, "alignment" refers to the placement of the frame in relation to the plot area. You select between Bottom, Corner (upper right corner), Top, Right, or Left.

Tip

You can also drag the legend's frame around to manually place it wherever you want it. Move it as you learned to move frames in Chapter 14.

Data Labels

Data labels aren't appropriate for every chart. In fact, so far you haven't used any of them at all in your sample charts! Data labels announce the value, percentage, series, and so on for a bar, slice, or other value marker. The best place to use them is on a pie chart because there's a fairly large expanse of area for each slice. Series and Percentage data labels are shown in Figure 15.18.

Figure 15.18 For some types of charts, data labels can help make the meaning more clear.

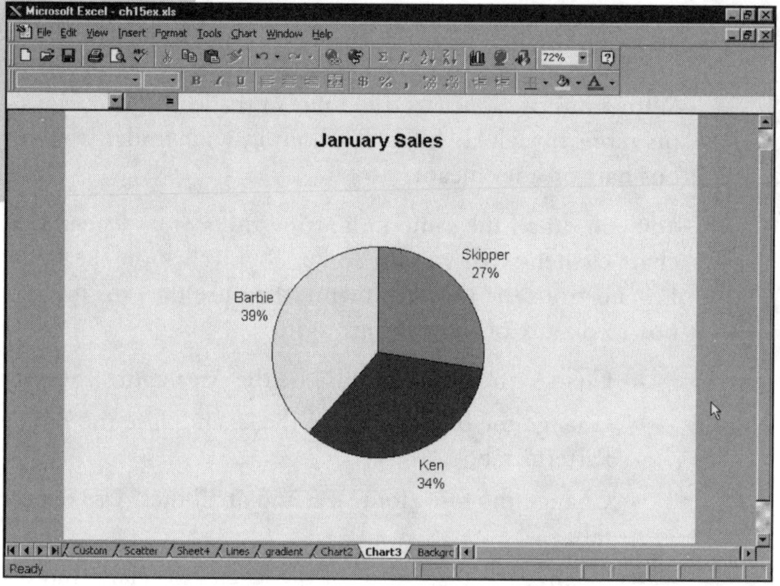

Note

Notice that Figure 15.18 doesn't contain a legend. It doesn't contain a legend because the data labels convey the legend information.

To add data labels to your chart, follow these steps:

1. Right-click the chart area and choose Chart Options from the shortcut menu.
2. Click the Data Labels tab (see Figure 15.19).
3. Click the option button for the kind of labels you want:
   - **None.** The default; no labels.
   - **Show Value.** Shows the actual value from the cell that the chart takes its information from.
   - **Show Percent.** Shows what percentage of the whole each series represents.

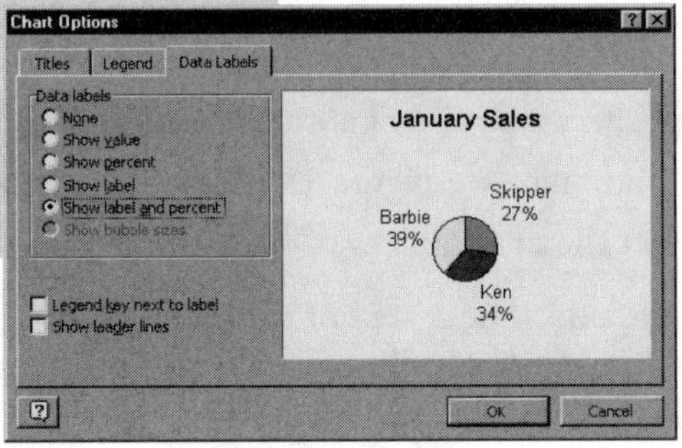

Figure 15.19 Choose what type of labels you want to appear on your chart.

- **Show Label.** Shows the label from the legend next to the series.
- **Show Label and Percent.** A combination of Show Percent and Show Label. (This is what you see in Figure 15.18.)

4. If you are using Show Label or Show Label and Percent, you don't need the legend, so click the Legend tab and deselect the Show Legend check box.
5. Click OK. Your labels appear on the chart.

Gridlines and Walls

Gridlines help the readers' eyes follow across the page. Gridlines are related to the axes. Both vertical and horizontal gridlines are available for your use. *Walls* are the space between the gridlines formatted in a different color than the plot area. Set the Walls area to None, and good-bye walls. (Don't you wish tearing down walls was always that easy?)

Note

To set the walls' formatting, right-click the wall and select Format Walls. Then choose the wall formatting in the Pattern tab of the Format Walls dialog box that appears.

In most cases, the default gridlines Excel adds work well. However, sometimes you might want to make the lines thicker or a different color, or turn them off altogether.

Displaying or Hiding Gridlines

To change which gridlines are displayed, follow these steps:

1. Right-click the chart area and choose Chart Options.
2. Click the Gridlines tab (see Figure 15.20).
3. Select or deselect the check boxes to turn on/off the gridlines.
    - **Category Axis.** These are not normally used, but if you want them, select either Major Gridlines or Minor Gridlines or both.
    - **Value Axis.** Normally just Major Gridlines are shown here, but if you want to see minor ones too, select the Minor Gridlines check box.
    - **Series Axis.** Some 3-D charts use this axis too. It is not available in Figure 15.20.

Figure 15.20 You can turn on/off selected gridlines here.

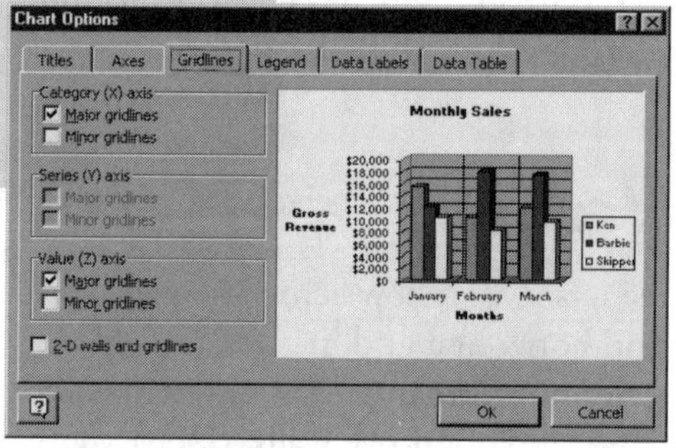

4. (Optional) To make the walls and gridlines 2-D on the 3-D chart, select the 2-D Walls and Gridlines check box.
5. Click OK.

Formatting Gridlines

You can format gridlines the same way you format other objects on a chart. Right-click a gridline and select Format Gridline. Any changes you make affect all gridlines of that type (for example, all horizontal major ones).

When you open the Format Gridlines dialog box, you see two tabs. One is Scale, which is the same as the Scale settings for the axis that that gridline touches. Any changes made in one place will be reflected in the other.

The other tab is Patterns (see Figure 15.21), and the controls there are the same as the controls you saw earlier for changing a border. The only difference is that the None option is grayed out. That's because you can't turn off gridlines from here. You must use the procedure outlined earlier in this section.

Figure 15.21 Change the color and thickness of your gridlines from here.

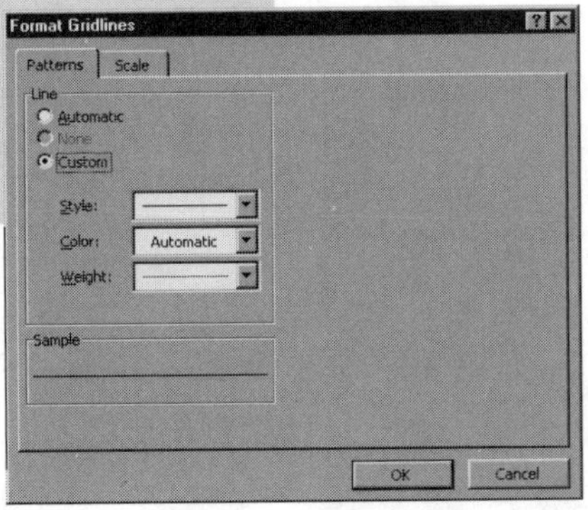

Formatting the Data Series

Now comes the fun part. You get to change the colors of the bars, lines, or slices; move them around; and otherwise tinker.

To format a data series, right-click on the bar, slice, or whatever, and choose Format Data Series from the shortcut menu. Then, depending on what type of chart you have, you will see different tabs with which you can modify the series' appearance.

Patterns and Colors

The first stop is the Patterns tab. This is just like the Patterns tab you worked with for backgrounds (refer to Figure 15.4), and the controls all work the same way. There is only one small addition: the Invert If Negative check box. This swaps the foreground and background colors if the number represented by the data series is negative. It applies to pies, bars, columns, and areas.

Note

The colors you choose on this tab apply only to the particular series that you right-clicked if there is more than one in your chart. That's because you will want to select the colors for each series separately instead of having them all be the same color.

Shape

On the Shape tab, you get to choose what shape your bars or columns will be (see Figure 15.22). Why settle for an ordinary bar? Have some fun with these. The choice you make here applies to only the data series you right-clicked on, so each series can have its own shape in the chart if you want.

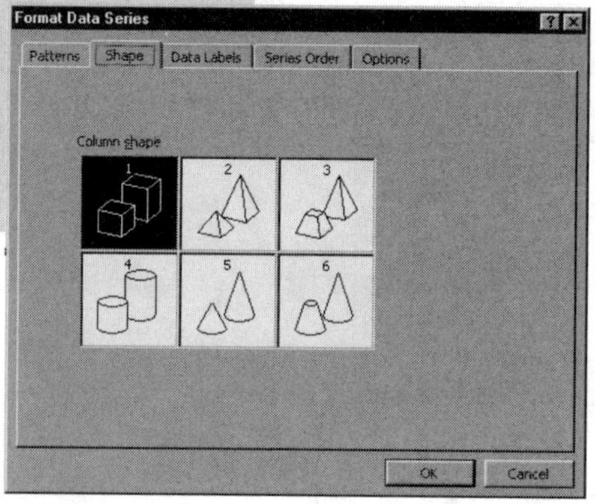

Figure 15.22 On the Shape tab, you can choose among several bar or column shapes.

Data Labels

The Data Labels tab contains the same basic controls as the Data Labels tab you worked with in the Chart Options dialog box (refer to Figure 15.19), except these controls apply only to the selected data series. You could use these, for example, to add data labels only for the series that you want to spotlight.

Series Order

On the Series Order tab (see Figure 15.23), you can change what order the series appear in on the chart. By default, they appear in the same order as they appear on the worksheet, but you may have a reason for wanting them switched on the chart, if nothing else for aesthetic purposes.

To change the series order, click on the series to be moved on the Series Order list and then click the Move Up or Move Down button to move it.

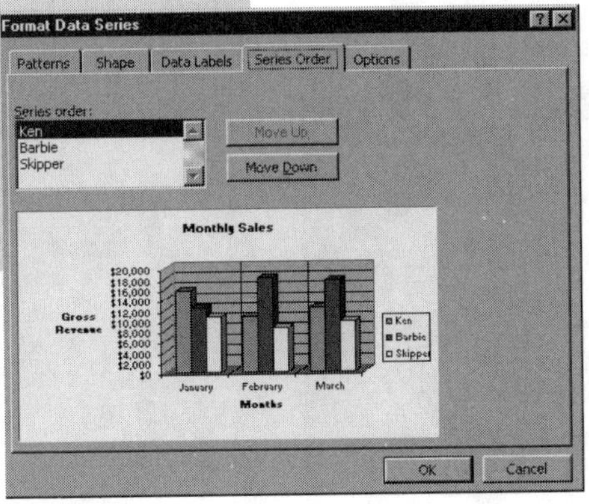

Figure 15.23 Change the order in which the series appear on the chart from the Series Order tab.

Options

The Options tab is different for different chart types. It contains options specific to that type. For example, Figure 15.24 shows the options for a column chart. You can set the gap between bars and the overall chart depth. Figure 15.25 shows the options for a pie chart. Here you can set the angle of the first slice, effectively rotating the slices so that any slice is at any position you want. Other chart types have other options you can explore on your own.

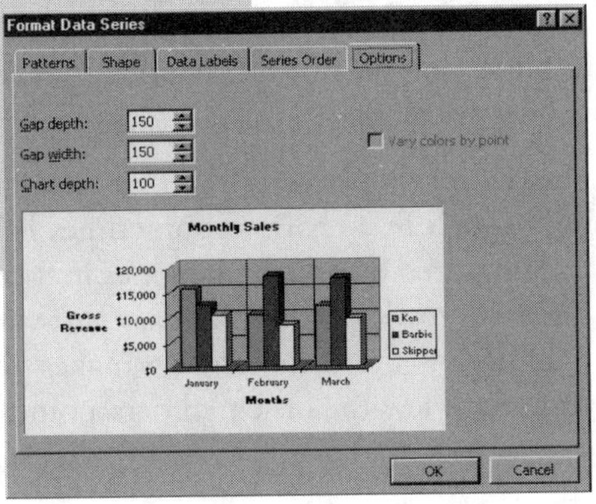

Figure 15.24 The Options tab for column and bar charts enables you to set the gaps between bars.

Figure 15.25 The Options tab for pie charts enables you to specify the angle of the first slice.

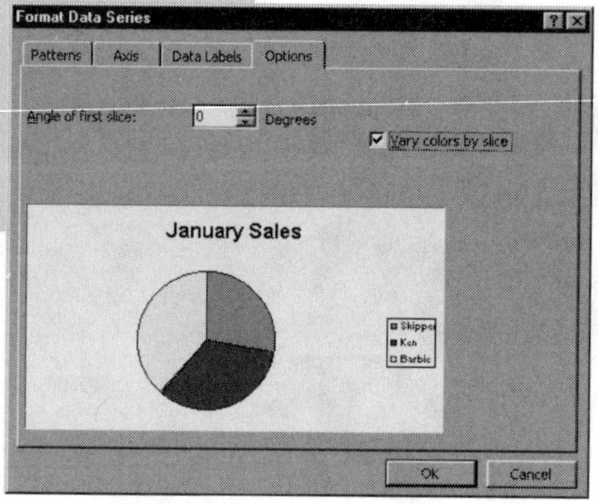

There is also a Vary Colors By Slice check box on the Options tab for pie charts. Leave this checked! If you unmark it, all the slices will be the same color, and you won't be able to tell them apart, even with a legend.

Changing the 3-D View

This feature is a little bit advanced, but can be a real lifesaver when you have a 3-D chart that needs some tweaking.

Not all of Excel's charts turn out perfectly the first time. Excel can't anticipate how your data is going to look in a chart, so sometimes in a 3-D chart some of the data bars or lines are obscured by other, taller ones in front of them. For example, in Figure 15.26, the back row's value for January isn't visible because the middle row is too tall. Modifying the 3-D settings makes the chart appear at a different angle, bringing into view the obscured data point.

To change the 3-D view, follow these steps:

1. Right-click on the chart area, plot area, or walls and choose 3-D View from the shortcut menu.
2. In the 3-D View dialog box (see Figure 15.27), click the buttons to change the view, and then click Apply to try out the settings (drag the title bar of the dialog box to move it out of the way as needed):

Rotating Pie Slices: A Real-World Example

A few years back, I was administering a program in which I had to provide monthly reports showing a breakdown of the percentage of users in certain categories. I used a pie chart for this, but there were many categories, and the pie slices were rather thin. The labels often got cut off or ran into each other like this:

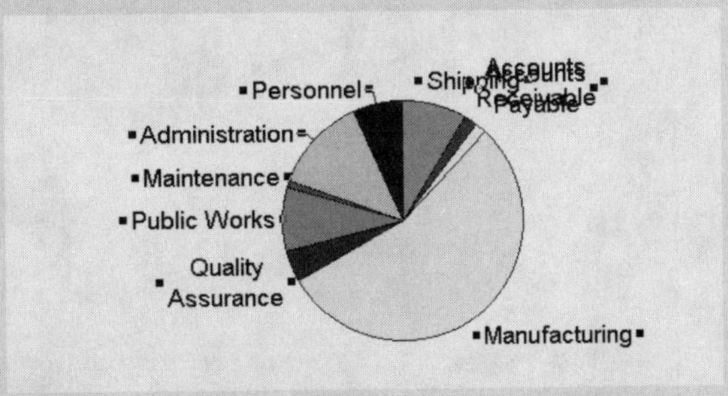

I solved the problem by adjusting the Angle of First Slice until the pie rotated enough that the thinner slices were on the sides, where there was more room for their labels.

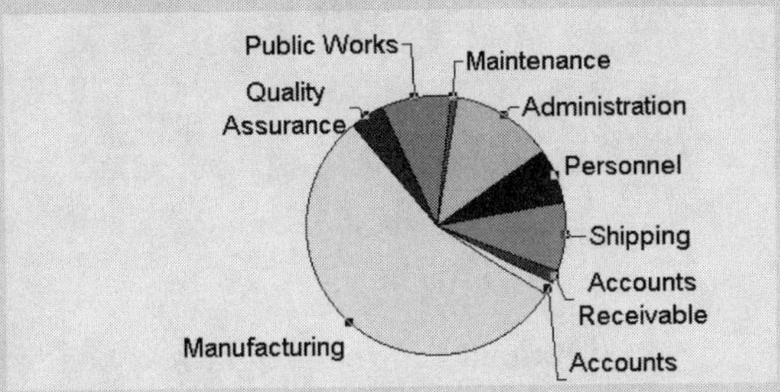

- Use the Elevation buttons to tilt the view up and down.
- Use the Perspective buttons to zoom the view in and out.
- Use the Rotation buttons to rotate the chart. When you rotate a chart so much that the walls will be in the way, the walls move to the opposite side. (Convenient, eh?)

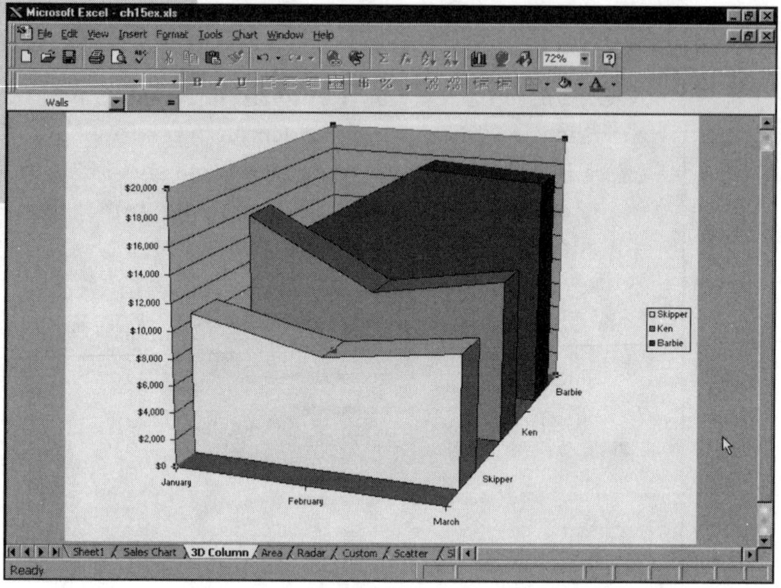

Figure 15.26 This chart could benefit from some 3-D setting changes to make the back row more readable.

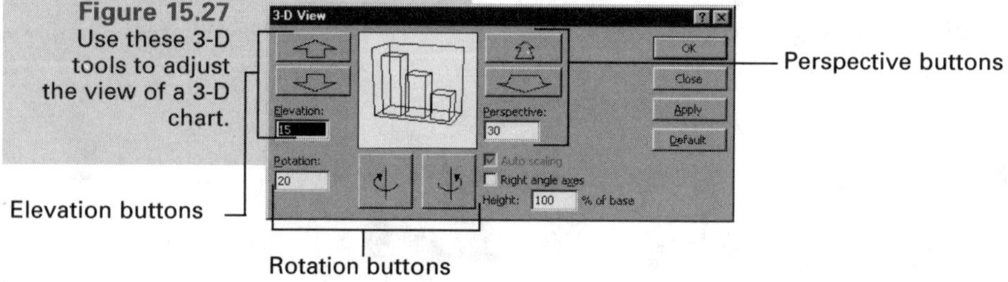

Figure 15.27 Use these 3-D tools to adjust the view of a 3-D chart.

3. (Optional) In the Height text box, enter a percentage of the base width to represent the height of the chart. The default is 100; a setting of less than that will make a short, squat chart, whereas a setting of more than that will make a taller, thinner chart.
4. When you are satisfied with your settings and have tested them out by clicking Apply, click OK. Figure 15.28 shows the chart from Figure 15.26 adjusted so that all data points are visible.

Figure 15.28
Now each series is completely visible, thanks to some 3-D adjustments.

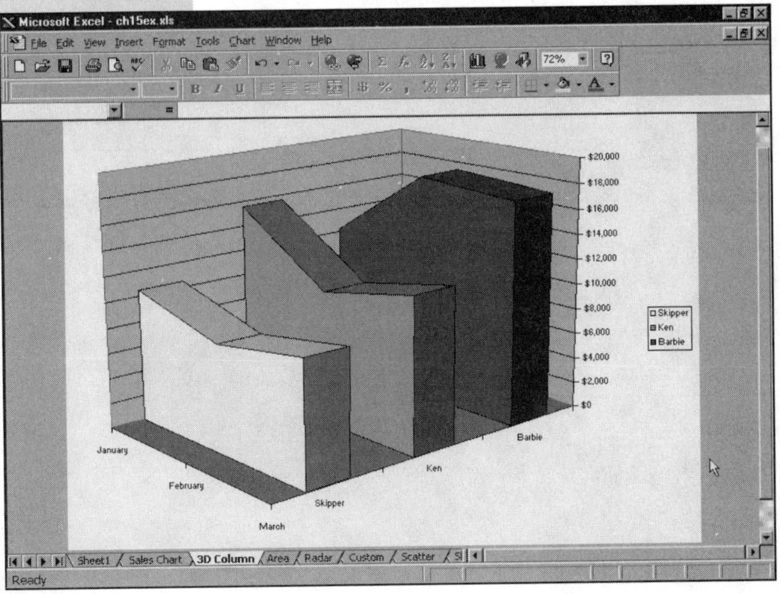

16

Incorporating Graphics in Your Worksheet

In This Chapter

- Adding Premade Clip Art and Pictures
- Including Sounds and Video Files
- Drawing Your Own Graphics
- Modifying Text with WordArt
- Using Microsoft Map to Show Geographical Data

Strictly speaking, nothing in this chapter is absolutely necessary. It's all about dressing up your worksheets with pictures, fancy lettering, maps, and multimedia components (like sounds and videos). And you can certainly present effective data without any of those things. But if you want to dazzle your reader as well as inform, you've come to the right place.

Introducing the Clip Gallery

In previous versions of Excel, inserting clip art, sounds, videos, and pictures was kind of a hodge-podge affair. There were separate commands for each type of insertion, and the procedure worked differently for each too. With Excel 97, Microsoft has pulled together all these elements in one convenient location: the Clip Gallery.

The Clip Gallery (see Figure 16.1) has four tabs, one for each type of file. You can organize frequently used files through the Clip Gallery, import from various sources (including the Internet), and create categories to keep your files neatly sorted. You'll learn to do all these things in this chapter.

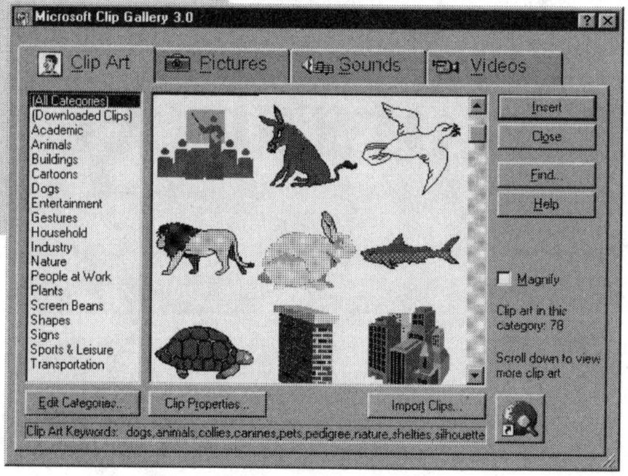

Figure 16.1 In the Clip Gallery, each of the various types of multimedia files has its own tab.

Why would you insert a clip? Here are some reasons:

- Clip art (premade art that comes with Excel) can dress up a boring worksheet. For example, images of smiling employees shaking hands can drive home a message of teamwork.
- Scanned pictures from your own company can make a worksheet seem more personal to the reader. For example, you could scan in pictures from the charitable events your company sponsored to include with your financial data on those events, helping the reader understand why the money was spent.
- Video clips can illustrate procedures in a worksheet that's distributed on disk rather than printed. For example, you could include a video clip of a manufacturing process along with process productivity data.

- Sound clips can provide additional information. For example, a recording of a bird call could accompany data on the sightings of that bird, or a voice-over explanation from the CEO could enhance a quarterly report to employees.

As you work, you will likely find many more reasons to use clips in Excel in your own organization.

Opening the Clip Gallery

No matter what kind of clip you want to insert, you open the Clip Gallery by telling Excel that you want to insert Clip Art. (Don't worry if you want to insert a video, sound, or picture instead—it's just a menu command, and it doesn't lock you into inserting only clip art.)

To open the Clip Gallery, follow these steps:

1. Display the worksheet where you want the clip inserted. (Clips float on top of the sheet, like charts, instead of being attached to a particular cell.)
2. Choose Insert, Picture, Clip Art.
3. If a dialog box appears telling you that additional clip art is on the CD and your CD is handy, go ahead and put it in your CD-ROM drive. (If it's not handy, don't worry about it.) Then click OK.

In the dialog box in step 3, there is a Don't Remind Me Again check box. If you select this check box, you won't see the dialog box in the future—step 2 will take you directly to the Clip Gallery.

Inserting a Clip into Your Worksheet

No matter what type of clip you want (clip art, sound, video, or picture), you insert it in your worksheet the same way. Follow these steps:

1. Click on the tab for the type of clip you want.
2. Click on the category of clip you want from the Categories list. Or, to see all clips, select All Categories from the list, as shown in Figure 16.2.
3. Click on the clip you want. If it's a sound or video, you can click Play to get a preview of it before you insert. (The Play button doesn't appear on the Clip Art and Picture tabs.)
4. Click Insert. The Clip Gallery closes, and your clip appears in your worksheet. If it's a sound or video, an icon represents it on the worksheet.

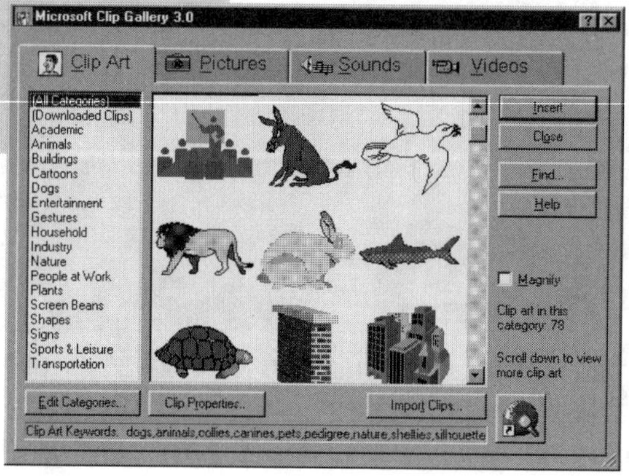

Figure 16.2 Click the clip you want, and then click Insert.

Importing Clips

When you first use the Clip Gallery, there may not be anything on the Pictures, Sounds, and Videos tabs, and most of the buttons may be grayed out. That's all right—it's just that no clips are imported yet. Excel comes with much clip art already imported, but you must import the other clip types yourself.

To try out importing, import all the bitmap files in your Windows folder, making them available for use in Excel.

Hands On: Importing Bitmap Files from Windows

Windows 95 comes with several bitmap images (albeit small ones) that it uses as wallpaper. Although you will probably not use these as pictures in Excel very often, they make excellent practice files. Import them into the Clip Gallery now:

1. If the Clip Gallery isn't open, choose Insert, Picture, Clip Art.
2. Click the Pictures tab.
3. Click the Import Clips button. The Add Pictures to Clip Gallery dialog box appears.
4. Change the drive and folder to display the contents of the Windows folder (see Figure 16.3).
5. Click on Black Thatch, and then hold down the Shift key while you click on Waves. This selects all the files in-between those two.
6. Click the Open button. A Clip Properties dialog box appears for Waves, as shown in Figure 16.4.

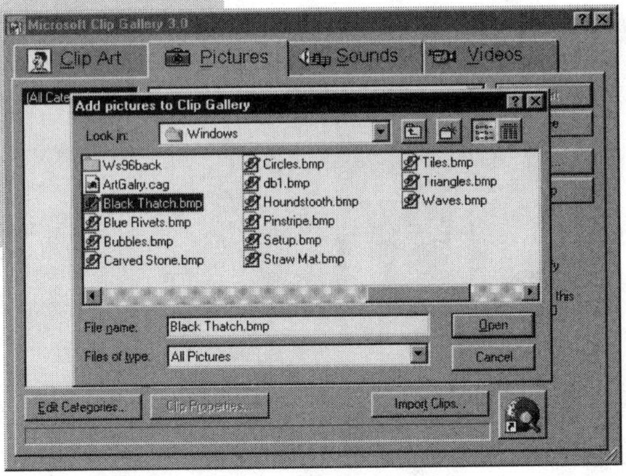

Figure 16.3 You'll find some .BMP (bitmap) images to practice with in the Windows folder.

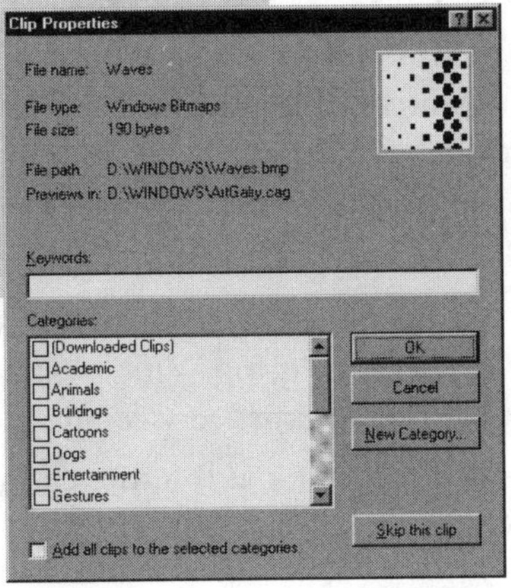

Figure 16.4 For each imported clip, you must give Clip Gallery some information.

7. Create a new category to hold these Windows bitmap files. Click on the New Category button.
8. Type **Windows 95 Bitmaps** in the New Category Name text box and then click OK. Windows 95 Bitmaps now appears on the Categories list, with its check box marked.
9. Type **Wallpaper** in the Keywords text box because these bitmaps were originally designed to be used as wallpaper in Windows 95.
10. Click the Add All Clips to the Selected Categories check box.
11. Click OK. All the bitmap images appear on the Pictures tab of the Clip Gallery, as shown in Figure 16.5.

You can follow the same procedure shown in the preceding Hands On to import any kind of file as a clip: video, sound, picture, or additional clip art.

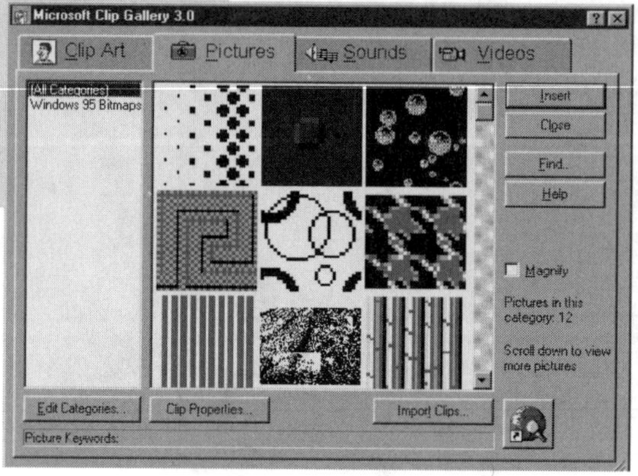

Figure 16.5
Now you can use any of these pictures in Excel through the Clip Gallery.

Getting More Clips from the Internet

Find it Online

Microsoft has a Web site on the Internet where you can download additional clips from (http://www.microsoft.com/clipgallerylive/). They include sounds, videos, pictures, and clip art. To get them, you must have a way to connect to the Internet (an online service or a dial-up or network Internet connection). To see what's available, follow these steps:

1. Establish your Internet connection. This may involve starting your online service software and connecting, or using Windows 95's Dial-Up Networking to connect to your Internet service provider.
2. Minimize the software used to make the Internet connection.
3. Start Excel, or switch back to it if it was already open.
4. Choose Insert, Picture, Clip Art. The Clip Gallery appears.
5. Click the tab representing the type of clip you want to import.
6. Click the globe button in the bottom right corner of the Clip Gallery.
7. If you see a dialog box telling you that you should click OK to browse the Web, do so. (You may not see this dialog box at all, depending on your setup.) Your browser opens, and the Clip Gallery Live page loads.
8. Read the licensing agreement in the left pane and then click the Accept button to move on. The upper right pane changes to show the controls in Figure 16.6.
9. Click the Browse or Search button to choose how you want to use the site. For this example, choose Browse.

SEE CHAPTER 21 TO LEARN MORE ABOUT USING EXCEL WITH THE INTERNET.

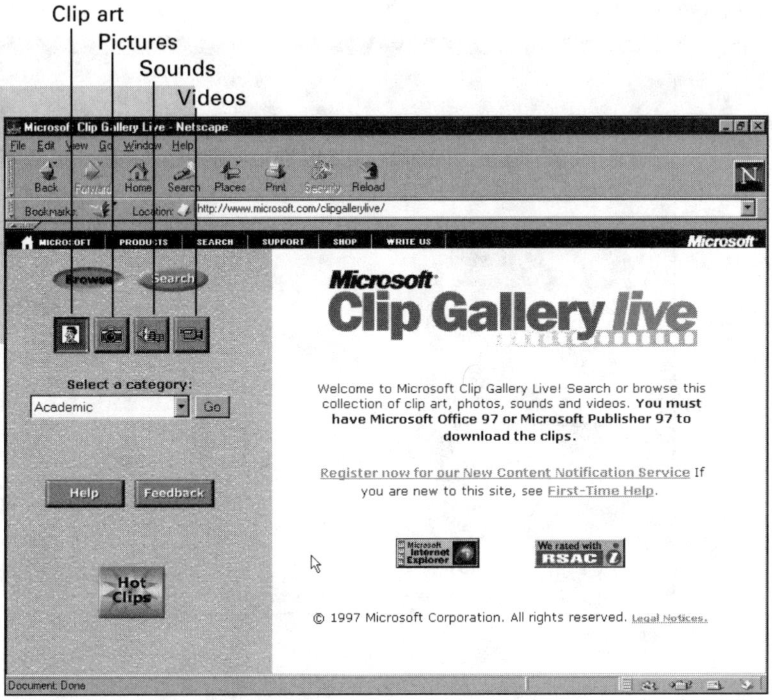

Figure 16.6 Microsoft's Clip Gallery Live page enables you to browse the available clips or search by keyword.

10. Click the button that indicates what kind of clips you are looking for. From left-to-right, they are Clip Art, Photos, Sounds, and Videos. For this example, choose Videos.
11. Open the Select a Category drop-down list and choose a category that you're interested in. For this example, choose Office.
12. Click Go. The top left pane changes to show the available clips in that category (see Figure 16.7). If more clips are in the selected category than can be displayed at once, you can see the next group by clicking the right-arrow button under the clips. (In Figure 16.7 there are only three.)
13. Click the hyperlink (the underlined name) of the clip to start downloading it to your computer. It may take a few minutes, depending on the size of the clip and the speed of your connection. When it transfers, the Clip Gallery reappears on your screen with the new clip added on the appropriate tab in the Downloaded Clips category.
14. Jump back to your browser and get more clips if you want. When you are finished, terminate your Internet connection and jump back to the Clip Gallery to use your new clips.

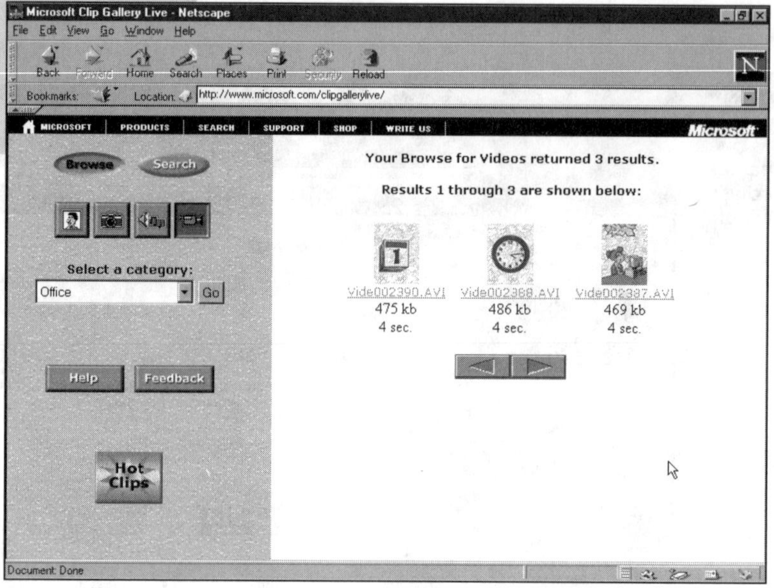

Figure 16.7 The available clips are shown in little preview windows.

Recategorizing Clips

Is it necessary to recategorize clips? Usually not, if you don't have too many of them. You can usually find the clip you want just by browsing in the Clip Gallery. But if you want to be meticulous about your clip filing system, or if you need to manage a large number of clips, you might want to pay attention to the categories and move things around to make the categories more logical.

In the Hands On procedure earlier in the chapter, you saw how you can create a new category on-the-fly as you import a clip. But you can also move an existing clip from category to category, and even make a clip appear in several categories. Follow these steps:

1. In the Clip Gallery, click on the clip you want to recategorize.
2. Click the Clip Properties button. The Clip Properties dialog box appears (see Figure 16.8).
3. Select or deselect check boxes for the various categories to choose which categories the clip will appear in.
4. (Optional) If you need to create a new category, click the New Category button, type a name for it, and click OK.
5. When you are finished with that clip, click OK to close the dialog box.

Figure 16.8 You can change what categories a clip appears in from the Clip Properties dialog box.

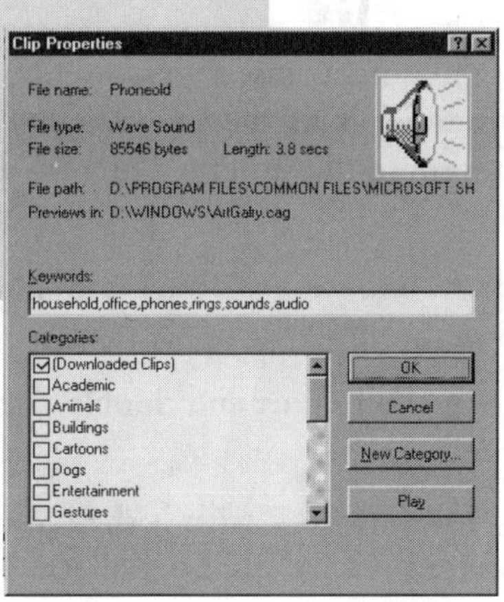

You can also manage the categories as a group, rather than as associated with an individual clip. This enables you to rename and delete categories. To do this, follow these steps:

1. From the Clip Gallery, click the tab for the type of clips for which you want to edit the categories. (There are separate categories for each clip type.)
2. Click the Edit Categories button. The Edit Category List dialog box appears (see Figure 16.9).

Figure 16.9 You can change and delete categories from the Edit Category List dialog box.

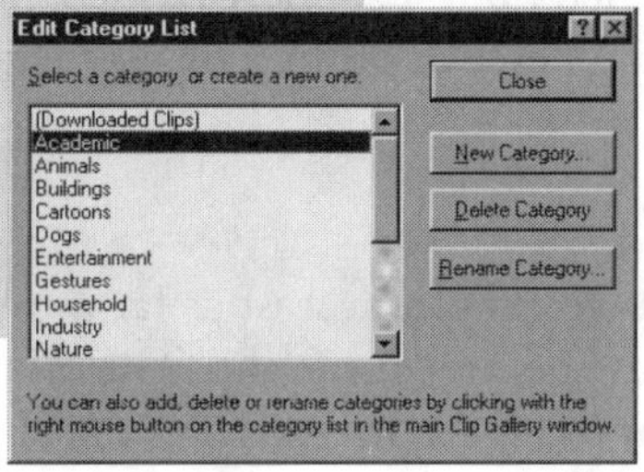

3. Select the category you want to act upon.
4. To rename the category, click the Rename Category button. Type a new name in the dialog box that appears and then click OK.
5. To delete the category, click the Delete Category button.
6. Select another category and rename or delete it if needed; when you're finished, click Close.

Inserting a Picture from a File

Sometimes you may just want to quickly insert a picture in your worksheet, without going to the trouble of adding it to the Clip Gallery. For such situations, Excel offers the following procedure that inserts a picture directly from a file on disk into Excel:

1. Select the worksheet where you want to add the graphic file.
2. Choose Insert, Picture, From File. The Insert Picture dialog box appears.
3. Locate the picture you want to import and double-click on it. The picture appears in your worksheet.

After the picture is inserted, you can work with it the same way that you would work with a picture you inserted with the Clip Gallery. The following section explains your options.

Working with Clips in a Worksheet

After you place a clip onto your worksheet, you can do a variety of things to it. The exact things you can do depend on what kind of clip it is. You can't do much with a sound clip other than move it around and resize its icon. With pictures and clip art, you can do more editing, including resizing and changing the colors in some cases. In the following sections you'll learn to move and modify clips.

Activating a Sound or Video Clip

Pictures and clip art just sit there, but a sound or video clip is expected to perform. To play one of these, double-click on its icon or image in the worksheet.

Moving a Clip Around

A clip is just like a chart on a worksheet, at least as far as moving it around goes. To move a clip, point the mouse pointer at the clip. The mouse pointer changes to a four-headed arrow, as shown in Figure 16.10. Drag the clip to a new location.

Resizing a Clip

To resize a clip, click on it to select it. Selection handles (white boxes) appear in its corners, like the ones shown in Figure 16.10. When you point your mouse pointer at a selection handle, it changes to a double-headed arrow. Drag from there to resize the clip.

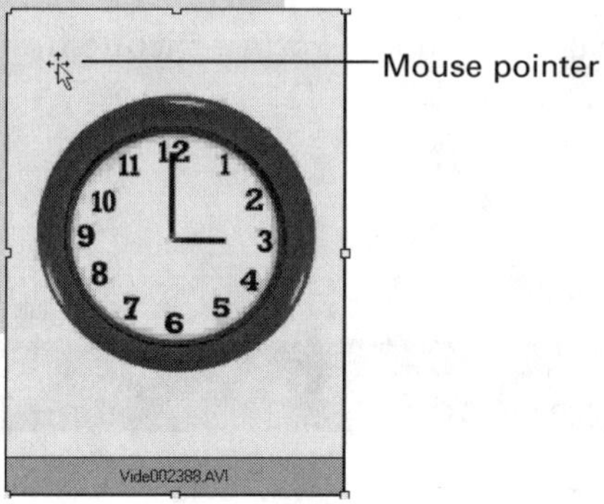

Figure 16.10 When you point at a clip, the mouse pointer changes to show you that you can move it by dragging.

To resize proportionally, so that the clip does not become distorted, drag one of the corners rather than one of the sides.

Using the Picture Toolbar

The Picture toolbar contains buttons that help you change how a clip appears in your worksheet. Even if a clip is not, strictly speaking, a picture (for example, if it's a video or sound clip), it still has an icon or image that represents it on the worksheet. That means that you can use the Picture toolbar to control how that icon or image appears.

To display the Picture toolbar, right-click the clip and choose Display Picture Toolbar from the shortcut menu. The Picture Toolbar appears. Table 16.1 explains the Picture toolbar controls.

One of the most useful—and easy to use—controls is the Image Control button. You can set any image instantly to color, grayscale, or black and white, or set it up as a watermark (a faint image that appears behind your work, like a company logo on stationery). Figure 16.11 shows the same image with each of the Image Control settings.

Modifying an Image with the Format Picture Dialog Box

There is a whole set of controls for modifying images in Excel. You can access the controls for a particular image by selecting the image and then doing any of the following:

- Click the Format Picture button on the Picture toolbar.
- Right-click the image and choose Format Picture from the shortcut menu.
- Choose Format, Picture.
- Press Ctrl+1.

Table 16.1 The Picture Toolbar Buttons

Button	Name	Purpose
	Insert Picture From File	Opens the Insert File dialog box so that you can insert a picture.
	Image Control	Lets you choose from four modes: Automatic (usually color), Grayscale, Black and White, and Watermark. These are shown in Figure 16.11.
	More Contrast	Increases the difference between the lights and darks.
	Less Contrast	Decreases the difference between the lights and darks.
	More Brightness	Makes the colors in the picture brighter.
	Less Brightness	Makes the colors in the picture darker.
	Crop	Changes the mouse pointer to a cropping tool, with which you can exclude parts of the image.
	Line Style	Changes the thickness/style of the border surroun-ding the clip.
	Format Picture	Opens the Format Picture dialog box (discussed later in this chapter).
	Set Transparent Color	Sets one color in the picture to be transparent. (Available only for bitmap pictures that do not already have transparency settings and for some, but not all, clip art).
	Reset Picture	Returns the picture to its default values.

Figure 16.11 Use the Image Control button on the Picture toolbar to set an image to one of four modes.

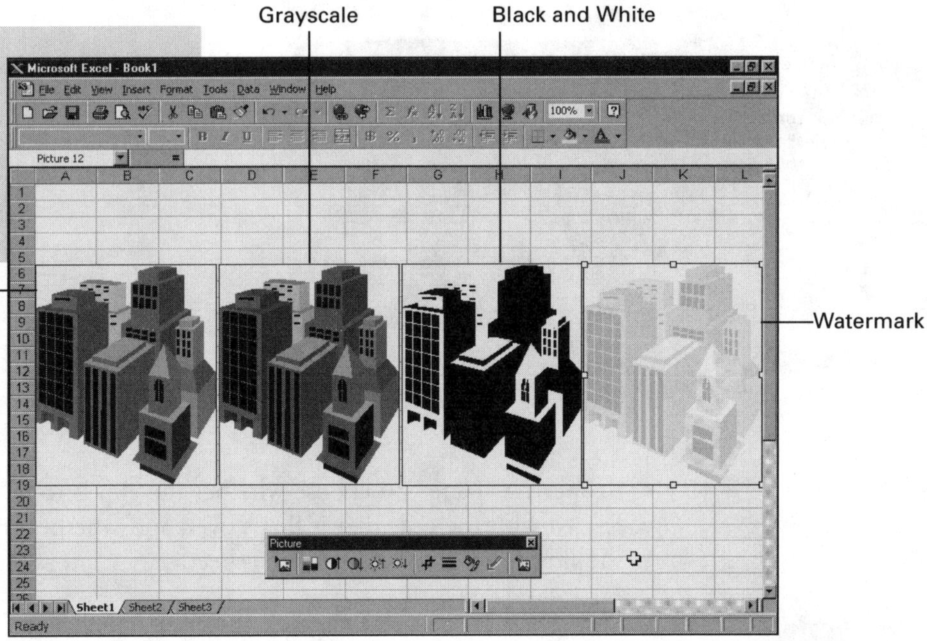

On the Format Picture dialog box (see Figure 16.12), you'll find these tabs:

- **Colors and Lines.** Here you choose the color and thickness of the border surrounding the clip. In the Fill section, you can also select a background color for the image, or select None for a transparent background.

Tip

Transparent backgrounds look especially good on images with many jagged or pointed edges. The transparent background allows the cells behind the image to be seen, so that it looks like the image has been drawn directly onto the worksheet. This effect is not as dramatic if the image is squared-off and blocky.

SEE CHAPTER 22 FOR MORE INFORMATION ABOUT WORKBOOK AND WORKSHEET PROTECTION.

- **Size.** On this tab, you can enter precise size settings (height and width) for the image, and choose whether to preserve the aspect ratio (the relationship of height to width).
- **Picture.** The Picture tab contains controls for cropping, brightness, and contrast. The Color drop-down list here corresponds to the Image Control button on the Picture toolbar.
- **Protection.** Only one thing is on this tab: a Locked check box. If Protection is turned on for the worksheet, this check box controls whether this image is protected.

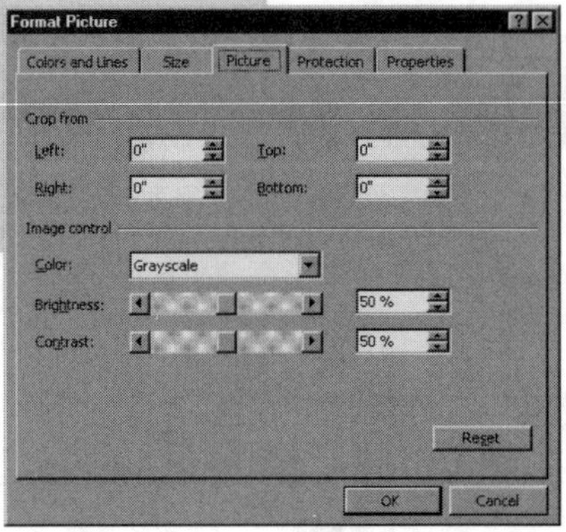

Figure 16.12 Use the Format Picture dialog box to fine-tune settings for your picture.

- **Properties.** Here you choose whether the clip is to be moved and/or resized with the cells that it floats over, and whether the clip's image should print when you print the sheet.

Tip

If the clip is an image, you will probably want it to print with the sheet. However, if the clip is a sound or video, its effect will be lost in the printout, so you will probably not want it to print.

Drawing Your Own Graphics

If you are an artist or if you just need a few simple shapes, you may be able to draw what you need with the Drawing toolbar. This is the same Drawing toolbar that's available in all Office products, so if you have used it in Word or PowerPoint, you have a head-start in learning.

To display the Drawing toolbar, right-click on any toolbar and choose Drawing from the shortcut menu. It appears at the bottom of the screen, as shown in Figure 16.13.

Figure 16.13 The Drawing toolbar, ready for action.

Drawing Simple Shapes and Lines

Two types of tools are on the Drawing toolbar: tools that draw shapes and tools that manipulate shapes. Because you can't manipulate a shape before you've drawn it, you'll look at the drawing tools first:

Icon	Name
	Line
	Line with arrow
	Rectangle
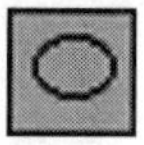	Ellipse

The procedure is basically the same for all these tools, although it may take you a bit of practice to master them:

1. Display the worksheet on which you want to draw.
2. Click the drawing tool you want.
3. Point the mouse pointer where you want the line or shape to begin.
4. Hold down the mouse button and drag to where you want the line or shape to end.
5. Release the mouse button to view the finished line or shape.

If you double-click instead of click in step 2, you can repeat the procedure from step 3 to draw more of the same shape. Otherwise you must go back to step 2 each time.

Placing AutoShapes on the Worksheet

AutoShapes are predrawn shapes that function like the lines and boxes that you draw. They're great for people who want shapes like arrows and starbursts but aren't coordinated enough to draw them (or simply don't have the time to waste). To use an AutoShape, follow these steps:

1. Display the worksheet on which you want to place the AutoShape.
2. Click the AutoShapes button on the Drawing toolbar. A menu pops up listing categories of shapes.
3. Point your mouse at the category you want (for example, Block Arrows). A menu of the available shapes in that category appears (see Figure 16.14).

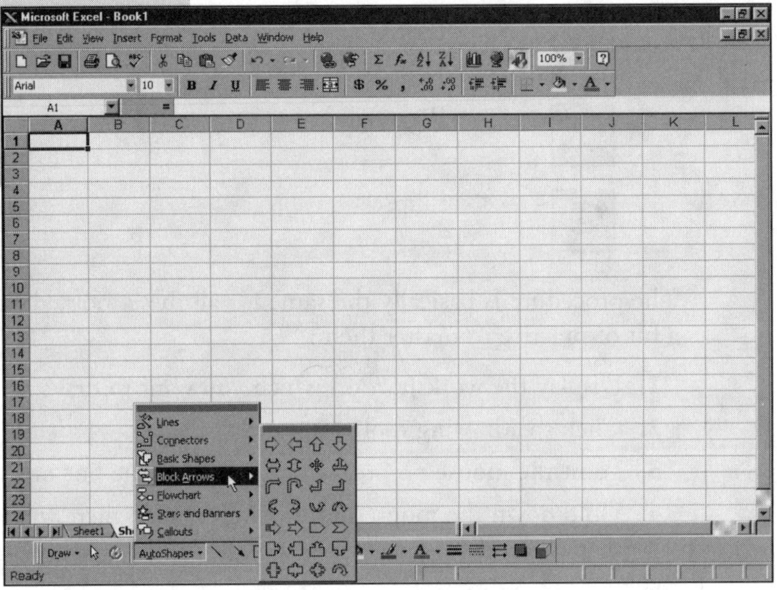

Figure 16.14 Choose the category of AutoShape you want and then the shape itself.

4. Click on the shape you want. Your mouse pointer turns into a crosshair.
5. Drag on the worksheet to draw a box where you want the shape to appear. When you release the mouse button, the shape appears on your worksheet.

Manipulating Lines and Shapes

Many of the basics for working with the lines and shapes you draw are the same as working with clips (which you learned about at the beginning of this chapter). For example, to move a line or shape, simply click on it to select it and then position the mouse pointer over it so that your pointer becomes a four-headed arrow. Then drag the line or shape to its new position.

Resizing a line or shape is the same as resizing a clip too: point to one of the line or shape's selection handles and drag it to change the line or shape.

Copying and Deleting Drawn Objects

You can copy lines and shapes the same way that you copy anything else in Excel:

1. Select the object.
2. Choose Edit, Copy, click the Copy button on the toolbar, or press Ctrl+C.
3. Select where you want it to go.
4. Choose Edit, Paste, click the Paste button, or press Ctrl+V.

Deleting is just what you'd expect too: select the object and then press the Del key on the keyboard.

Rotating and Flipping Drawn Objects

Suppose that you've drawn an arrow that points up with the AutoShape feature, but you want it to point down. No problem—just flip it. To flip a drawn object:

1. Select the drawing.
2. Click the Draw button on the Drawing toolbar. A menu appears.
3. Point to Rotate or Flip on that menu. Another submenu appears.
4. Choose Flip Vertical or Flip Horizontal, depending on what you're after. (In this example, to turn the arrow upside down, choose Flip Vertical.)

As you saw while you had the menu open, the Rotate or Flip submenu also has commands for Rotate Right and Rotate Left. You can use these to rotate your shape 90 degrees.

If you want to control the precise amount of rotation, use the Free Rotate feature:

1. Choose Draw, Rotate or Flip, Free Rotate, or click the Free Rotate button on the Drawing toolbar (see Figure 16.15). The selection handles around the shape turn into green circles.
2. Position the mouse pointer over one of those circles, so that the mouse pointer turns into a circular arrow. Then drag that selection handle to rotate the shape to the exact position you want.
3. Click anywhere away from the shape to finish.

Modifying How a Drawn Object Appears

On the Drawing toolbar are several tools that control how a drawing appears. Table 16.2 show the buttons on the Drawing toolbar.

Figure 16.15 Drag the round green selection handles to rotate the shape.

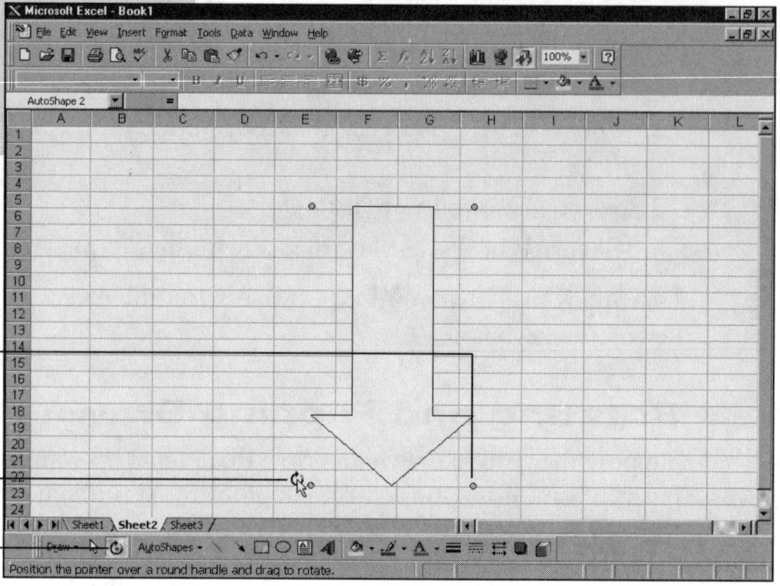

Tip: You can access all the controls from the Drawing toolbar in a more formal form, with more precise controls, by right-clicking on the shape or line and then choosing Format AutoShape from the shortcut menu. (It doesn't matter whether you actually created it with the AutoShapes button; Excel considers all shapes and lines AutoShapes after they're drawn.)

Making Fancy Text with WordArt

All the Office programs (including Excel) come with a mini-application called WordArt that helps you make interesting looking text. You can take a standard line of text and bend it, squeeze it, or twist it into a form that will make your reader pay attention. Figure 16.16 shows some WordArt text.

Caution: **Be careful not to overuse WordArt. Used sparingly, it adds interest to your text, but used too frequently, it can become jarring and annoying to the reader.**

Table 16.2 Drawing Toolbar Buttons

Button	Name	Description
	Fill Color	Open the drop-down list to choose a fill color, and then click the button to apply the color to the selected shape. (Does not work with lines.)
	Line Color	Open the drop-down list to choose a line color and then click the button to apply the color to the line or shape. (If working with a shape, it changes the outline color around the shape.)
	Line Thickness	Select the line or shape, and then open this drop-down list and select the line thickness to use. If applied to a shape, it changes the border around the shape.
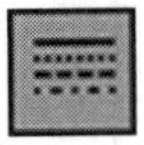	Line Style	Select the line or shape, and then open this drop-down list and select the line style (dotted, dashed, and so on). If applied to a shape, it changes the border.
	Arrow Style	Select the line, and then open this drop-down list and select the type of arrow to use (including None to remove an arrow). (Doesn't work with shapes.)
	Shadow	Select the shape, and then click this button to open a list of shadow types. Click on the one you want to apply it. (Doesn't work with lines.)
	3-D	Select the shape, and then click this button to open a list of 3-D types. Click on the one you want to apply it. (Doesn't work with lines.)

You can create a piece of WordArt easily using some standard settings and then refine it later to be exactly what you want. Follow these steps to create some WordArt:

1. Display the worksheet where you want to place the WordArt.
2. Click the WordArt button on the Drawing toolbar (the one with the crooked A on it). The WordArt Gallery dialog box appears (see Figure 16.17).
3. Select one of the gallery designs for your WordArt. If there isn't one that's exactly what you want, pick something similar; you can modify it later.
4. Click OK. The Edit WordArt Text dialog box appears (see Figure 16.18).
5. Type the text you want in the Text box. (You can make multiple lines by pressing Enter at the end of a line.)

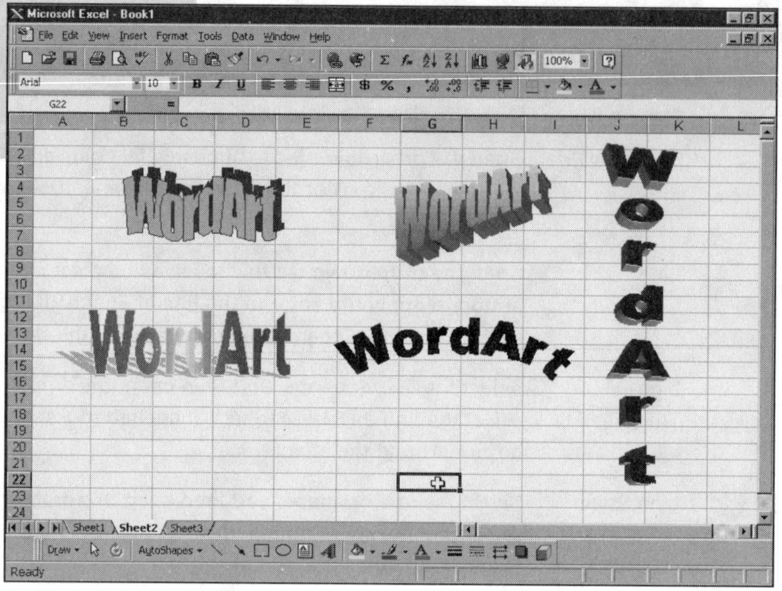

Figure 16.16 Here are some examples of what WordArt can do.

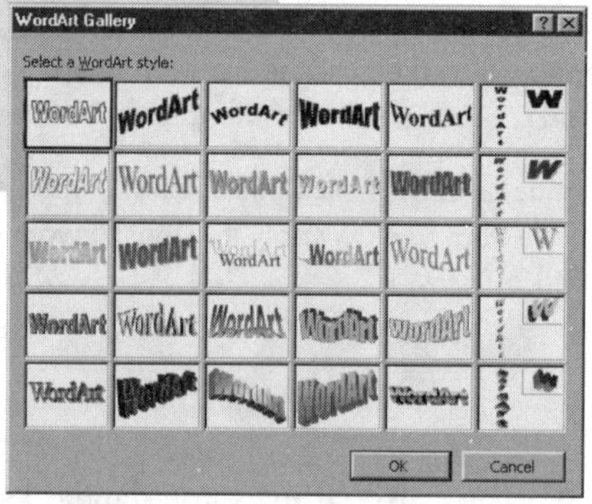

Figure 16.17 Choose a design from the WordArt Gallery.

Note

Don't type too long a phrase for WordArt. WordArt looks best with short words or phrases. More than three words is too much and doesn't look very good.

6. Click OK when you're finished typing. The finished WordArt appears on your worksheet (see Figure 16.19).

Figure 16.18 Type the text you want to use in your WordArt.

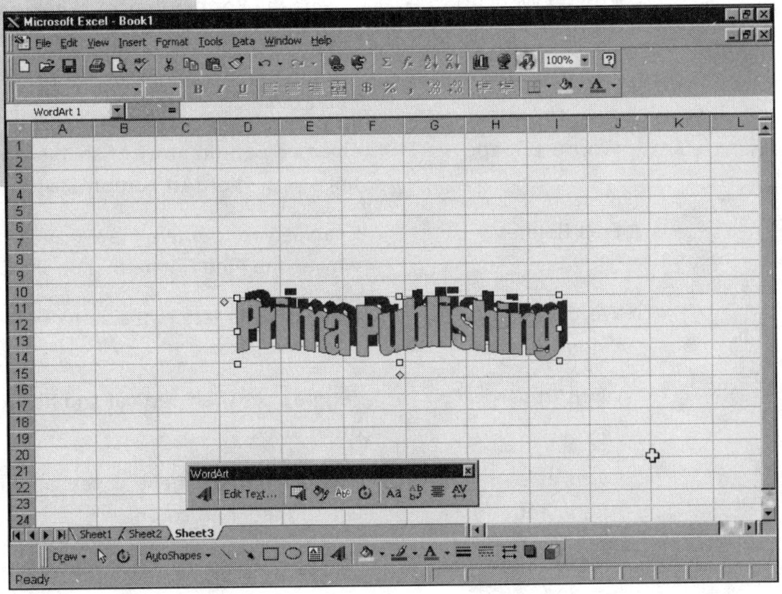

Figure 16.19 The finished WordArt appears in the worksheet along with the WordArt toolbar.

Editing Your WordArt

WordArt has its own toolbar, made especially to help you make changes to your WordArt objects. It appears automatically when you create a piece of WordArt. (You can see it in Figure 16.19.) Table 16.3 explains what these buttons are for.

To edit a piece of WordArt, double-click it. This displays the WordArt toolbar (if it isn't visible already) and the Edit WordArt Text dialog box. When you are finished making changes to the WordArt, click outside it to deselect it. Like any other drawn object, you can drag it around on the worksheet to reposition it, or resize it using the selection handles in the corners.

Table 16.3 WordArt Toolbar Buttons

Button	Name	Description
	Insert WordArt	Opens the WordArt Gallery dialog box for a new WordArt object.
Edit Text...	Edit Text	Reopens the Edit WordArt Text dialog box (refer to Figure 16.18).
	WordArt Gallery	Reopens the WordArt Gallery dialog box for the existing WordArt object.
	Format WordArt	Opens the Format WordArt dialog box, where you can change the lines and colors used. (The tabbed sections are the same as the ones in the Format Picture dialog box.)
	WordArt Shape	Opens a pop-up array of shapes you can choose to have your WordArt conform to.
	Free Rotate	Enables you to rotate the WordArt (works the same way as the Free Rotate tool on the Drawing toolbar).
	WordArt Same Letter Heights	Makes all the letters the same height.
	WordArt Vertical Text	Toggles between vertical and horizontal text orientation.
	WordArt Alignment	Opens a pop-up menu of text alignments (centered, left aligned, and so on).
	WordArt Character Spacing	Changes the spacing between letters.

Mapping with Microsoft Map

Microsoft Map is a powerful little program that comes free with Excel. It takes your data and, when possible, matches it up with a map and plots it there. Clear as mud, eh? Well, have you ever watched the network news on Election Night? They have a map of the United States, and as each state's precincts report in, they color each state either red or blue depending on which candidate won that state.

Someone behind the scenes plugs in the numbers of electoral votes for each candidate, and then the computer figures out whether that state belongs to one candidate or the other or whether it's too close to call. Microsoft Map is the same sort of program that does this on TV, and you can create your own at home.

Here are some other ideas for using a mapping program like Microsoft Map:

- Showing how many salespeople your company has in each state
- Showing which states have the most sales of your product
- Highlighting countries where there is opportunity for expansion of your product line
- Identifying the most important cities in a sales territory

Hands On: Creating an Election Map

Now's your chance to be just like those big network guys. Create a map listing some Presidential election results. (You can make the party you like best win!) Even though this is just an exercise, it gives you a peek at what Microsoft Map can do.

Note

The examples I'm using here are totally fictitious, including the number of electoral votes for the states. But then, you probably knew that. In real life, the Republicans would never be able to take Indiana <wink>.

1. On a blank worksheet, enter the data in Figure 16.20. You're going to do just a few states for this example. (If you have a strong party affiliation, feel free to give more to your party!)
2. Select the entire block, including the column labels.
3. Click the Map button on the Standard toolbar (looks like a globe). The mouse pointer changes to a crosshair.
4. On the worksheet, draw a large rectangle, like the one in Figure 16.21. This will hold the map of the United States.
5. When you release the mouse button, the Multiple Maps Available dialog box appears. Choose United States (AK & HI Inset) and click OK. Microsoft Map opens and creates the map, as shown in Figure 16.22.

Figure 16.20 Use this sample data to make your map. You can change the numbers if you like to make your party win!

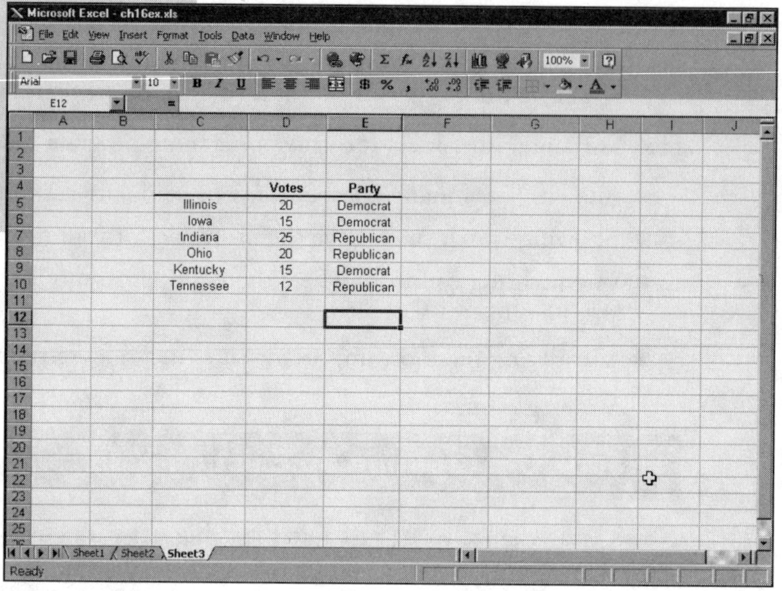

Figure 16.21 Make your rectangle about the same size as the one shown here.

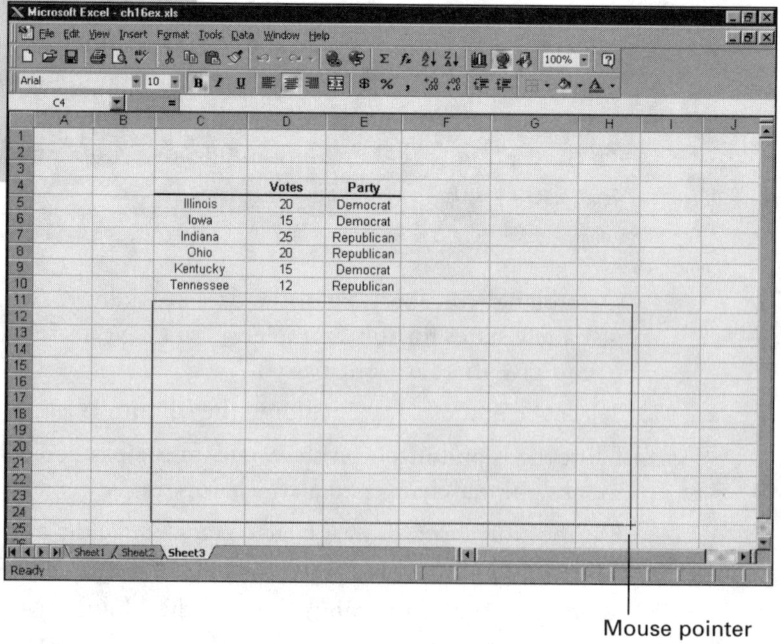

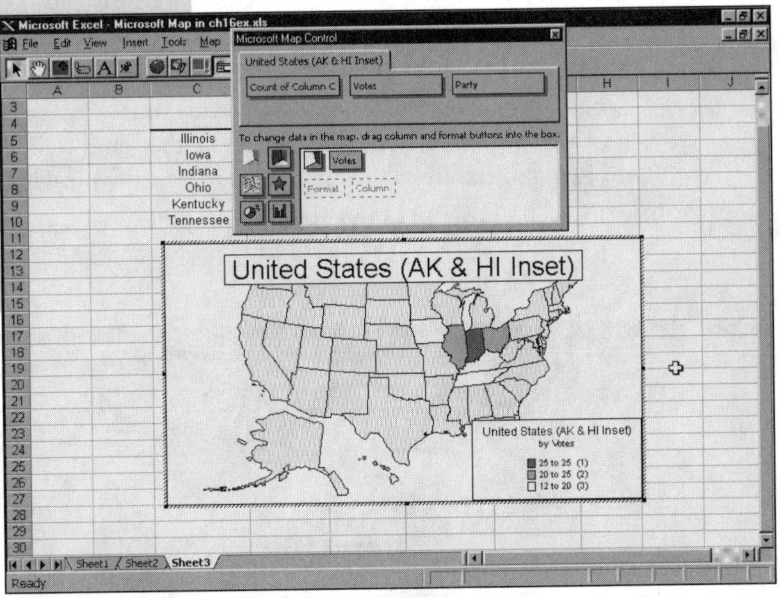

Figure 16.22 Microsoft Map does not always guess what you want correctly. Here, it assumed you wanted the map to show how many electoral votes each state has.

Microsoft Map has tried to guess at what you wanted, as you can see in Figure 16.22, but it's not quite right. You want to know which party won which state, so you want to use column D, not C. That means you'll need to work with the Microsoft Map Control window to tell the program what you want to show on your map.

6. In the Microsoft Map Control window, point to the gray Votes box in the center (white) area, so that your mouse pointer turns into a hand with a handle.
7. Drag Votes out of the white area, until your mouse pointer turns into a trash can, and drop it. Now you should be left with two gray dotted boxes in the white area: Format and Column, as shown in Figure 16.23.

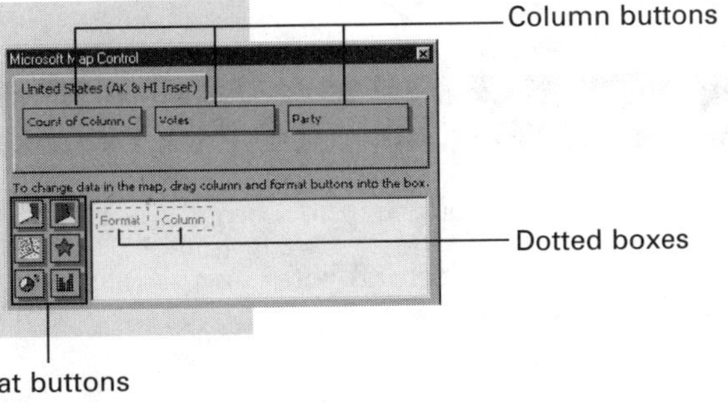

Figure 16.23 After you drag Votes out of the white area, you're left with just the dotted gray placeholders.

8. Now you need to add the Party column to the box. Position your mouse pointer over the gray Party box at the top of the dialog box, and drag it into the white area and drop it there.

   That's more like it! Microsoft Map adds the Category Shading button next to Party, and the map changes to show the states claimed by the Democrats in Red and the Republicans in Green, as shown in Figure 16.24.

9. Close Microsoft Map by clicking on the worksheet outside the map.

Figure 16.24 Now the map shows the data you wanted to see!

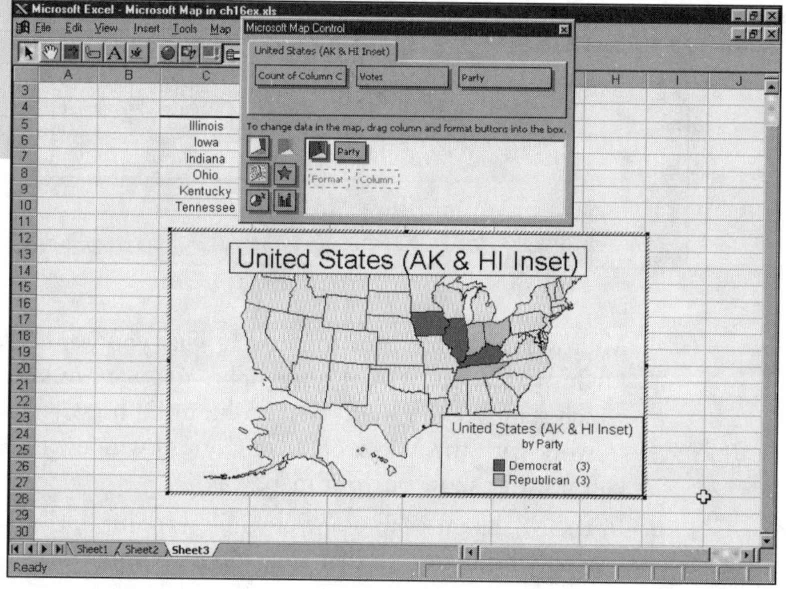

This map is a graphic that you can treat like any other graphic. Use the skills you have learned earlier in this chapter to move it, resize it, and so on. Click it to select it and drag it around, resize it, and so on, or double-click it to activate it so that you can edit it some more in Microsoft Map.

Hands On: Editing a Map

Now add some features to your map to learn about the editing controls.

It would be nice to see the electoral votes on the map, not just what party won. Add the numbers from column D (the Votes column).

1. Double-click on the map to reopen Microsoft Map.
2. Choose Tools, Labeler. The Map Labels dialog box appears.
3. Select the Values From option button.
4. Open the Values From drop-down list and select Votes.
5. Click OK to close the dialog box.
6. Now click on each state in turn. When you click on a state, you add the number from the Votes column to it. Figure 16.25 shows all the states from your worksheet labeled with the number of electoral votes.

   Now make those numbers a little smaller and less obtrusive.

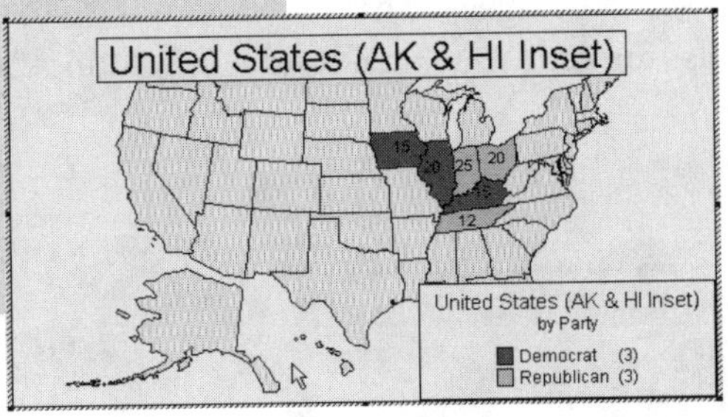

Figure 16.25 Now each state shows not only who won (by color), but the number of electoral votes.

7. Click on the Arrow button (the leftmost button) on the Microsoft Map toolbar. The mouse pointer changes to an arrow.
8. Right-click on one of the numbers and choose Format Font from the shortcut menu.
9. In the Font dialog box (which is the same one you're accustomed to seeing), decrease the number in the Size box. If it's at 8 (the smallest the list goes), manually type in **6**. Click OK when you're finished.
10. Repeat steps 8 and 9 for each number until they are all made smaller.

    The title of the map is United States (AK & HI Inset). This isn't the best title possible: anyone can plainly see what it's a map of. A better title would be "Election Results By State." So change the title to that.
11. Double-click on the words United States (AK & HI Inset), and then drag the mouse across the words to highlight them.
12. Type **Election Results By State** and press Enter.
13. Right-click on the title you typed and choose Format Font.
14. In the Size text box, change the number to 14. Then click OK. Now the title is correct and a manageable size.

15. Point the mouse pointer at the title, so that the pointer turns into a four-headed arrow and drag the title to center it over the map.

    While you're at it, make the legend box smaller and the map frame larger so that the legend doesn't obscure poor Florida, at least not altogether. You know how to resize an object:

16. Drag the bottom selection handle of the map frame down about two rows' worth, increasing the height of the frame.
17. Click on the legend box in the bottom right corner. Selection handles appear in its corners.
18. Drag the top left corner of the legend box down toward the bottom right corner until the legend no longer obscures all of Florida. (It's okay if it still covers a little of it.)

Finally your map is finished! Your final results should look something like Figure 16.26.

Figure 16.26 The finished map with a resized, renamed title.

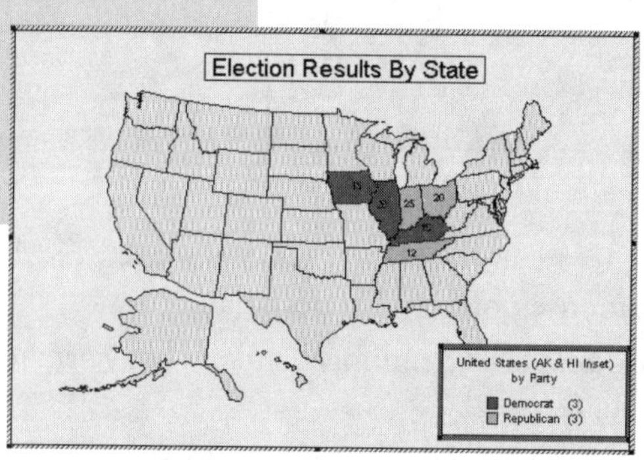

You can do much more with Microsoft Map. This little tutorial only skimmed the surface! Check out the help system in Microsoft Map (choose Help, Microsoft Map Help Topics when a map is activated) to learn more about this interesting program.

Note

Microsoft Map is useful, but it is no substitute for a full-featured mapping program like the ones you can purchase separately. For information about one such product line, MapInfo, choose Help, How To Get More Data. MapInfo offers many additional maps for Microsoft Map, as well as more program features.

PART V

What Else Can Excel Do?

17

Using Excel as a Database

IN THIS CHAPTER

- Creating a Database in Excel
- Understanding Relative and Flat File Databases
- Creating Field Names, Fields, and Records
- Using a Data Form to Enter Data
- Attaching a Data Validation to Database Cells
- Creating Simple Formulas that become Calculated Fields in the Database

A simple definition of an Excel *database* is a group of related information stored and managed on a worksheet. A database can be a list of people and their telephone numbers, an inventory, or a shopping list. What you do with the database is up to you, but Excel has incorporated features that simplify managing data.

Defining a Database

If you can type a list in Excel, you can create a database. That's because in Excel, a simple *list* is also a database. Beginning with Excel 5, Microsoft decided that the word database might be intimidating to some so they changed the terminology to *list management.* Whether you call it a list or a database, in Excel it's the same thing.

THE PROCESS OF IMPORTING AND EXPORTING DATABASES IS COVERED IN CHAPTER 20.

Before you learn how easy it is to create a database in Excel, you should understand the difference between a *flat file database* and a *relational database.* All databases in Excel are of the flat file variety. A flat file database is a list of data kept in one table. In Excel, this table is a contiguous range of cells (rows and columns). A relational database stores information in multiple tables and can be queried to display data from one or more tables. Microsoft Access and Visual FoxPro are relational databases.

Two types of databases are used in Excel. An *internal database* is a list that is kept in Excel. An *external database* imports data from other applications into Excel.

Creating an Excel Database: Dos and Don'ts

There's a secret to creating good databases in Excel that even some experienced spreadsheet developers don't seem to understand, or at least don't always follow. The secret is planning. Take a moment to think about what you want to accomplish with the database. Will the database need to be sorted or searched, and will others use it? How can you make the data easy to read and use? If you want to start off on the right foot, spend some time planning the database.

When creating a database in Excel:

- Keep the database separate from other lists on the worksheet. It's best to have only one database per worksheet.
- Avoid storing important information to the left or right of the database. When the database is filtered to look at only data that meets a specified criteria, information will be hidden.
- Blank rows in an Excel database could cause problems when working with the database. If a blank row is placed between the field name and the data, Excel cannot detect the field names as the header for the database. Blank rows between records cause Excel to conclude that it's found the end of your database.

- Use one row for field names. Names on more than one row are not recognized.
- Format the field name as bold or a different format than the data. Excel attempts to use this formatting change to distinguish between field names and data.
- Avoid using dates, formulas, or blank cells as field names.
- Make the database easy to read. Don't use too many fonts and colors. Keep squinting to a minimum by maintaining a readable font size.
- A worksheet is limited to 65,536 rows and 256 columns. That's a lot of potential for managing data, but if you use all this space, your computer will run out of memory. Either Excel will slow to a crawl, or you'll receive an out of memory error, and the application will shut down. If size is an issue consider using a relational database such as Access or Visual FoxPro.

Setting Up Field Names

One of the most important steps to creating a database is deciding what fields to use. The terms *field*, *field name*, *record*, and *database range* are used extensively in this chapter. A definition of each is shown in the following table:

Term	Definition
Field	A column within a database that contains one type of data, such as a phone number.
Field name	A unique column label for a field in the database, such as "City." Each field name must be placed in a separate cell, and all field names appear in the same row.
Record	A row within the database. In a contact database, for example, all the information on one contact (name, address, phone, and so on) represents a single record.
Range	The area that makes up the entire database. The database range includes field names and data.

ENTERING AND EDITING DATA IS COVERED IN CHAPTER 7.

After you enter field names in the worksheet, Excel automatically recognizes the list as a database. Figure 17.1 shows a database with five field names and four records. The field names show what type of information is being managed. To follow along with the exercises in this chapter, create the database shown in Figure 17.1.

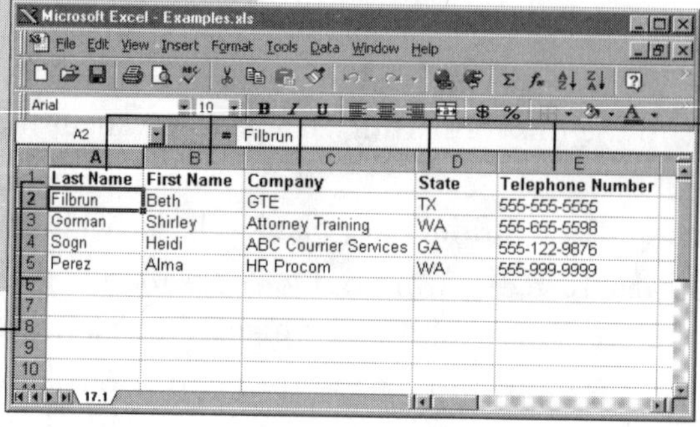

Figure 17.1 The field names are entered in row one and formatted differently from the data that is entered under it.

If a field name is too long to fit in one cell, consider formatting the text to wrap. Choose Format, Cells, click the Alignment tab, and select Wrap Text. Then click OK.

Entering and Editing Data

The most common way to enter and edit data is to type or edit the data directly in the worksheet cells. To create a new record, select the first empty cell in the database and begin typing. Press the Tab key to enter the data and move one cell to the right; press Enter to move to the cell below the active cell.

You can tell Excel to move a different direction when you press Enter. Choose Tools, Options, and click the Edit tab. Select a different option for Move Selection After Enter. Then click OK.

To edit a record, select the cell to be modified and type the new information. Once the Enter or Tab key is pressed, the modified data will replace existing data. To edit a portion of the data, select the cell and use the formula bar to edit. This process is shown in Figure 17.2.

To navigate between fields and records in a database, use the keys listed in Table 17.1.

Leading spaces in any cell will cause problems with how a database is sorted. Sorting is covered in Chapter 18.

Figure 17.2
Select the data to be modified in the formula bar and edit the data.

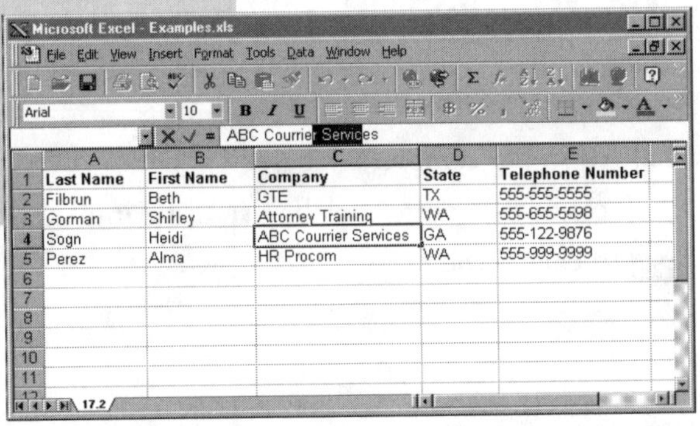

Table 17.1 Navigational Keys

Direction	Key(s)
One cell to the right	Tab or →
One cell to the left	Shift+Tab or ←
One cell down	Enter or ↓
One cell up	Shift+Enter or ↑
First field in a record	Home
Select an entire row	Shift+Spacebar, or click row number
Select an entire column	Ctrl+Spacebar, or click column letter
Select the entire database range	Ctrl+Shift+*

AutoComplete

AutoComplete is a tool that scans data previously entered for repeating characters. If a match is detected, Excel attempts to complete the word for you. If the word shown is not the one you want, finish typing and press the Enter key. AutoComplete is shown in Figure 17.3.

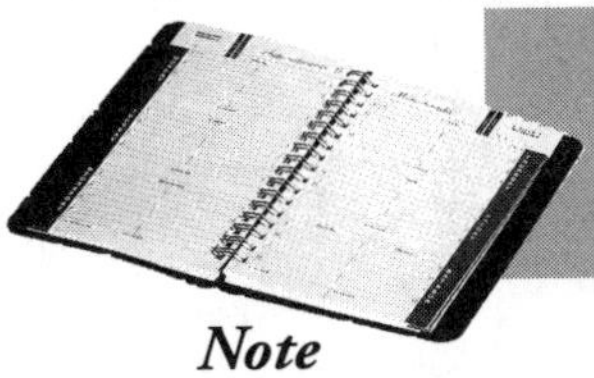

Note

AutoComplete only works down columns, not across rows, nor will it work if there are blank cells above the new column entry.

Hands On: Using AutoComplete to Enter Data

To use AutoComplete, follow these steps:

1. Select cell A6 in the sample database.
2. Type **G**. Excel finds a match in the list and completes the name `Gorman`.
3. Press Esc to cancel the entry.

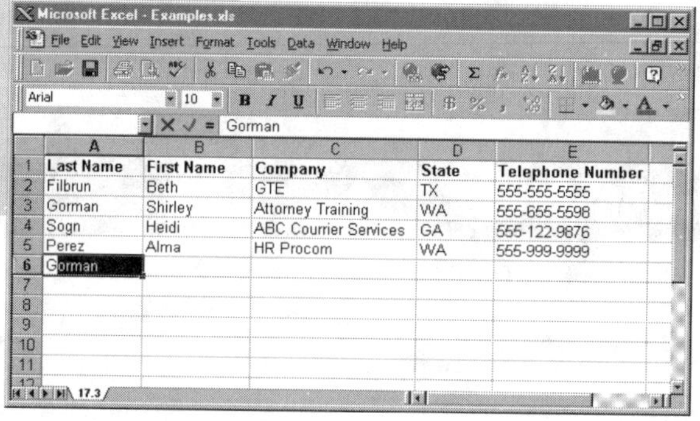

Figure 17.3 The Auto-Complete feature quickly fills in repeated entries in a column.

Excel attempts to match the entry to existing data within the database. If it finds a match, it completes the word for you. If you agree with Excel's suggestion, press Enter.

When Excel detects two fields with the same beginning letter(s), an alphabetical search is performed for the first unique character in each word.

Pick from List

The Pick from List feature provides a list of previously entered data from a column. Pick from List is accessible by right-clicking on a cell in the database and selecting the Pick from List command.

Hands On: Using the Pick from List Feature to Enter Data

To use Pick from List, follow these steps:

1. Right-click on cell A6 in the sample database.

2. Choose Pic<u>k</u> from List. The drop-down list box shown in Figure 17.4 shows all previously entered data fields for the Last Name column.
3. Select Gorman.

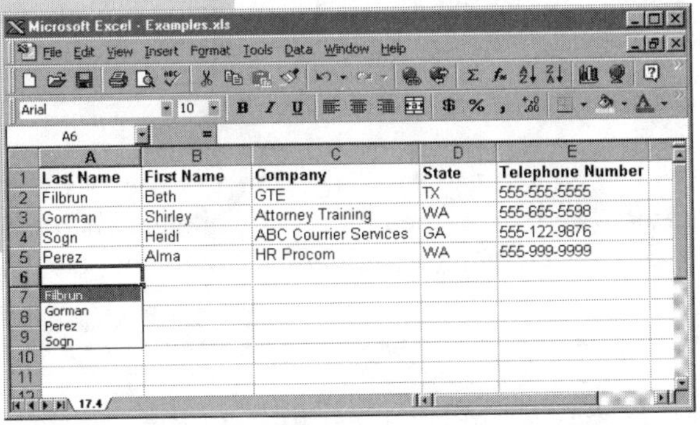

Figure 17.4 All data fields previously entered appear in a list box to enable a quick selection.

Using a Data Form to Enter Data

Most often, data is entered and edited directly in worksheet cells. However, Excel provides a feature that displays a form in which you can view, enter, edit, and search records in the database.

A *data form* is a dialog box that displays up to 32 fields. Each field has an edit box next to it where information is typed. The buttons on the right side of the dialog box perform actions on the database. Figure 17.5 shows a data form.

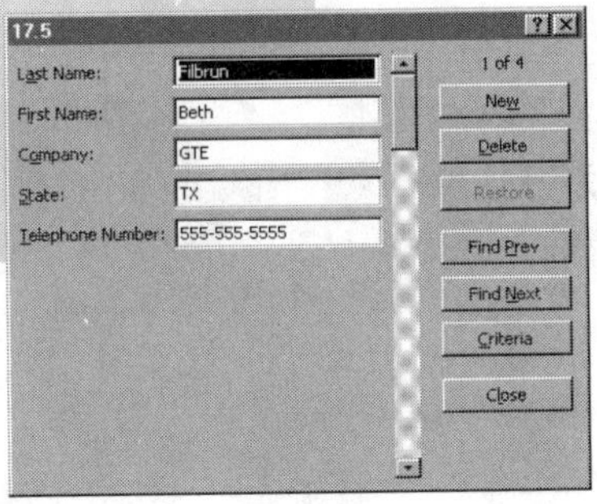

Figure 17.5 Manipulating data is made easy with data forms.

Hands On: Displaying a Data Form

To display a data form:

1. Select cell A2 in the sample database.
2. Choose Data, Form. The Data Form dialog box appears, displaying data for the first record in the database.
3. To close the data form, click Close.

Tip

The name of the data form comes from the worksheet name. To change the worksheet name, close the data form, double-click the sheet tab, type a new name, and press Enter.

Field names are the only requirement for activating a data form although it's easier if you have at least one record in the database. When no records are present, Excel displays the message box shown in Figure 17.6. If you see this dialog box, click OK to accept the first row of data as field names.

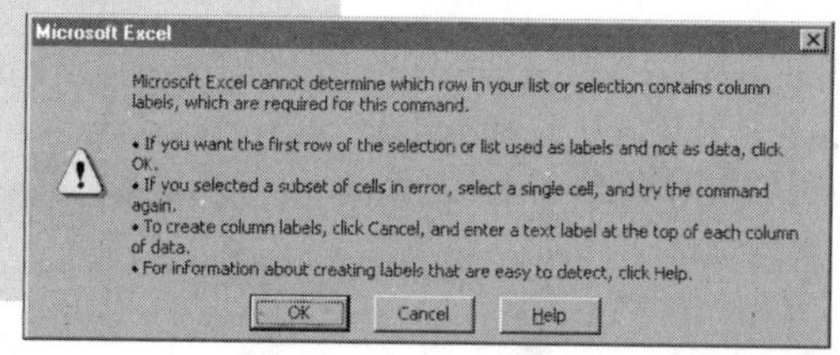

Figure 17.6 When Excel doesn't detect field names, you must point them out.

Note

Hidden columns do not appear on the data form. When a field is a calculation (a calculation contains a formula), there is no edit box, and the field cannot be edited directly from within the form. To edit a calculated field, you must close the data form and edit the formula directly in the worksheet.

Hands On: Entering Data in a Data Form

You use the New button in a data form to add new records. Excel clears the display, if necessary, and prepares the form for new information.

To create a new record using the data form:

1. Select cell A2 in the sample database.
2. Choose Data, Form to display the data form.
3. Click New.
4. Type your last name, first name, company, state, and telephone number in the appropriate text boxes.
5. Click Close to close the data form (and see the new record in the database).

Tip

Press Tab to move to the next text box in the data form; press Shift+Tab to move to the previous text box.

If the New button is clicked again, the previous record is not overwritten, but added to the database. Each new record you add using the data form expands the database range; there is no limit to the number of records that can be entered using a data form.

The Restore button in the data form cancels any changes made to the current record (except deletions) prior to closing the data form. If you make changes, go to another record and then return, you cannot restore the original record.

The Delete button deletes the currently displayed record permanently. If you accidentally delete a record using the data form, you cannot get it back.

To repeat a field from the previous record, click in the field to be repeated and press Ctrl+Shift+ ".

Editing Data in a Data Form

The data form can also be used to edit records in the database. The position of the record is shown in the top right corner of the data form, just above the New button (refer to Figure 17.5). The first number is the position of the current record on the worksheet. The second is the total number of records in the database.

Hands On: Editing Data in a Data Form

To edit data in the data form, follow these steps:

1. Display the data form, if necessary.
2. Click the Find Next or Find Prev button to move between records.
3. Select a text box and edit the contents with the new information.
4. Click Close.

Searching the Database Using a Data Form

The Criteria button in the data form enables a search for records that match criteria that you define. When the data form is in Criteria mode, the word `Criteria` is displayed in the top right corner of the data form, above the New button. Notice the button in the Criteria position is now Form. Click the Form button to cancel the search and return to the data form.

Hands On: Specifying Search Criteria in the Data Form

To enter criteria:

1. Open the data form, if necessary.
2. Click the Criteria button.
3. Select the Company field.
4. Type **HR Procom**. If you are unsure of the complete word or number you want to search for, type as much information as you can to narrow the search. (The letters **HR** could be entered instead, and the search would still execute correctly.) Figure 17.7 shows the data form Criteria search.

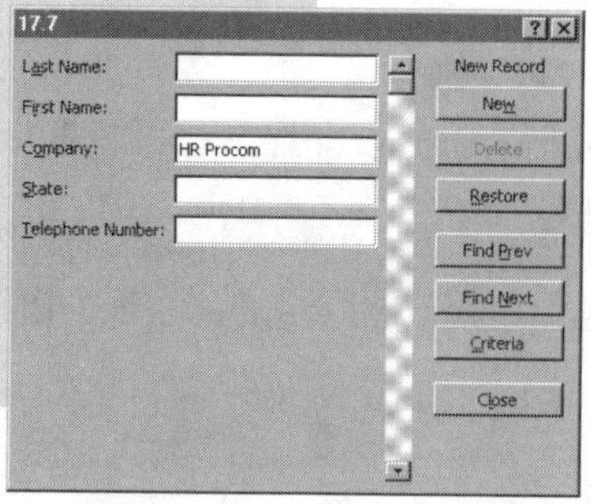

Figure 17.7 The criteria form is similar to the data form in appearance, however, it is used for searching the database

5. Click the Find Next or Find Prev button to begin the search and move through the records that match the defined criteria.
6. Click Close when you're finished.

You can enter criteria in any field within the data form to find records that match the request. Defining criteria can filter the list to group records that meet a certain set of requirements. The preceding example executed an alphabetical search. Mathematical operators can also be used to establish search criteria.

Criteria	Example
Alphabetical search	Attorney
Wild card search such as *Att	Finds Attorney and Attention
Equal to a value or field	=10000
Greater than 100,000	>100000
Less than 100,000	<100000
Relational value within the field	<>100000

Note

The criteria engine on the data form does not enable you to search a field for multiple responses. For example, if you want to search for all your clients in both Washington and Oregon, you could not do so in the data form dialog box. This search must be executed with AutoFilter or Advanced Filter. These tools are covered in Chapter 18.

Using Microsoft Access Forms in Excel

If you're an experienced Access user and have the application installed on your computer, you can build a form for data entry in that application and use it with a database in Excel.

Excel 97 and Access 97 include new Wizards that can help create data forms with built-in design templates. The process is slower than when a form is created in

Excel because you're working with two fairly memory extensive applications. Access builds the form and embeds a button object on the worksheet, which enables you to toggle between the Access form and the Excel worksheet.

If you're interested in creating more elaborate forms, check out what Microsoft Access 97 has to offer, or build a custom data form on a worksheet in Excel using the Forms toolbar. For information on how to use the Forms toolbar see online help and search the topic Forms, Creating.

To enable the creation of Access forms, you must have installed and activated the Microsoft AccessLinks add-in. To find out whether AccessLinks is installed on your computer, from within Excel, choose Tools, Add-Ins. If AccessLinks does not appear in the list of Add-ins, you will need to install it. To install an add-in that was not installed during setup, close all open programs. Go to the Control Panel and then double-click the Add/Remove Programs icon. If you installed Microsoft Office, click Microsoft Office on the Install/Uninstall tab and then click Add/Remove. If you installed only Microsoft Excel, click Microsoft Excel on the Install/Uninstall tab and then click Add/Remove.

Creating Calculated Fields

FORMULAS ARE COVERED IN CHAPTER 8.

When fields in the database contain formulas, they are considered *calculated fields*. You can tell when a cell contains a formula because formulas always begin with an equal sign. Many types of worksheet functions can be used in formulas within a database. The most common functions are covered in this section.

The list in Figure 17.8 shows the sales and expenses for several outdoor equipment companies. The formula in cell D2 calculates the Revenue for Rock Climbers Emporium by subtracting the expense amount from sales.

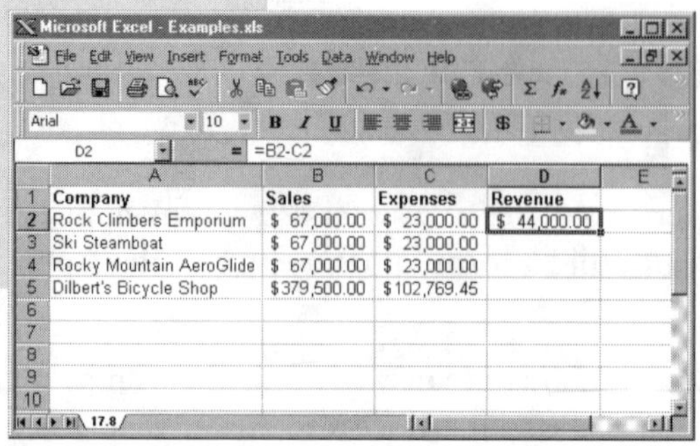

Figure 17.8 The formula in cell D2 subtracts the value in cell C2 (Expenses) from the value in cell B2 (Sales).

When you are working with a database, Excel 97 can use field names within a formula without having to create defined names. An example of using field names in a formula is shown in Figure 17.9.

Figure 17.9
Field names can be used to build formulas.

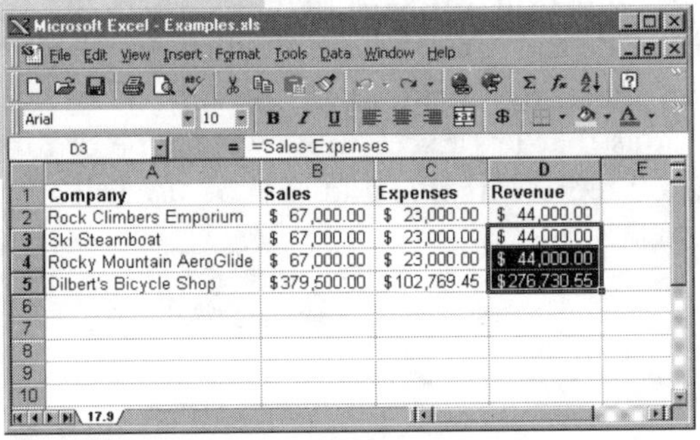

Hands On: Using Field Names in Calculated Fields

To calculate with field names:

1. Select another worksheet in the workbook and enter the data as shown in Figure 17.8 (except for formulas in the range D2:D5).
2. Click cell D2.
3. Type **=Sales-Expenses** and press Enter.
4. Click cell D2 again.
5. Position the pointer over the fill handle in the bottom right corner of the cell. The mouse pointer should appear in the form of a thin, black plus sign.
6. Click and drag to cell D5; then release the mouse button. The formula fills down the column.

Using field names to create formulas helps to track what information is being calculated. These formulas are dynamic and change if supporting values change. For example, if a number in the sales column is edited, the formula updates without further intervention. Building formulas with field names helps to identify what fields are being calculated and is known as *self-documentation* with formulas.

Creating Formulas in a Database

Five common worksheet functions are used in worksheets and databases. These are SUM, AVERAGE, MINIMUM, MAXIMUM, and SUBTOTAL. In addition to these functions, built-in functions work specifically with a database. All database functions begin with the letter "D" (such as DSUM).

The following function table shows five common functions and how they are used in a formula.

The SUBTOTAL function works differently than the other functions in the table. The items inside the parentheses are called *arguments*, and the SUBTOTAL function requires more arguments than the rest. The 9 argument is one of 11 Summary Functions that lets Excel know what type of formula to create. In the following table, a 9 represents that addition be used.

Function	Example
SUM	=SUM(A1:A5)
AVERAGE	=AVERAGE(A1:A5)
MINIMUM	=MIN(A1:A5)
MAXIMUM	=MAX(A1:A5)
SUBTOTAL	=SUBTOTAL(9,A1:A5)

For information on using Summary Functions choose Help, Contents and Index; click the Index tab and type **Summary Functions** in the edit box. Click the Display button to view the Help topics.

Database Functions

In addition to common worksheet functions, 13 additional worksheet functions are designed to work with databases. You can access these functions in the Paste Function dialog box, shown in Figure 17.10. A list of the database functions and a description of each of these functions appears in Table 17.2.

To use the database functions:

1. Select a blank cell next to any cell of the database.
2. Choose Insert, Function, or click the Paste Function button on the Standard toolbar. The Paste Function dialog box appears.
3. In the Function Category list, select Database. The Database function names now appear on the right side of the Paste Function dialog box.

4. Select a function (such as DAVERAGE) from the Function Name list and click OK.
5. The Formula Palette appears. At this point, specify the arguments for the function and then click OK when you are finished.

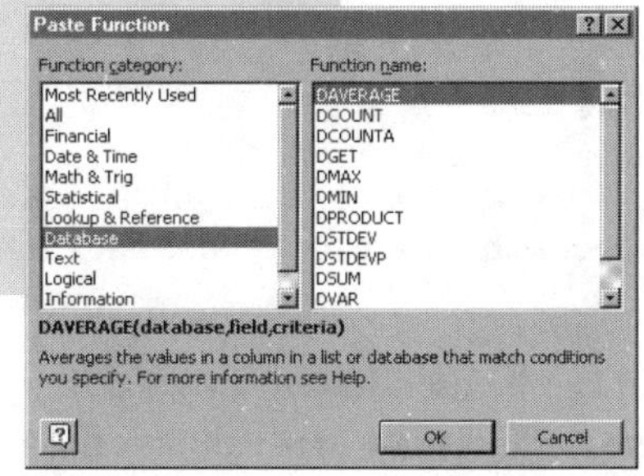

Figure 17.10 Many built-in worksheet functions can be accessed from this dialog box.

Table 17.2 Excel's Database Functions

Function	Description
DAVERAGE	Averages columns of numbers that match the conditions that you specify.
DCOUNT	Counts the cells that contain a number that you specify.
DCOUNTA	Counts non-blank cells.
DGET	Extracts a single record from a database that matches the conditions that you specify.
DMAX	Returns the largest or maximum value in a specified field.
DMIN	Returns the smallest or minimum value in a specified field.
DPRODUCT	Multiplies the fields in the database that meet a specified condition.
DSTDEV	Returns the standard deviation based on a sample from the database.
DSTDEVP	Returns the standard deviation based on the entire population of selected database entries.
DSUM	Adds the number values in a specified field.
DVAR	Estimates the variance based on a sample from selected database entries.
DVARP	Calculates the variance based on the entire population of selected database entries.
GETPIVOTDATA	Returns the data stored in a pivot table. This is a new database function in Excel 97.

Note

Help is available through every step of building the function. Click the button in the lower left corner of the Paste Function dialog box or the Formula Palette to display the Office Assistant.

Using Data Validation

When you create a database for others to use, you lose control over what gets typed into the fields. This opens the door for typos that can destroy the integrity of your collected data.

Data validation is a tool that can be used to restrict what is entered into a cell. Earlier versions of Excel had the capability of data validation but not without writing a macro to do so. Excel 97 takes the programming element out of applying data validation and has placed this useful tool as a command on the Data menu.

Figure 17.11 shows a database where column B must have a particular type of data entered. This is a good candidate for applying data validation.

Figure 17.11
Data validation restricts what is entered into a cell.

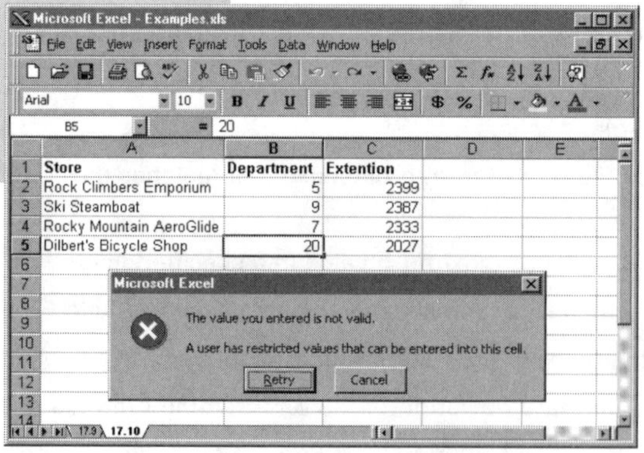

To set data validation:

1. Select column B, the column containing data you want to validate.
2. Choose Data, Validation. The Data Validation dialog box appears.

All data types except for the Any Value type require additional information. A completed Data Validation dialog box is shown in Figure 17.12.

Note

The Data Validation dialog box has three tabs: Settings, Input Message, and Error Alert. The Settings tab defines what data type is permitted in the field. Click the drop-down arrow for Allow and select Whole Number. Other types of entries that can be restricted are Any Value, Decimal, List, Date, Time, Text Length, and Custom.

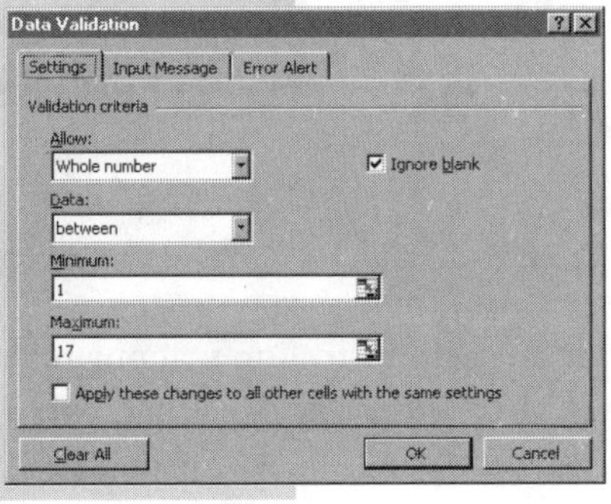

Figure 17.12 The Settings tab in the Data Validation dialog box provides options to designate what type of value is permitted in the cell as well as to set conditions on the value.

The Data Validation dialog box contains options to Ignore Blank fields and to Apply These Changes to All Other Cells with the Same Settings.

1. Click the drop-down arrow under Data and select Between.
2. Type **1** in the Minimum text box and type **17** in the Maximum text box.
3. Click OK to close the Data Validation dialog box.
4. Select cell B4 and Type **20**. Press the Enter key.

When data validation is set up correctly, an error message appears with a warning when data entered does not meet the restricted data type. The error message is a good start but doesn't inform the user what data type is accepted.

To specify an input and error message:

1. Select column B and choose Data, Validation.
2. Click the Input Message tab.
3. In the Title text box, type **Restricted Entry**.
4. In the Input Message text box, type **Enter a whole number between 1 and 17.**

5. Click the Error Alert tab.
6. Make sure that the Show Error Alert After Invalid Data Is Entered check box is selected.
7. Click the Style drop-down arrow. The error message can appear in a Stop, Warning, or Information format. To preview the appearance of each message box, select each type.
8. Add a Title and Error Message.
9. Click OK to close the Data Validation dialog box.

To clear previously entered validation for the active cell(s), click the Clear All button in the Data Validation dialog box.

Database Tricks

There are a few things that are helpful to know about that don't fall under normal chapter headings. These I consider tricks learned over the years.

Parsing Data

Database information will not always be presented to you in an optimal format. A common mistake is putting the name of a person in one cell. Sure, the database is smaller because fewer fields are used, but it's pretty tough to sort by last name if the first name also appears in the cell. Data that contains spaces or symbols to separate words can be parsed within seconds.

Hands On: Parsing Data to Separate Columns

To learn how to parse data to separate columns, follow these steps:

1. Type your full name in a cell on a worksheet as you would if you were closing a letter. An example of this is **Joannie B. Goode**.
2. Select the cell that contains the name and choose Data, Text to Columns.
3. If spaces separate the first and last name, select the Fixed Width option. For names that are separated by symbols such as commas (Goode,Joannie,B), select Delimited. In this example, select Fixed Width.
4. Click the Finish button. The data is parsed into separate columns.

Checking the Used Range of a Database

When data is entered in a worksheet and then deleted, the used range of the database does not automatically reset. This can cause the file size of the worksheet to be larger than it should. To check the last cell of a database range, press Ctrl+End.

If the cell selected is not the last cell in the database, you can reset it. Follow these steps:

1. Press Ctrl+End to find the last used cell in the worksheet.
2. Select entire rows between where your database actually ends and the cell that Excel selects as the last cell.
3. Choose Edit, Delete.
4. Repeat steps 2 and 3 for columns, if necessary.
5. Save and close the workbook. When you reopen the workbook, the used range will be reset to the correct position.

18

Working with Database Data in Excel

In This Chapter

- Sorting Data
- Searching for Records that Match Criteria
- Using AutoFilter and Advanced Filter
- Creating Automatic Subtotals and Outlining the Database
- Creating and Using PivotTables

What good is data on a worksheet if you can't make sense of it? Excel includes built-in tools to help manage and analyze data. In fact, there's no better spreadsheet program on the market for this purpose. Excel can sort, search, and filter data as well as add automatic subtotals, outline, and create PivotTables. The PivotTable feature alone is worth reading this chapter.

Sorting the Database

Databases are created to manage information. Sorting helps by arranging data in a logical order that you define prior to the sort. A database can be sorted by toolbar buttons or through a dialog box, each yielding a different result.

To follow along with the examples used in this chapter, create the database shown in Figure 18.1.

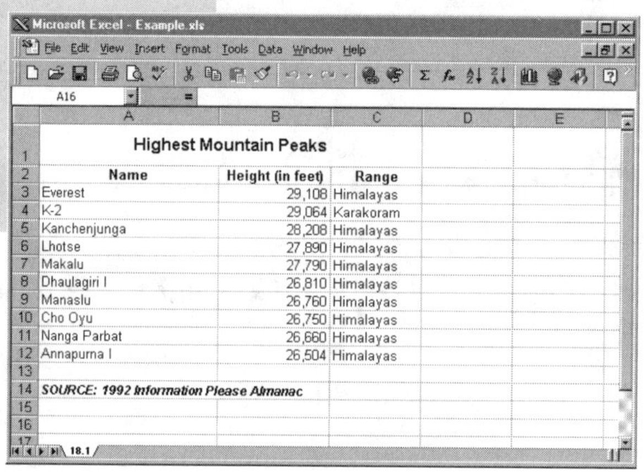

	A	B	C
1	Highest Mountain Peaks		
2	Name	Height (in feet)	Range
3	Everest	29,108	Himalayas
4	K-2	29,064	Karakoram
5	Kanchenjunga	28,208	Himalayas
6	Lhotse	27,890	Himalayas
7	Makalu	27,790	Himalayas
8	Dhaulagiri I	26,810	Himalayas
9	Manaslu	26,760	Himalayas
10	Cho Oyu	26,750	Himalayas
11	Nanga Parbat	26,660	Himalayas
12	Annapurna I	26,504	Himalayas
13			
14	SOURCE: 1992 Information Please Almanac		

Figure 18.1 The Highest Mountains Peaks database is used in the examples throughout this chapter.

ENTERING AND EDITING DATA IS COVERED IN CHAPTER 7.

Sorting with Toolbar Buttons

Two buttons on the Standard toolbar provide a shortcut to performing simple sorts. These sorts are limited because they can sort by one column of data in ascending or descending order. The ascending button has the AZ button face, whereas the ZA button sorts in descending order.

THE STANDARD TOOLBAR IS COVERED IN CHAPTER 1.

Be careful not to select multiple cells in the database when sorting. When multiple cells are selected, only that data is sorted while the supporting data remains in place. If you're not careful, your data could become scrambled. To sort a database, click in one cell only, and the surrounding list will be included when the sort button is clicked.

If you've sorted incorrectly, click the Undo button that has a backward arrow on the button face or choose Edit, Undo Sort.

More Complex Sorts

Suppose that you need to sort the database by the highest mountain peak and then by name. When more than one field is to be sorted, use the Sort dialog box. The Sort dialog box shown in Figure 18.2 allows data to be sorted by up to three fields at a time. One sort field is required; the two others in the dialog box are optional.

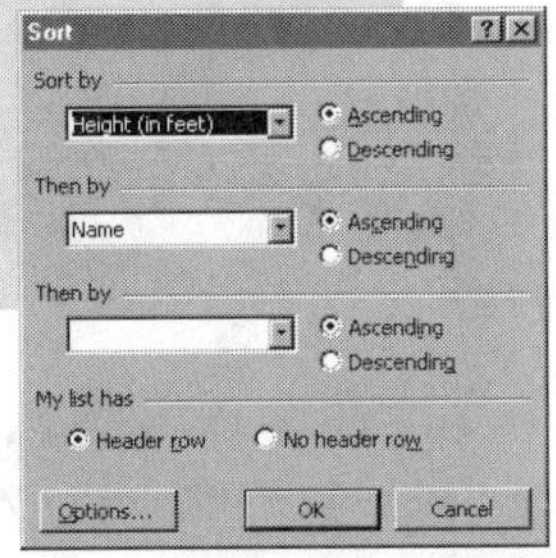

Figure 18.2 The Sort dialog box presents the option to sort by three fields.

Hands On: Sorting Data on Multiple Fields

To sort by multiple fields:

1. Select cell A3 in the Highest Mountain Peaks database.
2. Choose Data, Sort.
3. Click the drop-down arrow next to the first Sort By option and select the Height (in feet) field.
4. Select the option for Descending in the Sort By section.
5. Click the first Then By drop-down arrow and select the Name field.
6. Check the My List Has section and make sure that the Header Row option is selected. If Excel doesn't detect a change in format for field names, the headings will be sorted into the database.
7. Click OK. The sorted database is shown in Figure 18.3.

The new arrangement of the database may not be what you expected. When multiple fields sort the database, it sorts the least important field first. The Height (in feet) field was sorted before the Name field and therefore treated as the less important of the two fields.

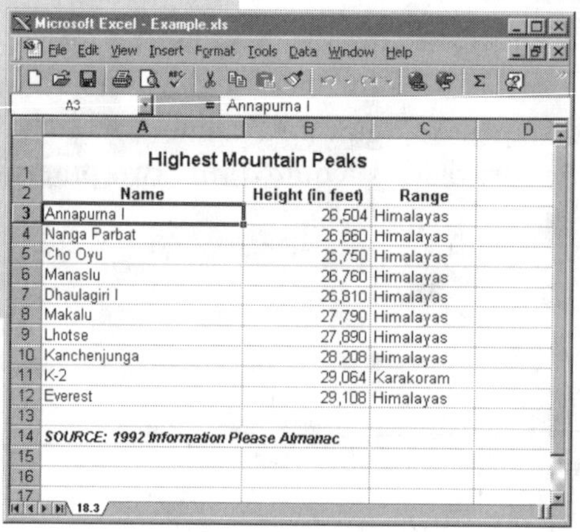

Figure 18.3 Sorting records can yield unexpected results when the order of importance is improperly entered.

To sort the database by more than three fields, sort the list twice beginning with the least important.

Retaining the Original Sort Order

Before you sort, think about whether the database needs to be restored to its original order. If this is a possibility, you'll want to add a column next to the data and place sequential numbers in it *before you sort for the first time.*

Hands On: Returning the Database to the Original Order

To track the original order of the database:

1. Select cell B2.
2. Choose Insert, Column.
3. In cell A2, Type **Record** and format the font as bold.
4. Enter a **1** in cell A3 and a **2** in cell A4.
5. Select cells A3 and A4. Place the mouse over the bottom right portion of the cells until a thin, black plus sign appears.
6. Drag the mouse to cell A12 to fill the numbers from 1 to 10.
7. Select cell A3 again.

8. Hide the column of data by choosing Format, Column, Hide.
9. Sort the database by choosing Data, Sort.
10. Sort by Name in Descending Order and set the other two drop-down boxes to None. Click OK.
11. Unhide the hidden column by pressing Ctrl+A to select the entire worksheet and then choosing Format, Column, Unhide.

The data has been sorted in Figure 18.4 but can quickly be restored to the original sort by sorting the Record field in ascending order.

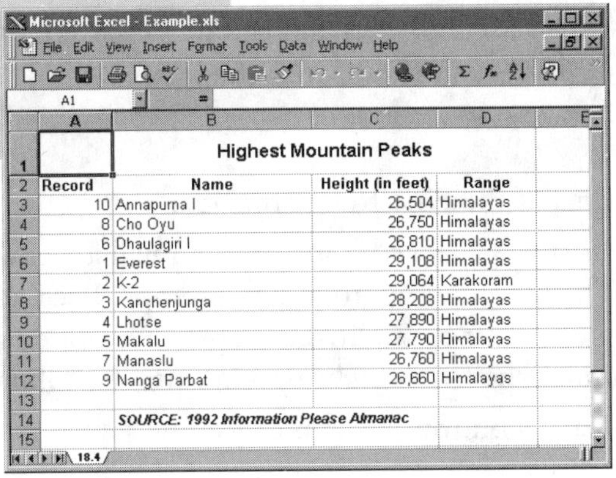

	A	B	C	D
1		Highest Mountain Peaks		
2	Record	Name	Height (in feet)	Range
3	10	Annapurna I	26,504	Himalayas
4	8	Cho Oyu	26,750	Himalayas
5	6	Dhaulagiri I	26,810	Himalayas
6	1	Everest	29,108	Himalayas
7	2	K-2	29,064	Karakoram
8	3	Kanchenjunga	28,208	Himalayas
9	4	Lhotse	27,890	Himalayas
10	5	Makalu	27,790	Himalayas
11	7	Manaslu	26,760	Himalayas
12	9	Nanga Parbat	26,660	Himalayas
13				
14		SOURCE: 1992 Information Please Almanac		
15				

Figure 18.4
A new sort order with traces back to the original.

Sorting Options

Several factors can affect how a list is sorted. One is leading spaces, the other capitalization. The Sort Options dialog box is shown in Figure 18.5 and provides the option to sort by capitalization by checking the Case Sensitive option. If this setting is active, fields that begin with lowercase letters are sorted and placed before those same letters capitalized.

Hands On: Viewing the Sorting Options

To view sorting options:

1. Select cell A3 and choose Data, Sort.
2. Click the Options button on the Sort dialog box.

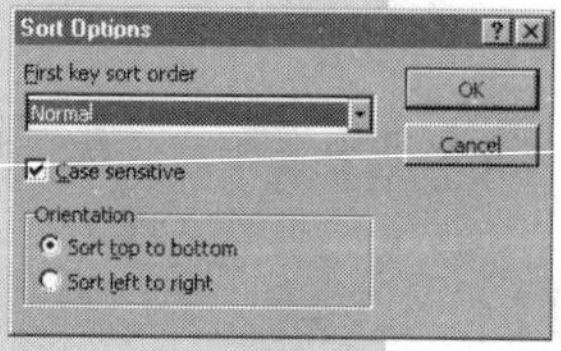

Figure 18.5
The Sort Options dialog box provides three options for determining how a database is sorted.

Note

The Sort Options dialog box allows for case sensitive and custom sort orders to be used when sorting the database. The First Key Sort Order is for sorting by built-in and custom lists. Creating custom lists is covered later in this chapter.

3. Select Normal as the First Key Sort Order.

   If Case Sensitive is checked, capitalization will affect the way the database is sorted. The Orientation group box prompts Excel to Sort Top to Bottom, or Sort Left to Right. The top to bottom option sorts rows by a single column. The left to right option sorts the columns by a single row.

4. Click the Cancel button twice to cancel the sort.

Creating a Custom Sort Order

You've seen how Excel can sort by alphabet or number. It can also sort by built-in and custom lists. Excel comes with a built-in list of days and months in the full word and abbreviated form. If a built-in list is detected, Excel attempts to use it as a sorting preference instead of an alphabetized sort.

Hands On: Viewing the Custom Lists

To view the built-in lists:

1. Select a cell in the database.
2. Choose Data, Sort.
3. Click the Options button.
4. Under First Key Sort Order, click the drop-down arrow and view the available choices. Selecting an item in the list will instruct Excel to use it as a sort order.

5. Click the Cancel button twice to close each dialog box and cancel the sort.
6. Save this worksheet. You'll use it again later in the chapter.

Creating a Custom List

Sometimes a database should not be sorted in ascending or descending order but in an order that you create. For example, a distribution list can be used to trace the progress of a report throughout your department.

Hands On: Adding a Custom List of Planets

To create a custom list:

1. Create a new worksheet.
2. Type the following list of planets in cells A1 through A9.

Cell Location	Information To Enter
A1	Mercury
A2	Venus
A3	Earth
A4	Mars
A5	Jupiter
A6	Saturn
A7	Uranus
A8	Neptune
A9	Pluto

3. Select cells A1 through A9 and choose Tools, Options, and select the Custom lists tab.
4. Locate the Import button in the bottom right portion of the Options dialog box shown in Figure 18.6. The Import list from cells text box should contain the text $A$1:$A$9. This is the location of the custom list on the worksheet. If the text box is empty, click on the worksheet and use the mouse to select the list of planets.
5. Click the Import button. The custom list is added to the Options dialog box and can be used as a sort preference later.
6. Click OK to close the Options dialog box.

Sorting by Custom Lists

You only have to enter a custom list once. The list is kept in a global file and is available in any Excel workbook.

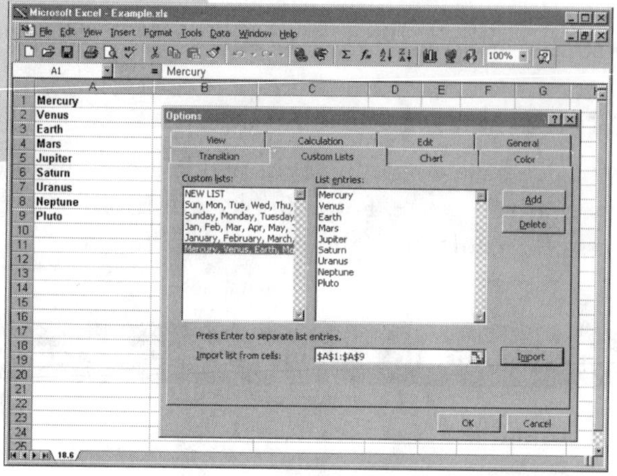

Figure 18.6
Custom lists can be imported from any Excel worksheet.

Hands On: Sorting Data in a Custom List

To sort using a custom list:

1. Select any cell in the database.
2. Choose Data, Sort.
3. Click the Options button.
4. Click the drop-down arrow under the First Key Sort Order section.
5. Select the custom list of planets. Click the OK button twice to sort.

Custom lists can be used for more than defining sort order. If you find yourself typing the same list repeatedly, create a custom list, type one word from the list on a worksheet and use the fill handle to drag down using AutoFill to show the rest of the list entries.

AutoFilter

There are times when you don't want to see all the data in the database. Excel has an AutoFilter tool that finds and displays a subset of the database temporarily hiding the rest of the data.

Hands On: Applying an AutoFilter to the Database

To apply an AutoFilter:

1. Activate the Highest Mountain Peaks database and select any cell within the database range.
2. Choose Data, Filter, AutoFilter. Small arrows have been added to the right side of each field name. The arrows are used to filter data for the column.
3. Click the arrow next to the Range field.
4. Select Himalayas from the drop-down list. The list is filtered to show mountain peaks only in the Himalayan range, as shown in Figure 18.7.

Figure 18.7
AutoFilter hides the rows of records that are not in the Himalayas.

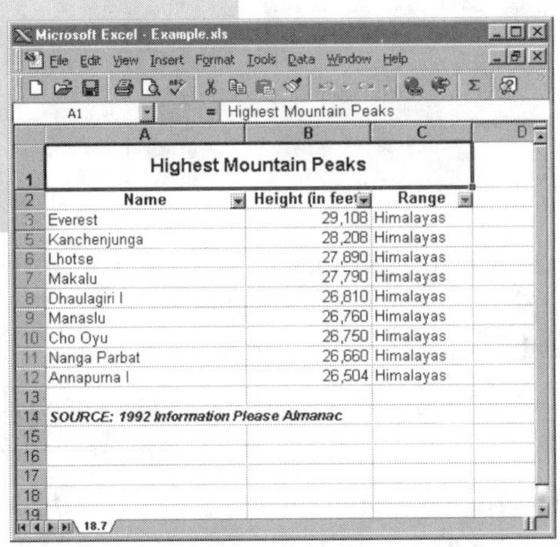

5. To turn off the AutoFilter, choose Data, Filter, AutoFilter again.

When a field is filtered, the arrow changes color to differentiate it from the non-filtered columns of data. AutoFilter can find the Top 10 entries, blanks and non-blanks if they exist, but the real power behind AutoFilter comes from creating custom filters.

Note

There is an undocumented but important improvement to AutoFilters in Excel 97. In previous versions, AutoFilter still showed inapplicable data when a list was filtered by one field and the drop-down arrow was clicked on another. By making Excel AutoFilter smarter, the feature has become much more powerful.

Hands On: Creating a Custom AutoFilter

To create a custom AutoFilter:

1. Apply AutoFilter by choosing Data, Filter, AutoFilter.
2. Click the arrow next to the Height (in Feet) field to view the filters for this field.
3. Select Custom from the drop-down list. The Custom AutoFilter dialog box is shown in Figure 18.8.

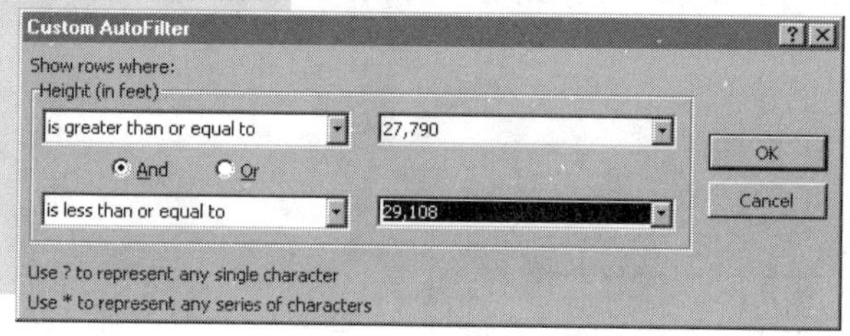

Figure 18.8 Custom filters allow you to filter and compare multiple items of data.

Search criteria can be entered into the Custom AutoFilter dialog box to search for multiple items. This example uses AutoFilter to find all mountain peaks between 27,790 and 29,108 feet.

4. Click the first drop-down arrow and select Is Greater Than Or Equal To.
5. Select Is Less Than Or Equal To in the bottom text box.
6. Type **27,790** into the top right text box and **29,108** in the one below it. If you don't want to type the number, click the drop-down arrow next to each text box and select from the list.
7. Click OK to filter the database.

In Figure 18.9 the database is filtered to show only a subset of the records.

The operators used within the Custom AutoFilter dialog box include:

Equals	Does Not Equal
Is Greater Than	Is Greater Than or Equal To
Is Less Than	Is Less Than or Equal To
Begins With	Does Not Begin With

Ends With	Does Not End With
Contains	Does Not Contain

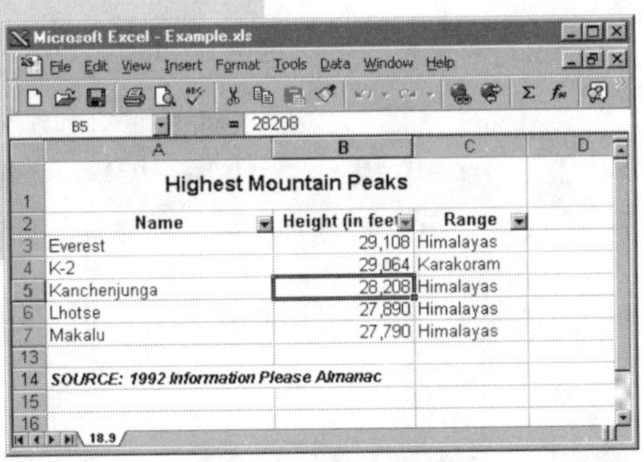

Figure 18.9 Rows that don't match the criteria are temporarily hidden.

If you don't know the full spelling of a word that you want to search for, use the wild card character *. For example, if you don't know how to spell Himalayas or don't care to, Type an **H*** in the right section of the dialog box and have it return all items that contain the letter *H*. The *?* wild card character searches for all words that match the one letter that is replaced by the question mark. An example of creating a wild card search with the question mark is typing **D?N**. This searches for records that contain the *d* and the *n* and have a single character between them. This search could return the constants *Dan*, *Don*, *Den*, and so on.

Wild Card Character	**Action**
?	Finds a single character
*	Represents any series of characters

Filtered lists remain filtered until turned off or changed to show All from the filtered column.

Note

Advanced Filter

To filter multiple fields, find unique records, or copy the results of a filter to a different location, use Advanced Filter.

Advanced Filter requires a criteria range to be set on the worksheet and set apart from the database where information is stored. Avoid using any rows that are used or adjoining the database. A good place for the criteria range is above the table separated by at least one blank row. This enables the criteria and database to be seen together on the same worksheet without interfering with one another.

Note

AutoFilter must be turned off to activate Advanced Filter.

Figure 18.10 shows a criteria range at the top of a worksheet.

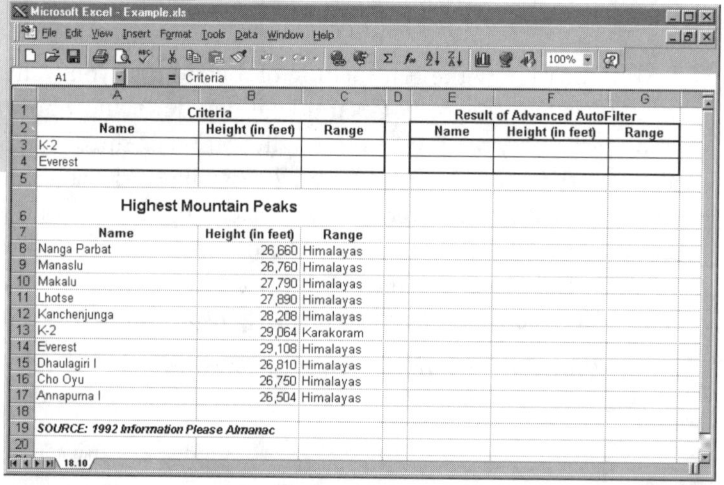

	A	B	C	D	E	F	G
1	Criteria				Result of Advanced AutoFilter		
2	Name	Height (in feet)	Range		Name	Height (in feet)	Range
3	K-2						
4	Everest						
5							
6	Highest Mountain Peaks						
7	Name	Height (in feet)	Range				
8	Nanga Parbat	26,660	Himalayas				
9	Manaslu	26,760	Himalayas				
10	Makalu	27,790	Himalayas				
11	Lhotse	27,890	Himalayas				
12	Kanchenjunga	28,208	Himalayas				
13	K-2	29,064	Karakoram				
14	Everest	29,108	Himalayas				
15	Dhaulagiri I	26,810	Himalayas				
16	Cho Oyu	26,750	Himalayas				
17	Annapurna I	26,504	Himalayas				
18							
19	*SOURCE: 1992 Information Please Almanac*						
20							

Figure 18.10
The criteria range is visible but separated from the data by a blank row.

Hands On: Setting Up a Criteria Range

To set up the criteria range:

1. Activate the Highest Mountain Peaks database.
2. Select rows 1 through 4. Do this by clicking on the row number at the left side of the row. Four rows are selected to insert the same number of rows in step 3.
3. Choose Insert, Rows and add 4 blank rows at the top of the worksheet.

4. Select and copy the field names in cells A7:C7. The field names in the criteria range must be an exact match to the ones in the database.
5. Select cell A2 and choose Edit, Paste.
6. The borders are optional in this exercise but may help to set off the cells that make up the criteria range.

Hands On: Entering the Criteria

With the criteria range prepared, define the criteria to be used in Advanced Filter:

1. Type **K-2** in cell A3 and **Everest** in cell A4.
2. Select cell A8 or any cell within the database.
3. Choose Data, Filter, Advanced Filter. The Advanced Filter dialog box shown in Figure 18.11 appears.
4. Select Copy to Another Location in the Action group box. If this option is not selected, the original list will be filtered in place much like the effect of AutoFilter where rows that don't match the criteria are hidden.

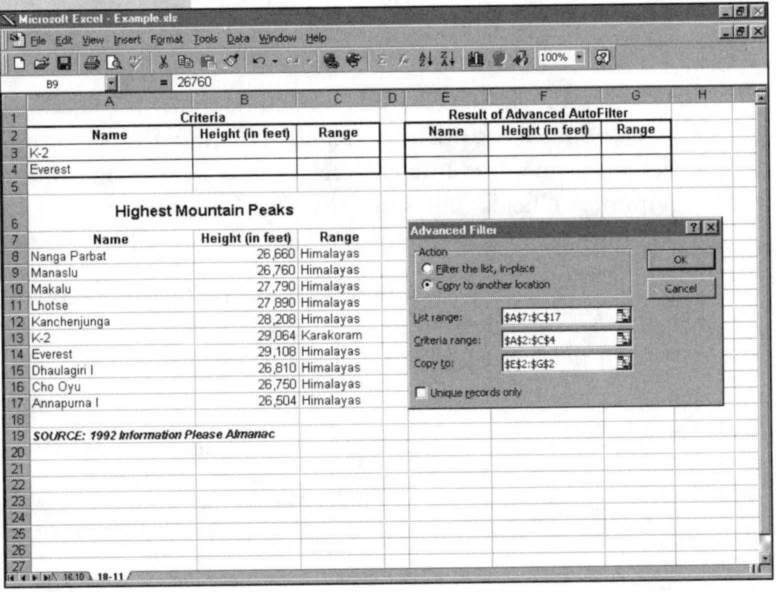

Figure 18.11 Data can be filtered in place or to a new location. If filtered in place, the data is not overwritten, just hidden from view.

5. Enter the following information if necessary:

List Range:	**$A$7:$C$17**
Criteria Range:	**$A$2:$C$4**
Copy To:	**$E$2:$G$2**

6. Click OK to create the Advanced Filter. The results of the Advanced Filter are shown in Figure 18.12.

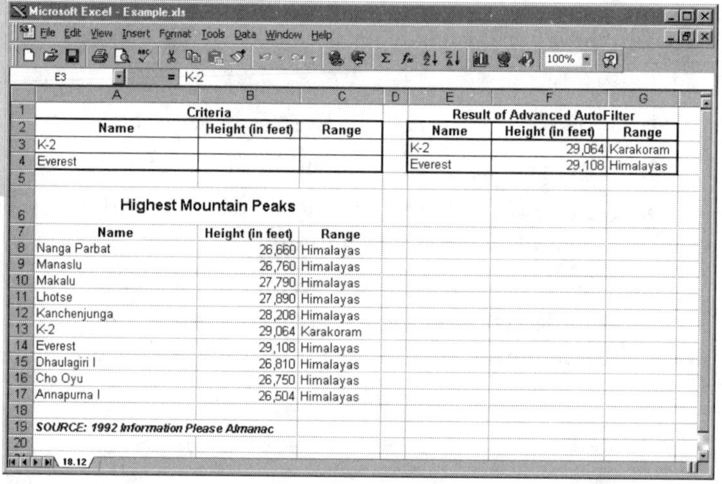

Figure 18.12 Any record found to match the criteria is copied to the designated worksheet range.

When information is placed on one line under the criteria headers, the list will be filtered for all records that match the criteria in that line. If several criteria are defined as in our example, Excel performs a search to find the records that match both of the fields independently. Excel performs an OR operation to display all records where the Name field contains the word K-2 *or* Everest.

If the data is a range of numbers, use mathematical operators to search for the value. An example of this might be to find all fields >=28,208. This statement will find all fields greater than or equal to twenty-eight thousand, two hundred and eight.

The list of mathematical operators and their functions:

Operator	**Function**
=	Equal to
<	Less than
<=	Less than or equal to
>	Greater than

Operator	Function
>=	Greater than or equal to
<>	Not equal to

Tip

You can use Advanced Filter to remove all the duplicate records from a list. Copy the data to a new location (no duplicates), delete the original source, and then copy back the Filtered data.

To learn more about AutoFilter and Advanced Filter see Excel's online Help.

Adding Subtotals to a Database

The capability to add subtotals to a database is extremely useful when attempting to manage and analyze data. The subtotals are embedded onto the worksheet and are fairly automated. The database shown in Figure 18.13 is used for this exercise. Before applying any subtotals, the database must be sorted.

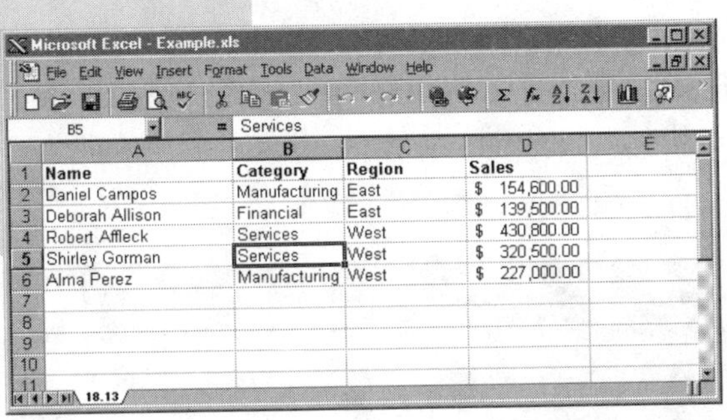

Figure 18.13 Applying subtotals is useful when using Excel as a reporting tool.

Hands On: Adding Subtotals to the Database

To add subtotals to a database:

1. Select a cell within the sorted database.
2. Choose Data, Subtotals to display the Subtotals dialog box. When a cell within the database is selected prior to choosing Subtotals, Excel automatically selects the database range of the active cell. Figure 18.14 shows the Subtotal dialog box.

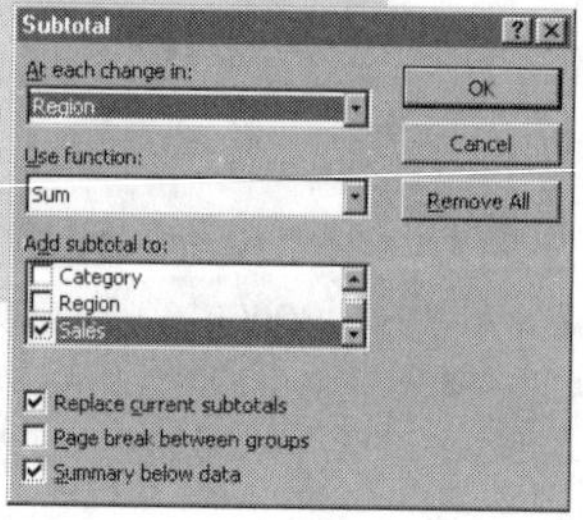

Figure 18.14 Subtotals are based on a change in a specified field.

Without much assistance, the Subtotals feature inserts a formula after each change in field.

3. Set up the following criteria:

At each change in:	**Region**
Use function:	**Sum**
Add subtotal to:	**Sales**

Subtotals can be added to any or all fields in the database. Place a check mark next to any field name in the Add Subtotals To list box. Accept the defaults at the bottom of the dialog box and click OK to apply subtotals.

When subtotals are created, Excel displays the database in an outline view. The outline numerical controls show the level of subtotals within the database. Figure 18.15 shows the same database with added subtotals.

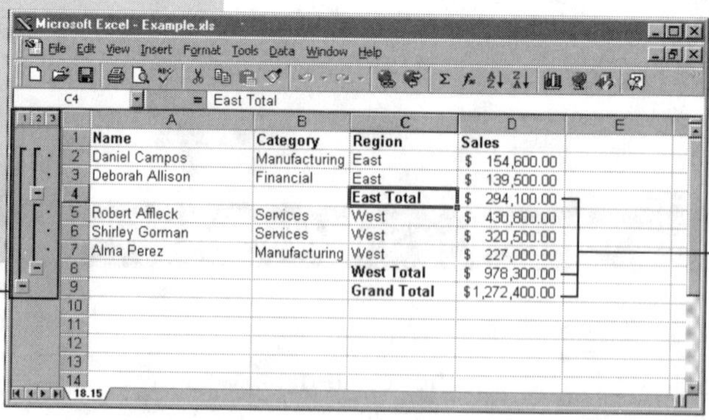

Figure 18.15 The subtotals are added at each change in a field that you specified in the Subtotal dialog box.

Outline controls

Subtotals

The numbers in the upper left portion of the worksheet represent a different layer of the applied subtotals. In the example database, level 1 is the grand total; two represents the next level of subtotals; and three will expand the database to the fullest extent. The numbers and each of the plus and minus signs can be clicked to display different views of the data's organization.

To remove subtotals from the database choose Data, Subtotals and click the Remove All button.

PivotTables

PivotTables are the ultimate in reporting tools and could possibly be the best feature in Excel. If you've ever been tasked with creating a presentation based on data and the data changes half way through the project, you'll appreciate the beauty and flexibility that a PivotTable provides.

Microsoft defines a PivotTable in online help as an interactive table that quickly summarizes, or cross-tabulates, large amounts of data. You can rotate its rows and columns to see different summaries of the source data, filter the data by displaying different pages, or display the details for areas of interest.

Note

There is much information about PivotTables that cannot be summarized in a segment of a chapter. Excel's online Help is full of useful information, tips, and tricks about creating and using PivotTables.

The specifications of a PivotTable have been greatly improved in Excel 97. Table 18.1 shows all specifications for creating and using PivotTables.

Table 18.1 PivotTable Specifications

Specification	Limit
Maximum number of PivotTables on a sheet	Limited by available memory
Maximum number of items in a PivotTable	8,000
Maximum number of pages in a PivotTable	8,000
Maximum number of row or column fields in a PivotTable	Limited by available memory
Maximum number of page fields in a PivotTable	256 (or available memory)
Maximum number of data fields in a PivotTable	256
Maximum number of calculated item formulas in a PivotTable	Limited by available memory

Creating a PivotTable

The process of creating a PivotTable is made easy with the PivotTable Wizard. The Wizard walks you through a series of steps to build the PivotTable from your database.

Hands On: Creating a PivotTable in the Database

To create a PivotTable:

1. Select any cell in the database.
2. Choose Data, PivotTable Report. The PivotTable Wizard - Step 1 of 4 dialog box is shown in Figure 18.16.

Figure 18.16 Step 1 of the PivotTable Wizard prompts for the type of location holding the data.

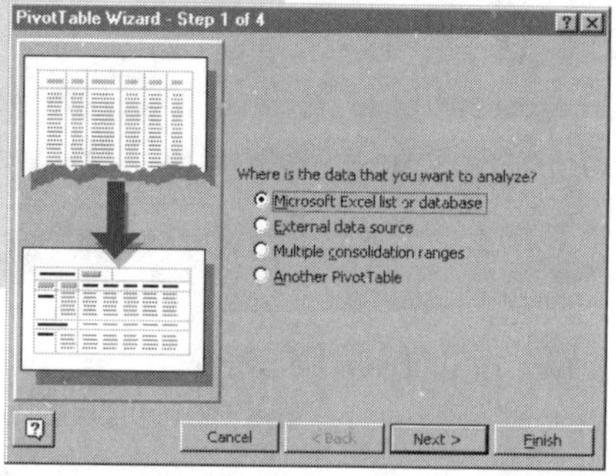

Note

PivotTable data can reside in external sources, an Excel worksheet, consolidated ranges, or in other PivotTables.

The database doesn't have to be in Excel; it can be in an external data source such as Microsoft Access or FoxPro. The database can even reside in multiple consolidated ranges or in another PivotTable.

3. Select the first option, Microsoft Excel List or Database and click the Next button.

4. Step 2 of the PivotTable Wizard shown in Figure 18.17 defines the location of the data. The location can be typed into the text box or selected with the mouse. The Collapse Dialog button located at the right of the Range text box helps you select cells on the worksheet by hiding a large portion of the PivotTable Wizard - Step 1 of 2. When the Collapse Dialog button is clicked, the dialog box is collapsed to show only the cell range text box and hides the rest of the dialog box. When you finish selecting the range on the worksheet, click the button again to display the entire dialog box. Click the Next button.

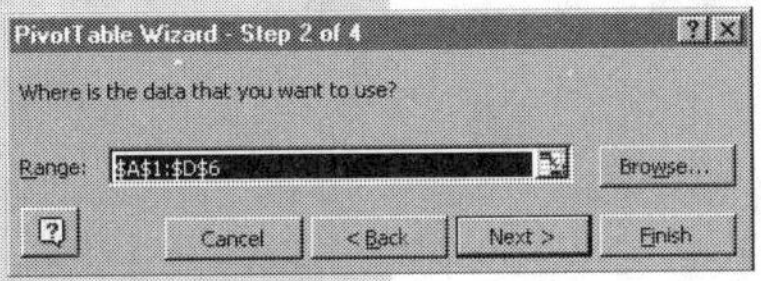

Figure 18.17 To enter the location, type directly into the text box or click on the worksheet and select the range with the mouse.

5. The PivotTable Wizard - Step 3 of 4 dialog box shown in Figure 18.18 builds the layout of the PivotTable. Click and drag each of the following field name labels to the correct position on the diagram. When a Page field is added to a PivotTable, the item will have a drop-down arrow next to the field name. The arrow works much like an AutoFilter where only certain data is displayed to show a subset of the database. The Row and Column fields control how the PivotTable is laid out. The only required field for a PivotTable however is to include at least one Data field.

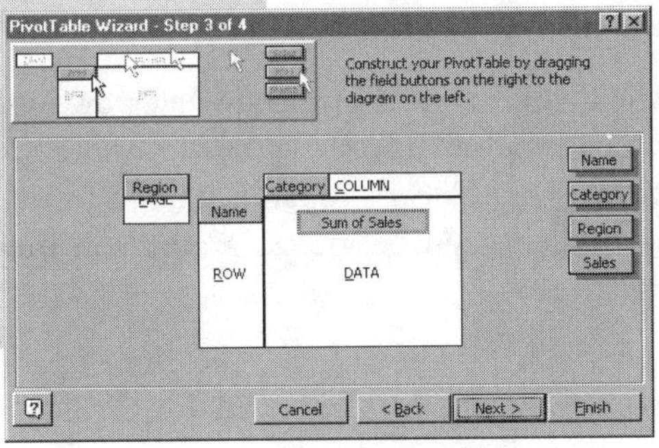

Figure 18.18 Drag field names from the right side of the dialog box to position on the diagram to construct the layout of the PivotTable.

Field Name	Position
Region	Page Field
Name	Row Field
Category	Column Field
Sales	Data Field
Page	Shows data for one item at a time
Column	Shows items in the field as column labels
Row	Shows items in the field as row labels
Data	Shows data for one item at a time in the table. Different functions and formatting can be applied to the data fields in a PivotTable.

6. Click the Next button to move to Step 4 in the PivotTable Wizard shown in Figure 18.19.

Figure 18.19 Step 4 assigns options for how the PivotTable will appear and function.

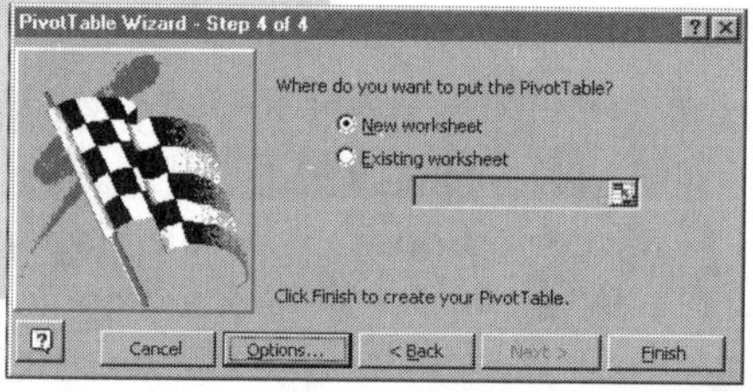

7. Keep the default selection to create the PivotTable on a New Worksheet.
8. Click the Options button and review the available options.
9. Click OK and then click Finish to create the PivotTable.

Figure 18.20 shows the newly constructed PivotTable.

The Page field of the PivotTable has a drop-down arrow to the right of it. Use this arrow to filter the data much like applying an AutoFilter. Although this is a nice presentation, it doesn't show half the capabilities of a PivotTable. The beauty of a PivotTable is how the fields can be moved around on the worksheet to change how the data is organized.

When you create charts on the PivotTable, the chart dynamically updates when the PivotTable changes. PivotTables are ideal for displaying presentations on a computer monitor, and they save paper in the process.

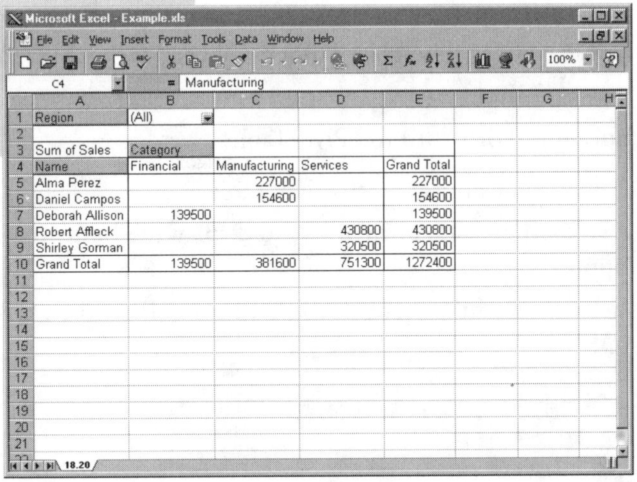

Figure 18.20 The PivotTable has one page, column, row, and data field.

Modifying the Layout of a PivotTable

To change the layout of the PivotTable:

1. Click and hold down the mouse button on the Category column field.
2. Drag the Category column field underneath the Region field and release the mouse button. Figure 18.21 shows the new layout of the PivotTable.

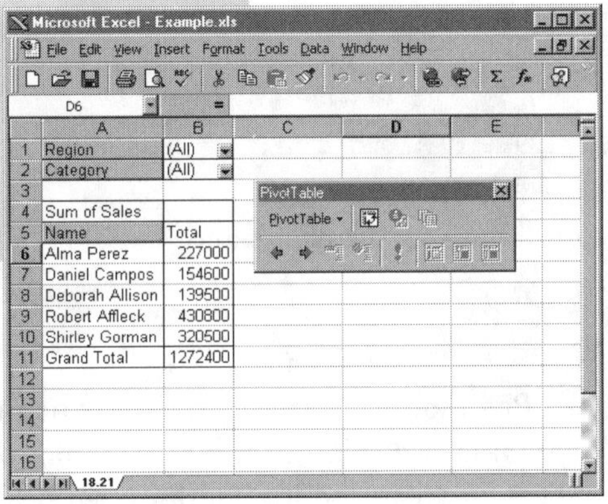

Figure 18.21 Rearranging the PivotTable is as simple as dragging one field to another location.

To remove a field from the PivotTable, click and drag the field name away from the PivotTable. When the mouse is over an unused area, an X will appear through the PivotTable field. If the mouse is released over this area, the PivotTable field will no longer appear within the construct of the PivotTable but will not be deleted from the original database.

The example PivotTable is functional, but you can jazz it up a bit by applying an AutoFormat. To illustrate the potential of using a PivotTable as a reporting tool, a dynamic chart will be placed alongside the PivotTable. The finished product is shown in Figure 18.22.

To apply AutoFormat to the PivotTable:

1. Select any cell within the PivotTable.
2. Choose Format, AutoFormat to display the built-in formatting that can be applied.
3. Select Colorful 2 from the Table format list. Click OK.

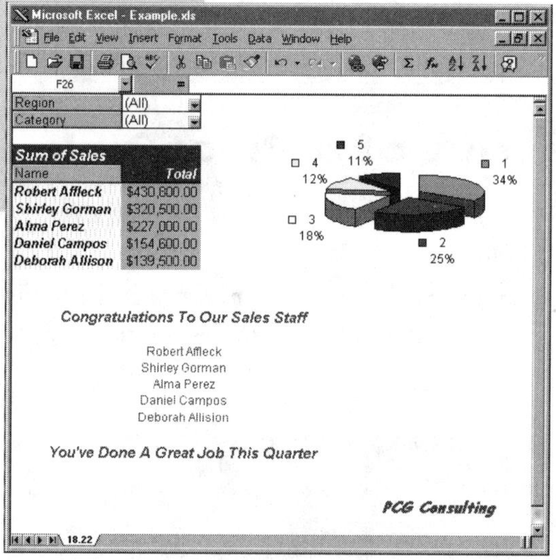

Figure 18.22 The PivotTable is formatted and ready to be used in any board of directors meeting.

Now you're ready to roll with an attractive and flexible PivotTable.

Editing a PivotTable

Because the layout of a PivotTable is flexible, so should being able to add or modify data. When a PivotTable is displayed, the PivotTable toolbar should be also. This toolbar has a bevy of features for working with PivotTables including refreshing the data. If you prefer using the menu commands, PivotTables can be updated by choosing Data, Refresh Data.

To add information to an existing PivotTable, open the worksheet where the data is stored and insert a row in the PivotTable source range. The PivotTable will keep track of these additions (or deletions) as long as both the source range and PivotTable are open when the changes are made.

If the database length has changed, you may need to go back a step or two in the PivotTable Wizard to change the range of the database. The Excel OFFSET function can be used to make a database range dynamic. For help on using the OFFSET function see Excel's online Help or help within the Function Wizard.

19

Making the Most of Excel's Tools

In This Chapter

- Using Goal Seek
- Applying Solver to Find Results for Complex Problems
- Using Scenario Manager to Perform What-If Analysis on Worksheet Data
- Using AutoSave and Analysis ToolPak to Increase the Functionality of Excel

You don't have to be a scientist or mathematician to use the analysis tool features in Excel. If you know what you want to accomplish with your data, you can follow Excel's step-by-step instruction help to construct formulas and functions to solve business problems.

Goal Seek

Goal Seek is a handy tool that can be used for determining a specific result for one cell by adjusting the value in another cell. This sounds complicated, but it's one of the easiest Excel tools to learn and use.

You decide to buy a car. The maximum monthly car payment can be up to $375.00. The current interest rate is 6%, and you are not providing a down payment. You would like to pay the car off in three years. What is the maximum that you can spend on a new car? You can use Goal Seek to solve problems like this, as you'll see in upcoming exercises.

Goal Seek is started by selecting a cell that contains a formula and choosing Tools, Goal Seek. The Goal Seek dialog box is shown in Figure 19.1.

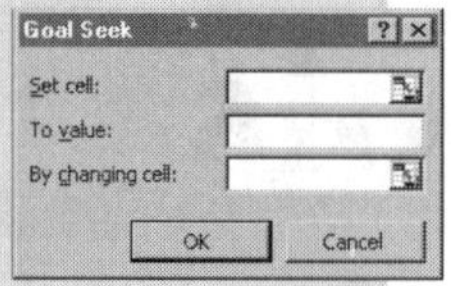

Figure 19.1 The Goal Seek dialog box has three text boxes, Set Cell, To Value, and By Changing Cell.

The Set Cell text box must contain a formula and is the cell that you want to find a solution for. The To Value cell is the target value that you want to solve for. The By Changing Cell text box is the cell value changed to find the result.

Hands On: Using Goal Seek

ENTERING AND EDITING DATA IS COVERED IN CHAPTER 7.

If you want to determine the amount that you can afford to spend on a new car or house, you can use Goal Seek.

1. Create a new worksheet with the information shown in Figure 19.2.
2. From cell B5 choose Insert, Function to display the Paste Function dialog box. Select the Financial Function Category from the left side of the Paste Function dialog box and PMT function from the Function Name list on the right.
3. Click OK to display the PMT Formula Palette.

Figure 19.2 Goal Seek will be used with the PMT function to determine the maximum purchase price for a new car.

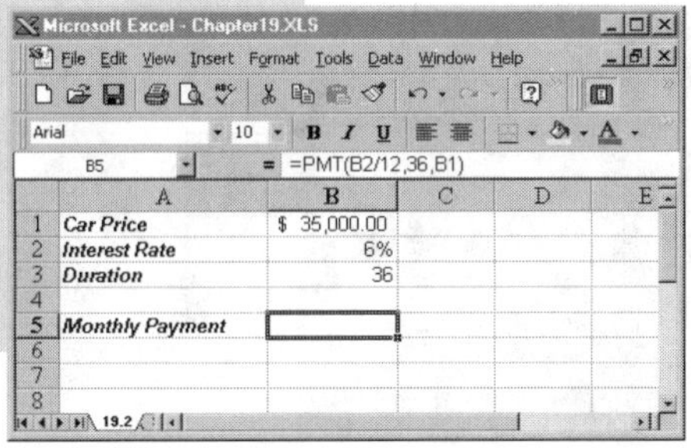

A shortcut to opening the Paste Function dialog box is to press Shift+F3.

4. Type **B2/12** in the Rate text box, **12*3** (or **36**) in Nper, and **B1** in the PV text box.

Note

Rate **is the interest rate per period (or years). To find the monthly interest rate, the percentage is divided by 12.**

Nper **is the total number of payments to be made for the loan. If the duration of a loan is three years, multiply three by the number of months (or payments) to be made in a year.**

5. Click OK and then press Enter to complete the PMT formula.
6. Choose Tools, Goal Seek to display the Goal Seek dialog box shown in Figure 19.3.
7. In the Set Cell text box you can either select cell B5 on the worksheet, or Type **B5** directly into the text box.
8. In the To Value text box Type **375.00**.
9. In the By Changing Cell text box, you can either select cell B1 on the worksheet, or type **$B$1** directly into the text box.
10. Click OK to process Goal Seek and to display the solution dialog box shown in Figure 19.4.

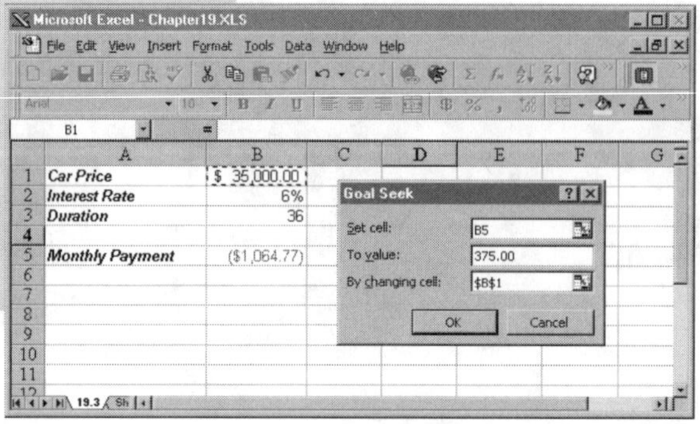

Figure 19.3
Goal Seek solves the problem backwards, taking known data and searching for missing variables.

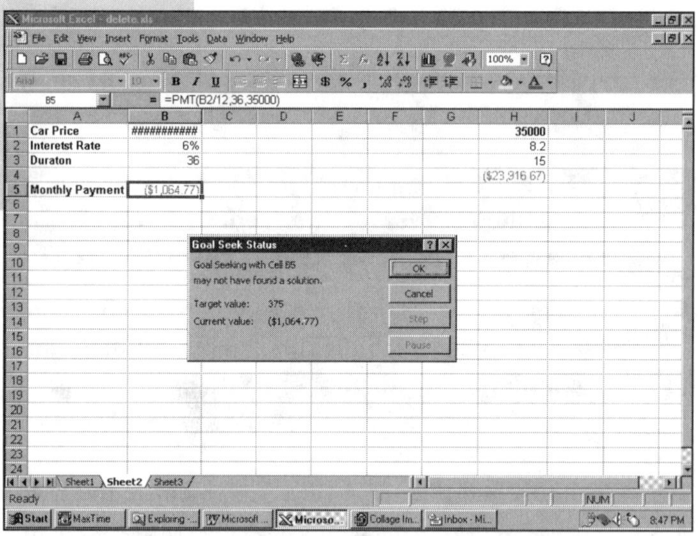

Figure 19.4
After Goal Seek is complete, it lets you know whether a solution was found.

11. To accept the solution, click OK. The Cancel button returns the original values to the worksheet.

Goal Seek determines that the maximum purchase price for the car is $12,326.63.

CHARTS AND THE CHART WIZARD ARE COVERED IN CHAPTER 14.

Hands On: Charting and Goal Seek

If you use charts to present the car purchase case study, you can use the chart to directly manipulate values and activate Goal Seek.

1. Select cells A5:B5.
2. Click the Chart Wizard toolbar button on the Standard Toolbar or choose Insert, Chart.
3. Click the Finish button to bypass the remaining Chart Wizard steps and build the chart shown in Figure 19.5.

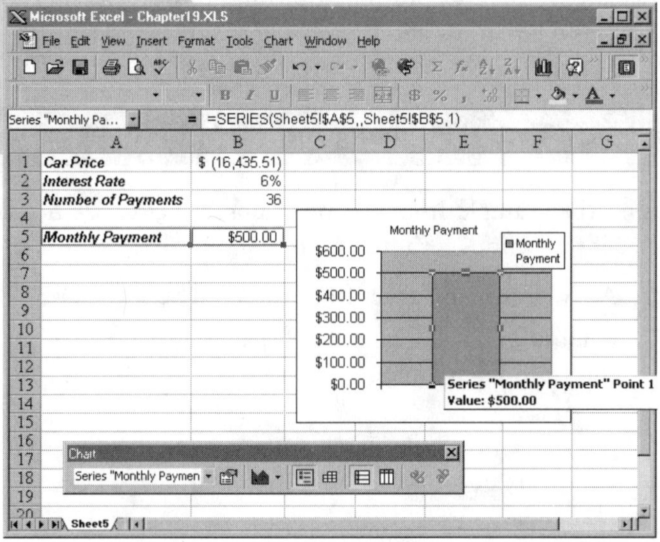

Figure 19.5 Drag the bar chart up or down to activate Goal Seek.

4. Click once on the Monthly Payment series, pause, and then click again. *Do not double-click.* The objective is to select the chart, but not to activate it. If the chart series is properly selected, the formula bar should contain the formula `=SERIES(Sheet5!$A$5,,Sheet5!$B$5,1)`, and small handles should appear around the selected data series.
5. Hover the mouse at the top of the bar until the mouse pointer changes to two arrows.
6. Click and drag the bar series up to `$500.00`. When the mouse is released, the Goal Seek dialog box appears.
7. In the By Changing cell text box, Type **B1**. Click OK twice.

The monthly payment value is changed to $500.00, and the maximum price of the car increases to $16,435.51.

Scenario Manager

The *Scenario Manager* is a tool used to create different views of set values to forecast different business scenarios. With Scenario Manager, you can create and switch between a group of scenarios such as present, best, worst, and likely case scenarios.

There are many reasons to use Scenario Manager in business. Scenario Manager is a valuable tool for projecting income and expense analysis data, financial and break-even planning, and forecasting trends.

Hands On: Using Scenario Manager

Using the example from the preceding exercise, use Scenario Manager to play what-if projections for interest rates of 3%, 5%, and 8.2%.

1. Activate the worksheet from the Goal Seek exercise.
2. Choose Tools, Scenarios to display the Scenario Manager dialog box shown in Figure 19.6.

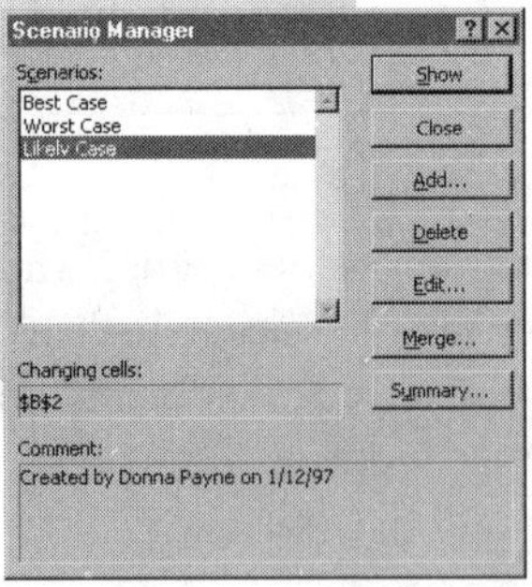

Figure 19.6 The Scenario Manager dialog box stores different scenarios for what-if analysis.

3. Click the Add button to create a new scenario. The Add Scenario dialog box appears. It doesn't matter which scenario you have initially selected.
4. Type **Best Case** in the Scenario Name text box and **$B$2** for Changing Cells. Click OK.
5. In the Scenario Values text box type **.03** and then click OK.
6. In the Scenario Manager dialog box, click the Add button again and create additional scenarios:

Scenario Name	By Changing	Scenario Values
Worst Case	$B$2	.082
Likely Case	$B$2	.05

7. After you've created the three scenarios, click the Show button in the Scenario Manager dialog box to display the scenario for each case, one at a time. You may need to move the dialog box to view the data.

Hands On: Creating a Summary Report

It is more practical to see all scenarios together where results and information can be easily compared. To do this, create a Summary Report.

1. Click the Summary button in the Scenario Manager dialog box. The Scenario Summary dialog box is now displayed.
2. A Scenario Summary or PivotTable report can be generated. Accept the default for Report Type and in the Result Cell Type **=$B$5**.

The Summary for the variable interest scenario is displayed in Figure 19.7. Each scenario is consolidated into one report.

To delete or edit a Scenario, activate the Scenario Manager dialog box and click the corresponding button.

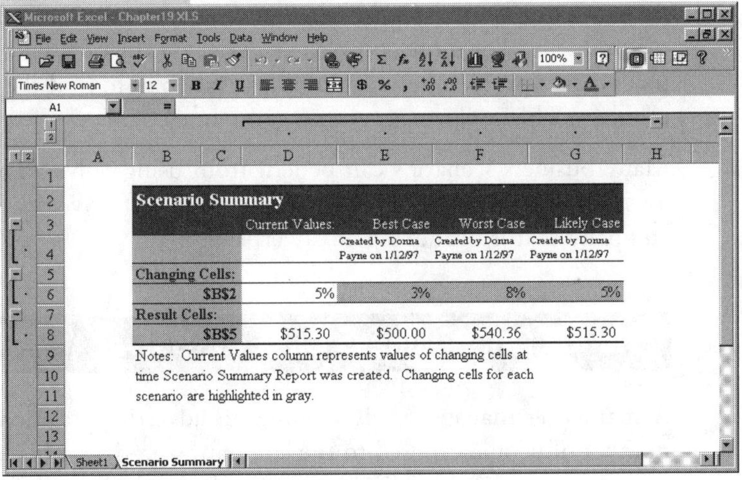

Figure 19.7 The Summary Report can be created in two formats, Summary Report or PivotTable.

Using Add-In Programs

Add-ins are programs that ship with Microsoft Excel and as the name implies, add functionality to the application. Add-in components are installed during the Excel installation and appear under the Excel Tools, Add-Ins menu when available.

Note

If the add-ins covered in this section are not loaded on your computer, click Start, Settings, Control Panel, and double-click on the Add/Remove Programs icon. Select Excel or Microsoft Office and click the Add/Remove button. Look in the components of Excel and find the Add-ins to install.

After an add-in is installed on your computer, it needs to be loaded. To load an add-in, choose Tools, Add-Ins and select the check box next to the add-in name; then click OK. All add-ins except those in the Analysis ToolPak add commands to the menu items.

Some of the more common add-ins are covered in this section. A table is provided for the add-ins not covered with the name of the add-in and a brief overview of its function. For more information on add-ins consult Excel's online help.

Solver

As you learned earlier in this chapter, Goal Seek is used to find solutions to simple problems. For more complex analysis, use the *Solver* add-in. Solver is a useful tool when a problem requires multiple variables to find the optimal solution to a problem. This tool can save time and money.

Many business scenarios can benefit from using Solver. The purpose of the following example case study is to develop an effective advertising strategy for a company that is producing an advertising plan.

Hands On: Business Case for Solver

A marketing manager is developing an advertising campaign to maximize the number of people exposed to the company's product while staying within a budget. The advertising mediums to be used are television and magazine. A decision must be made as to which mixture of advertising mediums is most beneficial to the company.

1. Create the worksheet shown in Figure 19.8.
2. Select cells A2 to B16. Choose Insert, Name, Create to display the Create Names dialog box. The Left Column option should already be checked. Click OK to create the defined names.

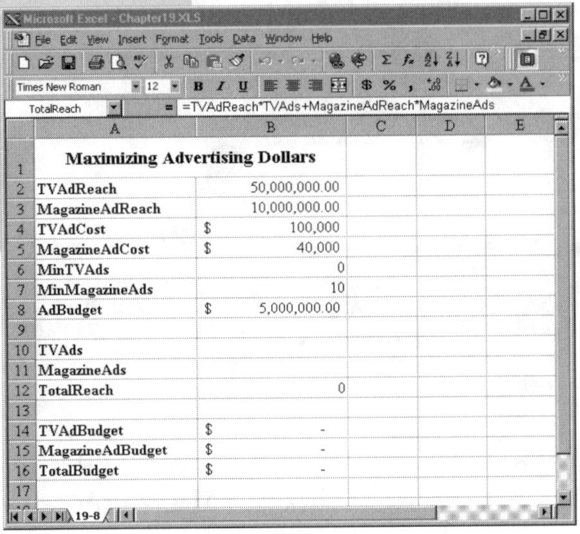

Figure 19.8 Solver uses calculations and limits to find solutions to business problems.

Tip

It's good practice to use defined names. The names are easier to understand when looking at the formula and can be self-documenting. The value of using defined names is illustrated as you build constraints in Solver.

3. In cell B12, type **=TVAdReach*TVAds+MagazineAdReach*MagazineAds** and press Enter.
4. In cell B14, type **=TVAds*TVAdCost** and press Enter.
5. In cell B15, type **=MagazineAds*MagazineAdCost** and press Enter.
6. In cell B16, Type **=TVAdBudget+MagazineAdBudget** and press Enter.
7. Select cell B9 and choose Tools, Solver to display the Solver Parameters dialog box shown in Figure 19.9.
8. In the Set Target Cell text box type **TotalReach** (do not press the Enter key).
9. The Equal To button selected should be Max.

10. Type **TVAds,MagazineAds** in the By Changing Cells text box. Click Add, and the Add Constraint dialog box shown in Figure 19.10 appears.

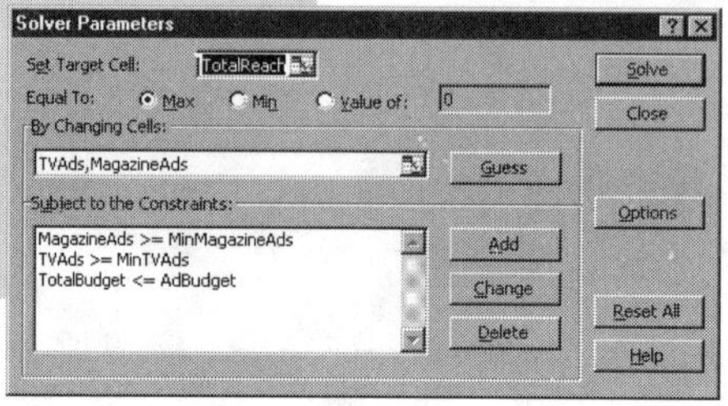

Figure 19.9 The Solver Parameters dialog box builds the business case scenario.

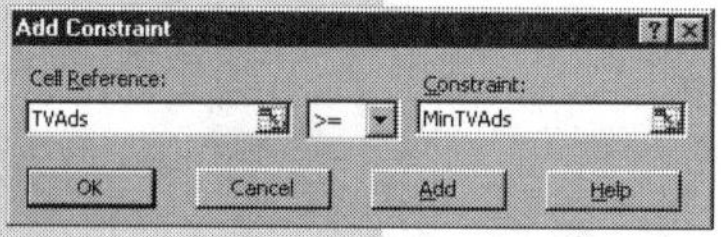

Figure 19.10 Multiple constraints to the problem can be added when using Solver.

11. In the Cell Reference text box type **MagazineAds**. If anything appears in this text box, select the text and then type over it.
12. Click the drop-down arrow between the two text boxes and set the value to greater than or equal to (>=).
13. Click OK to return to the Solver Parameters dialog box and add the following constraints. If you need help, revisit steps 10 through 13.
14. Add the following constraints using steps 10 through 12:

TVAds	>=	**MinTVAds**
TotalBudget	<=	**AdBudget**

15. Click OK to return to the Solver Parameters dialog box.

Note

The maximum number of adjustable cells in Solver is 200.

16. Click the Solve button. Solver displays the Solver Results dialog box and asks if you want to Keep the Solver Solution or Restore Original Values.

17. Accept the default settings and click OK. The solution that Solver has found to solve this problem is shown on the worksheet. Figure 19.11 shows that Solver has found the best possible way to spend the advertising budget based on the numbers in the worksheet.

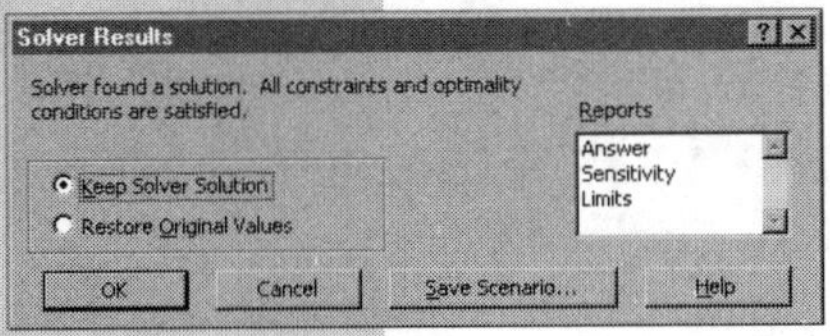

Figure 19.11 Solver determined the most effective way to divide the advertising medium for the company's budget.

Cells B10 and B11 show that the best combination of advertising for the company is 46 television and 10 magazine ads.

AutoSave

If your office building is prone to power failures or if you have the bad habit of not saving your Excel workbook regularly, consider activating the AutoSave add-in. This add-in functions the same way as the AutoSave feature in Microsoft Word, by automatically saving the file at a specified time interval.

Hands On: Enabling AutoSave

If you want your Excel workbook to automatically save after an interval of time, you can enable the AutoSave add-in.

1. Choose Tools, Add-Ins.
2. Place a check mark next to AutoSave and click OK.
3. Choose Tools, AutoSave to display the AutoSave dialog box shown in Figure 19.12.
4. The defaults are Automatic Save Every 10 Minutes, Save Active Workbook Only, and Prompt Before Saving. Click OK to accept the defaults and activate AutoSave.

Figure 19.12 The AutoSave add-in can prevent the loss of data in the event of a power failure.

5. To temporarily disable AutoSave, choose Tools, AutoSave and uncheck the Automatic Save Every check box.
6. To turn off the AutoSave add-in choose Tools, Add-Ins and uncheck the check box next to AutoSave.

Random Number Generator

Whether you want to create many random numbers for analysis or guess at winning lottery numbers, Excel has an add-in tool to generate random numbers in Excel.

The *Random Number Generator* is part of the Analysis ToolPak add-in and fills a range with unique random numbers using criteria that you define in the Random Number Generator dialog box.

FUNCTIONS AND FORMULAS ARE COVERED IN CHAPTER 8.

Hands On: Creating Random Numbers

If you want to create a list of random numbers, you can use the Random Number generator add-in from within Excel.

1. Create a new worksheet. Choose Tools, Add-Ins and click to place a check mark next to the Analysis ToolPak. Click OK to close the Add-Ins dialog box.
2. Choose Tools, Data Analysis to display the Random Number Generator shown in Figure 19.13.
3. In the Number of Variables text box type **1**. This is the number of columns to enter random numbers into.
4. In the Number of Random Numbers text box type **15**.
5. The Distribution should be set to Uniform.
6. Set the Parameters Value and Probability Input Range to between **10** and **50**.

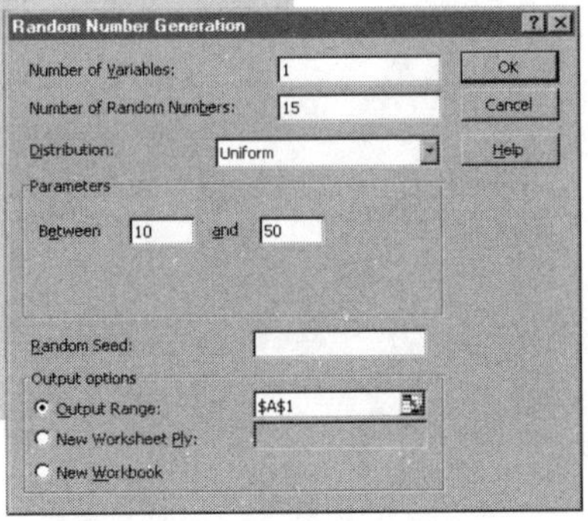

Figure 19.13 The Random Number Generator is a part of the Analysis ToolPak and can be used to create a list of random numbers.

7. Leave the Random Speed text box blank unless you want to use the random numbers over again each time.
8. Set the Output Range to **$A$1** and click OK to generate random numbers.
9. Select column A and choose Format, Cells, and Number. In the Format Cells dialog box, click the Number Category and change the Decimal Places to **0**. Click OK to format the random numbers to integers.

To generate random numbers that change with each recalculation use the =RAND() function.

Rank and Percentile

Another tool from the Analysis ToolPak is *Rank and Percentile*. This tool is extremely useful for teachers to generate quick reports using students' classroom grades. The Rank and Percentile add-in creates a report with the Point, Grade, Rank, and Percentile data in a matter of minutes.

Hands On: Using Rank and Percentile

The Rank and Percentile add-in is especially useful for teachers who need to create a ranking of student grades compared to other students in the class and then generate a percentile comparison.

1. Create a new worksheet using the data from Figure 19.14. The key for the grading scale is:

   Grades

   4 - A

   3 - B

   2 - C

   1 - D

   0 - F

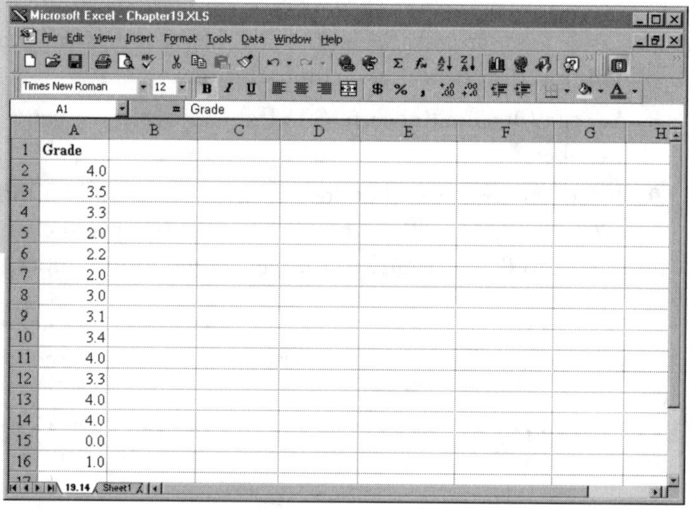

Figure 19.14 Rank and Percentile is useful for generating a quick report comparing and ranking like information.

2. Choose Tools, Data Analysis and select Rank and Percentile. Click OK to display the Rank and Percentile dialog box shown in Figure 19.15.
3. Set the Input Range to **$A$1:$A$16**.
4. The list is Grouped By Columns, and check the Labels in First Row box.
5. Set the Output Range to **$D$1**. Click OK to generate the Rank and Percentile report. Figure 19.16 shows the finished Rank and Percentile report.

The Point column is the original position of the grade on the worksheet. The Grade column groups and sorts grades in descending order. The Rank column shows how each student placed in comparison to other students. The Percent column is the calculated percentage that received each score.

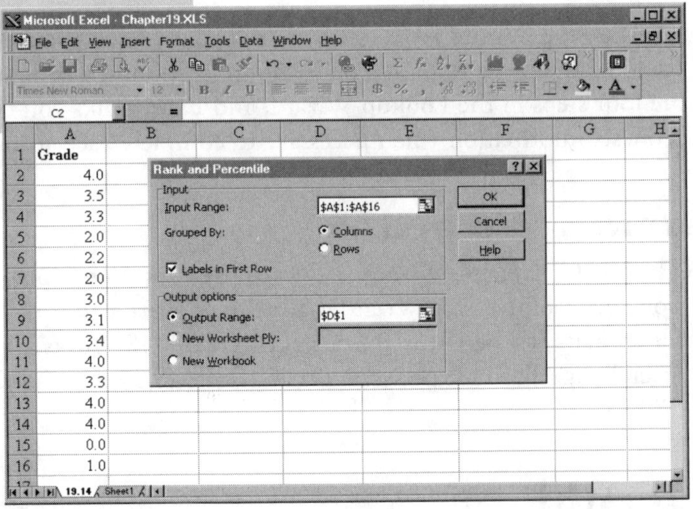

Figure 19.15
The Input Range is the data to be evaluated.

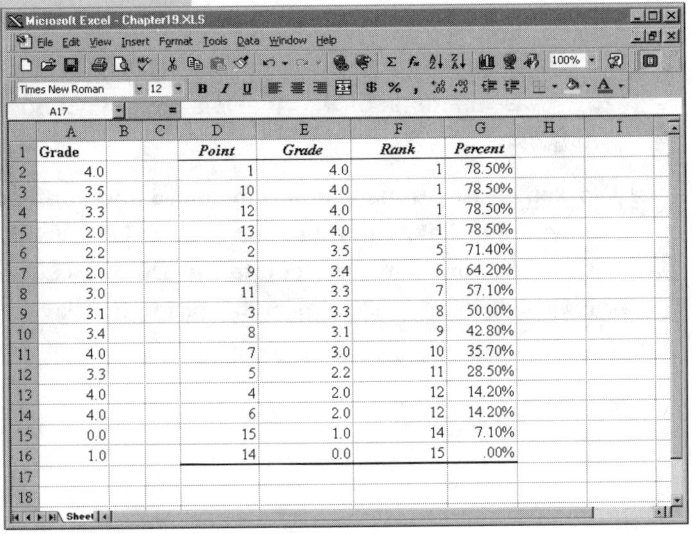

Figure 19.16
The Rank and Percentile add-in generates a table of values to compare student grades.

The New Wizard Add-Ins

New to Excel 97 are four Wizards listed under the Tools menu. These Wizards are Lookup, File Conversion, Web Form, and Conditional Sum. Two of the four Wizards are introduced in this section. For additional information on Add-Ins, see Excel's online help.

Lookup Wizard

The Lookup Wizard is accessed by choosing Tools, Wizard, Lookup and is used for looking up the value at a defined intersection in a table on a worksheet. There are four steps in the Lookup Wizard, and Excel walks you through each step and requests information when necessary to complete each formula.

File Conversion Wizard

The File Conversion Wizard is accessed by choosing Tools, Wizard, File Conversion and is a three-step Wizard that helps convert a group of files to Excel 97. The file formats can be Lotus 1-2-3, QPro/DOS, MS Works 2.0, dBase, SYLK, Data Interchange Format, previous versions of MS Excel, and Quattro Pro, 1.0/5.0 (WIN).

Other Excel Add-Ins

Many add-ins are not directly mentioned in this chapter that provide equally useful functions. Table 19.1 shows the remaining add-ins and their purpose.

Note

To access functions of the Analysis ToolPak choose Tools, Data Analysis.

Worksheet functions also are included and enabled with the Analysis ToolPak. The most common is NETWORKDAYS. NETWORKDAYS is used to calculate the workdays (Monday through Friday) between two dates, subtracting holidays.

Table 19.1 Other Excel Add-Ins

Add-In	Function/Purpose
AccessLinks	Lets you use Access forms and reports on Microsoft Excel data tables
Analysis ToolPak	Engineering, Statistical Analysis, and Financial Functions These functions include: Anova: Single Factor Anova: Two Factor with Replication Anova: Two Factor without Replication Correlation Covariance Descriptive Statistics Exponential Smoothing F-Test Two Sample for Variances Fourier Analysis Histogram Moving Average Regression Sampling t-Test: Paired Two Sample for Means t-Test: Two Sample Assuming Equal Variances t-Test: Two Sample Assuming Unequal Variances z-Test: Two Sample for Means
Internet Assistant Wizard	Converts Microsoft Excel tables and charts to HTML files
Microsoft Bookshelf Integration	Supports lookup reference in Excel and Copy to Excel in Bookshelf
MS Query add-in for Excel 5 compatibility	Works with Microsoft Query to gather external data
ODBC add-in	Allows you to use Open Database Connectivity (ODBC) function to connect to external data sources directly
Report Manager	Combines spreadsheet views with data scenarios to create and present reports
Template Utilities	Utilities used by Microsoft Excel
Template Wizard with Data Tracking	Creates form templates with data tracking
View Manager	Lets you create, define, and view different views on a worksheet
Update Add-in Links	Updates links to functions that were previously provided by add-ins to directly access the new built-in functions

20

Linking Excel with Other Applications

In This Chapter

- Exporting Data from Access to Excel
- Understanding OLE
- Linking Information from Microsoft Office Applications
- Embedding Information from Another Program
- Using Hyperlinks to Connect Documents

Although Excel is a powerful software package, no application can do everything. But when you use a software bundle like Microsoft Office that works well together, you can combine the best features from each application and make them available in another. In this chapter you'll explore how to share data between several applications and see how well the pieces to the puzzle fit together.

Note

You'll need Microsoft Office 97 Professional to complete the exercises in this chapter.

The first thing you're going to do is bring the data into Excel from Access. Next you'll learn about tools that work behind the scenes to make Office integration possible, and then you'll build the report using the rest of Microsoft Office.

Transferring Data from Access to Excel

Because Microsoft Access is a relational database, it stores and validates data well, and it doesn't have the row limitation that Excel does. However, no application is better than Excel at managing, manipulating, and displaying numerical analysis. Because Microsoft Access and Excel integrate well together, you can store the data in an Access database and bring it into Excel to do the number crunching.

Note

Excel has exceptional database capabilities also. When data is stored in an Excel spreadsheet, it is often referred to as being in a *flat file database*, meaning that the data is stored in one and only one table. Database applications such as Microsoft Access, SQL Server, and Visual FoxPro are relational databases that use multiple tables to store data.

Some tools in Excel work very well with databases. These tools include database functions, PivotTables, AutoFilter, and Automatic Subtotaling.

DATABASES ARE COVERED IN CHAPTER 18.

Hands On: Exporting from Access

Data can be exported from Access by using the File menu to save the file in an exportable format.

1. Open Access 97. When Microsoft Access is started, a dialog box appears prompting you to choose whether to open a Blank database, use the Database Wizard, or Open an existing one.

2. Choose to open an existing database and select the Northwind database from the bottom portion of the dialog box (see Figure 20.1); then click OK.

Note

The Northwind.mdb (database file) is located in the \Office \Samples directory of your Office 97 installation directory. If the Northwind database does not appear, you'll need to install the sample files available during the Microsoft Access 97 installation. To install these files close all open applications. Click the Start button and select Settings, Control Panel. Double-click the Add/Remove Programs icon. Select Microsoft Office (or Access with a Stand-alone installation) and follow the instructions for adding and removing components of the application.

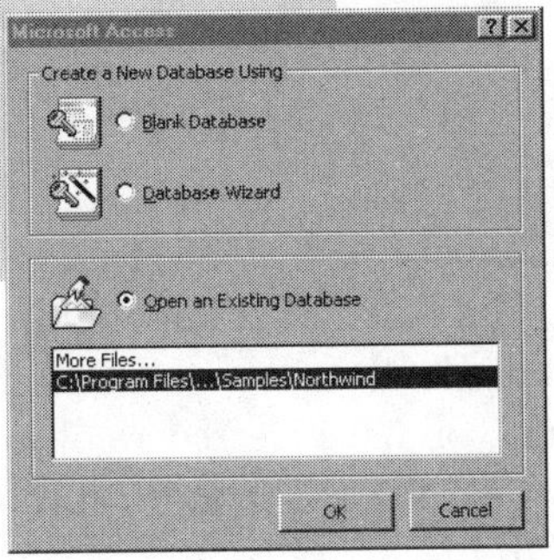

Figure 20.1 Three options are presented when you start Access.

3. Select the Order Details from the Tables tab and click the Open button.
4. When the Order Details table opens, choose File, Save As/Export.
5. Make sure that the To an External File or Database option button is selected and then click OK.
6. In the Save In text box, navigate to the My Documents folder on your C drive.
7. In the Save as Type text box, click the drop-down arrow and select Microsoft Excel 97.
8. Click the Export button to begin the export of data from the Northwind Access database to an Excel 97 workbook saved in the My Documents folder.

The Access file has been successfully saved and can be opened just as you can open any other Excel file.

Tip

Another way to bring data from Access into Excel is to choose Data, Get External Data, Create New Query or choose Data, Get External Data, Run Database Query (runs a previously created *.dqy query). Both of these create QueryTables.

This process opens a program called Microsoft Query (not installed with a Typical installation of Excel) that ships with Microsoft Office that can bring all or a subset of the data table into Excel.

Integration Tools

Some tools work behind the scenes of Microsoft Office to make integration possible. Information can be shared by copying and pasting, by embedding, and by linking between applications.

What Is OLE?

OLE is the acronym for *Object Linking and Embedding*, or a complicated description for the simple act of copying and pasting. By highlighting and copying information in one application, such as Excel, and then pasting that information in another application, such as Word, you have created an object. The result of pasting can take the form of the information itself or an icon showing the application that the information was copied from.

The difference between linking and embedding is simply a matter of where the information is stored. When an object is *linked*, it keeps a return address to the location it was copied from, which it uses to keep itself up-do-date. If you copy some of the Order Details numbers from an Excel workbook and paste them using a link into a Word document, any changes made to the workbook will automatically appear in the Word document. As long as the Word document can still find the Excel workbook it is linked to, your Order numbers will appear in Word.

The following examples illustrate the differences between sharing data by copying and pasting, linking, and embedding.

Copying and Pasting Data

When an object is copied and pasted between applications, the object becomes a part of the application that it is being copied into. For example, using the database that you transferred to Excel, you'll share data between Microsoft Word and Excel.

Hands On: Copying and Pasting Data between Applications

To copy data from Excel and paste it in a Word document, follow these steps:

1. Open the Order Details file that you saved in the preceding exercise (this is the file you exported from Access to Excel).
2. Select the range A1:E1 (the database headers).
3. Click the Bold button on the toolbar to distinguish the header information.
4. Select the range A1:E10.
5. Choose Edit, Copy, or click the Copy button on the Standard toolbar.
6. Open Microsoft Word.
7. In Word, choose Edit, Paste.

The pasted data from Excel has been changed into a Word table that can be edited directly from within Word. Figure 20.2 shows the copied and pasted data in Word.

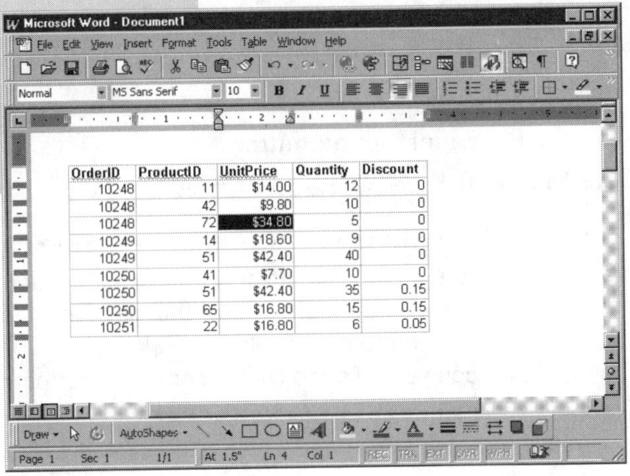

OrderID	ProductID	UnitPrice	Quantity	Discount
10248	11	$14.00	12	0
10248	42	$9.80	10	0
10248	72	$34.80	5	0
10249	14	$18.60	9	0
10249	51	$42.40	40	0
10250	41	$7.70	10	0
10250	51	$42.40	35	0.15
10250	65	$16.80	15	0.15
10251	22	$16.80	6	0.05

Figure 20.2 The data now has no connection to the original Excel file.

Linking Data

The same Excel worksheet data from the preceding example can be used to create a link between the Excel file and the Word file where the information is being pasted. This way, when the Excel file is changed, the link is maintained, and the new information is updated in the Word document when it is opened.

Hands On: Linking Data Between Applications

To link data from Excel in a Word document, follow these steps:

1. Open the Order Details file that you saved in the preceding exercise.
2. Select the range A1:E10.
3. Choose Edit, Copy or click the Copy button.
4. Switch to Microsoft Word.
5. Choose Edit, Paste Special. The Paste Special dialog box appears (see Figure 20.3).

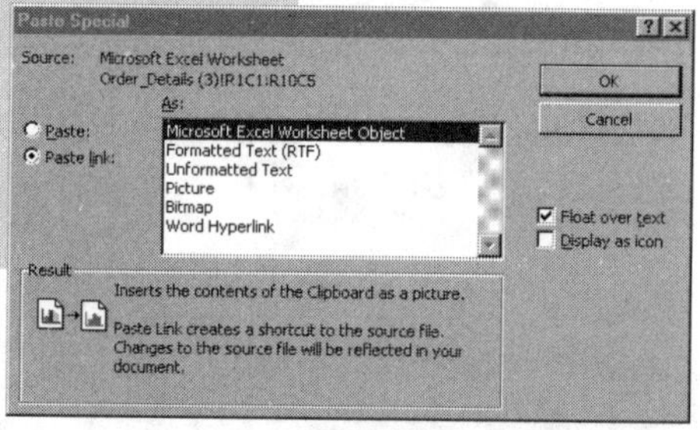

Figure 20.3 The Paste Link option creates a link between the object's old and new location.

6. Select the Paste Link option button.
7. Select Microsoft Excel Worksheet Object in the list box and click OK.

If you prefer to store the information as an icon in the new application, select the Display as Icon check box on the right side of the dialog box. This option is useful when you don't have much room to display the full contents of the linked information. When the user double-clicks the linked icon, the information appears.

8. Double-click the copied Excel data in the Word document as if you wanted to edit the data. The Excel window appears (see Figure 20.4).
9. Click anywhere outside the Excel information to return to Word.

Figure 20.4
The linked object remains in Word but is edited in-place using Microsoft Excel.

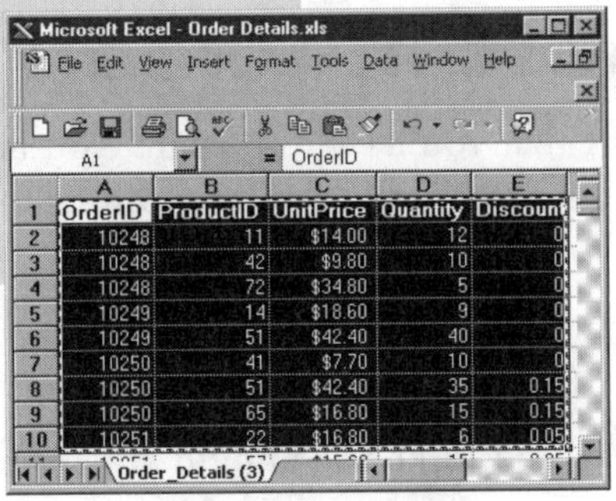

When the information is double-clicked, OLE kicks into action. OLE allows for in-place editing and activation of objects created in another OLE-compliant Microsoft Office application.

Embedding Information from Another Program

When the information you paste from one application to another cannot be dependent on another file always being present, then embedding is for you. If you copy those same numbers from Excel into Word and use an embedded paste, then all the Excel information is actually stored inside the Word document. The Word document can be sent via e-mail or other network device without losing its connection to the Excel workbook.

Hands On: Embedding Data Between Applications

To embed data from Excel in a Word document, follow these steps:

1. Open the Excel Order Details workbook.
2. Select the range A1:E10 and click the Copy button.
3. Switch to Microsoft Word.
4. Choose Edit, Paste Special.
5. Make sure that the Paste option is selected, and then choose Microsoft Excel Worksheet Object in the list box. *Do not* select Paste Link this time.
6. Click OK.

The information is embedded into the Word document and will no longer require being connected to the source document to be available. Also, because you embedded the object, you can change the information and formatting in the object using Excel without altering the object.

Generating a Report in Excel

Getting back to the report that you have to prepare, you have valid information that was exported from Access to Excel. Now you can take advantage of some of Excel's tools to make the report more presentable.

Note

The Excel Order Details workbook should still be open. If it's not, open it at this time.

Filtering the Database

AUTOFILTER IS COVERED IN CHAPTER 18.

You want to show how many orders came in at or above $250.00 in your report. To do this, you'll use the AutoFilter tool on the Excel database.

Hands On: Filtering Data and Charting the Filtered Data

To filter data in the database, follow these steps:

1. Select any cell in the database.
2. Choose Data, Filter, AutoFilter.
3. Click the drop-down AutoFilter arrow in cell C1 and select (Custom) from the list. The Custom AutoFilter dialog box shown in Figure 20.5 appears.
4. In the top left box, select Is Greater Than Or Equal To from the drop-down list.
5. In the top right box, type **250** and click OK. The list is filtered to show only orders equal to or greater than $250.00.
6. Select the cells A1:E2029, which make up the filtered database range.
7. Choose Edit, Copy.
8. Switch to Microsoft Word and choose Edit, Paste Special.

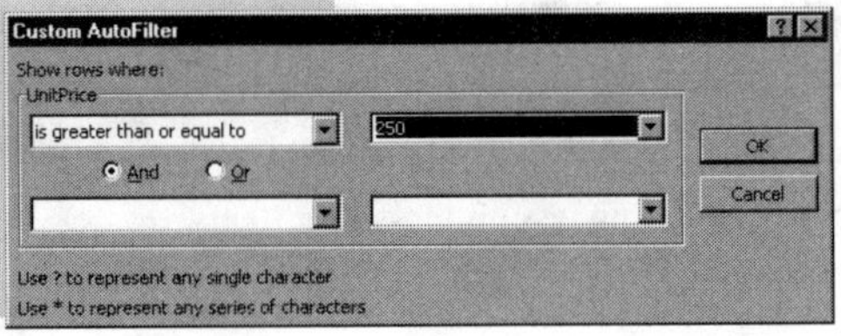

Figure 20.5 Use the Custom AutoFilter dialog box to specify how to filter the data.

9. Select Paste Link and Microsoft Excel Worksheet Object, and then click OK. The filtered list is copied (with a link) to the Word document.
10. Return to the Excel workbook leaving both documents open.
11. Select the range C1:D2029 (the list should still be filtered).
12. Click the Chart Wizard button on the Standard toolbar. Select a 3-D column chart and move through the Chart Wizard steps placing the chart on an existing worksheet next to the Orders list.
13. Select the chart and choose Edit, Copy.
14. Switch to Microsoft Word and choose Edit, Paste Special.
15. Select Paste, click Microsoft Excel Chart Object, and click OK. The chart appears in the document.

CHARTS ARE COVERED IN CHAPTER 14.

Adding Text to the Word Document

To add text between, around, or on top of objects, you can type directly, or use a text box object.

You can use the Text Box button on the Drawing toolbar to create a text box. Figure 20.6 shows the Word document with the database, chart, and minimal surrounding text.

Tip

I've added some pizzazz to the objects by applying a little formatting and some tricks learned over the years. The interior of the chart was selected, and a color was chosen for the background of the chart. The process was repeated on the exterior portion of the chart. The text box was selected, and the borders turned off by choosing Format, Text Box and changing to no border color.

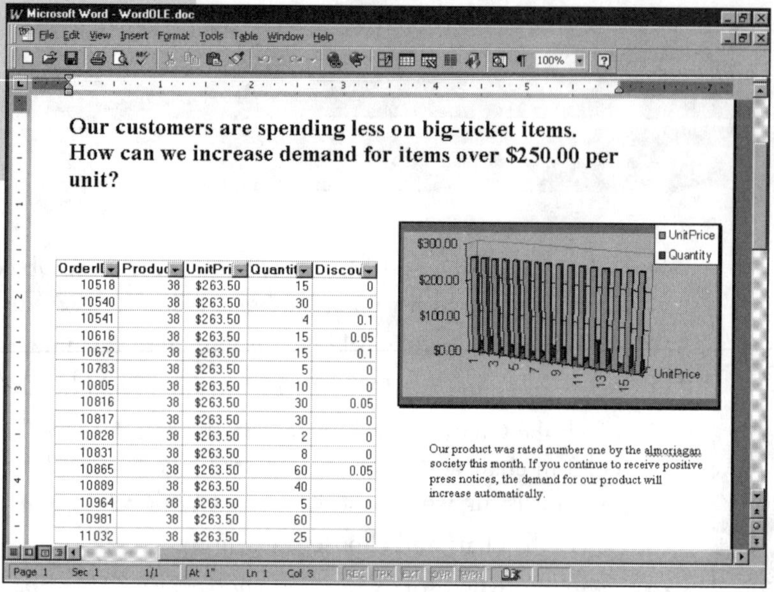

Figure 20.6 All objects can be moved around the page to change the layout.

Using Hyperlinks to Connect Documents

HYPERLINKS ARE COVERED IN DETAIL IN CHAPTER 21.

If you don't want to copy and paste or embed information from one document to another, you can create a *hyperlink*. A hyperlink is useful when information already exists in one place, and you want to use that information but don't want to have to reenter or copy and paste it into another document.

A hyperlink appears in the document and can be clicked on to jump to another cell, a range of cells, another document, or to the Internet if you have Internet access.

Wrapping It Up with PowerPoint

You've already created a report in Microsoft Word, but because you will be conducting a meeting with the sales force to discuss your findings, you'll need a presentation. PowerPoint makes it easy to create professional-looking presentations in a small amount of time.

To share information between Excel and other applications with PowerPoint, the same process of copying and pasting is performed.

Hands On: Sharing Data Between Excel and PowerPoint

To paste an Excel chart into a PowerPoint presentation, follow these steps:

1. Select the chart that you created in Microsoft Excel.
2. Choose Edit, Copy.
3. Choose Start, Programs and then select Microsoft PowerPoint.
4. Click the Blank Presentation option and then click OK.
5. Click the first slide (upper-left) corner and click OK.
6. Click on the Click to Add Title area and type **Sales Report Meeting**.
7. In the `Click to Add Sub-Title` area, type **Pacific Northwest Region**. Click on the white unused portion of the slide to deselect the subtitle.
8. Click Insert, New Slide and select the second row, fourth chart (title and chart slide), and click OK.
9. Click on the Click to Add Title area and type **High Dollar Item Sales**.
10. Choose Edit, Paste to paste the Excel chart into PowerPoint.
11. Save your work and close all documents and applications.

PowerPoint slides can be set up as animated, and you can create attractive background colors and themes to jazz up a presentation.

21

Using Excel with the Internet

In This Chapter

- Introducing Excel's Internet Features
- Checking Out the Web Toolbar
- Creating Hyperlinks in Cells
- Assigning Hyperlinks to Objects
- Creating Hyperlinks to Web Pages
- Exporting Excel Data to a Web Page
- Using the Internet Assistant Wizard
- Create Web Queries

An increasing number of people have created and maintain their own pages on the World Wide Web. It's no surprise then that Microsoft has designed components of Excel 97 to take advantage of Web tools used on the Internet and on corporate intranets.

Web Tools in Excel 97

A Web toolbar is included in each Office application. The toolbar includes components that can help to access and explore Web sites on the Internet or on your corporate intranet. There are three ways to display the Web toolbar:

- Click the Web Toolbar button on the Standard toolbar (the globe with two arrows).
- Choose View, Toolbars and select the Web.
- Right-click on any toolbar and click on Web.

Figure 21.1 shows the Web toolbar.

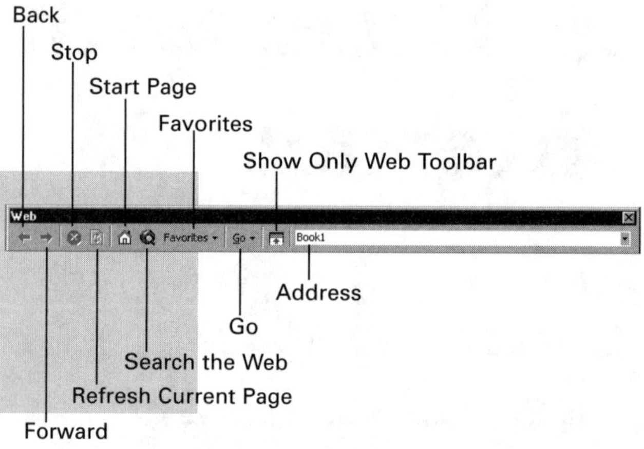

Figure 21.1
The Web toolbar is available in all Microsoft Office Applications except for Outlook.

Table 21.1 lists each toolbar button and its function.

Hyperlinks

A *hyperlink* (or *jump*) is a directional instruction to go to another location, whether it's a cell, the Internet, or a corporate intranet. This is a great way to move to pertinent cell or Web locations to show the workbook user information that would otherwise have been copied from one location into your workbook.

A hyperlink can be distinguished by a different color and underlined font. After the hyperlink is clicked, it changes color to show that the hyperlink location has been previously accessed.

Table 21.1 Web Toolbar Buttons

Toolbar Button	Function
Back	Goes back to the previous file or location in the list of the last 10 items that you jumped to.
Forward	Opens the next item in the list of the last 10 items that you jumped to.
Stop	Stops the jump process.
Refresh Current Page	Downloads the current page to refresh and show any changes or updates to the page.
Start Page	You can specify which page you will start from.
Search the Web	Opens a Search page that enables you to search the Web for phrases and text topics.
Favorites	Displays a list of commands to go to locations that you have added to a favorite folder. Favorites should include sites that you visit frequently.
Go	Displays a list of commands that help you navigate through Web pages and quickly go to your most recently viewed pages.
Show Only Web Toolbar	Hides all toolbars from view except the Web toolbar.
Address	Type an address of a location of a file or Web site that you want to go to or use the drop-down list to select a previously used location.

Hands On: Creating a Hyperlink to a Cell

A hyperlink can be created and assigned to any cell that when clicked goes to a defined location in any open Excel 97 workbook. The defined location can be to a cell or a range of cells. Hyperlinks can also be created in Word and PowerPoint.

1. Open an Excel workbook.
2. Choose Insert, Hyperlink to display the Insert Hyperlink dialog box shown in Figure 21.2. If you have not yet saved the workbook, Excel will prompt you to do so. If you do not want to save the workbook at this time, click the No button.
3. Click in the Named Location in File (optional) text box.
4. Click the Browse button (if you know the path of the file and its information, you can enter it in the text box directly without using Browse).
5. Select Sheet3 and click OK.

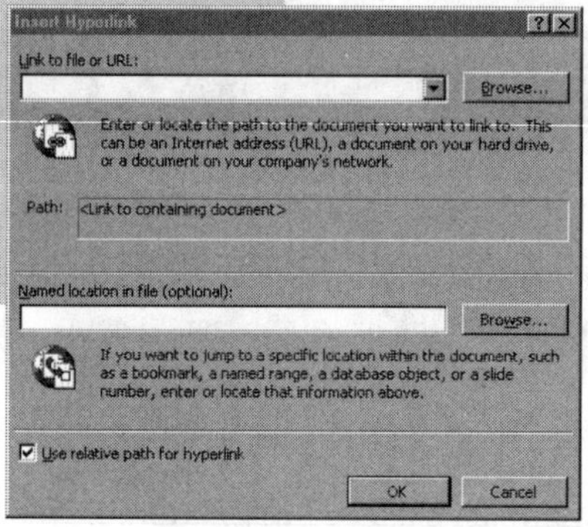

Figure 21.2 A hyperlink can be assigned to jump to a cell, object, defined name, or Internet site.

6. **Sheet3!A1** was entered into the text box. If cell A1 is the correct destination cell, click OK. Otherwise, select A1 in the text box and type the desired cell location. Click OK.

Note

To set the destination location to a range of cells in the Insert Hyperlink dialog box, type the range of cells instead of the single one. An example of this is Sheet3!A1:B5.

Back on the worksheet, you see the result of creating a hyperlink to a cell. Figure 21.3 shows the hyperlink created on the worksheet.

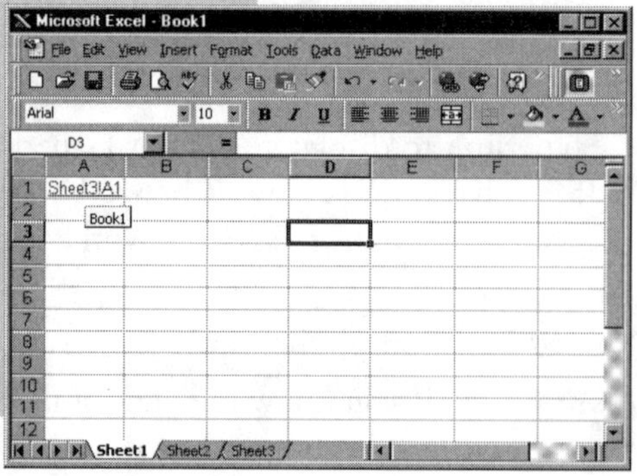

Figure 21.3 A hyperlink is displayed as blue underlined text until it is accessed. Once accessed, the hyperlink changes to an underlined maroon format.

Hands On: Creating Hyperlinks to Cells Using Defined Names

Displaying the label `Sheet3!A1` in a worksheet cell is not very descriptive. For more meaningful hyperlinks, use a defined name as a basis to be displayed in the cell.

1. Select Sheet2 in an Excel workbook.
2. Select cells D1:D5.
3. Choose Insert, Name, Define.
4. In the Names in Workbook text box type **Budget** and click OK to create the defined name using the selected cells.
5. Select Sheet1 and choose Insert, Hyperlink.
6. Click in the Named location in file (optional) text box and type **Budget**. Then click OK (or press Enter). The result is shown in Figure 21.4.

The defined name is placed in the cell rather than the cell address. This makes your worksheet more professional and more descriptive. When the budget hyperlink is clicked, cells D1:D5 on Sheet2 are selected.

Figure 21.4
Using defined names as hyperlinks is a good worksheet modeling tool.

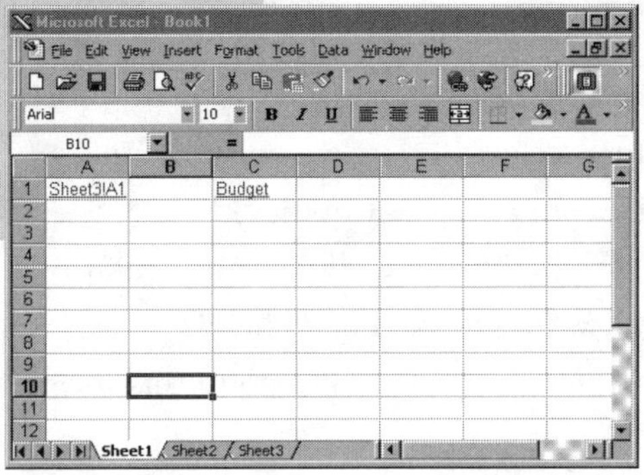

A new worksheet function has been added to the Paste Function dialog box to insert a hyperlink. The function arguments are the destination location and a "friendly name" that you would like to appear in the cell as the hyperlink text. In most cases you create hyperlinks as described in this section. Calling the Hyperlink function is for users familiar with creating and implementing advanced worksheet functions in Excel. For additional information, see help in the Paste Function dialog box or online help.

If you have access to the World Wide Web, you can create hyperlinks to sites on the Internet. There are two ways to do this, by creating a link to a URL, or by setting the Hyperlink base property in a workbook.

The difference between the two is that a hyperlink base property will assume that you are starting from the same Web site each time when using the workbook and requires only the htm file be entered as the hyperlink.

Hands On: Hyperlinks to Web Sites

The easiest way to create a hyperlink to the Internet is to follow the same procedure as creating a link to cells in a workbook, only with the Internet, a URL is specified.

Note

I've created several Web site pages that will be used throughout this chapter. If you have Internet access, feel free to browse the pages. Information and sample Excel files will be placed on the Web site regularly.

1. Connect to the Internet.
2. Start Microsoft Excel and create a new workbook.
3. Select a blank cell in an Excel workbook.
4. Choose Insert, Hyperlink, and click in the Link to File or URL text box.
5. Type **http:\\www.dpayne.com** and click OK.
6. Click on the hyperlink in the cell to go to this site on the Internet.

Note

You will need Internet access and Microsoft Internet Explorer 3.0 or later to follow the Internet examples in this chapter.

7. After checking out the Excel Web site, disconnect from the Internet and return to the Excel workbook example.

You can define the starting point for hyperlinks that point to files or Internet sites. You might use this feature when a workbook contains hyperlinks to multiple pages on one Web site. Instead of typing the full URL path to each hyperlink, you need only do it once as a base property to the workbook. The Properties dialog box is shown in Figure 21.5.

1. In the workbook to contain the hyperlinks to the Internet, choose File, Properties.
2. Click the Summary tab.

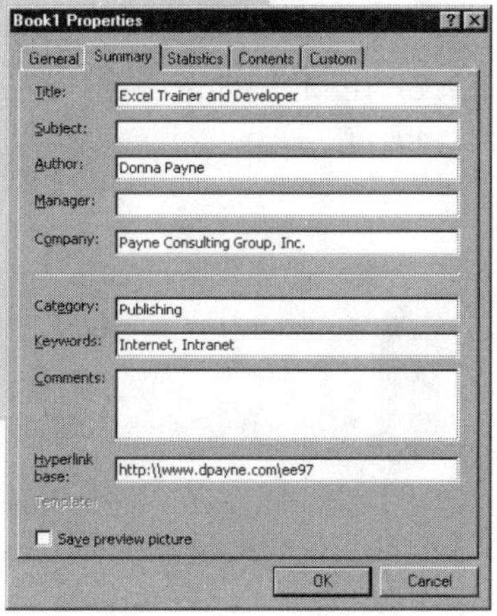

Figure 21.5 Create a base property hyperlink to avoid having to type the complete path to a site every time you create a hyperlink in the workbook.

3. Locate the Hyperlink Base text box and type **http:\\www.dpayne.com\ee97**.
4. Click OK to close the Properties dialog box.
5. Select any blank cell on the worksheet.
6. Choose Insert, Hyperlink, and in the File or URL text box type **welcome.htm**.
7. Click OK to close the dialog box.
8. Click the `welcome.htm` hyperlink to go to that page on the Web site dpayne.com.
9. Disconnect from the Internet and return to the Excel workbook example.
10. Close the workbook. There is no need to save this workbook.

Instead of assigning a hyperlink to a cell, you can use graphic objects that act as buttons to take you to the destination of the hyperlink. This is a sharp way to create links without having obvious hyperlinks in the workbook.

Hands On: Assigning a Hyperlink to a Graphic Object

You can create an object or use an existing one. Because the WordArt features are enhanced in Excel 97, in the exercise that follows you'll create a WordArt object and assign a hyperlink to it.

1. Open a new Excel workbook.
2. Choose View, Toolbars, and make sure that there is a check mark next to Drawing. If not, click on the Drawing command to enable the Drawing toolbar.
3. Click the rotated A button on the Drawing toolbar. This displays the WordArt Gallery shown in Figure 21.6.

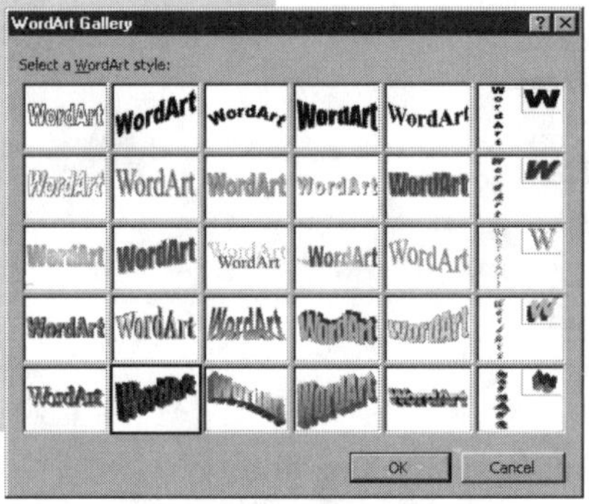

Figure 21.6 Create a base property hyperlink to avoid having to type the complete path to a site every time you create a hyperlink in the workbook.

4. Select any style from the Gallery and click OK.
5. In the Edit WordArt Text dialog box, type your name and click OK.
6. The graphic should be selected but if it's not, click once. Handles should surround the object when the object is properly selected.
7. Choose Insert, Hyperlink and select the Named Location in File text box.

The keyboard shortcut to inserting a hyperlink is Ctrl+K.

8. Click Browse, select Sheet2, and change the reference to D4.
9. Click OK twice to close the dialog boxes.
10. Click on the graphic object to go to the hyperlink cell D4.

Internet Assistant Wizard

If you have your own Web site or a corporate intranet site, you can enable the Internet Assistant Wizard to save Excel files in an HTML (Web) format. HTML files can be loaded onto the Web and can be displayed and accessed by other users.

The Internet Assistant Wizard is an add-in that must be enabled. Once enabled, the Save as HTML command is added to the File menu. The Wizard walks you through a series of dialog boxes to help you build the HTML file.

Hands On: Enabling the Internet Assistant Wizard Add-In

To save an Excel document in an HTML file format, you'll need to make sure that the Internet Assistant Wizard add-in is loaded.

1. Choose Tools, Add-Ins.
2. Place a check mark in the box next to Internet Assistant Wizard.
3. Click OK.

Note

If the Internet Assistant Wizard is not displayed in the list of Add-Ins, you'll need to install it from the Control Panel and Add/Remove Programs icon.

Hands On: Saving an Excel File as an HTML Document

When the add-in is loaded, you can save any Excel worksheet or chart to an HTML format by choosing the Save As HTML command from the File menu.

1. On a new Excel worksheet, type any data into several cells.
2. Select the cells that contain data on the worksheet.
3. Choose File, Save As HTML, and click OK. The Internet Assistant Wizard Step 1 of 4 dialog box appears (see Figure 21.7).

Note

If you have the Excel 97 Office Assistant enabled, it will appear asking if you need help with the feature. Click Yes to receive help, No to proceed without further assistance from this tool.

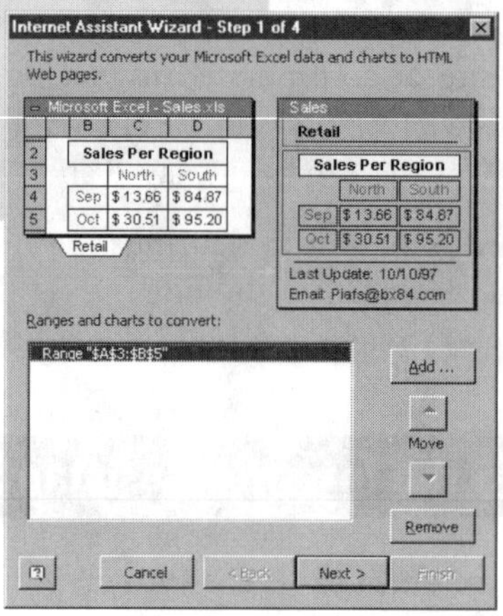

Figure 21.7 Graphical illustrations show how the file is processed.

Because you previously selected the cells that contain your data, the Ranges and Charts to Convert reference is already added. You can add, remove, and change the position of the range and charts to be converted by clicking the buttons on the dialog box.

4. Click the Next button to move to Step 2 of 4 of the Internet Assistant Wizard (shown in Figure 21.8).

   The first option button prompts you to decide whether to Create an Independent, Ready-to-View HTML Document That Contains Your Formatted Data (Header, Table, and Footer Will Be Created). If this option is chosen, the dialog box shown in Figure 21.9 appears.

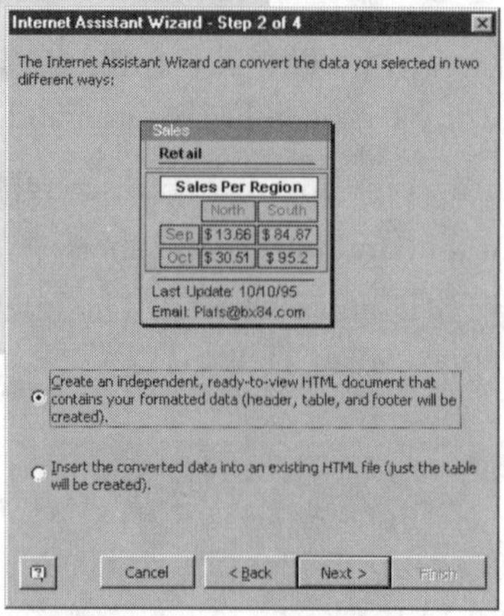

Figure 21.8 The data can be converted in two different ways. Step 2 of 4 asks which way to convert the data.

Figure 21.9 This dialog box prompts you for information about the header and footer that you want in this document.

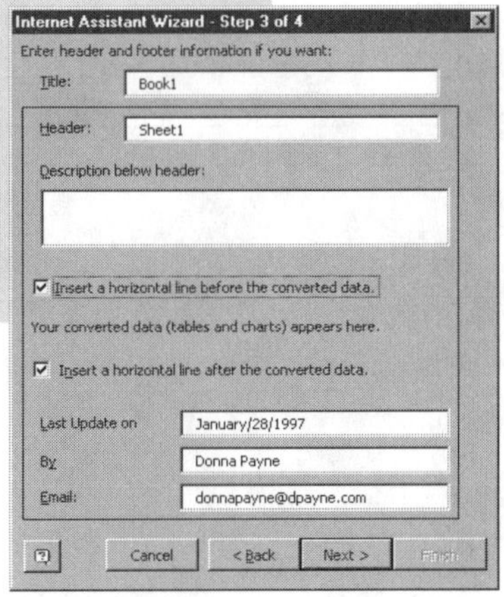

Note

If the second option in Step 2 of 4 was selected (to Insert the Converted Data into an Existing HTML File (Just the Table Will Be Created), the dialog box shown in Figure 21.10 appears.

5. Click the Next button to move to the Internet Assistant Wizard shown in Figure 21.11.

Figure 21.10 This dialog box prompts whether to open the file directly, or to open the file from a FrontPage Web.

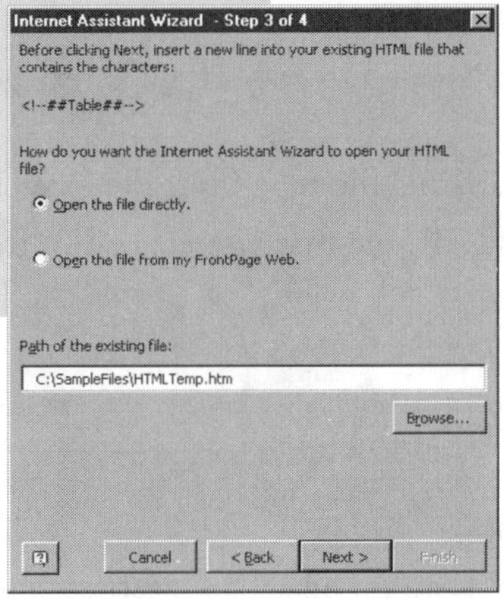

Figure 21.11
The Step 4 of 4 dialog box prompts to select which code page to use and how to save the file.

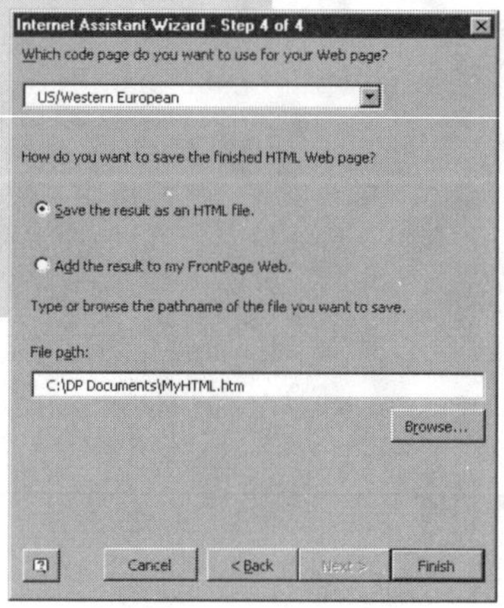

6. Click the Finish button to save the document as an HTML file and close the Internet Assistant Wizard dialog box.
7. Close the Excel workbook.

Hands On: Opening an HTML File

The Internet Assistant Wizard can also be used to import HTML files. In the previous exercise, you created an HTML file. In this exercise, you'll use the Internet Assistant Wizard to open it in Microsoft Excel 97.

1. Choose File, Open.
2. In the Open dialog box, locate the Files of Type text box and click the drop-down arrow.
3. Select the HTML Documents file type from the list.
4. Locate and select the HTML file that you created in the previous exercise.
5. Click the Open button.
6. Close the Excel workbook.

Web Queries

Excel 97 provides the capability to go onto the Internet, query information, and return it to the Excel 97 worksheet. To create a Web query, you must have access to the Internet or a corporate intranet.

A common query in the business community is tracking the progress of stocks on the New York Stock Exchange. A query uses a text file that has instructions on how to query different sites. These text files have the .IQY (some pronounce this *icky*) file extension.

Several sample Web queries (.IQY files) ship with Microsoft Excel 97. They are located in the folder where you installed Office 97 in a Queries folder.

Hands On: Creating a Web Query

The following exercise leads you through the steps to creating a Web query.

1. Choose Data, Get External Data.
2. Click the Run Web Query command.
3. Locate the sample queries in the Office, Queries folder on your computer.
4. Select the Get More Web Queries.iqy file. This file will provide additional examples of queries on the Web.
5. Click the Get Data button. The Returning External Data to Microsoft Excel dialog box (shown in Figure 21.12) appears.
6. Select the first option to place the data into an Existing Worksheet. The active cell is selected by default. If you want to change it, click in any cell on the worksheet or type the cell address in the text box and click OK.

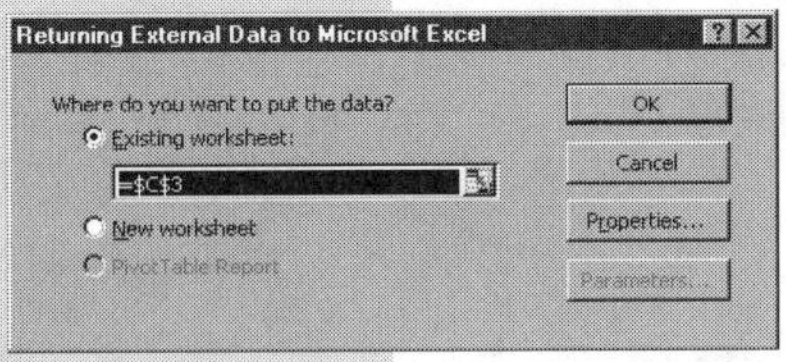

Figure 21.12 You are prompted to select where to put the data being returned from the Web query.

If you have an Internet connection, Excel 97 will attempt to locate the Web query that you have selected. The Get More Queries site contains .IQY links to many companies, data files, and reports. Each site is shown as a hyperlink and can be accessed by clicking the link.

Find it Online

The Get More Queries Web page is available at the time of the release of Office 97. Web pages are notorious for being moved or deleted. If you experience an error when trying to access this site, go to http://www.microsoft.com/excel/webquery/samples/htm.

Some exercise from this chapter can be found online at http:\\www.dpayne.com/ee97.

Tips, Tricks and FAQs can be found at http:\\www.dpayne.com.

The Microsoft Excel Newsgroups provide quick access to Excel gurus where you can submit a question and receive answers from the experts. The Excel Newsgroup URL is http://www.microsoft.com/MSExcelSupport/default-news.htm.

Microsoft on the Web

If you have a Web browser installed on your computer, you will find a new set of commands enabled on your Help menu. These commands help you search the Microsoft Web site to find and download useful information as well as free stuff from Microsoft.

Choose Help, Microsoft on the Web. Table 21.2 describes each command on this menu and its function.

Although this chapter covered a lot of material on how to use the Internet features in Excel 97, many more advanced topics were not covered. For more information on using the Internet features in Excel, see online help, or the Microsoft Web site on the Internet.

Table 21.2 Microsoft on the Web Commands

Command	Function
Free Stuff	Download free templates, patches, add-ons, files, and utilities that work with the Microsoft Office application.
Product News	Excel's Home Page. If you select Product News in Word or any other Office application, that product's home page is displayed.
Frequently Asked Questions	The FAQ or most frequently asked questions page.
Online Support	An online support mechanism maintained by Microsoft support engineers.
Microsoft Office Home Page	The home page for all Microsoft Office applications.
Send Feedback	If you've ever wanted to send comments, bug reports, or feature suggestions to Microsoft, here's your opportunity to do so by sending a feedback form.
Best of the Web	Contains links to other Web sites.
Search the Web	Displays a search page to search the Web.
Web Tutorial	A tutorial on using the Web.
Microsoft Home Page	The parent of all Microsoft home pages on the Web. This page has links to Product, Sales, Support, Conferences, Training, and even Employment at Microsoft pages. You'll also find Newsgroup links from this page. Many newsgroups provide quick answers by industry recognized experts on Microsoft products. Although the newsgroups are facilitated by peer-to-peer interaction, many of the Microsoft MVPs (most valuable professionals) are authors of best-selling computer software books and well-respected software experts.

22

Sharing a Workbook with Multiple Users

In This Chapter

- Setting Up a Shared Workbook
- Editing and Reviewing Changes
- Tracking and Resolving Conflicts
- Reviewing Change History
- Applying Protection to Shared Workbooks

If you work with other people on the same Excel files, you can take advantage of the shared workbook feature in Excel 97. Although shared workbooks were available in Excel 7, the functionality has been greatly improved. For example, Excel can now track who makes changes to the workbook, what the changes are, and when they occur.

Overview of a Shared Workbook

A *shared workbook* is an Excel file that has been set up to allow for simultaneous multiple user input. You can do many (not all) of the same types of things in a shared workbook that you can in a regular Excel workbook. As each user saves, the changes are saved and tracked with the workbook.

ENTERING AND EDITING DATA IS COVERED IN CHAPTER 7.

There are many circumstances when creating shared workbooks can be beneficial and time saving. For example, a company must create a budget for the coming year, and each department manager must submit her own set of numbers, but ultimately, the numbers must come together to form a corporate budget.

Before shared workbooks, one person would be designated as the person responsible for maintaining the master budget workbook. He would often have to rekey numbers increasing the potential for error. With shared workbooks, this problem has been eliminated.

Hands On: Setting Up a Workbook as Shared

The example in the exercise that follows is of a training company that has an inventory of manuals and videos. Multiple users will access and change the workbook as the inventory changes.

1. Create a new workbook and a worksheet; enter the information for the Inventory Control Log shown in Figure 22.1.

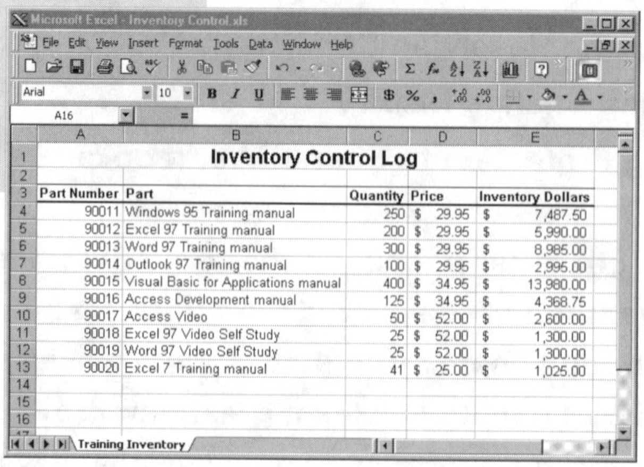

Figure 22.1 The sample workbook will be used to track changes to the worksheet.

2. Choose Tools, Share Workbook and select the Editing tab shown in Figure 22.2.
3. Select the option to Allow Changes By More Than One User at a Time. This Also Allows Workbook Merging. Workbook merging is covered later in this chapter.

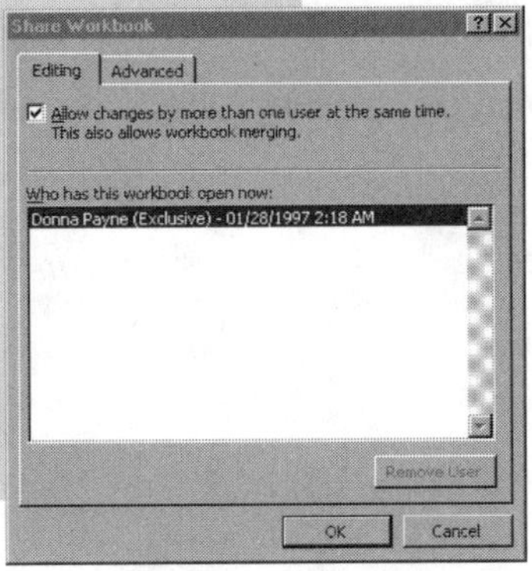

Figure 22.2 The Editing tab is used for setting up and monitoring the shared workbook, the Advanced tab is used for setting properties of the shared workbook.

4. Click OK. When you share a workbook for the first time, you're prompted to save and name the file.

Note

If other people will share the workbook, save it to a common shared folder either on the network or on your computer.

5. Name the file **Inventory Control** in a folder of your choosing. Click the Save button to save the shared workbook.

Note

The title bar should display `Microsoft Excel - Inventory Control.xls [Shared]`. The workbook is not successfully shared if the word `Shared` doesn't appear in brackets beside the name of the workbook.

Limitations to a Shared Workbook

When a workbook is shared, you may notice that some features are not available:

- Merge cells
- Define or apply conditional formats
- Set up data validation
- Insert or delete blocks of cells (although you can delete rows and columns)
- Insert or change charts, pictures, objects, hyperlinks, or PivotTables
- Use drawing tools
- Assign passwords to protect individual worksheets or the entire workbook
- Change existing passwords
- Use scenarios
- Group and outline data
- Insert automatic subtotals
- Create data tables
- Make changes to dialog boxes
- Write, view, record, assign, or change a macro

You may want to consider using these features prior to sharing your workbook, or after unsharing the workbook. (Unsharing the workbook has consequences.)

Editing a Shared Workbook

Shared workbooks are edited the same way nonshared workbooks are, by typing the new data directly into the cell and saving the workbook. When workbooks are shared, multiple users can edit the same workbook and even the same data at the same time.

Each time the workbook is saved, all changes made to the workbook are updated. If a workbook is undergoing heavy edits by multiple users, it's a good idea to save often to see other changes as they occur.

Note

To make changes to a shared workbook created in Excel 97, you must use Excel 97. You cannot use earlier versions.

Reviewing Edits to the Shared Workbook

After changes have been made and saved to the shared workbook, they can be shown either on the worksheet that contains the data, or on a new conflict history worksheet.

Hands On: Reviewing Changes in a Shared Workbook

To show changes to the data directly on the worksheet:

1. Choose Tools, Track Changes, Highlight Changes. The Highlight Changes dialog box is shown in Figure 22.3.

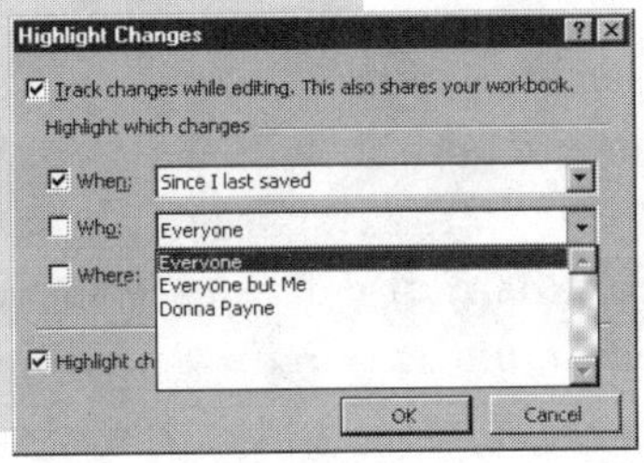

Figure 22.3 The Highlight Changes dialog box provides options for how changes to the file are viewed and updated.

The When check box lets you show only the edits made on the worksheet during a time interval you specify).

The Who check box lets you view the edits made by specific users of the shared workbook. The workbook includes the names of all users who have accessed and changed the workbook as well as the Everyone and Everyone But Me option.

The Where check box lets you look at the changes made to a specific portion of the worksheet by asking you to specify a range.

2. Uncheck the When option and click OK.
3. Point to the cell that was edited, which is now highlighted, and a revision comment as shown in Figure 22.4 appears indicating the change, who made it, and when the change occurred.

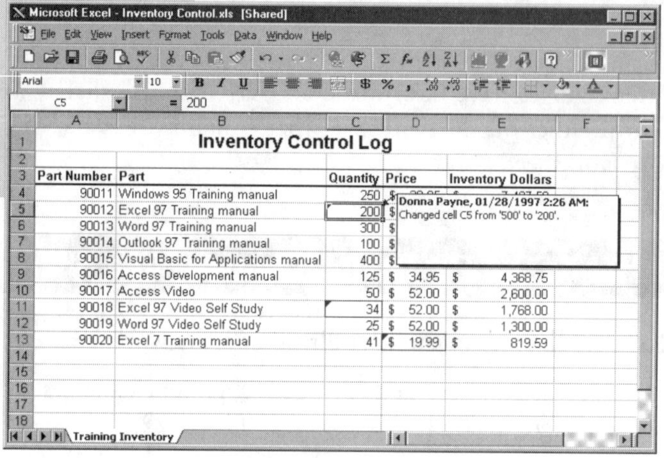

Figure 22.4 Several users have updated this file. Their edits are shown in the highlighted cells.

Note

The edits from each user of the workbook appear in a different color. Excel outlines the cell border with the color for each user and places a triangle shape in the upper left corner of the cell that has been changed. A comment or cell note is associated with the cell that displays the name of the person who made the edit, the date and time the edit was made, and the actual change in the data. The information is displayed by hovering (the mouse pointer) over the highlighted cell without clicking the mouse button. The tracking highlights can be hidden at any time.

4. Choose Tools, Track Changes, Highlight Changes and uncheck the option to Highlight Changes On Screen.
5. Click OK to close the dialog box.

The Change History

Excel will silently keep track of the change history of the shared workbook. The change history appears on a separate worksheet titled History when the option to display it is enabled.

Hands On: Viewing the Change History

To display the change history:

1. Choose Tools, Track Changes, Highlight Changes.
2. Select the option to List Changes on a New Sheet.
3. Click OK.

The change history worksheet appears in Figure 22.5.

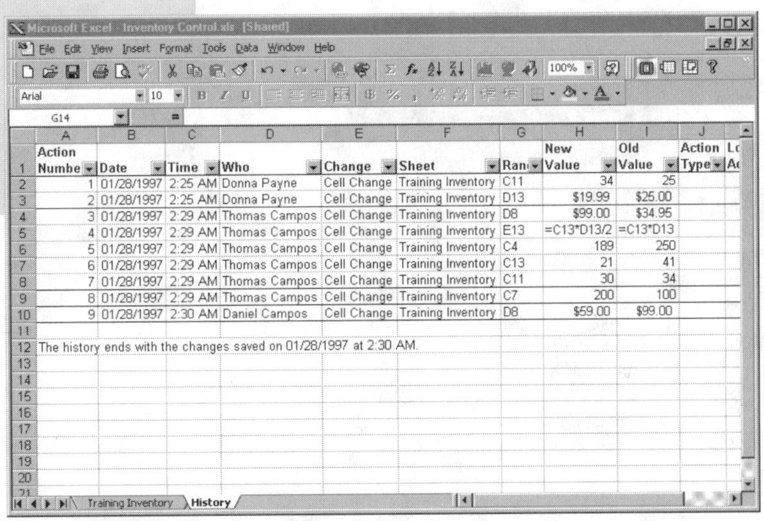

Action Numbe	Date	Time	Who	Change	Sheet	Ran	New Value	Old Value	Action Type	Lo A
1	01/28/1997	2:25 AM	Donna Payne	Cell Change	Training Inventory	C11	34	25		
2	01/28/1997	2:25 AM	Donna Payne	Cell Change	Training Inventory	D13	$19.99	$25.00		
3	01/28/1997	2:29 AM	Thomas Campos	Cell Change	Training Inventory	D8	$99.00	$34.95		
4	01/28/1997	2:29 AM	Thomas Campos	Cell Change	Training Inventory	E13	=C13*D13/2	=C13*D13		
5	01/28/1997	2:29 AM	Thomas Campos	Cell Change	Training Inventory	C4	189	250		
6	01/28/1997	2:29 AM	Thomas Campos	Cell Change	Training Inventory	C13	21	41		
7	01/28/1997	2:29 AM	Thomas Campos	Cell Change	Training Inventory	C11	30	34		
8	01/28/1997	2:29 AM	Thomas Campos	Cell Change	Training Inventory	C7	200	100		
9	01/28/1997	2:30 AM	Daniel Campos	Cell Change	Training Inventory	D8	$59.00	$99.00		

The history ends with the changes saved on 01/28/1997 at 2:30 AM.

Figure 22.5 All changes to the shared workbook are tracked in the change history worksheet.

The change history worksheet is organized as a database with the AutoFilter feature applied. This enables quick sorting and searching by clicking on the drop-down arrow and selecting the criteria that you are searching for from the list.

The fields for the history sheet are:

- **Action Number.** Assigns a sequential number to each edit.
- **Date and Time.** The calendar date and time when an edit was made to the worksheet.
- **Who.** The person who edited the workbook.
- **Change.** The type of change that was made to the worksheet.
- **Sheet.** The name of the worksheet that was edited.
- **Range.** The cell location of the edited information.

- **New Value and Old Value.** New data entered into the cell and old data that has been replaced by the New value.
- **Action Type and Losing Action Type.** If there was a conflict, how it was resolved.

Setting Options for Managing Changes

Excel lets you designate how changes are processed and how long a change history is stored with the workbook.

These settings are available on the Advanced tab of the Share Workbook dialog box shown in Figure 22.6.

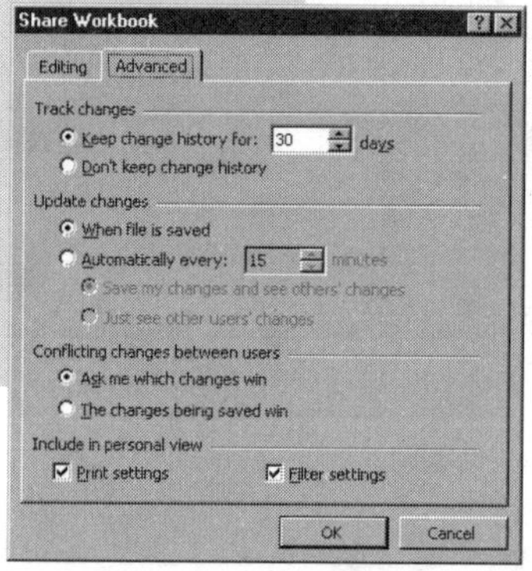

Figure 22.6 You can automate the settings for shared workbooks through the Share Workbook dialog box.

Hands On: Changing Shared Workbook Settings

To change the settings of the shared workbook:

1. Choose Tools, Share Workbook.
2. Click the Advanced tab. The Advanced tab has four sections that control how the workbook is maintained:
   - The Track Changes section controls how long the change history of the workbook is saved. The first option asks you to specify a number of days to save the change history of the workbook. The second option is selected when you do not want to save changes to the shared workbook.

Note

The number of days to keep a change history must be between 1 and 32,767. The default number of days is 30.

- The Update Changes section specifies how and when the file is saved and the changes updated.
- The third section, Conflicting Changes Between Users, manages how conflicting information is processed. For example, you can set the option to be prompted when a conflict occurs, or to accept the changes that are being saved without further user intervention.
- The Include in Personal Settings section allows each user to create and store his own Print and Filter Settings so that when the workbook is opened, the user sees his preferred view of the document, not the preferred view of the last person who saved the files.

Resolving Conflicts

Conflicts occur when multiple users enter different values in the same cell location and then save the workbook. When Excel detects a conflict, the Resolve Conflicts dialog box appears. This dialog box asks you to resolve the conflict by showing you your changes and the conflicting ones. The last person to save decides which changes to keep in the event of a conflict.

The buttons that appear in the Resolve Conflicts dialog box are Accept Mine, Accept Other, Accept All Mine, Accept All Others, and Cancel. Unless you've set up the Advanced tab of the Share Workbook dialog box to resolve conflicts automatically, this dialog box will appear when a conflict occurs.

Note

The option The Changes Being Saved Win in the Advanced tab of the Share Workbook dialog box automatically replaces conflicting changes with your own changes each time you save.

Accepting and Rejecting Revisions

You can review, reject, or accept changes made to the shared workbook by stepping through the revisions made to the workbook or by accepting or rejecting all.

1. Choose Tools, Track Changes, Accept or Reject Changes. The Select Change to Accept or Reject dialog box is shown in Figure 22.7.

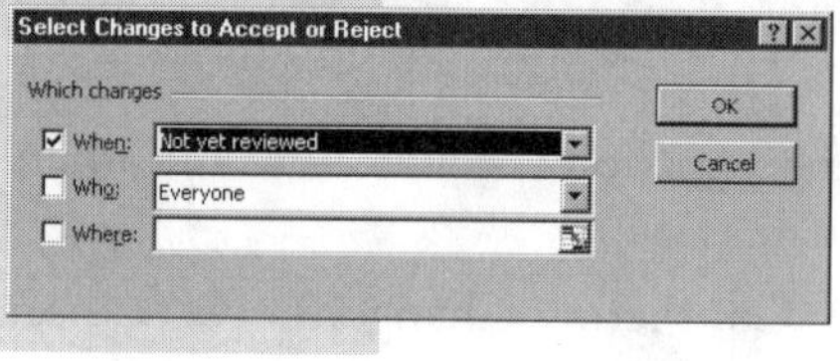

Figure 22.7
You can review changes made by all users of the workbook or selected users.

2. Click the Cancel button to close the Accept or Reject dialog box.

Another way to maintain a shared workbook is to turn on the change history for the shared workbook and distribute the workbook to multiple users by e-mail or other methods of distribution. After editing, these copies can be gathered together and combined into one single file.

To merge the changes of multiple workbooks:

1. Open the shared workbook that you want to gather the changes into from the other workbooks.
2. Choose Tools, Merge Workbooks. You'll be prompted to save the workbook; click OK.
3. Select any files that need to be merged into the current document and click OK. You can use the Ctrl or Shift keys to select multiple files at once to be merged.

For Excel to merge the changes, all workbooks must meet the following criteria:

- Be copies of the same workbook.
- Have a different file name.
- Have no password protection, or duplicate passwords.
- Original workbook must have been shared prior to copies being distributed.
- Prior to making and distributing copies of the workbook, the change history setting must have been enabled.
- The number of days to save in the change history settings must not have been exceeded.

Monitoring Access of a Shared Workbook

You can monitor who currently has the shared workbook open by accessing the Editing tab on the Shared Workbook dialog box.

To find out who is working on the file:

1. Choose Tools, Share Workbook and select the Editing tab from the Share Workbook dialog box.
2. The Who Has This Workbook Open Now section displays the names of all users who currently have the shared workbook open.

Anyone with the workbook open can disconnect a user from the shared workbook by clicking the Remove User button.

Clicking the Remove User button causes the disconnected user to lose all changes made to the shared workbook that have not been saved. The disconnected user can save the workbook by choosing File, Save As and merging the changes with the shared workbook when it becomes available. Notify users prior to disconnecting them to avoid data loss.

3. Click the Cancel button to close the Share Workbook dialog box.

The Who Has This Workbook Open Now information is extracted from the user name section of the Options dialog box. To verify this information choose Tools, Options, General and User Name.

Protecting the Shared Workbook

You can limit what a user can do to the shared workbook by applying password and Sharing with Track Changes protection. Revisions made to the shared document are tracked in the change history of the workbook, and this history cannot be removed without unsharing the workbook and providing a password to do so. The Protect Shared Workbook dialog box is shown in Figure 22.8.

Note

The password must be set up prior to sharing the workbook.

To protect the shared workbook:

1. Choose Tools, Protection, Protect Shared Workbook.
2. Click the Sharing with Track Changes option.
3. Click OK to close the dialog box.

Figure 22.8
You can review changes made by all users of the workbook or selected users.

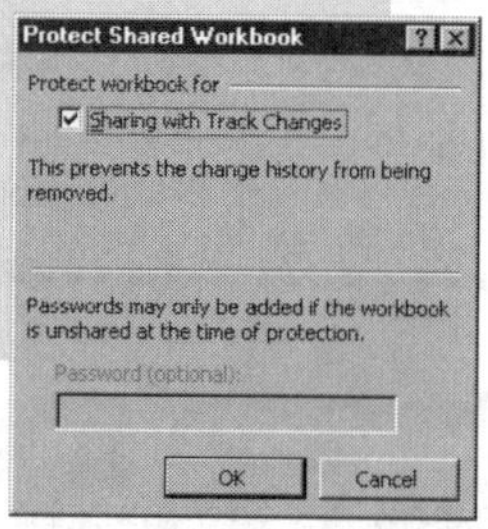

Attaching Comments

ENTERING AND EDITING COMMENTS IS COVERED IN CHAPTER 7.

In addition to tracking and highlighting changes made to the workbook, you can insert comments in a shared workbook. Comments are useful for explaining why certain edits were made to the data.

To insert comments in a shared workbook:

1. Select a cell to add a comment to.
2. Choose Insert, Comment.
3. Type the comment to be added in the comment box.

Tip

The keyboard shortcut to insert a comment in the active cell is Shift+F2.

To edit a comment:

1. Select the cell that contains the comment to be edited.
2. Choose Insert, Edit Comment.

Appendices

A

Installing Excel 97

In This Appendix

- Understanding the Installation Process
- Installing Excel
- Installing Excel as Part of Microsoft Office
- Adding and Removing Excel Components
- Installing Internet Explorer

Excel 97 may come to you in one of two ways: as a stand-alone product or as a part of the Microsoft Office 97 package. In this appendix we'll look at both possibilities as well as how to install extra components you may need eventual-

What Does Installing Do?

In the old days (1985 or so), a computer program could fit—uncompressed—on a single floppy disk. That was good because most computers didn't have hard disks back then. You just popped the floppy into your drive and ran the program right from there.

Nowadays, of course, that could never happen. Big, feature-rich programs like Excel take up tens of megabytes of space. You can't just pop in the disk Excel came on and run it—you first have to run the setup program.

The setup program does several things:

- It decompresses the compressed files. (Files on the installation disk are squashed so that more of them will fit on the disk.)
- It creates the appropriate folder structure on your hard disk.
- It copies the files needed to run Excel onto your hard disk.
- It adds a shortcut to Excel to your Start menu.

Tip

Office 97 and Excel 97 do provide an option to run the applications directly from the CD, saving disk space on your PC. (It runs slower that way, but it does work.) However, to set this up, you must still run the setup program, as you learn to do later in this appendix.

Excel or Office?

Some people buy Excel as a stand-alone product; others acquire it as part of the Microsoft Office suite of programs. The installation program works pretty much the same way no matter which version you have. The real difference is in what gets installed.

If you bought the Microsoft Office 97 version, when you run the setup program it installs all the Office components, not just Excel. Office comes with a variety of tools, including Word (a word processor), PowerPoint (a presentation graphics program), and Outlook (a scheduling and planning tool). The professional edition also comes with Access (a database). Installing all these tools is fine if you have enough disk space, but if you don't, you will want to use the Custom setup procedure described in the following section to exclude the components you won't ever use.

Installing Excel

As I said, the installation procedure itself is the same no matter whether you have the Office 97 or Excel 97 version. That's because the same tasks need to be done no matter what is getting copied to your hard disk: the Setup program needs to know who you are, what components you want, and where you want them stored. The following steps walk you through the procedure—follow them, or just follow along with the prompts on your screen.

1. Close all open applications.
2. Insert the Microsoft Office 97 or Microsoft Excel 97 CD in your CD-ROM drive, or the first diskette in your floppy disk drive. A dialog box opens automatically.

Note

If you don't see a dialog box automatically when you insert the CD, your computer may not be set up to Autorun CDs. Double-click the My Computer icon on the desktop and double-click the CD drive's icon. Then locate and double-click the Setup icon. Then catch up to the rest of us at step 4.

3. Click the Install Microsoft Office button (or the Install Microsoft Excel button, if you're installing the stand-alone version).
4. At the Welcome dialog box, click Continue.
5. In the Name and Organization Information dialog box, enter your name and organization. Then click OK.
6. When asked to confirm your name and organization, click OK again.
7. If you're asked for the CD key, find it on the sticker on the back of the jewel case and enter it. It may be an 11-digit or 20-digit number. Then click OK.
8. Next you see your product ID number. It consists of your version number plus the CD key number that you just entered. Write it down on your registration card and then click OK.
9. Choose the drive and folder into which Microsoft Office is installed (or Excel, if installing the stand-alone version). The default is the Program Files folder on the same drive that Windows is installed on (see Figure A.1). Click OK to accept that (recommended), or click Change Folder and select a new location.

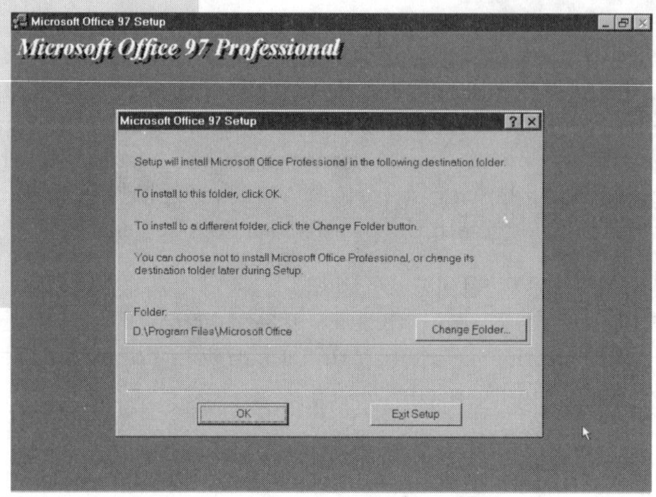

Figure A.1 Accept the directory chosen by the installation program by clicking OK, or click Change Folder and choose your own.

10. Choose the type of installation you want by clicking the appropriate button:

    - **Typical.** Installs the most common components. This is the easiest method, and most users will be happy with the options installed.
    - **Custom.** Enables you to choose exactly which components you want. This is for experienced users and those who are installing Office and don't use certain Office products at all.
    - **Run from CD-ROM.** Sets up the program(s) to run mostly from the CD. Because it copies very few files to your hard disk, it's ideal for users who are very short on disk space; however, it requires that the CD be in the drive whenever Excel (or another Office component) is running.

    If you chose Typical or Run from CD-ROM, skip to step 14. If you chose Custom, the Microsoft Office 97 Custom dialog box appears (see Figure A.2).

11. You see a series of components with check boxes. A check in a white-background box means all options for that component will be installed. A check in a gray-background box means that only some of the component's options will be installed. Use these methods to choose which components and options you want:

    - To select all components, click the Select All button. This is the best way to go if you have plenty of disk space and aren't sure which features you'll be using.

Figure A.2 Click the check boxes to select or deselect categories and options.

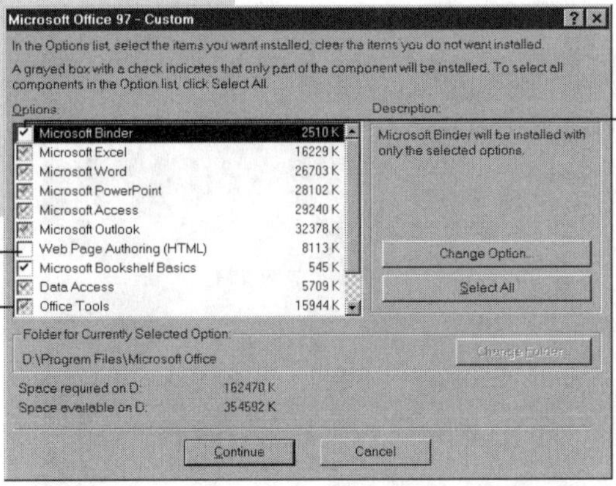

Completely selected

Unselected

Partly selected; click the Change Option button for details.

- To deselect an entire component, click its check box to remove the check mark. For instance, if you are using the Microsoft Office version and you don't want PowerPoint to be installed at all, remove the check mark next to PowerPoint. Do the same for any other Office components you don't want.
- To choose which options of a component are installed, click the component and then click Change Option. A dialog box appears, showing the options for that component, each with its own check box that you can use to turn it on or off. Click OK to return to the main screen. Refer to Table A.1 (in the next section) for some ideas about what to select.

12. When you finish selecting options, click Continue.
13. If the installation program finds old Office or Excel components, it asks whether you want to remove them. Click Yes. (Any data files you had will remain, even if you delete the old program.)
14. Wait for the setup program to copy the files (see Figure A.3). When you see the message `Microsoft Office 97 Setup was completed successfully.` (or Excel, as the case may be), click OK. You are now ready to use Microsoft Excel.

On some computers, you may be asked to restart before using the software. If you see a dialog box asking whether you want to restart now, click Yes. Do not try to use the software without restarting the computer if restarting has been suggested; it will not work properly.

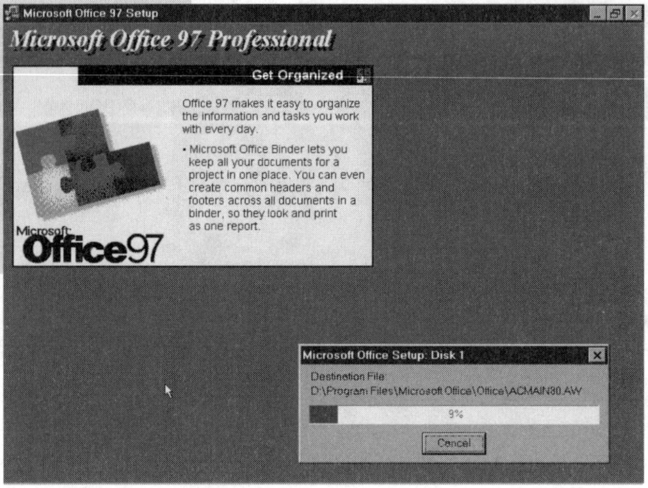

Figure A.3 It takes several minutes for the setup program to copy its files; a progress bar at the bottom of the screen shows how far it has progressed.

Custom Installation: Some Advice

It's hard to know exactly which options to choose in a Custom installation if you're a beginner. Table A.1 provides some ideas of some components you might want that are not installed by default. Table A.1 is based on the Office version of the software, but the options are similar for the stand-alone version.

Table A.1 Excel Options Not Installed by Default That You Might Want

Component (Office version)	Option	Comments
Excel	Spreadsheet Templates	The Expense Report Template and Purchase Order Template are not installed by default.
Excel	Add-Ins	Install the File Conversion Wizard if you have a group of files you will be converting to Excel format.
Excel	Spreadsheet Converters	The Quattro Pro 1.0/5.0 (Win) converter is not installed by default.

Component (Office version)	Option	Comments
Web Page Authoring (HTML)	(No options)	If you plan to create Web pages, you will definitely need these tools. Excel is not the best tool for creating Web pages, but you may need to convert some existing data to HTML format to include on your company's Web site.
Office Tools	Microsoft Office Shortcut Bar	(Office version only) This is not installed by default, although it was in previous releases of Office. If you're accustomed to using it, install it.
Converters and Filters	Text	I recommend that you install all of these. You never know what text file formats you may encounter.
Converters and Filters	Graphics	I also recommend that you install all of these.

Installing Internet Explorer

If you use the Internet (or if you want to learn), you may find Microsoft's *Web browser*, Internet Explorer 3.0, useful. After you run the Excel or Office installation program, an icon appears on your desktop called Setup for Microsoft Internet Explorer 3.0. That icon makes it easy to install the program.

Note

A Web browser enables you to view graphical content on the Internet. To use it, you must have an Internet connection. You can get an Internet connection by subscribing to the Microsoft Network; the easiest way to get that subscription is to double-click the Microsoft Network icon on your desktop and follow the prompts.

Follow these steps to install Internet Explorer:

1. Double-click the Setup for Microsoft Internet Explorer 3.0 icon on your desktop.
2. A dialog box asks whether you want to install the program. Click Yes.
3. Read the licensing agreement and then click I Agree.
4. Wait for the setup program to install the files you need. If you see the Version Conflict dialog box asking you whether you want to keep an existing file, click Yes.
5. At the message `Do you want to restart your computer now?`, click Yes.

After your computer restarts, you are ready to use Internet Explorer. You can use it through your Microsoft Network account or with any other Internet connection. For more information about the Internet, see Chapter 21.

B

Using the IntelliMouse with Excel

In This Appendix

- Understanding the IntelliMouse
- IntelliMouse Operations in Excel 97
- Exploring Additional IntelliMouse Functions

The Microsoft IntelliMouse is a pointing device that's like a regular mouse, but with some special features that make it easier to use Microsoft Office and some other Windows-based products that support its enhancements. If you use it with a product that doesn't recognize its special features, it works just like any other regular mouse. You can buy it along with the Microsoft Office 97 upgrade, or you can purchase it separately for about $70. Many new PC manufacturers are also including it with their new sys-

How to Use the IntelliMouse in Excel

Like any other mouse, the IntelliMouse includes a primary (left) and secondary (right) mouse button. The difference between the IntelliMouse and a standard mouse is the wheel located between the left and right mouse buttons.

You can either rotate or click (press and release) the IntelliMouse wheel depending on what feature you want to use. Rolling the wheel forward or back zooms in and out, or scrolls through the worksheet or chart sheet. The wheel on the IntelliMouse scrolls three rows per wheel rotation. When you click the wheel and drag, the mouse scrolls through the worksheet continuously.

Tip

The IntelliMouse can zoom the worksheet between 10% and 100%. If you use the IntelliMouse to zoom more often than you use it to scroll, you can change an option in Excel so that the wheel automatically zooms rather than scrolls. Choose Tools, Options and then select the General tab. In the Settings area, select the Zoom on Roll with IntelliMouse check box. Click OK to close the Options dialog box.

The IntelliMouse adds functionality to Excel and other Office 97 applications. Table B.1 describes how the IntelliMouse operates with Excel 97.

Table B.1 IntelliMouse Operations in Excel 97

Excel Operation	Mouse Motion
Scroll continuously in a worksheet	Click and hold the wheel and drag the mouse pointer in the direction that you want to scroll. When you drag, the mouse pointer changes to a directional arrow with a dot to indicate which way you are scrolling.
Scroll several rows at a time	Rotate the wheel forward (without clicking anything) to move up a few rows or back to move down a few rows. For this feature to work properly, make sure that the Zoom on Roll with IntelliMouse option is not selected (choose Tools, Options and click the General tab).

Excel Operation	Mouse Motion
Speed up scrolling on a worksheet	Click and release the wheel button and move the mouse pointer in the direction that you want to go to.
Zoom in on a worksheet	If the Zoom on Roll with IntelliMouse check box is selected (choose Tools, Options and click the General tab), move the wheel forward. If this option is not selected, hold down the Ctrl key and move the wheel forward.
Zoom out on a worksheet	If the Zoom on Roll with IntelliMouse check box is selected (choose Tools, Options and click the General tab), move the wheel back. If this option is not selected, hold down the Ctrl key and move the wheel back.
Show/hide details in an outline	Select a cell with data in the outline and then hold down the Shift key and roll the wheel forward to show more detail or back to hide details.
Show/hide details in a PivotTable	Select a row field in the PivotTable. Hold down the Shift key and roll the wheel forward to show detail or back to hide details.

Additional Features of the IntelliMouse

There are a few other settings for the Microsoft IntelliMouse. They are not connected directly to Excel, but they are worth exploring because of their value in making the IntelliMouse more convenient for you to use.

You'll need to install the IntelliPoint software before using this section. It comes with the IntelliMouse.

Hands On: Exploring the IntelliMouse Settings

To begin using some additional IntelliMouse capabilities, follow these steps:

1. Open the Control Panel on your computer.
2. Double-click the Mouse icon. The Mouse Properties dialog box contains new tabs with setting options for the IntelliMouse.

3. Select the Wheel tab. This tab contains the two check boxes for enabling the wheel and wheel button. These are on by default, but you can deselect either check box to turn off the features. If you do so, the IntelliPoint mouse will work the same as a normal mouse.
4. Select the Productivity tab. This tab contains one of my favorite features of this mouse, the Odometer option. The odometer tracks how far you have moved the mouse pointer since a specific date. To reset the mouse odometer, click the Reset button. You would be surprised how quickly your daily mouse use adds up.
5. The ClickLock check box enables the mouse button to be clicked once and then locked into place so that you can drag objects and text, and work with menus easier. To release the mouse lock, click the mouse button again. This is a nice feature for people who have trouble with the drag operation (either they have some disability or they just can't master the action of dragging with the mouse button held down).
6. When you are finished making your selections, click OK.

The IntelliMouse pointing device is an effective tool to use with Excel and Microsoft Office. Once you begin using it, you won't want to be without it.

C

Excel 97 Functions

In This Appendix

Here is a complete list of the functions Excel 97 offers. There are more than 300 functions in all.

Excel groups its functions into categories, to make it easier for you to find the function you need. That way, if you know you are looking for engineering functions, you don't have to wade through a list of logical functions, for example. For more information about a particular function, see the Function Wizard in Excel or the Office Assistant or Help system.

Note

Some of these functions come in the Analysis ToolPak. If a function that you need is not available, run the Setup program to install the Analysis ToolPak. After you install the Analysis ToolPak, enable it with the Tools, Add-Ins command. Add-Ins are covered in Chapter 19.

Note

Whenever you insert a function with the FunctionWizard, it inserts the leading equals sign (=) automatically for you. If you are typing a function manually, however, you must not forget this sign, or Excel will interpret the function line as text.

Database Functions

REFER TO CHAPTER 8 FOR INFORMATION ON ENTERING AND USING FUNCTIONS IN EXCEL.

`DAVERAGE(database,field,criteria)`

Averages the values in a column in a list or database that match conditions you specify.

`DCOUNT(database,field,criteria)`

Counts the cells that contain numbers in a column in a list or database that match conditions you specify.

`DCOUNTA(database,field,criteria)`

Counts all the nonblank cells in a column in a list or database that match conditions you specify.

`DGET(database,field,criteria)`

Extracts a single value from a column in a list or database that matches conditions you specify.

`DMAX(database,field,criteria)`

Returns the largest number in a column in a list or database that matches conditions you specify.

DMIN(database,field,criteria)

Returns the smallest number in a column in a list or database that matches conditions you specify.

DPRODUCT(database,field,criteria)

Multiplies the values in a column in a list or database that match conditions you specify.

DSTDEV(database,field,criteria)

Estimates the standard deviation of a population based on a sample, using the numbers in a column in a list or database that match conditions you specify.

DSTDEVP(database,field,criteria)

Calculates the standard deviation of a population based on the entire population, using the numbers in a column in a list or database that match conditions you specify.

DSUM(database,field,criteria)

Adds the numbers in a column in a list or database that match conditions you specify.

DVAR(database,field,criteria)

Estimates the variance of a population based on a sample, using the numbers in a column in a list or database that match conditions you specify.

DVARP(database,field,criteria)

Calculates the variance of a population based on the entire population, using the numbers in a column in a list or database that match conditions you specify.

GETPIVOTDATA(pivot_table,name)

Returns data stored in a PivotTable.

Date and Time Functions

DATE(year,month,day)

Returns the serial number of a particular date.

DATEVALUE(date_text)

Returns the serial number of the date represented by date_text.

`DAY(serial_number)`

Returns the day of the month corresponding to serial_number.

`DAYS360(start_date,end_date,method)`

Returns the number of days between two dates based on a 360-day year (twelve 30-day months), which is used in some accounting calculations.

`EDATE(start_date,months)`

Returns the serial number that represents the date that is the indicated number of months before or after a specified date (the start_date).

`EOMONTH(start_date,months)`

Returns the serial number date for the last day of the month that is the indicated number of months before or after start_date.

`HOUR(serial_number)`

Returns the hour corresponding to serial_number.

`MINUTE(serial_number)`

Returns the minute corresponding to serial_number.

`MONTH(serial_number)`

Returns the month corresponding to serial_number.

`NETWORKDAYS(start_date,end_date,holidays)`

Returns the number of whole working days between start_date and end_date.

`NOW( )`

Returns the serial number of the current date and time.

`SECOND(serial_number)`

Returns the second corresponding to serial_number.

`TIME(hour,minute,second)`

Returns the serial number of a particular time.

`TIMEVALUE(time_text)`

Returns the serial number of the time represented by time_text.

`TODAY( )`

Returns the serial number of the current date.

WEEKDAY(serial_number,return_type)

Returns the day of the week corresponding to serial_number.

WEEKNUM(serial_number,return_type)

Returns the week number in the year corresponding to serial_number.

WORKDAY(start_date,days,holidays)

Returns a number that represents a date that is the indicated number of working days before or after start_date.

YEAR(serial_number)

Returns the year corresponding to serial_number.

YEARFRAC(start_date,end_date,basis)

Calculates the fraction of the year represented by the number of whole days between two dates (the start_date and the end_date).

Engineering Functions

BESSELI(x,n)

Returns the modified Bessel function, which is equivalent to the Bessel function evaluated for purely imaginary arguments.

BESSELJ(x,n)

Returns the Bessel function.

BESSELK(x,n)

Returns the modified Bessel function, which is equivalent to the Bessel functions evaluated for purely imaginary arguments.

BESSELY(x,n)

Returns the Bessel function, which is also called the Weber function or the Neumann function.

BIN2DEC(number)

Converts a binary number to decimal.

BIN2HEX(number,places)

Converts a binary number to hexadecimal.

BIN2OCT(number,places)

Converts a binary number to octal.

COMPLEX(real_num,i_num,suffix)

Converts real and imaginary coefficients into a complex number of the form x + yi or x + yj.

CONVERT(number,from_unit,to_unit)

Converts a number from one measurement system to another.

DEC2BIN(number,places)

Converts a decimal number to binary.

DEC2HEX(number,places)

Converts a decimal number to hexadecimal.

DEC2OCT(number,places)

Converts a decimal number to octal.

DELTA(number1,number2)

Tests whether two values are equal.

ERF(lower_limit,upper_limit)

Returns the error function integrated between lower_limit and upper_limit.

ERFC(x)

Returns the complementary ERF function integrated between x and infinity.

FACTDOUBLE(number)

Returns the double factorial of a number.

GESTEP(number,step)

Tests whether a number is greater than a value.

HEX2BIN(number,places)

Converts a hexadecimal number to binary.

HEX2DEC(number)

Converts a hexadecimal number to decimal.

HEX2OCT(number,places)

Converts a hexadecimal number to octal.

IMABS(inumber)

Returns the absolute value (modulus) of a complex number in x + yi or x + yj text format.

IMAGINARY(inumber)

Returns the imaginary coefficient of a complex number in x + yi or x + yj text format.

IMARGUMENT(inumber)

Returns the argument as an angle expressed in radians.

IMCONJUGATE(inumber)

Returns the complex conjugate of a complex number in x + yi or x + yj text format.

IMCOS(inumber)

Returns the cosine of a complex number in x + yi or x + yj text format.

IMDIV(inumber1,inumber2)

Returns the quotient of two complex numbers in x + yi or x + yj text format.

IMEXP(inumber)

Returns the exponential of a complex number in x + yi or x + yj text format.

IMLN(inumber)

Returns the natural logarithm of a complex number in x + yi or x + yj text format.

IMLOG10(inumber)

Returns the common logarithm (base 10) of a complex number in x + yi or x + yj text format.

IMLOG2(inumber)

Returns the base-2 logarithm of a complex number in x + yi or x + yj text format.

IMPOWER(inumber,number)

Returns a complex number in x + yi or x + yj text format raised to a power.

IMPRODUCT(inumber1,inumber2,...)

Returns the product of 2 to 29 complex numbers in x + yi or x + yj text format.

IMREAL(inumber)

Returns the real coefficient of a complex number in x + yi or x + yj text format.

IMSIN(inumber)

Returns the sine of a complex number in x + yi or x + yj text format.

IMSQRT(inumber)

Returns the square root of a complex number in x + yi or x + yj text format.

IMSUB(inumber1,inumber2,...)

Returns the difference of two or more complex numbers in x - yi or x - yj text format.

IMSUM(inumber1,inumber2,...)

Returns the sum of two or more complex numbers in x + yi or x + yj text format.

OCT2BIN(number,places)

Converts an octal number to binary.

OCT2DEC(number)

Converts an octal number to decimal.

OCT2HEX(number,places)

Converts an octal number to hexadecimal.

Financial Functions

ACCRINT(issue,first_interest,settlement,rate,par,frequency,basis)

Returns the accrued interest for a security that pays periodic interest.

ACCRINTM(issue,maturity,rate,par,basis)

Returns the accrued interest for a security that pays interest at maturity.

AMORDEGRC(cost,date_purchased,first_period,salvage,period,rate,basis)

Returns the depreciation for each accounting period (French accounting system).

AMORLINC(cost,date_purchased,first_period,salvage,period,rate,basis)

Returns the depreciation for each accounting period (French accounting system).

`COUPDAYBS(settlement,maturity,frequency,basis)`

Returns the number of days from the beginning of the coupon period to the settlement date.

`COUPDAYS(settlement,maturity,frequency,basis)`

Returns the number of days in the coupon period that contains the settlement date.

`COUPDAYSNC(settlement,maturity,frequency,basis)`

Returns the number of days from the settlement date to the next coupon date.

`COUPNCD(settlement,maturity,frequency,basis)`

Returns a number that represents the next coupon date after the settlement date.

`COUPNUM(settlement,maturity,frequency,basis)`

Returns the number of coupons payable between the settlement date and maturity date, rounded up to the nearest whole coupon.

`COUPPCD(settlement,maturity,frequency,basis)`

Returns a number that represents the previous coupon date before the settlement date.

`CUMIPMT(rate,nper,pv,start_period,end_period,type)`

Returns the cumulative interest paid on a loan between start_period and end_period.

`CUMPRINC(rate,nper,pv,start_period,end_period,type)`

Returns the cumulative principal paid on a loan between start_period and end_period.

`DB(cost,salvage,life,period,month)`

Returns the depreciation of an asset for a specified period using the fixed-declining balance method.

`DDB(cost,salvage,life,period,factor)`

Returns the depreciation of an asset for a specified period using the double-declining balance method or some other method you specify.

`DISC(settlement,maturity,pr,redemption,basis)`

Returns the discount rate for a security.

DOLLARDE(fractional_dollar,fraction)

Converts a dollar price expressed as a fraction into a dollar price expressed as a decimal number.

DOLLARFR(decimal_dollar,fraction)

Converts a dollar price expressed as a decimal number into a dollar price expressed as a fraction.

DURATION(settlement,maturity,coupon yld,frequency,basis)

Returns the modified duration for a security with an assumed par value of $100.

EFFECT(nominal_rate,npery)

Returns the effective annual interest rate, given the nominal annual interest rate and the number of compounding periods per year.

FV(rate,nper,pmt,pv,type)

Returns the future value of an investment based on periodic, constant payments and a constant interest rate.

FVSCHEDULE(principal,schedule)

Returns the future value of an initial principal after applying a series of compound interest rates.

INTRATE(settlement,maturity,investment,redemption,basis)

Returns the interest rate for a fully invested security.

IPMT(rate,per,nper,pv,fv,type)

Returns the interest payment for a given period for an investment based on periodic, constant payments and a constant interest rate.

IRR(values,guess)

Returns the internal rate of return for a series of cash flows represented by the numbers in values.

MDURATION(settlement,maturity,coupon,yld,frequency,basis)

Returns the Macauley duration for an assumed par value of $100.

MIRR(values,finance_rate,reinvest_rate)

Returns the modified internal rate of return for a series of periodic cash flows.

NOMINAL(effect_rate,npery)

Returns the nominal annual interest rate, given the effective rate and the number of compounding periods per year.

NPER(rate,pmt,pv,fv,type)

Returns the number of periods for an investment based on periodic, constant payments and a constant interest rate.

NPV(rate,value1,value2,...)

Calculates the net present value of an investment by using a discount rate and a series of future payments (negative values) and income (positive values).

ODDFPRICE(settlement,maturity,issue,first_coupon,rate,yld, redemption,frequency,basis)

Returns the price per $100 face value of a security having an odd (short or long) first period.

ODDFYIELD(settlement,maturity,issue,first_coupon,rate,pr, redemption,frequency,basis)

Returns the yield of a security that has an odd (short or long) first period.

ODDLPRICE(settlement,maturity,last_interest,rate,yld, redemption,frequency,basis)

Returns the price per $100 face value of a security having an odd (short or long) last coupon period.

ODDLYIELD(settlement,maturity,last_interest,rate,pr, redemption,frequency,basis)

Returns the yield of a security that has an odd (short or long) last period.

PMT(rate,nper,pv,fv,type)

Calculates the payment for a loan based on constant payments and a constant interest rate.

PPMT(rate,per,nper,pv,fv,type)

Returns the payment on the principal for a given period for an investment based on periodic, constant payments and a constant interest rate.

PRICE(settlement,maturity,rate,yld,redemption,frequency,basis)

Returns the price per $100 face value of a security that pays periodic interest.

PRICEDISC(settlement,maturity,discount,redemption,basis)

Returns the price per $100 face value of a discounted security.

PRICEMAT(settlement,maturity,issue,rate,yld,basis)

Returns the price per $100 face value of a security that pays interest at maturity.

PV(rate,nper,pmt,fv,type)

Returns the present value of an investment.

RATE(nper,pmt,pv,fv,type,guess)

Returns the interest rate per period of an annuity.

RECEIVED(settlement,maturity,investment,discount,basis)

Returns the amount received at maturity for a fully invested security.

SLN(cost,salvage,life)

Returns the straight-line depreciation of an asset for one period.

SYD(cost,salvage,life,per)

Returns the sum-of-years' digits depreciation of an asset for a specified period.

TBILLEQ(settlement,maturity,discount)

Returns the bond-equivalent yield for a treasury bill.

TBILLPRICE(settlement,maturity,discount)

Returns the price per $100 face value for a treasury bill.

TBILLYIELD(settlement,maturity,pr)

Returns the yield for a treasury bill.

VDB(cost,salvage,life,start_period,end_period,factor,no_switch)

Returns the depreciation of an asset for any period you specify, including partial periods, using the double-declining balance method or some other method you specify.

XIRR(values,dates,guess)

Returns the internal rate of return for a schedule of cash flows that is not necessarily periodic.

`XNPV(rate,values,dates)`

Returns the net present value for a schedule of cash flows that is not necessarily periodic.

`YIELD(settlement,maturity,rate,pr,redemption,frequency,basis)`

Returns the yield on a security that pays periodic interest, such as bonds.

`YIELDDISC(settlement,maturity,pr,redemption,basis)`

Returns the annual yield for a discounted security.

`YIELDMAT(settlement,maturity,issue,rate,pr,basis)`

Returns the annual yield of a security that pays interest at maturity.

Information Functions

`CELL(info_type,reference)`

Returns information about the formatting, location, or contents of the upper-left cell in a reference.

`ERROR.TYPE(error_val)`

Returns a number corresponding to one of the error values in Microsoft Excel.

`INFO(type_text)`

Returns information about the current operating environment.

`ISBLANK(value)`

`ISERR(value)`

`ISERROR(value)`

`ISLOGICAL(value)`

`ISNA(value)`

`ISNONTEXT(value)`

`ISNUMBER(value)`

`ISREF(value)`

`ISTEXT(value)`

These functions all test the type of a value or reference and return TRUE or FALSE.

ISEVEN(number)

Returns TRUE if number is even, or FALSE if number is odd.

ISODD(number)

Returns TRUE if number is odd, or FALSE if number is even.

N(value)

Returns a value converted to a number.

NA( )

Returns the error value **#N/A**.

TYPE(value)

Returns the type of value.

Logical Functions

AND(logical1,logical2,...)

Returns TRUE if all its arguments are TRUE; returns FALSE if one or more arguments is FALSE.

FALSE( )

Returns the logical value FALSE.

IF(logical_test,value_if_true,value_if_false)

Returns one value if a condition you specify evaluates to TRUE and another value if it evaluates to FALSE.

NOT(logical)

Reverses the value of its argument.

OR(logical1,logical2,...)

Returns TRUE if any argument is TRUE; returns FALSE if all arguments are FALSE.

TRUE( )

Returns the logical value TRUE.

Lookup and Reference Functions

ADDRESS(row_num,column_num,abs_num,a1,sheet_text)

Creates a cell address as text, given specified row and column numbers.

AREAS(reference)

Returns the number of areas in a reference.

CHOOSE(index_num,value1,value2,...)

Uses index_num to return a value from the list of value arguments.

COLUMN(reference)

Returns the column number of the given reference.

COLUMNS(array)

Returns the number of columns in an array or reference.

HLOOKUP(lookup_value,table_array,row_index_num,range_lookup)

Searches for a value in the top row of a table or an array of values, and then returns a value in the same column from a row you specify in the table or array.

HYPERLINK(link_location,friendly_name)

Creates a shortcut or jump that opens a document stored on a network server, an intranet, or the Internet.

INDEX(array,row_num,column_num)

Returns the value of a specified cell or array of cells within array.

INDEX(reference,row_num,column_num,area_num)

Returns a reference to a specified cell or cells within reference.

INDIRECT(ref_text,a1)

Returns the reference specified by a text string.

LOOKUP(lookup_value,lookup_vector,result_vector)

Looks in a one-row or one-column range (known as a *vector*) for a value and returns a value from the same position in a second one-row or one-column range.

LOOKUP(lookup_value,array)

Looks in the first row or column of an array for the specified value and returns a value from the same position in the last row or column of the array.

MATCH(lookup_value,lookup_array,match_type)

Returns the relative position of an item in an array that matches a specified value in a specified order.

OFFSET(reference,rows,cols,height,width)

Returns a reference to a range that is a specified number of rows and columns from a cell or range of cells.

ROW(reference)

Returns the row number of a reference.

ROWS(array)

Returns the number of rows in a reference or array.

TRANSPOSE(array)

Returns a vertical range of cells as a horizontal range, or vice versa.

VLOOKUP(lookup_value,table_array,col_index_num,range_lookup)

Searches for a value in the leftmost column of a table, and then returns a value in the same row from a column you specify in the table.

Math and Trigonometry Functions

ABS(number)

Returns the absolute value of a number.

ACOS(number)

Returns the arccosine of a number.

ACOSH(number)

Returns the inverse hyperbolic cosine of a number.

ASIN(number)

Returns the arcsine of a number.

ASINH(number)

Returns the inverse hyperbolic sine of a number.

ATAN(number)

Returns the arctangent of a number.

ATAN2(x_num,y_num)

Returns the arctangent of the specified x- and y-coordinates.

ATANH(number)

Returns the inverse hyperbolic tangent of a number.

CEILING(number,significance)

Returns number rounded up, away from zero, to the nearest multiple of significance.

COMBIN(number,number_chosen)

Returns the number of combinations for a given number of items.

COS(number)

Returns the cosine of the given angle.

COSH(number)

Returns the hyperbolic cosine of a number.

DEGREES(angle)

Converts radians into degrees.

EVEN(number)

Returns number rounded up to the nearest even integer.

EXP(number)

Returns e raised to the power of number.

FACT(number)

Returns the factorial of a number.

FLOOR(number,significance)

Rounds number down, toward zero, to the nearest multiple of significance.

`GCD(number1,number2,...)`

Returns the greatest common divisor of two or more integers.

`INT(number)`

Rounds a number down to the nearest integer.

`LCM(number1,number2,...)`

Returns the least common multiple of integers.

`LN(number)`

Returns the natural logarithm of a number.

`LOG(number,base)`

Returns the logarithm of a number to the base you specify.

`LOG10(number)`

Returns the base-10 logarithm of a number.

`MDETERM(array)`

Returns the matrix determinant of an array.

`MINVERSE(array)`

Returns the inverse matrix for the matrix stored in an array.

`MMULT(array1,array2)`

Returns the matrix product of two arrays.

`MOD(number,divisor)`

Returns the remainder after number is divided by divisor.

`MROUND(number,multiple)`

Returns a number rounded to the desired multiple.

`MULTINOMIAL(number1,number2,...)`

Returns the ratio of the factorial of a sum of values to the product of factorials.

`ODD(number)`

Returns number rounded up to the nearest odd integer.

`PI( )`

Returns the number 3.14159265358979, the mathematical constant π, accurate to 15 digits.

`POWER(number,power)`

Returns the result of a number raised to a power.

`PRODUCT(number1,number2,...)`

Multiplies all the numbers given as arguments and returns the product.

`QUOTIENT(numerator,denominator)`

Returns the integer portion of a division. Use this function when you want to discard the remainder of a division.

`RADIANS(angle)`

Converts degrees to radians.

`RAND( )`

Returns an evenly distributed random number greater than or equal to 0 and less than 1.

`RANDBETWEEN(bottom,top)`

Returns a random number between the numbers you specify.

`ROMAN(number,form)`

Converts an arabic numeral to roman, as text.

`ROUND(number,num_digits)`

Rounds a number to a specified number of digits.

`ROUNDDOWN(number,num_digits)`

Rounds a number down, toward zero.

`ROUNDUP(number,num_digits)`

Rounds a number up, away from 0 (zero).

`SERIESSUM(x,n,m,coefficients)`

Returns the sum of a power series based on a formula.

`SIGN(number)`

Determines the sign of a number.

`SIN(number)`

Returns the sine of the given angle.

`SINH(number)`

Returns the hyperbolic sine of a number.

`SQRT(number)`

Returns a positive square root.

`SQRTPI(number)`

Returns the square root of (number * π).

`SUBTOTAL(function_num,ref1,ref2,...)`

Returns a subtotal in a list or database.

`SUM(number1,number2,...)`

Adds all the numbers in a range of cells.

`SUMIF(range,criteria,sum_range)`

Adds the cells specified by a given criteria.

`SUMPRODUCT(array1,array2,array3,...)`

Multiplies corresponding components in the given arrays and returns the sum of those products.

`SUMSQ(number1,number2,...)`

Returns the sum of the squares of the arguments.

`SUMX2MY2(array_x,array_y)`

Returns the sum of the difference of squares of corresponding values in two arrays.

`SUMX2PY2(array_x,array_y)`

Returns the sum of the sum of squares of corresponding values in two arrays.

`SUMXMY2(array_x,array_y)`

Returns the sum of squares of differences of corresponding values in two arrays.

TAN(number)

Returns the tangent of the given angle.

TANH(number)

Returns the hyperbolic tangent of a number.

TRUNC(number,num_digits)

Truncates a number to an integer by removing the fractional part of the number.

Statistical Functions

AVEDEV(number1,number2,...)

Returns the average of the absolute deviations of data points from their mean.

AVERAGE(number1,number2,...)

Returns the average (arithmetic mean) of the arguments.

AVERAGEA(value1,value2,...)

Calculates the average (arithmetic mean) of the values in the list of arguments.

BETADIST(x,alpha,beta,A,B)

Returns the cumulative beta probability density function.

BETAINV(probability,alpha,beta,A,B)

Returns the inverse of the cumulative beta probability density function.

BINOMDIST(number_s,trials,probability_s,cumulative)

Returns the individual term binomial distribution probability.

CHIDIST(x,degrees_freedom)

Returns the one-tailed probability of the chi-squared distribution.

CHIINV(probability,degrees_freedom)

Returns the inverse of the one-tailed probability of the chi-squared distribution.

CHITEST(actual_range,expected_range)

Returns the test for independence.

CONFIDENCE(alpha,standard_dev,size)

Returns the confidence interval for a population mean.

`CORREL(array1,array2)`

Returns the correlation coefficient of the array1 and array2 cell ranges.

`COUNT(value1,value2,...)`

Counts the number of cells that contain numbers and numbers within the list of arguments.

`COUNTA(value1,value2,...)`

Counts the number of cells that are not empty and the values within the list of arguments.

`COUNTBLANK(range)`

Counts empty cells in a specified range of cells.

`COUNTIF(range,criteria)`

Counts the number of cells within a range that meet the given criteria.

`COVAR(array1,array2)`

Returns covariance, the average of the products of deviations for each data point pair.

`CRITBINOM(trials,probability_s,alpha)`

Returns the smallest value for which the cumulative binomial distribution is greater than or equal to a criterion value.

`DEVSQ(number1,number2,...)`

Returns the sum of squares of deviations of data points from their sample mean.

`EXPONDIST(x,lambda,cumulative)`

Returns the exponential distribution.

`FDIST(x,degrees_freedom1,degrees_freedom2)`

Returns the F probability distribution.

`FINV(probability,degrees_freedom1,degrees_freedom2)`

Returns the inverse of the F probability distribution.

`FISHER(x)`

Returns the Fisher transformation at x.

FISHERINV(y)

Returns the inverse of the Fisher transformation.

FORECAST(x,known_y's,known_x's)

Calculates, or predicts, a future value by using existing values.

FREQUENCY(data_array,bins_array)

Calculates how often values occur within a range of values, and then returns a vertical array of numbers.

FTEST(array1,array2)

Returns the result of an F-test.

GAMMADIST(x,alpha,beta,cumulative)

Returns the gamma distribution.

GAMMAINV(probability,alpha,beta)

Returns the inverse of the gamma cumulative distribution.

GAMMALN(x)

Returns the natural logarithm of the gamma function, G(x).

GEOMEAN(number1,number2,...)

Returns the geometric mean of an array or range of positive data.

GROWTH(known_y's,known_x's,new_x's,const)

Calculates predicted exponential growth by using existing data.

HARMEAN(number1,number2,...)

Returns the harmonic mean of a data set.

HYPGEOMDIST(sample_s,number_sample,population_s,number_population)

Returns the hypergeometric distribution.

INTERCEPT(known_y's,known_x's)

Calculates the point at which a line will intersect the y-axis by using existing x-values and y-values.

KURT(number1,number2,...)

Returns the kurtosis of a data set.

LARGE(array,k)

Returns the k-th largest value in a data set.

LINEST(known_y's,known_x's,const,stats)

Calculates the statistics for a line by using the "least squares" method to calculate a straight line that best fits your data, and returns an array that describes the line.

LOGEST(known_y's,known_x's,const,stats)

In regression analysis, calculates an exponential curve that fits your data and returns an array of values that describes the curve.

LOGINV(probability,mean,standard_dev)

Returns the inverse of the lognormal cumulative distribution function of x, where ln(x) is normally distributed with parameters mean and standard_dev.

LOGNORMDIST(x,mean,standard_dev)

Returns the cumulative lognormal distribution of x, where ln(x) is normally distributed with parameters mean and standard_dev.

MAX(number1,number2,...)

Returns the largest value in a set of values.

MAXA(value1,value2,...)

Returns the largest value in a list of arguments.

MEDIAN(number1,number2,...)

Returns the median of the given numbers.

MIN(number1,number2,...)

Returns the smallest number in a set of values.

MINA(value1,value2,...)

Returns the smallest value in the list of arguments.

MODE(number1,number2,...)

Returns the most frequently occurring, or repetitive, value in an array or range of data.

NEGBINOMDIST(number_f,number_s,probability_s)

Returns the negative binomial distribution.

NORMDIST(x,mean,standard_dev,cumulative)

Returns the normal cumulative distribution for the specified mean and standard deviation.

NORMINV(probability,mean,standard_dev)

Returns the inverse of the normal cumulative distribution for the specified mean and standard deviation.

NORMSDIST(z)

Returns the standard normal cumulative distribution function.

NORMSINV(probability)

Returns the inverse of the standard normal cumulative distribution.

PEARSON(array1,array2)

Returns the Pearson product moment correlation coefficient, r, a dimensionless index that ranges from -1.0 to 1.0 inclusive and reflects the extent of a linear relationship between two data sets.

PERCENTILE(array,k)

Returns the k-th percentile of values in a range.

PERCENTRANK(array,x,significance)

Returns the rank of a value in a data set as a percentage of the data set.

PERMUT(number,number_chosen)

Returns the number of permutations for a given number of objects that can be selected from number objects.

POISSON(x,mean,cumulative)

Returns the Poisson distribution.

PROB(x_range,prob_range,lower_limit,upper_limit)

Returns the probability that values in a range are between two limits.

QUARTILE(array,quart)

Returns the quartile of a data set.

RANK(number,ref,order)

Returns the rank of a number in a list of numbers.

`RSQ(known_y's,known_x's)`

Returns the square of the Pearson product moment correlation coefficient through data points in known_y's and known_x's.

`SKEW(number1,number2,...)`

Returns the skewness of a distribution.

`SLOPE(known_y's,known_x's)`

Returns the slope of the linear regression line through data points in known_y's and known_x's.

`SMALL(array,k)`

Returns the k-th smallest value in a data set.

`STANDARDIZE(x,mean,standard_dev)`

Returns a normalized value from a distribution characterized by mean and standard_dev.

Note

Some functions have two versions, one ending with A and one not (for example, STDEV and STDEVA). The "A" versions are used if you need compatibility with Lotus 1-2-3. The functions both do exactly the same thing in Excel itself.

`STDEV(number1,number2,...)`

Estimates standard deviation based on a sample.

`STDEVA(value1,value2,...)`

Estimates standard deviation based on a sample.

`STDEVP(number1,number2,...)`

Calculates standard deviation based on the entire population given as arguments.

`STDEVPA(value1,value2,...)`

Calculates standard deviation based on the entire population given as arguments, including text and logical values.

`STEYX(known_y's,known_x's)`

Returns the standard error of the predicted y-value for each x in the regression.

TDIST(x,degrees_freedom,tails)

Returns the Student's t-distribution.

TINV(probability,degrees_freedom)

Returns the inverse of the Student's t-distribution for the specified degrees of freedom.

TREND(known_y's,known_x's,new_x's,const)

Returns values along a linear trend.

TRIMMEAN(array,percent)

Returns the mean of the interior of a data set.

TTEST(array1,array2,tails,type)

Returns the probability associated with a Student's t-Test.

VAR(number1,number2,...)

Estimates variance based on a sample.

VARA(value1,value2,...)

Estimates variance based on a sample.

VARP(number1,number2,...)

Calculates variance based on the entire population.

VARPA(value1,value2,...)

Calculates variance based on the entire population.

WEIBULL(x,alpha,beta,cumulative)

Returns the Weibull distribution.

ZTEST(array,x,sigma)

Returns the two-tailed P-value of a z-test.

Text Functions

CHAR(number)

Returns the character specified by a number.

CLEAN(text)

Removes all nonprintable characters from text.

CODE(text)

Returns a numeric code for the first character in a text string.

CONCATENATE(text1,text2,...)

Joins several text strings into one text string.

DOLLAR(number,decimals)

Converts a number to text using currency format, with the decimals rounded to the specified place.

EXACT(text1,text2)

Compares two text strings and returns TRUE if they are exactly the same (including case), FALSE otherwise.

FIND(find_text,within_text,start_num)

Finds one text string (find_text) within another text string (within_text), and returns the number of the starting position of find_text, from the leftmost character of within_text.

FIXED(number,decimals,no_commas)

Rounds a number to the specified number of decimals, formats the number in decimal format using a period and commas, and returns the result as text.

LEFT(text,num_chars)

Returns the first (or leftmost) character or characters in a text string.

LEN(text)

Returns the number of characters in a text string.

LOWER(text)

Converts all uppercase letters in a text string to lowercase.

MID(text,start_num,num_chars)

Returns a specific number of characters from a text string, starting at the position you specify.

`PROPER(text)`

Capitalizes the first letter in a text string and any other letters in text that follow any character other than a letter.

`REPLACE(old_text,start_num,num_chars,new_text)`

Replaces part of a text string with a different text string.

`REPT(text,number_times)`

Repeats text a given number of times.

`RIGHT(text,num_chars)`

Returns the last (or rightmost) character or characters in a text string.

`SEARCH(find_text,within_text,start_num)`

Returns the number of the character at which a specific character or text string is first found, reading from left to right.

`SUBSTITUTE(text,old_text,new_text,instance_num)`

Substitutes new_text for old_text in a text string.

`T(value)`

Returns the text referred to by value.

`TEXT(value,format_text)`

Converts a value to text in a specific number format.

`TRIM(text)`

Removes all spaces from text except for single spaces between words.

`UPPER(text)`

Converts text to uppercase.

`VALUE(text)`

Converts a text string that represents a number to a number.

D

Glossary

‘ (Apostrophe). Typed before a string of digits, it tells Excel to consider those digits to be *text*, not a *number*.

#. Used singly, it precedes a formula error message. Examples include `#NAME?` and `#REF!`. If several appear in a row (`####`) it indicates that the cell is too narrow to display its numeric content.

?. In a formula, denotes an *absolute reference.*

3-D. An effect used with pictures to add the appearance of depth (three dimensions) using shading.

3-D range. A range of cells that spans more than one worksheet in a workbook.

A

Absolute reference. A cell reference in a formula that remains fixed when the formula is moved to a different cell. Absolute references are denoted by dollar signs in formulas, like this: =$C$5.

Active cell. The cell in which the cell cursor is resting.

Active workbook. The workbook that is currently “on top” if more than one workbook is open.

Active worksheet. The worksheet that is currently "on top," being displayed.

Alignment. The arrangement of text or an object in relation to a document's margins or the edges of a cell in a table. Alignment can be left, right, centered, or justified.

Applet. A small software program provided with Excel that allows you to perform additional operations, such as Microsoft Map for creating data maps.

Auditing. Checking a worksheet for formula errors.

AutoComplete. A feature of Excel that completes your typing based on what you have already typed in that worksheet.

AutoCorrect. A feature of Excel that corrects common spelling mistakes (such as "teh" for "the") automatically.

AutoFill. A feature of Excel that attempts to fill in a series of cells for you based on what you have entered in adjacent cells.

AutoFit. An Excel feature that automatically widens a column to accommodate its longest entry.

AutoFormat. An Excel feature that applies predefined sets of formatting to a worksheet's rows and columns.

Automatic Recalculation. The default recalculation setting in Excel, wherein formula results are updated immediately when changes are made to the values in referring cells.

AutoShape. A set of automated drawing shapes.

AutoSum. An Excel feature that adds a column or row of numbers quickly.

Axis (pl. axes). In a graph, one of two value sets (see also y-axis and x-axis).

B

Bar chart. A type of chart that uses horizontal bars of varying lengths to represent values. When the bars are vertical, it's called a *column chart* in Excel; however, some people refer to both types as bar charts.

Bitmap. A type of graphic image made up of individual colored dots that form a picture.

Bold. A style applied to text to make the font lines thicker.

Border. A visible line surrounding text or objects.

Break. An instruction embedded into an Excel worksheet that indicates a change, such as a Page Break to start a new page.

C

Cascade. To arrange the windows in Excel so that the title bars align diagonally from top left to bottom right.

Cell. The area where a row and column in an Excel worksheet intersect.

Chart. Also called *graph*. A visual representation of numerical data.

ChartWizard. An Excel feature that makes it easy to create a chart from worksheet data.

Circular reference. A formula reference that refers to its own cell. For example, A1=A1+1.

Click. To press and release the left mouse button once.

Clip art. A ready-made drawing that can be inserted in an Excel worksheet.

Clip Gallery. Excel's clip management program, enabling you to categorize and organize pictures, clip art, video clips, and sound files.

Clip Gallery Live. Microsoft's Web page devoted to providing free downloadable extra clips for use in Office programs.

Clipboard. A holding area in Windows where material that is *cut* or *copied* is placed until you are ready to *paste* it.

Collapse Dialog button. A button in a dialog box that, when clicked, shrinks the dialog box out of the way so that you can select cells to reference in one of the dialog box's controls.

Column. A set of cells running vertically down a worksheet.

Column chart. A type of chart that uses vertical bars of varying lengths to represent values. This is sometimes called a *bar chart.*

Comma style. A style applied to Excel cells that formats the content with commas every third digit for ease of reading.

Command button. A button in a dialog box that issues a command (like Close or Save) or opens another dialog box.

Comment. A note attached to a cell that is intended for on-screen reference only. When you position the mouse pointer over the corner of the cell, the comment appears.

Conditional formatting. Formatting that is applied only when the content of a cell meets certain conditions (for example, is greater than 0).

Contrast. The amount of black and white in a picture that can be adjusted to modify the image's seeming brightness.

Copy. To copy the contents of cells or an object to the *Clipboard.*

Crop. A tool used to erase portions of a picture.

Cut. To move the contents of cells or an object to the *Clipboard.*

D

Data. Information, which can be either numerical or textual.

Data form. A form used to enter, edit, or view individual database records.

Data series. In charts, elements that represent a set of data, such as a pie segment, lines, or bars.

Data table. A grid accompanying a chart that shows the data on which the chart was based.

Dependent. A formula that depends on another formula to calculate its result. For example, if cell C3 contains a formula and cell D5 references that formula, the formula in C5 is dependent upon the one in C3.

Desktop. The main area of Windows where you can open and manage files and programs.

Dialog box. A window that appears during some procedures in Excel that allows you to make settings by entering text, selecting things from lists, or checking boxes or buttons.

Docked. A toolbar that is "fastened" at the top or bottom (or left or right)of the Excel window. Docked toolbars have no title bar of their own. Also called *Floating.*

Double-click. To press and release the left mouse button twice quickly in succession.

Doughnut chart. A variation of a pie chart that shows the data as percentages of a whole ring-shaped object.

Drag. To press and hold down the left mouse button while moving the mouse.

Drag and drop. A method of moving text or objects by clicking on an object with a mouse, dragging it to a new location, and releasing the mouse button to drop it into its new location.

E

E-mail. Electronic mail. Messages distributed and received over a computer network or system of networks, such as the Internet.

Ellipses. Three dots. Whenever you see ellipses after a command, it means that the command opens a dialog box.

F

Field. A placeholder for corresponding data that will be automatically inserted, such as a date and time field.

Fill. To place a color or line pattern in the interior of an object, such as a square or cell of a table. Also, an Excel command that repeats information from one cell in multiple other cells with a single command.

Font. A design set of letters, symbols, and numbers.

Footer. Text entered in a footer placeholder, which is automatically placed at the bottom of each document page.

Format. To add or change settings for font, font style, color, and line style to text or an object.

Format Painter. A feature of Excel that allows you to easily copy all formatting applied in one set of text to any other text.

Formula. A mathematical expression that performs a calculation on one or more fixed numbers and/or cells' contents.

Formula bar. The on-screen area where the formula in a cell appears when that cell is active.

Formula Palette. An Excel feature that provides help entering functions from the worksheet window.

Free rotate. See *Rotate.*

Freeze. To keep certain rows or columns on-screen while others around them scroll.

Full Screen view. A special Excel view that hides all screen elements except the workbook and the menu bar, for maximum use of the screen in editing.

Function. A special formula built into Excel. Functions typically help the user perform more complex operations than he/she could easily write formulas for from scratch.

G

General. Excel's term to refer to the default formatting or alignment of a cell. If a cell contains no formatting, it is considered to use the General format.

Gradient. A shading effect that moves from lighter to darker in such a way that it suggests a light source shining on the object containing the gradient.

Graph. Also called *chart.* A visual representation of numerical data.

Graphics. A file containing visual data, such as a line drawing, rather than text.

Graphics file format. Individual systems of storing graphics file data. Graphics file filters are required to read various graphics file formats; Excel comes with several built in.

Grayed out. Unavailable. Commands and buttons that cannot be used immediately appear gray (rather than normal black) to indicate this.

Grayscale. A process used in printing documents that utilizes shades between white and black to enhance computer graphics printouts.

Gridlines. The lines dividing rows and columns in a worksheet. On a chart, gridlines in the walls help the eye follow the values on the chart.

H

Handle. Small squares that appear when you select an object that allow you to resize it. Also called a *selection handle* or *resizing handle.*

Header. Text entered in a header placeholder, which is automatically placed at the top of each document page.

Highlight. A feature that places colored highlighting on-screen for selected text.

Home page. The hypertext document on the World Wide Web that appears when you first open your Web browser. Also refers to the top page on someone's Web site. Also called a *Start page.*

HTML. Hypertext Markup Language. The language used to create hypertext.

Hyperlink. Any underlined text or hyperlink object created using hypertext that a computer user can click on with a mouse, causing a different hypertext document to display.

Hypertext. Text that functions as a hyperlink.

I

Image control. A Word feature used to adjust the appearance of pictures relative to grayscale settings.

Indent. To set text away from a margin or the edge of a cell by a specific distance.

Insertion point. The blinking vertical line that indicates where typed text will appear when you are editing cell data.

IntelliMouse. A new mouse from Microsoft that has a rolling wheel in the center that controls Zoom and some other features such as navigating.

Internet. A globally connected system of computer networks allowing online access to various types of documents such as graphics and hypertext documents.

Intranet. A hypertext-linked network of limited scope, such as within a company.

Italic. A font style that applies a slanted effect to text.

J

Jump. Within a hypertext system, to move from one hypertext document to another using hyperlinks.

Justify. One type of alignment that spreads letters in a cell so that they are spaced out between the left and right sides of the cell.

L

Label. A descriptive text element added to a chart to help the reader understand a visual element. Also refers to row or column headings.

Landscape. Orientation of a document so that, when printed, text runs from left to right along the longer edge of a piece of paper.

Left-aligned. Text that aligns with the left margin of the cell, box, or other location where it is placed.

Legend. In a chart, a feature that defines the relationship of the graphic symbols to the data elements for the reader.

Line style. Effects using width, arrows, and dashes that can be applied to a line.

Locking. Specifying that certain cells cannot be changed.

M

Macro. A method of recording and playing back a series of keystrokes or commands using a software program's command language. Excel uses the Visual Basic for Applications command language for macros.

Manual recalculation. If Excel is set for Manual recalculation, you must press the F9 key to update formulas based on the changes made to the cells they refer to. See *Recalculation.*

Margin. A border that runs around the outside of a document page, in which nothing will print.

Maximize. To expand a window to fill the entire screen.

Media Player. A Microsoft Windows accessory program for playing multimedia files.

Menu. A list of commands you can choose from.

Menu Bar. The bar across the top of the Excel window containing the names of the available drop-down menus.

Microsoft Map. An auxiliary program that works with Excel to help you plot data geographically on a map.

Minimize. To shrink a window to an icon on the desktop or in the application window.

N

Named range. See *Range name.*

Normal view. Excel's default view, in which you can see the rows, columns, toolbars, and menus on-screen normally.

Number. Excel sees a string of text as a number if it contains only digits and number symbols like a period, dollar sign, or comma. Otherwise, it sees it as *text*. You can force Excel to see digits as text by preceding them with an apostrophe.

O

Object. Any graphic, drawing, chart, or other file placed within an Excel worksheet.

Office Assistant. A feature of Excel 97 for Windows that allows you to enter questions in natural English language sentences.

OLE. Object Linking and Embedding. Microsoft Corporation's standards built into Windows that allow the embedding of a document created in one software application in a document created in another software application. OLE also allows the establishment of a relationship (link) between the embedded data in one document to the original data.

Option buttons. A set of buttons in a dialog box from which only one may be selected at a time. Also called *Radio buttons*.

Order of precedence. The order in which Excel calculates the math operators in formulas. First is exponentiation, followed by multiplication and division, followed by addition and subtraction.

Orientation. A setting that designates whether a document will print with text running along the long or short side of a piece of paper. See *Landscape* and *Portrait*.

P

Page break. An instruction that can be embedded into an Excel worksheet to instruct Excel to print on a new page at that point.

Page Break Preview. A view in Excel that is commonly used for determining and checking where page breaks will fall.

Page setup. The collection of settings that relate to how the pages of your document are set up, including margins, orientation, and the size of paper each page will print on.

Password. A word selected by an Excel user to protect a document; after a document is protected, the correct password must be entered to open or modify that document.

Paste. To place text or an object into a worksheet from the Windows *Clipboard.*

Paste Function. An Excel tool that helps you enter functions by providing the proper arguments and advice.

Paste link. To place a copy of a file in an Excel worksheet while establishing a link with the original file.

Pattern. An arrangement of dots or lines that can be used to fill the center of an object.

Pie chart. A round chart type in which each pie wedge represents a value.

Plot area. The portion of a chart where the actual graphic is contained that shows the data.

Portrait. An orientation that places text from left to right along the shorter side of a piece of paper.

Precedent. A reference in a formula that refers to an earlier formula in the worksheet. For example, if cell C3 contains a formula and cell D5 references cell C3, the formula in C3 is a precedent.

Print area. The specified range of cells that you choose to be printed. Unless you set it up otherwise, the print area is the active worksheet.

Print Preview. An Excel feature that enables you to see a preview of how your printed document will look on-screen before you print it.

Properties. Characteristics or settings for a device, file, or program.

Protect. To make settings so that only someone with the correct password can modify an Excel workbook.

R

Radio buttons. See *Option buttons.*

Range. A rectangular block of cells consisting of at least one cell.

Range name. A meaningful name you assign to refer to a specific range.

Recalculation. Updating the results of formulas as the cells they are based on change contents. Calculation can be either *manual* or *automatic.*

Redo. To restore an action you have undone using the Undo command.

Relative reference. A cell reference in a formula that changes if you move the formula. In other words, the reference is relative to the position of the formula in the worksheet. Compare to *Absolute reference.*

Restore. To change a minimized or maximized window back to its original size (opened but not filling the entire screen).

Revisions. Highlighting effects applied to indicate any changes in text from one version of a worksheet to another. See also *Tracking revisions.*

Right aligned. Text that is lined up with the right side of a tab setting or cell.

Right-click. To press and release the right mouse button once.

Right-drag. To press and hold down the right mouse button while you move the mouse.

Rotate. To move an object along a 360 degree path. When the rotation can be any amount, Excel refers to it as *Free rotate.*

Row. A set of cells running from left to right across a worksheet.

S

Save As. To save a previously saved worksheet with a new name or properties.

Scan. To electronically record a hard copy image as a graphics file; this file can then be opened and manipulated within software such as Excel.

ScreenTip. A Help feature that displays the name of a tool in a small box when you move your pointer over the tool.

Scroll. To move the on-screen display to view different parts of the worksheet.

Scroll bar. A screen element used with a mouse for navigating around a worksheet horizontally or vertically.

Series. In a worksheet, a series is a regular progression of values from one cell to the next (like 100, 200, 300). In a chart, a series is a group of values (for example, the sales figures for a particular salesperson for a series of months).

Shading. A pattern ranging between white and black that fills an object.

Shadow. A drawing effect that appears to place a shadow alongside an object.

Sheet. Another name for *Worksheet.*

Shortcut. An icon that refers to a program or data file in Windows.

Shortcut keys. Keys you can press as a shortcut to choosing a command from a menu. For example, Ctrl+C is the shortcut key combination for the Edit, Copy command.

Shortcut menu. The menu that appears when you right-click an object in Excel (or in Windows 95).

Sort. To arrange data alphanumerically in either ascending (A-Z) or descending (Z-A) order.

Sound Recorder. A Microsoft Windows accessory program that can be used to record, edit, and play back sound files.

Spelling checker. A feature of Excel that checks the spelling of words in your worksheet against a dictionary and flags possible errors for correction.

Split. To divide the Excel window into two panes and show a different part of the workbook in each pane.

Spreadsheet Solutions. Sophisticated templates Excel provides that help you generate common business forms like invoices and purchase orders.

Stacked bar chart. A bar chart variation wherein multiple series are stacked upon one another to show the whole. For example the sales for three salespeople might be stacked into a single bar to show the total sales.

Start page. The hypertext document on the World Wide Web that will display when you first open the Web from Excel. Also refers to the top page on someone's Web site. Also called a *Home page.*

Status bar. An area at the bottom of Excel that provides information about the workbook, such as what worksheet, row, and column your cursor is currently resting in.

Style. A predefined set of formats that you can apply to text all at once.

Submenu. A menu within a menu.

Symbol. A typeface that uses graphics like circles, percent signs, or smiling faces in place of letters and numbers.

T

Tab scrolling buttons. The arrow buttons at the bottom left corner of the workbook window that control which sheet tabs are visible.

Tabs. Markers at the bottom of a workbook or the top of a dialog box that represent the pages available for viewing.

Template. A predefined collection of formatting and style settings on which you can base a new document.

Text. If the data you enter contains any characters that disqualify it from being considered a number, Excel considers it text. Excel can display text but cannot perform calculations on it. Only *Numbers* can be calculated.

Texture. A predesigned background that comes with Excel that makes your workbook or chart appear to be sitting on a surface like brick, marble, wood, or some other material.

Text wrap. This feature forces newly entered text in a cell to wrap to the next line when the insertion point reaches the right edge of the cell.

Tile. To arrange multiple windows so that each window fits on-screen without overlap.

Title bar. The colored bar across the top of a window that tells the program's name.

Toolbar. A group of buttons (tools) representing commonly used commands. Toolbars can be *docked* or *undocked (floating).*

Toolbar button. A graphic representation used on toolbars to represent the various functions performed when those buttons are pressed with a mouse.

Tracking revisions. A feature that allows you to keep a record of changes to an Excel worksheet or compare one document with another.

U

Undo. To reverse the last action performed.

Undocked. Toolbars that are not fastened to the top or bottom (or right or left) of the screen, but float freely in their own window. Also called *floating.*

Uppercase. A capital letter.

V

View. In software, various displays of documents or information that allow you to perform different tasks or see different perspectives on information. Excel has two views: Normal and Page Break Preview.

Virus. A computer program that attaches itself to other programs and replicates and/or causes system problems.

W

Watermark. A shading effect for pictures, which makes them appear to be a background impression, like a watermark impression on fine stationary.

Web. See *World Wide Web.*

What's This? A part of the Excel Help system; after you choose What's This? from the Help menu, your pointer changes to a question mark, and you can click on any on-screen element to receive an explanation of that element.

Wizard. A feature that walks you through certain procedures, producing something, such as a table, letter, or chart, based on answers you give to questions and selections made in Wizard dialog boxes.

WordArt. An application included with Excel used for adding special effects to text, such as curving the text.

Workbook. An Excel file containing one or more tabbed worksheets.

Worksheet. A tabbed page in an Excel workbook containing a grid of *rows* and *columns* that form *cells.*

World Wide Web. A hypertext system of documents transmitted and accessed over the Internet.

Wrap. See *Text wrap.*

X, Y, Z

X-axis. In a chart, the horizontal value axis.

Y-axis. In a chart, the vertical value axis.

Zoom. To modify view settings so that what you are seeing on your screen is a percentage (larger or smaller) of a worksheet's actual size.

Index

Numbers and Symbols

A

G

J

K

L

M

N

Q

R

S

U

V

W

X

Y

Z

Send Us YOUR COMMENTS

Dear Reader:

Thank you for buying this book. In order to offer you more quality books on the topics ***you*** would like to see, we need your input. At Prima Publishing, we pride ourselves on timely responsiveness to our readers' needs. If you'll complete and return this brief questionnaire, ***we will listen!***

Name: (first) ________ (M.I.) ____ (last) ________

Company: ________ Type of business: ________

Address: ________ City: ______ State: ____ Zip: ____

Phone: ______ Fax: ______ E-mail address: ________

May we contact you for research purposes? ❑ Yes ❑ No

(If you participate in a research project, we will supply you with your choice of a book from Prima CPD)

❶ How would you rate this book, overall?

- ❑ Excellent
- ❑ Very Good
- ❑ Good
- ❑ Fair
- ❑ Below Average
- ❑ Poor

❷ Why did you buy this book?

- ❑ Price of book
- ❑ Content
- ❑ Author's reputation
- ❑ Prima's reputation
- ❑ CD-ROM/disk included with book
- ❑ Information highlighted on cover
- ❑ Other (Please specify): ________

❸ How did you discover this book?

- ❑ Found it on bookstore shelf
- ❑ Saw it in Prima Publishing catalog
- ❑ Recommended by store personnel
- ❑ Recommended by friend or colleague
- ❑ Saw an advertisement in: ________
- ❑ Read book review in: ________
- ❑ Saw it on Web site: ________
- ❑ Other (Please specify): ________

❹ Where did you buy this book?

- ❑ Bookstore (name) ________
- ❑ Computer Store (name) ________
- ❑ Electronics Store (name) ________
- ❑ Wholesale Club (name) ________
- ❑ Mail Order (name) ________
- ❑ Direct from Prima Publishing
- ❑ Other (please specify): ________

❺ Which computer periodicals do you read regularly? ________

❻ Would you like to see your name in print?

May we use your name and quote you in future Prima Publishing books or promotional materials?

❑ Yes ❑ No

❼ Comments & Suggestions: ________

PLEASE
PLACE
STAMP
HERE

PRIMA PUBLISHING
Computer Products Division
701 Congressional Blvd., Suite 350
Carmel, IN 46032

---

8 Where do you use your computer?

Work	❑ 100%	❑ 75%	❑ 50%	❑ 25%
Home	❑ 100%	❑ 75%	❑ 50%	❑ 25%
School	❑ 100%	❑ 75%	❑ 50%	❑ 25%

Other ______________________________

9 How do you rate your level of computer skills?

- ❑ Beginner
- ❑ Advanced
- ❑ Intermediate

10 What is your age?

- ❑ Under 18
- ❑ 18-24
- ❑ 25-29
- ❑ 30-39
- ❑ 40-49
- ❑ 50-59
- ❑ 60-over

11 I would be interested in computer books on these topics

- ❑ Word Processing
- ❑ Networking
- ❑ Desktop Publishing
- ❑ Database
- ❑ Spreadsheets
- ❑ Web site design

Other ______________________________

SAVE A STAMP

Visit our Web Site at: **http://www.primapublishing.com**
and simply fill in one of our online Response Forms

To Order Books

Please send me the following items:

Quantity	Title	Unit Price	Total
______	______________________________	$ ______	$ ______
______	______________________________	$ ______	$ ______
______	______________________________	$ ______	$ ______
______	______________________________	$ ______	$ ______
______	______________________________	$ ______	$ ______

Shipping and Handling depend on Subtotal.

Subtotal	Shipping/Handling
$0.00–$14.99	$3.00
$15.00–$29.99	$4.00
$30.00–$49.99	$6.00
$50.00–$99.99	$10.00
$100.00–$199.99	$13.50
$200.00+	Call for Quote

Foreign and all Priority Request orders:
Call Order Entry department
for price quote at 916/632-4400

This chart represents the total retail price of books only (before applicable discounts are taken).

Subtotal $ ______

Deduct 10% when ordering 3-5 books $ ______

7.25% Sales Tax (CA only) $ ______

8.25% Sales Tax (TN only) $ ______

5.0% Sales Tax (MD and IN only) $ ______

Shipping and Handling* $ ______

Total Order $ ______

By Telephone: With MC or Visa, call 800-632-8676, 916-632-4400. Mon-Fri, 8:30-4:30.
WWW {http://www.primapublishing.com}

Orders Placed Via Internet E-mail {sales@primapub.com}

By Mail: Just fill out the information below and send with your remittance to:

Prima Publishing
P.O. Box 1260BK
Rocklin, CA 95677

My name is ______________________________

I live at ______________________________

City ______________________ State ______ Zip ______

MC/Visa# ______________________ Exp. ______

Check/Money Order enclosed for $ ______________ Payable to Prima Publishing

Daytime Telephone ______________________________

Signature ______________________________

Other books from Prima Publishing, Computer Products Division

ISBN	Title	Price	Release Date
0-7615-0801-5	ActiveX	$40.00	Available Now
0-7615-0680-2	America Online Complete Handbook and Membership Kit	$24.99	Available Now
0-7615-0915-1	Building Intranets with Internet Information Server and FrontPage	$45.00	Available Now
0-7615-0417-6	CompuServe Complete Handbook and Membership Kit	$24.95	Available Now
0-7615-0849-X	Corporate Intranet Development	$45.00	Available Now
0-7615-0743-4	Create FrontPage Web Pages in a Weekend	$29.99	Available Now
0-7615-0692-6	Create Your First Web Page in a Weekend	$29.99	Available Now
0-7615-0969-0	The Essential Office 97 Book	$27.99	Available Now
0-7615-0695-0	The Essential Photoshop Book	$35.00	Available Now
0-7615-0752-3	The Essential Windows NT Book	$27.99	Available Now
0-7615-0427-3	The Essential Word 97 Book	$24.99	Available Now
0-7615-1008-7	Excel 97 Visual Learning Guide	$16.99	Available Now
0-7615-1013-3	Hands-On Java	$40.00	Spring '97
0-7615-1046-X	Hands-On Visual Basic 5	$40.00	Spring '97
0-7615-1005-2	Internet Information Server 3 Administrator's Guide	$40.00	Available Now
0-7615-0815-5	Introduction to ABAP/4 Programming for SAP	$45.00	Available Now
0-7615-0901-1	Leveraging Visual Basic with ActiveX Controls	$45.00	Available Now
0-7615-0690-X	Netscape Enterprise Server	$40.00	Available Now
0-7615-0691-8	Netscape FastTrack Server	$40.00	Available Now
0-7615-0852-X	Netscape Navigator 3 Complete Handbook	$24.99	Available Now
0-7615-1162-8	Office 97 Visual Learning Guide	$16.99	Spring '97
0-7615-0759-0	Professional Web Design	$40.00	Available Now
0-7615-0773-6	Programming Internet Controls	$45.00	Available Now
0-7615-0914-3	Programming ISAPI with Visual Basic 5	$40.00	Spring '97
0-7615-0780-9	Programming Web Server Applications	$40.00	Available Now
0-7615-0063-4	Researching on the Internet	$29.95	Available Now
0-7615-0686-1	Researching on the World Wide Web	$24.99	Available Now
0-7615-0769-8	VBScript Master's Handbook	$45.00	Available Now
0-7615-0684-5	VBScript Web Page Interactivity	$40.00	Available Now
0-7615-0903-8	Visual FoxPro 5 Enterprise Development	$45.00	Available Now
0-7615-0814-7	Visual J++	$35.00	Available Now
0-7615-0726-4	Webmaster's Handbook	$40.00	Available Now
0-7615-0751-5	Windows NT Server 4 Administrator's Guide	$50.00	Available Now
0-7615-1007-9	Word 97 Visual Learning Guide	$16.99	Available Now
0-7615-1083-4	WordPerfect 8 Visual Learning Guide	$16.99	Spring '97

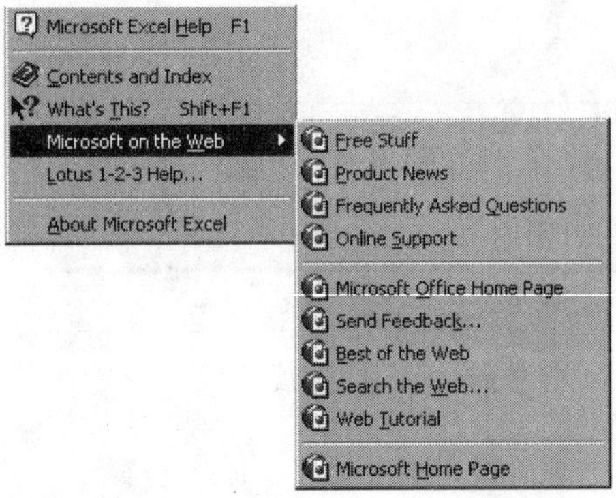

Microsoft

Free Stuff

- Download new queries
- Get additional templates
- Download a free Web Connectivity set

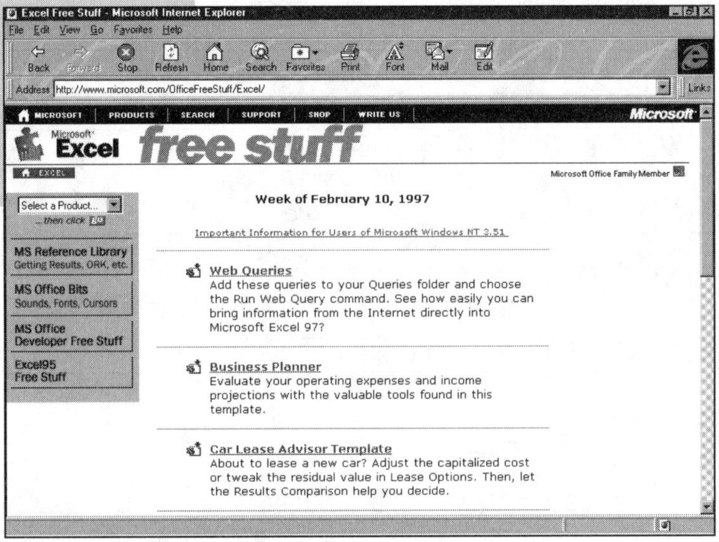

Frequently Asked Questions

- Hotlinks to the Microsoft Knowledge Base
- Answers to the most common user questions
- Information about using new features

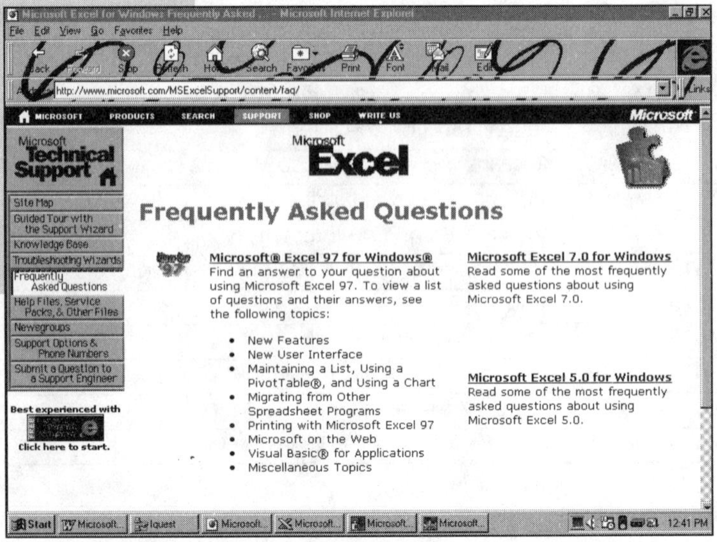